Annual yacht races off Key West. ROBONEAL.COM

Aerial of Key West. ROBONEAL.COM

Old Seven Mile Bridge (foreground) leads to historic Pigeon Key. ROBONEAL.COM

Snorkeling off of Rock Key near Key West. ROBONEAL.COM

Parked for the evening on Islamorada on a full moon night (long exposure). ROBONEAL.COM

Exploring the National Marine Sanctuary off of Key Largo in a glass-bottomed boat. FLORIDA KEYS NEWS BUREAU/MONROE COUNTY TDC

Kayaking in the mangroves. ROBONEAL.COM

Snorkelers enjoying the sunset at Bahia Honda. ROBONEAL.COM

Bird dog. ROBONEAL.COM

You never know who you might meet. RON ARMSTRONG

Parading down Duval Street during the Conch Republic Celebration. ROBONEAL.COM

Key West rooster. ROBONEAL.COM

Fort Jefferson, Dry Tortugas National Park. ROBONEAL.COM

Dolphin Research Center on Grassy Key. ROBONEAL.COM

The famed Turtle Hospital in Marathon. FLORIDA KEYS NEWS BUREAU/MONROE COUNTY TDC

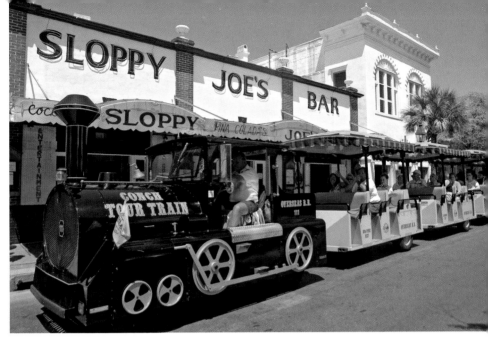

Ride a Conch Train in Key West. FLORIDA KEYS NEWS BUREAU/MONROE COUNTY TDC

Check out the many galleries scattered throughout the Keys.
FLORIDA KEYS NEWS BUREAU/MONROE COUNTY TDC

Sunsets take center stage at mile marker 8 leading into Key West. ROBONEAL.COM

Floating the day away at Fort Zach. ROBONEAL.COM

Sandbars near Calda Bank off Key West. ROBONEAL.COM

Sundown on Florida Bay in Key Largo. ROBONEAL.COM

Marker buoy designating the southernmost point. ROBONEAL.COM

INSIDERS' GUIDE® SERIES

INSIDERS' GUIDE® TO
FLORIDA KEYS AND KEY WEST

FIFTEENTH EDITION

JULIET DYAL GRAY

INSIDERS' GUIDE

GUILFORD, CONNECTICUT
AN IMPRINT OF GLOBE PEQUOT PRESS

.

All the information in this guidebook is subject to change. We recommend that you call ahead to obtain current information before traveling.

INSIDERS' GUIDE

Copyright © 2010 by Morris Book Publishing, LLC

Editor: Kevin Sirois
Project Editor: Lynn Zelem
Layout: Kevin Mak
Text Design: Sheryl Kober
Maps: XNR Productions, Inc. © Morris Book Publishing, LLC

ISSN 1529-174X
ISBN 978-0-7627-6015-2

Printed in the United States of America
10 9 8 7 6 5 4 3 2

For our good friend, Nancy Toppino, who loved the Florida Keys and Key West. She took pride in this guide, which she authored for many years. She was sweet, wonderful to work with, and one of a kind. We miss her dearly.

—The editors at Globe Pequot Press

CONTENTS

CONTENTS

Directory of Maps

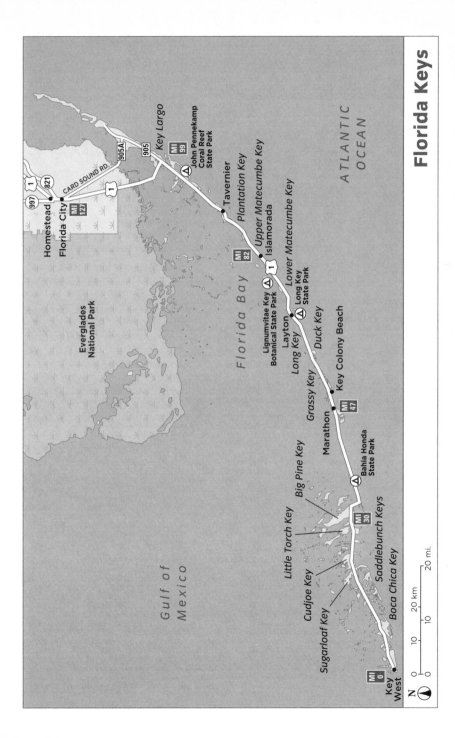

Florida Keys

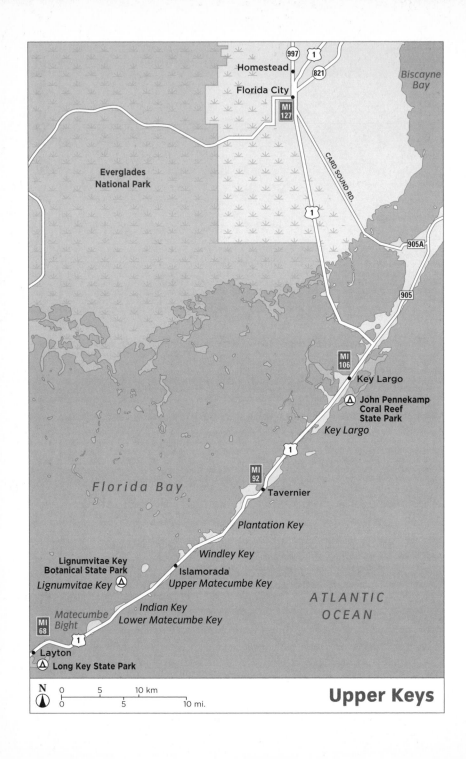

Upper Keys

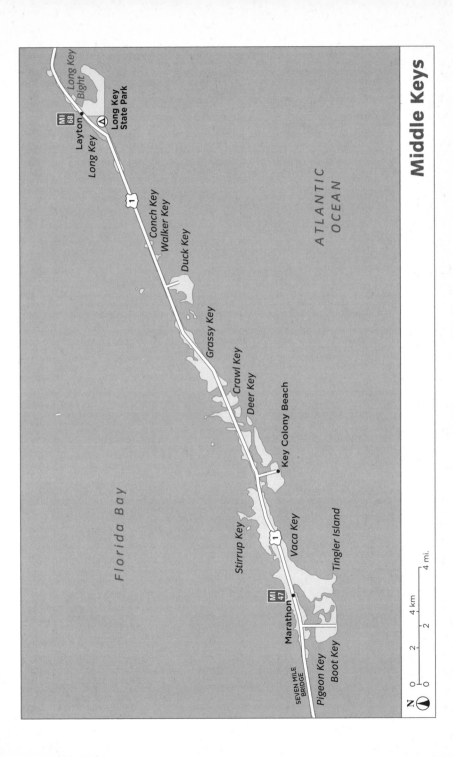

Middle Keys

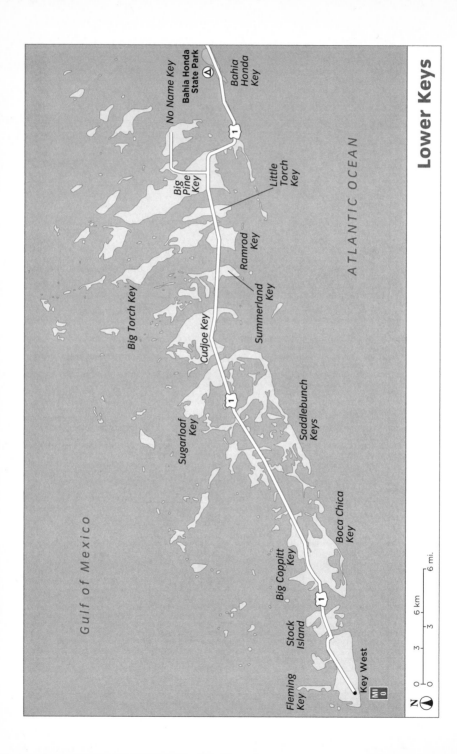

Lower Keys

Gulf of Mexico

Fleming Key

Stock Island

Key West

Big Coppitt Key

Boca Chica Key

Saddlebunch Keys

Sugarloaf Key

Big Torch Key

Cudjoe Key

Summerland Key

Ramrod Key

Little Torch Key

Big Pine Key

No Name Key

Bahia Honda State Park

Bahia Honda Key

ATLANTIC OCEAN

N

MI 0

0   3   6 km

0   3   6 mi.

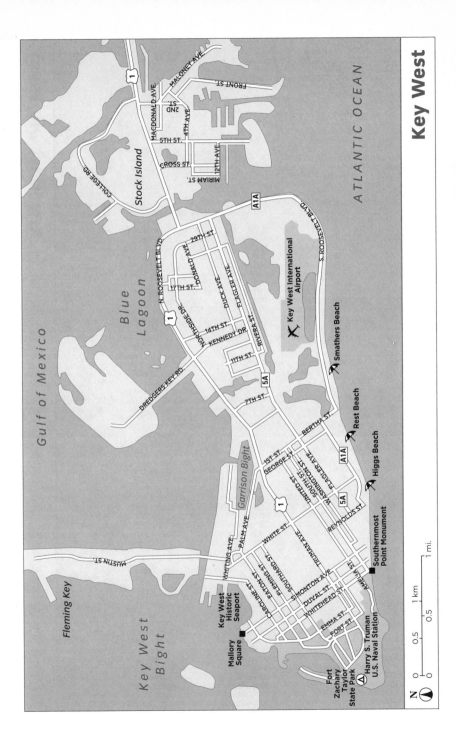

Key West

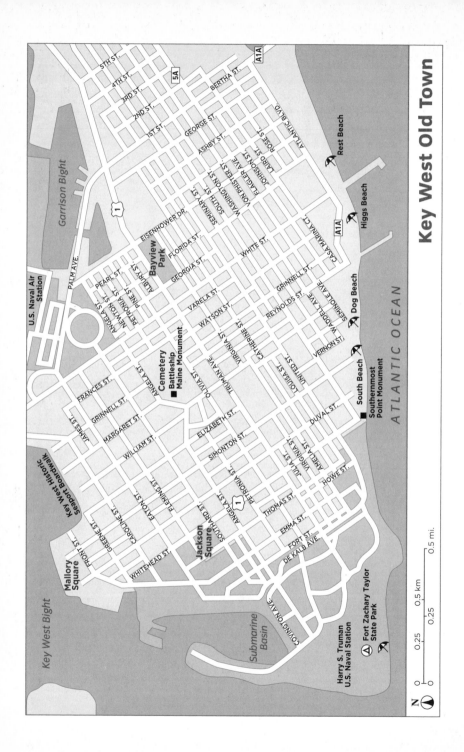

Key West Old Town

ABOUT THE AUTHOR

Juliet Dyal Gray is a native Floridian who writes about the Florida Keys for many national publications including *Delta Sky* magazine. Her writing career has taken her on many journeys including snorkeling around the islands of the Galapagos and on safari in South Africa. In addition to writing, Juliet also produces theater with Broadway Theatre Project. Juliet writes from her home in Key West, Florida.

ACKNOWLEDGMENTS

I am extremely grateful to the amazing people in the Florida Keys who tolerated and answered my many questions during the research of this book. My eternal thanks also to my family and close friends including my parents, Jake and Kay Dyal, and my husband, Christian Gray, for all their support. I am especially grateful for the wisdom of the late Nancy Toppino, without whom this book would not have been possible. As I continue to live and work in the Florida Keys, I am also truly thankful to be a permanent Insider in Paradise.

—JDG

PREFACE

Forget the black-and-white world you leave behind. When you arrive in the Florida Keys, life suddenly turns into Technicolor, and it doesn't take a twister to lead you to the lush Emerald City of Oz. Settle yourself in. Take Toto along, too.

Nowhere else on earth is there an Eden such as ours, where all are admitted freely and via so many varied means. Ours is the land of dreamers, doers, and do-si-doers, of train makers, treasure trovers, and time-honored tranquility. There are no Munchkins along the yellow brick road that unites each of our magical isles and then appends us to the mainland. In the Florida Keys everyone and everything is larger than life.

Look closely, and the enigmatic view from afar becomes as lucid as the crystalline waters of the Atlantic Ocean and the Gulf of Mexico that envelop us. From coconut palms to cormorants, you'll see that we are more than the Duval Street party scene in Key West. We are angelfish and anemones, gorgonians and groupers, lobsters and lizardfish, sponges and stone crabs. We're a thriving city of marine creatures commuting daily from North America's only barrier reef, approximately 6 miles offshore, to sweeping underwater meadows of turtle grass near shore where we forage and feed.

By day we are the golden sun that rises over the ocean, glows brightly, and then, in ardent shades of red, dips ever-so-gently beneath the gulf horizon. As darkness enfolds the Florida Keys, we are the cornucopia of stars that seem to gleam more brilliantly here in our endless skies than anywhere else.

We are a necklace of tiny pearl islands tenuously strung together by 42 majestic bridges and the dream of one man, Henry Morrison Flagler. We're divers and diesel mechanics, anglers and archaeologists, sailors and salvagers, cruisers and commercial fishermen, boaters and bartenders, gunkholers and guides, restaurateurs and real estate agents, hoteliers and hostesses. And our heart is in the sea.

We are hardwood hammocks, tropical pinelands, and mangrove islets. Unique in the universe, we are diminutive key deer, sour key limes, and endangered Key Largo wood rats. We are nesting great white herons, communal white pelicans, and showy roseate spoonbills. Creatures great and small, we are bonefish and billfish, sharks and stingrays, sea turtles, manatees, and dolphins. And because we vigilantly guard our copious treasures, we are the Florida Keys Wild Bird Center, Reef Relief, the Turtle Hospital, The Nature Conservancy, and the Reef Environmental Education Foundation. At last we have a brain.

Whether you mistakenly believe that you lack a heart . . . a brain . . . the nerve . . . you're sure to unearth it all, along with a deeply enriched spirit, on your journey through the mysteries, rich history, and legends of the Florida Keys. Experience all the marvels of this awe-inspiring Oz. You'll never want to click your ruby slippers, sandals, or bare feet—or board a plane, boat, or automobile—heading for home. One visit is, after all, what led so very many of us to become Insiders. Welcome to this side of the rainbow. We are the Florida Keys.

HOW TO USE THIS BOOK

Here at the southernmost tip of the continental United States, the serpentine Overseas Highway fuses many of our 800-plus islands with ligaments of vaulted bridges and concrete connective tissue.

Ours is a marriage of land and sea. To merely introduce you to the topside society of the Florida Keys would neglect the flamboyant and fascinating communities living below. This guide lifts the curtain, bringing the many facets of our watery stage to life. We treat you to our unique geology and colorful history. We introduce you to the flora and fauna of the habitats of our tropical ecosystem. And we take you where you may have never been before—fishing, diving, and boating in our waters.

We'll help you sate your appetite with listings of restaurants, seafood markets, and specialty food shops. We'll show you where the action is with the rundown on attractions, recreation sites, festivals and special events, and nightlife of the Keys. We'll offer myriad alternatives for you to rest your weary head: hotels, motels, inns, guesthouses, and condos; campgrounds; even resort marinas and anchoring-out spots for your motor or sailing yacht. Landlubber or seafarer, everything you need to know is in the *Insiders' Guide to Florida Keys and Key West*.

One thing you can count on about the Florida Keys is that the people living in Paradise, while seemingly laid back, are actually extremely pro-active and easily galvanized when it comes to defending our fragile ecosystem. For example, when news of the Gulf Oil Spill hit the Keys in 2010, locals created adopt-a-mangrove and shore watch volunteer groups to keep the areas clean and report any oil sightings in the area. Many also took Hazardous Waste Operations and Emergency Response Standard courses so they would be authorized to volunteer in case an oil cleanup was necessary. Throughout the threat of the oil spill, the Florida Keys remained in business and hopeful that the currents would not bring the deadly oil to our pristine waters. To learn more about the oil spill and its effects on the Florida Keys, visit www.fla-keys.com/oilspill or www.noaa.gov.

To navigate this book, begin with the assumption you are traveling "down the Keys," that is, from Key Largo to Key West. We have organized our information by descending mile marker. Mile markers are those small green signs with white numbers you'll see posted at the sides of the Overseas Highway (US 1). We have designated mile-marker addresses as either oceanside (on your left as you travel down the Keys) or bayside (on your right as you go toward Key West). At Key West, which is MM 0, locations are stated using street names.

Most chapters have several parts. A general preface to the subject matter acquaints you with aspects of the topics common to all areas of the Florida Keys. This is followed by specifics for the Upper Keys (MM 106 on Key Largo to MM 70 on Long Key), Middle Keys (MM 70 to MM 39 on Ohio Key), Lower Keys (MM 39 to Stock Island), and finally Key West, the entrance to which is actually about MM 5 on Stock Island, although mile marker appellations are not used in Key West.

When making phone calls from outside the area, note that the area code in the Florida Keys is 305. When using the main local carrier, BellSouth, you can call anywhere in the Florida Keys at no charge.

Throughout all the chapters we have sprinkled Insiders' tips, extracted from those in the know (with a little arm-twisting). You'll find enlightening Close-ups chock-full of information on everything from where to find the best food festivals to details about our amazing and rich history. And just so you will be sure to understand the language, we have included a glossary of Keys-speak.

Moving to the Florida Keys or already live here? Be sure to check out the blue-tabbed pages at the back of the book, where you will find the **Living Here** appendix that offers sections on relocation, real estate, retirement, education, health care, and media.

You hold in your hand a passport to the Florida Keys. We help you hit the road, explore the sea, and speak the language of the natives. Locals call this Paradise. Judge for yourself.

HISTORY

The saga of the Keys, like the livelihoods of its inhabitants, tethers itself first, foremost, and forever to the sea. Our fragile strand of coral beads, which arcs southwest from the U.S. mainland to within 100 miles of Cuba, has been for eons at the mercy of the elements. Nature determined, more than humans ever did, the course of our history. That is, until one man accomplished what natural forces could not: He connected the islands to each other and to the mainland United States.

We will chronicle the Florida Keys, therefore, as a man-made triptych, highlighting the eras before, during, and after Henry Flagler's Florida East Coast Railroad Extension refashioned the subsequent history of the region.

PROLOGUE
Native Americans and the Spanish

The earliest recorded evidence of a Native American population in the Keys is estimated to be around A.D. 800, when maritime Indians populated the islands. Kitchen middens, or mounds of fish and sea-turtle bones and conch shells, can be found throughout the Keys. Archaeologists believe that although ancient villages may have existed thousands of years before this time, the rising sea level has buried these settlements beneath the ocean.

Historians cannot agree on which tribes of **Native Americans** inhabited the Florida Keys in the ensuing centuries. The Tequestas, Calusas, Matecumbes, Caribbean Island tribes, and Seminoles from the mainland are all mentioned, although no archaeological evidence is conclusive. Widely accepted, however, is the notion that the Native Americans were seafarers by necessity and initially friendly to the white explorers they encountered.

Ponce de León garnered the credit for naming the Florida Keys "Los Martires" in 1513 during his exploration of the Gulf of Mexico. Legend maintains that the string of rock islands looked to him like suffering martyrs from his vantage point at sea. The Spanish took interest in the Native Americans of Los Martires in the centuries that followed but had no desire to seize their rocky islands. Priests from Havana attempted to convert the Native Americans to Catholicism. Some say this was an attempt not to save their souls but to teach them to be friendly to the crews of the Spanish ships and to hate the French and English, Spain's enemies who also were attempting to explore the New World. Spain's overriding interest in the Florida Keys at this time simply was to protect their fleet of treasure ships voyaging past its shores en route from Mexico and Cuba to the mother country.

The Gulf Stream: Treasure Highway

Long before the Overseas Highway became the main road of the Florida Keys, another highway controlled the islands' destiny: the great, blue river-in-the-Atlantic—the **Gulf Stream.** (The warm water of the Gulf Stream, the temperature of which varies greatly from surrounding waters, flows in a northerly direction between the Keys and Cuba, up the northeast coast of the United States, and then turns toward the east where it crosses the Atlantic Ocean to the European continent.) **Conquistadores, explorers,** and **adventurers** capitalized on the pulsing clockwise current (2 to 4 knots) to carry them swiftly back to Europe, where they unloaded the harvested riches of the New World at the feet of greedy monarchs.

The **Spanish** were the first to send their treasure-laden ships on this precarious route past our island chain, which is protected from the ocean's fury by a barrier coral reef (see the Diving and Snorkeling chapter). The Gulf Stream, which is not a definitive channel, winds an uneven course about 45 miles wide just outside the reef. Bad weather or bad judgment dashed the hopes, dreams, and cargo of hundreds of ships against this unforgiving coral graveyard.

It was the Native Americans who initially took advantage of this unexpected shipwrecked bounty, but **salvaging** became big business in the Keys with the arrival of the **Bahamian Conchs** (see The Wrecking Industry in this chapter). The passing ships inspired piracy from many nations, particularly the English, who lurked in the cuts and channels between the islands waiting to raid the ships' caches of gold and silver.

The Native Americans learned the ways of the Europeans, trading with the Spanish in Havana by means of large oceangoing canoes, pirating English ships, and free-diving to salvage the cargo of their wrecked vessels. The white man's diseases, however, greatly reduced Native American numbers. In 1763 Spain gave Florida to England in exchange for Cuba. At this time the last of the indigenous Native American families fled to Havana, fearing retribution for the cruelty they had heaped upon the British sailors found dashed upon the reef and stranded.

Key West

A time-honored story persists that warring tribes of mainland **Seminoles** and island **Calusas** had one final battle on the southernmost island of our chain of keys. Spanish conquistadores purportedly found the island strewn with bleached bones of the Native Americans and called the key **Cayo Hueso** (pronounced KY-o WAY-so), or "island of bones." Bahamian settlers pronounced the Spanish name as **Key West.**

Settled long before the other keys in the chain, Key West was very much a maritime frontier town by the 1820s, booming with sea-driven industries. Ships sailing out of Key West Harbor set across the Florida Straits to Havana, their holds filled with the fish, sea turtles, and sponges harvested along the length of the Keys. A lively fishing trade with Cuba continued into the 1870s. The melting pot of Key West included seamen from many cultures: African-American Bahamians, West Indian African Americans, Spanish Cubans, and white Bahamians of English descent.

Key West was incorporated in 1828. Within 10 years it was the largest and wealthiest city in the territory of Florida, even though it could be reached only by ship, a geographic fact of life that continued until **Henry Flagler's Florida East Coast Railroad Extension** was finished in 1912. But it was the very waters isolating Key West from the rest of the world that contributed to its wealth.

Piracy

When the United States gained possession of Florida and the Florida Keys in 1821, the island of Key West took on a strategic importance as a U.S. naval base. **Lieutenant Matthew Perry,** who was assigned to secure the island for the United States, deemed Key West a **safe, convenient,** and **extensive harbor.** It became the base of operations to fight the piracy that ravaged the trading vessels traveling the Gulf Stream superhighway and those heading through the Gulf of Mexico to New Orleans. English, French, and Dutch **buccaneers** had threatened the Spanish treasure galleons in the 18th century. In the early days of the 1800s, Spanish **pirates,** based mainly in Cuba, hid among the islands of the Keys and preyed on all nations, especially the United States. Using schooners with centerboards that drew only 4 to 5 feet of water, the pirate ships dipped in and out of the shallow cuts and channels to avoid capture.

i The battleship USS *Maine* sailed from Key West Harbor to Havana Harbor in Cuba, where the ship exploded and sank in 1898. The ship's gun site hood is located at the Florida Keys Historical Military Memorial at Mallory Square in Key West. Crewmen from the disaster are buried in the Key West Cemetery, and the investigation took place in the Key West Customs House.

In 1830 **Commander David Porter** was sent to Key West to head up an antipiracy fleet and wipe out the sea jacking from the region. Commandeering barge-style vessels equipped with oars, Porter and his crews were able to follow the sea dogs into the shallow waters and overtake them. After 1830 the area was safe from banditry once again.

The Wrecking Industry

Whereas the Gulf Stream was once the sea highway carrying Spanish treasure galleons back to Europe, in the 18th and 19th centuries the route was traversed in the opposite direction. Trading vessels sailed from New England ports to the French and British islands of the West Indies and the Antilles, hugging the shoreward edge of the Gulf Stream so as not to have to run against its strong northerly currents. They often ran aground on the reef, giving birth to a lucrative **wrecking industry** that salvaged silks, satins, lace, leather, crystal, china, silver, furniture, wine, whiskey, and more.

After the United States took possession of Florida in 1821, Key West became an official wrecking and salvage station for the federal government, which sought to regulate and cash in on the lucrative trade that until this time was going to Nassau or Havana. Salvage masters had to get a license from a district court judge, proving that they and their salvage vessels were free of fraud. By 1854 wrecking was a widely practiced profession in the Keys. Fleets of schooners patrolled the Keys from Biscayne to the Dry Tortugas. First they would assist the shipwrecked sailors, then try to save the ship (there was no Coast Guard in those days).

Unlike early unregulated times, the wreckers couldn't just lay claim to the ship's cargo for themselves. They were paid off in shares of the bounty. During peak wrecking years, 1850 to 1860, nearly one ship per week hit the reefs, some with cargo valued in the millions of dollars.

Although by 1826 some of the reefs along the length of the Keys were marked by lighthouses or lightships, most remained treacherous and claimed many cargoes, particularly in the Upper Keys where the Gulf

Stream meanders close to the reef. Stories have endured throughout the years that some of the more enterprising and unscrupulous wreckers even changed or removed navigational markers or flashed lights in imitation of a lightship to lure an unsuspecting vessel to its demise on a shallow shoal so they could salvage the cargo. The construction of additional **lighthouses** along the reef in the mid-1800s improved navigation to the point that the wrecking industry gradually faded away by the end of the 19th century.

Sponging

Sponging developed quickly in the Keys after the area became part of the United States, maturing into a commercially important industry by 1850.

Sponge harvesting initially was accomplished from a dinghy: One man sculled while the other looked through a glass-bottomed bucket. The spotter held a long pole with a small, three-pronged rake on one end used to impale the sponge and bring it into the boat. On shore the sponges were laid on the ground to dry in the sun so that the living animal within would dehydrate and die. The sponges then were soaked for a week and pounded on a rock or beaten with a stick to remove a blackish covering. Cleaned of weeds, washed, and hung to dry in bunches, the sponges were displayed for sale.

Cubans, Greeks, and **Conchs** harvested the sponges as fast and furiously as they could, with little regard for how the supply would be maintained, and it inevitably began to diminish. The Greeks began diving into deeper waters for the sponges, much in demand on the world market by 1900, and eventually moved to Florida's west coast at **Tarpon Springs,** where the sponging was more bountiful.

By 1940 a blight had wiped out all but about 10 percent of the Keys' sponge population. Although sponges again grow in our waters, commercial sponging is no longer a viable industry as synthetic sponges have absorbed the market.

i The colorful history of the Florida Keys comes alive at www.mile-markers.org in a marvelous virtual road trip. Learn about the people, places, and history of the Keys through photos and postcards. This fascinating presentation of history and legend comes courtesy of the Monroe County Public Library, Florida International University, the Florida Center for Library Automation, and the Historic Florida Keys Foundation.

Cubans and the Cigar Industry

Cuba, closer to Key West than Miami is, has always played a role in the historical evolution of the Keys. Cuban fishermen long frequented the bountiful Keys waters, and in the 19th century, Cuban émigrés brought new life and new industry to Key West. **William H. Wall** built a small **cigar** factory in the 1830s on Key West's Front Street. It was not until a year after the Cuban Revolution of 1868 when a prominent Cuban by the name of **Señor Vicente Martínez Ybor** moved his cigar-making factory to Key West from Havana, that the new era of cigar manufacturing began in earnest.

E. H. Gato and a dozen or so other cigar-making companies followed Martínez Ybor. And an influx of Cuban immigrant cigar workers "washed ashore," joining the melting pot in Key West. **Tobacco** arrived in bales from Havana, and production grew until factories numbered 161, catapulting Key

West to the rank of cigar-making capital of the United States. Though the manufacturers moved their businesses to Key West to escape Cuban **tariffs** and the cigar-makers' union, the unions reestablished themselves in Key West by 1879, and troubles began anew.

The industry continued to flourish in Key West until its peak in 1890, when the city of Tampa offered the cigar manufacturers lower taxes if they would move to the **Gulf Coast swamplands,** an area now called **Ybor City.** With this incentive, the cigar-making industry left the Keys, but many of the Cuban people stayed, creating a steady **Latin influence** on Key West that has endured to this day.

The Salt Industry

Early settlers of Key West and Duck Key manufactured **sea salt** beginning in the 1830s, using natural salt-pond basins on both islands. Salt was essential for preserving food in those days because there was no refrigeration. Cut off from tidal circulation except during storms, the **salt ponds** were flooded with seawater and then allowed to evaporate. The resulting **salt crystals** were harvested.

Capricious weather often flooded the salt ponds with fresh water, ruining the salty "crop." By 1876 the salt industry no longer existed in the Keys. The destructive forces of repeated hurricanes made the industry economically unfeasible.

Homesteading the Keys

Bahamians also homesteaded other keys in the early 19th century, settling in small family groups to farm the thin soil. Familiar with cultivating the unique land of limestone islands, the Bahamians worked at farming **pineapples, key limes,** and sapodillas, called **"sours and dillies."**

Many believe **Indian Key** was the first real settlement in the Upper Keys. By 1834 it had docks, a post office, shops, and a mansion belonging to the island's owner, **Jacob Housman.** It became the governmental seat of Dade County for a time, but attacks from mainland Native Americans proved an insurmountable problem for this little key (see the Attractions chapter). Through the ensuing decades, Bahamian farmers homesteaded on **Key Vaca, Upper Matecumbe, Newport** (Key Largo), **Tavernier,** and **Planter.** By 1891 the area that is now **Harry Harris Park** in Key Largo had a post office, school, church, and five farms (see the Recreation chapter).

The census on any of these keys varied widely over the course of the century, and little is known as to why. For instance, Key Vaca had 200 settlers in 1840, according to Dr. Perrine of Indian Key, but by 1866, a U.S. census revealed an unexplained population of zero for Key Vaca.

i Key West was once the largest manufacturer of cigars in the United States. In 1915 Key West had 29 cigar factories, employing 2,100 workers, who hand-rolled 62,415,000 stogies from imported Cuban tobacco.

FLAGLER'S FOLLY: THE FLORIDA EAST COAST RAILROAD EXTENSION

The dream of one man changed the isolation of the Florida Keys for all time. Native New Yorker **Henry Flagler,** born in 1830 and educated only to the eighth grade, established the **Standard Oil Company** with **John D. Rockefeller** in 1870 and became a wealthy, well-respected businessman. In 1885 he purchased a short-line railroad between Jacksonville and St. Augustine and began extending the rails southward toward Miami, then only a small settlement.

Flagler's vision of his railroad project went beyond Miami, however. He wanted to connect the mainland with the deep port of Key West, a booming city of more than 10,000 people, in anticipation of the growing shipping commerce he thought would be generated by the opening of the Panama Canal in the early years of the 20th century. He may even have set his sights on eventually connecting Key West with Cuba.

i In 1885, a trolley line was established in Key West known as the Key West Street Car Association. The open-sided wooden cars had four benches and were pulled by two mules. In 1898, the Key West Electric Company bought the line and ran ten-bench cars that operated on existing broad-gauge tracks using power from a double-wired overhead system.

By 1904 the railroad extended to Homestead, at the gateway to the Keys. The year 1905 saw the commencement of what many perceived as an old man's folly: a **railroad** constructed across 128 miles of rock islands and open water, under the most nonidyllic conditions imaginable, by men and materials that had to be imported from throughout the world. Steamships brought fabricated steel from Pennsylvania, and cement from Germany and Belgium was used to create concrete supports below the waterline. Cement for above-water concrete came from New York State, sand and gravel from the Chesapeake, crushed rock from

the Hudson Valley, timbers and pilings from Florida and Georgia, and provisions from Chicago. Barges carried fresh water from Miami to the construction sites. Nothing was indigenous to the Keys except the mosquitoes and the sand flies.

By 1908 the **first segment,** from Homestead to Marathon, was completed, and **Marathon** became a boomtown. Ships brought their cargoes of Cuban pineapples and limes here, where they were loaded onto railway cars and sent north. (The railroad turnaround was at the current site of **Knight's Key** campground.) Railroad workers used **Pigeon Key** (see the Attractions chapter) as a base for further railway construction.

The 7-mile "water gap" between Marathon and **Bahia Honda** took some engineering prowess to overcome, and the completion of the project was severely hampered by several devastating hurricanes in 1909 and 1910. But on January 22, 1912, Henry Flagler—by then age 82—finally rode his dream from Homestead to Key West. He traveled across 42 stretches of sea, more than 17 miles of concrete viaducts and concrete-and-steel bridges, and more than 20 miles of filled causeways, ultimately traversing 128 miles from island to island to the fruition of his vision. He entered Key West that day a hero. He died the following year probably never knowing that his flight of fancy changed the course of the Florida Keys forever.

Flagler's railroad, called the **Key West Extension,** made Key West America's largest deepwater port on the Atlantic Coast south of Norfolk, Virginia. Trade with the Caribbean increased, and Key West flourished for 23 years, recovering from the loss of the sponge and cigar industries. The Florida East Coast Railroad Company completed construction of Key West's first official tourist hotel, the **Casa Marina,** in 1921. **La Concha** was built in 1928.

In 1923 Monroe County appropriated funds to construct a road paralleling the railroad. The bumpy rock road crossed Card Sound with a long area of fill and a wooden bridge. Half a dozen humpback bridges crossed the creeks and cuts on **Key Largo.** Extending the length of Key Largo, the road continued across **Plantation Key, Windley Key,** and **Upper Matecumbe.** At the southern end of our island chain, a narrow, 32-mile road connected Key West with **No Name Key** off **Big Pine Key.** A car ferry service provided the waterway link between the two sections of roadway by 1930, which traversed what we now call the Upper and Lower Keys.

By 1934, the failing economy prompted the **Federal Emergency Relief Administration** to step in and they commenced development and promotion of Key West as a magnet for increased tourism in the Keys.

i It was in 1962, in the salt ponds near the Key West International Airport, the Casa Marina Hotel, White Street Pier, and Smathers Beach, that the U.S. Army poised Hawk missiles 6 inches above sea level. They were aimed at Cuba following the threat of nuclear war with Russia that threatened our nation. Once the threat was removed from Cuba, the sites were abandoned in 1979. Traces of old bunkers, buildings, and towers still exist. Go to www .missilesofkeywest.com for more on this scary event in recent American history.

To that end, developers began building bridges to connect the **Middle Keys** to each other and to the two sections of finished roadway. A "bonus army" of World War I veterans was employed to accomplish this momentous task. However, in 1935 Mother Nature reasserted her authority and once again charted the destiny of our islands. On Labor Day, what today we would call a **Category Five hurricane** hit the Upper and Middle Keys, destroying much of Flagler's railroad. Hundreds of lives were lost when the 17-foot storm surge hit the crew working on a bridge at Islamorada.

Because of mismanagement and lack of foreign freight heading northward from Cuban and Caribbean ports, the railroad was already in receivership. The railroad chose not to rebuild, citing financial difficulties. By this time it had become cheaper to haul cargo by truck than by train. The county's **Overseas Road and Toll Commission** purchased the right-of-way from the Florida East Coast Railroad and converted the single-track railway trestles, which remained intact after the hurricane, into two-lane bridges for automobiles. The highway from Homestead to Key West opened for traffic in 1938.

EPILOGUE

In the late 1930s, the U.S. Navy, stationed in Key West, began construction of an 18-inch pipeline that carried fresh water from wells in Homestead to Key West. The naval presence in Key West grew with the beginning of **World War II,** when antisubmarine patrols began surveillance of surrounding waters. The navy also improved the highway to better accommodate the transfer of supplies for its military installation. The Card Sound Road was bypassed. The new road, which followed the old railroad bed, now is known as **the "Stretch."** By 1942 the Keys enjoyed fresh water and electricity service, and the **Overseas Highway** (US 1) officially opened in 1944, ushering in a new era of development that continues to this day.

After World War II the Florida Keys became more and more popular as a sportfishing destination, and fishing camps dotted the shores from the Upper Keys to Key West. Still a rather remote, primitive spot to visit, the Keys nevertheless continued to evolve into a desirable tourist terminus, and Key West burgeoned as a port of call. Also contributing to Key West's rebirth was the discovery of pink gold: shrimp. Fishermen who had caught a shark in the waters between Key West and the Dry Tortugas found the fish's stomach filled with large pink shrimp. This led to the discovery of a bountiful shrimping area off the Tortugas, and the Key West "pinks" shrimping industry was spawned in the Florida Keys. It is still a viable occupation as far up the Keys as Marathon.

From 1978 to 1983 the old rail-bed conversion bridges were retired. Modern concrete structures, some four lanes wide, now span our waters. Most mind-boggling as an engineering feat is the seemingly endless Seven Mile Bridge, which connects the once insurmountable watery gap between Marathon and Bahia Honda Key. Many of the old bridges have been recycled as fishing piers, but others still stand, abandoned and obsolete alongside their successors, crumbling reminders of the Keys' not-so-distant past.

By the 1980s the Florida Keys had emerged as a tourist-driven economy. Tourism remains the major industry of the Keys today, with the water-based attractions of Key West topping the list of popular agendas.

Of growing concern is the effect the influx of visitors will ultimately have on the delicate balance of habitats within the tropical ecosystem of the Florida Keys (see the Area Overview chapter). The jury is still out. Will humans or Mother Nature determine the postscript for Paradise?

AREA OVERVIEW

Make no mistake, the sea is in charge here and always has been. Throughout the ages, the fluctuation of the sea has determined the fate of the coral islands we call the Florida Keys and will dictate its future as well. Put into simple perspective, sea level has been rising for the past 15,000 years, and the rate appears to be increasing due to the long-range effects of global warming. Just imagine: A 6-foot rise in sea level would eliminate all of the Lower and Middle Keys except Key West. The Upper Keys, being somewhat higher, would escape extinction for a time. But if sea level increases by 15 feet, the string of islands known as the Florida Keys will be reduced to a couple of tiny islets, and the majority of Paradise will be lost once again to the sea.

To be in the Florida Keys is to become one with nature, for the Keys offer unparalleled opportunities to be in direct daily contact with her substantial bounty. You'll know what we mean the moment you crest the first of the 42 bridges now spanning our islands and feel the vast power of the surrounding seas. Gaze down on our string of coral pearls from the air and you'll see that the Keys look insignificant juxtaposed against the encompassing Atlantic Ocean and Gulf of Mexico.

Insiders' Guides to other locales will introduce you to the lay of the land. But to gain an understanding of our world, which we reverently refer to as "Paradise," you must be forearmed with the scope of our waters, for all things revolve around the sea here. We will acquaint you with our climate, weather, and the multiple interrelated habitats of our tropical ecosystem—the only such ecosystem in the continental United States.

HABITATS OF THE FLORIDA KEYS

The word *tropical* generally refers to plants and animals living in the latitudes between the Tropic of Cancer in the Northern Hemisphere and the Tropic of Capricorn in the Southern Hemisphere. The Florida Keys are somewhat north of the Tropic of Cancer, but the warming influence of the nearby Gulf Stream assures us the benefits of a tropical climate.

Our natural flora grows nowhere else in North America, and the combination of our eight interrelated habitats and the creatures dwelling therein is truly unique.

The Land

Hardwood Hammocks
When the coral reef emerged from the sea eons ago and calcified into limestone bedrock, floating debris accumulated on it, decomposed, and gradually evolved into a thin layer of soil. Seeds from the hardwood forests of the Yucatan, Honduras, Nicaragua, South America, and the Caribbean Islands were carried to the Florida Keys by the winds of hurricanes, the currents of the Gulf Stream, migrating birds, and eventually even

humans. Thus, the vegetation of the Florida Keys is more common to the tropical Caribbean Basin than to the adjoining temperate areas of mainland Florida.

Found throughout the Keys, these West Indian tropical hardwood hammocks nurture highly diverse communities of rare flora and fauna—more than 200 species—some found nowhere else in the United States. The hammocks (originally an Indian word meaning "shady place") also shelter a variety of endangered species.

Most of the hardwood hammocks of the Keys were cleared years ago to supply the wood for shipbuilding and home building and to clear the land for planting pineapples or citrus as a commercial venture. But several good examples of West Indian hardwood hammocks still flourish in the Keys. The largest contiguous hammock in the continental United States is on North Key Largo. Known as the Key Largo Hammock State Botanical Site, it encompasses 2,700 acres. A dense understory of plants, shrubs, and vines adapts to the shady conditions on the hammock floor. And wildflowers must reach for the sky under the shady foliage top hat of the hammock, often turning into creeping vines.

The Key Largo wood rat, an endangered species that looks more like a big-eared Disney mouse than a London sewer rat, joins the Key raccoon, the Key cotton mouse, opossums, gray squirrels, and an assortment of migratory birds amid the flora of the hammocks. The 16-inch-long rodent, found only in the hammocks of North Key Largo, has been dubbed a "pack rat" because it likes to collect empty shells, aluminum pop-top tabs, and the colorful rings from plastic milk bottles.

i With 42 bridges connecting the Florida Keys, 15 percent of travel time is spent on bridges. The longest bridge is Seven Mile Bridge and the shortest is Harris Gap Bridge, a mere 37 feet long.

The Pinelands

Pinelands in the Lower Florida Keys differ from the vast forests you may have seen in other areas of the United States. Adapting to growing conditions with limited fresh water, the tall, spindly trees are small in girth and sparsely foliated. Primarily found on Big Pine Key, these South Florida slash pines mingle with an understory of silver palms and brittle thatch palms, both of which are rare outside the Keys and protected under the Preservation of the Native Flora of Florida Act. Among the 7,500 protected acres in the Lower Keys, other pinelands grace No Name Key, Little Pine Key, Cudjoe Key, Sugarloaf Key, and Summerland Key.

The most famous pineland resident in the Lower Keys is undoubtedly the key deer, a subspecies of the Virginia white-tailed deer, found nowhere else in the world. These tiny deer, each about the size of a large dog, attempt to coexist with human inhabitants who have taken over much of the unpreserved woodlands of the Lower Keys. However, the diminutive animals frequently venture out of the woods and onto the Overseas Highway, where they are often struck and killed by vehicles. For that reason, speed limits through Big Pine Key are reduced (45 mph daylight, 35 mph nighttime) and strictly enforced by law enforcement officials.

In 1957 the National Key Deer Refuge was established in Big Pine Key to ensure a sheltered natural habitat for the endangered species. About 800 key deer exist in the Lower Keys today. The key deer feed on red and black mangroves, thatch palms, and a variety of native berries. While they can tolerate small quantities of salt in brackish water, fresh water is essential to their survival. No official records document the origin of the key deer in the Florida Keys, but it is widely believed they migrated from the mainland as white-tailed deer when the seas receded. When sea level rose again during the current interglacial epoch, the deer were trapped in their pineland habitat. Over time their diminutive stature evolved as an adaptation to their sparsely vegetated environment.

The Shoreline

Mangrove Habitats

Called the island builders, mangroves comprise the predominant shoreline plant community of the Florida Keys, protecting the landmass from erosion. Able to establish itself on the coral underwater bedrock or in the sand, the mangrove's root structure traps, holds, and stabilizes sediments. Over time the infant mangrove habitats establish small islets such as those you'll see peppering Florida Bay and the oceanside near-shore waters. Mangrove habitats bordering the Keys filter upland runoff, maintaining the water quality of our seas.

The leaf litter that falls from the red mangroves decomposes in the tangle of its prop roots, forming a critical base in the food chain that supports the myriad species of the marine community inhabiting shoreline waters. Important as a breeding ground and nursery for juvenile spiny lobster, pink shrimp, snook, mullet, tarpon, and mangrove snappers, the mangroves also shelter these sea creatures from their predators. (See the Diving and Snorkeling chapter and the Fishing chapter for more on the fascinating underwater creatures living here.)

Great rookeries of wading and shorebirds roost and nest on the canopy of broad leaves of the mangrove habitats, creating a virtual aviary in every uninhabited islet (see the Gunkholing section in this chapter for our bird-watching primer). Three kinds of mangroves thrive in the Florida Keys. The distinctive high-arching prop roots of the red mangrove enable the plants to exchange gases and absorb oxygen from the seawater. Long, pencil-like seedpods, called propagules, develop during the summer and drop off the mangroves in the autumn, floating upright hither and yon with the tides. Eventually snagged on a branch or caught against a rock, the seedling establishes itself by growing prop roots, and a key is born.

The black mangrove, with dark, scaly bark, grows in the high-tide zone. The white mangrove, smallest of the three species, looks like a shrub with broad, flat, oval leaves and grows above the high-tide line along with stands of buttonwood trees.

> **i** Cuba is closer to Key West than Miami is. Cuba sits roughly 90 miles off the southern tip of Key West, while Miami is 130 miles north of "the Rock."

Sand Beach Habitats

Most of the islands of the Florida Keys have a limestone rock shoreline, but Long Key, Bahia Honda Key, and small portions of the shoreline of Lower Matecumbe have beaches of sand consisting not of quartz but of tiny fossils. These minuscule remains of calcareous, lime-secreting marine plants and animals are broken down by wave action upon the sea bottom. Only keys that have a break in the offshore reef line or are near a deep tidal channel receive enough sediment to build a natural beach. Fronted in most cases by beds of sea grass, the Keys' beaches always have a "weed line" on shore made up of remnants of turtle grass, manatee grass, or sargassum weed washed up with the tide.

The natural beaches of the Keys don't have sand dunes but rather more bermlike mounds. Sea oats grow in the sand, helping to hold the particles together. State law mandates that you may not pick sea oats at any time.

i Mallory Square in Key West isn't the only public place to view our world-famous sunsets. Many ocean-going vessels offer sunset cruises and if you are a land lover, head up the Keys. On Big Pine Key, Bahia Honda State Park on the beach offers an unobstructed scenic view. Head on up to Marathon and stop at the entrance to the old Seven Mile Bridge for the nightly celebration where gazers can see the Florida Straits and the Atlantic Ocean.

The Sea

Sea-Grass Habitats

In the shallow near-shore waters of the ocean or Florida Bay, sediments build up on the limestone bedrock sea bottom, supporting a variety of sea grasses that perform an integral function in our tropical ecosystem. Sea grasses grow entirely under water, one of the few flowering plants to do so. Most prevalent of the sea grasses in the Florida Keys are the sweeping meadows of turtle grass, which have interlocking root systems that burrow as deep as 5 feet into the sediment. The wide, flat blades, often more than

12 inches long, break the force of the waves and slow current velocity.

The turtle grass traps marine sediments and silt carried in and out on the tides, allowing them to settle to the bottom. This natural filtration system clarifies the water and enhances coral growth in the nearby reef habitat. The sunken pastures of turtle grass and the less abundant shoal grass and manatee grass, which have rounded leaves and weaker root systems, become very dense, providing food and shelter for marine life at all levels of the food chain (see the Fishing chapter for more on the species dwelling within).

More than 80 species of resident and migratory coastal birds forage the sea grasses, feeding on fish and invertebrates of the habitat (see the Gunkholing section in this chapter for our bird-watching tips).

Hardbottom Habitats

Wave action and tidal currents sweep the limestone bedrock of the near-shore sea-bottom habitats nearly clean, permitting no sediment buildup. Algae, sponges, gorgonian corals, and stony corals attach themselves directly to the bedrock. Snapping shrimp often make their homes within the sponges; they make a popping sound with their large snapping claw to repel predators. More seaward of the near-shore waters, colonies of soft corals dominate the underwater hardbottom landscape. A feathery fairyland blooms like a backstage theater costume room.

Tentacled anemones also call the hardbottom habitat home and peacefully coexist with conchs and tulip snails, the spiral-striped, spindle-shaped mollusks. The much-sought-after stone crabs and juvenile spiny lobsters try to stay out of sight here (see the Diving and Snorkeling chapter). Boat wakes, anchor damage, and collection of sea creatures by divers and snorkelers threaten the hardbottom habitats.

Coral Reef

Extending 200 miles, from Fowey Rocks near Miami to the Dry Tortugas, our living coral reef habitat—the only one in the continental United States—is a national treasure. The reef, composed of the limestone remains of colonies of individual animals called polyps, plays host to an unbelievable assortment of marine creatures, fish, and vegetation (see the Diving and Snorkeling chapter and our Fishing chapter). The coral reef habitat, together with the mangrove and sea-grass habitats, is the breeding ground for 70 percent of the commercial fishing industry's catch.

This wave-resistant barrier, which protects the sea-grass meadows from erosion and heavy sedimentation, is particularly beautiful off the Upper Keys. The landmass of Key Largo shields the coral habitat from changing water temperatures and sediments that emanate from Florida Bay through the tidal channels of the Middle and Lower Keys. Though it rigidly protects the shoreline of the Florida Keys from tropical storms, the coral reef itself is a fragile habitat. Field studies since 1984 have indicated some coral die-off and the sometimes fatal bleaching or discoloration of the corals in select areas of the Keys' barrier reef. Excessive nutrients in the water due to land-based pollution will degrade water quality and foster the growth of algal blooms, which screen the sunlight, robbing the coral of the oxygen that is necessary for healthy development.

Humans constitute one of the reef's most destructive threats. Anchor damage, boat groundings, and snorkelers and divers touching, collecting, or stepping on the delicate organisms can cause injury and certain death to the reef. See Protectors of Paradise in this chapter for more information on how you can help preserve and protect our reefs while still enjoying them.

Bare-Mud and Bare-Sand Bottom Habitats

Along the barrier reef, skeletons of reef plants and animals form areas of open, bare-sand sea bottom, inhabited by species of algae, sea urchins, snails, clams, and worms that serve as the food train for visiting starfish, conch, and finfish. Similar belts or patches of bare-mud bottom habitats, both oceanside and in Florida Bay, support a like assemblage of marine creatures. Joining this group are burrowing shrimp, whose tunneled dwellings leave telltale mounds in the mud.

A Gunkholing Primer

Rachel Carson may have said it all in *The Edge of the Sea:* "I doubt that anyone can travel the length of the Florida Keys without having communicated to his mind a sense of the uniqueness of this land of sky and water and scattered mangrove-covered islands."

Nowhere will you be more aware of our quintessence than when you are gunkholing. Here in the Florida Keys, gunkholing simply means slipping off land in a small dinghy, canoe, sea kayak, or shallow-draft skiff equipped with a push pole and tranquilly gliding through our shallow, mangrove-lined inshore waters in search of sightings of indigenous birds and aquatic creatures. Though the dedication to spotting feathered friends may be referred to as "birding" or "bird-watching" in some areas of the country, here in the Keys another arena of fascinating marine creatures presents itself in the shallow waters of our flats. You can easily gunk-hole on your own without a guide, or you can sign up for a guided ecotour (see the Recreation chapter).

Hundreds of virgin mangrove islets sprinkle the inshore waters of the inhabited Keys, often serving as giant rookeries for shorebirds and wading birds that are attracted to the abundant chow wagon beneath the surface of the water. Look to our Recreation chapter for information on renting a kayak, canoe, or small skiff. See the Attractions chapter for descriptions of the wildlife refuges of the Florida Keys, many of which encompass myriad outlands. And most important, read on for a primer of the most frequently encountered species on a gunkholing expedition in our tropical ecosystem.

Nature's Aviary

When gunkholing around the mangrove islets in search of wild birdlife, be sensitive to the presence of nesting birds. Do not anchor within 200 feet of an island, and keep noise to a minimum so as not to frighten the birds. If you do happen to flush a bird from its nest, move away from the nest area so that the bird will swiftly return to guard its young. Here are several species you can expect to spot:

- **Brown Pelican**—Some say the brown pelican's mouth can hold more than its stomach can, but this common resident of the Florida Keys will push this theory to the limit given half a chance. The brown pelican will dive from 20 to 30 feet above the sea, entering the water like a competing Olympian and scoring with freshly caught fish every time. You'll see these cute, personality-packed

fish-beggars everywhere, especially hanging out at fishing marinas. Look for them on their favorite gravity-defying perches atop mangroves or feathery Australian pines.

- **American White Pelican**—With a wingspan of 10 feet, the white pelican is more than a bird of a different color. These winter visitors to the Florida Keys (they are frequently spotted in Montana in the summer months) live a much different lifestyle than their brown cousins. Completely white except for black-tipped wings and long yellow beaks, white pelicans live together in flocks in the uninhabited wild of the backcountry keys. The white pelicans, far from the panhandling ways of the browns, are cooperative feeders, congregating as a team on the water's surface and herding fish into an ever-narrowing circle where the group will dine. Look for white pelicans at Little Arsnicker or Sandy Keys in the Upper Keys backcountry.

- **Cormorant**—Cormorants by the thousands inhabit rookeries in the mangroves of the unpeopled islands. These large-bodied, hook-billed black birds, consummate fish-catchers all, will launch themselves in attempted flight at the first inkling of an approaching gunkholer, often hitting the water in a brief belly flop before gaining momentum to become airborne. Like the lesser-seen anhinga, or water turkey (more prevalent in the Everglades), the cormorant's plumage becomes waterlogged, which facilitates diving and swimming skills in its endless search for fish. You'll often see the birds perched on poles and buoy markers, wings outstretched in a drying maneuver. Cormorants swim with only their necks and heads visible above the water.

- **Snowy Egret and Great Egret**—Plume hunters nearly eradicated the egret population at the turn of the 20th century, for the birds' magnificent snow-white aigrettes were high fashion in the millinery industry. The egrets achieve their feathery plumage only in breeding season, so it was easy for the hunters to kill the birds in their nests. Both snowy and great egrets thrive once again in the Florida Keys. Distinguished from their cousins the great white herons, which also grace the shorelines of the Keys, the white egrets have black legs with yellow feet and black bills. Though both egrets display magnificent white plumage, the snowy egret is about half the size of the great egret.

- **Great White Heron**—Formerly considered a separate species from the great blue heron encountered in many parts of the United States, what we commonly call the great white heron is actually the white "morph," or color phase, of the great blue. Found only in the tropical ecosystem, this large white heron, more than 4 feet tall, is not as fearful of humans as other species, and is often seen in backyards and other inhabited areas. You'll be able to tell a great white heron from a great egret because the heron has long yellow legs and a yellow beak. The heron still-hunts for its food: Standing stiffly at full alert, the heron stalks a prey of fish, frogs, or lizards; it then stabs the prey with its beak, flips the prize whole into its narrow throat, and swallows it in one long neck-expanding gulp. Herons and egrets build their lofty stick nests atop the mangroves of remote rookery keys.

- **Roseate Spoonbill**—A rare sighting in the Florida Keys, the roseate spoonbill, or pink curlew, is more common in the upper Florida Bay near Flamingo in Everglades National Park. Like the great white heron and egret, it also was slaughtered to near extinction in the early 1900s for its brilliant pink plumage, which was used for ladies' hats. The roseate spoonbill moves its large spatulate bill from side to side under water in the shallows, searching for minnows and small aquatic creatures. This distinctive bird is costumed like a vaudeville dancer—pink body accented by an orange tail, a bare greenish head, bright red shoulder and chest patches, and a black-ringed neck.

- **White Ibis**—Common in the Florida Keys, the white-plumed ibis bears black-tipped wings, most apparent when spread in flight, a distinctive scarlet, down-curved bill, and red legs. You'll often see young ibises, which are brown, in a flock of their white brethren, searching for aquatic insects, crabs, shrimp, and small snakes. The ibis was once worshipped in Egypt as a bird-headed god, and the pharaohs were buried alongside a mummified ibis. Killing an ibis for any other purpose was an offense punishable by death.

- **Osprey**—The high platform-topped poles you may see along the Overseas Highway have been erected for the osprey, which builds its bulky nest atop, laying three eggs out of harm's way each breeding season. Look up when trying to spot these fish-eating birds in the wild as well, for their nests will be constructed on the very pinnacles of the trees. Resembling a bald eagle, the osprey can be distinguished by a black streak behind each eye.

- **Magnificent Frigatebird**—The graceful, effortless flight of the frigatebird, or man-o-war bird, often heralds fish below, for this coastal forager is constantly on the lookout for finned pleasures. Often known to harass other seabirds until they drop their catch, the piratical frigatebird catches the spoils midair. Having a wingspan greater than 7 feet, the frigatebird inflates its throat sac and floats on air currents, its deeply forked, scissorlike tail a distinctive sight.

- **American Bald Eagle**—Once endangered nearly to the point of extinction, American bald eagles have made a recovery all across the United States due to preservation efforts. Look for the bald eagle's distinctive white head and tail high in the mangroves of uninhabited keys in Florida Bay, where they build their nests. Fish dominate their diet, and it is not uncommon for the bald eagle to steal the catch of a neighboring osprey.

Nature's Aquarium

As you gunkhole through our shallow sea-grass, mud, sand, and hardbottom habitats surrounding mangrove areas of our uninhabited keys, you may observe life below the surface of the water. Be sure to wear polarized sunglasses and proceed in a shallow-draft craft.

- **Starfish**—Commonly adorning the sandy bottom areas or sea-grass meadows of the shallow waters are cushion sea stars, often referred to as "starfish." These heavy-bodied, orange-brown creatures with five thick, starlike arms don't look alive, but they are.

- **Loggerhead Sponge**—The most common sponge you will see from your small skiff or while snorkeling in these waters is the loggerhead sponge, a barrel-shape sponge easily identified by the dark holes in its upper surface.

- **Stingray**—This unusual creature, shaped like a diamond or disk, often lies motionless on the ocean bottom, partially buried in the sand. The ray has eyes and breathing holes on its topside, with its mouth positioned on the underside to feed off the seafloor. When frightened, the stingray will swim away, its huge, winglike fins flapping in gentle undulation.

- **Horseshoe Crab**—You'll quickly spot the distinctive spikelike tail and smooth, horseshoe-shaped body shell of this 300-million-year-old species as the crab forages the sea-grass habitat for algal organisms.

- **Sea Turtle**—Keep a close lookout for the small head of the giant sea turtle as it pops out of the water for a breath of air. Loggerheads can remain submerged for as long as three hours. Green turtles, once commonplace here but overharvested for use in soup, for steaks, in cosmetic oils, and for leather, are rarely encountered today. The sea turtles' front appendages have evolved into flippers.

- **Manatee**—On a lucky day, you may catch a rare glimpse of the timid West Indian manatee, or sea cow, a docile aquatic mammal that likes to graze on the turtle-grass flats. The brownish gray manatee has armlike flippers, a broad, spoonlike tail, and an adorable wrinkled face. It can grow to 15 feet long, weighing in at nearly a ton. Protected as an endangered species, the manatee often rolls on the water's surface for air and cannot swim rapidly enough to avoid collision with oncoming boaters, a constant source of peril (see the Boating chapter for regulatory information).

- **Bottlenose Dolphin**—A more frequent sight on a gunkholing excursion is that of bottlenose dolphins, which you probably remember as the "Flipper" performers of marine parks. Seen in free-swimming pods in open waters, the graceful dolphins undulate through the waves with rhythmic regularity, and they are sometimes curious enough to approach your boat.

- **Fish of the Flats**—Alert attention to underwater movements in the sea grass of the flats may net you a sighting of a baby black-tip or bonnethead shark, a nurse shark, barracuda, bonefish, and more. See The Flats section of the Fishing chapter for descriptions of the finned treasures lurking beneath the shallows.

WEATHER AND CLIMATE

The mild tropical climate of the Florida Keys has no equal in the United States. In fact, neither frost, nor ice, nor sleet, nor snow visits our islands.

Temperature

The proximity of the Keys to the Gulf Stream in the Straits of Florida and the tempering effects of the Gulf of Mexico dictate that average winter temperatures vary little more than 14 degrees from those of the summer months. Average year-round temperature is about 75 degrees. Cold, dry air moving down from the north in the winter is greatly modified by the gulf waters over which it passes. And southeasterly trade winds and fresh sea breezes keep summer temperatures from ever reaching the triple-digit inferno experienced by the Florida mainland. The water and land heat and cool at different rates, creating thermal currents that air-condition the Keys.

Rainfall

The Florida Keys experience two seasons: wet and dry. From November through April, the sun shines abundantly and less than 25 percent of the year's precipitation falls, usually associated with a cold front in the dead of winter. May through October is the rainy season, when nearly three-quarters of our annual rainfall occurs during brief daily showers or thunderstorms. But these percentages are deceiving; our climate is really quite dry. Average rainfall in the winter is less than 2 inches a month; summer months see closer to 4 to 5 inches of rain.

i The long blue line that divides part of the new Stretch from Florida City to Key Largo is not just any "blue line." Famed artist Wyland (a resident of Islamorada; see Arts and Culture chapter) was asked by the Florida Department of Transportation to choose a color for this otherwise dull 3-foot-high line of concrete. He chose "Belize Blue" from his personal color book, and explained that it represented the color of the Florida Keys.

Hurricanes

The piper must be paid for this idyllic climate, and hurricanes have always been a key ingredient in our tropical mix. The potentially deadly weather systems move westerly off the African coast during hurricane season (officially June 1 to Nov 30 but most prevalent in Aug and Sept) and generally turn north near the Lesser Antilles, often heading our way.

Hurricanes have been harassing visitors to our shores for centuries. In 1622 at least five ships of the Spanish Tierra Firma Fleet wrecked as a result of a hurricane west of the Dry Tortugas. One of the most famous of these ships, the *Atocha*, was discovered and salvaged in 1985 by Mel Fisher (see Mel Fisher Maritime Heritage Society and Museum in the Attractions chapter). The New Spain Armada suffered a fatal blow by a hurricane in 1733, when 17 of 21 galleons struck the reefs of the Upper Keys, spewing treasure cargo amid the coral.

Key West suffered a devastating hurricane in 1835, but the hurricane of 1846 is considered the city's most severe. Key West residents pluckily rebuilt after these hurricanes and through the repeated hammerings of 1909, 1910, 1914, and 1919. On Labor Day 1935, a Category Five hurricane tore through the Upper Keys and Lower Matecumbe, totally destroying the area, including Flagler's Florida East Coast Railroad Extension. Five hundred people lost their lives in the high winds and 7-foot tidal surge in Lower Matecumbe alone. Experts estimate that the Labor Day hurricane packed winds of between 200 and 250 miles per hour. In comparison, Hurricane Katrina's winds, which devastated much of Mississippi and Louisiana in 2005, hit 140 miles per hour at landfall.

On August 29, 1960, an African storm caused an airplane crash near Dakar, Senegal, Africa, killing 63 people. Three days later this storm system was officially named Donna by the National Hurricane Center, which was formed in 1955 in Miami. By September 9, Donna's eye, which stretched 21 miles wide, passed over the region, bringing horrendous winds that effectively leveled the area from Marathon to Lower Matecumbe. Tides in Marathon were more than 9 feet high, and the surge in Upper Matecumbe topped 13 feet. Tea Table Bridge washed out, the freshwater pipeline broke in six places, and electricity was out. Donna ranks among the most destructive storms in U.S. history.

Three hurricanes have hammered the Florida Keys in recent years. Hurricane Georges, a strong Category Two hurricane with sustained winds of 105 mph, wreaked havoc from the Middle Keys to Key West on September 25, 1998. The massive cleanup and repair effort took residents nearly a year, but courtesy of La Niña, a wet summer in 1999 restored most of the lost foliage to its former glory. Then on October 15, 1999, Hurricane Irene battered the Keys with 75 mph winds and dumped 10 to 20 inches of rain on the still-recovering islands. And on October 24, 2005, the Lower Keys had an uninvited tourist by the name of Wilma. This Category Five hurricane, with winds of 125 mph, inundated a large portion of the Lower Keys. An accompanying storm surge of 10 feet from the Gulf of Mexico flooded and destroyed everything in its path.

Visitors to the Florida Keys during hurricane season should heed official warnings to evacuate our islands in the event of a potential hurricane. Because we have only one main artery linking our islands to the mainland (the Overseas Highway), it takes 22 to 26 hours of crawling, bumper-to-bumper traffic to clear residents and visitors out of the Florida Keys. Officials warn that storm-watching during a hurricane is not a diversion to be considered here. A sizable hurricane will cut off all services in the Keys and communications to the outside world.

PROTECTORS OF PARADISE

The natural wonders that make up the Florida Keys have good friends in the following organizations, which oversee efforts to protect the region's environment as best they can.

National Marine Sanctuary

In 1990 President George H. W. Bush signed into law the Florida Keys National Marine Sanctuary and Protection Act, designed to protect our spectacular marine ecosystem. The resulting Florida Keys National Marine Sanctuary encompasses 2,800 square nautical miles, incorporating within its boundaries the previously formed Key Largo National Marine Sanctuary (1975) and the Looe Key National Marine Sanctuary (1981). The Florida Keys National Marine Sanctuary engulfs all of the Florida Keys, including the Marquesas Keys and the Dry Tortugas, and surrounding waters. In an effort to provide a secure habitat for the marine flora and fauna that make the Florida Keys so special, the protection act immediately prohibited oil drilling within the sanctuary and created an "area to be avoided" (ATBA) for large ships in our waters.

Ecologists hope that the access restrictions and activity regulations in select areas of the Florida Keys National Marine Sanctuary will help protect sensitive areas of the ecosystem. Furthermore, professionals feel that, with minimal human contact, areas of high ecological importance will evolve naturally and those areas representing a variety of habitats will be sustained. This zoning program will be monitored for revision every five years (see the Boating chapter for more information on specific regulations and restrictions). For more information, call the Florida Keys National Marine Sanctuary Headquarters at (305) 809-4700 or visit www .floridakeys.noaa.gov.

The Nature Conservancy

The Nature Conservancy established a Florida Keys program in 1987 to protect the health and extraordinary diversity of our tropical ecosystem. This nonprofit conservation group states its mission as "preserving plants, animals, and natural communities that represent the diversity of life on Earth by protecting the lands and waters they need to survive." The Conservancy's work includes monitoring, management, and stewardship actions in the water and on the land; advocacy efforts; and support for volunteer programs. The conservancy established the Florida Reef Resilience Program to develop strategies to improve the health of our fragile coral reefs. This program includes a coral restoration project, which, in addition to reseach, establishes underwater nurseries to help grow coral. As of this writing, four in-water coral nurseries exist, with more on the way in the coming years. For more information about the Nature Conservancy, please call the Keys program office at (305) 745-8402 or visit their Web site at www .nature.org.

Reef Relief

Reef Relief, a Key West–based nonprofit group of volunteers founded in 1987, works toward the preservation and protection of the coral reef habitat of the Florida Keys. The group's first project was to install more than 100 mooring buoys, which, when used properly, eliminate anchor damage at the reef. The Florida Keys National Marine Sanctuary maintains the mooring buoys.

Another part of Reef Relief's mission is public awareness and education regarding the living coral reef habitat. To this end, each year the organization sponsors a cleanup

Close-up

Sunrise, Sunset

In the Florida Keys we justifiably lay claim to the most spectacular sun awakenings and finales in the universe. Anglers rise early enough to witness the brilliant fireball burn its way out of the ocean, its igneous shafts dramatically piercing the clouds overhead. Divers relish the midday sun's intense rays, which light up the ocean waters like a torch, illuminating the colorful corals below. Sunbathers lie prone on pool decks and man-made beaches, soaking in the solar rays, storing up some much-needed vitamin D.

But our sunsets take center stage in the twilight hours. Both visitors and residents jockey for an unobstructed vantage point from which to watch the smoldering orange ball ooze into the sea like a sphere of molten lava. Flotillas of small boats drift anchorless in the gulf waters . . . waiting. Travelers pull their autos off the Overseas Highway and stand at the water's edge, their awestruck attention riveted on the setting sun. Key West even has a daily sunset celebration ceremony at Mallory Square, complete with fire-eaters, jugglers, and Keys buskers of every shape and description.

If you are vigilant, you may see the green flash, a brilliant, emerald-colored spark of light that occasionally appears just as the sun melts into the sea. The rare sighting lasts only a second or less and has inspired legends the world over. According to the *Boston Globe*, "The green color results from the refraction, or bending, that sunlight undergoes as it passes through the thick layers of atmosphere near the horizon. Blue and green wavelengths of light are refracted the most, just like in a prism, so the setting sun appears to have a very thin blue-green fringe on its top edge. This fringe is hidden by the glare from the rest of the sun until all but the last of the sun's rim is blocked by the horizon."

In the Florida Keys the sun sets over the Gulf of Mexico. The day must be clear, and the sun must meet the horizon through a cloudless sky to reveal the green flash. Although sighting a green flash is a singular phenomenon akin to spotting a comet or a shooting star, every sunset is reason for celebration in the Florida Keys.

campaign that attracts hundreds of volunteers. They comb shorelines and out-islands and dive the reef, collecting trash and storm-driven debris. For more information, contact Reef Relief Environmental Center and Headquarters, 631 Greene St., Key West, (305) 294-3100, www.reefrelief.org.

Turtle Hospital

Located near MM 48.5, Bayside, in Marathon is the famed Turtle Hospital, a turtle rapid-care center and recovery room run as a labor of love by Ritchie Moretti since 1986. In the winter of 2009 to 2010, the Turtle Hospital took in more than 200 sea turtles at one time, which were ailing due to the unseasonably cold weather. Local veterinarians volunteer their time, often performing complicated turtle surgery on fibro-papilloma tumors, impactions, and shell fractures caused by hit-and-run boating injuries. After surgery, the turtles are moved to the recovery room, some in outdoor tanks and the rest in the property's original saltwater pool.

i **Key West is famous for a lot of things and having a tree take national honors is just another feather in our city's cap. On the corner of Leon and Washington stands a green buttonwood (which is really an American sycamore) that is the largest in the country. For more information on the buttonwood, contact the Key West Garden Club at (305) 294-3210 or visit www.keywestgardenclub.com.**

More than 5,000 schoolchildren visit the Turtle Hospital every year, learning about the fascinating reptilian order *Chelonia*. The general public visits, too. The Turtle Hospital offers a 45-minute guided educational experience three times daily. The tour requires reservations and, since this is a working hospital, cancellations occur due to turtle emergencies and/or weather. For more information, visit www.turtlehospital.org or call (305) 743-2552.

GETTING HERE, GETTING AROUND

You are headed for the Florida Keys. Whether you travel by land, by sea, or by air, you must conform to some strict, uncompromising standards that your travel agent may have neglected to tell you.

First, remove your socks. You won't need them here. Don your shorts. They are *de rigueur*. Slip on those shades. How else can you see? And reset your watch. The pace is slower here—you're on Keys time now.

Things really are different here. Our single main street stretches 126 miles—from Florida City to Key West—and dead-ends at the sea. Our 42 bridges span the kissing waters of the Atlantic Ocean and the Gulf of Mexico, from Key Largo to Key West. And our Keys communities resound as distinctively as the ivories of a piano. So come on down. We're playing your song.

BY AIR

Commercial Flights

KEY WEST INTERNATIONAL AIRPORT
3491 South Roosevelt Blvd., Key West
(305) 296-5439
www.keywestinternationalairport.com
The facility doubled in size to 50,000 square feet in 2009 following an extensive renovation garnering a $31 million price tag. The airport can now accommodate many more passengers traveling in and out of the southernmost city. The Conch Flyer restaurant/lounge has propellers from actual airplanes hanging out of the wall. In back of the massive cocktail bar are loads of pictures and memorabilia of Key West history. The bar stools are designed with propellers as legs to support the seats. The food is really great, too. Although Key West is the Florida destination of choice for thousands of visitors each year, do not expect to arrive here via commercial jetliner. Air service to this island in the sun is of the commuter variety. The planes are small, and flights are often overbooked during peak seasons, especially in Jan and Feb, so be sure to arrive early to check in for your flight.

If you are meeting a flight, short-term metered parking is available. You may also park in the long-term lot. Weekly rates are available.

Avis, Budget, Dollar, and Hertz rental cars are available at the airport terminal; Alamo and Enterprise are just a courtesy call away (see listings in our Rental Cars section in this chapter). Whenever possible, make reservations for your vehicle in advance. Taxis stand by in front of the airport awaiting each flight, and many hotels offer complimentary shuttle service.

Flights into and out of Key West are provided by the following airlines:

- **American Airlines,** (800) 433-7300; www .aa.com
- **Cape Air,** (305) 293-0603, (800) 352-0714; www.flycapeair.com. Provides scheduled service between Key West and Fort Myers.
- **Continental Airlines,** (800) 523-3273; www.continental.com
- **Delta Air Lines,** (800) 221-1212; www .delta.com
- **SeaCoast Airlines,** (866) 302-6278; www .seacoastairlines.com. Provides scheduled service between Key West and St. Petersburg/Clearwater.
- **US Airways,** (800) 428-4322; www.usair .com

i A Russian–made 1972 Antonov AN-24 Air Cubana was hijacked from Havana in 2003 and flown to Key West by architect Adermis Wilson Gonzalez with 32 passengers aboard. Purchased by someone at auction, then left in airport storage for years, the plane is now used as a permanent training tool for airport emergency crews.

MIAMI INTERNATIONAL AIRPORT
4200 NW 21st St., Miami
(305) 876-7000
www.miami-airport.com
An international airport offering flights on most major airline carriers, Miami International Airport is accessible from either I-95 or Florida's Turnpike via Highway 836 and LeJeune Road. You can rent a car (see the listing in this chapter for contact information) and drive the distance to the Keys. Miami to Key Largo is approximately 60 miles; to Islamorada, 80 miles; to Marathon, 115 miles; to Big Pine, 130 miles; to Key West, 160 miles.

FORT LAUDERDALE–HOLLYWOOD INTERNATIONAL AIRPORT
100 Terminal Dr., Fort Lauderdale
(866) 435-9355
www.fortlauderdaleinternational airport.com
Smaller than Miami International, this airport off I-595 offers fewer flight options but is hassle-free when compared to Miami. To drive to the Keys from Fort Lauderdale–Hollywood International Airport, follow signs to Florida's Turnpike via I-595. Driving from Fort Lauderdale–Hollywood International Airport will add about 45 more minutes to your total trip.

Private and Charter Aircraft

AIR KEY WEST
3491 South Roosevelt Blvd.
(at Key West International Airport)
(305) 923-4033
www.airkeywest.com
Fully certified, licensed, bonded, and insured as an FAA air carrier, Air Key West can take you away to other U.S. cities, the Bahamas, or the Caribbean. This aircraft charter service offers affordable rates and professional, reliable service.

MARATHON JET CENTER
MM 52 Bayside, Marathon
(305) 743-1995
www.marathonjetcenter.com
Located at the west end of Florida Keys Marathon Airport, Marathon Jet Center is a flight-based operation that caters to general aviation and light aircraft. It offers a maintenance facility on the premises and sells 100 low-lead (LL) and Jet A fuel. Tie-down fees are charged per overnight or per month. Marathon Jet Center offers aircraft for rent and also gives aerial tours of the Middle Keys and the reef.

Directions to the Keys

Directions from Miami International Airport via Florida's Turnpike:

Take LeJeune Road south to Highway 836 West. As you approach the ramp, get in the right-hand lane. Be aware, however, that a frontage-road access just before the sign and arrow often lures confused first-timers into turning too soon. The ramp is actually just after the sign and arrow. Follow Highway 836 West to Florida's Turnpike South, Homestead. Continue on Florida's Turnpike until it ends in Florida City at US 1. Continue south on US 1 to the Keys.

from Miami through Card Sound and Barnes Sound and down the length of the Keys in the Florida Bay/Gulf of Mexico. Or parallel the oceanside shores following Hawk Channel, a well-marked route protected by the reef.

Long a bustling port, Key West Harbor is still busy—full of commercial traffic, tourist-filled tour boats, and visiting cruise ships. If you choose to navigate your motor or sailing craft to Key West from the Atlantic, come in through the main ship channel, which is marked S.E. CHANNEL on the charts. From the gulf take the N.W. Channel until it intersects with the main ship channel. You can anchor out in protected areas of the harbor or put into one of the comprehensive Key West marinas.

For complete information on arriving and vacationing on your pleasure craft, see our Cruising chapter.

SEACOAST AIRLINES
3491 South Roosevelt Blvd.
(at Key West International Airport)
(866) 302-6278
www.seacoastairlines.com

Enjoy flightseeing trips in a relaxed atmosphere on SeaCoast Airlines from Key West to St. Petersburg/Clearwater. SeaCoast Airlines also offers charters to other Florida cities.

BY SEA

Visit the Florida Keys as the pirates and buccaneers did before you: by sea. Revel in the beauty of these sea pearls, strung together by the wisp of the Overseas Highway. Your perspective of the Keys will be different when viewed from our waters. Navigate your motor or sailing craft through the Intracoastal Waterway, which extends

KEY WEST EXPRESS
100 Grinnell St.
(888) 539-2628
www.seakeywestexpress.com

Key West Express is a fun alternative for traveling to and from Key West for visits to Ft. Myers and Marco Island. Operating four vessels daily and offering the only high-speed ferry service to these points, you can stay for a few hours or a couple of days in these locations. Two vessels are docked in Ft. Myers under the San Carlos Sky Bridge, at Fishermen's Wharf; the 140-foot *Atlanticat Catamaran* has two enclosed, climate-controlled cabins, sundeck, satellite TV, full galley, and bar. The 170-foot *Key West Express*, with full state-of-the-art electronics and amenities, alternates trips but shares the same schedule as the *Atlanticat Catamaran*. They depart Ft. Myers at 8:30 a.m., arrive in Key West at noon, depart Key West at 6 p.m., and arrive at Ft. Myers at 9:30 p.m.

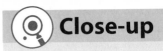 **Close-up**

Keys-Speak Glossary

backcountry—shallow sea-grass meadows and mangrove islet waters of Florida Bay

bayside—anything on the opposite coast from the Atlantic; for instance, Florida Bay in the Upper Keys, the Gulf of Mexico in the Middle and Lower Keys

bight—a body of water bounded by a bend or curve in the shore; several are found in Key West

bluewater—deep, offshore waters of the Atlantic Ocean

bubba—slang for best friend, buddy

chickee—an open-sided, thatched-roof hut commonly found near the water's edge that is used as shelter from the sun

coconut telegraph—local gossip about any subject, person, place, or thing

Conch (pronounced "konk")—a descendant of the original Bahamians who settled the Keys; a person born in the Florida Keys

conch—meat of a marine mollusk used in chowder and fritters; once a staple in the diet of early Conchs and Keys-dwelling Native Americans, now an endangered species that may not be harvested in the Keys

conch cruiser—a bicycle that is painted and decorated with outrageous artwork and embellishments

con leche—this is the fuel that keeps the locals humming: hot coffee with steamed milk and sugar

Duval crawl—the notorious bar-hopping Key West scene from one end of Duval Street to the other

Fat Albert—two large, white blimps tethered on Cudjoe Key (MM 23) that the U.S. Government uses to track aircraft, boat traffic (especially for drug enforcement), and weather by radar. Fat Albert is also used to broadcast TV Marti—a TV station targeted toward audiences in Cuba.

flats—shallow, near-shore waters of the Atlantic

freshwater Conch—a person who has lived in the Florida Keys for at least seven years

gunkhole—to explore the shallow, near-shore waters and mangrove islets in a shallow-draft craft in search of birdlife and marine species

hammock—an elevated piece of bedrock covered with a hardwood tropical forest; also a woven lounger strung between two palm trees

Keys disease—the party life in the Keys has a tendency to have a lengthy duration; starting early in the day to late at night, drinks and other vices can be a 24/7 lifestyle

mile marker or MM—the green-and-white signs along US 1 that mark miles, in descending order, from Florida City (MM 127) to Key West (MM 0)

no-see-ums—tiny, biting flies with a hot, painful stinging bite

oceanside—anything on the Atlantic coast of the Keys

Paradise—the Florida Keys

puddle jumpers—small commercial planes that fly in and out of the Key West airport and carry passengers to major airport hubs

the Rock—slang for the Florida Keys, usually uttered by locals heading for the mainland: "I need to get off the Rock."

the Stretch—this is not an aerobics move but the "stretch" of highway (US 1) that leads into and out of the Keys, from MM 123 near Florida City to MM 105 in Key Largo

Only in season, the 130-foot *Whale Watcher* is docked at the Marco River Marina, in Marco Island, with five jet drive motors, two climate-controlled enclosed cabins, sundeck, full galley, and bar. The ship leaves Marco Island at 8:30 a.m., arrives at Key West at 11:30 a.m., and leaves Key West at 5 p.m., arriving at home port at 8 p.m. There is a full galley and bar that is cash only aboard all of these vessels.

BY LAND

The Overseas Highway tethers our islands to the mainland like one long anchor line. Addresses along this common main street are issued by mile markers, designated as MM. Commencing with MM 126 in Florida City and culminating with MM 0 in Key West, small green markers with white numbers are posted every mile.

The Overseas Highway actually curves and drifts toward the southwest, rendering it all but impossible to refer to directions as "north to here" or "south to there." Here in the Keys everything is grounded by a mile marker, and you'll note that we orient most of the addresses we give in this book by mile marker.

As you head toward Key West, mile marker numbers descend in order. Anyplace on the right side of the road bordering Florida Bay or the Gulf of Mexico is referred to as bayside. The opposite side of the road, bordering the Atlantic Ocean, is therefore called oceanside. So addresses on the Overseas Highway will usually be referred to by both mile marker number and a bayside or oceanside distinction.

The old saying, "All roads lead to the sea," could very well have been written about the Keys. The occasional side street you might encounter on one of our wider islands—such as Key Largo, Marathon, or Big Pine

Key—will terminate at the bay, the gulf, or the ocean after only a few blocks.

Key West, the southernmost point in the continental United States, slumbers closer to Havana than it does to Miami—when it sleeps, that is, which is not all that often. In Keys-speak, this is where the action is.

Although nearly 28,000 people make Key West their home, this island still retains a small-town charm. The quaint Old Town area remains essentially a charming, foliage-canopied grid of streets lined with gingerbread-trimmed frame structures that evoke a succession of bygone eras and a cache of simmering secrets. This area, by the way, boasts the largest collection of frame structures in a National Register historic district of any city in Florida—nearly 3,000—and some architectural elements that are found nowhere else in the world.

The Mid Town area is predominantly residential. New Town takes in the shopping centers and fast-food and hotel chains along North Roosevelt Boulevard on the gulf side and across the island to the airport and beaches along South Roosevelt Boulevard on the Atlantic side.

Old Town, destination of choice for most visitors to Key West, is accessed from the Overseas Highway by either North Roosevelt Boulevard (US 1) to Truman Avenue or South Roosevelt Boulevard (A1A) along the beach to White Street. From White Street, Southard Street runs one way toward the heart of Old Town. Fleming Street is one way leading the opposite direction.

Old Town is anchored by Duval Street, which has been dubbed "the longest street in the world" because it runs from the Atlantic to the Gulf of Mexico. It is actually only a little more than a mile long. Although finding your way around Key West is not difficult, the narrow, often one-way streets—combined with a proliferation of tourist-driven rental cars and scooters in peak seasons—can make driving around this island both frustrating and time-consuming. Old Town is best explored on foot or by bicycle.

Key West provides public bus service and several other unique modes of transportation, which we describe in this chapter.

Rental Cars

Public transportation in the Keys is practically nil. You really need a car to get around, unless you are staying strictly in Key West. Most rental car agencies are at the airports in Fort Lauderdale, Miami, or Key West. Some pick up and deliver vehicles. Reserve your automobile before you arrive in the Keys—availability in peak seasons is often limited—at one of the following agencies:

ALAMO RENT A CAR
2516 North Roosevelt Blvd.
(888) 826-6893
www.alamo.com

AVIS RENT A CAR
3491 South Roosevelt Blvd.
(at Key West International Airport)
(305) 296-8744 or (800) 831-2847
www.avis.com

BUDGET CAR & TRUCK RENTAL
3491 South Roosevelt Blvd.
(at Key West International Airport)
(305) 294-8868 or (800) 527-0700
www.budget.com

DOLLAR RENT A CAR
3491 South Roosevelt Blvd.
(at Key West International Airport)
(305) 296-9921 or (800) 800-4000
www.dollar.com

ENTERPRISE RENT-A-CAR
2516 North Roosevelt Blvd.
(305) 292-0220 or (800) 736-8222
www.enterprise.com

HERTZ RENT A CAR
3491 South Roosevelt Blvd.
(at Key West International Airport)
(305) 294-1039 or (800) 654-3131
www.hertz.com

THRIFTY CAR RENTAL
3491 South Roosevelt Blvd.
(at Key West International Airport)
(305) 294-8644 or (877) 283-0898
www.thrifty.com

TROPICAL RENTALS
1300 Duval St.
(305) 294-8136
www.tropicalrentacar.com

Taxi Service

If you don't have your own automobile or haven't rented a car for the duration of your visit, you may find yourself in need of ground transportation within the Keys. Be aware that the fare could get pricey (sometimes approaching the cost of a daily rental vehicle), especially if you are traveling any distance. But if you need a lift, try one of these.

Upper Keys:
- **Key Largo Cabs,** (305) 451-9700 or (305) 852-8888
- **Mom's Taxi,** (305) 852-7999 or (305) 453-4049

Middle Keys (Marathon):
- **Action Taxi,** (305) 743-0077
- **On Time Taxi,** (305) 289-5656
- **Friendly Cab Company,** (305) 289-5454

Lower Keys:
- **Sugarloaf Key Taxi,** (305) 745-2319
- **Sunset Taxi,** (305) 872-4233

Other Key West Taxis:

- **A Airport Cab Company,** (305) 292-1111
- **Five 6's Cab Company,** who have "gone green" with hybrids, (305) 296-6666, www .keywesttaxi.com
- **Friendly Cab Company,** (305) 295-5555

i Everyone has heard of the Blue Ridge Parkway, Route 66 and the Las Vegas Strip. These are each designated as one of America's Byways, according to the National Scenic Byways Program—in 46 states there are 150 such roads. Now, US 1 has officially become one of America's Scenic Byways. Visit www.byways.org for more information.

Airport Limousine and Shuttle Service

In the event you are stranded without transportation to either of the mainland airports, alternative transport is available. These companies offer a variety of services, often also catering to private groups and functions. Prices and services vary, and the following are dependable options in the Florida Keys: **Keys Shuttle** (305-289-9997, 888-765-9997; www.keysshuttle.com) and **Sea the Keys** (305-896-7013; www.keywestdaytrip.com).

Bus Service

GREYHOUND BUS LINES
Miami International Airport, Miami
Key West International Airport, Key West
(800) 231-2222
www.greyhound.com
Greyhound bridges the gap in mass ground transit from Key West to Miami and beyond. Greyhound departs Miami International Airport for the Key West depot, which is housed in the Adam Arnold Annex at the airport,

usually twice a day, seven days a week, The trip will take 4 hours, 30 minutes from Key West to Miami International by Greyhound Bus. Fares to and from Miami International Airport depend on embarking and disembarking sites. Greyhound schedules and fares are subject to change. Be sure to confirm your specific travel arrangements when purchasing tickets.

DADE-MONROE EXPRESS
(305) 770-3131
www.miamidade.gov/transit
Miami-Dade Transit (MDT) provides bus service from Florida City to the City of Marathon at MM 50. The route designation is #301. Stops are Key Largo MM 95, Tavernier MM 90, and Islamorada MM 74.

LOWER KEYS SHUTTLE
(305) 809-3910
www.monroecounty-fl.gov
Lower Keys Shuttle operates between Key West and Marathon, connecting with the Dade-Monroe Express in the City of Marathon at MM 50. This provides the link between Key West and Florida City. Scheduled stops are Key West MM 3, Boca Chia MM 8, Big Coppitt MM 10, Bay Point MM 15, Sugarloaf MM 17, Cudjoe Key MM 22.5, Summerland MM 25, and Big Pine MM 30.

CITY OF KEY WEST DEPARTMENT OF TRANSPORTATION
627 Palm Ave.
(305) 293-6426
www.keywestcity.com
Public transport city buses circle the island of Key West several times a day along color-coded routes. Signs at all of the bus stops sport colored dots to indicate the routes they serve.

Remember that this is an island where the buses traverse in a great big circle. You simply cannot get lost if you stay on a particular bus since it will eventually return to the stop where you boarded it. For more information call the Key West Department of Transportation (KWDOT).

On weekdays, bus service starts as early as 5:30 a.m. and continues until 11:30 p.m.; on weekends and holidays, the hours may be shorter and the stops less frequent, depending on the route. A complete timetable and route map is available from KWDOT. "BOB" is the Bikes on Buses program. This allows customers to take their bicycles on the bus at no additional cost by securing them onto a bike rack attached to the front of the bus.

Alternative Key West Transportation

CONCH TOUR TRAIN
303 Front St.
(305) 294-5161 or (800) 868-7482
www.historictours.com/keywest
Take a train ride around Key West and travel through time as you learn about this historic city. Enjoy open-air seating with a personal narrative from the driver of the train. Departing every 30 minutes, the tour lasts 1.5 hours and there is only one stop toward the end of the ride. Adult tickets are $29, kids 4 to 12 years pay $14, and for kids under 4, the ride is free. Buying tickets online will save you about 10 percent. NOTE: The Conch Trains that you see chugging around town are bona-fide touring vehicles; you cannot get on and off a Conch Train at will. See our Attractions chapter for further information on this and other tours.

OLD TOWN TROLLEY TOURS OF KEY WEST
3840 North Roosevelt Blvd.
(305) 395-4958 or (800) 213-2474
www.historictours.com/keywest
Listen to a narrative of historic Key West on this continuous loop tour, learning as you go. Although this transportation option is promoted and sold as a 90-minute tour, with over 100 points of interest, you can hop on and off the trolley as many times per day as you wish. It's one hassle-free way to shop, dine, or take in the myriad attractions Key West has to offer.

You can park your car free at the Key West Welcome Center (3840 North Roosevelt Blvd., 800-284-4482; www.keywestwelcome center.com), where you can also buy tickets and board the trolley. Day-trippers will find the welcome center readily accessible upon entry into Key West. Bear right and follow the signs for US 1. The welcome center is on the left side of the road. Park your car, then grab a trolley and let your conductor spirit you around Key West. You can also pick up the trolley at Mallory Square beginning at 9 a.m. daily. The trolley disembarks at 12 different stops including Mallory Square, Historic Key West Seaport, Crowne Plaza La Concha, and the Southernmost Point. Trolleys stop at each location every 30 minutes.

i The Florida Keys have sights fit for a queen! In 1991, Queen Elizabeth II and Prince Philip spent a weekend cruising the Florida Keys on board their ship the HMY *Britannia*. In Key West, they toured Fort Jefferson National Monument at the Dry Tortugas.

Cost of the trolley tour is $29 per day for adults and teens, $14 for children ages 4 through 12. Children age 4 and younger ride free. Buying tickets online will save you about 10 percent.

Mopeds, Scooters, and Electric Cars

Key West is the perfect place to explore by moped or electric car, although we wouldn't recommend riding in the Mallory Square/lower Duval Street area or along North Roosevelt Boulevard, which are heavily congested with people, automobiles, and delivery trucks. The egg-shaped electric cars are eerily quiet and understandably slow. They seat two or four, have no doors, and top out at 25 mph, making them ideal for an island where the speed limits never go above 35. Many places rent a choice of mopeds, electric cars or bicycles by the hour, day, overnight, or week (see our Recreation chapter for information on bicycle rentals).

Some companies consider a daily rental to be 24 hours; others cap the day at 8 hours. Inquire when you call. Some rental agencies even have double scooters that seat two; it is illegal to carry a passenger on any other kind. The following Key West companies rent a full range of vehicles:

- **Adventure Scooter & Bicycle Rentals,** 611 Front St., (305) 293-9955
- **A & M Rentals,** 523 Truman Ave., (305) 294-8888
- **Moped Hospital,** 601 Truman Ave., (305) 296-3344
- **Pirate Scooter Rentals,** 401 Southard St., (305) 295-0000
- **Randall J's Scooter Rentals,** 505 Greene St., (305) 296-0208
- **Sunshine Rentals,** 1910 North Roosevelt Blvd., (305) 294-9990
- **Tropical Rentals,** 1300 Duval St., (305) 294-8136

PARADISE PEDICAB
401 Southard St.
(305) 292-0077
Take a tour of Key West the slow-and-easy way in a velotaxi, better known as a pedicab. These bicycle-powered vehicles are a great way to feel the warm breeze on your face and breathe in the tropical air as your cyclist narrates the sights. A most unique mode of transportation in this most unique town.

Are We Almost There?

Driving in the Keys takes time and patience. Speed limits are strictly enforced and in some areas, 45 mph is as fast as the law allows. Here are approximate drive times from various locations. (Please note that times may vary due to weather and road conditions):

Miami to Big
Pine Key . . . . 2.5 hours

Key West to West
Palm Beach. . . . . 5 hours

Key West to Miami. . . . 3.5 hours

Marathon to Orlando . . . 7 hours

Key West to Fort
Lauderdale . . . . 4 hours

Key West to Naples . . . 5.5 hours

For you road warriors:

Key West to Anchorage,
Alaska (4,020 miles) . . 81 hours

Foot Power

Strolling Key West is a great way to work off the pounds you'll be packing on by grazing the tempting kiosks, juice bars, ice-cream shops, restaurants, and, of course, bars of Key West. The sidewalk-lined streets in Old Town often front little-known lanes where unusual shops or galleries hide beneath ancient foliage. You'll miss these—and much of the mystery and charm of this southernmost city—if you don't get out of your car and walk a bit.

Key West Parking

Parking is plentiful and free of charge in the Keys, until you visit Key West. Ask any Key West local if there's a downside to living in Paradise and he or she will almost always complain about parking. There are simply too many cars in Old Town Key West and too few places to put them. And because the permanent population of this tiny island keeps growing and most visitors either arrive by car or rent a vehicle when they get here, the parking problem isn't going away anytime soon.

Patrons of the shops and restaurants in Duval Square (1075 Duval St.) will find free parking available in an adjacent lot accessed from Simonton Street. Free parking for patrons of some Duval Street restaurants, shops, and bars may also be available in designated lots off either Whitehead or Simonton Streets, both of which run parallel to Duval. Metered curbside parking is, of course, available on several downtown streets, including Duval, Whitehead, and Simonton, as well as along most of the streets that intersect them. Special curbside parking areas are designated for scooters and mopeds; do not leave vehicles on the sidewalk.

In the past, tourists who wanted to avoid feeding meters and didn't mind a little extra walk could simply secure a free curbside parking spot in the many residential Old Town neighborhoods several blocks off Duval. No more. In an effort to appease Key West residents who complained about having to park several blocks from their homes because tourists had taken their curbside spots, the city of Key West has a resident parking program.

Here's how parking in residential Old Town works: Curbside spots along many Old Town streets have been ruled off with white paint and marked with the large white letters spelling out RESIDENTIAL PARKING. In order to park your vehicle in one of these spots, your car must display either a Monroe County license plate or a residential parking permit (available from the city of Key West with proof of residence).

If you park in one of the residential parking spaces and your car does not show the proper proof of residence, you may return to find it gone. Your illegally parked vehicle will likely have been towed to the city's impound lot on Stock Island. To retrieve it, you will have to have cash—no checks or credit cards are accepted.

If you want to be right in the thick of things, you will either have to feed a meter or pay to park in a lot. The city is now equipped with machines on parts of Duval and Southard streets that allow you to pay for hours at a time via credit card and place the receipt on your dashboard, thus eliminating the need for coins. The traditional meters still exist as well. Meter maids (and men) regularly patrol the streets of Key West at all hours, and tickets are liberally distributed. All-day parking is available for more reasonable prices at several privately owned lots on either side of Duval Street; watch for the lot attendants holding cardboard signs. You might also consider one of the convenient parking facilities described below.

i In 1931 travelers on the Overseas Highway (US 1) would drive to No Name Key, then ferry to Key Vacas, on to US 1 to Grassy Key, and a ferry would then go to Lower Matecumbe Key and on to Card Sound Road to the mainland.

KEY WEST BIGHT PARKING LOT
Corner of Caroline and Margaret Streets
(305) 809-3864
Located adjacent to the attractions at Key West Historic Seaport, this open-air lot offers full-day parking for a maximum of $16.25. If you just need to run a quick errand, you can park here for an hourly charge. The fully automated lot is accessible 24 hours to cars, motorcycles, and scooters only; no RVs, trailers, or buses permitted.

MALLORY SQUARE PARKING LOT
Corner of Wall and Front Streets
(305) 292-8158
www.keywestcity.com
This parking lot abuts the cruise-ship dock off Wall Street in the Mallory Square area and is convenient to all the west-end attractions and the sunset celebration. Through the years, however, it has been reduced in size to accommodate the enlarged and improved Mallory Square, so parking space is limited. Rates run $4 per hour, day and night or $32 for 24 hours. The lot is open from 8 a.m. until midnight. Cars, motorcycles, small trucks, and vans are welcome; campers, RVs, buses, and trailers are not.

OLD TOWN PARKING GARAGE
Key West Park N' Ride
300 Grinnell St.
(305) 293-6426
www.keywestcity.com
The Old Town Parking Garage offers you the chance to find one of 250 covered parking spaces at a reasonable rate anytime, day or night. Cars, small trucks, and motorcycles are welcome here. For $2 an hour ($13 maximum), you can park and then ride one of the shuttles to the downtown area several blocks away. Don't misplace your ticket, though, or you will incur a $20 fee. There is no extra charge for the shuttle when you show your ticket; a shuttle ride will cost 50 cents per person without the ticket. If your stay will be long-term, choose the monthly rate of $99 plus tax.

ACCOMMODATIONS

From luxury resorts to little-known hideaways, the Florida Keys' myriad accommodations suit every vacation fantasy and budget. What began in the 1930s as a small
assortment of fishing camps experienced a renaissance after World War II ended. Henry
Flagler's railroad and the creation of the Overseas Highway had made our islands more
accessible, but residents still relied on cisterns for fresh water until water lines were
installed to service the Key West naval base during World War II. The availability of fresh
water made our region a more civilized and desirable vacation destination, and in the
1950s and 1960s, when motoring became a popular means of travel, hotels and motels
sprang up throughout our islands.

OVERVIEW

In this chapter we escort you through some
of the Florida Keys' more outstanding facilities. Our selections are based on attributes
of rooms, service, location, property, and
overall ambience. Listed by descending mile
marker number beginning with Key Largo in
the Upper Keys and heading down the Keys
to Big Coppitt, these facilities encompass
a wide assortment of styles and rates. We
have included directions for those establishments located off the Overseas Highway
that may be difficult to find. In the Key West
section, we switch to alphabetical order;
we also provide a separate section of inns
and guesthouses in our southernmost city,
with a corresponding pricing code for those
accommodations.

LOCATION AND AMENITIES

Like our Conchs (those of us born in the Keys)
and Keys characters (those of us who were
not), accommodations in the Florida Keys
are highly individualistic. Most are situated

on the Florida Bay, the Gulf of Mexico, or the
Atlantic Ocean. We commonly refer to the
Atlantic as "oceanside." For simplicity's sake
in this chapter, we refer to the bayside and
gulfside as "bayside."

Oceanside accommodations offer exotic
sunrises and proximity to dive sites, oceanside flats, and blue-water locations for sportfishing. Water access is generally deeper on
the oceanside than in the bay, affording
boaters and sailors more options. Bayside
lodgings can boast of our spectacular Keys
sunsets, which sink into the placid skinny
waters of the gulf like a meltdown of molten
lava. Some hotels, motels, resorts, and inns
sit alongside inland canals or marina basins,
and many of our waterfront facilities are
accessible by boat.

Many of our small mom-and-pop lodgings you will see lining the Overseas Highway
were primarily built in the 1950s and 1960s
as fishing camps. These facilities offer basic,
affordable rooms and efficiencies, some with
screened patios. Mom-and-pop motels often

draw cost-conscious families, last-minute travelers, anglers, and scuba divers—those active, outdoorsy types seeking nothing more than a bed and a shower. These motels have a high return rate.

Also individually owned, but often with more expansive waterfront properties and recreational amenities, are facilities that offer a potpourri of accommodation options, ranging from sleeping rooms to efficiencies to multiple-bedroom apartments, often within one property. Many sleeping rooms provide mini-refrigerators and have balconies, while efficiencies offer abbreviated kitchens as well. Suites, villas, and cottages will allow you the space to spread out a bit and to cook a meal or two "at home" when the mood hits. They usually have a sleeper sofa in the living space and a full kitchen. These accommodations often maintain freshwater swimming pools, hot tubs, and guest laundry facilities. If they don't offer on-premises water sports, these recreational activities are almost always located nearby.

Our large comprehensive resorts offer all the amenities of a mom-and-pop facility and then some. From fitness to child-care centers and concierge to room service, these hotels cater to families and honeymooners, business travelers and sports enthusiasts, power players and movie stars. You'll find tennis courts and water sports, fishing charters and dive excursions. Some offer optional conference rooms or a variety of travel/sport packages. Couples often opt for romantic weddings and honeymoons amid our tropical breezes, lush foliage, crystalline seas, and magnificent sunsets.

Whether the accommodations are large, small, or somewhere in between, all of our guest properties exude a casual, barefoot ambience. To one degree or another, all

Ecotourism in the Keys

Ecotourism is on everyone's mind. More and more companies are "going green" worldwide and this includes properties in the Florida Keys. Meeting the criteria means purchasing renewable energy, recycling, installation of low-flow shower heads, energy-efficient lighting, energy efficient appliances, upgrading air-conditioning filters, using environmentally friendly cleaning products, and in the case of the Hyatt, using natural woods for room furnishings. In addition to the entire Southernmost Hotel Collection, over 600 resorts in Florida have completed the Florida Department of Environmental Protection's Certified Green Lodging Program and are designated as such. For a complete list of designated properties in the Keys, visit www .floridagreenlodging.org. To learn more about companies that are going green in the Keys, visit www .keysglee.com.

bestow the uninterrupted escape for which the Florida Keys has always been known.

RESERVATION AND CANCELLATION POLICIES

During high season and special events, our facilities are almost always full. You might benefit from a no-show on a walk-in basis late at night, but we suggest reserving and confirming dates, accommodations, and prices two to three months in advance. More desirable facilities fill up more rapidly, and special events sometimes require one-year advance planning.

To avoid potential complications, be sure to inquire about all details of your accommodations when making reservations and confirmations. Obtain a confirmation number and the full name of the person who takes your reservation.

If you are planning to arrive at one of our resort marinas by sailing or motor yacht, be sure to read our Cruising chapter first. Dockage space for transient cruisers is at a premium at these desirable establishments and is often booked a year in advance during high season. Be sure to ascertain water depth and size restrictions of the marina before you venture here in your vessel. Many of our recommended accommodations offer marina facilities where you may bring your own trailered boat and, for a small daily fee, secure dockage of your craft for the duration of your stay. The boat basins of these facilities are usually not as deep as the resort marinas that accommodate large vessels and therefore are more suitable for shallow-draft boats. Those accommodations offering accessibility by boat have been noted throughout.

Check-in time typically is after 3 p.m., and check-out is between 10 and 11 a.m. Some facilities levy an extra charge if you occupy your room after check-out time. But in some cases, the management is prepared to keep your luggage safe while you soak in a few extra rays before catching that flight home. They may even have a room designated for you to shower and change in before you leave. It is always better to inquire than to ignore posted check-out times.

RATE INFORMATION

Rate structures for Keys lodgings vary nearly as much as the accommodations themselves, but you can draw a few generalizations. Rates fluctuate by season and depend largely upon the size of the accommodation and its proximity to the water.

High season (Dec through Apr) supports the highest rates. High-season rates usually prevail during sport lobster season at the end of July (a near holiday in the Keys; see the Diving and Snorkeling chapter), Fantasy Fest in October (our southernmost decadent version of Mardi Gras; see our Annual Events chapter), and most national holiday weekends. You must make reservations well in advance of your visit during any of these times. Many facilities fully book available accommodations one year in advance for high season and the holidays.

A second season commences in May and continues through the summer months, attracting vacationers seeking to escape the steamy heat of the rest of Florida and the Deep South. Rates during this period are generally slightly less than high season.

Low season is September, bringing a savings of about 20 percent off high-season rates.

Rates for motel or sleeping rooms, which typically hold two double beds, are based on single or double occupancy. Additional guests are charged a supplementary fee, but motels impose a maximum occupancy for each room.

Children younger than age 13 frequently are permitted to stay for free when accompanied by an adult. Cribs and cots often are provided at no charge or at a minimal additional cost.

Condominiums, villas, and cottages generally establish a weekly rate per unit, but many also offer a three- or four-night package as well, which is priced per night.

Accommodations of like rating will command differing prices, depending upon how close they are to the waterfront and what kind of view they offer. If you prefer accommodations overlooking the bay or ocean, ask for a bayfront or oceanfront room. Sometimes waterfront means a canal or lagoon. Be sure to query. Water view does not necessarily mean that your room will be on or facing the water, but as a general rule, water view is less expensive and provides at least a glimpse of the bay or ocean. Garden views and nonwaterfront accommodations, often just a short walk to water's edge, are priced even lower.

We suggest you shop around for exact daily or weekly rates and vacancies. Be sure to ask if the facility offers any discounted rates. Sometimes you can luck into a short-term discount or sport package that will be just what you are seeking.

In all cases, rates are quoted for the high season. Prices for motel- or sleeping-room facilities are figured on a double-occupancy average rate per night. Villas, efficiencies, and condominium units, which generally establish rates per unit rather than per person, will be quoted as such. And even though these units traditionally are rented by the week, we have computed our code on an average daily rate so that you can compare apples with apples.

It is not uncommon to find accommodations that run the gamut of several price-code categories all at the same place. The code will indicate if you can expect a range of space and pocketbook possibilities. (Accommodations in Key West generally are more expensive than the rest of the Keys; therefore, we have established a separate pricing key for Key West accommodations.)

Price Code

Price codes are high-season rates figured without additional fees, such as room service and calls, and without the 12.5 percent room tax. Our recommended accommodations accept major credit cards unless otherwise specified.

$	$55 to $99
$$	$100 to $150
$$$	$151 to $250
$$$$	$251 and higher

THE FLORIDA KEYS

Upper Keys

At the top of the Keys, **Key Largo,** home of **John Pennekamp Coral Reef State Park,** bustles with an energetic crowd of divers and snorkelers in all seasons. The orientation here is definitely geared toward the underwater treasures of the coral reef that lies just 4 miles offshore. Many motels and resorts in this area offer diving and snorkeling packages.

The settlement of **Tavernier** snuggles between Key Largo and Islamorada. This quiet area is known for its historic qualities. Dubbed the Sportfishing Capital of the World, **Islamorada** stretches from **Plantation Key** at mile marker 90 to **Lower Matecumbe Key** at mile marker 73. This village of islands, incorporated in 1998, is renowned for its contingent of talented game-fishing guides (see the Fishing chapter) and prestigious fishing tournaments.

The Upper Keys pulsates with tiki bars and watering holes as well as an array of fine restaurants (see the Restaurants and Nightlife chapters). Excursions to historic **Indian Key** and **Lignumvitae Key** and visits to **Theater of the Sea,** which offers dolphin and sea mammal shows and allows guests to swim with the dolphins, rate high on the list of things to do for families and sports enthusiasts alike (see the Attractions chapter).

AZUL DEL MAR $$$–$$$$
MM 104.3 Bayside, Key Largo
(305) 451-0337
www.azulhotels.us

Featured in *Travel + Leisure's* "The World's Greatest Hotels, Resorts and Spas" in 2009, Azul del Mar is one of a pair of sibling hotels on opposite ends of the Florida Keys. Picture yourself in either one of these two exceptional properties (see Azul Key West in this chapter), offering options from both ends of "Paradise" and a beautiful drive in between. Upon your arrival, the hushed silence of Azul del Mar is all around you. The sprawling lawn that flows to the private beach that rolls into the Gulf of Mexico sets the mood at this adults-only property. The sea views, and tropical gardens overflowing with palms, orchids, frangipani, and mahogany trees set the tone for embracing you into Azul's Zen-like atmosphere. Rooms feature soft beds with down comforters; sleek kitchens with microwaves, fridges, mini-dishwashers, and coffeemakers; and TVs, CD players, and DVD players to watch movies from their in-house library. Aveda products are located in the bath, and pastries, yogurt, and coffee packets are offered to guests in the mornings. There is no formal dining area at Azul, but they do have gas grills for guests, and there are many fine restaurants in the local vicinity. The unhurried sense you will have is as if you have stepped into another world.

AMY SLATE'S AMORAY
DIVE RESORT $$–$$$
MM 104.2 Bayside, Key Largo
(305) 451-3595 or (800) 426-6729
www.amoray.com

About 80 percent of the guests at Amy Slate's Amoray Dive Resort are divers, and in 2008 this resort was rated "Best in the Keys" by *Scuba* magazine for diving. An eclectic collection of plantation-style villas springs to life daily as the undersea enthusiasts rustle about, eager to embark on the resort's 45-foot *Amoray Diver* for the half-hour ride to John Pennekamp Coral Reef State Park (see the Diving and Snorkeling chapter). Amy Slate's Amoray owes its name in part to *People* magazine. The publication sent a writer to Key Largo to cover an Amy Slate underwater wedding "crashed" by a moray eel, and thus coined the term "That's Amoray."

The rooms here are named for tropical fish. Varying in size, amenities, and price, the rooms range from the standard motel variety to small apartments with full kitchens. The accommodations all have ceiling fans and feature tile floors, queen-size beds, and daybeds. Two-story, two-bedroom, two-bath duplexes accommodate as many as eight guests; they offer full kitchens and screened porches with personal hammocks. Some accommodations afford partial water views. A pool and hot tub front Florida Bay, and a bayfront sundeck and small sandy area at the water's edge sport a picnic table, barbecue grill, and hammock, allowing for swimming, snorkeling, and fishing. Continental breakfast and Wi-Fi are included in the room rate. Boat slips are available.

MARRIOTT KEY LARGO BAY
BEACH RESORT $$$–$$$$
MM 103.8 Bayside, Key Largo
(305) 453-0000 or (888) 236-2427
www.marriottkeylargo.com

Bayside sunset views and a primo location near John Pennekamp Coral Reef State Park mark only two of a multitude of pluses at the Marriott Key Largo Bay Beach Resort. The 153 hotel rooms of this Key West–style resort vary in view (bay view and deluxe bay view cost more), but all include a room safe, minibar, pay-per-view in addition to free cable television, hair dryer, coffeemaker, iron, and ironing board. All but 30 rooms have patios or balconies.

Rooms are equipped with voicemail and a dataport with free Wi-Fi. For more spacious quarters but more dearly priced, 20 suites—1,200 square feet apiece—have a full kitchen, a full bathroom, a queen-size sleeper sofa in the living room, and two bedrooms, one with a king-size bed and one with two double beds. Wraparound patios provide panoramic views of Florida Bay and its famed sunsets. For the royal treatment, the resort also offers one 1,400-square-foot penthouse suite, which, in addition to the amenities of the other suites, features a Roman tub in the master bedroom as well as a bath and a half.

Treat yourself to libations or dining at one of Marriott Key Largo Bay's restaurants or bars—Gus' Grille (see the Restaurants chapter); Breezer's Bar and Grille (see the Nightlife chapter); or Flipper's Poolside Tiki Bar.

The resort also features two fitness areas with state-of-the-art equipment and offers a full-service complete day spa as well as therapeutic sea-breeze-kissed massage in a private open-air tiki hut. A boutique shop in the lobby called By the Way will lure the shopaholics. Pirate Island Divers provides on-premises water-sports selections ranging from diving, snorkeling, parasailing, and glass-bottomed boat excursions to boat or personal watercraft rentals.

Fishing charters can be booked through the hotel as well. Boat dockage is available for guests' vessels at no extra charge.

TARPON FLATS INN $$$
MM 103.5 Oceanside, Key Largo
(305) 453-1313 or (866) 546-0000
www.tarponflats.com

Standing on the banks of Largo Sound, this romantic bed-and-breakfast tantalizes your every dream. The three-story sunshine yellow B&B offers modern accommodations with a Caribbean flair decorated in a Victorian theme that beckons you at every turn. A fishing camp in the 1960s and '70s, the resort comes complete with its own beach! British Colonial mahogany furniture is the decor in suites and rooms. The four full suites feature queen-size beds and queen-size sofa beds, satellite TV, high-speed Wi-Fi Internet, and fully equipped kitchens. In synch with nature, the verandas off the rooms frame luscious views of Largo Sound and the John Pennekamp Coral Reef State Park (see the Campgrounds and Cruising chapters). Tarpon Flats Inn's marina can accommodate your boat or charter one for some of the best fishing and fun in the Keys. Let a guide zip you through the blue waters of the Gulf Stream to Adams Cut, where you can reel in trout, redfish, bonefish, and snook. Cruising out to the backcountry of Florida Bay or the Atlantic Ocean, you can land wahoo, tuna, sailfish, and tarpon. Fishing not your thing? The inn can arrange snorkel and dive trips, or just go along for a ride and bring your camera for some dazzling photos to show folks back home.

JULES' UNDERSEA LODGE $$
MM 103.2 Oceanside, 51 Shoreline Dr., Key Largo
(305) 451-2353
www.jul.com

For a unique experience that is one to write home about, Jules' Undersea Lodge has to be near the top of the list. You actually dive 21 feet beneath the surface of the sea to enter this lodge. This only underwater hotel in the world is under the surface of a tropical mangrove of the Emerald Lagoon. The cottage-size building has hot showers, a well-stocked kitchen (with refrigerator and microwave), books, music, and video movies. As you snuggle in your bed, you can view the sea life that appears at the windows of this aquatic habitat.

Dive certification is offered at the facility and individuals must meet the requirements of the Professional Association of Diving Instructors (PADI) and Discover Dive in order to stay in the lodge.

HAMPTON INN KEY LARGO $$$
MM 102 Bayside, Key Largo
(305) 451-1400
www.hilton.com

Not far from John Pennekamp Coral Reef State Park, Dolphin Cove, Theater of the Sea, Florida City Outlet Mall, and the Everglades National Park, you will discover Key Largo's Hampton Inn Resort. There are only 100 rooms, newly decorated with a quiet tropical coolness, each offering flat-screen TVs, free Wi-Fi, a refrigerator, microwave, coffeemaker, and a wet bar. Each guest room has either a private balcony or patio that opens directly to the heated pool, beach, or surrounding tropical gardens. Breakfast is included in your stay at this pet-friendly location and dining is strictly a light approach, with Islander's Cafe serving light bites and cocktails in the lobby.

LARGO LODGE $$
MM 101.7 Bayside, Key Largo
(305) 451-0424
www.largolodge.com

A secluded, romantic, rainforest setting greets you at this "old island–style" hideaway. At Largo Lodge a collection of six cottages, one efficiency, one bay unit, and one garden unit resides among three acres of lush, tropical gardens overflowing with bromeliads, orchids, and trickling water fountains. A quiet and spacious sandy pier faces the waters of Florida Bay, where you can relax and read, swim, picnic, or simply worship the sun. And you may meet one of the wild bird contingents that frequent the premises.

Each one of the cottages features a living room, one bedroom with two queen beds, and a combination kitchen/dining area. All units are located in the garden, a short distance from the sandy beach and waterfront. The efficiency has one queen bed, equipped kitchen, bath, and outside patio seating. The garden unit is near the waterfront and has one queen bed, microwave, half-size refrigerator, coffeemaker, and a private deck with a seating area overlooking the gardens. The bay unit has a king size bed, sliding glass doors with a waterfront view, half-size refrigerator, coffeemaker, microwave, and your own private deck with outdoor waterfront seating. Boat dockage is available, but you should launch your boat at a public ramp (see our Boating chapter) and bring it around to Largo Lodge, because the lush tropical plantings make it difficult to maneuver a trailer. Guests must be over age 16 and no pets are allowed.

ACCOMMODATIONS

i The Monroe County Tourist Development Council can help you find the perfect spot to rest your head as well as help you plan your entire Florida Keys vacation. Call them toll-free at (800) 352-5397 or visit www.fla-keys.com.

MARINA DEL MAR RESORT
AND MARINA $$–$$$$
MM 100 Oceanside, 527 Caribbean Dr., Key Largo
(305) 451-4107
www.marinadelmarkeylargo.com

The Marina Del Mar Resort and Marina, on a quiet, dead-end street along an ocean-fed canal and boat basin, draws an active boating, fishing, and diving crowd. This facility shares the same marina as its sister properties—Holiday Inn Key Largo Resort and Ramada Resort and Marina.

The 76 rooms are bright and modern with tile floors, ceiling fans, white wicker furnishings, and bold tropical accents and feature king-size beds or two double beds. Some also have whirlpool tubs, complete kitchens, and private waterfront balconies. All are equipped with ironing boards and irons. A complimentary continental breakfast is offered daily, and restaurants and attractions are nearby. Deep-sea charter fishing boats are docked behind the Marina Del Mar. The hotel also maintains two tennis courts and a small fitness room with Nautilus equipment.

Overlooking the heated swimming pool, complete with brick sundeck and hot tub, is Coconuts, a casual indoor-outdoor restaurant (see the Restaurants and Nightlife chapters).

The resort's marina attracts long-term and transient cruisers (see our Cruising chapter). A snorkeling excursion vessel and a glass-bottomed tour boat, which both offer daily trips to the coral reefs, are berthed here as well. Next door a full-service dive center offers resort and open-water diving instruction and certification. This is a pet-friendly resort.

HOLIDAY INN KEY LARGO
RESORT AND MARINA $$–$$$$
MM 99.7 Oceanside, Key Largo
(305) 451-2121 or (800) 843-5397
www.holidayinnkeylargo.com

If action is what you seek on your vacation, the 130-room Holiday Inn, situated on a busy boat basin, bustles with activity from dawn until dark. You'll find charters for snorkeling, diving, fishing, sunset cruises, and sailing excursions emanating from the docks that run between the Holiday and its sister hotels, the Ramada Key Largo Resort and Marina Del Mar Resort and Marina (see separate listings). Together they compose the Key Largo Resorts.

Bogie's Café offers indoor or outdoor dining for breakfast, lunch, or dinner. The Tiki Bar serves light fare all day while live music percolates poolside on weekend evenings. You'll find a small "marketessen" in the lobby for sandwiches, pastries, juice, soda, and bottled water.

Rooms at the Holiday Inn face lush tropical gardens or the harbor, and the colorful accents in each room reflect the flora that flourishes outside the tinted glass doors. Rooms feature modern bathrooms, king-size beds, floor-to-ceiling beveled mirrors, and great vacation amenities such as coffeemakers, hair dryers, mini-refrigerators, ironing boards and irons, cable TV with HBO guest choice movies, and voicemail. There is a fitness center on property as well as a Jacuzzi for your post-workout recovery.

Palm trees, frangipani, and bougainvillea

weave a foliage trail between the two heated pools and the hot tub, and chickees and tropical waterfalls pepper the property. Docked canalside at the Holiday Inn are two famous boats: the original *African Queen* from the legendary movie of the same name and the *Thayer IV* from the motion picture *On Golden Pond.*

RAMADA KEY LARGO RESORT
AND MARINA $$-$$$$
MM 99.7 Oceanside, Key Largo
(305) 451-3939 or (800) 272-6232
www.ramadakeylargo.com

Sister hotel to the Holiday Inn and Marina Del Mar Resort and Marina, the Ramada exudes a quieter, more laid-back ambience. Reciprocal privileges exist among the three facilities, so guests may enjoy dining at or room service from Bogie's Cafe and Coconuts, as well as the Tiki Bar. The newly redecorated 88 rooms and five king Jacuzzi suites of this resort have all the amenities you would expect. The spacious rooms have king-size beds or two queen beds, a private balcony, coffeemaker, fridge, cable TV/HBO, hair dryers, and iron and ironing boards. The king suites have a queen pullout sofa, and all rooms open onto a private patio or balcony. A continental breakfast is served daily and tickets for the casino cruise are on sale here as well. The Ramada wraps around a small, private kidney-shaped swimming pool for your enjoyment.

BAYSIDE INN KEY LARGO $$-$$$
MM 99.5 Bayside, Key Largo
(305) 451-4450 or (800) 242-5229
www.baysidekeylargo.com

Located on beautiful Florida Bay in the heart of Key Largo, this location is an ideal getaway. 56 bright, tropical-themed guest rooms with two double beds overlook the bay. The inn is under new management and the entire resort has received a complete makeover and renovation. One-Bedroom Waterfront Suites feature a full kitchen, a living room with a king-size Murphy bed, dining room, private bathroom, a bedroom with a king-size bed, pull out queen couch, and a private balcony overlooking the pool, beach, and sunsets. Bay View Rooms offer a full waterfront view, surrounded by tropical gardens and palm trees. Each room has a king-size bed with beach, waterfront, and sunset views and small refrigerator and microwave. The Island View Rooms include either a double or a king-size bed, a sitting/dining area, microwave, and small refrigerator. In addition to the new rooms, there is also now a fitness center, an on-site laundry facility, and a fabulous sushi restaurant called Sushi Nami, which is open for lunch and dinner.

THE PELICAN KEY LARGO
COTTAGES ON THE BAY $-$$
MM 99.5 Bayside, Key Largo
(305) 451-3576 or (877) 451-3576
www.hungrypelican.com

Murals of manatees, pelicans, roseate spoonbills, and egrets decorate the outside walls of the one-story "old Keys" buildings at the Pelican, which are linked by masses of bougainvillea. All 23 rooms have tropical furniture and accents. The grounds of the property have loads of tropical greens and flowers for you to enjoy. Each unit is air-conditioned and has a small refrigerator, private bathroom with a shower, tile floors, and Internet access. Some have kitchens as well. The Roseate Waterfront Suite has one king-size bed, two double beds, and a full kitchen. It connects to the Sailaway, which has one king-size bed, one sleeper sofa, a microwave, and a refrigerator. All have TVs and DVD players, and there is a coin-operated laundry facility available.

Situated on Florida Bay, the Pelican has two fishing piers. You'll be able to swim or snorkel between the piers, but the facility does not have a swimming pool. You may launch your boat from the Pelican's boat ramp, and dockage for small boats is free for guests. Use of paddleboats, canoes, and kayaks is complimentary. The property sports a large chickee for lounging, and barbecue pits are scattered about.

SUNSET COVE BEACH RESORT $-$$
MM 99.3 Bayside, Key Largo
(305) 451-0705 or (877) 451-0705
www.sunsetcovebeachresort.com

Concrete camels, elephants, lions, tigers, and leopards lurk on the grounds of the Sunset Cove Motel, incongruously poised among cottages and waterfront suites. Don't worry, they are only life-size painted statues of the African beasts, remnants of a former owner's travels and hobbies. All the pet-friendly units at Sunset Cove are individually decorated, most still sporting 1950s and 1960s decor and furnishings, and offer a variety of bedding options, tile floors, and dated but clean, functional private baths. The cottages also have full kitchens. Each unit showcases wall murals of exotic flora and fauna, painted by area artists.

Down at the waterfront on Florida Bay, you'll enjoy free use of paddleboats and canoes. The beach is peppered with lounge chairs and barbecue grills if your idea of recreation is more reclined. A large thatched chickee with a stone waterfall in the middle of the property creates an island ambience. Guests are welcome to use Sunset Cove's boat ramp, and boat dockage for vessels up to 20 feet in length is available at no extra

charge. Maid service is not available; fresh towels must be obtained at the office. Sunset Cove does not have a swimming pool. Guests enjoy a free continental breakfast.

KONA KAI RESORT $$$$
MM 97.8 Bayside, Key Largo
(305) 852-7200 or (800) 365-7829
www.konakairesort.com

Lost in a cluster of mom-and-pop motels toward the southern end of Key Largo sits a truly intimate, adults-only gem known as Kona Kai. This is a small, quiet tropical resort, sure to dissolve your city cares. Near the facility's tennis court, the owners have planted an exotic tropical fruit garden of lichis, guava, starfruit, sapote, Florida pistachios, jackfruit, and more. Guests are free to help themselves to samplings of the tropical fruits.

Gardens throughout the two-acre property of winding walkways showcase palm trees, hibiscus, and bromeliads, plus heliconia and birds-of-paradise. An orchid shadehouse features various species of exotic blooms. The gardens have been featured on HGTV's *Secret Garden Show*.

An elevated heated (in winter) swimming pool and a hot tub are accented by a magnificent circular staircase and paverstone deck, as well as a thatched-palm chickee; a glass-block wall shelters a saltwater pond with a waterfall. Lounge chairs, picnic tables, barbecue grills, a hammock, and a fiberglass Ping-Pong table sit close to Kona Kai's white-sand beach, which is guarded by a stone alligator. You'll be able to snorkel, swim, and fish off a platform at the end of a dock, and a paddleboat, kayak, and other water "toys" are available free of charge.

Kona Kai's 11 intimate, cottage-style suites and guest rooms are decorated with flair, style, and attention to every detail. All units feature double-, queen-, or king-size beds. Suites have ceiling fans, tile baths and floors, glass-block showers, antiques, DVD players, Wi-Fi, and eclectic design accents. Many also have a full-size sleeper sofa or futon, and some units have full kitchens complete with Noritake china and matching flatware. Those without kitchens have small refrigerators and coffeemakers. Each room is named for a tropical fruit. Just look for the corresponding icon on the tile under the outside lantern to your room. Keeping with this theme, in the bathroom you'll find fruit-scented soaps, shampoos, and skin lotion that keep with the tropical fruit theme. Rooms, some of which are connected, offer either courtyard or full waterfront views. Kona Kai is a nonsmoking establishment.

A small, lovely fine-art gallery on the property exhibits the work of world-renowned artists (see the Arts and Culture chapter). Many of the original paintings from the gallery are hung in the individual guest suites as well and can be purchased. An outdoor dive station with rinse and soak tanks, an outdoor shower, and open-air lattice lockers are just down the walkway. Kona Kai can accommodate five boats with up to a 2-foot draft.

MARINER'S RESORT VILLAS
AND MARINA $$$–$$$$
MM 97.5 Oceanside, Key Largo
(305) 853-1111
www.keyscaribbean.com
Developed by Keys Caribbean Resorts, this gated resort on 16 lush acres brimming with coconut palms, bougainvillea, and mangrove trees is as private as it gets. Beautiful townhomes and villas allow their guests all the comforts of a private residence but with all the amenities of a resort. Classic Caribbean color schemes throughout each haunt, along with a 43-slip marina to accommodate your nautical adventures with direct access to the Atlantic Ocean, give you a feeling of being on an island. Nearby is the famous John Pennekkamp Coral Reef State Park (see Recreation chapter), or ask the "Adventure Concierge" to plan an outing of diving, fishing, snorkeling, ecotours, parasailing, or jet skiing.

On the premises are two pools—one of which is a 7,800-square-foot, oceanfront lagoon-styled pool that has two zero-entries—a Jacuzzi, clubhouse, fitness center, two tennis courts, a professional dive shop, and just about any kind of water sport you can imagine. Be sure to enjoy the Coral Jacuzzi Grotto for a relaxing treat! Mariner's Resort offers packages for weddings and family reunions.

KEY LARGO GRANDE RESORT
AND BEACH CLUB, A HILTON
RESORT $$$–$$$$
MM 97 Bayside, Key Largo
(305) 852-5553 or (800) 445-8667
www.hilton.com
This luxury resort lounges on 12.5 acres in a lush hardwood forest along the Gulf of Mexico. Accommodations are comfortable for both business or leisure travel with nature trails, private beach, exciting water sports, sport fishing, two heated pools (family and adult), fitness, sauna, whirlpool facilities, outdoor lighted tennis court, two on-site restaurants, a 10,000-square-foot meeting/event space, and for guests arriving by boat, there is the 21-slip docking facility at the marina—all for your entertainment and enjoyment while here in the Florida Keys.

With 190 rooms and suites, there is something here for everyone's budget. The

Key Room has a queen bed, marble bath, and private balcony. The Canopy View Room offers views off the balcony of tropical foliage with a fridge and a king or queen bed. The Grand View frames quiet vistas of Florida Bay from the balcony with a king or queen bed. In the Grand Suites are in-room Jacuzzi, king bed, sleeper sofa, fridge, and views of Florida Bay. All rooms have modern tropical decor, custom bedding, in-room coffeemaker, refreshment centers, room service, Wi-Fi (for an extra fee), voicemail, in-room movies, and video games. There are also numerous mealtime options on-property.

Splashes Pool Bar has grab-and-go food for lunch and dinner, the newly renovated Treetops Bar & Grill offers dining with a Mediterranean and Caribbean twist for breakfast and dinner, and the Waves Beach Bar is the best place to enjoy lunch or an afternoon cocktail.

DOVE CREEK LODGE $$$
MM 95 Oceanside, Key Largo
(305) 852-6200 or (800) 401-0057
www.dovecreeklodge.com
The Dove Creek Lodge was established to create an atmosphere for the serious fishing person. Any type of Florida Keys fishing obsession is met here with enthusiasm because they can handle any request, can place you on the water with a guide, and can suggest the correct tackle to turn that passion into reality. Offering fly-fishing for bonefish out on the flats, bill fishing, reef/spear fishing, snorkeling, off shore/deep sea fishing, diving, fly-fishing for beginners, ecotours, or just exploring the backcountry, Dove Creek Lodge lives up to its reputation. For beginners or pros, they also can sign you up for all the major fishing tournaments in the Keys, which run from Apr through Dec.

The amenities on-site are lodge rooms with mini-fridge and balcony, one- and two-bedroom suites, or luxury suites. In the luxury suites you have a full kitchen and screened patio; one of the two has an 8-foot pool table! The Lodge also houses a full tackle shop to outfit you with all the proper gear. The property sits right next door to one of the best seafood establishments in the Keys, Snapper's Waterfront Restaurant (see Restaurant and Nightlife chapters), where they say "our seafood is so fresh we have to change the menu daily 'cause we don't know what's coming in off the boats." You can arrive by land or sea for your stay. Dove Creek Lodge offers family and wedding packages and group rates. No pets or smoking allowed.

OCEAN POINTE SUITES $$$
MM 92.5 Oceanside, 500 Burton Dr.,
Tavernier
(305) 853-3000 or (800) 882-9464
www.opsuites.com
Directly on the Atlantic Ocean, this tropical, contemporary three-story, all-suite stilt condominium complex boasts 240 units with gingerbread-trimmed balconies facing the water. Suites at Ocean Pointe are individually owned and decorated, but, for the most part, expect to find tropical prints with wicker and rattan furnishings. The spacious one- and two-bedroom units (two full baths) feature whirlpool tubs, complete kitchens with microwave and coffeemaker, washer and dryer, living rooms with sleeper sofas, and private balconies.

Just outside your door are nature walks, a private beach, a large heated swimming pool, barbecue grills, picnic areas, beach volleyball courts, and lighted tennis courts. The 70-acre property also has a playground, a boat ramp capable of handling watercrafts up to 28 feet, and a marina. If you feel like a bite, head for the Waterfront Cafe for breakfast, lunch, afternoon snack, or a light dinner. Kayak and canoe rentals also are available.

To reach Ocean Pointe, head toward the ocean at Burton Drive (mile marker 92.5), where signs lead to Harry Harris Park. Follow Burton Drive about a quarter mile, turn right into the Ocean Pointe complex, and pass the guardhouse. Signs will guide you to the manager's office.

ATLANTIC BAY RESORT $$–$$$$
MM 92.5 Bayside, 160 Sterling Rd., Tavernier
(305) 852-5248 or (800) 937-5650
www.atlanticbayresort.com

Atlantic Bay Resort enjoys three acres of prime bayfront property, planted with palms and bougainvillea, and features a large beach area peppered with chaise lounges and barbecue grills, Adirondack beach chairs, and hammocks. Unique to this property is a special feature of Florida Bay called the "deep hole," where depths drop dramatically to 20 feet right off-shore. A coral rock ledge shelters lobsters and starfish and a regiment of sergeant-major fish, which keep company with mangrove snappers and parrotfish. This assortment of marine life as well as a sunken Haitian raft makes for dynamic snorkeling.

The Atlantic Bay Resort offers 19 efficiencies, cottages, or suites for up to four persons, all with full kitchens for self-catering convenience, free Wi-Fi, and hardwood or tile floors. The units are tropically furnished with colorful upholstered rattan and wicker. The Royal Caribbean Suite is located directly on the white sandy beach, and features two bedrooms and a private deck overlooking the bay. The master bedroom has a view of the bay and a king-size bed, while the

second bedroom (queen) features a view of the tropical garden area with private tiki hut and deck. The Caribbean Cottages are a little farther back from the water and enjoy views of either the heated swimming pool or Florida Bay. Each cottage has individual tiki hut porches, a full kitchen, living room, and separate bedroom with a king-size canopy bed. One-bedroom efficiencies are housed in a two-story, motel-style building toward the back of the property. Each unit has a full kitchen, living room with futon, and a separate bedroom with a king-size bed or twin beds.

Atlantic Bay Resort maintains two boat ramps and a 100-foot dock. Boat dockage and use of the boat ramp are available to guests at no extra charge. Guests enjoy complimentary use of rowboats and paddleboats during their stay. To find this resort, turn onto Sterling Road at mile marker 92.5 and proceed toward Florida Bay.

LOOKOUT LODGE RESORT $$–$$$
MM 87.7 Bayside, Islamorada
(305) 852-9915 or (800) 870-1772
www.lookoutlodge.com

Situated next to mile marker 88, one of the Upper Keys' most distinguished restaurants (see the Restaurants chapter), Lookout Lodge is a clean, modestly priced motel of Spanish-influenced architecture. The resort's nine basic rooms—featuring decidedly 1960s decor and amenities—come in four styles: studios with one double and one twin-size bed; studios with two double beds and a patio; and one- and two-bedroom suites. Suites each include a queen-size sleeper sofa. Cribs, side rails, and rollaway beds are provided at no additional cost. All suites have kitchenettes, tile floors and baths, voicemail telephones, and ceiling fans. Three afford full water views. A limited number of small pets are allowed.

Steps lead from the resort's raised man-made beach to the bay for swimming and snorkeling. The property features gas grills, picnic tables, a thatched-palm chickee, and lounge chairs, but no swimming pool. Dock space, available at an additional fee, is limited and must be reserved in advance. A dive/snorkel boat on premises takes guests to the reef. Two weeks' advance cancellation is required.

PELICAN COVE RESORT
AND MARINA $$$–$$$$
MM 84.5 Oceanside, Islamorada
(305) 664-4435 or (800) 445-4690
www.pcove.com
Perched beside the Atlantic Ocean, Pelican Cove Resort—constructed in concrete with a tin roof and Bahamian shutters—ensures an ocean view from almost every one of its 63 rooms. The nonsmoking resort offers a choice of accommodations ranging from standard rooms with one or two queen-size beds, mini-refrigerators, and coffeemakers, to efficiencies and one-bedroom hot tub suites, each with its own balcony. Efficiencies and suites have full modern kitchens with curved breakfast bars and either two queen-size beds or a queen-size bed and sleeper sofa. Some hotel rooms and suites connect, all units feature tropically inspired furnishings, and a few have been designated as pet-friendly.

Behind the resort, steps connect the raised man-made beach to the ocean, where dredging for a once-used quarry has caused waters to run 30 feet deep. A swimming pool with sundeck, outdoor cabana bar and cafe, poolside hot tub, volleyball net, playground, and water-sports concession all front the beach. Complimentary coffee and juice are offered in Pelican Cove's office 24 hours a day, and a complimentary continental breakfast is served daily. Children younger than age 17 stay free at Pelican Cove. Sandbox toys for children are available in the office. Limited boat dockage is available to guests at an additional fee. Reservations must be made in advance.

CHESAPEAKE BEACH
RESORT $$$–$$$$
MM 83.4 Oceanside, Islamorada
(305) 664-4662 or (800) 338-3395
www.chesapeake-resort.com
The elegant Chesapeake Beach Resort hugs the Atlantic on six and a half acres of lushly landscaped grounds. This pristine three-story 65-unit resort boasts 13 villas, 44 guest rooms, and eight suites. The Chesapeake sports two heated pools, a hot tub, tennis courts, on-site laundry facilities, and an outdoor gym shaded by a tiki hut as well as a 700-foot sunning beach and a saltwater lagoon. Suites and villas offer full kitchens and have balconies or screened porches. The higher-priced units also feature whirlpool bathtubs, king-size beds, queen-size living-room sleepers, two televisions, and wet bars. The one- and two-bedroom suites even have a Jacuzzi in the bedroom.

Fishing, snorkeling, diving, and para-sailing excursions can be booked on the premises as well as sunset cruises. You can rent kayaks and powerboats of up to 33 feet. Chesapeake also provides a boat ramp and boat dockage. Chesapeake provides a playground for children, who can stay for free if they are younger than age 13.

OCEAN DAWN SUITES $$$–$$$$
MM 82.9 Oceanside, Islamorada
(305) 664-4844 or (866) 540-5520
www.oceandawnsuites.com

Nothing looks like a million dollars in decorating until you have spent a million dollars! The owners of Ocean Dawn Suites started out just giving this property a facelift, but when the zeros started adding up, this once eight-room lodge reopened after a complete renovation with style and pizazz, containing marble bathrooms, porcelain floors, custom furniture, and 40-inch flat-TV screens. Outdoors, guests will enjoy a new clay tennis court, pool, croquet lawn, and a man-made beach, just yards from the Atlantic Ocean. It's ideal for intimate wedding parties, offering a bridal suite featuring a private balcony, kitchen, and Jacuzzi.

CASA MORADA $$$–$$$$
MM 82.2 Bayside, 136 Madeira Rd.,
Islamorada
(305) 664-0044 or (888) 881-3030
www.casamorada.com

Tucked on the shores of Florida Bay, out of the fray of US 1 on a residential street, this all-suites hotel exudes the charm of a Mediterranean villa. The 16 suites, each unique, have private terraces or semiprivate gardens overlooking the water and are decorated with a mixture of wrought-iron and mahogany furniture, which was exclusively created for Casa Morada. Unusual memorabilia from throughout the world accent the rooms. Rooms have cable TV, phones with modem ports, refrigerators, electric kettle coffee/tea setup, electronic safes, and hair dryers.

Cross a small, circa-1950 bridge to a private island and you'll find a sandy playground with a pool, secluded cabana, and terrace with breakfast, lunch, and beverage service. Continental breakfast is complimentary as are yoga classes held at 8:30 a.m. Wed through Sun. To find Casa Morada, turn in at the Lorelei Restaurant sign and follow Madeira Road into a quiet, residential neighborhood.

CHEECA LODGE & SPA $$$$
MM 82 Oceanside, Islamorada
(305) 664-4651 or (800) 327-2888
www.cheeca.com

Majestically sprawling amid 27 manicured, tropical acres with more than 1,100 feet of beachfront, Cheeca Lodge & Spa creates a vacation enclave you may never want to leave. An errant ember from a cigarette caused a New Year's Eve fire that closed Cheeca for most of 2008, leading to an extensive renovation on the property. Follow the winding drive through splashes of bougainvillea beneath towering coconut palms, stroll across the courtyard between an avenue of date palms, and enter an island lobby alive with bromeliads and potted palms. All 203 spacious guest rooms and one- or two-bedroom suites sport tropical themes and colors that reflect the sun and the sea of the Florida Keys. Tennis Villas, Golf Villas, Lake Villas, and Ocean Villas offer full kitchens.

Four Jacuzzis are sprinkled around the property, tucked privately amid lush tropical foliage. Many rooms have balconies that overlook the ocean or across the grounds of the resort; some units have screened porches. Focused on fishing, families, and the environment, Cheeca Lodge & Spa offers an overflowing cache of recreational options. A saltwater lagoon is stocked with tropical fish for easy on-site snorkeling. A fishing pier juts out into the ocean, where guests can dock boats with up to a 3-foot draft or just drop a line and try their luck.

Two pools grace the premises, a freshwater option to the sand beach and seductively salty Atlantic. Guests enjoy Cheeca's six Har-Tru tennis courts, nature trails, and water sports offering envirotours of the Everglades, as well as kayaking and windsurfing.

While here as a guest, be sure to enjoy the 5,700-square-foot luxury Spa at Cheeca. This spa is available to guests for full-line skin care, body treatments and scrubs, wellness classes, and young adult spa treatments. Massage therapies include stone massage, Thai table, refloxology, lomi lomi, myofascial release, deep tissue, mother earth, and Swedish.

The award-winning children's club, Camp Cheeca, keeps the kids happily occupied with specially designed, environmentally inspired activities (see the Kidstuff chapter). Note that Cheeca Lodge & Spa charges a daily resort fee that covers housekeeping gratuity, in-room coffee and tea, in-room bottled water, use of the spa fitness center, daily newspaper, fishing poles for the pier, golf clubs, sea kayaks, bikes, pool floats, cabanas, use of tennis courts and racquets, local phone calls, 800 calls, and incoming and outgoing faxes.

THE MOORINGS VILLAGE
RESORT $$$–$$$$
MM 81.5 Oceanside, 123 Beach Rd.,
Islamorada
(305) 664-4708
www.themooringsvillage.com

The Florida Keys may be Paradise, but the Moorings Village is utopia. The 18 cottages and homes are peppered throughout 18 acres of a former oceanfront coconut plantation; hammocks laze between majestic palms; winding, floral-draped trails emit the essence of gardenia; and canoes and skiffs dot the 1,100-foot white-sand beach as if guests simply washed ashore. The exquisitely elegant Moorings Village maintains a low, laid-back profile, creating an inimitable tropical ambience not readily found in the Florida Keys.

Cottages range from one to three bedrooms with one to three-and-a-half baths. The four original cottages, which have been completely renovated, date from the 1930s; newer buildings were completed in 1992. All are white with Bahamian shutters and trimmed in bright Caribbean colors. The cottages, which are named for some of Islamorada's pioneers, feature complete kitchens, telephone and television, and bathrooms with handpainted tiles. Most units have plantation-style porches as well as washers and dryers. The newer cottages offer luxurious soaking tubs and oversize shower stalls. Only the four original Moorings cottages can be rented by the night (two-night minimum). The rest require a one-week minimum stay.

Guests enjoy use of sailboards and kayaks, a 25-meter lap pool, and tennis court. Citrus trees are sprinkled about the lush bougainvillea-bedecked grounds. Pristine and private, the Moorings Village rates as one of the best-kept secrets in the Keys.

KON-TIKI RESORT $$–$$$
MM 81.2 Bayside, Islamorada
(305) 664-4702
www.kontiki-resort.com

Kon-Tiki's pebbled walkways, private patios, and cottages consistently attract anglers and families alike. The resort's quiet, U-shaped property boasts a shuffleboard court, chickee, pier, private beach on Florida Bay, park benches, and a brick barbecue. The primary attraction here, though, is the saltwater pond stocked with all sorts of tropical fish. Guests are invited to don snorkel and mask and take an underwater look-see. Accommodations feature bright, clean, and comfortable motel units, fully equipped efficiencies, and one-bedroom apartments, most of which have private patios or screened porches. Two-bedroom, two-bath apartments and three-bedroom, three-bath villas, priced according to size, accommodate as many as six. Kon-Tiki offers a heated pool and a boat ramp and dockage for vessels up to 24 feet long at no extra charge.

LA SIESTA RESORT & MARINA $$
MM 80.2 Oceanside, Islamorada
(305) 664-2132
www.lasiestaresort.com
Tucked away amidst the palm trees and the tropical foliage, you'll find La Siesta Resort & Marina. There are a few options for lodging on the property, including one-, two- and three-bedroom cottages and suites. All offer a fully equipped kitchen, cable television, phone, heat and air conditioning, daily maid service, and complimentary use of bicycles and fishing gear. The Insider tip here is to request cottage 101. It has been newly renovated with a navy-and-white nautical theme replete with white wainscoting and framed photos of fishing expeditions from yesteryear hanging on the walls. Cottage 101 also has a flat-screen TV, king-size bed, Mitchell Gold sleeper sofa, and a personal patio with a view of the marina and ocean beyond. And then there is the best amenity of all—your own personal hammock under the palm trees. Sure, there are water sports and a heated pool on-site as well, but the hammock beckons. How can you resist?

HAMPTON INN & SUITES $$$–$$$$
MM 80 Oceanside, Islamorada
(305) 664-0073 or (800) 426-7866
www.hamptoninn.com
Situated directly at ocean's edge, the Hampton Inn offers 59 suites, 16 standard rooms, and four wheelchair-accessible rooms with vistas of our endless sparkling sea. Suites feature one or two bedrooms, one or two baths, sleeper sofas in the living rooms, and full kitchens (coffee and popcorn are supplied every day). Cable television and pay-per-view movies entertain in each unit and suites have two televisions. The fresh furnishings of the Hampton Inn reflect island ambience with fabrics of pastels and teal amid light rattan.

The common lobby area of the Hampton sports a fishing theme—giant mounted dolphin, wahoo, and tarpon; carved wood piscatory reliefs; bronze game-fish sculptures. Tables and comfy chairs flank a keystone fireplace, which is more decorative than functional, given the balmy Keys weather. A complimentary continental breakfast buffet is served here daily.

Outside, guests enjoy a heated pool and spa, tiki bar, and palm-laden, sandy sunning area. A dock jutting out into the Atlantic affords boat dockage for small vessels, but be aware that depths fall to a scant 18 inches at low tide. You'll find a complete selection of water sports on premises, including snorkel or dive excursions, parasailing, and fishing charters. The popular Outback Steak House (305-664-3344) also is on the premises.

BREEZY PALMS RESORT $–$$$
MM 80 Oceanside, Islamorada
(305) 664-2361
www.breezypalms.com
Quaint coral buildings with turquoise doors, trim, shake roofs, and screened porches

mark Breezy Palms Resort, a cozy place nestled on 320 feet of oceanfront. The brightly wallpapered motel rooms, efficiencies, apartments, and cottages are clean, spacious, and well appointed, featuring rattan furniture and colorful island floral prints. Chickees and copious coconut palms pepper the property, which sits directly on the Atlantic Ocean and sports a sandy beach as well as a swimming pool. A brick barbecue, picnic table, and volleyball net add to the amenities; dockage is available for an additional fee. No straight inboards or personal watercraft, such as JetSkis or WaveRunners, are permitted. Breezy Palms is accessible by boat. Children younger than age 13 stay free.

WHITE GATE COURT $$–$$$
MM 76 Bayside, Islamorada
(305) 664-4136 or (800) 645-4283
www.whitegatecourt.com
A touch of understated European elegance marks the restored villas and bungalows at White Gate Court, situated on three acres abutting the placid Gulf of Mexico. These 1940s-era Conch cottages survived the hurricane of 1961 and decades of neglect before receiving tender loving care from owner Susanne Orias DeCargnelli, a native of Hungary who spent many years in South America. Painted cheerful yellow and white inside and out, the seven private units exude a rustic Old World charm. Spacious interiors feature rough-plastered walls; fresh tile and lightly stained wood-plank floors; fully equipped, stylistically European white kitchens; and sparkling modern bathrooms. Beds are covered with exquisite individualized quilts. All units have covered porches and outdoor tables and chairs. Some even feature rope hammocks.

White iron gates guard this tropical hermitage, fronting a long, narrow driveway lined with palm trees, oleanders, and white coach lamps. Lounge chairs pepper a 200-foot white-sand beach where guests enjoy swimming and snorkeling in the sandy-bottom gulf; White Gate Court does not have a pool. A finger dock stretches into the water for fishing, and tiki torches and barbecue grills are available for an evening cookout. A guest laundry also is provided. Pets and children are welcome.

CORAL BAY RESORT $$$$
MM 75.6 Bayside, Islamorada
(305) 664-5568
www.thecoralbayresort.com
Coral Bay Resort's three motel rooms, 11 efficiencies, and two villa suites are secreted away in white-trimmed, pastel pink, air-conditioned Conch–style cottages, each with a lazy-days front porch. A painted icon distinguishes each unit, creating a virtual school of tropical fish. The fresh interiors sparkle with light furniture, pastel fabrics, and tile floors. A selection of South Florida art adorns the walls. A variety of bedding options is available. The efficiencies feature full kitchens, and each villa suite also provides a living area with a sleeper sofa.

You'll enjoy Coral Bay's heated pool as well as the sandy beach on the Gulf of Mexico that is peppered with lounges and chickees. Fishing and snorkeling in the 14-foot-deep saltwater tidal pool are excellent. The pier itself has built-in seating and a fish-cleaning station. Guests can dock their own vessels for free or use the resort's paddleboat for exploration. Waters beyond the dock are illuminated at night, so the seaside fun doesn't have to end at sunset.

TOPSIDER RESORT $$$
MM 75.5 Bayside, Islamorada
(305) 664-8031 or (800) 262-9874
www.topsiderresort.com

The 20 octagonal, elevated time-share villas at Topsider Resort flank a wood boardwalk that marches from the secluded parking lot to the crystalline waters of the Gulf of Mexico. Ablaze with gumbo-limbos, crotons, and bougainvillea, the grounds of the Topsider create a rainforest mystique, even though the resort itself is right off the Overseas Highway. Units are identical in layout. Each features two bedrooms, two baths, a dining area, living room, and full kitchen. Ceiling fans, washer and dryer, and ground-level storage are standard. The units are updated on a rotating basis. Be sure to inquire as to when your unit was last renovated before booking.

Guests at Topsider Resort enjoy an elevated pool and spa, a tennis court, children's swings and slides, grills, picnic tables, and bayfront wood lounges for sunning on the sandy lagoonside beach. Free boat dockage is available on Topsider's long pier. Minimum stay here is three nights, but most guests opt for a week's sabbatical. No pets, please.

CALOOSA COVE RESORT $$$
MM 73.8 Oceanside, Islamorada
(305) 664-8811
www.caloosacove.com

An irregularly shaped condominium complex set apart from civilization on a 10-acre parcel of prime oceanfront property, Caloosa Cove offers 30 spacious, light, and bright efficiencies and one-bedroom suites. Suites offer eat-in kitchens, spacious bedrooms, and living rooms with sofa beds. Each efficiency is a large one-room unit with an eat-in kitchen, queen-size bed, and love seat. All are decorated with tropical rattans and

pastels. A covered deck that looks directly at the Atlantic fronts every unit.

Caloosa Cove's large irregular-shaped pool, surrounded by extensive decking and thatched-palm chickees, sits directly on the ocean's edge, affording endless vistas of the beyond. The grounds encompassing the coral-laden exterior of Caloosa Cove burgeon with mature tropical plantings.

Activities and amenities on condo premises include shuffleboard and basketball courts, a barbecue area, lighted tennis courts, a full-service marina, fishing charters, and boat and bicycle rentals. The nearby Safari Lounge serves your choice of cocktails.

Middle Keys

The Middle Keys, known locally as the "heart of the Keys," stretch from the Long Key Bridge to the Seven Mile Bridge. Long, Conch, Duck, and Grassy Keys lead the way to the string of bridge-connected islands known as the incorporated city of Marathon.

Basing your accommodations in the Middle Keys offers some distinct advantages. The barrier reef sheltering the prolific fishing waters of the Atlantic supports a plethora of marine life and harbors a number of primo shipwrecks for divers (see the Diving and Snorkeling chapter). Fishing in the Middle Keys rivals that of the famed Islamorada, a well-kept secret. From flats to backcountry, bluewater to bridges, you won't hear too many tales of the "one that got away" here (see the Fishing chapter).

Marathon currently offers one golf course, the nine-hole Key Colony Beach public course.

Marathon has a movie theater, too (cinemas are few and far between in the Keys). This quirky little theater, which shows first-run movies that change weekly, seats viewers in movable, swivel barrel chairs that surround small round tables designed to hold your popcorn and soda. (See the Recreation chapter for details on golf, tennis, movie theaters, and more.)

The **Dolphin Research Center** on Grassy Key is a must-do regardless of where your accommodations might be. And in Marathon, **Crane Point Museum and Nature Center** will captivate the whole family, as will historic **Pigeon Key,** at the end of a length of the old Seven Mile Bridge accessed at mile marker 47 (see the Attractions chapter). **Sombrero Beach** in Marathon, a very nice man-made public beach, provides endless ocean vistas to all.

Needless to say, like the rest of the Keys, this whole area is packed with recreational water options from party fishing boats and glass-bottomed reef excursions to personal watercraft and sea kayak rentals. Parasailing and ultralight rides are available here as well (see the Recreation chapter).

The pace is less tiki-bar frenetic here than in the Upper Keys. The sidewalk rolls up at a relatively early hour. But this area will appeal to families with children as well as serious anglers and divers who, after a day on or under the water, relish a relaxing dinner at one of the many top-notch restaurants and then a nocturnal refueling of energy for whatever tomorrow may bring.

LIME TREE BAY RESORT $$$
MM 68.5 Oceanside, Long Key
(305) 664-4740 or (800) 723-4519
www.limetreebayresort.com
Located on the "island" of Long Key amongst 100 palm trees, the Lime Tree Bay Resort is a true gem. In addition to the idyllic location, the property also contains a pool that sits right on the water's edge, and tiki huts,

hammocks, and barbecue areas all dot the property. Take a swim in one of the two pools, snorkel right off the beach, or take out one of the complimentary sea kayaks. Each of the rooms and suites features free Wi-Fi and handsome tropical furnishings like Mexican-tile flooring and paddle ceiling fans. This beautiful resort has received a Superior Small Lodging Award and offers different packages throughout the year, so be sure to ask if they are running any specials.

BAY VIEW INN MOTEL
AND MARINA $$–$$$
MM 63 Bayside, Conch Key
(305) 289-1525 or (800) 289-2055
www.bayviewinn.com
Located in the heart of fishing island Conch Key, with views of the Gulf of Mexico, the brightly colored Bay View Inn Motel and Marina is a quiet retreat from the busy crowds of larger resorts. The inn offers free Wi-Fi, free boat dockage, a swimming pool, and a variety of accommodations: rooms, efficiencies, and family suites. Some of the efficiencies and rooms are situated at the waterfront on the marina and have individual grills for that daily catch or late night dining. Regular rooms come with refrigerators, cable TV, and two queen-size beds. The efficiencies, which also sleep four, come with kitchenettes to support family-style vacations. The Bay View can arrange for Jet Ski, kayak, and boat rentals so you are sure to enjoy the great outdoors during your stay.

CONCH KEY COTTAGES $$–$$$$
MM 62.3 Oceanside, Walker's Island
(305) 289-1377 or (800) 330-1577
www.conchkeycottages.com
Step back in time as you drive across the narrow causeway from the Overseas

Highway into Keys past. Lovingly restored beyond their former grandeur, the pastel, gingerbread-trimmed Conch Key Cottages—like an upended basket of Easter eggs—are as unique as the conch shells for which they're named.

The wood-paneled Coquina, resting at water's edge, provides king-size beds in each of its two voluminous bedrooms. A walled patio with a hot tub and gas grill maximizes your privacy, and the sizable, well-equipped kitchen might even entice you to cook during your holiday. The largest cottage, the King's Crown, is about 1,200 square feet of living space, with a king-size bed in one bedroom and two queen-size beds in the other, plus a living room, dining room, kitchen, and one and a half baths. The Whelk, Queen, and Fighting Conch cottages each fringe the living/dining/kitchen combo room with a queen-size bedroom, one bathroom, and a massive, screened porch overlooking a primo bonefish flat. The honeymoon cottage, the Baby Conch, miniaturizes the features of the others, but the custom-painted lamps and specially made furnishings mirror the details of its more capacious relatives.

A small swimming pool sits amid towering palms, and several varieties of bananas hang at the ready for guest consumption. Plantings reflect the owners' philosophy of growing old-fashioned vegetation that attracts birds and butterflies.

Conch Key Cottages maintains a boat ramp and marina that can accommodate an 8-foot draft. Guests may dock their vessels at no extra charge. So you are sure to bring those freshly caught snappers to the table, there is a fish-cleaning station complete with water and electricity. Guests enjoy the use of a complimentary two-person kayak for the entire duration of their stay.

HAWK'S CAY RESORT AND MARINA $$$–$$$$
MM 61 Oceanside, Duck Key
(305) 743-7000 or (888) 313-5749
www.hawkscay.com

In 2008, it took $35 million for this resort to kick it up a few notches and polish Hawk's Cay's grandeur. Mount the steps to the tiled veranda, its Bahama fans slowly stirring the subtropical air over the wicker settees. Pass into the palm-filled lobby and out the other side to . . . the Caribbean? Like Alice passing through the looking glass, you will adjust your perspective, slow down, kick back, and recharge your batteries at this rambling Caribbean-style resort. Gracious yet low-key, opulent but subdued, Hawk's Cay's 60-acre facility encompasses one of the five islands of the Duck Key configuration.

Accommodations in the main building offer guest rooms that are gardenview, oceanview, and poolview. These newly decorated accommodations are richly appointed West Indies elegance offset by local art and photography reflecting the charms of the Florida Keys. The Premium Lanai Suites and Junior Suites offer Egyptian linens, some with separate living areas with sleep sofas, chairs, a writing desk, and views off balconies of the water and views of Duck Key. The Duck Key Villas at Hawk's Cay offer guests the option of self-contained vacation homes. These two-story, Key West–style abodes all offer full kitchens, living rooms, covered porches, washers and dryers, ceiling fans, and flat-screen televisions. The Duck Key Villas have two bedrooms and one and a half baths. The more spacious Hawk's Cay Villas offer two bedrooms, a den, and two and a half baths as well as an optional private tropical spa pool on a porch overlooking a canal. Unique to this Keys property is the saltwater lagoon, belted by a man-made, sandy beach, which borders the canal entrance to Hawk's Cay Marina boat basin (see the Cruising chapter).

When you've had enough of doing nothing at all—lazing around the lagoon, the family or adults-only pools, or the hot tub—check out the diversions. Observe the ongoing dolphin discovery program at Dolphin Connection (see the Attractions chapter). Book a fishing or diving charter or a sunset sailing cruise. Sign up for parasailing or sailing instruction, or rent a sea kayak for a self-guided ecotour through the backcountry waters (see the Fishing, Recreation, Boating, and Area Overview chapters). Work out at the Indies Club recreation and fitness center. Or swing your racquet in the tennis garden, participating in lessons, roundrobins, or just whacking returns at the ball machine.

Hawk's Cay also houses the Calm Waters Spa where services vary daily and all are accompanied by access to the candlelit whirlpool, eucalyptus steam room, and dry sauna.

The popular restaurants Alma and Tom's Harbor House on the premises whet any appetite (see our Restaurants chapter). Children fare equally well at Hawk's Cay. Camp Hawk, the Cove, and AquaJam all guarantee that Mom, Dad, and the kids all find a holiday wonderland (see the Kidstuff chapter).

GULF VIEW WATERFRONT RESORT $$$
MM 58.5 Bayside, Grassy Key
(305) 289-1414 or (877) 289-0111
www.gulfviewwaterfrontresort.com
This small, private resort hosts 11-unit accommodations that include guest rooms with refrigerators and microwaves as well as one- and two-bedroom apartments with full-size kitchens. Clean, bright furnishings make this a wonderful middle Keys location for families where they also welcome your pet. On the property is a lovely freshwater heated pool, boat ramp, dock, and even a putting green for the land lovers. Swing low in a hammock or sit under one of the tiki huts and gaze out over hundreds of palm trees surrounded by beautiful tropical vegetation. For the more active guest, bikes are available for rent, and complimentary kayaks, canoes, and paddleboats are just begging to be used in the clear blue Keys waters.

BONEFISH RESORT $$-$$$
MM 58 Oceanside, Grassy Key
(305) 743-7107 or (800) 274-9949
www.bonefishresort.com
Family owned and lovingly cared for, Bonefish Resort is one of those little gems reflecting old Florida Keys. This true motel is a "happy camper" resting among coconut palms, banana trees, hibiscus flowers, and tropical gardens. Open the handpainted door to your efficiency or room and step into a bright, fun space. The deluxe efficiency has one queen bed, one double plus a futon, full kitchen, private deck/patio, and barbecue grill. The efficiency offers two queen beds, full kitchen, and outdoor area. Guest rooms have one double bed and furnishings to suit. Walk the white sandy beach and come back for a swim in the pool or enjoy the picnic area. Rent a tandem kayak or pedal boat, then take a stroll and retire to a hammock or an old-fashioned swing. Truly a Keys kind of day!

RAINBOW BEND RESORT $$$-$$$$
MM 58 Oceanside, Grassy Key
(305) 289-1505 or (888) 929-1505
www.rainbowbend.com

Fire up a 15-foot Boston Whaler and head for the flats, for at Rainbow Bend each day of your stay entitles you to four free boating hours. Use of canoes, kayaks, and paddleboats is also complimentary. Stretched across two and a half acres of palm-speckled oceanfront beach, Rainbow Bend presents a mixed bag of accommodations, ranging from large sleeping rooms and efficiencies to oceanfront one- and two-bedroom suites. Small pets are allowed for an additional fee.

Relax under chickees on the lounges and Adirondack chairs that pepper the beach. If fresh water appeals to you, dip into the large pool and hot tub that edge the property. A long, wooden pier extends into the shallow ocean waters, where you can drop a line or dock your own small watercraft for the duration of your stay.

The Hideaway Cafe, which overlooks the beach, offers lunch and dinner (see our Restaurants chapter). A complimentary breakfast is served here each morning.

YELLOWTAIL INN $$-$$$
MM 58 Oceanside, Grassy Key
(305) 743-8400 or (800) 605-7475
www.yellowtailinn.com

Cute, quaint, charming, and reminiscent of old Keys style. This description of the Yellowtail Inn fits this property to perfection. Here you can rent rooms, efficiencies, cottages, and suites. The rooms offer a microwave in a kitchenette, queen bed, and a private patio. The efficiencies have a queen bed, sleeper sofa, and full kitchen. The cottages have a sunroom, queen bed, sleeper sofa, full kitchen, and a private patio. The suites have two bedrooms and two baths with full kitchens, dishwasher, dining area, sleeper sofa, and private balcony and private patio. All of the accommodations are decorated in Keys

tropical casual with the light and airy colors of carefree sunny days. On the lovely grounds is a heated swimming pool, fishing pier, small private beach, and barbecue grills. Kayak and pedal boats, fishing and snorkeling gear, and bikes can round out your daily activities. After all these activities, it is nice to know there is a coin laundry facility on the grounds!

WHITE SANDS INN $-$$$
MM 57.6 Oceanside, Grassy Key
(305) 743-5285
www.whitesandsinn.com

Hugging a prime piece of direct ocean frontage on Grassy Key, the pale-pink-and-white White Sands Inn houses seven one-room units—four efficiencies and three sleeping rooms—and the Tree Top Terrace suite, which has two bedrooms with two singles and a king-size bed, living room, full kitchen, and a private deck. The other units have tile floors and remodeled bathrooms, two queen-size beds, and crisp bedding. The rooms are air-conditioned, and some sport ceiling fans as well. Efficiencies feature fully equipped kitchens, but even the sleeping rooms are fitted with mini-refrigerators, coffeemakers, and microwaves, so you can self-cater if you wish.

The Sunrise Beach House at the White Sands Inn is a three-unit house at ocean's edge that enjoys sweeping vistas of the Atlantic and a heated swimming pool. One unit features three bedrooms, one bath, a living room with queen-size futon, and a fully equipped kitchen. The second unit features a king-size bed, bath, and mini-refrigerator, microwave, and coffeemaker. The third unit offers a queen-size bed, a full kitchen, and a sitting area with a queen-size futon.

The White Sands Inn rests amid towering coconut palms at water's edge, where

ACCOMMODATIONS

sparkling white imported sand forms a beach. Grills are available, and a large picnic table rests under a thatched chickee. The ambience at this intimate hideaway is casual and friendly. A long, curved pier stretches out into the ocean, where kayaks, a rowboat, and a paddleboat are docked for free usage by guests. At low tide the near-shore waters abutting the inn recede, forming a natural sandy beach. You can walk for miles along the sandy flats. And rumor has it that bonefish lurk at the edge of the flat, just ripe for the catching!

COCOPLUM BEACH AND
TENNIS CLUB $$$$
MM 54.5 Oceanside, 109 Coco Plum Dr., Marathon
(305) 743-0240 or (800) 228-1587
www.cocoplum.com

If you want quiet, find the elusive Cocoplum Beach and Tennis Club. Hidden among 53 varieties of palm trees and other tropical plantings, the pod of 20 three-story, art deco–colored "mushrooms" bestows a true island ambience. The endless ocean stretches to tomorrow, ribboned in a blue-to-green prism. Each octagonal villa—ringed with sliding doors to a wraparound deck and screened porch—houses two bedrooms, two baths, and a family room with sleeper sofa, wet bar, two TVs, and two telephones, and is nonsmoking. Each unit has a dining room and a full-size kitchen, complete with a microwave oven, blender, and coffeemaker. Guests enjoy use of a private utility room and washer and dryer on the lower level of each unit.

Cocoplum Beach and Tennis Club has planted a fruit-and-spice park that sports banana trees, citrus, and Key lime trees. Guests are invited to freely pick any of the ripe fruit and enjoy the tastes of the tropics. Loll by the illusion-edge swimming pool, which is surrounded by paver-stone decking. Or pop into one of the blue cabanas sprinkled about the sandy beach area. The hot tub awaits your tired muscles after a few hours of spirited tennis or beach volleyball. Or just fold yourself into one of the many secluded hammocks and take a snooze.

Reservations for seven nights are preferred, but three- to six-night stays are available, space permitting. Prices vary by proximity to the ocean. Extended stay discounts of 14 days or more are available in certain periods.

SEA ISLE CONDOMINIUMS $$–$$$
MM 54 Oceanside, 1101 West Ocean Dr., Key Colony Beach
(305) 743-0173 or (877) 743-0173
www.seaislecondos.com

The sandy beach and ocean views distinguish this 24-unit condo resort. Three tri-level, white buildings, one behind another, line Sea Isle's narrow strip of Key Colony Beach. Built in the late 1960s and individually owned and decorated, the furnishings of these spacious two-bedroom, two-bath apartments swing widely among styles of ensuing decades. Nevertheless, all necessities for a sun-filled, fun-filled vacation are provided: a heated swimming pool, shuffleboard, gas grills, picnic tables, lounge chairs, and chickees. Stroll down Key Colony's "condo lane" to the public golf course and tennis courts or head into Marathon for a selection of boating, fishing, and diving activities (see chapters devoted to those subjects). Reservations require a one-week minimum stay.

KEY COLONY BEACH MOTEL $
**MM 54 Oceanside, 441 East Ocean Dr.,
Key Colony Beach
(305) 289-0411**

Sitting proudly beside the ocean in Key Colony Beach—often called "condo row"—the modest Key Colony Beach Motel provides simply furnished rooms, each featuring two double beds, a refrigerator, and an excellent location. A lovely, palm-lined, sandy beach fronts this two-story white motel, which also has a heated swimming pool. All you need here is a towel, some sunscreen, and a good book.

CONTINENTAL INN $$–$$$
**MM 53.8 Oceanside, 1121 West Ocean
Dr., Key Colony Beach
(305) 289-0101 or (800) 443-7352
www.marathonresort.com**

Don your mask, fins, and snorkel, because a small, rocky formation at the edge of Continental Inn's beach supports an aquarium of marine life. Located on the coveted sandy stretch of Key Colony Beach, this condominium resort, with its white-stone balustrade, looks faintly Mediterranean. Gulls and terns dart about the oceanfront chickees as guests drink in the limitless vistas of the Atlantic. These individually owned, simply decorated, one-bedroom efficiencies flank a large, heated swimming pool. A small kitchen/dining/sitting area adjoins each bedroom and bathroom unit. Two two-bedroom apartments, each of which has a full living room with a sofa and a full eat-in kitchen, provide more spacious quarters for up to four people. You can play the links at the nearby public golf course, head for the tennis courts, or take your kids to a nice playground (see the Recreation chapter). No boats or trailers are allowed.

CORAL LAGOON RESORT
AND MARINA $$$–$$$$
**MM 53.5 Oceanside, Marathon
(866) 904-1234
www.corallagoonresort.com**

These 25 Key West–style villas and detached marina homes that are as pretty as a picture with white picket fences and wood shutters on six acres next to the Boat House Marina (see the Boating chapter). The two-story homes offer an open floor plan with three bedrooms, two and a half baths, and luxury interiors with peaceful tropical colors and tasteful decorations. You'll enjoy the full gourmet kitchens, washers and dryers, Wi-Fi, cable, a film library for your viewing pleasure, housekeeping services, and wonderful water views from the first- and second-floor private porches. The resort rents these homes daily, weekly, or monthly.

Boaters at the Coral Lagoon Resort will be thrilled with the Boat House, a full-service marina adjacent to the resort with options of dry storage or wet slips that can accommodate boats up to 50 feet in length. This property allows easy access to the Atlantic Ocean for excellent blue water offshore fishing and the Gulf of Mexico for thrilling backcountry wreck fishing and boating.

INDIGO REEF RESORT $$$–$$$$
**MM 53 Bayside, Marathon
(305) 853-5000 or (866) 643-5397
www.indigoreefresort.com**

Built on 15 acres in the heart of Marathon, this waterfront enclave with classic Florida Keys architecture and lush tropical landscaping is every vacationer's dream. 67 "homes" are casually themed with three bedrooms, two and a half baths, gourmet kitchens, plasma TVs, and Wi-Fi, with first- and second-level porches for maximum water views. On the property is a waterfront swimming pool, and a full service private spa can be arranged by appointment in your villa.

The marina was built with anglers and boaters in mind with easy access to the Gulf of Mexico and tropical reefs, private boat slips just steps away from each home, and an on-site dock master. Guests can also avail themselves of the services of the Adventure Concierge Program for personalized dive, snorkel, boat, and fishing trips.

TROPICAL COTTAGES $$$
MM 50.5 Bayside, Marathon
(305) 743-6048
Built in 1952, Tropical Cottages considers itself a "vintage Florida Keys resort." This enchanting hideaway caters to honeymooners, weddings, reunions, and small groups (adults only; no one under the age of 18). Nestled in a tropical cove that opens into the Gulf of Mexico, the location provides a kayak launch area, boat ramp, and dockage. It is adjacent to the Florida Keys Land and Sea Trust, offering kayak trails, which makes for quiet exploring of backcountry and calm waters. (Don't forget to put snorkeling on your list as well.) Each cottage becomes your personal hideaway, complete with private bath and dressing area and landscaped lanai with outdoor shower and patio for dining. Units are nicely decorated with wicker/rattan furniture, king- or queen-size canopy beds, and ceiling fans. There is also, if you must, air-conditioning. You may book by the night, week, month, or season. Included in your dream vacation at Tropical Cottages are fresh flowers and chilled champagne (upon arrival with reservations), daily housekeeping (upon request), and complimentary use of the resort's bikes, rowboats, canoes, and sea kayaks. Also, one of their special touches is a treasure map to

help you uncover natural bathing beaches, scenic bike paths, and picnic spots, with a bonus of restaurant and shopping tips. The memories of your stay will be anything but concrete and neon, but at least this place has electric lights and running water, along with lots of laid-back charm.

THE REEF RESORT $$–$$$
MM 50.5 Bayside, Marathon
(305) 743-7900
www.thereefatmarathon.com
As you drive through Marathon, you may spot what looks like a cluster of beige spaceships hugging Florida Bay. No, the aliens have not landed. These 22 octagonal villas, suspended on "landing" shaft stilts, actually provide a luxurious Keys getaway. Each villa features the same floor plan—two bedrooms, two baths, a full kitchen, and living room with sleeper sofa. The open ceiling vaults around a spoked, central fulcrum. Each unit has a washer and dryer. Lushly landscaped grounds on six acres, surrounding the two tennis courts, belie the fact that the Reef Resort borders the Overseas Highway. Bicycles, canoes, paddleboats, and rowboats are available at no extra charge for guests who can tear themselves away from the swimming pool. Picnic tables, grills, and chickees on the waterfront inspire a cookout at sunset. The Reef Resort's marina offers dockage for your boat of 25 feet or less (5-foot draft at low tide). Rentals are available for the week or the month.

SOMBRERO RESORT AND
  LIGHTHOUSE MARINA $$–$$$
MM 50 Oceanside, 19 Sombrero Blvd.,
Marathon
(305) 289-7662 or (800) 433-8660
www.sombreroresort.com

Sombrero Resort and Lighthouse Marina flank Boot Key Harbor and an adjoining inland canal. Sombrero offers efficiencies and condominium accommodations with all the amenities of a resort. Though not on the ocean, this destination resort, located in the heart of Marathon between the Overseas Highway and the oceanfront Sombrero Beach, allows you to be within steps of all the action, yet bathed in a laid-back and relaxing atmosphere. The 93 suites and efficiencies are situated in two three-story white buildings with covered parking beneath. A typical one-bedroom condominium is light, bright, and clean, featuring a living room with sleeper sofa, dining area, kitchen, bedroom with a king-size bed, and a full bathroom with shower. Some units have two double beds. Connecting doors may be opened between units if desired.

A keystone deck surrounds the large swimming pool, complete with tiki bar for that midafternoon tropical libation. A game room, also poolside, will amuse the kids with billiards, table soccer, and video arcade games. You'll be able to improve your tennis on the four lighted courts, get your daily workouts in the exercise room, and pamper yourself in the salon and spa. Sombrero Resort and Lighthouse Marina maintains a marina and a boat ramp. Guests may launch their boats at their ramp and secure dockage at one of the slips for an additional fee per day based on availability. Boats and trailers may be kept in the parking lot.

i If you are not staying at one of the large resort properties in the Keys, no big deal! Their restaurants and bars still offer an excellent atmosphere for socializing. Typically, establishments have casual eats at an outside bar, and in many cases reservations are not necessary.

BANANA BAY RESORT
& MARINA $$–$$$
MM 49.5 Bayside, Marathon
(305) 743-3500 or (866) 689-4217
www.bananabay.com
This dazzling 10-acre plantation-style resort on Florida Bay keeps Banana Bay Resort & Marina true to its reputation as a popular destination. The spacious rooms of the two residential areas—Island House and Marina Bay House—feature upscale island-style rattan furnishings and Bahama shutters. The grounds are ancient: gnarled trunks of massive royal poinciana trees, 20-foot traveler's palms, and mature bird-of-paradise plants. And don't miss the bananas, 15 varieties tucked between towering scheffleras and gumbo-limbos, papayas, and staggering banyan trees. A resident hawk makes regular passes at the small goldfish pond, hoping for an unsuspecting appetizer.

Don't let this quiet island charm fool you. There is plenty to do besides loll by the L-shaped swimming pool or soak in the hot tub. Banana Bay offers an on-premises playland: tennis, parasailing, sea kayaking, sailboarding, or rentals of personal watercraft, sailboats, and more from Fish-n-Fun Boat and Watersport Rentals. Banana Bay offers popular island wedding packages, including a choice of romantic settings for the ceremony.

THE BLACKFIN RESORT
AND MARINA $–$$$
MM 49.5 Bayside, Marathon
(305) 743-2393 or (800) 548-5397
www.blackfinresort.com
Accommodations at the 35-unit Blackfin Resort and Marina fall into a number of comfortable, affordable configurations: doubles, each of which features a queen-size bed

and small sitting area; singles, which are smaller rooms than the doubles but still are equipped with queen-size beds; and king rooms, which have king-size beds and love-seats. Some mini-refrigerators are available for these rooms. Blackfin also offers six cozy single efficiencies, queen-size bedrooms with kitchenettes that are comfortable for two adults; two large efficiencies, each of which features a big kitchen, dining area, and two queen-size beds; and one very large two-bedroom apartment, a 1,600-square-foot unit that offers a separate kitchen and dining room, two baths, and a porch.

Blackfin sits on four and a half acres abutting the Gulf of Mexico. The grounds are peppered with poinciana, gumbo-limbo, strangler fig trees, and curving coconut palms. Stone paths wind through gardens of tropical flora.

On a remote point of land at the end of the marina marked by a miniature light-house, guests enjoy a 600-foot, man-made, sandy beach sprinkled with lounge chairs, picnic tables, barbecue grills, and a thatched chickee. A freshwater pool overlooks the gulf. The placid waters of the gulf shelter a potpourri of tropical fish, a virtual aquarium for anglers and snorkelers.

A large marina accommodates guests' vessels at an additional charge. The resort lies just 2 nautical miles from the Seven Mile Bridge for easy access to the Atlantic for fishing or diving. Benches and a fish-cleaning station at the marina are well utilized by anglers. Personal watercraft and kayak rentals are available on-premises. Also on the premises are the Hurricane Grille restaurant and a jazz/blues bar with live entertainment.

CRYSTAL BAY RESORT $$-$$$
MM 49 Bayside, Marathon
(305) 289-8089 or (888) 289-8089
www.crystalbayresort.com

The best-kept secret in Marathon is hereby out of the bag! Situated in the heart of the city on the Gulf of Mexico, Crystal Bay Resort offers reasonably priced lodging in Conch-style bungalows. Crystal Bay Resort has 26 units, which include spacious sleeping rooms, efficiencies, a studio, and a full apartment. The bungalows and guest rooms, with many bedding configurations, are a vision of whites and pastels and feature tile floors, new or updated baths and kitchens, and stenciled walls.

Dotted with hammocks, coach lights, and a gazebo, the grounds stretch from the Overseas Highway back to the placid waters of the gulf. Children enjoy an extensive sandbox play yard complete with state-of-the-art, climb-upon equipment. Adults like the picnic area, which is peppered with brick barbecue grills. And everyone loves the free-form swimming pool and water-fall. Equipped with fiber-optic lighting, the waters change colors in the evening, creating a kaleidoscopic effect that carries on where the spectacular sunset left off. Chaise lounges and chickees are sprinkled about the water's edge, and a small marina basin allows easy access to explore surrounding waters. Guests may launch their boats here; dockage is an extra fee. A fishing pier, complete with cleaning station, juts offshore.

**TRANQUILITY BAY BEACH
  HOUSE RESORT** $$$$
MM 48.5 Bayside, Marathon
(305) 289-0888 or (866) 643-5397
www.tranquilitybay.com

Tranquility Bay Beach House Resort is owned and operated by the Singh Company. This company has developed some of the most successful properties in the Florida Keys (see Parrott Key Resort, this chapter), and this location is yet another jewel in their crown. Combining vacation-home ownership or weekly rentals with luxury resort surroundings is just one of the highlights of this beautiful resort. Built on 12 acres overlooking the aquamarine Gulf of Mexico, Tranquility Bay is your own little "private island." Magnificent palm trees appoint the sand dunes, where sea oats sway in warm breezes. A two-and-a-half-acre white sandy beach sparkles in the sunlight. The beach houses are decorated with tropical cottage flair, offering a choice of two or three bedrooms. The floor plan has great rooms, one and a half baths, gourmet kitchens, two porches, and plasma TVs. Twenty-four-hour room service and daily maid service are available.

Tranquility Bay can help you produce the wedding of your dreams, assisted by their specialists on staff. You can hold a reception or meeting on their 3,000-feet Great Lawn or have an intimate dinner for two. Part of your stay should include their Island Spice Private Spa, which offers in-home treatments. Be sure and catch a sunset or two at TJ's Tiki Bar, which is perched on the beach. Tranquility Bay has a supervised children's program called Keys Kids Adventure Camp. Upon check-in let the Adventure Concierge create an outing that offers everything under the sun and sea! This is a nonsmoking resort property.

BLUE WATERS RESORT MOTEL $–$$
MM 48.5 Bayside, Marathon
(305) 743-4832 or (800) 222-4832
www.bluewatersresortmotel.com

You'll enjoy a Mediterranean feeling here at Blue Waters Resort Motel, for the white-stucco buildings, gray-tile roofs, and bright, turquoise-blue doors evoke visions of Greece. Two banks of motel units, some with efficiency kitchens, flank the parking lot. The rooms feature two double beds or a king-size bed. For a real getaway, try renting one of their Island Homes. This is a 1,400-square-foot house floating on the water! It has two bedrooms with queen beds, two and a half baths, and a fully appointed kitchen. A raised swimming pool affords a view of a small boat basin on the gulf where guests may dock their boats for a small additional charge per day.

THE HAMMOCKS AT MARATHON $$$
MM 48.2 Bayside, Marathon
(305) 743-9009 or (800) 456-0009
www.bluegreenrentals.com

Perched in lush tropical foliage with the Gulf of Mexico at your doorstep, the Hammocks at Marathon offers you an escape from the real world. Wildlife of parrotfish, tarpon, and lobster are in the clear waters of the lagoon. You glimpse egrets, pelicans, and herons among the mangroves. Palm trees and tiki huts dot the landscape, which also features a pool and hot tub to take you away. Lodging options include studio rooms (without kitchens); one bedroom, one bath, and kitchen; or two bedrooms, one and a half baths, and kitchen. On the property, Barnacle Barney's Tiki Bar & Grill overlooks the marina, with full bar and menu to satisfy. Be sure to order the Lobster Reuben, their specialty. Barney's also celebrates the famous Florida Keys sunsets with the firing of a cannon as the sun sizzles into the cool Gulf waters. Water sports and fishing abound to keep your appetite humming. Sorry, no dock space; neither boat parking nor trailers permitted.

Lower Keys

The Lower Keys, sleepier and less densely populated than the Middle or Upper Keys, distinguish themselves with acres and acres of shallow-water turtle-grass flats and copious uninhabited mangrove out-islands. This is a gunkholing bonanza. The Lower Keys are surrounded by the **Great White Heron National Wildlife Refuge,** a large area in the Gulf of Mexico encompassing tiny keys from East Bahia Honda Key to the Content Keys to Cayo Agua and the Bay Keys. **Big Pine Key** is the home of the **National Key Deer Refuge,** a preserved area of wilderness sheltering our diminutive key deer.

Fishing is outstanding here, though ocean access is more limited. The Lower Keys can also boast of the **Looe Key National Marine Sanctuary,** one of the best snorkeling and diving reefs in the world. (See the Area Overview and Diving and Snorkeling chapters for details.)

Accommodations are scattered all throughout the Lower Keys, where campgrounds tend to dominate (see the Campgrounds chapter if you'd like to camp in the area). Most of the accommodations here started as fishing camps decades ago and have been updated to varying degrees. Several wonderful bed-and-breakfast inns are tucked away on a little-known oceanfront road, offering seclusion, privacy, and limitless vistas of the sea.

Crowning the assets of Lower Keys accommodations is **Little Palm Island,** a premier resort that rules in a class by itself. Whatever your lodging choice in the sanctuaries of the Lower Keys, your proximity to Key West more than makes up for any tourist attractions or nightlife that may be lacking here.

BARNACLE BED & BREAKFAST $–$$
1557 Long Beach Dr., Big Pine Key
(305) 872-3298 or (800) 465-9100
www.thebarnacle.net

The Barnacle Bed & Breakfast lolls on a serene stretch of beach that extends out into the Atlantic. Constructed as three rotated, star-shaped levels, the Barnacle is a study in contradictions. The generous Tarpon and Dolphin rooms on the second level, with two queen-size beds per room, open to a foliage-filled atrium that houses the hot tub. Comfortably furnished with ceiling fans, a sofa, television, table, and chairs, the atrium serves as a common room. Guests meet here each morning for a complimentary breakfast buffet. The Blue Heron cottage perches in an outbuilding, where its stained-glass windows and private porch lend a romantic perspective. Both the Blue Heron and the Ocean room (which nearly rests on the sand) have kitchens, living rooms, private entrances, and patios. A circular stairway crawls to the Crow's Nest, a cozy little room located above the atrium with a skylight window.

Guests enjoy use of kayaks, bicycles, snorkeling gear, and barbecue grills. Children younger than age 16 are not permitted. Smoking is permitted only outside the guest rooms. Finding Long Beach Road is a little tricky: Turn left at Big Pine Fishing Lodge, mile marker 33, oceanside, and proceed about 2 miles.

DEER RUN BED & BREAKFAST $$
MM 33 Oceanside, Long Beach Dr.,
Big Pine Key
(305) 872-2015
www.deerrunfloridabb.com

The diminutive key deer really do have the run of this Florida Cracker–style home, for they stroll the grounds like boarded guests.

Owner Sue Abbott met the herd years ago when she first bought the property, and they've remained fast friends ever since. Staying at Deer Run is akin to vacationing in a nature preserve. The self-proclaimed "Mother Teresa of wildlife," Abbott hand-raises macaws, and at least half a dozen cackle in a wild cacophony around the property.

If you love animals and eccentricity, the three diverse units at Deer Run emanate a homey, folksy appeal. Two of the three rooms have a private entry and bath. A king-size bed fills the lower-level oceanfront room, which sports a large screened porch. A small, affordable room-without-a-view is accessed from the side yard. And in the upper level of the main house, a queen-size bed distinguishes the oceanfront third bedroom. Bathroom facilities are the conventional hallway variety.

The peaceful beach, only 50 feet beyond a raised hot tub, fronts a productive bonefish flat. After you've visited with the animals, wade out and spot a tailing fish. Breakfast is served on the veranda, overlooking the ocean. Deer Run caters to adults. Smoking is not permitted. A three-night minimum is required on holidays. Payment must be made in cash or traveler's checks; credit cards are not accepted. To find Long Beach Road, turn left at Big Pine Fishing Lodge, mile marker 33, oceanside, and proceed about 2 miles.

OLD WOODEN BRIDGE GUEST COTTAGES AND MARINA $$
MM 30.5 Bayside, 1791 Bogie Dr., Big Pine Key
(305) 872-2241
www.oldwoodenbridge.com
Since the 1950s, this family-owned/operated marina has been a haven for locals and visitors alike. The Old Wooden is tucked away at the foot of the bridge that connects Big Pine Key to No Name Key. The bridge was wooden when the camp was built, but it has since been replaced with a concrete structure. Hurrah for progress, but Insiders are happy some things do not change—like the utter authenticity of old Florida Keys flavor in this family-friendly location.

The Old Wooden Bridge sits on Bogie Channel, where you can access both the Gulf of Mexico and the Atlantic Ocean. There is nothing fancy or pretentious about this place. There are 14 one- and two-bedroom cottages, with tile floors. Cottages are decked out in wicker furniture; finishing out the floor plans are kitchens with stoves, microwaves, and utensils; cable TV; Internet access; and air-conditioning. On the property there are campsites and picnic and barbecue areas where key deer roam free. The full-service marina supplies folks with gas, tackle, bait, and rental boats. They also have a family-size swimming pool, along with game and recreation rooms and RV and tent campsites.

PARMER'S RESORT $–$$$
MM 28.5 Bayside, 565 Barry Ave., Little Torch Key
(305) 872-2157
www.parmersplace.com
Originally a fishing camp in the 1930s, Parmer's Resort is something of an institution in the Lower Keys. The 43 units in 13 buildings sprinkled over the five-acre property have copped the monikers of the fish, birds, and flora populating the Florida Keys. From the Grunt, Hibiscus, and Flamingo to the Permit, Spoonbill, and Jasmine, the homey 1960s-style units differ widely in both size and amenities. Small, medium, and large motel rooms, standard and small efficiencies,

cottages, and one- and two-bedroom apartments are all clean and simple.

Fronting Big Pine Channel, Parmer's offers boat dockage at a small additional fee, but there is no beach. A free-form swimming pool anchors the center of the property. You'll need to use a pay phone to call the office, and you must pick up after yourself or pay a fee for maid service. But you can always stoke up the barbie, because Parmer's loans small gas grills to cook your catch of the day. A complimentary continental breakfast is served daily.

LITTLE PALM ISLAND $$$$
**MM 28.5 Oceanside, Little Torch Key
(305) 515-4004 or (800) 343-8567
www.littlepalmisland.com**

Little Palm Island continues to dazzle its guests with barefoot elegance beyond your wildest imagination. An exquisite resort encapsulated on its own five-acre island, 3 miles offshore from Little Torch Key, Little Palm is the centerpiece of the jeweled necklace of the Florida Keys. And like all really fine gems, a stay here carries a hefty price tag. Elevated, thatched-roof bungalows, reminiscent of the South Pacific, shelter Little Palm's privileged guests. Each villa has an elegant yet cozy sitting room, complete with a stocked minibar. The bedroom's king-size bed is romantically draped in mosquito netting. A lavish dressing room with vanity and a luxurious terracotta-tile bathroom sporting an indoor whirlpool and privately fenced outdoor shower complete the suite. To top it all off, add optional massages, facials, pedicures, manicures, and body treatments, either in your suite or at SpaTerre. Two Island Grand Suites provide the ultimate creature comforts—his and hers bathrooms, slate floors, sweeping front porch, and a private

outdoor hot tub that looks out at the placid surrounding waters.

The island restores your soul as well. Television sets, telephones, and alarm clocks are banned, ensuring your escape from reality. Curving coconut palms and flourishing flora pepper the grounds surrounding the villas. At Little Palm Island you can elevate doing nothing at all to an art form. The unhurried pace encourages serious lounging beside the free-form pool, atop the crystal sand beach, or enveloped in a two-person hammock. You'll find a meditative Zen garden secreted away deep within the 5.5 acres of island. If the sun is too much for you, stop in at the 600-volume reading library, find a good book, and sit a spell.

When you've unwound at last and you're ready to function vertically once again, the island offers a cornucopia of diversions. Play with Little Palm's complimentary toys—surf bikes, day sailers, kayaks, canoes, a Hobie Cat, and snorkeling and fishing equipment. Rent a pontoon boat or a nifty Sun Cat motorized lounge chair and gunkhole around the surrounding miniature mangrove islets. Dive Looe Key National Marine Sanctuary or hire a backcountry guide and fish for tarpon, permit, or bonefish. Head offshore with a sportfishing captain and catch that marlin. And if you are really adventurous (and your pocketbook is limitless), Little Palm will shuttle you to a deserted island by seaplane for a tropical tryst.

Access to Little Palm Island is provided from its mainland substation at Little Torch Key. Their luxurious launch transports guests to and from the resort. The 40-foot cruiser, *Woodson*, with two main cabins decked out in teak, polished brass, and mahogany trim, assures a glamorous arrival to the dock. Meals are taken in the outstanding gourmet dining room (see the Restaurants chapter) and all-inclusive packages are available.

A Noble House resort, Little Palm Island and its restaurant garner a myriad of awards and accolades from rating services and publications all over the world, consistently ranking in the top 10. But Insiders know Little Palm Island is number one in the Florida Keys. (Children younger than age 16 are not permitted.)

KEY WEST

This diverse, charming, historic city is considered one of the nation's top travel destinations. Key West's accommodations range from the comfort of a standard motel room to the luxury of a private suite in a historic inn. In this section we escort you through a variety of facilities. Our selections are based on attributes of rooms, service, location, and overall ambience. All facilities have air-conditioning, cable television, and telephones unless stated otherwise.

Price Code

Daily rates for the high season for double occupancy are categorized in the price code. Because many facilities offer a variety of accommodations within one property, we have provided a range, the first to indicate the rate for a typical room and the second for more complex units, such as apartments and suites. Prices indicated in the key do not include the 12.5 percent room tax, room service, or added fees for phone calls, rollaway bed, crib rentals, and other incidentals. In most cases an additional per-person charge is levied when occupancy exceeds two. Off-season rates are typically lower, and in some cases dramatically less. Off-street parking is usually available for guesthouses at about $5 per day.

$	$100 to $150
$$	$151 to $200
$$$	$201 to $300
$$$$	$301 and higher

Motels, Hotels, and Resorts

Hotels, motels, and resorts on this island tend to be so pricey that it is difficult to find a room for less than $100 during the high season. During Fantasy Fest (see the Annual Events chapter) in October and Christmas week, rates jump even higher.

Some chains and individually owned motels along North Roosevelt Boulevard offer waterfront accommodations. Those accommodations near the city's shopping centers and fast-food restaurants in New Town are somewhat removed from the charm of the city's historic district, the hustle and bustle of Duval Street, and public beaches.

Motels

BEST WESTERN HIBISCUS MOTEL $–$$
1313 Simonton St.
(305) 294-3763 or (800) 780-7234
www.bestwestern.com
As Best Westerns go, this independently owned affiliate is small and understated. It is also one of few chains or franchises within Key West's historic Old Town. Of concrete-block construction, the Hibiscus has 61 units, including standard rooms and five one-bedroom efficiencies. Standard rooms are relatively large with two queen-size beds, while efficiencies offer separate bedrooms and kitchens. Decor is bright and clean and features wood furnishings, carpeting, and coordinating wallpaper and bedspread

patterns. All units overlook either the motel's heated swimming pool and hot tub or the street and a variety of palms. Bicycles are available for rent, and cribs are an additional cost per night. Four people can share a room at the given rate. Breakfast is included.

BLUE MARLIN RESORT MOTEL $–$$
1320 Simonton St.
(305) 294-2585 or (800) 523-1698
www.bluemarlinmotel.com

With its reasonable rates, heated swimming pool, and off-street parking spaces that allow you to pull the car fairly close to your door, the Blue Marlin is a good choice for families who want to be near the action but don't want to pay dearly for the privilege. This two-story, pink cement-block structure is not luxurious, but the 54 rooms—all of which overlook the pool—are carpeted, clean, bright, and spacious. All rooms come equipped with a refrigerator; 10 have kitchenettes.

The best thing about the Blue Marlin, perhaps, is its location. It's tucked just a block off Duval Street on the Atlantic side of the island. The Southernmost Point and South Beach are about three blocks away; other downtown attractions such as the Hemingway House, Key West Lighthouse, and even Mallory Square (on the gulf side of the island) are within a reasonable walking distance. There's no restaurant on the premises, but several reasonably priced eateries, including a 24-hour Denny's, and a convenience store are located nearby. No more than four people may occupy a room here. No cots are available.

COMFORT INN AT KEY WEST $–$$
3824 North Roosevelt Blvd.
(305) 294-3773 or (877) 424-6423
www.comfortinn.com

Guests at the two-story Comfort Inn have a choice of 100 rooms housed in three buildings. Options include a room with two double beds or a few larger rooms with king-size beds. The rooms are carpeted and have comfortable furnishings; rollaways are provided upon request to a limited number of rooms. Smoking and nonsmoking rooms are available, as are wheelchair-accessible facilities. The motel is less than half a mile from the Stock Island Bridge and rooms face either the pool or the parking lot. All have free Wi-Fi. Those on the second floor share a common balcony.

The motel offers complimentary continental breakfast and maintains a large outdoor swimming pool surrounded by concrete decking. Scooter rentals are on the premises, and public transportation is available. Complimentary hot and cold beverages are served in the lobby throughout the day.

COURTYARD KEY WEST
WATERFRONT MARRIOTT $$–$$$
3031-41 North Roosevelt Blvd.
(305) 296-6595 or (888) 869-7066
www.marriott.com

This property faces the Gulf of Mexico side of Key West in "New Town," just 10 minutes away from all the downtown activity. On site is a junior Olympic pool, Jacuzzi, and tiki bar (serving lunch and cocktails). Laze on a sunbathing beach or walk along a 300-foot observation boardwalk. Check into your room with king or queen size beds, all with patios or balconies. Family suites are available with microwave, fridge, and a pull-out queen sofa. Courtyard Key West has a meeting room that can seat up to 35 people, ideal for small gatherings, and offers free Wi-Fi. A complimentary shuttle runs to and from downtown from 8 a.m. to 11 p.m. and there is a strict nonsmoking policy at the Courtyard.

FAIRFIELD INN & SUITES BY MARRIOTT KEY WEST $-$$
2400 North Roosevelt Blvd.
(305) 296-5700 or (800) 228-2800
www.fairfieldinnkeywest.com

Fairfield Inn's easygoing prices and comfortable, well-kept facilities make this one of Key West's popular choices with vacationers. The motel offers 100 standard rooms and 32 suites throughout three two-story buildings, newly remodeled at a price tag of $7.5 million. Standard rooms primarily are furnished with two double beds, each with a comfortable, pillow-top mattress; suites with varying amenities, including kitchens or kitchenettes and king-size beds, are other options. Fairfield Inn offers two swimming pools, gas grills, a tiki bar, volleyball court, and guest laundry facilities. A separate concessionaire offers on-premises scooter rentals. Complimentary continental breakfast is offered daily, and covered parking spaces are available.

Hotels

BEST WESTERN KEY AMBASSADOR RESORT INN $$
3755 South Roosevelt Blvd.
(305) 296-3500 or (800) 432-4315
www.keyambassador.com

The Key Ambassador Resort Inn consists of a cluster of two-story buildings scattered across seven acres of profuse tropical gardens punctuated by palm trees and hibiscus across the road from the Atlantic Ocean. Every room has a private balcony, and all 100 units have pleasant views of the garden, the harbor, the pool, or the ocean. Rooms

are decorated in "Key West tropical"—light wood furnishings and floral bedspreads and drapes—and the walls are hung with the works of local artists. Floors are a combination of tile and pastel carpeting, and guests have a choice of two double beds or a king-size bed. Each unit is equipped with a mini-refrigerator.

Central to Best Western Key Ambassador and overlooking the ocean is a (heated in winter) swimming pool with a sundeck. A small bar and grill sits beside it. For do-it-yourselfers, a cookout area offers barbecue grills and outdoor tables and chairs. Other amenities include guest laundry facilities and a daily complimentary continental breakfast. From the Key Ambassador, it's a 10-minute walk to Smathers Beach and 2 miles to historic Old Town. Scooter rentals are available next door or the front desk staff can arrange for a trolley tour. Pets are not permitted here.

CROWNE PLAZA KEY WEST LA CONCHA $$-$$$$
430 Duval St.
(305) 296-2991 or (800) 745-2191
www.laconchakeywest.com

If you truly want to stay where the action is, you can't do better than this. Not only is La Concha the tallest building on the island of Key West, but it's also situated smack-dab in the center of the busy Duval Street scene. Originally opened to great fanfare in 1926, La Concha has, throughout the years, played host to a wide variety of guests, including royalty, presidents, and Pulitzer Prize–winning authors. Hemingway mentions it in one of his novels, and legend has it that Tennessee Williams completed the award-winning play *A Streetcar Named Desire* while in residence here.

Like the island itself, La Concha has weathered many changes and has undergone numerous face-lifts. Today its 150 guest rooms and 10 suites have a casual yet elegant feel. Each is furnished in 1920s art deco style, with wicker chairs, poster beds, floral bedspreads, lace curtains, and period antiques. Many rooms overlook either the never-ending parade of activity on Duval Street or the pool terrace. The spacious pool, set amid lush island foliage, features a multilevel sundeck and tiki bar serving snacks and tropical libations.

The hotel's Jack's Seafood Shack, which opens directly onto Duval Street, serves breakfast buffet, lunch, and dinner and features nightly entertainment. And for you coffee lovers, the only Starbucks on the island is located in the building as well. The Old Town Trolley stops at the door of La Concha, and the island's favorite haunted attraction, Ghost Tours of Key West, leaves nightly from the lobby (see the Attractions chapter).

This hotel's most notable feature, perhaps, is its seventh-floor wraparound observation deck. The Top not only offers a bird's-eye perspective on downtown Key West, but it is also one of the best places in town to view the sunset. You're well away from the craziness down at Mallory Square and while you're drinking in all that beauty, you can be drinking a cocktail, cold beer, or soda as well. A full bar at the Top is open limited hours around sunset each evening and serves cocktails and appetizers.

THE INN AT KEY WEST   **$$$**
3420 North Roosevelt Blvd.
(305) 294-5541 or (800) 330-5541
www.theinnatkeywest.com
With dazzling landscaping and interior decorating, using a tropical theme in their rooms

and suites, the Inn at Key West has set the stage for your enchanting vacation plans. The inn is conveniently located along North Roosevelt Boulevard and only 3 miles from Duval Street. With 105 rooms, this complex can accommodate a getaway for 2 or a family reunion for 20. All rooms, decorated in Tommy Bahama furnishings, have cable TV, climate control, and luxurious bathrooms. Choice rooms offer private balconies where you can take in a wandering tropical breeze from the Gulf of Mexico. On premises is the largest tropical freshwater pool in Key West. Creatively landscaped foliage and vegetation surround a lively full-service tiki bar. The Inn at Key West houses the casual open-air Café at the Inn, which is under the umbrella next to the bar. You can enjoy breakfast buffet and lunch till early afternoon or Sunday brunch (sorry, no alcohol till noon in the Keys on Sunday). Concierge services are available for booking everything from sightseeing tours to sports activities.

PEGASUS INTERNATIONAL
HOTEL   **$–$$**
501 Southard St. (corner of Duval)
(305) 294-9323 or (800) 397-8148
www.pegasuskeywest.com
Located on a busy corner in the heart of downtown Key West, Pegasus International Hotel offers 30 rooms with various bedding combinations, including two double beds, a queen-size bed, or a king-size bed. The rooms are tastefully appointed in tropical decor. Rates are reasonable, especially considering the hotel's prime location, which is within easy walking distance of Mallory Square and the restaurants and bars on lower Duval Street, plus the fact that parking is free. Amenities here include a swimming pool, hot tub, and sundeck, all located on

the second floor and all overlooking bustling Duval Street. Aside from the complimentary continental breakfast, there are no on-premises food outlets at Pegasus; however, several restaurants are conveniently located within a block or two.

PELICAN LANDING
RESORT & MARINA $$$$
915 Eisenhower Dr.
(305) 293-9730 or (888) 822-5840
www.keywesthideaways.com
You've found your home away from home in the inconspicuous gulfside Pelican Landing, a concrete-block condominium and marina complex on Garrison Bight. Among the 16 units, guests are offered a choice of standard rooms with two double beds or one-, two-, or three-bedroom suites. All accommodations are decorated according to the taste of their individual owners. Suites have balconies overlooking the marina, and those on the fourth (top) floor are duplex-style with either loft bedrooms or two enclosed, second-story bedrooms. Large sliding glass doors with vertical blinds lead to furnished balconies, and all suites have washer-dryers. Suites have king-size beds in the master bedroom, two double beds in the second and third bedrooms, and queen-size sleeper sofas. Some suites have hot tubs. A one-bedroom penthouse suite is among the most romantic.

Pelican Landing's heated swimming pool is surrounded by a sundeck. Gas barbecue grills and a fish-cleaning station are available for guests. The facility is boat accessible by powerboat only, because a fixed bridge offers only an 18-foot clearance. The marina offers 15 boat slips accommodating vessels up to 35 feet with a 12-foot beam. All guests have off-street parking. Charter fishing boats are just across the dock. Pets are welcome.

SOUTHERNMOST HOTEL $–$$$
1319 Duval St.
(305) 296-6577 or (800) 354-4455
www.southernmostresorts.com
Gingerbread architectural detail and native flora come together at Southernmost Hotel, reminding visitors that they have reached an eclectic city on an island. Situated just across from Southernmost on the Beach, Southernmost Hotel's six buildings are surrounded by ample parking and are trimmed with exotic plants, flowers, and trees. One of the hotel's two swimming pools sits in the center of the parking lot, concealed by lush greenery and a wall. The courtyard features the main pool, surrounded by decking, and a hot tub. Each pool has its own outdoor tiki bar. The 127 guest rooms have either two double beds or a king- or queen-size bed; some rooms include sleeper sofas. A large room with two double beds and a kitchen serves as the facility's one and only efficiency. Some rooms have private balconies. Scooter and bicycle rentals and concierge services are available. The tiki bars serve light bites for breakfast and lunch. Southernmost Hotel is wheelchair accessible and offers smoking and nonsmoking rooms.

SOUTHERNMOST ON
THE BEACH $–$$$$
508 South St.
(305) 296-6577 or (800) 354-4455
www.southernmostresorts.com
So you want to stay right on the beach? At a gorgeous property? Then book your reservation at the Southernmost on the Beach. New in 2009, this 80-room lodging will pamper you and your party. Suites are 400 square feet

with 13 oceanfront and 48 oceanview rooms. On site is a private pier and a pool with pool bar, and you can wine and dine at the Southernmost Beach Café. Duval Street is just a block away, but once on this lovely resort, you will think you are on a deserted island.

Full-Service Resorts

BEACHSIDE MARRIOTT $$$$
3841 North Roosevelt Blvd.
(305) 296-8100 or (800) 546-0885
www.beachsidekeywest.com
Proudly standing sentinel at the entrance to Key West on Roosevelt Boulevard is the Beachside Marriott. With no expenses spared, this upscale property is impressive. There are 222 rooms, all dressed up in designer furniture, flat-screen TVs, and marble, marble to marvel you, everywhere! Elegance abounds here, but still with a Key West charm about the property. The 5,600-square-foot ballroom can handle any event, and if you wish to impress your best friends and family, they can land at the helicopter pad on the lobby roof.

There is a heated pool on the grounds flanked by lush tropical foliage, rooftop sundecks, and a small beach for midnight strolls. Head to the Blue Bar by the pool for casual afternoon refreshments. Then for evening, glide indoors to the swank Tavern N Town restaurant set with white tablecloths, French china, and classic dishes of foie gras and grilled duck. You get the picture!

CASA MARINA RESORT AND
  BEACH CLUB $$$$
1500 Reynolds St.
(305) 296-3535 or (800) 303-5717
www.casamarinaresort.com
The Waldorf Astoria Collection is now the proud owner of the grand dame of hotels in the Florida Keys, the Casa Marina Resort and Beach Club. Construction of the hotel dates back to 1918, after railroad magnate Henry Flagler envisioned a resort for wealthy snowbirds. This still holds true today. The beautiful property is a Florida Keys fairy tale, a legend that has hosted the likes of baseball great Lou Gehrig, actress Rita Hayworth, and President Harry Truman.

Built of poured concrete with walls 12 to 22 inches thick, the structure has withstood many a storm and come away only ruffled. Sleek guest rooms, suites, and public areas; two new pools; private cabanas; new landscaping; and a private water walkway to the Atlantic Ocean await guests. Its location on the largest private beach in Key West, minutes from Old Town and Duval Street and three minutes from the Key West International Airport, makes this laid-back, elegant hotel an ideal choice.

Offering timeless, tasteful luxury in all of its 311 guest rooms, the resort includes 72 suites on four floors. Wi-Fi connection is available throughout the hotel, as well as 11,000 square feet of event space accommodating up to 500 people. There are 12 meeting/event rooms and a health club with massage, sauna, and salon services. Motor scooters and bicycles can be rented. Lighted tennis courts with lessons are available. The Sun-Sun Beach Bar and Grill is nestled between the beach and pool area for a romantic breakfast, lunch, or dinner. The Rambler Lounge is a full bar with nightly entertainment and, of course, room service for guests. The Strip House restaurant, located a short stroll away at the sister property, the Reach Resort (see listing in this chapter), is the hot spot in Key West for a top-notch steak with all the trimmings.

DOUBLETREE GRAND
KEY RESORT $$$-$$$$
3990 South Roosevelt Blvd.
(305) 293-1818 or (800) 222-8733
www.doubletreekeywest.com

Just when locals thought the island of Key West simply could not support one more hotel, along came this luxury resort. Grand Key Resort boasts 216 guest rooms in a variety of configurations, from connected double queen-size rooms to luxurious suites. The property is tucked between two condominium complexes on the north side of the island, not far from Key West International Airport. Rooms overlook the parking lot on one side and the salt ponds that border the airport on the other; if you're lucky enough to be on one of the upper floors, you might have a pretty decent view of the Atlantic Ocean and Smathers Beach in the distance.

Everything at Grand Key is spanking clean and bright. All of the rooms are appointed in the casually elegant tropical style that has become the hallmark of upscale hotels in Key West. All of them feature a full complement of guest amenities, including mini-fridges, coffeemakers, hair dryers, in-room safes, ceiling fans, bathrobes, cable TV with HBO, and in-room movies. A focal point in the lobby is the 25,000-gallon aquarium that stretches from floor to ceiling and is filled with the kind of colorful fish you would likely see in their natural habitat on a trip to the reef.

The Palm Haven Restaurant, which overlooks the pool at the far end of the lobby, serves island fare. Snacks and tropical libations are available at an open-air bar positioned poolside. A large deck and plenty of white rocking chairs beckon sun worshipers. An on-premises gift shop, meeting facilities, and concierge services are available.

Children are welcome here. In fact, those younger than age 18 stay free with parents, and nature-based programs are planned to keep them entertained.

HYATT KEY WEST RESORT
AND SPA $$$-$$$$
601 Front St.
(305) 809-1234 or (888) 591-1234
www.keywest.hyatt.com

Fronting on the Gulf of Mexico, the five-story Hyatt Key West, with a $10 million redesign project, is a three-building, 118-unit complex of standard rooms, junior suites, and standard suites, all with sliding glass doors and private balconies. Rooms overlook the city, pool, or Gulf of Mexico. Fully carpeted except for tile entranceways, standard rooms generally face the city and have one king-size bed or two double beds, fully stocked minibars, hair dryers, coffeemakers, irons, and ironing boards. Some have ceiling fans, and bathrobes are provided upon request. A variety of suites feature panoramic views of the gulf. Junior suites (L-shaped with a small sitting area and no dividing walls) and standard suites (one-bedroom units with a door separating the bedroom from the living area) are all fully tiled and boast the same amenities as standard rooms. Junior suites also have whirlpool tubs. Furnishings all are primarily light oak accented by wicker and rattan; bed coverings and draperies are in tropical prints. Wall hangings feature colorful local and Caribbean scenes.

Hyatt has an outdoor swimming pool and hot tub, two restaurants, a small health club, two dive boats, a charter fishing boat, and a 68-foot sailing yacht for afternoon snorkeling and early-evening sunset sails. The Hyatt operates their Jala Spa to soothe and pamper their guests. Also available are the use of an on-site fitness center, water sports, and scooter and bike rentals, and the hotel has a small private beach. A three-tier sundeck overlooks the beach, and the resort's own SHOR American Seafood Grill (see the Restaurants chapter) is a great place to enjoy the sunset. Concierge, room service, and laundry valet are available. The Hyatt has smoking and nonsmoking rooms and wheelchair-accessible facilities. The resort offers special packages throughout the year, so inquire when you call to make reservations.

OCEAN KEY RESORT
AND SPA $$$-$$$$
Zero Duval St.
(305) 296-7701 or (800) 328-9815
www.oceankey.com
Part of the Noble House family of resorts, Ocean Key is a large resort with an intimate flavor. From their rooms and balconies, Ocean Key guests can see the water, our famous sunsets, and offbeat Mallory Square entertainers, all without the hassle of crowds. Among the 100 units in this five-story resort are guest rooms and one- and two-bedroom, two-bath suites furnished with laminated wood and other lightweight furnishings. Ceiling fans are standard. Standard guest rooms all feature tiled floors and one queen-size bed, plus a queen-size pullout sofa in the sitting area. Kitchens and living rooms in all suites are tiled, and bedrooms are carpeted. Other features include oversize baths and private hot tubs, kitchens, living rooms with sleeper sofas, and private balconies. One-bedroom suites have a king-size bed. Two-bedroom units have a king-size bed in the master bedroom and a queen-size bed in the second bedroom. Penthouse suites, the most expensive units in the facility, feature

full kitchens with microwaves, washers, and dryers.

On the premises are the Sunset Pier, which has a full bar, waterfront dining, and live entertainment nightly; the Hot Tin Roof restaurant (see our Restaurant chapter); the poolside Liquid Lounge bar, only open to resort guests; and a marina with fishing, snorkeling, dive charter boats, and a glass-bottomed tour boat. Other amenities include valet laundry, room service, and concierge service. The hotel honors requests for nonsmoking rooms. Children younger than age 12 stay free when accompanied by an adult. Ocean Key Resort does not provide cots. Cribs are provided free upon request.

Ocean Key Resort and Spa offers its tranquil Spa Terra for its guests. This serene escape is a 2,550-square-foot Indonesian-inspired spa. The theme of this facility originated at the sister property, famed Little Palm Island Resort (see listing in this chapter) located on Little Torch Key.

This resort offers many fun and exciting packages for guests, so be sure to inquire when making your reservation. Oscar–winning actress Meryl Streep was spotted here in a large-hat-and-sunglasses disguise, enjoying a brief vacation with family in tow, and country chanteuse Shania Twain (with posse) also checked in for a weekend visit.

ORCHID KEY INN $$$-$$$$
1004 Duval St.
(305) 296-9915 or (800) 845-8384
www.orchidkey.com
Something old is new and grand again. Built in the 1950s, the Key Lodge Motel had the perfect location but needed to be brought up to date. Tucked between old conch houses and storefronts, the new owners (they also own the Almond Tree Inn,

see listing in this chapter) have brought this 24-room property back to life in a big way. After massive renovations made while maintaining the original footprint, the Orchid Inn is open and warmly greets guests. Terrazzo tile floors and fabrics reminiscent of the '50s are tastefully done with muted walls and white bedding accented with teal green and blues. The guest rooms have the original tongue-and-groove ceilings, painted white to give the space a light, airy feel. Each room also has a small kitchenette counter with microwave, mini-fridge, and coffeemaker. Local artists' works hang on the walls to reinforce the Key West theme. The owners have outfitted the resort with Energy Star appliances and low-flow fixtures. Fabrics, towels, and rugs are all made from sustainable resources with the countertops and flooring made from 75 percent recycled content. Even the wood furniture, from Indonesia, is produced from eco-friendly mindi wood, which is similar to American oak, but sustainably harvested. The outdoor water features have recycled water from an underground reservoir while the landscaping uses native materials that are drought-resistant. The pool has a dramatic sunning shelf and the hot tub features a tiled wall with a purple orchid mosaic and a rain waterfall. Near the pool is a bar, where guests are served drinks in the afternoon and evening and a continental breakfast in the morning. This property is centrally located for all activities in Old Town Key West, so you can walk or ride bikes to restaurants, shops, and activities.

PARROT KEY
HOTEL & RESORT $$$–$$$$
2801 North Roosevelt Blvd.
(305) 809-2200 or (866) 643-5397
www.parrotkeyresort.com

This newcomer to Key West has 97 rooms, four pools, and a sunning beach, is a few minutes from downtown Old Town, and is on the Gulf of Mexico. Owned by the Singh Company (same owners of Tranquility Bay Beach House Resort, this chapter), the Parrot Key Resort is straight out of a travel magazine. Each private three-story unit offers two or three bedrooms, three and a half baths, designer kitchens with signature stainless steel appliances, granite countertops, and two private porches. The interiors are decorated in a seaside cottage motif with original Florida Keys art for accents, fine linens, and king beds.

On the third floor of each guesthouse is the media/game room, outfitted with Xbox 360, a 37-inch LCD TV, Bose surround sound system, extensive games, and two Renegade game chairs. Tropical landscaping hides you away with lush gardens and sunbathing terraces surrounding two sides of the resort. There is a full conference center on the property and a casual dining facility steps from the pool. Parrot Key Resort is a smoke-free environment, both inside and out.

PIER HOUSE RESORT
AND CARIBBEAN SPA $$$–$$$$
1 Duval St.
(305) 296-4600 or (800) 723-2791
www.pierhouse.com
For more than 40 years, the Pier House has offered luxury lodging in Key West. The resort has recently undergone a renovation and rooms have views of the Gulf of Mexico, the swimming pool, or the city. Rooms overlooking the pool and the gulf have sliding glass doors and private balconies, and those facing the water may look out on the beautiful Key West Harbor or on sunbathers along a portion of the resort's private

beach. Standard in all rooms are minibars, coffeemakers, and hair dryers. Lush tropical foliage and brick paving surround the swimming pool and outdoor hot tub. The resort's beach and a secluded island glisten in the distance.

The Pier House is also host to the Caribbean Spa, a full-service spa that offers fitness facilities, facials, massages, a hair salon, and various manicures and pedicures. Room service is available and a concierge will arrange for additional needs. The hotel also features a restaurant called HarborView Café and the Chart Room Bar (see the Nightlife chapter). Off-street parking is abundant. Rates are based on double occupancy; each additional person is charged an additional fee per night.

THE REACH RESORT $$$-$$$$
1435 Simonton St.
(888) 318-4316
www.reachresort.com

Splendor by the sea is what visitors to the Reach Resort will discover. Newly aquired by the Waldorf Astoria Collection, this resort offers miles of ocean water to view and a glistening white-sand beach with sounds of rolling waves. All 226 guest rooms and suites have been recently renovated and are furnished with sunny lemon-colored walls and terra-cotta tiled floors with Caribbean artistic touches and private balconies. Island View rooms feature comfortable accommodations, balcony, and wet bar plus the usual amenities. Ocean View rooms give guests an ocean view or tropical pool view, private balcony, sofa bed, and wet bar. Boutique suites house the same features as Ocean View rooms but with in-room movies and plush bedding. Ocean View Boutique suites offer the same additional touches but with a living area and full sleeper sofas.

The resort has an outdoor swimming pool, hot tub, and full water-sports concession for rafts, parasailing, personal watercraft rentals, and more right on the beach. The Strip House restaurant, known for its amazing steak dinners (see our Restaurants chapter) sits on the first floor with stunning ocean views and dining inside and out. Room service, valet laundry service, and concierge services are available, along with complimentary transportation to and from Key West International Airport. Facilities at the neighboring sister property, the Casa Marina Resort, are open to all guests (see separate listing).

SHERATON SUITES
KEY WEST $$$-$$$$
2001 South Roosevelt Blvd.
(305) 292-9800 or (800) 452-3224
www.sheratonkeywest.com

Situated across from Smathers Beach, the brightly colored three-story, 180-unit Sheraton is a luxurious all-suite facility built around an expansive concrete sundeck and a swimming pool. The roomy suites (550 square feet) here are decorated in relaxing tropical teals, peaches, and lavenders and are furnished in colorful wicker. Walls feature bright Caribbean-colored borders; floors are carpeted; and rooms are furnished with refrigerators and wet bars, minibars, microwaves, and coffeemakers. Most offer king-size beds and whirlpool tubs, and those facing the pool and ocean have sliding glass doors leading to furnished balconies. Suites have irons and ironing boards, built-in hair dryers, and two televisions—one in the bedroom and another in the living room.

The Coral Crab Café restaurant offers breakfast, lunch, and dinner. A hot tub by the pool accommodates eight, and lounge chairs and pool towels are provided.

Sheraton Suites offers guests complimentary shuttle service to and from Key West International Airport as well as transportation to Mallory Square (see the Attractions chapter).

The staff at the guest activities desk will assist you in planning fishing and diving excursions, restaurant bookings, and more. On the premises are a fitness center, 1,100 square feet of banquet meeting space, and a gift shop. Guest laundry facilities are available, and off-street parking is plentiful. The Sheraton Suites is a pet-friendly resort as well. Animals weighing less than 80 pounds are welcome.

For information about accommodations in Key West—whether you're looking for a quaint guesthouse or a full-service resort—contact the Accommodation Center, www.accommodationskeywest.com; Rent Key West, www.rentkeywest.com; or the Innkeepers Association, www.keywestinns.com.

SUNSET KEY GUEST COTTAGES $$$-$$$$
245 Front St.
(305) 292-5300 or (888) 477-7786
www.sunsetkeyisland.com

The guest cottages at Sunset Key are an extension of the Key West Hilton Resort and Marina, tucked away on an island directly across the harbor from the main hotel, overlooking Mallory Square. Access is strictly by private launch, which operates 24 hours a day between Sunset Key and the Hilton marina.

Nestled amid swaying palms and lush flowering hibiscus, the cottages offer an opportunity to truly get away from the hustle and bustle of Duval Street, yet still enjoy the heart of Key West. You may come and go

from Sunset Key at will, of course, but you truly never have to leave at all. The emphasis here is on privacy and service; if whatever you require is not on the island, rest assured that it can be delivered posthaste from Key West. Cottages feature a beachfront, ocean view, or garden view, with beachfront being the most expensive. Rates are structured on a per-cottage basis, and up to six guests may share a single cottage. Interiors feature separate living and dining areas and bedrooms with either double or king-size beds; every bedroom has its own bath stocked with hair dryer, bathrobes, and plush, oversize towels. The decor has a distinctly Caribbean flavor—ceramic tile floors, pastel accents, ceiling fans, and comfortable, casual, whitewashed furnishings. Airy living rooms open onto private verandas, and kitchens are fully stocked with select foods and beverages and the requisite utensils for preparing and serving your own meals. Each has a microwave/convection oven, coffeemaker, toaster, refrigerator, and dishwasher.

Guests will find a limited selection of groceries at the island outpost market; however, grocery delivery service from Key West is also offered for more extensive orders. If you'd prefer to leave the cooking to someone else, simply walk a few steps to the full-service gourmet restaurant, Latitudes (see the Restaurants chapter), or arrange for a private chef to prepare a meal in your own kitchen. Room service is also available. Oprah Winfrey once rented all of Sunset Key to host her 44th birthday party. Famous faces were everywhere in Key West that weekend.

In addition to a white-sand beach, the island features a freshwater pool, hot tub, two tennis courts, and a health club. No cars are permitted on Sunset Key. However, parking is available in the Key West Hilton garage. Reservations for specific cottage assignments are accepted but not guaranteed; cottages are assigned on a first-come, first-served basis upon arrival. All cottages are nonsmoking.

TRUMAN HOTEL   **$$$–$$$$**
611 Truman Ave.
(305) 296-6700 or (866) 487-8626
www.trumanhotel.com

If you like the convenience of your hotel being within walking distance to all the major attractions, including Duval Street, then book your stay at the newly expanded Truman Hotel. 21 rooms, including a cottage that sleeps eight, have all been redone. Rooms have been appointed with king-size or double beds with flat-screen TVs, iPod and MP3 connections, refrigerators, and Wi-Fi. Baths with glass tile walls, mahogany vanities, and glass sinks that "float" atop marble surfaces flow with the cool blues, browns, and creams for room accents. An open courtyard with tables and chairs for reading or sunning is very inviting. The pool, replete with relaxing underwater jets, is surrounded by palm trees and lounge chairs and is the perfect place to unwind before cocktail hour. This is a nonsmoking hotel. Harry and Bess would approve!

THE WESTIN KEY WEST
  RESORT AND MARINA   **$$$–$$$$**
245 Front St.
(305) 294-4000 or (866) 716-8108
www.westinkeywestresort.com

The bayfront Westin was designed so that all rooms provide views of the pool, the bay, or the marina and its surrounding waters. Guests here also are provided launch service to a relatively secluded beach at Sunset Key (see separate listing). The two buildings that make up the Westin have 178 rooms; one structure has only nonsmoking rooms. The three-story building overlooks the marina; the other, a four-story structure, sits adjacent to Mallory Square. Situated in historic Old Town near the old Custom House, the Westin and its grounds are surrounded by brick walkways. Sliding glass doors framed by wooden shutters open onto private terraces. Textured interior walls boast sconces; floors feature stone tiles. Bleached oak and stone furnishings and handpainted walls welcome visitors to the hotel lobby.

On premises are a swimming pool, hot tub, and sundeck area; fitness facilities; a restaurant offering indoor and outdoor dining; and a sunset deck and lounge. Meeting space is available for large groups.

B&Bs, Inns, and Guesthouses

Key West's Conch-style mansions and captains' and cigar-workers' homes date from the 1800s, and many have been marvelously restored to accommodate a thriving tourist industry. Close to 100 intimate hideaways are tucked along the streets, avenues, and lanes of Key West's Old Town, and these charming, romantic inns, bed-and-breakfasts, and guesthouses provide a sense of history, tranquillity, and intimacy within the active city.

You'll find few waterfront or water-view guesthouse accommodations. Rather, rooms enjoy tranquil garden views or views of the ever-changing, active streetfront. French doors tend to lead to private verandas with picket fences overlooking lush courtyards where deluxe continental breakfasts, full breakfasts, and afternoon cocktails frequently are served beside peaceful swimming pools, goldfish ponds, or hot tubs. Some guesthouses provide passes that allow use of beach, spa, and fitness facilities at some of the island's full-service resorts.

Key West welcomes diversity, and some guesthouses cater primarily or exclusively to gay travelers. Others are considered all-welcome or gay-friendly. In a separate section at the end of this chapter, we highlight primarily and exclusively gay retreats, many of which maintain clothing-optional policies. In fact, a few seemingly conservative guesthouses and inns on the island have begun to incorporate a clothing-optional policy, therefore, it is always a good idea to call ahead and check with the property before finalizing your reservation.

Rates quoted by inns typically are based on double occupancy, and additional guests pay anywhere from $10 to $50 extra per night. Rooms do have a maximum capacity. Inquire about this and all other details when you call to make reservations. If you are certain you'll need full telephone service in your room, check, too, to determine if your service is designed both for call-ins and call-outs.

Pets tend to be more welcome in Key West guesthouses than in hotels or other accommodations throughout the Florida Keys and Key West, but be sure to ask when making your reservation. We will note where pets are permitted. A flat fee or refundable deposit may be required.

As a general rule, guesthouses are for adults only. If a particular property welcomes children, we'll tell you. Otherwise, you may assume that you should either leave the kids at home or look elsewhere in this chapter for kid-friendly accommodations.

The city's high season is typically December through April, and room rates are even higher—with minimum stays

required—during special events and holidays. If you come to Key West for Fantasy Fest in October or during Christmas week in December, the minimum stay may be set at six to seven nights. If you plan to be in Key West at either of these times, you should call and reserve your room at least six months to a year in advance.

At last count, the Key West phone book had listings for close to 100 guesthouses and inns. We have done our best to provide a representative sampling. For a complete list of accommodations, contact the **Key West Information Center** at (305) 292-5000 or the **Key West Chamber of Commerce** at (305) 294-2587 or (800) 527-8539.

ALMOND TREE INN $$–$$$
512 Truman Ave.
(305) 296-5415 or (800) 311-4292
www.almondtreeinn.com

The Almond Tree Inn sits at the historic crossroads of Truman Avenue and Duval Street in Old Town Key West. Lush tropical landscaping surrounds the 22 elegant, amenity-filled rooms. A tranquil waterfall is on the property and sundecks surround the pool. Private, off-street parking assures convenience away from the well-traveled Old Town location. All rooms have TV, voicemail, coffeemakers with gourmet coffee, mini-refrigerators, and microwave ovens. A complimentary continental breakfast is served daily, and beer and wine are offered in the afternoon underneath the pavilion. Some rooms are deluxe king, some rooms are premium king with a king-size bed and a sleeper sofa, and oversize guest rooms have two queen-size beds and a sleeper sofa. All rooms are non-smoking and guests must be age 25 or older unless accompanied by an adult.

AMBROSIA HOUSE $$–$$$$
622 Fleming St.
(305) 296-9838
www.ambrosiakeywest.com

As its name implies, Ambrosia is like a deliciously flavored tropical oasis. This delightful bed-and-breakfast compound is really a combination of six restored properties on two acres. The compound consists of six carefully restored buildings nestled among lush tropical landscaping and clear, cool ponds. Located in the heart of Old Town Key West, just a block and a half off Duval, Ambrosia is convenient to shopping, restaurants, and nightlife. The accommodations include suites, town houses, and a stand-alone cottage. Town houses have full living rooms, complete kitchens, and spiral staircases leading to master suites with vaulted ceilings and private decks. The cottage, which overlooks a dip pool, is a perfect family retreat; it has two bedrooms, two baths, a living room, and full kitchen. Honeymoon suites have four-poster canopy beds and in-room Jacuzzis. All rooms and suites feature individual entrances with French doors opening onto private verandas, patios, or gardens. The walls are adorned with the original works of Key West artists; the beds are dressed in designer linens. Guest amenities include refrigerators, coffeemakers, portable phones, ceiling fans, and cable TV. Large sunning areas, a lap pool, and hot tub are also available. Children are welcome, as are pets.

ANDREWS INN & GARDEN COTTAGES $$–$$$
Zero Whalton Lane
(305) 294-7730 or (888) 263-7393
www.andrewsinn.com

You might have to search a bit to find this place, but once you do we guarantee you won't want to leave. After a day at the beach or a night on Duval, this tiny inn offers a welcome little slice of tranquillity that is tough to beat. Andrews Inn is practically in Hemingway's backyard. You'll find it tucked behind his former house—the only thing that separates the two is a brick wall—on a shaded narrow lane between Duval and Whitehead Streets. Guest rooms here are named for settings in Hemingway's books, such as Paris and Pamplona. They all have vaulted ceilings, a queen- or king-size bed, TV, phones, and private bath. Just outside your door, you'll find a lush tropical garden and comfortable lounge chairs situated around a cool, refreshing pool. You're assured of privacy here all right, but we should warn you about the neighbors because you're almost certain to have a visit from at least one of them. A representative from that gang of six-toed cats that reside next door at the Hemingway House is likely to wander over to say hello.

Andrews Inn offers complimentary mimosas and continental breakfast each morning and cocktails by the pool every afternoon. If you're lucky and you're able to snag one of the inn's limited off-street parking spaces, you can just abandon your car for the full length of your stay. Andrews Inn is within easy walking distance of most Key West restaurants, bars, and attractions.

THE ARTIST HOUSE $–$$$$
534 Eaton St.
(305) 296-3977 or (800) 582-7882
www.artisthousekeywest.com

With the addition of guest suites a block away from the original property, Artist House now offers accommodations at two levels—in a charming turn-of-the-last-century Victorian mansion and in modern, tastefully appointed villas. The one you choose is a matter of personal taste. What the Artist House Guest Villas might lack in Old World charm, they more than make up for by being exceptionally bright and roomy. Each of the six suites have been recently renovated and includes a fully equipped kitchen with microwave, stove, and refrigerator and a separate bedroom with a queen-size bed and cable TV. The three rooms in the house have been renovated as well. Private sundecks, a heated swimming pool, and a reserved parking space for each guest round out the amenities.

Legend has it that this 1890 Victorian mansion, formerly the home of Key West painter Eugene Otto, is haunted by the ghost of Otto's deceased wife, whose burial place in the Key West cemetery lacks a tombstone. Some guests claim they have seen Mrs. Otto on a winding staircase in a room on the second floor.

If you'd care to learn more about this somewhat peculiar family, you will find Eugene Otto's paintings on display at the East Martello Museum. At the Key West City Cemetery (see the Attractions chapter), the former artist's tombstone is surrounded by those of his pet Yorkshire terriers. Ironically, pets are not allowed at the Artist House or Villas these days. However, children age 10 and older are permitted.

AUTHORS OF KEY WEST
GUESTHOUSE $-$$
725 White St.
(305) 294-7381 or (800) 898-6909
www.authorskeywest.com
Visiting writers to Key West often select this private three-building compound as their outpost. Each has his or her favorite room, and each room is named for one of Key West's legendary authors, such as Ernest Hemingway or Tennessee Williams. Look for memorabilia on the author of your choice. The main two-story, eight-room house is tucked neatly behind a cement wall. Lined with lush tropical foliage, it boasts a two-sided sundeck. Two poolside Conch houses, built around the turn of the 20th century, are available for rent; these one-bedroom homes feature queen-size beds and full kitchens. Both have small private porches. Rooms within the main house are equally diverse, offering views of the street, the sundeck, or the gardens. Continental breakfast is served daily in the lounge or by the swimming pool. The inn provides off-street parking, and bicycles are available for rent. Pets are not permitted. Note that the entrance to Authors is on Petronia Street.

AZUL KEY WEST $$$-$$$$
907 Truman Ave.
(305) 296-5152 or (888) 293-2985
www.azulhotels.us
Here is the other bookend of Azul properties mentioned early in this chapter (see Azul del Mar). This graceful Queen Anne mansion, built for wealthy cigar baron Walter James Lightbourn, was completed in 1903. In 1992 it was transformed into a hotel, and in 2007 the home was beautifully restored to its current charming splendor. Listed on the National Register of Historic Places, Azul Key West offers guests stylized bedrooms with flat-screen TVs, Wi-Fi, and a shimmering pool. Breakfast fare is a "Tropical Continental" featuring fruit, yogurt, and cereal. Book the room that takes you up two flights of stairs to the treetops. Spend a night among the stars and clouds that is as close to heaven as this "paradise" can get you.

THE BANYAN RESORT $$$-$$$$
323 Whitehead St.
(305) 296-7786 or (866) 371-9222
www.banyanresort.com

The Banyan Resort is a collection of eight beautifully preserved and refurbished Conch-style homes, five of which are listed on the National Register of Historic Places. One of these buildings formerly served as a cigar factory. The homes boast 38 contemporary studios, suites, and duplexes, with full kitchens. Some units have been sold as condominiums; others are available as time-shares and guest accommodations. Studios are least expensive, and rates increase with size: one bedroom, one bath; two bedrooms, one bath; and two bedrooms, two baths. All accommodations have French doors leading to private patios and verandas that overlook award-winning gardens. Included among the gardens are jasmine, frangipani, hibiscus, ixora, rare orchids, palm and fruit trees, and two magnificent 200-year-old banyan trees. The Tiki Bar serves drinks and light bites throughout the day. Bicycle rentals are available on the premises. Children, with restrictions, are permitted. Limited off-street parking is available at an additional charge.

BLUE PARROT INN $-$$$
916 Elizabeth St.
(305) 296-0033 or (800) 231-2473
www.blueparrotinn.com

Built in 1884 with wood pegs that are more hurricane friendly than nails, the Blue Parrot Inn offers nine guest units. Rooms vary in size, number of beds, and decor. The only blue parrot in residence here is a stuffed one; however, the cats you'll see wandering the grounds are very much alive. A large Irish room with two double beds features Celtic prints and green accessories; the flamingo room, with a queen-size bed, is flocked with feathers and photographs of the famed Floridian birds. Still others remain true to this guesthouse's name through parrot-print bedspreads. All rooms have phones and most have mini-refrigerators.

Out back, a heated swimming pool surrounded by extensive decking sets the scene for a leisurely continental breakfast consisting of fresh fruit, bagels, English muffins, and home-baked quiche or fruit breads served every morning. A tremendous staghorn fern strung along branches of a gumbo-limbo tree makes a magnificent garden centerpiece. The atmosphere at the Blue Parrot is friendly and intimate. Guests must be at least 16 years of age and no pets are allowed. Curbside parking is free; off-street parking is available for an extra charge.

CASA 325 $$-$$$
325 Duval St.
(305) 292-0011 or (866) 227-2325
www.casa325.com

Casa 325 offers one- and two-bedroom suites in a vintage Victorian building that has been recently restored and decorated in a tropical island theme. Suites feature queen-size beds, kitchenettes with refrigerators, microwave, wet bar, and ceiling fans. A center courtyard showcases gardens and a swimming pool.

CENTER COURT HISTORIC
  INN & COTTAGES $-$$$$
915 Center St.
(305) 296-9292 or (800) 797-8787
www.centercourtkw.com

Center Court is a fine example of the historic preservation for which Key West is so justly famous. Nestled on a quiet, inconspicuous lane just half a block from Duval Street, the main guesthouse, constructed in 1874, is surrounded by a collection of former cigar-makers' cottages. Owner-operator Naomi Van Steelandt enrolled in construction courses so that she could carry out the restoration, which won two Historic Preservation Awards of Excellence in 1994. Walls are pastel-colored and feature original local art. Guest rooms are cozy and sleep two to six. Rooms are stocked with beach bags, beach towels, and other goodies. Each cottage has its own bright and cheerful personality, as well as a fully stocked kitchen, barbecue grill, and private hot tub.

The main building houses a spacious, airy breakfast room; dining takes place out on the back porch overlooking a swimming pool, spa, and exercise pavilion. Two cottages are set beside a lily pond. A spiral staircase alongside one of these cottages leads to a clothing-optional sundeck. Breakfast is complimentary for guests in rooms; cottage guests have the facilities to fix their own. Children are allowed in the cottages and suites. Pets are permitted for an additional fee per night. Van Steelandt also performs and coordinates weddings and makes honeymoon arrangements. For information, call her at the numbers shown above.

CHELSEA HOUSE $$–$$$
707 Truman Ave.
(305) 296-2211 or (800) 549-4430
www.historickeywestinns.com
Built in 1870 for a British ship captain who hauled tobacco from Havana and later became the first general manager of Duval Street's La Concha Hotel, Chelsea House was later converted to a guesthouse by the captain's grieving widow to provide lodging to Key West's military visitors. The Conch-style mansion serves as the main guesthouse. And with the addition of a pool

house, garden rooms, and suites building, the total number of units now stands at 19. Each has 10-foot-high ceilings and individualized decor. Guest rooms in the main house feature hardwood floors and heavy mahogany and oak period furnishings. Poolhouse rooms open directly onto the sundeck, and the garden rooms feature raised decks with rocking chairs for lounging. All rooms are furnished with antiques and feature private baths, ceiling fans, refrigerators, and complimentary bath amenities. Some have private or shared porches, oversize tubs, and cathedral ceilings. Unlike the Red Rooster (Chelsea House's more casual sister hotel, described later in this chapter), this is co-owner Jim Durbin's showpiece, boasting four-poster beds and armoires plus nightly turndowns and fresh pool towels.

A full acre of property, shared with the neighboring Red Rooster, is likely the largest of all of Key West's guesthouse properties. Here, a private garden with massive palms and flowering plants forms an L-shaped alcove visible from the windows, French doors, and balconies of some rooms in the main house. Every room at Chelsea House either has a balcony or opens onto the pool area.

A daily continental breakfast is served in an enclosed poolside cafe, and clothing is optional on a secluded elevated sundeck. Also available for topless lounging at this adults-only inn are the gardens, deck, pool, and cabana areas. Off-street parking provides a space for every guest. With prior approval, pets are accepted.

THE CONCH HOUSE
HERITAGE INN $–$$$
625 Truman Ave.
(305) 293-0020 or (800) 207-5806
www.conchhouse.com

Since the 1800s, this historic two-story estate has been passed on from generation to generation. The current owners are Sam Holland Jr. and his mother, Francine Delaney Holland. She is the great-granddaughter of Cuban émigré Carlos Recio, a close friend of Cuban revolutionary Jose Martí. The inn is listed on the National Register of Historic Places and combines Old World decor with modern amenities. The five bedrooms in the main house feature high ceilings, wood shutters, wraparound porches, and picket fences. A poolside cottage offers three guest rooms decorated with Caribbean prints and wicker. Guests may have their continental breakfast in the dining room or on the veranda. Children older than age 12 are permitted at the inn.

CUBAN CLUB SUITES $$–$$$$

LA CASA DE LUCES $–$$$

DOUGLAS HOUSE
  GUEST ROOMS $$–$$$$
419 Amelia St.
(305) 294-5269 or (800) 833-0372
www.casadeluces.com

Cuban Club Suites, La Casa De Luces, and Douglas House Guest Rooms share guest check-in and lobby facilities on Amelia Street, but Cuban Club Suites is actually in a separate building at 1102 Duval St. These two-story luxury suites are condominiums occupying second and third floors above boutiques that are open to the public.

A large living area, full kitchen, bath, and bedroom with a queen-size bed occupy the main level of the two-bedroom suites. An oversize loft area above the main level is furnished either with a queen- or king-size bed and features a second bath and a small private sunning deck. One-bedroom suites have a large living area, full kitchen, and half bath on the first floor; the second-floor loft has a queen-size bed, full bath, and small sunning deck. All suites have washers and dryers and are furnished primarily with light wicker furnishings or heavy wood furnishings accented by antique reproductions.

At the less exclusive La Casa De Luces (English translation: house of lights) are eight units ranging from two small rooms sharing a bath to large garden suites with king-size bed, living room, washer-dryer, and full kitchen. Most rooms are furnished with lightweight wicker furnishings and tropical prints; all have exterior access via private verandas. Complimentary continental breakfast is delivered to guest rooms each morning, and within the La Casa De Luces lobby is a small museum illustrating the rich Cuban history of both buildings. Neither facility has a swimming pool, but guests are provided passes to a nearby resort. Off-street parking is available. Families are welcome. Dogs are permitted if management is notified at the time the reservation is made.

Douglas House is a collection of six Victorian homes, four of which are more than 100 years old. Each house contains 2 to 5 spacious units for a combined total of 15. Standard rooms and one-bedroom suites are furnished with a queen-size bed or two double beds; suites have a full kitchen. All units have private baths and outdoor entrances, and each unit is furnished differently. Some are carpeted with standard wood furnishings; others have hardwood floors and wicker furnishings. Suites have French doors opening to a private deck, patio, or balcony. Some suites have loft-style bedrooms.

Within the compound are two swimming pools and a hot tub surrounded by gardens. Continental breakfast is served poolside each morning, and coffee perks throughout the day. Pets are permitted. Children younger than age 12 are not allowed during the high season.

CURRY MANSION INN $$-$$$$
511 Caroline St.
(305) 294-5349 or (800) 253-3466
www.currymansion.com

Curry Mansion Inn's chief claim to fame is its location on the grounds of the estate that once belonged to the Currys, Florida's first homegrown millionaire family. Situated on Caroline Street, just a few steps off Duval, the 22-room mansion was begun by William Curry in 1855 and completed by his son Milton in 1899. Innkeepers Al and Edith Amsterdam purchased the property in 1975. Edith runs a blog on the inn's Web site so you can read about all the latest goings-on in Key West and at the inn. Curry Mansion is today a museum, housing a selection of turn-of-the-20th-century furnishings and memorabilia from Key West's heyday as the richest city in America (see the Attractions chapter). It is also the centerpiece for a guesthouse that is consistently rated among the best in Key West.

Guests at the Curry Mansion Inn do not actually stay in the mansion; they do, however, have full access to it. Guest accommodations consist instead of 28 rooms adjacent to the mansion, most of which open onto a pool and all of which are surrounded by the lush foliage that characterizes the Curry estate. All of the rooms feature wicker furnishings, antiques, and ceiling fans; the beds are draped in handmade quilts. Modern amenities include private baths, wet bars, small refrigerators, air-conditioning, cable television, and telephones.

A complimentary breakfast buffet is offered poolside each morning; complimentary cocktails are served each evening from 5 to 7 p.m. The inn's heated pool and hot tub are open 24 hours. Ask about beach privileges at nearby oceanfront resorts; Curry Mansion Inn has agreements with several.

A particularly appealing feature of this guesthouse is its location—right in the heart of downtown Key West. The restaurants, bars, shops, and other Duval Street attractions are just steps away; parking is plentiful.

CYPRESS HOUSE $-$$$$
601 Caroline St.

CYPRESS HOUSE GUEST STUDIOS $-$$$
613 Caroline St.
(305) 294-6969 or (800) 525-2488
www.cypresshousekw.com

The 40-foot heated lap pool surrounded by lush tropical gardens on the grounds of this 100-year-old mansion is among the largest at any of Key West's inns. The New England–style, three-story home, constructed of cypress, is listed on the National Register of Historic Places and is a noted attraction along the Conch Train tourist route (see the Attractions chapter). Rebuilt in the wake of the fire of 1886 that consumed much of Key West, the facility was originally owned by Richard Moore Kemp, a shipbuilder and naturalist credited for the discovery of the ridley turtle (now known as the Kemp's ridley turtle). Twenty years after Kemp built his own home, he added another house to the property for his daughter and son-in-law, a pioneer Key West sponger.

Connected by a wooden fire escape, the two homes share a sundeck. Rooms throughout the structures feature 12-foot-high ceilings and wood floors with area rugs.

In-room telephones allow for outside calling, and most rooms have queen-size beds and ceiling fans. Six of 16 rooms have private baths. A handpainted floral ceiling border accents one room, and all are furnished with period antiques. Porches on the first and second floor are accessible to guests. A breakfast buffet featuring home-baked goods is served poolside, as is a nightly complimentary cocktail hour with beer, wine, and snacks.

Pets are not permitted, but you are invited to pet the resident dog and cat in case you miss your own. Four luxury suites and two guest rooms distinguish Cypress House Guest Studios (formerly William Anthony House), located three doors up the street at 613 Caroline St. Amenities include sitting and dining areas, private baths, kitchenettes, air-conditioning and heating, cable TV, and phones. However, it's not the usual amenities that will draw you in to the aura of idyllic retreat, but the spa, pond, deck, and delightful gardens.

DUVAL HOUSE $$-$$$$
815 Duval St.
(305) 292-9491 or (800) 223-8825
www.duvalhousekeywest.com
This two-story inn may be set on busy Duval Street, but its pigeon plums, banyans, heliconia, and hibiscus successfully guard it from intrusion. Lounge poolside amid traveler's palms and light jazz music, linger on a shady hammock, or chat with others in a gazebo by the fishpond. The inn's breakfast room maintains a library of books, board games, magazines and newspapers, and a weather chart listing temperatures throughout the world.

In the 1880s Duval House was inhabited by cigar workers. Today the 28 standard

and deluxe rooms and apartments are furnished with English antiques, white wicker, and French doors. All are air-conditioned. Locally made frangipani soap is placed in each bathroom. Most rooms have color television, and some feature elegant poster beds and private porches. All except the two apartments and two front rooms look out onto the gardens. If you visit Duval House, look for Mush, the resident cat, who receives letters from former guests throughout the world.

EDEN HOUSE $-$$$$
1015 Fleming St.
(305) 296-6868 or (800) 533-5397
www.edenhouse.com
For years Eden House was known as a no-frills, low-budget hangout for writers, intellectuals, and Europeans. Over the past few years, owner Mike Eden has added several enhancements.

Constructed of wood and concrete, the facility categorizes units by luxury rooms and efficiencies (two of them have sleeping lofts); private rooms and efficiencies with bath or shower; semiprivate rooms with shared baths; and European rooms with double or twin-size beds, a sink, and a bath and shower in the hall. Most other units feature queen-size beds. Prices descend respectively. Accommodations are decorated in light, subdued colors and tropical prints and furnished with a mix of wicker and rattan. Many units have French doors leading to porches and decks near the center of the facility, where gardens surround a swimming pool, hot tub, and gazebo.

Children are permitted, but pets are not. Bicycle rentals are available and guests are treated to a cold drink at check-in. Be sure to check out the elevated sundeck and hammock area, but tread softly. Those tanning bodies are likely to be sound asleep. Eden House is a smoke-free facility.

THE FRANCES STREET
BOTTLE INN $–$$
535 Frances St.
(305) 294-8530 or (800) 294-8530
www.bottleinn.com

Tucked away in a quiet residential neighborhood on the edge of Old Town, this charming inn takes its name from the owner's collection of antique bottles and cobalt-blue glassware displayed in every window and along several interior shelves. The trim, white frame structure was once a corner grocery store and boardinghouse. The atmosphere here is quiet and intimate. The Bottle Inn has just eight guest rooms, each with private bath, air-conditioning, and color television. White wicker chairs line a gracious porch across the front of the house, and in the lush tropical gardens, a complimentary continental breakfast is served each morning under the poinciana trees. Concierge service is available. Although the grounds are too small to allow for a pool, there is a hot tub. If you're looking for a guesthouse experience well removed from Duval, yet still within walking distance of most Old Town attractions, you'll find excellent value here. This is a pet-friendly inn.

THE GARDENS HOTEL $$$$
526 Angela St.
(305) 294-2661 or (800) 526-2664
www.gardenshotel.com

In 1930 the late Key West resident Peggy Mills began collecting various species of orchids from Japan, Bali, and other exotic parts of the world. As neighboring homes were placed on the market, Mills would

purchase and level them, adding to her garden until it encompassed a full city block. Before Mills passed away, her garden gained the attention of botanists worldwide and national magazines. These gardens have been restored to much of their original splendor. The Gardens Hotel is a member of Small Luxury Hotels of the World.

A complex of five guesthouses and a carriage house, the hotel offers 17 units, including a pair of two-bedroom suites, set around a tiki bar, swimming pool, hot tub, fountain, and a winding path of bougainvillea, orange, jasmine, palm, mango, breadfruit trees, and more. The architecture is classic, and rooms are furnished with mahogany reproductions from Holland and floral chintz.

Floors are hardwood, bathrooms marble with whirlpool tubs, and walls are decorated with original Key West scenes painted by equestrian Peter Williams. All rooms have garden views, and fountains throughout the grounds enhance the sense of tranquillity. Each room has a television, coffeemaker, minibar, and private porch. All except the historic rooms and the master suite have separate entrances and private porches.

HERON HOUSE $$–$$$$
512 Simonton St.
(888) 861-9066

HERON HOUSE COURT
412 Frances St.
(800) 932-9119
www.heronhouse.com

Centered on a 35-foot swimming pool, decorated with a mosaic of a heron, and a Chicago brick patio and sundeck, every one of the 23 rooms at the Heron House features unique woodwork and stained glass created by local artists. Platform-style oak beds are handcrafted, and all accommodations have

French doors leading to private porches or balconies overlooking the English-style country gardens. This historic facility was built prior to the turn of the last century. It offers basic, upper-standard, and deluxe rooms. All are spacious with incredibly high ceilings and double, queen-size, or king-size beds. Deluxe rooms and junior suites have wet bars, futon sitting areas, and mini-refrigerators. Coffee is served in the breezeway. A private sundeck is clothing optional. Heron House accepts children older than age 15. The Heron House also has a sister property known as Heron House Court. The Heron House Court is similarly styled and resides in a 1900s-era building that is listed on the National Register of Historic Places. The 14 rooms and two suites offer king- or queen-size beds and include Crabtree & Evelyn bath products. There is a heated outdoor pool and hot tub on the property and guests enjoy complimentary continental breakfast and beer and wine during happy hour on the weekends.

ISLAND CITY HOUSE HOTEL $$–$$$
411 William St.
(305) 294-5702 or (800) 634-8230
www.islandcityhouse.com

At Island City House, two 1880s homes and a cypress wood house designed to resemble a cigar factory encompass an Old World–style enclave lined with brick walkways and lush tropical gardens. Wood decking surrounds the hot tub and swimming pool tucked neatly at one end of the compound; the swimming pool has a tiled alligator motif at the bottom. Central to Island City House is its charming courtyard patio, where antique iron benches and bistro-style tables are set around a fountain and fishpond. This is the setting for the daily continental breakfast.

Island City House itself is a Conch-style mansion originally built for a wealthy merchant family. Here, guests choose from 12 one- and two-bedroom parlor suites with kitchens and antiques that provide a New England maritime feel. The Arch House, the only carriage house in Key West, maintains six studio and two-bedroom suites decorated with casual furnishings of rattan and wicker. At the Cigar House, built on a cistern and the former site of a cigar factory, spacious suites feature plantation-style decor that combines antique furnishings with wicker and rattan. The homes have hardwood floors throughout, and many rooms feature French doors leading to private patios and decks.

Children are permitted; those younger than age 12 stay free. Bicycle rentals are available on the premises, and a complimentary breakfast is served in the garden each morning.

THE KEY WEST BED & BREAKFAST—
   THE POPULAR HOUSE $–$$$
415 William St.
(305) 296-7274 or (800) 438-6155
www.keywestbandb.com

When strong winds blow through the city of Key West, you can feel the three-story Key West Bed & Breakfast move with them, for this 1890 home was built by shipbuilders skilled in crafting structures able to weather any storm.

With the exception of one suite, all of the inn's eight guest rooms feature a mix of bright colors, elegant Victorian furnishings, exposed Dade County pine, and 13-foot ceilings. Most have queen-size beds, and third-floor suites in the dormered attic offer a choice of two magnificent views. The back suite has French doors leading to a private deck and is decorated in more muted tones because it gathers color from the backyard's flowering trees, including a wild orchid tree that produces rich purple flowers. The suite at the front of the house is noted for its 5-foot arched Palladian window, which provides a view of the sunset above the city's rooftops and trees.

Continental breakfast, including freshly baked goods and freshly squeezed orange juice, is served outdoors, where tables and chairs line the backyard wood deck. All rooms are air-conditioned, and most have ceiling fans. The inn has no televisions or telephones except for a community telephone to which all guests are provided access.

Two of the inn's four porches are furnished with a swing and double hammock, and the oversize backyard hot tub is also used as a dip pool.

LA MER HOTEL AND
DEWEY HOUSE $$$–$$$$
504/506 South St.
(305) 296-6577 or (800) 354-4455
www.southernmostresorts.com
La Mer Hotel and Dewey House are Key West's only oceanfront bed-and-breakfasts. These two properties have the same owner but are marketed as individual luxury getaways, with distinctly different names. Connected by swaying tropical green gardens with palm trees, a fountain, a dipping pool, and loads of romantic charm, these properties offer a splendid way to spend memorable days and nights in the Florida Keys. La Mer is a turn-of-the-20th-century Conch house with 11 rooms. Each room is elegantly decorated with private balconies or patios. The Dewey House was once home to John Dewey, educator and philosopher, and remained a private residence until 1997. Both properties feature marble bathrooms (some with Jacuzzi tubs), classic furnishings, mini-fridges, Wi-Fi, laundry services, king, queen, or two double beds, and privileges to Southernmost Hotel and Southernmost on the Beach.

While here, you will be treated to deluxe continental breakfast, and afternoon tea served with fresh fruit and cheese. Both properties are nonsmoking; guests must be 18 years of age, and no pets are permitted. Both La Mer and Dewey are steps from lively Duval Street, but far enough away for you to enjoy the tranquil atmosphere of these two classic properties.

LIGHTHOUSE COURT $$$
900 Whitehead St.
(305) 294-9588 or (800) 549-4430
www.historickeywestinns.com
Established as a guesthouse in 1984, the Lighthouse Court is a historic compound of 10 Conch houses dating from 1820 to 1920. Covering half a city block in Old Town, the location of this compound is ideal for sightseeing. It is directly next door to the Lighthouse Museum, across the street from the Ernest Hemingway house, and a block away from lively Duval Street. The half-acre grounds of the property offer many relaxing spaces to explore. Snuggle on a swing on one of the quaint porches, or follow the charming brick paths to find tree swings and hammocks. Chaise lounges and a sundeck beckon you out of the heat of the tropical sun. All of this, with the Key West Lighthouse as a backdrop. The 40 rooms that make up Lighthouse Court are Key West charming. All are tailored to couples, with room offerings of full-, queen-, and king-size beds. The room decorations are embellished with tropical colors and open onto the courtyard. If you really want to embody the aura of old

Key West, reserve the Hemingway Retreat. The penthouse at the Lighthouse Court is named after their famous neighbor and overlooks his Key West home. This suite has views of the lighthouse from the living room, sundeck, and bedroom. 1,000 square feet of space houses a plasma TV, gourmet kitchen, dining area, and loft bedroom. All of the suites are nonsmoking.

THE MARQUESA HOTEL $$$–$$$$
600 Fleming St.
(305) 292-1919 or (800) 869-4631
www.marquesa.com
In 2009, *Conde Nast Traveler* named the Marquesa on their "Gold List of the World's Best Places to Stay." This cluster of homes dates from the 1880s. Each standard room, deluxe room, junior suite, standard suite, and terrace suite is furnished with ceiling fans and an eclectic collection of antique English and West Indian reproductions that evoke the ambience of an exquisite English plantation. Accommodations are spacious, with oversize marble baths. Many rooms feature French doors and private porches overlooking two pools and the garden. At the east end of the garden, brick steps accented by a fountain lead to a newer building of complementary architecture. Breakfast (available for a nominal fee) includes a feast of baked goods fresh from the oven of the highly praised Cafe Marquesa (see the Restaurants chapter).

THE MERMAID AND
THE ALLIGATOR $$–$$$
729 Truman Ave.
(305) 294-1894 or (800) 773-1894
www.kwmermaid.com
In the enclave known as the heart of Key West's historic district, this charming and inviting 1904 Victorian home awaits its guests.

Full breakfast is served, and in the evening guests can enjoy a complimentary glass of wine poolside. Located an easy three-block walk to Duval Street, you are close enough to all attractions but far enough away to enjoy a relaxing atmosphere. Among the bonuses of staying at the Mermaid and the Alligator are the resident pooches Caya and Havana. These lovely, friendly, adorable, jet black flat coat retrievers will welcome you and put a smile on your face.

OLD TOWN MANOR   . $$$–$$$$
511 Eaton St.
(305) 292-2170
www.oldtownmanor.com
Listed on the National Register of Historical Homes, written about in *Key West Gardens and Their Stories* by Janis Frawley-Hold and featured in *Everyday with Rachel Ray* magazine, Old Town Manor still remains a peaceful bed-and-breakfast with grandeur. Built in 1886 in Greek revival style, there are two significant buildings on the property. One is the three-story home and the other is a carriage house that at one time served as a dry goods store. This property was one of Key West's first ornamental gardens, and today the century-old palms still stand.

Steps off Duval Street, in the hub of Old Town, the last century has caught up to this one. The place is delightfully furnished, using the practice of feng shui with touches in keeping with the history of the past. Free DVDs, Wi-Fi, and all the other expected comforts await the traveler. Continental breakfast is included with your room.

THE PALMS HOTEL $$
820 White St.
(305) 294-3146 or (800) 558-9374
www.palmshotelkeywest.com

The main Conch-style house with its wrap-around porches was built in 1889. It features Caribbean influences and is listed on the National Register of Historic Places. In the 1970s the hotel added an L-shaped structure built in a complementary style around a large heated swimming pool. All 20 rooms are painted in pastels and furnished with wicker and Caribbean-style decor; rooms in the main house have separate access to the porch. Most have queen- or king-size beds or two double beds. Some floors are carpeted, some are tiled, and several rooms in the main house feature all-wood flooring. Private entrances, private baths, and ceiling fans are standard. A deluxe continental breakfast is served each morning at the full-service poolside tiki bar, and the large heated swimming pool is open around the clock. The Palms has a small parking lot on the street directly behind the hotel; on-street parking is also available. Children are permitted; pets are allowed with advance approval.

THE PARADISE INN $$$$
819 Simonton St.
(305) 293-8007 or (800) 888-9648
www.theparadiseinn.com
Style and distinction mark the 15 suites and three cottages of the Paradise Inn. Two of the three cottages are refurbished Conch houses; the rest are recently built two-story buildings of coordinating architecture. Painted white with Caribbean-blue Bahamian shutters, all units have high ceilings, large marble baths, natural oak flooring, and unique window dressings that combine stagecoach and handkerchief valances with wood mini-blinds. French doors lead to outdoor porches in all but one cottage, and the interior decor features distressed pine, botanical prints, and pale shades of tan.

Rooms have queen- and king-size wrought iron and California sleigh beds.

The inn's diverse gardens, designed by award-winning landscape architect Raymond Jungles of Coral Gables, feature Barbados cherry and avocado trees and bromeliads. Even the pool and hot tub, separated by a lily pond, evoke luxury. Children are permitted. A complimentary breakfast is served in the lobby.

PILOT HOUSE GUESTHOUSE $$–$$$
414 Simonton St.
(305) 293-6600 or (800) 648-3780
www.pilothousekeywest.com
This 100-plus-year-old Conch-style home provides rooms and suites that mix antique furnishings with functional pieces and tropical rattan prints. Once a three-bedroom home, the guesthouse's floor plan has been altered so the first-floor library and dining room now accommodate a guest room and two two-bedroom suites. Suites on the second floor are furnished with its original family in mind. Built by the late Julius Otto, son of a prominent Key West surgeon, the 3,000-square-foot mansion served as a winter retreat. Julius's brother Eugene inherited the Artist House (see listing in this chapter) around the corner, and the yards of the two Otto homes almost back each other. Here in the gracious Pilot House, curved archways lead from one room to another, and moldings are massive but not overpowering.

Frangipani and royal poinciana trees thrive in the yard, and a gumbo-limbo grows through the roof of what is known as this facility's spa building. Set along the brick-patio backyard is a Spanish-style stucco cabana building that offers six suites with queen- and king-size beds, full kitchens, and in-room hot tubs. Furnishings in the cabana are contemporary white wicker amid adobe-colored walls. Mirrors are abundant, and 6-square-foot open showers have sleek European-style showerheads jutting from the ceilings. Passageways rather than doors create privacy for each area of these suites, and all entrances face the swimming pool.

Most rooms in the main house have balconies but are accessed through a formal entrance, and all rooms have kitchenettes, ceiling fans, and private baths. The inn does not provide breakfast, but restaurants are nearby. The backyard swimming pool, at 15 feet by 30 feet, is larger than most in Key West, and an in-ground spa for 12 is sheltered from the sun by a tin roof with lattice and the aforementioned gumbo-limbo tree that grows through the roof. Both are clothing optional. No off-street parking is provided.

ROSE LANE VILLAS   **$$-$$$**
522-524 Rose Lane
(305) 292-2170
www.roselanevillas.com

The Rose Lane Villas are actually in a treasure of a home built in 1886 for Dr. William Warren. This charming oasis greets you when you step onto the front porch, and the cheery wicker furniture beckons you to stay and rest a spell. Steps from throbbing Duval Street, you feel a million miles away from it all, here in the seclusion of the Rose Lane Villas. Offering one-, two-, and three-bedroom villas with kitchens complete with full refrigerators, cooktop range, microwave, coffeemaker, and all essentials. Rooms have cable TV, DVD and movie rentals, and a welcome basket from the owners filled with coffee, tea, bottled water, and snacks. If you just want to read a book or nap, outside by the in-ground pool is the perfect spot to capture a few rays.

SANTA MARIA SUITES
RESORT   **$$$-$$$$**
1401 Simonton St.
(305) 296-5678 or (866) 726-8259
www.santamariasuites.com

An island unto itself, steps away from vivacious Duval Street and minutes from the Atlantic Ocean, you'll discover Santa Maria Suites Resort. Voted as one of the "12 Sexiest Hotels" by *Forbes Traveler*, this "uptown" resort in is definitely a dream come true! 35 luxurious two-bedroom, two-bath suites with glass front balconies overlooking a sensual pool surrounded by exotic tropical greenery are stunning. All suites have state-of-the-art kitchens with wine chillers, flat-screen TVs, Wi-Fi, housekeeping, washer and dryer, and private parking. Put on those Jimmy Choos and pop that bottle of Cristal—this modern and chic Santa Maria Suites Resort is one to savor. The resort also houses the chic sushi restaurant Ambrosia (see the Restaurants chapter).

SIMONTON COURT HISTORIC
INN AND COTTAGES   **$-$$$**
320 Simonton St.
(305) 294-6386 or (800) 944-2687
www.simontoncourt.com

Situated on two acres of property that once boasted a cigar factory, Simonton Court offers 10 varied structures among a number of buildings. The inn's four outdoor swimming pools once served as cisterns. Simonton Court's original building is a Victorian-esque mansion with maritime influences, including a widow's walk. Built by a judge in the late 1880s and known as the Mansion, it now houses the most luxurious rooms and suites on the property. Some of Simonton Court's guest rooms are furnished in period antiques and have green marble bathrooms and large terraces; others offer Caribbean-style decor. One has a spa tub and includes the widow's walk.

A two-story clapboard building with porches, once the actual cigar factory, is now known as the Inn. Within the Inn today are nine rustic old Key West–style rooms paneled with Dade County pine and featuring high ceilings and heavily shuttered windows. When closed, the shutters effectively bar the heat. Rooms here range from basic units with king-size beds to a triplex with kitchen, bedroom, and living-dining area. All rooms at the Inn have hardwood floors and private baths. On the "rustic" side are Simonton Court's two-story cottages. Decorated with antique bamboo furnishings and brightly colored handmade fabrics, interiors are bright and airy. The first floor of each cottage has a kitchenette with microwave (no oven) and a queen- or king-size bed. Attic-style lofts with skylights are furnished with two double beds. Still another building, known as the Manor House suite, offers a spacious two-bedroom complex with full kitchen and living room and a private outdoor pool. Simonton Court's two-story Townhouse Suites are extremely plush, decorated in Grand Floribbean–style antiques and white linens. The first floor has a living room, a bedroom with queen-size bed, a private patio, and a bath with shower. A similar floor plan upstairs is enhanced by vaulted ceilings, skylights, and a spa tub. Both floors have separate entrances via a private balcony or brick patio so that only half the town house can be rented if desired. Town house guests enjoy their own semiprivate swimming pool.

Simonton Court's tropically landscaped gardens, antique brick pathways, swimming pools, and hot tub all come aglow at night, when lighting emphasizes all the right places.

SOUTHERNMOST POINT GUEST HOUSE $–$$$
1327 Duval St.
(305) 294-0715
www.southernmostpoint.com

Throughout Key West, you will discover all kinds of things dubbed "the southernmost"—a southernmost hockey rink and Southernmost Motel, for instance. The Southernmost Point Guest House, across from the Southernmost House, is a showy, three-story, Conch-style mansion built in 1885 for E. H. Gato Jr., son of Key West's first cigar manufacturer. The home is notable for its wraparound porches and private balconies, some of which afford partial ocean or garden views. Rooms come in varying sizes, but all have private entrances, private baths, and ceiling fans. The Ernest Hemingway suite is a deluxe efficiency, with two double beds, designed with a junglelike theme in honor of the legendary author's ardor for hunting, but most rooms are furnished either with queen-size or double beds and antiques with a tropical flair. Some rooms have kitchenettes, and the largest of all is the two-bedroom master suite with queen-size bed in the master bedroom, with a pullout sleeper sofa and a private balcony that offers a partial view of the Southernmost Point (see the Attractions chapter). Suite No. 6 is a duplex composed of portions of the home's second and third floors, and suite No. 5 features a king-size bed and a private porch with a swing.

All guests are given a key to the hot tub (large enough for 12 people). Lounge chairs are provided amid the guesthouse's tropical gardens of banana, coconut palm, breadfruit, and mango trees.

ACCOMMODATIONS

SPEAKEASY INN $–$$$
1117 Duval St.
(305) 296-2680
www.speakeasyinn.com

The Speakeasy, a turn-of-the-20th-century inn, offers spacious rooms in its main Duval Street house plus three spacious suites in a back-alley building along Amelia Street. The original building was the home of Raul Vasquez, a cigar selector at the Gato cigar factory whose true passion was rumrunning between Key West and Cuba. The newer building, built as a residence for the owner's stepdaughter, offers what is referred to as the Gallery Suite, considered to be the best offering in the house. The large, apartment-size unit has a queen-size bed and sleeper sofa and features beamed ceilings, hardwood floors, track lighting, and patio doors leading to a private deck and yard. This and other rooms at Speakeasy also are appointed with private tiled baths, refrigerators, wet bars, and ceiling fans. First-floor rooms feature queen-size beds and private patios. Those on the second floor offer queen- or full-size beds but lack a wet bar. And room No. 2 in the main house features an elegant claw-foot bathtub.

TRAVELERS PALM INN AND GUESTHOUSES $–$$$
915 Center St.
(305) 304-1751 or (800) 294-9560
www.travelerspalm.com

The newly renovated Travelers Palm consists of three new cottages that are all now completely eco-friendly. Owners Roxanne Fleszar and Michel Appellis met on the property in 1996 and eventually purchased it in 2000. They have recently completed the extensive renovations, which garnered them a Certificate of Excellence from the Historic Florida Keys Foundation. Captain's Quarters is the largest and most modern of the cottages and can accommodate up to four people. This two-bedroom, two-bath cottage also features a full kitchen, living room, and dining room with a front porch and side decks that contain a gas grill. All the cottages have access to the on-site solar heated pool replete with stone waterfall.

WEATHERSTATION INN $$–$$$$
57 Front St.
(305) 294-7277 or (800) 815-2707
www.weatherstationinn.com

Nestled deep within one of Key West's premier residential communities, Weatherstation Inn could easily be considered one of this town's best-kept secrets in luxury guesthouse accommodations. Guests here are just 2 blocks off bustling Duval Street, but they'd never know it. Rarely does any sound intrude. Opened in 1997, this two-story, eight-room guesthouse sits on the grounds of the Old Navy Yard inside the gated Truman Annex compound and just down the street from Harry Truman's Little White House. The beach at Fort Zachary Taylor is a short walk away (see the Attractions chapter). Motorized access is limited to the residents of the Annex, and so within these gates, life is always quiet and serene.

With its glistening hardwood floors and elegant island furnishings, the inn calls to mind the plantation homes of days gone by in the British and Dutch West Indies. The balconies and decks overlook lush tropical landscaping, and from the second-floor rooms guests can catch an occasional glimpse of the cruise ships arriving in the harbor just beyond. Amenities here include a heated pool, concierge service, and complimentary continental breakfast.

WESTWINDS INN $-$$
914 Eaton St.
(305) 296-4440 or (800) 788-4150
www.westwindskeywest.com

This complex encompasses a 22-room, two-story New England–style home, two-story Conch houses, and poolside cottages. The majority of guests are couples. Room decor is wicker throughout, with queen-size beds in suites, private entrances to the cottages and Conch houses, and some furnished private and shared porches. Painted in various shades of pastels, all rooms provide a feel of tropical ambience, with ceiling fans and carpeted floors. Some rooms in the main house share a bath. Suites include one-bedroom cottage and Conch units with kitchenettes and kitchenless accommodations that sleep several guests.

In back of the compound, brick walkways wind through gardens of hibiscus, bromeliads, and other flowers and shrubs, and the kidney-shaped swimming pool with waterfall is sizable. Continental breakfast is served poolside.

Gay Guesthouses
ALEXANDER'S GUESTHOUSE $$-$$$
1118 Fleming St.
(305) 294-9919 or (800) 654-9919
www.alexhouse.com

The main three-story building of Alexander's, a Conch–style design, was built around the turn of the past century and has since been renovated. Two additional two-story Conch houses combine for a total of 17 guest rooms. This guesthouse, which attracts both gay men and women, is gay owned and operated. The rooms at Alexander's are relatively basic, equipped with queen-size beds. All rooms have private baths, and two share shower facilities. Deluxe rooms, some with

private porches and patios, have king-size beds. For larger accommodations, opt for a more luxurious suite with king-size bed and queen-size sleeper sofa. Some rooms feature hardwood floors, while others are completely carpeted. Throughout the inn, eclectic local art mixes with poster prints. A highlight is the cobalt-blue, tiled swimming pool surrounded by lush tropical flora. Second- and third-level tanning decks are clothing optional. An expanded continental breakfast is served by the pool each morning; wine and cheese are offered every evening.

BIG RUBY'S GUESTHOUSE $$-$$$
409 Applerouth Lane
(305) 296-2323 or (800) 477-7829
www.bigrubys.com

Formerly the home of a sea captain, the main guesthouse at Big Ruby's, like its two additional on-premises structures, is New England–style clapboard architecture on the outside with contemporary styling on the inside. Seventeen rooms of varying sizes and decor feature clean lines, hardwood floors, and Simmons Beautyrest mattresses in a variety of sizes. Refrigerators, ceiling fans, robes, and beach towels are standard in all rooms. All three buildings of this exclusively gay male and female property share a clothing-optional sunning yard and swimming pool. An outdoor rain-forest shower amid the vines allows for rinsing before and after swimming.

Continental and full cooked-to-order breakfasts are served poolside, as are wine and juice in the early evening. Big Ruby's is set back about 20 feet from the narrow, one-way lane through which it is accessed, and all three buildings are surrounded by orchids and bougainvillea. Balconies on the third floor are set amid the trees, and the grounds are so lush that the second-floor porch does not even allow a view of the street. Limited off-street parking is provided on a first-come, first-served basis.

i Household pets are members of the family, but traveling with them can create a dilemma. Here in the Florida Keys, which is one of the pet loving capitals of the world, you will find properties that welcome one and all. In the Upper and Middle Keys, try Key Largo Grande, Casa Morada, Blackfin Resort, and the White Gate Court. In Key West, consider the Westin Key West, Francis Street Bottle Inn, Chelsea House, Key West Hideaways, the Old Town Manor, and Rose Lane Villas. View www.aaa.com for more listings.

EQUATOR RESORT $$–$$$
818 Fleming St.
(305) 294-7775 or (800) 278-4552
www.equatorresort.com

The building that houses this state-of-the-art, all-male resort looks as though it might have been around for a while, but it is new. It was simply designed to blend with the surrounding structures in this Old Town neighborhood. When it came to guest rooms, the architects opted for upscale with no attempts at conserving space. All 18 rooms are bright and spacious, each featuring Mediterranean tile floors, incredibly comfortable beds, in-room refrigerators, genuinely ample closets, and plenty of walking-around space. Some have special luxuries like wet bars and two-man whirlpool bathtubs.

Common areas are equally well appointed, with a clothing-optional pool, eight-man outdoor whirlpool, lush tropical gardens, a sundeck, and covered patio. A complimentary full breakfast is served daily; complimentary cocktails and snacks are offered every evening except Sunday. All guest rooms are nonsmoking; however, most of them open directly to private decks or balconies where smoking is permitted.

OASIS GUESTHOUSE AND CORAL TREE INN $$–$$$
822 and 823 Fleming St.
(305) 296-2131 or (800) 362-7477
www.keywest-allmale.com

With its Main, Lopez, and Margaret Houses, the Oasis offers 20 guest rooms on three fronts that share a yard: The Main House faces Fleming Street; Lopez House faces Lopez Lane; and Margaret House looks toward Margaret Street. Guests at the facility, which caters to gay men, check in at Main on Fleming. Oasis offers a range of accommodations, including standard rooms with one queen-size bed or two double beds, poolside rooms with queen-size beds and living rooms, and a penthouse on the second, and top, floor of Margaret House. All rooms feature updated furnishings and custom drapes and matching bedspreads in tropical or paisley prints. Some rooms have baths with whirlpool tubs; still others share a bath. The pool and the sundeck surrounding it are clothing-optional.

Also owned by Oasis proprietors is Coral Tree Inn across the street. This handsome 11-room facility is designed to reflect an upscale European retreat. Also catering to gay men, Coral Tree Inn is in a tranquil setting in Old Town. Rooms here feature a queen-size bed or two double beds. They have porches and balconies facing either the pool or Fleming. Penthouse suites are on the third floor. The clothing-optional Coral Tree

Inn has a 24-man hot tub and sunning area, and guests here and at Oasis share facilities.

Both establishments are known for hospitality. A bottle of wine welcomes guests upon arrival; continental breakfast is served each morning. Tropical cocktails are offered by the pool each afternoon, and wine and hot hors d'oeuvres are served in the evening.

PEARL'S RAINBOW $-$$$
525 United St.
(305) 292-1450 or (800) 749-6696
www.pearlsrainbow.com

Lesbian owned and operated, Pearl's Rainbow is one of only a handful of exclusively female resorts in Key West. Men, children, and pets are not permitted here. Pearl's Rainbow includes two clothing-optional swimming pools, two hot tubs, and 38 guest rooms. All standard guest rooms at Rainbow House feature queen-size beds, private baths, TV, air-conditioning, and ceiling fans. The priciest accommodation is a deluxe poolside suite consisting of a king bedroom, private bath, and separate living room with big-screen TV. Pearl's Rainbow is located half a block off Duval on the ocean side of the island. Shops, bars, and restaurants are within a reasonable walking distance.

RESTAURANTS

Take in the glorious sights in the Florida Keys, then treat your taste buds to a culinary holiday they will never forget. We are an island of restaurants offering stone crabs, yellowtail snapper, cracked conch, ropa vieja, picadillo, queen of all puddings, and key lime pie.

Surrounded by water, the Florida Keys yields a bounty that easily could qualify as the eighth wonder of the world. We confidently can boast that nowhere else in the continental United States—oh, why not say it, the universe even—will you find fresher, more innovatively prepared fish and seafood than in our restaurants. Be sure to sample our special natural resources, served any way you like. We import a few raw materials in the feather and flesh categories as well, so your palate will be truly well rounded. (For preparing your own fare, see the Specialty Foods, Cafes, and Markets chapter.)

Enjoy the relaxed atmosphere of our restaurants, where even the most upscale dining carries a laid-back apparel code. Be it a roadside cafe or a resort dining room, you need dress no more formally than "Keys casual," typically an ensemble of shirt and shorts, shoes, or sandals. Men may leave their sport jackets at home, and don't even think about bringing a suit to the Keys unless it is the swimming variety. The same code applies to women; we don't discriminate here. The occasional restaurant, such as Cheeca Lodge, Pierre's, or Little Palm Island, affords you the chance to dress up a bit more if you like—long slacks for the gentlemen, perhaps an island-style dress for the ladies. But the choice is yours.

The appearance of a restaurant's decor doesn't hold to the strict expectations of other parts of the country, either. You'll find that the most unassuming hole-in-the-wall cafe, diner, or bistro may serve the best food in town. Don't drive by. Some of our culinary treasures are hidden away off the beaten track. We'll help you find them.

OVERVIEW

You may find our specialties, from fish to fowl, a trifle confusing. We will translate the Keys-speak. We have organized the restaurants of the Keys from Key Largo to Key West by descending mile marker and have located them as oceanside or bayside. In the Key West section, we offer a cuisine-oriented arrangement with restaurants listed alphabetically.

Free on-site parking is available at virtually all our recommended establishments in the Upper, Middle, and Lower Keys. However, most restaurants in Key West do not have on-site parking. Most restaurants suggest that you make reservations, especially during the high season. Those that do not take reservations will be noted.

Many restaurants serve limited alcoholic beverages. You may infer that unless we specify that an establishment offers a full-service bar—usually the larger restaurants or resort facilities—only beer and wine will be served.

Handicap accessibility varies greatly in restaurants throughout the Keys. While many of our establishments are at ground level, and some second-story locations within large resorts may have elevators, steps sometimes must be negotiated and some bathrooms may be too tiny to accommodate a wheelchair. If this is of particular concern to you, be sure to call the restaurants to see exactly what arrangements might be made to fit your needs.

Unless otherwise specified, you may assume that our recommended restaurants are air-conditioned. Those that provide outdoor seating or accessibility by sea will be highlighted. Children are generally welcome in Florida Keys restaurants. The odd exceptions or age restrictions will be stated.

The dollar sign price code indicated in each restaurant listing will help you gauge the cost of your dining experience (see key below). Some of our restaurants include soup or a house salad with an entree; at others, entrees are strictly a la carte. Most of our restaurants accept major credit cards but rarely a personal check. If plastic is not acknowledged, we alert you in advance so that you won't be caught short of cash.

Price Code

Our price-code rating reflects the cost of dinner entrees for two, without cocktails, appetizers, wine, dessert, tax, or tip.

$................. **Less than $25**
$$ .... **$25 to $40**
$$$ .... **$41 to $60**
$$$$ .... **More than $60**

THE FLORIDA KEYS

Upper Keys

ALABAMA JACK'S $
1500 Card Sound Rd. (Oceanside)
Key Largo
(305) 248-8741
www.alabamajacks.com

There are a couple of reasons why one drives the back door into the Florida Keys. Card Sound Road, north of Key Largo, offers incentives to take this scenic excursion. The traffic is not as heavy, the wildlife are more prolific (crabs run across the road, crocs occasionally appear, and the birds are bountiful), and you can eat at Alabama Jack's. No trip to the Florida Keys is complete without stopping at this Caribbean honky-tonk. Key West may have Margaritaville, but the rest of us can boast about this local favorite. Don't be turned off by the outside of the place; it's what's inside that makes this a true Keys treasure. Alabama Jack's is rated to have the best Conch fritters and Key lime pie by everyone who manages to find the place. It sits on the water where you can feed the fish, check out the mangroves, and enjoy the friendly Keys attitude of the staff.

GILBERT'S RESORT $
Tiki Bar and Restaurant
MM 107.9 Bayside, Key Largo
(305) 451-1133
www.gilbertsresort.com

Gilbert's Waterfront Tiki Bar and Restaurant is not to be missed. The owners pride themselves on their Old World menu and old Keys charm. Starting at lunchtime, the restaurant offers daily specials—authentic German schnitzel dinners on Monday, all-you-can-eat shrimp on Wednesday, and a German buffet tempts you with all the sauerbraten, goulasch soup, and Bitburger beer you can hold on Thursday. Of course, Gilbert's also has Keys seafood and steak, but if you are missing hearty ethnic classics, look no farther. They also offer a raw bar throughout the week and a bountiful breakfast buffet every Sat and Sun.

THE BUZZARDS ROOST $
MM 106.5 Oceanside, Key Largo
(305) 453-3746
www.buzzardsroostkeylargo.com

"You hook it and we'll cook it," say the owners of this casual waterfront restaurant in Key Largo. You can also come by boat (GPS coordinates are N 25.10.237, W 80.22.285) if you really want to have a waterfront experience. If the fishing wasn't that great on your outing, they offer some tasty menu items that will surely fill your tank. One of the best appetizers is corny blue crab cakes. This is blue crab meat blended with veggies and roasted corn served with remoulade sauce. The catch of the day is prepared grilled, blackened, Jamaican jerked, broiled, fried, or sautéed in lemon butter and wine. Buzzards Roost also serves garlic Conch steak and Florida oysters. Seafood Fra Diablo is fish, shrimp, and scallops in spicy marinara sauce served over linguini. If you don't like seafood, they are proud of their fabulous steaks that will please any size appetite.

SUNDOWNERS ON THE BAY $$
MM 104 Bayside, Key Largo
(305) 451-4502
www.sundownerskeylargo.com

One of Key Largo's most popular places to enjoy the sunset, this open and airy—yet cozy and intimate—establishment overlooks the azure expanse of Blackwater Sound. On the light side, Sundowners' Key Largo fish sandwich wins raves—fresh fish grilled and topped with sautéed onions and American cheese on a kaiser roll. If you prefer a more elaborate meal, try the locals' favorite, Mahi Mahi Meuniere—crispy fish topped with white wine and Key lime butter. Friday night is an all-you-can-eat fish-fry extravaganza, and all the tables are set with fresh flowers for evening dining. A large bar, adjoining the indoor dining area, is available for dinner service as well, and busy evenings tend to run on the loud side. The patio and deck afford more privacy. Sundowners offers a full bar and is open for lunch and dinner. Reservations are recommended. The restaurant is accessible by boat.

SEÑOR FRIJOLES $
MM 103.9 Bayside, Key Largo
(305) 451-1592
www.senorfrijolesrestaurant.com

Don your sombrero for a taste of Mexico by the sea—Keys style. Señor Frijoles sits on Florida Bay next to Sundowners and offers popular Tex-Mex fare, such as burritos, enchiladas, and quesadillas. But you'll also find some jazzed-up Conch Republic versions, such as blackened tuna tacos filled with crispy cabbage, pico de gallo, and chipotle sour cream with black beans and rice on the side. Feeling parched? Señor Frijoles offers seven different mouthwatering margaritas made with freshly squeezed lime juice as well as many other tropical libations and Mexican beers with which you can toast the fabulous Keys sunset. Señor Frijoles is accessible by boat and open for lunch and dinner daily.

GUS' GRILLE $$
MM 103.8 Bayside, Key Largo
(at Marriott Key Largo Bay Beach Resort)
(305) 453-0000
www.marriottkeylargo.com

This restaurant serves "Floribbean" dinner specialties such as pan seared yellowtail snapper lightly blackened with garlic mashed potatoes, white wine caper sauce, and cilantro tomato salsa. The executive chef creates your meal right before your eyes in an open kitchen, an upmarket grill-style presentation reminiscent of a tony trattoria. Unobstructed views of Florida Bay and the famous Keys sunset are available from virtually every seat in the house. Booths line the window walls of the light and airy dining room; outdoor patio dining is also available. Walk over the suspension bridge from Gus' Grille to Breezers Bar and Grille for great drinks with luscious sunset views. Open daily for breakfast, lunch, and dinner, Gus' has wheelchair-accessible facilities and an elevator. You can dock your boat at the Marriott while you enjoy your meal at Gus', but reservations for both slips and tables are recommended.

NUM THAI RESTAURANT & SUSHI BAR $$
MM 103.2 Bayside, Key Largo
(305) 451-5955

If your taste for Asian food hovers around Thailand or Japan, Num Thai can offer you the best of both worlds: spicy Thai curries and noodle dishes or sushi, sashimi, and traditional Japanese dishes. The restaurant basks in the glow of deep-teal-colored walls covered with Asian accents while a sushi bar affords one and all the opportunity to watch the masters at work. Japanese offerings include temaki, cone-shaped hand rolls; hosomaki, medium rolls cut into bite-size pieces; a wide assortment of sushi, by the piece or in dinner combos; and tempura. Or enjoy Thai satays; spicy beef salad; seafood, chicken, or beef curries; or volcano jumbo

shrimp, grilled and fired with chili sauce. Pad Thai proves to be a hefty portion.

Open for lunch Mon through Fri and dinner every day, Num Thai accepts reservations for parties of more than five. American and Oriental beers, wine, plum wine, and sake all are offered.

CAPTAIN SHON'S SEAFOOD GRILL & PUB $$
MM 103 Bayside, Key Largo
(305) 453-4000

If it is edible and comes from the sea, Captain Shon's has it on their massive menu. They have been in the business of smoked salmon and seafood processing since 1974, so they know a bit about "la mer." Top dishes are the Key West homemade shrimp cakes, wild Carribbean jumbo conch fritters, and Old English–style fresh seafood and chips. The open-air dining room has swirling fans to keep you comfortable. Their beer menu lists more than 100 brands, so that will keep you reading at least until dessert arrives!

THE FISH HOUSE RESTAURANT & SEAFOOD MARKET $$
MM 102.4 Oceanside, Key Largo
(305) 451-4665
www.fishhouse.com

The scent of freshly prepared seafood lures patrons into this campy nautical establishment, which is bedecked with fishnets, mounted fish, buoys, and twinkling fish lights. Seafood is the name of the game here, and the food doesn't disappoint. The extensive menu features smoked fish done on the premises and the local favorite salad, Jean's Greens—romaine lettuce, fried onion rings, and crumbled bleu cheese served with homemade Catalina dressing. The Fish Matecumbe, a mouthwatering combo of the fresh catch of the day topped with tomatoes, shallots, capers, fresh basil, olive oil, and lemon juice and broiled to perfection, is also always a favorite. The Fish House food is as memorable as "The Fish House Gang" that serves it—most of them have been there since it opened in 1987. The Fish House is open for lunch and dinner daily and reservations are not accepted.

i The Florida Keys is a unique place to live and visit. We are also unique in that most of our creature comforts are provided to us by air, sea, or land. In other words, practically everything is imported except our weather and friendly folks.

THE FISH HOUSE ENCORE RESTAURANT, SUSHI BAR & LOUNGE $$$
MM 102.4 Oceanside, Key Largo
(305) 451-0650
www.fishhouse.com

The owners of the perennially popular Fish House, C. J. Berwick and Doug Prew, have opened Encore, an upscale fine-dining restaurant that tingles the taste buds and scintillates the senses. From the baby grand piano to the long mahogany bar, the decor is elegant, but you do not need to be similarly attired to dine here. Keys casual is good enough! An outdoor patio invites dining amid lush tropical vegetation in all seasons (unobtrusive heaters warm things up on those occasional cool nights in Dec and Jan). You'll find plenty of fish on the menu, such as the wildly popular Fish Matecumbe from sibling restaurant the Fish House alongside 13 other fresh fish dishes. Encore offers a great selection from the land, too, such as chicken breast hand breaded with Japanese

breadcrumbs and a 24-ounce mouthwatering bone-in ribeye steak. Appetizers, soups, and salads are inventive, and the signature dessert, White Chocolate Baby Grand, is enough to share and still satisfy your sweet tooth. After dinner, stop at the piano bar, where you can enjoy tunes from Sinatra to Billy Joel. And, on some lucky evenings, you might even catch a local or two playing along on their own instruments. Encore is open daily for dinner only. Reservations are suggested for Fri and Sat nights.

HOBO'S CAFÉ $
MM 101.7 Oceanside, Key Largo
(305) 451-5888
www.hoboscafe.net

This place use to look like a hobo on the outside, but now there's nothing but a "homey" feeling about its digs. Keys casual is the norm with shirts and shoes the required dress, but if you have socks on, you are overdressed. They want you relaxed so that you can wolf down their home-cooked burgers, sweet potato fries, garlic wings, fish sandwiches, and salads and finish things off with a slice of their mouth-pleasing Key lime pie. An Insiders' secret is out about one of the best locals' place in the Upper Keys.

UPPER CRUST PIZZA $$
MM 101.6 Oceanside, Key Largo
(305) 451-4188

Long a favorite pizza restaurant in Marathon, Upper Crust moved up the Keys several years ago and is now winning raves in Key Largo. You can build your own thick-crust pizza with an array of ingredients, but the House Deluxe is a combination you won't want to miss—pepperoni, sausage, mushroom, green pepper, onion, black olives, extra sauce, and extra cheese. Upper Crust also serves a large variety of pasta dishes and subs and offers daily specials that are difficult to pass up. Upper Crust is open daily for lunch and dinner.

TOWER OF PIZZA $
MM 100.6 Bayside, Key Largo
(305) 451-1461

Antipasto, Greek salad, minestrone, and a potpourri of great pasta dishes vie with fantastic pizza at Tower of Pizza establishments. Sauces and dough here are homemade, and cheeses are fresh. Locals particularly like the Sicilian-style pie, but you can build your own from a long list of tantalizing ingredients. Delivery is free with a minimum order. The second location is at MM 81.5 Bayside in Islamorada (305-664-8216). Both Towers are open every day for lunch and dinner.

COCONUTS RESTAURANT & NIGHT CLUB $$
MM 100 Oceanside, Marina Del Mar Resort and Marina
528 Caribbean Dr., Key Largo
(305) 453-9794
www.coconutsrestaurant.com

This vibrant outdoor restaurant, cornered between Key Largo Harbor and the swimming pool of Marina Del Mar Resort and Marina, offers lively after-hours entertainment and a variety of culinary specialties, among them fresh seared ahi tuna and crispy coconut shrimp with Malibu rum dipping sauce. Coconuts' signature dish is Yellowtail Largo—yellowtail snapper sautéed with artichoke hearts, shrimp, capers, and garlic in a lemon white-wine sauce. After dinner, head for Coconuts' indoor nightclub and dance the night away or sit back and enjoy the live entertainment (see the Nightlife chapter). Coconuts has a full bar, is open

for lunch and dinner, and is accessible by boat. Reservations are accepted for parties of more than nine. To reach Coconuts, head toward the ocean on Laguna at MM 100; the restaurant is about a quarter mile in on the left.

CAFÉ LARGO $$
MM 99.5 Bayside, Key Largo
(305) 451-4885
www.keylargo-cafelargo.com

This vibrant, third-generation owned restaurant has been serving up home-style Italian specialties in the upper Keys for almost 20 years. The DiGiorgio family offers everything Italian, from pasta to pizza, along with some local delicacies thrown in for good measure. The expansive and diverse menu includes the popular Parmigian Fried Portabella Stix appetizer, tender osso bucco with mushroom risotto, and Florida lobster stuffed with crabmeat and baked with sweet butter and white wine. Specialty drinks include a Key Lime Pie Martini and freshly made sangria by the glass. Café Largo has a full bar and extensive wine list, and is open daily at 4:30 p.m.

BAYSIDE GRILLE $$
MM 99.5 Bayside, Key Largo
(305) 451-3380
www.keylargo-baysidegrill.com

Situated at the end of a winding drive behind Café Largo and perched on the very edge of Florida Bay, Bayside Grille commands one of the premier waterfront vistas in the Keys. Small, casual, and bistro-ish, the open-air Bayside Grille's layout of tables fronted by glass pocket doors enables all diners to drink in the shimmering blue sea while partaking of a palate-tingling selection of offerings. Seafood reigns here—Key West garlic shrimp, island seafood curry, and seafood enchiladas are favorites. But landlubbers will also find a good selection of certified Angus burgers, New York strips, and flank steak and flavorful grilled chicken entrees and pasta dishes. Bayside Grille offers a full bar and the restaurant serves lunch and dinner daily.

DJ'S DINER AND COFFEE SHOP $
MM 99.4 Oceanside, Key Largo
(305) 451-2999
Established in 1958, DJ's regulars claim "they serve the best breakfast in town," so you'd best be hustling on over to get a table. DJ's serves daily lunch specials, too, like the highly praised blackened tuna Caesar wrap, but no dinners. So, get up early, have a *big* appetite, and enjoy this bright spot in the Upper Keys.

MRS. MAC'S KITCHEN $
MM 99.4 Bayside, Key Largo
(305) 451-3722
www.mrsmacskitchen.com
You don't show up here for the looks of the place. If good home cooking is what you want and you're craving plenty of carbs, this is the place to satisfy all of the above. The house is old, bedecked with antiquated license plates that only add to the well-seasoned charm of this Key Largo legend. The menu is long, the sandwiches are hearty, the conch chowder authentic, and the nightly specials will bring you back—to Mrs. Mac's! Open for breakfast, lunch, and dinner. Closed Sunday.

HARRIETTE'S $
MM 95.7 Bayside, Key Largo
(305) 852-8689
This popular roadside diner–style restaurant offers reasonably priced home-style meals in a simple setting. Tables and chairs surround counter dining; local arts and crafts on consignment provide the decor. Harriette's specialty? Ensuring that no guest leaves the restaurant hungry. Open only for breakfast and lunch, Harriette's serves filling omelets, oversize homemade biscuits with sausage gravy, burgers, and hot and cold sandwiches. The restaurant caters primarily to a repeat local crowd, so lunch specials change daily. Look for comfort food at Harriette's: meat loaf, pork chops, stuffed peppers, roast pork, and chicken and dumplings. Open seven days a week from 6 a.m. to 2 p.m. Reservations are not accepted; no credit cards.

SNAPPER'S WATERFRONT
RESTAURANT $$
MM 94.5 Oceanside
139 Seaside Ave., Key Largo
(305) 852-5956
www.snapperskeylargo.com
Lots of action in a frenzied atmosphere, but worth it! The best part of Snapper's is sitting out on the deck near the water overlooking Snapper's Marina next to the food, that is, which is Old Florida and Bahamian cuisine at its best with Asian influences. Sample some Applewood Smoked Bacon Wrapped Scallops, Lynda's Infamous Chicken Wings, which have been marinated in Caribbean rum, or the local favorite—Matt's Shrimp Fritters with ponzu dipping sauce. For a sweet and savory entrée, try the Kung Pao Shrimp—stir fried Gulf shrimp sautéed with green peppers, onions, mushrooms and cashews in a Szechuan sauce served on a bed of Jasmine rice. Snapper's offers an extensive raw bar as well as sandwiches, burgers, and many selections for landlubbers. There's a lot of action and a frenzied atmosphere, but it's worth the visit. Weekends feature live entertainment nightly in season. The restaurant serves lunch and dinner seven days a week

and brunch on Sundays, and is accessible by boat. Reservations are accepted.

CRAIG'S RESTAURANT $$
MM 90.5 Bayside, Tavernier
(305) 852-9424

Chef-owner Craig Belcher opened his name-sake establishment in 1981 with his signature sandwich, which he bills as "World Famous Fish Sandwich." A diner-style restaurant with an all-day menu, Craig's tries to please every palate, be it down-home or gourmet. The Jon Chicken Sandwich, a grilled chicken breast with Dijon mustard, Cajun seasoning, melted cheese, grilled onions, grilled mush-rooms, and bacon, puts a little pep in the ubiquitous *poulet*. Open seven days a week for breakfast, lunch, and dinner, Craig's does not accept reservations.

OLD TAVERNIER RESTAURANT $$
MM 90.1 Oceanside, Tavernier
(305) 852-6012

One of the Upper Keys' most popular estab-lishments for over 20 years, the Old Tavernier marries the Mediterranean and the Carib-bean with a continental flair to create a singular cuisine. Diners enjoy traditional Ital-ian pasta favorites such as pasta primavera, baked ziti, fettuccine Alfredo, or chicken or veal Parmesan. Opt for a culinary adven-ture with a Greek style whole yellowtail pan-seared, baked, and drizzled with olive oil, oregano, and lemon and served with rice and seasonal vegetables. Guests have the option of dining indoors—where white linen tablecloths are aglow with candles and watercolor sailboat scenes dot the walls—or outdoors on a balcony overlooking a narrow canal. Old Tavernier has a full bar and wine list, and is open daily for dinner only. The restaurant is accessible by boat.

BOARDWALK PIZZA $
MM 88.8 Bayside, Tavernier
(305) 853-3800
www.boardwalkpizzainthekeys.com

Easy living and easy eating are what makes life in the Keys so popular. Boardwalk Pizza creates handmade pizza and bakes the pies in a stone-lined pizza oven. This is a small eatery that is big on taste. Locals rave about the crust, characterized as neither thick nor thin, but light, fluffy, and tender. You'll also find cheesesteaks, subs, calzones, and pasta here. This pizzeria is open daily for lunch and dinner.

MARKER 88 $$$
MM 88 Bayside, Islamorada
(305) 852-9315
www.marker88.info

Book your reservation at this restaurant and come face-to-face with a famous Islamorada culinary landmark. Combining bayside ambi-ence with innovative preparation of the Keys' freshest bounty, Marker 88 will not disap-point. Established in 1978 by German-born, Swiss-trained André Mueller, who made the cuisine legendary, the restaurant is popu-lar with presidents—such as George H. W. Bush—and local patrons alike.

Marker 88's cuisine is legendary. Favor-ite dishes include sustainable seafood items like the onion crusted mahi mahi served with toasted onions and a white wine, Key lime juice, and butter sauce. Another swoon-worthy dish is the locally caught poached Florida lobster served with drawn butter. The wine list has more than 250 entries, so you are sure to find the right one to complement your meal. Dessert hits the mark also. Try the Key lime baked Alaska, with ice cream and Key lime filling topped with meringue. As sophisticated as the Marker 88 cuisine may be, decor here is charmingly rustic: Wood tables are made of hatch covers lifted from boats. Tiffany lighting provides a soothing romantic setting, as do the views of Florida Bay. Marker 88 is surrounded by heavy tropical vegetation and rambling docks, and a deck laden with wood outdoor tables and chairs provides the perfect setting for a predinner sunset toast or a starlit after-dinner drink. This boat-accessible restaurant maintains a full bar and is open daily for lunch and dinner. Reservations are recommended.

SMUGGLERS COVE RESORT
AND MARINA $$
MM 85.5 Bayside, Islamorada
(305) 664-5564
www.smugscove.com

If you want to find a good place to eat, ask a local. Smugglers Cove, a locals' favorite in Islamorada, puts on no pretensions. What they do put on, however, is a great fish sandwich, among other entrees, that draws raves. Options include peel-and-eat shrimp, oysters on the half shell, chicken wings, and even a kid's menu. What Smugglers lacks in decor and ambience, they make up for in taste. Smugglers Cove is open seven days a week for lunch and dinner and is boat accessible.

ISLAND GRILL $$-$$$
MM 85.5 Oceanside, Islamorada
(305) 664-8400
www.keysislandgrill.com

Don't pass up the opportunity to stop here if you see the parking area full. Cruise the parking lot to find a spot because this is one of those "don't judge a book by its cover" places. If the hostess tells you there is a wait, go to the bar and play a couple of ring-toss or pirate-dice games and have a cold,

---

Music, Mambo, and Mojitos

Conga lines with salsa music playing from the *Buena Vista Social Club*, cigar smoke curling around the lights with mojitos (pronounced moh-hee-tohs) in hand, you have the setting for a night on the town in tropical south Florida. Ernest Hemingway is reported to have enjoyed more than one of these drinks that originated in Havana, Cuba, at the Le Bodeguita del Medio hotel. Today, the mojito is showing up in bars across the country including the Keys. A similar American drink, the mint julep, is made with Kentucky bourbon in place of Cuban rum. The mojito lists five ingredients: powdered sugar, lime juice, mint leaves, white rum, and club soda. Place leaves in a tall ("Collins") glass, squeeze 2 ounces lime juice, add 1 teaspoon sugar, mash together, add crushed ice, then pour in 2 ounces rum and top with 2 ounces club soda. Put on a fedora or stiletto heels and mambo the night away.

---

tall Key West Sunset Ale. If you are seated inside at the Island Grill, ask for a table near the ceiling-to-floor window area, which will put you right along the canal facing Snake Creek. Outdoor tables are the best choice because you are actually on the dock area of the restaurant. The menu is swimming with seafood, and Island Grill is one of the best places to try an appetizer of spicy seared tuna nachos served over fried wontons with a seaweed salad amid ginger and sweet soy dressing. This dish is so mountainous that it could pass for an entree! Entrees include Low Country shrimp and grits, black Angus New York strip steak, and Island Grill seafood pasta. Youngsters might like the chicken sandwich or fried fish selections. Open daily for breakfast, lunch, and dinner, but early arrival for any meal is suggested due to parking limitations.

BRAZA LEÑA BRAZILIAN
STEAKHOUSE $$–$$$
MM 83.5 Bayside, Islamorada
(305) 664-4940
www.brazalena.com
This upscale *churrascaria* (Brazilian steakhouse) has *gauchos* dashing to your table with swords of beef, lamb, pork, and poultry. This all-you-can-eatery has more meat than you see at some food stores! Along with this showy presentation is a really delicious salad bar brimming with almost 50 different items from vegetables to seafood. Braza Leña is a fun place to go with great atmosphere. Another location is at 421 Caroline St. (305-432-9440). The Islamorada location is open Tues through Sun for dinner and the Key West location is open daily for dinner.

ZIGGIE AND MAD DOG'S $$
MM 83 Bayside, Islamorada
(305) 664-3391
www.ziggieandmaddogs.com
Steaks, chops, and seafood are on the menu at this newly renovated Keys landmark. Partners Randy Kassewitz and Miami Dolphins football player Jim "Mad Dog" Mandich have taken this historic property (originally built in the 1930s) and turned it into a fine dining establishment offering "something for every

palate." Menu items include grilled duck breast served with warm lingonberry sauce, delicious baked jumbo shrimp with mango and crab stuffing, and grilled double bone pork chop glazed with plum and port wine. The wine list is extensive. And while the décor may have changed, not to worry— the fish stories still abound in the chic bar area. (Be sure to ask the bartender about Al Capone playing cards in the back room.) Open daily for lunch and dinner, reservations recommended.

LORELEI RESTAURANT $$$

LORELEI CABANA BAR $
MM 82 Bayside, Islamorada
(305) 664-2692
www.loreleifloridakeys.com
The legend of Lorelei maintains that a nymph's sweet, lyrical singing lured sailors to shipwreck on a rock. Today's Lorelei lures you to a primo perch on the very edge of Florida Bay, where you'll relish breakfast, lunch, or dinner daily as well as those other munching hours in between. Come by boat, if you like, because the Lorelei also maintains a marina where you'll be able to rub shoulders with some of the Keys' renowned fishing guides. The Cabana Bar breaks the day starting at 6 a.m., then serves a casual lunch menu from 11 a.m. to 9 p.m., offering live entertainment nightly starting just before sunset. The air-conditioned Lorelei Restaurant's seafood-inspired menu makes a gustatory decision a difficult task. Landlubbers are accommodated with steak, chicken, ribs, and pasta offerings. The Lorelei Restaurant is open daily for dinner. Early-bird specials are offered from 5 to 6 p.m. Lorelei's family menu offers seven complete meals for $15.95 each, a real value.

ATLANTIC'S EDGE $$$

NIKAI SUSHI $$$

TIKI BAR $$

Cheeca Lodge & Spa, Islamorada
MM 82 Oceanside
(305) 664-4651
www.cheeca.com

The fine-dining room at Atlantic's Edge restaurant located in the Cheeca Lodge & Spa has panoramic vistas of the Atlantic Ocean, with seating indoors and out. Some of the selections on the gourmet menu are Florida Keys barrel fish with Parmesan risotto, wild mushrooms, greens, and a lemon-thyme sauce, or the whole fried Florida Keys fresh fish served with chili aioli, citron vinaigrette, and house-made tartar sauce. Also available to tempt your palate is a bone-in filet mignon with Vidalia onion gratin, asparagus, and island peppercorn sauce. Atlantic's Edge is open for breakfast, lunch, and dinner nightly, offering libations from a full bar.

The Nikai Sushi restaurant features an abundance of fresh sushi options from five different types of tartars to maki and vegetable rolls to specialty rolls like the Keysy Japanesy—a coconut shrimp and avocado roll topped with escolar tartar tempura crunchies and a Key lime glaze. Nikai is open for lunch and dinner with a selection of Japanese sakis and wine.

At the Tiki Bar, share plates of Key West peel-and-eat shrimp, a California roll brought over from Nikai, or a crispy wood-fired flatbread, topped with Florida tomatoes, buffalo mozzarella, fresh basil, and sea salt. The Tiki Bar is located on the beach, serves speciality cocktails from the full bar, and is open all day every day of the week.

CHANTICLEER SOUTH $$$–$$$$

81671 Old Hwy., Johnson Road, Islamorada
(305) 664-0640
www.chanticleer-south.com

The South of France comes to South Florida in a big way. Chef Jean-Charles Berruet left his Chanticleer on Nantucket Island and opened this top-notch French dining experience in Islamorada. Must-try tidbits are Gaspacho de Crabe (the classic soup garnished with crab meat), classical-style shimp bisque, and foie gras en turrine served with sweet fruit compote and brioche toast. Entrees complemented by the wine list include dishes of duck, escargots, snapper, lobster, or the French requisite coq au vin. Expect classic French dishes with a regional twist emphasizing the local vegetables and bounty from the sea. Chanticleer South is open for dinner Wed through Sun and reservations are recommended.

KAIYO $$$

MM 81.7 Oceanside, Islamorada
(305) 664-5556
www.kaiyokeys.com

Kaiyo's delightful blend of "Florida Asian" results in an exciting presentation of sushi and Keys-inspired dishes. Ones to try are the crispy pork and ginger dumplings with sesame dipping sauce and the whole tempura-fried yellowtail served with rice, bok choy, and three different sauces. Also not to be missed are Kaiyo's sakes. One that is fabulous is the sake margarita, served with a salt rim and key lime, on the rocks or frozen. Sake it to me! Kaiyo's has 12 types of saki, Kirin beer, and special teas. From the menu (fastened to a wooden board held by a bamboo rod) to the amenities (hot towels served before dining) to the decor (the restaurant is awash in varying hues of blues and purples punctuated by upscale Asian accents), Kaiyo pays exquisite attention to the details. A massive mosaic depicting the tropical reef and its creatures, based on Chef Dawn Sieber's love of sea glass, dominates the sushi bar room. And where did the restaurant's unusual name come from? In Japanese *kai* means "small body of water" and *yo* means "large body of water." In its cuisine and its ambience, Kaiyo, situated in Islamorada between the Atlantic Ocean and the Gulf of Mexico, successfully marries the mystique of Asia with the mystery of the sea. Kaiyo is open for lunch and dinner daily. The restaurant does not accept reservations or large groups.

MORADA BAY BEACH CAFÉ $$–$$$
MM 81.6 Bayside, Islamorada
(305) 664-0604
www.moradabay-restaurant.com
Leading the Purple Isle's culinary lineup, Morada Bay Beach Café in Islamorada delivers a tapas-style selection of appetizers and eclectic entrees in the most seductive of atmospheres. From the bark-chip parking lot, past a huge copper urn filled with bougainvillea petals, to the cobblestone brick entrance under a thatched-roof canopy—Morada Bay Beach Café neglects no detail of ambience. Pastel beach tables and low Adirondack-style chairs pepper a wide expanse of sandy beach (imported from the Bahamas) that fronts the gentle waters of Florida Bay. Curving palms and tiki torches complete the outdoor illusion. You'll be happy to know the food at Morada Bay Beach Café is as imaginatively designed as the decor. The Thai style dolphin fingers, ahi tuna tartare, Morada Bay crab cakes, and to-die-for seared tuna rolls all shine from the tapas menu. If you prefer a traditional dining

entree instead of the wonderful array of light noshes, any of Morada Bay Beach Café's fresh fish selections—all imaginatively prepared—will more than satisfy your taste for the sea. Morada Bay Beach Café finishes you off with some calorie-loaded ammunition. Save room for dessert if you are able. This is the perfect place to watch the sunset, as the restaurant perches at the edge of Florida Bay and recognizable musicians often stop by for a lively impromptu set while vacationing in the Keys. Morada Bay Beach Café is open for lunch and dinner daily.

PIERRE'S RESTAURANT $$$$
MM 81.6 Bayside, Islamorada
(305) 664-3225
www.pierres-restaurant.com
Magazine shoots and movie stars can be seen here, but the real star attraction at Pierre's is the cuisine. Sharing the same beach, sunset, and ambience with the more casual Morada Bay Beach Café, Pierre's is the place to go for a romantic, deep-pocket dining experience. Flickering candlelight and comfy leather sofas greet you in the downstairs lounge area for predinner libations, and a covered porch welcomes you to sit a spell on cushioned wicker chairs and watch the famed Keys sunset. Walk up the sweeping curved staircase, however, and your dining adventure begins. The decor, tropically British colonial, is elegant yet casual. Dine indoors or out on the covered porch. Check your almanac and join in the upscale monthly full-moon beach party held here. Torches, live music, and special tropical drinks are a sure bet to get you moonstruck or howling at the moon! The culinary stars shine with such signature dishes as Florida Keys ogfish Meuniere, Tempura Lobster Tail, and a constantly changing rotation of

the chef's creative offerings. Pierre's is open every evening for dinner only.

ISLAMORADA FISH COMPANY $–$$
MM 81.5 Bayside, Islamorada
(305) 664-9271
www.ifcstonecrab.com

Islamorada Fish Company, primarily a seafood market that opens at 9 a.m., also serves lunch and dinner daily until 9 p.m. Eat indoors at the Island Conch House Eatery or outside under umbrella tables that perch on a peninsula jutting into Florida Bay. Islamorada Fish Company's restaurant is so popular that it is not unusual to wait an hour or more for a table. But don't worry. The restaurant abuts World Wide Sportsman's cavernous sports emporium, so you can browse your wait away or sit in a rocking chair on the store's porch, look at the sunset, and wait for your name to be called. (See the Specialty Foods, Cafes, and Markets chapter for more information.)

GREEN TURTLE INN $$
MM 81.2 Oceanside, Islamorada
(305) 664-2006
www.greenturtlekeys.com

Sid and Roxie's Green Turtle Inn availed itself to an eager public in 1947. The building had already survived the deadly 1935 Labor Day hurricane, but after Hurricane Wilma visited the Keys in 2005, the white wooden structure shuttered its doors. In 2007, new owners with a new vision for the restaurant brought this phoenix-from-the-ashes story to life. Today, the Sid and Roxie's Green Turtle Inn sign has been restored and proudly hangs outside. The location now showcases three businesses in harmony: the Green Turtle Inn, Sandy Moret's Florida Keys Outfitters (see the Fishing chapter), and the Wyland

Art Gallery. At the Turtle, you can expect a "traditional Keys menu with flair." The "traditional" aspect features stone crab claws, Keys lobster, jumbo shrimp, or catch of the day. The "flair" guise stars alligator or conch steak and turtle or conch chowder. The 50-seat restaurant with open kitchen, full bar with tasting stations, catering, gourmet to go, and a Green Turtle Inn product line makes this a hot hangout in the Upper Keys. Breakfast, lunch, and dinner await you seven days a week.

UNCLE'S RESTAURANT $$$
MM 80.9 Oceanside, Islamorada
(305) 664-4402
www.unclesrestaurant.com

Mexican tiles, ceiling fans, stained glass, candlelit tables, soft music, and original paintings of Keys flora and fauna set the stage for fine dining at Uncle's. And if you'd prefer to sit under the stars, Uncle's will accommodate you, for it also serves dinner at tables sprinkled on an outdoor deck. Uncle's cuisine sparkles with a decidedly Mediterranean flair. Seafood selections are many, including fish du jour prepared eight different ways, and there are chicken, veal, beef, pasta, and "Heart Smart" selections as well. Uncle's offers an extensive wine list and full bar, and is open daily, except Sun, for dinner only. They will happily cook your catch for a fraction of the normal dinner price.

LAZY DAYS RESTAURANT $$
MM 79.9 Oceanside, Islamorada
(305) 664-5256
www.lazydaysrestaurant.com

Lazy Days provides the ideal setting for kicking back, gazing over the sparkling blue Atlantic, and dining on a revolving selection of seafood offerings. The elevated plantation-style building with turquoise roof, French doors, and wraparound balcony is, indeed, designed for lazy days, for it perches directly on the shoreline of the ocean. During the winter season all doors are open, and Bahama fans circulate the fresh ocean air inside and out. Brass hangings and rich tropical foliage enhance the dining room.

Because of this setting, Lazy Days has been featured on the Food Network as one of the best scenic spots on the water to dine. Some of the menu favorites, such as cracked conch served fried or sautéed with Key lime or garlic butter or jumbo stuffed shrimp baked with crabmeat stuffing and topped with béarnaise sauce and Key lime butter are house standouts. Lazy Days serves lunch and dinner daily and is accessible to boats with a 2- to 3-foot draft.

Middle Keys

ALMA/TOM'S HARBOR HOUSE
RESTAURANT $$$–$$$$
MM 61 Oceanside, Hawk's Cay Resort, Duck Key
(305) 743-7000
www.hawkscay.com
Alma is a world-class Latino-themed restaurant with an intimate decor. The adjoining bar is the Bar at Alma, which features a white marble bar at which you can savor drinks and try their outstanding tequila and rum collection. Mojitos anyone? (See sidebar in this chapter.) If you plan on coming by boat, call the marina in advance to secure a slip (see Cruising chapter). Alma is open for dinner only seven days a week. Tom's Harbor House Restaurant offers casual seaside dining on a spacious waterfront deck. But don't let the casual atmosphere fool you. The head chef, Charlotte Miller, has won awards for her

seafood dishes, so expect to be wowed by the water. Tom's Harbor House is open daily for dinner and offers live entertainment on the weekends.

THE WRECK & GALLEY GRILL
AND SPORTS BAR $–$$
MM 59 Bayside, Grassy Key
(305) 743-8282
Nautically decked out with photos of some of the dive wrecks in the Keys, The Wreck & Galley Grill ranks as a top-notch Middle Keys watering hole. Buffalo wings here—billed as the largest in the Keys—live up to their hype. Burgers are made from black Angus beef, and Jamaican jerk chicken and grilled or blackened fish sandwiches have won raves from the locals. All-you-can-eat nights include fried fish and French fries on Wed and Sat, and prime rib on Fri. This is the perfect place for a beer and a bite and to take the kids.

HIDEAWAY CAFE $$$–$$$$
MM 57.75 Oceanside, Grassy Key
(at Rainbow Bend Resort)
(305) 289-1554
www.hideawaycafe.com
The only thing rivaling the direct ocean vistas at Hideaway Cafe is the cuisine. Sure to please the foodie in you, the Hideaway also will intrigue the diner who likes to pig out: The Hideaway Rib Steak is large enough to serve a family of four, and the seafood Wellington is a dream! Other favorites include seafood crepes—a seafood combo rolled in a homemade crepe—topped with flamingo sauce, and seafood puttanesca—shrimp, scallops, and shellfish in a red, spicy sauce. Top off your dinner with Bananas a la Hideaway—sautéed bananas in brown

sugar and banana liquor. What a gourmet surprise! Hideaway Cafe is open daily for lunch and dinner. The service is "relaxed," so plan to drink in the view along with your libations. Reservations are recommended.

THE ISLAND FISH COMPANY
TIKI BAR & RESTAURANT $-$$
MM 54.5 Bayside, Marathon
(305) 743-4191

Perched on a narrow spit of land jutting out into the Gulf of Mexico, The Island Fish Company provides one of the most scenic sunset spots in the Middle Keys and some doggone great food to boot. Whether you feel like a margarita and some nachos, gulf oysters on the half shell, a grilled grouper sandwich, a bowl of conch chowder, or a more substantial meal, Island Fish Company doesn't disappoint. Try the conch ceviche, tender, Key lime–marinated unforgettable pieces of conch with onions and peppers in a lime vinaigrette served with tortilla chips, or the Buffalo shrimp, flash fried Key West pink shrimp tossed in hot pepper sauce and served with ranch dressing and a fried jalapeño pepper.

Tables are of the picnic or patio varieties, supercasual. Kids love playing in the open-air terrain. You can come to the Island Fish Company in a shallow-draft boat and dock alongside the restaurant. The restaurant is open for lunch and dinner daily and reservations are not accepted.

CABANA BREEZES $-$$
MM 54.5 Oceanside, Key Colony Beach
(305) 743-4849
www.cabanabreezes.com

Famous bandleader Guy Lombardo once owned this popular landmark back in the 1950s. Different names (the Colony House and the Shamrock) may have come and gone, but the outstanding food and service remain the same. The oceanfront tiki bar with entertainment brings in the crowds, but it is the masterful selections in the cabana that keep this eatery at the top of the locals' hit parade. Menu toppers range from beer battered fish and chips to the new heart healthy tuna steak sandwich—grilled tuna steak thinly sliced on a roll with wasabi mayo and pickled ginger—to filet mignon pan seared with a mushroom, shallot, peppercorn Cabernet demi glaze. A daily happy hour and live entertainment Thurs through Sun nights ensure that Cabana Breezes remains as popular and lively as ever.

KEY COLONY INN $$
MM 53.5 Oceanside, 700 West Ocean Dr.,
Key Colony Beach
(305) 743-0100
www.kcinn.com

The Key Colony Inn is a favorite dining haunt of residents and visitors alike. Besides the varied menu selections—75 entrees—of Italian-style pasta, veal, and chicken dishes, Key Colony Inn offers innovative presentations of Florida Keys seafood, steaks, and interesting daily specials. Diners agree, portions here are large, and you'll get a lot of bang for your buck. If dinner conversation is important, request a corner table, which may be a bit quieter, because ceiling acoustics in Key Colony Inn do not filter the noise of a room full of chattering diners. Or if the weather is fine, and it usually is, sit outside on the covered veranda. The restaurant features a full-service bar. Key Colony Inn is open for lunch and dinner daily. This place is always packed, lunch or dinner. Reservations are suggested year-round.

FRANK'S GRILL $$
MM 52 Bayside, Marathon
(305) 289-7772
Finding the place makes you work up an appetite, but it's worth looking. Turn at 113th Street and look for the sign. Frank is proud of his restaurant, and he proves it with signature dishes of Italian-American selections. Fish is grilled or blackened, and the catch of the day served Française style is a standout, as is the duck a l'orange. Friendly prices and nice owners make this a winner. Be sure to make a reservation as Frank's Grill fills up fast! Frank's is open for lunch and dinner Mon through Fri and dinner on Sat.

LEIGH ANN'S COFFEE HOUSE $
MM 51.5 Oceanside, Marathon
(305) 743-2001
www.leighannscoffeehouse.com
This popular coffeehouse is quaintly closeted in a pale-peach and white Key West–style building on the Overseas Highway. With French doors flung open wide, tile floors, tropical plants, and an eclectic array of rustic furniture and Keys art, this is coffeehouse à la Keys. Chic, clean, and packed with personality, Leigh Ann's food is pretty good, too. Homemade soups rival sandwiches on bagels, croissants, and sub rolls. Specials are made in small batches to ensure freshness. You can get an upscale pizza and a selection of salads as well. And don't forget the coffee. Choose among cappuccino, mocha coolers, muddy mocha, or macchiato. And Leigh Ann's serves beer and wine as well. This is a happening place! Leigh Ann's is open for breakfast and lunch until mid-afternoon daily.

HERBIE'S $–$$
MM 50.5 Bayside, Marathon
(305) 743-6373
Ask anyone: Herbie's is classic Keys. This roadhouse–style watering hole—two simple rooms and a porch with a large bar area and picnic tables—attracts a loyal contingent of locals and snowbirds alike. The conch chowder here is outstanding—packed with conch and chunks of potato. You can order fried shrimp, clam, oyster, or fish baskets or platters, or opt for burgers, dogs, and conch or fish sandwiches. Dinner specials are surprisingly sophisticated, and portions are generous. Herbie's will also cook your catch if you've had a lucky day on the water. Herbie's is open for lunch and dinner from Tues through Sat. The restaurant is not air-conditioned and does not accept reservations or credit cards.

i Florida Keys chefs use mixed elements of Asian, Latin American, and traditional American cuisine to create a unique style they call Floribbean cuisine.

THE WOODEN SPOON $
MM 50.5 Oceanside, Marathon
(305) 743-8383
You can't beat this no-nonsense eatery. The Wooden Spoon fires up the stove at 5 a.m. and the crowd is there to start their day. Hearty breakfasts attract many an Insider, fishing folks, tourists, and anyone else lucky enough to roll in the door. You can get box lunches to go if you're heading somewhere. The staff whips around the place at a hectic pace while remaining friendly and happy, and the doors are shut right after lunch. Not to worry—they'll be there tomorrow if you missed your chance today!

PANDA HOUSE $
MM 50 Bayside, Marathon
(305) 743-3417

One cannot live by Florida Keys seafood alone! This Marathon Chinese restaurant opened its doors in 1997, and the locals pack this place. Their enormous all-you-can-eat lunch buffet is not to be believed. Open seven days and free delivery in Marathon. The menu boasts Szechuan, Hunan, and Cantonese cuisines. The friendly staff gets right to the business of making sure your plate is full and you do not leave hungry. It's an ideal spot for families and if you have a crowd to feed.

BARRACUDA GRILL $$–$$$
MM 49.5 Bayside, Marathon
(305) 743-3314
Imaginative preparation and presentation showcase the entrees at the Barracuda Grill, a small, lively bistro in the heart of Marathon. Tantalizing stars of the menu are often the char-grilled veal chop, a 22-ounce rib-eye steak, roasted rack of lamb with black raspberry sauce or a sauté of portobello mushrooms, and mangrove snapper with mango salsa. A daily changing menu of the chefs' creative interpretations rivals the old favorites. Barracuda also offers a great children's menu with kid-friendly dishes such as Oodles of Noodles, Fish Have Fingers, and One Big Fish. Not your typical family restaurant, at Barracuda Mom and Dad can dine sumptuously and keep their kids happy, too. Barracuda Grill opens for dinner Mon through Sat at 5:55 p.m. Reservations are not taken. This popular spot fills up quickly, especially in high season, so come early if you don't want to wait for a table.

THE STUFFED PIG $
MM 49 Bayside, Marathon
(305) 743-4059
www.thestuffedpig.com

During high-season mornings you'll see a line of hungry diners outdoors reading newspapers and patiently awaiting admittance to the inner sanctum of the Stuffed Pig. This popular cafe packs 'em in for hearty country breakfasts. Try the Pig's Breakfast: two eggs, two pancakes, two sausages, two slices of bacon, potatoes, and toast. Or a Pig's Omelet, a four-egg wonder with the works. If you adhere to less porcine standards, the veggie and egg-substitute omelet will hold the cholesterol. The Stuffed Pig also serves lunch. The Stuffed Pig is open seven days a week at the crack of dawn (5 a.m.; an hour later on Sun). They close at 2 p.m. Mon through Sat and at noon on Sun. No reservations or credit cards are accepted.

KEYS FISHERIES
MARKET & MARINA $–$$
MM 49 Bayside, at the end of 35th Street, Marathon
(305) 743-4353 or (866) 743-4353
www.keysfisheries.com
For more than 30 years Keys Fisheries Market & Marina has been the Middle Keys' answer to the quaint, picturesque, eat-the-seafood-right-off-the-boat dining experience. Diners order their selections from an outdoor window, then carry trays to picnic tables overlooking a small marina harbor. You must help yourself to soft drinks, fast-food style. Though the place is rustic and informal, the fish doesn't get any fresher than this, because Keys Fisheries is just that, a working fishery and fish market (see the Specialty Foods, Cafes, and Markets chapter). Your wisest choices here will be local Keys seafood—such as grouper, yellowtail snapper, or mahi mahi—lobster bisque or chowder, Key West shrimp, and in season, the freshest stone crabs in Marathon served hot or cold, cooked right off the boat.

Keys Fisheries Market & Marina is open for lunch and dinner daily.

ANNETTE'S LOBSTER & STEAK HOUSE $$–$$$
MM 49 Bayside, Marathon
(305) 743-5516

An extensive menu and hearty portions distinguish this Marathon steak-and-seafood restaurant. Annette's sports a nautical decor with dark paneling, wood-plank floors, and memorabilia from the sea. The restaurant offers a smoking and a nonsmoking room, which are separated by a huge salad bar. You'll enjoy choosing from the vast selection of pastas, steaks, seafood, and, of course, lots of lobster. Signature dishes include horseradish grouper and a 20-ounce cowboy steak, which is an Angus bone-in rib eye. Annette's will also cook your catch for you. Ask for the macadamia nut–encrusted rendition. A new addition is the stone grill. Your food is cooked on granite stones and brought tableside, stones and all. Annette's places dessert selections on the menu's first page, so you are sure to be tempted and forewarned to save room. Annette's Lobster & Steak House is open daily for lunch and dinner.

BUTTERFLY CAFÉ $$$
MM 48.5 Bayside, Tranquility Bay
Beachfront Hotel & Resort, Marathon
(305) 289-0888
www.tranquilitybay.com/dining.htm

Housed in the main building of the lovely Tranquility Bay Beachfront Hotel & Resort (see Accommodations chapter), this fine restaurant is truly "Keys casual" with a traditional flair. Its chic but casual design, with white tablecloths and open, airy, high ceilings flowing out onto a large veranda with breathtaking views of gulf sunsets, only enhances the fare. Tropical world cuisine blended with exotic spices and fresh local catches is in evidence on the menu. The Sunset Sweet Potato Bisque, the Mango BBQ Quail, and the horseradish-crusted grouper served with leeks and citrus salad are all excellent choices. A fitting finish would be the TDF (to-die-for) sticky toffee pudding. Don't count the calories—this is why you are on vacation! The Butterfly Café is open for breakfast, lunch, dinner, and Sunday buffet. A children's menu is available, and reservations are required for all seatings.

BURDINES WATERFRONT AND CHIKI TIKI BAR & GRILLE $
MM 47.5 Oceanside, Marathon
(305) 743- 5317
www.burdineswaterfront.com

Take a break and go to this fun-to-be-in-the-Keys eatery. Burdines sits on a channel into Boot Key Harbor, and the view is as good as the food. The Chiki Tiki Bar & Grill sits on the second floor where you enjoy ocean breezes with a true Keys decor. The service is friendly and you are made to feel welcome and appreciated. The menu holds a bountiful selection, from Fresh Fish Sandwiches to Green Chili Cheeseburgers. They also dish out some great Cuban selections, such as black beans and rice served with a flour tortilla. If you order nothing else, be sure to get the skinny French fries. They are hand-cut and served with their famous "fry dust." This will put a smile on your tan face. The Chiki Tiki Bar & Grille is open for lunch and dinner daily and is accessible by boat.

PORKY'S BAYSIDE $
MM 47.5 Bayside, Marathon
(305) 289-2065
www.porkysbaysidebbq.com

Looks aren't everything! This tiny, open-air restaurant sits on the water with a picturesque setting among the lobster traps on the commercial fishing docks. Porky's is known for humdinger barbecue and their all-you-can-eat ribs specials every Tues and Wed night. Touted as "swinin' and dinin'," Porky's serves breakfast, lunch, and dinner every day and has live music every night from 6:30 to 9 p.m. Reservations for large parties only are accepted. No credit cards.

The Lime of the Keys

Key lime fruit is very small (1 to 2 inches), round, and a greenish-yellow color at maturity. The tart juice extracted from the limes goes on and into almost everything edible, from fish to salads, drinks, meats, and, of course, desserts. The Key limes were grown in southern Florida and the Florida Keys until the 1926 hurricane wiped out the citrus crop. The trees were replaced with a Persian lime, and most remaining Key lime trees were found throughout backyards in the Florida Keys. But commercial production of the Key lime trees is once again happening on a small scale, and Key limes do seem to be making a slight comeback as a Florida crop in recent years. Once you have tasted a true Key lime, any other lime will pale in comparison.

Lower Keys

ROB'S ISLAND GRILL $

**MM 31.5 Bayside, Big Pine Key
(305) 872-3022
www.bigpinekey.com/pages/robs_
island_grill.htm**

To locals this is a watering hole where everyone knows your name, what you like to eat, and what you like to watch on the sports channel. To Keys visitors, it's a great restaurant offering sports, spirits, and dynamite eats. You can get soups made from scratch, baskets of fried shrimp, chicken, or fish or come on Mexican Night on Monday or Key West Shrimp Night on Thursday and try the evening special. If you only want a sandwich, how about the Dolphin Reuben made with rye bread and topped with Swiss cheese and coleslaw? Or maybe you have a taste for house-made spinach artichoke dip? If your favorite team is losing and you're too depressed to be social, call ahead for takeout. This food could restore your good mood! Rob's is open for lunch and dinner every day but Tues.

NO NAME PUB $

**MM 31 Bayside, North Watson
Boulevard, Big Pine Key
(305) 872-9115
www.nonamepub.com**

This funky, one-of-a-kind establishment bills itself as "a nice place . . . if you can find it." And you might not find it without a little Insider knowledge. The No Name Pub—a pale yellow building with teal trim that looks like a house in a residential neighborhood—is topped with a small sign declaring its beginnings in 1936. And North Watson Boulevard is off the beaten track, too. Turn west at the traffic light at MM 31 in Big Pine (the only light from Marathon to Stock Island) onto Key Deer Boulevard. Proceed to Watson Boulevard and take another right. At the fork in the road, bear right, heading toward No Name Key. Go across a humpback bridge and past a residential subdivision. Just before the No Name Bridge across Bogie Channel, the pub will be on your left, all but hidden under a canopy of large trees.

Although the pizza is a star culinary attraction at No Name Pub, the decor and local Keys characters distinguish it from other pizza establishments. The interior is literally wallpapered with dollar bills auto-graphed by diners of years past. Be sure to scope out the barstools; no two of them stand at the same height. Those that are too short for the bar have 4-by-4-inch blocks of wood nailed to the bottoms of their legs. The management brags: "Friendly people, lousy service, great food!" The famous pizza is deep dish and arrives at your picnic table steaming hot; let it cool a bit to avoid burn-ing your palate. You'll taste a jolt of oregano, and the cheese is so thick it will drip down your chin with every bite. Yummm! No Name Pub is open seven days a week for lunch and dinner from lunchtime until "whenever."

BIG PINE RESTAURANT & COFFEE SHOP $
MM 29.5 Bayside, Big Pine Key
(305) 872-2790

The Big Pine Restaurant, sitting next to Big Pine Key's post office, has served this com-munity since the 1950s. Now new owners have given the restaurant a face lift and enlarged the menu, which still highlights traditional American fare: breakfasts of eggs, pancakes, or cereal; lunches of sandwiches or swell burgers; and classic dinners featuring steak, chicken, or fish. New choices include smoked fish, chicken, or ribs. Stop in and sit

awhile, visit with the Big Pine Key regulars—and enjoy the food! Open Tues through Sat for breakfast, lunch, and dinner and Sun for breakfast and lunch. Closed Mon.

PARROTDISE WATERFRONT BAR & GRILLE $$
MM 28.5 Bayside, 183 Barry Ave., Little Torch Key
(305) 872-9989
www.parrotdisewaterfront.com

Situated high above Big Pine Channel on the gulf, the pavilion-like interior is true Keys atmosphere for a casual feast with a diverse menu. A local favorite is the mahi mahi fingers, lightly broiled and served with fruit chutney. The seared tuna with sesame seeds served with ginger, wasabi, and soy is a real crowd pleaser. The Parrotdise offers a full-service bar. The bar and grill is open daily for lunch and dinner.

LITTLE PALM ISLAND RESORT & SPA $$$$
MM 28.5 Oceanside, Little Torch Key
(305) 872-2551 or (800) 343-8567
www.littlepalmisland.com

Dining at Little Palm Island is pure magic . . . romance with a capital R. You step into a fairy tale the moment you check in at the main-land substation on Little Torch Key to await your luxurious launch, the *Woodson*, that will spirit you to the island. The 15-minute boat ride to Little Palm Island simply heightens the anticipation. As you arrive at the island's dock, you'll spot the Great House nestled amid towering coconut palms. Once a rustic fishing-camp retreat, the Great House now houses Little Palm Island's world-renowned restaurant.

You may dine beneath the stars under a palm tree, at water's edge alongside the beach, on the outside wood deck, in the covered open-air porch, or indoors in air-conditioned comfort. Wherever you choose to partake of Little Palm's gourmet repast, you will be pampered with exquisite food and unobtrusive service. Classic European preparations fused with Floridian, Caribbean, and Pan-Asian flavors are the tantalizing offerings from the chef. Insiders know this translates into the meal of a lifetime. Little Palm offers libations from a full-service bar and maintains an extensive wine list.

Little Palm Island accepts a limited number of reservations from the general public for lunch and dinner daily. Sat and Sun, a tropical buffet-style brunch from 10:30 a.m. to 2:30 p.m. with a bloody Mary and champagne bar replaces the luncheon offerings. Call well in advance to secure a booking and reserve a space on the complimentary launch. You will be seated immediately upon disembarking. You may come to Little Palm Island on your own boat, but be sure to make slip reservations in advance (see our Cruising chapter). Children must be age 16 or older to dine at Little Palm Island.

BOONDOCKS GRILLE & DRAFT HOUSE $
MM 27.5 Bayside, Ramrod Key
(305) 872-4094
www.boondocks.us.com

Housing the largest miniature golf course in all of the Florida Keys, Boondocks is also home to a grill and draft house with an extensive menu. In addition to the daily happy hour special of 50 percent off all appetizers, like the crispy coconut shrimp and creamy smoked fish dip, Boondocks also offers drink and other food specials every weekday. Locals love the Patio Pig Pickin' Party every Fri from 3 to 6 p.m., but

no matter when you go, you will find a celebratiory atmosphere under the giant tiki hut that houses the restaurant and bar. They even have a Patio Pet Menu to ensure that Fido is as well fed as you are. Boondocks is open for lunch and dinner daily and has live entertainment on most nights of the week.

THE SQUARE GROUPER BAR AND GRILL $$
MM 22.5 Oceanside, Cudjoe Key
(305) 745-8880

Located midway between Key West and Big Pine, this establishment sets out to satisfy your hankering for memorable Keys cuisine. Conch and lobster fritters with Oriental dipping sauce are a crowd pleaser, and be sure to try the seared sesame-encrusted tuna. The catch of the day is prepared in a different manner nightly. A children's menu is available, and a dessert certain to bring out the fun in dinner for everyone is chocolate fondue with fresh fruit, marshmallows, and pound cake. Open wide and say *a-a-a-h!* The Square Grouper is open for lunch and dinner Tues through Sat, but make sure to call in advance as they have been known to close for a month or so during the slow summer season.

BUON APPETITO RISTORANTE ITALIANO $$
MM 21 Oceanside at 457 Drost Dr., Cudjoe Key
(305) 745-1711
www.buonappetitoinc.com

This is the real deal in Italian food. Worth a trip for the satisfying pastas, fine sauces, value priced specials, and eager-to-please service. Treat your taste buds to beef Carpaccio or pan-fried blue crab cakes. Move on to seafood pasta: linguine sautéed with calamari, shrimp, mussels, clams, and grouper, then topped with a tomato or white wine sauce. If you dare, you can end your meal with home-made tiramisu or cannoli. Buon Appetito is family owned and the experience is utterly authentic. Buon Appetito is open for dinner every day of the week except Tues.

MANGROVE MAMA'S
RESTAURANT $$
MM 20 Bayside, Sugarloaf Key
(305) 745-3030
www.mangrovemamasrestaurant.com
From US 1 you might miss Mangrove Mama's if you blink, because it looks tiny. What awaits you is a colossal culinary treat inside. This brightly hued Caribbean-style roadhouse offers a rustic old garden in the back where you can dine amid the banana trees. The old chairs are painted in a barrage of drizzled primary colors; ceramic fish sculptures adorn the walls. Bright tropical tablecloths cover the simple tables, and painted buoys hang from the trees and suspend from the rafters.

You'll find that seafood gets special treat-ment—steamed, baked, pan seared, grilled, stuffed with crabmeat, or rolled in coconut and deep-fried. Ribs are spicy, and scallops, chicken, steaks, and fresh fish march to a different drummer here, too. The restaurant serves lunch and dinner daily and brunch on Sun. Indoor dining is air-conditioned. In addition to a full-service bar, Mangrove Mama's has an extensive wine list. Reserva-tions are suggested for dinner.

BOBALU'S SOUTHERN CAFE $
MM 10 Bayside, Big Coppitt Key
(305) 296-1664
If inexpensive, stick-to-your-ribs food is what you're looking for, then look no more—you have come home. Appearances can

be deceiving, especially in the Florida Keys. Bobalu's may look a little shabby on the out-side, but the food and portions are anything but. The cuisine at Bobalu's is home-style, hearty, and southern. The menu includes such entrees as pot roast, pork chops, and authentic fried chicken. Side dishes like the mashed potatoes are the made-from-scratch kind, and desserts such as blackberry cob-bler and bread pudding will take you back to the days when families sat down together over Sunday dinner. The local favorite in both locations is the New Haven–style pizza, a Neapolitan-style pie with a crispier crust. Key West's favorite native son, Jimmy Buffett, has been known to dine at the Big Coppitt loca-tion on occasion and he even mentioned this place in his book *Where Is Joe Merchant?*

Bobalu's is open in Big Coppitt Tues through Sat for lunch and dinner and for Sunday brunch. Bobalu's is open at their second location in Key West at 404 Southard St. (305-293-3100) for lunch and dinner every day of the week.

KEY WEST

Some have called Key West the most success-ful melting pot in the United States. And no wonder. The southernmost city has a vibrant spirit that sparkles nowhere more brilliantly than in its cuisine. With restaurants as diverse and creative as a miniature Manhattan, Key West reflects the enduring ethnic traditions of generations past as well as the cutting-edge composition and presentation you would expect to find in major cosmopolitan cities worldwide. Add to all this gustatory wonder a dash of plain old Key West party and pizzazz, and you have a combination that is difficult to beat—anywhere! You can graze the side-walk cafes of Duval Street or drink and nosh at Key West's panoply of saloons. Sit beneath a canopy of poinciana trees to sample the upscale, up-to-the-minute cuisine or eat your way around the world without ever leaving our 8-square-mile island.

But while it's tough to find a bad meal in Key West, it isn't tough to find an expensive one. When it comes to dining out, our small town leans toward big-city prices. Even a simple hamburger can be costly here. But hey—you're on vacation. Just sit back, relax, and enjoy!

Whatever your pleasure, remember this is still the Keys. Dress code is always Keys casual; just make sure you wear a shirt and shoes with your shorts, and you're dressed for any occasion.

i If your dream dinner is a sunset lobster feast with your own personal chef aboard a 43-foot trimaran, hop aboard *Dreamchaser*, berthed at Key West Historic Seaport marina, for a four-course gourmet dinner topped off with one of our special Key West sunsets. You can make reservations by calling (305) 292-8667 or logging on to www.dreamchastercharters.com.

Key West has more than 150 restaurants, some say the most per capita in the United States. Many line the famed Duval Street; others are tucked away down tree-lined alleys or in unassuming residential-looking buildings. We will not highlight the national restaurant chains, most of which are in the newer sections of Key West along North Roosevelt Boulevard, because you are probably already familiar with their offerings. But we will assist you in finding those treasures known to locals—Insiders who keep their collective culinary finger on the pulse of the restaurant scene in Key West.

Our restaurants, like our people, defy easy classification. But we have divided the establishments into four categories to help you choose your dining preference: Key West Classics, those inimitable restaurants that the locals love and that you won't want to miss; Surf and Turf, primarily casually presented, simply prepared red meat and/or seafood; Island Eclectic, upscale gourmet dining of the modern American or new American cuisine genre, created with a tropical flair; and the Melting Pot, a potpourri of diverse ethnic offerings that spirit your taste buds to the far corners of the globe—the Americas, south of the border, the Continent, the Far East, and the islands. Restaurants are listed in alphabetical order in each category.

You will find that reservation policies vary in Key West. The more upscale the restaurant, the more likely you will need a reservation, especially in high season. If it's something you need to consider, we mention the restaurant's reservation policy in its description.

Unlike many restaurants in the rest of the Keys, most of those in Key West have full-service bars. We will highlight the ones that serve beer and wine only. On-site parking is a rarity among our recommended restaurants, most of which are in Old Town, where land is at a premium. In most cases you will need to park curbside on one of Key West's side streets or in a municipal or private lot (see our Getting Here, Getting Around chapter).

Unless stated otherwise, you may assume that restaurants are air-conditioned. Major credit cards and traveler's checks are widely accepted, but personal checks are not. And there is no restriction as to children dining in most establishments. Because restaurants in Key West's Old Town are often situated in 19th-century frame buildings that were formerly houses, wheelchair accessibility varies greatly. Sometimes steps must be negotiated, some bathrooms may be too tiny to accommodate a wheelchair, and separate nonsmoking sections may not always be available. If any of these anomalies is of particular concern to you, be sure to call the establishment to see exactly what arrangements might be made to fit your needs.

Price Code

Our price code mirrors that of the rest of the Florida Keys and is based upon dinner for two, without starters, dessert, alcoholic beverages, tax, or tip.

$................. Less than $25
$$ .... $25 to $40
$$$ .... $41 to $60
$$$$ .... More than $60

Key West Classics

A&B LOBSTER HOUSE   **$$**
700 Front St. (upstairs)
(305) 294-5880
www.aandblobsterhouse.com
A&B Lobster House, named for its original owners Alonzo and Berlin, is considered a Key West institution among seafood connoisseurs. Situated beside the water at the foot of Front Street, A&B offers a sumptuous selection of seafood as well as terrific views of the yachts moored at the Key West Historic Seaport.

In addition to Maine and Florida lobster served four different ways, the signature dish of sauteed jumbo scallops served with braised shiitake mushrooms, asparagus, and a lemon-garlic butter sauce is not to be missed. Steaks and pasta dishes are also available. Dine inside or outside on the wraparound porch; in either case, reservations are

suggested. After dinner, retire to Berlin's Bar to sample the fine selection of cigars and after-dinner drinks. A&B Lobster House is open daily from 6 p.m.; Berlin's opens at 5:30 p.m. for predinner cocktails.

ALONZO'S OYSTER BAR   **$–$$**
700 Front St. (downstairs)
(305) 294-5880
www.alonzosoysterbar.com
If you like oysters, Alonzo's is the place to go. You can order them up raw, on the half shell, baked, or batter dipped and fried. Check the chalkboard daily to find out where the oysters are from and what kind are available. This casual seaside eatery, situated downstairs from A&B Lobster House, also serves freshly shucked clams, lobster, conch, mussels, and a variety of dishes made with the native shrimp known as Key West pinks. If you're in the mood for a seafood soup besides chowder, try a bowl of the white clam chili. It's plenty filling but not as rich as its creamier cousin. Alonzo's serves lunch and dinner seven days a week and during happy hour, the entire right-hand side of the menu is half off. There's plenty of indoor and outdoor seating; reservations are not necessary. Free parking is available.

BLUE HEAVEN   **$$**
729 Thomas St.
(305) 296-8666
www.blueheavenkw.com
Blue Heaven—at various times a bordello, a pool hall, a railroad water tower, a cockfighting arena, a boxing ring (frequented by Papa Hemingway himself), and ice-cream parlor—is now a popular restaurant at the corner of Petronia and Thomas Streets. This throwback to the hippie era offers Caribbean and vegetarian cuisine in an unhampered

island setting. Situated in historic Bahama Village, Blue Heaven's ambience is as legendary as its cuisine. Roosters, hens, and chicks strut all around the picnic tables that fill Blue Heaven's backyard; so do the resident kitties. Jimmy Buffett's 1995 song "Blue Heaven Rendezvous" was inspired by this diamond in the rough and Kenny Chesney confessed to Oprah that it is his favorite restaurant.

Indeed, the magic is alive and well at Blue Heaven, where patrons enjoy specialties such as Jamaican jerk chicken, Caribbean bar-be-que shrimp, and locally caught seafood entrees. A dessert must-have is Banana Heaven, served with homemade vanilla ice cream. Sunday brunch at Blue Heaven, with diverse preparations of eggs, waffles, and pancakes—including the famous beer-batter and pecan varieties—draws crowds that line themselves up 'round the corner. Plan to wait at least an hour in high season. Blue Heaven has a full bar and serves liquor, wine, and beer. Blue Heaven serves breakfast with roosters, lunch under the shade, and dinner under the stars daily. Reservations are accepted for parties of 10 or more and besides the fowl, they have live entertainment.

B.O.'S FISH WAGON $
801 Caroline St.
(305) 294-9272
www.bosfishwagon.com

Almost any restaurant in Key West can make you a fish sandwich, but no one can make you a fish sandwich like Buddy Owen. He starts with Cuban bread, then piles the fresh fish and grilled onions so high, we dare you to try to get your mouth around it. Belly up to the counter and place your order for a fish sandwich grilled or fried; add sides like fries or onion rings only if you're really hungry.

The portions here are huge. The menu also features fish-and-chips, the ubiquitous conch fritters, burgers, and hot dogs. To quench your thirst, select from bottle or draft beer, wine by the glass (plastic, that is), sodas, or Key limeade.

While you're waiting for your sandwich to be delivered to your table, take a look around. The decor here can only be called Key West eclectic—fishing nets, lobster traps, a muffler shop sign, even an old pickup truck. B.O.'s has live music whenever the spirit moves them and is open for lunch and dinner Mon through Sat.

CAMILLE'S RESTAURANT $
1202 Simonton St.
(305) 296-4811
www.camilleskeywest.com

Their motto is "Exotic family cooking with no boundaries," and Camille's means it. The reasonably priced menu at this eclectic local favorite features a wide array of gourmet breakfast, lunch, and dinner specials; it changes daily and nightly. Stone-crab claw-meat cakes are grilled and served with spiced rum-mango sauce. A real crowd pleaser is Paradise Pasta—Key West pink shrimp, lobster, asparagus, and red and yellow peppers in a garlic Alfredo sauce. Weekend breakfast at Camille's is a particular treat, offering pecan waffles, an orgy of eggs Benedict, and eggs galore or eggs whatever—even egg white omelets if you are so inclined. And for lunch, the hand-pulled chicken salad sandwich is always a delicious choice.

Liquor and wine are offered, and the ambience is so friendly that tourists are treated like locals. Expect a wait—especially for breakfast. Camille's is open daily for breakfast, lunch, dinner, and happy hour. Reservations are a good idea.

HARPOON HARRY'S $
832 Caroline St.
(305) 294-8744
www.harpoonharrysrestaurant.com

Harpooned and hanging from the ceilings of this hometown-style diner is everything—including the kitchen sink. Across from Key West Historic Seaport, on the site of what was a small hospital-turned-barbershop, Harpoon Harry's combines Tiffany light fixtures with old roller skates, sleds, and carousel horses. Framed advertisements recall the days of Lucky Strike cigarettes, Mennen Toilet Powder, knee-highs, and antique cars. The restaurant's movie-star wall boasts Elvis, Sophia, and Lucy, and Desi. A case contains a collection of Mickey Mouse glasses, which are probably worth a fortune. It is, in fact, this original decor that drew The Travel Channel to Harpoon Harry's in 1995. Restaurateur Ronald Heck is the creative genius responsible for it. The owner of Michigan's Lighthouse Inn, Heck informed his Midwestern employees and patrons of the interior design plans he had for his new establishment, and they came bearing all sorts of amusements.

The luncheon menu at Harpoon Harry's is much less eccentric than the decor: Daily Blue Plate Specials consist of baked meat loaf or chicken pot pie made from scratch, and melt-in-your-mouth baked pork chops with mashed potatoes. Breakfast is highlighted by Harry's Special: two extra large eggs, two pieces of sausage, and bacon with ham, toast, and jelly served with home fries or grits. Two counters, booths, and tables are available daily for breakfast, lunch and dinner and there is free Wi-Fi in the restaurant. Reservations are not accepted.

i If you like to choose a restaurant by its bill of fare, grab a copy of *The Menu*. This quarterly restaurant guide, published by the *Key West Citizen*, features menus from more than 45 Key West eateries. You'll find free copies at hotels, attractions, grocery stores, and newsstands all around Key West. You can also visit their Web site: www.keywestmenu.com.

HOG'S BREATH SALOON $
400 Front St.
(305) 296-4222
www.hogsbreath.com/key-west

The name of this establishment may not be appealing, but its fish sandwiches—blackened or grilled with lemon—are. They're served up by the ton. Built to resemble an authentic surfer bar, Hog's Breath features lots of wood, including an African mahogany bar at which some guests are fortunate enough to land a seat. Mounted fish and surfboards hang from the walls, along with active water-related photographs. Not surprisingly, owner Jerry Dorminy of Alabama is a water-sports enthusiast. He originally established a Hog's Breath Saloon in Fort Walton Beach, Florida, in 1976, as a place where he and his friends could retreat after a day of fishing and sailing. In 1988, Dorminy opened Hog's Breath Key West. Here, nautical charts of Caribbean waters are lacquered onto wood tables, and patrons dine indoors or outside on a brick patio from which large trees sprout. In addition to the fish sandwich, Hog's Breath's smoked-fish dolphin dip and raw bar with oysters, shrimp, and stone crabs (in season) are extremely popular.

The restaurant's full-service bar features the medium-bodied Hog's Breath beer, brewed in the Midwest. In case you were wondering, the name of the joint comes from an old saying of Dorminy's grand-mother, that "hog's breath is better than no breath at all." The restaurant is open for lunch and dinner, and live bands play folk rock, rock, blues, and jazz throughout the day and evening. Reservations are not accepted.

JIMMY BUFFETT'S MARGARITAVILLE CAFE $
500 Duval St.
(305) 292-1435
www.margaritavillekeywest.com

Lunch really could last forever at Jimmy Buf-fett's Margaritaville Cafe, and patrons who steer here quite often remain throughout much of the day, regardless of whether or not they have amended their carnivorous habits. Margaritas are de rigueur and made fresh per order with Margaritaville tequila. In addition, there are plenty of Boat Drinks made with Margaritaville rum to whet your whistle. "Parrothead" and other island music plays in the background, and decorations include oversize props from stage settings of Buffett tours, including stuffed iguanas from "Off to See the Lizard," a mock-up ver-sion of his seaplane, a flying goose, and a big warm bun and a huge hunk of meat. The fixin's—lettuce and tomato, Heinz 57, and french-fried potatoes—are not forgotten. The casual and friendly Margaritaville, Buffett feels, combines his great love for music and food, both of which satisfy the soul.

Specialties of the house include Cheese-burgers in Paradise, blackened hot dogs, and the Delta Reuben, made with the catch of the day. Margaritaville is open for lunch and dinner daily and yes, Buffett himself has been known to stop by, cook a burger, and give an impromptu concert. Live music is offered nightly, beginning at 10:30 p.m. Reservations are not accepted, but those on the waiting list may shop for souvenirs in Buffett's adjacent store.

KELLY'S CARIBBEAN BAR, GRILL & BREWERY $
301 Whitehead St.
(305) 293-8484
www.kellyskeywest.com

Named after actress Kelly McGillis, this Carib-bean restaurant is on the site of the original Pan American World Airways offices. In 1927 Pan Am launched its first international air service from Key West, when mail was flown from the island's Meacham Field to Havana. The following year Pan Am began providing passenger service to Havana. A display of early photographs and memorabilia of Pan Am ser-vice from Key West line the room on the first floor. Outdoor dining is available on a stone patio with gardens. On the second floor Kelly's Clipper Club Lounge invites patrons to relax in an open-air gazebo-style setting where the lounge also hosts a number of performances, from burlesque shows to singer/songwriters.

Among the house specialties here are Kelly's Crab Cakes served with mango salsa and a spicy papaya remoulade and the lobster ravioli—lobster-stuffed ravioli with sundried tomatoes, in an orange-tarragon beurre blanc sauce. Kelly's Caribbean also is home to the Southernmost Brewery, which whips up an all-natural selection including Key West Golden Ale, Havana Red Ale, South-ern Clipper Wheat Beer, and Black Bart's Root Beer. The restaurant is open for lunch and dinner seven days a week. Reservations are accepted for parties of more than six.

LOBO'S GRILL $
5 Key Lime Square
(305) 296-5303
www.loboskeywest.com

Lobo's is where locals love to lunch. The menu includes burgers, nachos, quesadillas, and salads. But the real standouts are the roll-up sandwiches—a mix of meats, cheeses, fresh veggies, and spreads tucked tightly, then rolled, in a giant flour tortilla. Choose from such selections as the Delhi Chicken—curried chicken salad, Swiss cheese, sprouts, mango chutney, avocado, lettuce, and pineapple; or Porky's Nightmare—honey-baked ham, roast pork, bacon, cheddar, Swiss, lettuce, tomato, onions, and honey mustard. You can eat in or take out; call ahead for quick pickup or free delivery in Old Town. No credit cards.

PEPE'S CAFE & STEAKHOUSE $$
806 Caroline St.
(305) 294-7192
www.pepescafe.net

Billed as the "Eldest Eating House in the Florida Keys, established 1909," Pepe's is as beloved to Conchs and Key Westers as the Mallory Square sunset celebration. In the old commercial waterfront area of Old Town, Pepe's touts its gulf oysters, when available, as among its specialties: raw, baked, Florentine, Mexican, or Rudi style. Landlubbers are welcome at Pepe's as well. Options include New York strip steaks at 8, 12, and 15 ounces; filet mignon; pork chops; even barbecue. And Pepe's burgers sound as intriguing as they taste: White Collar Burger, Blue Collar Burger, Slit Ray Burger, and Patty Melt. Be sure to try a margarita here (the lime juice is squeezed fresh) and, for dessert, the brownie pie, served warm with ice cream—ask for Cuban coffee flavor instead of vanilla. Mmmmm! Pepe's serves early (mainly breakfast, 6:30 a.m. to noon), late (primarily dinner, after 4:30 p.m. to closing), and in between, predominantly oysters, soups, and sandwiches. One thing is for certain: No matter when you visit Pepe's,

you will not leave hungry. The restaurant is open every day. Patio dining is also available. Reservations are not accepted, and Pepe's is always packed just like your plate!

TURTLE KRAALS RESTAURANT
AND BAR $
231 Margaret St.
(305) 294-2640
www.turtlekraals.com

The recently reopened Turtle Kraals occupies the site of a former turtle cannery, hence the name—which essentially means "turtle pen." An open wood-fire grill has been added to the kitchen, causing Turtle Kraals to revamp its entire menu, and the results are mouthwatering. Start with the Bucket of Bones, spareribs that have been slowly cooked for up to 14 hours, or the mesquite grilled oysters on the half shell. Then move on to seafood specialties like the Best of the Bay, which includes half a Florida lobster tail, Key West pink shrimp, and oysters, all grilled on the open wood-fire grill and served with spicy butter for dipping. You can enjoy all these tasty treats inside in the dockside air conditioned restaurant or upstairs at the Tower Bar while watching the sun as it sets over the Key West Seaport. Turtle Kraals offers a huge selection of beer, and a full bar is available as well. Turtle Kraals is open daily for breakfast, lunch, and dinner.

Surf and Turf

THE COMMODORE WATERFRONT
RESTAURANT $$$
700 Front St.
(at Key West Historic Seaport)
(305) 294-9191
www.commodorekeywest.com

Tables covered in white linen are surrounded by mahogany paneling, brick walls, and lush greenery. Ceiling fans gently whirl and window walls look out onto the charming harbor of Key West Historic Seaport. The Commodore exudes the elegance of a fine ship, and the establishment offers some top-notch meat and seafood to match the refined ambience. Signature dishes abound. The Commodore Seafood Medley is lobster, shrimp, scallops, and mussels served in a light garlic sauce with vegetables while the New York strip is first seared to seal in the juices, then broiled and served with your choice of bearnaise, Roquefort, or au jus sauce and a baked potato. The Commodore serves dinner nightly. Reservations are recommended and free parking is available at A&B Marina.

CONCH REPUBLIC
SEAFOOD COMPANY $–$$
631 Greene St.
(305) 294-4403
www.conchrepublicseafood.com
From the look of this place—with its old wooden railings, weathered tin roof, and lazy, wobbly ceiling fans—you'd swear it had been in Key West for decades. Not so. The Conch Republic Seafood Company opened for business in the newly renovated Key West Historic Seaport in 1999.

As you've no doubt surmised, the menu here is heavy on seafood. Entrees include seared tuna steak, grilled double bone pork chops, and the local favorite stuffed shrimp—jumbo shrimp stuffed with lump crabmeat, wrapped with bacon topped with a sweet chili glaze and served with mango salsa, island rice, and greens. For starters, try the tempura-battered queen conch, lightly flash fried and served with orange horseradish marmalade. The full-service, 80-seat bar boasts one of the best rum selections

around—more than 80 varieties are available, along with 25 kinds of beer. The full menu is available daily from noon until 11 p.m. Live music is offered nightly, and happy hour is from 4 to 7 p.m. daily. Reservations are not necessary, and you need not ask for a waterfront table. Every seat has an open-air view of the harbor action. Check out the 80-foot aquarium stocked with local seafood that is the centerpiece of the restaurant, and don't miss the 1,200-pound antique still that stands behind the bar in honor of the rum-runners of yesteryear.

GUY HARVEY'S ISLAND GRILL $$
511 Greene St.
(305) 295-0019
www.guyharveysislandgrill.net
The name Guy Harvey (see the Arts and Culture chapter) needs no introduction to most folks. His love of the sea and its creatures makes this marine-life artist, biologist, and conservationist an international legend. His empire includes retail shops around the globe selling sportswear, T-shirts, and his art. In Florida they have even printed his art on two license plates, "Save Our Seas" and "Aquaculture." Now, Guy is getting his toes wet with Island Grill restaurants. Inside the building is a large saltwater fish tank and lots of fish mounts on the walls. Needless to say, Guy's artwork fills in the gaps. There are two bars here. One is built from the stern of a boat accented with tiles that make it seem to be canvassing the ocean waters. Seafood is the signature dish, with blue water crabs, oysters, and shrimp rounding it out. They offer sandwiches, burgers, and prime rib, and a children's menu is available. Open for lunch and dinner daily, one of their most popular eats is the cheesy garlic bread!

HALF SHELL RAW BAR $-$$
231 Margaret St.
(305) 294-7496
www.halfshellrawbar.com

The Half Shell Raw Bar is inches from the water and beyond casual. When the owners opened this seafood establishment in 1980, they dotted the all-wood walls with amusing license plates. Always consistent at Half Shell Raw Bar is its fresh seafood served on the casual, open-air waterfront. Located in Land's End Village at the Key West Historic Seaport, the restaurant is known for local seafood. The center of the action is Shucker's station, where mountains of oysters, clams, shrimp, and stone crabs are simply prepared, reasonably priced, and served with plastic utensils on paper plates at picnic tables. Half Shell carries stone crabs in season and Maine lobster. Its full bar offers beer, wine, and frozen drinks. Patrons may opt for outdoor dining on either a waterfront deck or a patio. Reservations are accepted for parties of more than six. Half Shell Raw Bar is open daily for lunch and dinner. Off-street parking is abundant.

HURRICANE HOLE WATERFRONT BAR AND SEAFOOD GRILL $
MM 4.5 Oceanside, Stock Island
(305) 294-0200
www.hurricaneholekeywest.com

Situated upon pilings overlooking Cowkey Channel, the location may look informal because it is inside the Hurricane Hole Marina compound, but what awaits the diner is one great meal. The atmosphere and dress code are Keys comfortable. The ample tables and room size of Hurricane Hole give it an airy feel even when the place is packed with folks. The menu is varied enough that it will please everyone's palate. The appetizers range from coconut shrimp to chicken tenders to bruschetta. The "Fresh Off the Hook" fish of the day is served five different ways, but the most popular entrees include the popular fish and chips. We recommend grabbing a bite after a day of kayaking or paddleboarding through the mangroves. No matter when you go, make sure to unhook your belt buckle at least two notches before you sit down to partake of your delightful meal! Hurricane Hole is open for lunch and dinner daily with happy hour specials.

MICHAELS $$$
532 Margaret St.
(305) 295-1300
www.michaelskeywest.com

Tucked away in a quiet Old Town neighborhood several blocks off Duval, this casual yet elegant little gem of a restaurant would be easy to miss, but we urge you not to. Since January 1997, owners Melanie and Michael Wilson have been serving up some of the best food on the island. Michael, the former corporate chef for the Chicago-based Morton's Steakhouses, knows how to cook a piece of beef. His prime beef is flown in fresh via FedEx from Allen Brothers in Chicago and his Filet al Forno, rubbed with roasted garlic and Roquefort, has garnered rave reviews and numerous awards. The menu also includes seafood and pasta specialties and a good selection of fondues is available in the Garden Bar. No matter which entree you select, be sure to save room for dessert. The Chocolate Volcano is a house specialty—it erupts at the touch of your fork!

Martini drinkers will appreciate the wide selection of concoctions including the traditional Presidential made with Grey Goose vodka and Epting's Espresso Martini, which includes Grey Goose vanilla vodka, kahlua, and espresso. And if martinis aren't your forte, there are plenty of other liquors to choose from as well as a wide selection of fine wines. Michaels is open nightly from 5:30 p.m. Reservations are recommended for both indoor and outdoor seating.

PRIME STEAKHOUSE $$$
951 Caroline St., Key West
(305) 296-4000
www.primekeywest.com

What a delightful surprise to enter the "Keys swank" atmosphere of Prime Steakhouse. The decor is nothing like the Technicolor offerings of other bars and restaurants in the Keys. What you notice first is the cool sensation of dark mahogany and richly upholstered booths. The tables are covered with crisp white linen cloths and tall drinking vessels. The staff is dressed all in black and the hushed atmosphere takes everyone down about two notches. Even though Prime Steakhouse has a limited menu, each and every selection is superb. They offer a local seafood special prepared Keys style, and their steak selections are outstanding. One of the house specialties is home-fried potatoes that are mashed and then fried. A feast in itself! Desserts are homemade Key lime pie with a nut-based piecrust and a to-die-for chocolate cake that is worth the calories. Enjoy the food and the loveliness of this elegant restaurant. Prime is open daily for dinner and reservations are recommended.

RUSTY ANCHOR RESTAURANT $$
MM 5 Oceanside, 5510 Third Ave.,
Stock Island
(305) 294-5369

Weigh anchor for a satisfying seafood meal at the Rusty Anchor, a casual seafood haven for the piscatorially inclined. You won't find fresher fish and seafood anywhere, for in the back of the Rusty Anchor is a commercial seafood market that supplies many of Key West's restaurants. The fish, lobsters, shrimp, and stone crab claws are delivered right from the boat (see our Specialty Foods, Cafes, and Markets chapter). The restaurant exudes a casual nautical atmosphere punctuated by rope-edged tables, wood buoys, nautical art prints, and photographs of the fishing fleets of old Key West. A 400-plus-pound marlin is mounted at one end of the dining room, and a couple of 15-pound lobsters grace the other walls.

Lunch and dinner are simply prepared. The saltwater fish is caught daily in the Key West area and generally is served broiled or fried. Try the teriyaki-grilled tuna sandwich on Cuban bread if it is offered as a special. If seafood is not your favorite, Rusty Anchor also serves burgers, steaks, and ribs. Food is presented picnic style on plastic plates, drinks in plastic cups, and beer out of the can. Open Mon through Sat for lunch and dinner, the Rusty Anchor does not require reservations. It's a great place to bring the kids.

SEVEN FISH $-$$
632 Olivia St.
(305) 296-2777
www.7fish.com

Don't be fooled by the name; this is a bistro you'll love to call your own. Although the seafood here is excellent, this restaurant, which is located at the corner of Olivia and Elizabeth Streets, has much more to recommend it. In addition to the freshest fish, the menu includes grilled chicken, meat loaf with mashed potatoes, and a New York strip steak cooked the way you like it. Salads—Three Cheese Caesar, mixed greens with balsamic vinegar, or roasted red pepper and goat cheese—are available in two sizes.

And for an additional charge, you can add grilled chicken or a crab cake to your greens if you like.

The environment at Seven Fish is cozy and friendly, the food flavorful and inexpensive. On the downside, Seven Fish is small—go early or you may have to wait—and the tables are quite close together. The restaurant is open nightly 6 to 10 p.m. except Tues. That's when the staff goes fishing. Reservations are recommended.

STRIP HOUSE $$$–$$$$
1435 Simonton St.
(305) 295-9669
www.striphouse.com

Dine outdoors or inside with an ocean view surrounded by luscious red décor and a collection of vintage Studio Manasse photographs from the 1900s with low lighting, and you have a tropical Strip House atmosphere that has all the fixings for a sensuous dinner. Enjoy their main dining room, bar, lounge, or two private dining areas for your evening's pleasure. The trend-setting steakhouse, named as one of America's 10 best in *GQ* magazine, features prime meats, goose fat potatoes, and truffle creamed spinach. Be sure and ask for their signature 24-layer chocolate cake—highly recommended! If that is too-o-o much then do go for the Australian Homemade Ice Cream offering. I won't even tell you how cool that is. This restaurant also services in-room menu items for the Reach Resort (see Accommodations chapter).

Island Eclectic

BAD BOY BURRITO $
1220½ Simonton St.
(305) 292-2697
www.badboyburrito.com

Hands down, this is the locals' favorite lunch in Key West, be it by delivery or sitting on a bar stool in the tiny establishment. It is hard to believe that a restaurant this small could pack such large flavors into its creations, but they do. Bad Boy's starts with organc flour tortillas, adds basmati rice and rattlesnake beans, and the rest is up to you. Try the veggie approach and add sautéed mushrooms, tomatilla sauce, shaved cabbage, shredded cheese, grilled green onions, and avocado. You will not be disappointed. Carnivore options include pork carnitas, duck, chicken, and seasoned ground Kobe beef. Bad Boy's also has items on the menu that don't require you to create, like the Cayo Hueso Fish Tacos and Disco Duck Quesadilla. No matter what you order, you will be glad you discovered Bad Boy Burrito. Bad Boy is open and delivers breakfast and lunch Mon through Sat from 10 a.m. to 6 p.m. No credit cards.

BAGATELLE $$–$$$
115 Duval St.
(305) 296-6609
www.bagatellekeywest.com

Incongruous amid the tourist trappings of lower Duval, Bagatelle sits reservedly amid the fray. Situated on two floors of a gracious old Key West home, Bagatelle serves fresh local ingredients with island inventiveness. Try the honey-fried lobster tail or the mojo-marinated free range chicken breast for something different. Or enjoy the avocado fan salad or the seafood chowder packed with shrimp, fish, and conch, a Bagatelle tradition since 1979.

Wraparound balconies on both levels afford outdoor dining, or you may choose to dine indoors where the decor favors that of a first-rate art gallery. Bagatelle is a premier spot from which to view the Fantasy

Fest Parade (see the Annual Events chapter). Reservations for the evening of Fantasy Fest should be made well in advance of the event, even up to a year. Bagatelle serves breakfast, lunch, and dinner daily. Reservations are suggested for dinner in all seasons at this popular restaurant, but at least a day in advance in high season.

BIG JOHN'S PIZZA $
1103 Kmart Shopping Center
(305) 293-9576
www.bigjohnspizzakw.com
If you don't feel like going out to a full-fledged restaurant, Big John's Pizza is an eatery located in a New Town shopping center where all the locals go to partake of the best pizza this side of Rome. Sure, there are the usual pizza-chain operations here, but this place is "where the locals know it's good." The couple who owns Big John's takes great pride not only in their food but also in their friendly and cheerful help. The establishment is newly renovated, bright, and pristine. The menu offers such fab choices as their homemade garlic knots, buffalo chicken salad, 20-inch pizzas, calzones, strombolis, and their world-class famous "Stuffed John," a double-crusted pizza stuffed with more ingredients than should be allowed! Big John's is open daily for lunch and dinner and offers free delivery anywhere in the city limits of Key West. A minimum order amount is needed for delivery beyond mile marker 2.

BISTRO 245 $$$
245 Front St.
(at the Westin Key West Resort and Marina)
(305) 294-4000
www.westinkeywestresort.com
Imagine, a Sunday brunch buffet table that is 70 feet long—so long you can barely see the other end! Dine indoors or out with a panoramic view of the Gulf of Mexico, all the while indulging in great Florida Keys cuisine. Regular menu offerings for breakfast, lunch, and dinner Mon through Sat, and the enormous food fest is Sun only.

CAFÉ MARQUESA $$$$
600 Fleming St.
(305) 292-1919 or (800) 869-4631
www.cafemarquesa.com
Golden walls covered with paintings, pastel tile floors, large mirrors, and a panoramic country-kitchen mural set the scene for one of the finest dining encounters in Key West. Café Marquesa, situated in the historic Marquesa Hotel, remains a consistent winner in the restaurant wars. Gracing the white linen tablecloths is an eclectic assortment of innovative dishes. The menu changes regularly, but specialties of the house have included Peppercorn Dusted Seared Yellowfin Tuna, Feta and Pine Nut Encrusted Rack of Lamb, and Grilled, Marinated Key West Shrimp. Café Marquesa, reminiscent of a European brasserie, oozes style. Reservations are highly recommended in all seasons. Café Marquesa serves dinner nightly.

HARBOURVIEW CAFÉ $
1 Duval St.
(at the Pier House Resort)
(305) 296-4600
www.pierhouse.com
This rendering of a classic setting is well worth the price of a dinner tab. Located in the Pier House Resort (see Accommodations chapter) the menu is full-blown "Floribbean" with all the trimmings. The restaurant lives up to its name with the stunning views of Key West Harbor.

Dine inside or out on the harbor and get your taste buds in gear with the Habana Cabana Pork Sliders, slow roasted pulled pork with tobacco onions on Hawaiian sweet rolls. Don't miss the white conch chowder—it will make you melt right into your entrée of yellowtail, mahi mahi, or salmon. The HarbourView serves breakfast, lunch, and dinner daily.

HOT TIN ROOF $$$
Zero Duval St. at Ocean Key Resort
(305) 296-7701 or (800) 328-9815
www.oceankey.com

The Hot Tin Roof name comes from Tennessee Williams's (a past resident of Key West) most famous play, *Cat on a Hot Tin Roof*. The dining room and outdoor deck enjoy panoramic views of Key West Harbor and its famed sunset. The chef has combined elements of South American, Asian, and French cuisine in an interpretation of flavors and attitudes of Key West he calls "Conch-fusion." Prime examples include the tapas options of the diver scallop with porcini dust and truffle emulsion and the ceviche served with candied sweet potatoes and corn nuts. The Stage Door Lounge serves themed signature cocktails and offers live jazz music some evenings as well. Hot Tin Roof is open for breakfast and dinner daily.

LATITUDES BEACH CAFE $$$
Sunset Key
(305) 294-4000
www.westinkeywestresort.com

When you think of dining seaside somewhere on a secluded island, this is the kind of place that comes to mind. Just five minutes across the water from the hustle and bustle of Mallory Square, the recently renovated Latitudes might just as well be half a world away. It is that peaceful, that serene. And as

near as we can tell, still largely undiscovered. Granted, it takes some planning to get here. You have to make a reservation, and you have to board a boat. But if what you seek is a quiet evening escape from the craziness of Key West, dinner at Latitudes on Sunset Key is well worth the effort.

Sunset Key is a private island, half of which is devoted to guest cottages, the other to pricey waterfront homes (see the Accommodations chapter and the Relocation and Vacation Rentals chapter for additional information). Island access is thus largely limited to residents. Launches for Sunset Key leave regularly throughout the day from the pier at the Westin Key West Resort and Marina at 245 Front Street. If you are not living or staying on the island, you must make a reservation for your meal at Latitudes with the Westin concierge to secure a boarding pass. Latitudes is open daily for breakfast, lunch, and dinner.

LOUIE'S BACKYARD $$$$
700 Waddell Ave.
(305) 294-1061
www.louiesbackyard.com

An enduring favorite among locals and visitors alike, Louie's Backyard combines island manor house ambience with cutting-edge cuisine. And though the exquisitely prepared, complex combination of ingredients that marks Louie's is often imitated elsewhere in Key West, this restaurant continues to shine. A sweeping veranda for outdoor dining overlooks Louie's "backyard," which is actually a prime piece of Atlantic oceanfront property. In the 1970s this spot was a favorite with next-door-neighbor Jimmy Buffett, who often played for his supper.

Dinner entrees span the globe, with fresh local seafood garnering center stage.

An equally innovative cuisine is offered on the lunch menu for nearly half the price of evening dining. Try lunch offerings such as Bahamian conch chowder with bird-pepper hot sauce; Asian chicken salad with green tea soba noodles, cucumbers, and a Thai peanut sauce; or the Not Just Any Fish Sandwich served with potato chips they make every morning. Sample dinner offerings include sautéed Key West shrimp with bacon, mushrooms, and stone-ground grits or grilled New York steak with artichokes and cippollini onions. The upstairs has been converted into the Upper Deck at Louie's Backyard offering a wine bar and small plates. Louie's Backyard serves lunch and dinner daily. Reservations are recommended in all seasons but especially in winter and on weekends. The Afterdeck outdoor oceanside bar is the locals' favorite place for a sundowner and is open all day and into the wee hours (see our Nightlife chapter).

i Hunter S. Thompson, an American journalist and author famous for his flamboyant writing style known as "gonzo journalism," lived in the Keys for part of his life. One of his favorite haunts was Louie's Backyard restaurant.

NINE ONE FIVE $$
915 Duval St.
(305) 296-0669
www.915duval.com

Snappy concept with gastronomical success! The chefs at nine one five have created dishes meant to mix and match and be served with wine. Upscale without being pretentious and loaded with atmosphere, housed in a stately Victorian home, this James Beard award-winning restaurant is the talk of the town. While you're waiting for your meal, try an appetizer like tuna dome made with dungeness crab with a lemon miso dressing, wrapped with sushi-grade ahi tuna. Don't miss the Devils on Horseback—bacon-wrapped dates stuffed with sweet garlic and served with a ginger soy dipping sauce. And for dessert, how about an artisan cheese plate replete with fresh Florida honeycomb? Post-dinner, head upstairs to Point Five (see our Nightlife chapter) and relax in the hip atmosphere of a wine bar with a cool DJ. Open nightly for dinner. Reservations suggested.

ROOF TOP CAFÉ $$$
310 Front St.
(305) 294-2042
www.rooftopcafekeywest.com

High amid the treetops, the Roof Top Café looks down on the tourist mecca along Front Street near Mallory Square. And although the restaurant bustles with dining activity, the atmosphere remains unhurried and removed from the fray. Diners may sit on a second-floor balcony, which extends on two sides of the building, under the canopy of ancient leafy trees. Inside, ceiling fans mounted on the white vaulted ceiling gently move the air about the open-air, pavilion-style dining room.

The cuisine, innovative in both composition and presentation, combines local piscatory resources with an international flair. Dinner creations have included mahi mahi with plantain and shrimp stuffing and mango coriander butter, chipotle-glazed roast pork tenderloin, and creamy wild mushroom risotto. Luncheon selections transcend the norm as well. Rooftop Cafe is open daily for breakfast, lunch, and dinner with a special sunset menu from 5:30 to 6:30 p.m. Reservations are strongly suggested for dinner in all seasons, especially at sunset.

SHOR AMERICAN
SEAFOOD GRILL $$$
601 Front St.
(305) 809-1234 or (888) 591-1234
www.keywest.hyatt.com

New contemporary decor has brought this popular hotel restaurant back into the spotlight for visitors as well as local diners. While sipping cocktails, enjoy a wall of windows that showcase the beautiful view of the Gulf of Mexico. Offering breakfast, lunch, and dinner, the chefs pride themselves on serving local fresh seafood such as seared sea scallops, shrimp cocktail, roasted lobster, and strawberry grouper (they also serve beef, pork, and chicken selections). Lighter fare of soups, sandwiches, and salads is equally appealing. Cap the meal with mango bread pudding or warm chocolate lava cake.

SQUARE ONE $$$
1075 Duval St.
(305) 296-4300
www.squareonerestaurant.com

Enjoy a touch of class and a bit of craziness, Manhattan style, at Square One, a casually sophisticated uptown bistro in Duval Square. Two enormous tropical floral murals flank the walls, offsetting the highly polished wood decor. The green carpet is mirrored in the green-rimmed chargers, which sit upon white linen tablecloths in the rich-looking dining room. Diners are treated to light piano music as they try a signature dish of slow-braised black Angus beef short rib, or one of the new "customized entrees." Lucky diners are offered meats, seafoods, sauces, and sides to choose from and the chef creates a truly original meal. Protein options include a whole florida yellow snapper and grass-fed black Angus tenderloin of beef with sauce options range from the classic bearnaise sauce to mint/parsley pesto.

Side offerings like the Yukon gold potato gratin and roasted baby mushrooms with rosemary and lavender round out the custom dish. Don't worry—a waiter is at the ready to guide you in the right direction should you need help.

Square One offers the option of outdoor dining in their tree-lined courtyard, and ample free parking is available. Square One serves breakfast, brunch, lunch, and dinner. Reservations are recommended.

Melting Pot

BLACKFIN BISTRO $
918 Duval St., Key West
(305) 509-7408
www.blackfinbistro.com

Stop into this classic bistro-style restaurant for a chance to relax and unwind afer the sensory overload of Duval Street. You won't find loud, tropical artwork stuffed into every corner here. Instead, rest your eyes on the soothing island photography, wine options written on a chalkboard, and fresh and clean lines of the cool bistro tables. And the food is just as lovely as the decor. From the yellowfin tuna burger to the cucumber shrimp sandwich, one bite is all it will take to figure out why the locals have embraced this new addition to Key West's eateries.

DION'S QUICK MART $
1127 Truman Ave., Key West
(305) 294-7572

Locals call Dion's Quick Mart a one-stop-shopping experience for your immediate needs. They sell everything from gas for your car to bread, milk, magazines, and the best fried chicken you have ever tasted. Forget about all the other brands of fried chicken you might have experienced in your travels, Dion's prides itself on quality, fresh, juicy, hot, crunchy, memorable chicken. You can smell the aroma of the fryers when you get near the place. It might be 6 a.m. by your watch, but your nose knows your taste buds are screaming "gimme some of that chicken" by the time your body reaches the counter. They also offer such other eats as fried okra and corn dog on a stick, but chicken is the code of the road here. Call ahead for large orders. Two additional locations in Key West are at 3228 Flagler Ave. (305-294-4574) and 5350 US 1 on Stock Island (305-296-9901). The location on Truman Avenue is open 24 hours, the shop on Flagler Avenue is open 6 a.m. to 11 p.m., and the Stock Island mart is open 6 a.m. to midnight.

SANTIAGO'S BODEGA $$
207 Petronia St.
(305) 296-7691
www.santiagosbodega.com

Tucked away on a small street with a neighborhood setting, you discover Santiago's Bodega. Wood floors, warm colors, and wide, open windows pouring out onto a porch for dining under gossamer lanterns capture the setting for this unique tapas experience. The food is fresh and simple with more than 30 selections on the menu including soups and salads. Smoked salmon carpaccio, fresh yellowfin ceviche, and the local favorite beef tenderloin topped with bleu cheese are on the offering. There are also loads of vegetarian dishes. Wine, beer, lovely sherry, and ports are also served. Service is charming and friendly. Open for lunch and dinner, but be mindful to make reservations—everyone wants a table!

SARABETH'S $$
530 Simonton St., Key West
(305) 293-8181
www.sarabethskeywest.com

There is a real Sarabeth, and she is an award-winning jam maker, pastry chef, and restaurateur. Not only does her "empire" include four locations in New York City and now Key West, but her legendary spreadable fruits and pastries can be purchased on her Web site as well as in her establishments. The restaurant group is well known for fresh, updated classic American cooking. The James Beard award-winning menus include from-scratch pancakes, salads, sandwiches, meat loaf, grilled meats, and fish. The coffee is served in cups so large they are called bowls. When you partake of any item, you are made to feel as though you are sitting in Sarabeth's personal kitchen where everything is created just for you. Seating, indoors or out, in this historic 1800s clapboard building is a wonderful way to make a Keys memory. Sarabeth's is open for breakfast and lunch Wed to Fri, brunch Sat and Sun, and dinner Wed to Sun. Reservations are suggested for parties of four or more.

South of the Border

CHICO'S CANTINA $$
MM 4.5 Oceanside, Stock Island
(305) 296-4714
www.chicoscantina.com
Mexican

Sit among giant cacti, Mexican tapestries, and a selection of south-of-the-border folk art at Chico's Cantina, a perennial favorite for Mexican cuisine. Open since 1984, this cantina knocks itself out with the freshest ingredients fashioned into off-the-charts homemade Mexican dishes. The food at Chico's is not your ordinary Mexican fare. Complimentary salsa is prepared with fresh tomatoes, onions, and peppers, creating the perfect balance between sweet and sassy. The salsa is so popular among locals that the restaurant sells the stuff in bulk. The sizzling fajitas—with a choice of vegetarian, chicken, beef, chicken-and-beef combo, shrimp, or shrimp-and-beef combo—are accompanied by fresh vegetables, cooked just until crispy. And the fish adobado, grilled in corn husks, packs just the right spicy zing. Daily specials usually highlight local seafood such as yellowtail snapper. Chile peppers rule the roost at Chico's Cantina. Not only is their subtle presence notable in the cuisine, but their icons appear on the curtains, as lights around the windows, even on ceramic pots. Chico's serves the same menu for both lunch and dinner. It's open daily. Beer and wine are served; takeout is available.

EL MESON DE PEPE   **$$**
410 Wall St.
(305) 295-2620
www.elmesondepepe.com
Cuban

Situated just off Mallory Square, El Meson de Pepe draws a large post-sunset crowd. A salsa band plays nightly as the sun sinks into the Gulf of Mexico, which adds to the festive and welcoming atmosphere. Look for Cuban-Conch classics on the menu— Mollete a la Pancho; Cuban bread stuffed with picadillo, a spicy combination of ground beef, capers, raisins, olives, and seasonings; and ropa vieja. Quench your thirst with Pepe's Lemonade, a refreshing cocktail made with Bacardi Limon, cranberry, and orange juice. El Meson de Pepe is open for breakfast, lunch, and dinner daily. Large groups are welcome, and reservations are appreciated but rarely necessary.

EL SIBONEY   **$**
900 Catherine St.
(305) 296-4184
www.elsiboneyrestaurant.com
Cuban

A cascade of bilingual chatter washes over the enthusiastic diners at El Siboney restaurant, an informal restaurant specializing in Cuban cuisine. The word Siboney is an alternate spelling of the Ciboney—Indians who occupied Florida and the Caribbean islands. Artwork depicting the Ciboney adorns the white walls of the restaurant. Red vinyl covers the simple cafe chairs, and your cutlery is served in a white paper bag. The food is top drawer all the way, though. Hot, buttery Cuban bread is immediately whisked to your table, and then begins the difficult decision of which taste-tempting delicacy to order. Portions are enormous at El Siboney; the same menu is offered at lunch or dinner.

We recommend one of the combination platters, especially if trying Cuban cuisine is a new experience for you: A platter of roast pork, black beans, yellow rice, and cassava is served heaped with raw onions. The pork melts in the mouth. Or try the roast pork accompanied with yucca and tamale; sounds similar, tastes totally different. You'll find myriad Cuban twists with beef, including the popular ropa vieja (shredded beef) and boliche (Cuban pot roast). Crab, shrimp, and chicken all get the wonderful Cuban garlic treatment, and you can choose paella for two persons. You can order an array of sandwiches or sides of tamale, yucca, black beans, platanos, and tostones. For a cocktail-with-a-kick, try the homemade sangria, and for dessert (if you have room) try the rice pudding, flan, or natilla. El Siboney is closed on Sunday. No credit cards.

JOSE'S CANTINA   **$**
800 White St.
(305) 296-4366
Cuban

Step inside this little neighborhood diner and you might believe you'd just walked in from the streets of Havana. The owners are Cuban, and so are most of the customers. But even if you don't speak Spanish, you're sure to receive a hearty *bienvenida* (welcome) here. The menus are in English, the waitstaff is bilingual, and the food is plentiful, delicious, and cheap.

Jose's has one of the best Cuban mixes on the island—that's a sandwich combination of ham and shredded pork on Cuban bread with lettuce, tomato, mayo, mustard, onions, and pickles. The dinners—Cuban variations on chicken, pork, and beef—come with the traditional black beans, yellow rice, and plantains. Beer, wine, and homemade sangria are available. Jose's is open for lunch and dinner, 365 days a year—yes, even Christmas. This restaurant is very small and, judging from the lack of parking spaces in the surrounding neighborhood at high noon and 7 p.m., quite popular. To avoid the congestion, plan to arrive a little ahead or well after peak dining periods. Reservations are not accepted and neither are credit cards.

OLD TOWN MEXICAN CAFÉ $
609 Duval St.
(305) 296-7500
www.oldtownmexicancafe.com
Mexican

Have a seat in the open-air dining room right on Duval Street or inside, tucked back away from the crowds. No matter where you sit, you are in for a fiesta of flavor. It all starts with the salsa. The freshly made salsa is so good here that when heading back to the mainland, locals first stop by Fausto's—the local grocery store that carries Old Town Mexican Café salsa by the pint—for the perfect hostess gift. But the salsa isn't the only reason to stop in. Authentic dishes like the tortilla soup and the enchiladas verdes keep locals coming back, along with the inventive veggie plates. Mango ice cream hits the spot as the perfect ending to the Mexican feast. Old Town Mexican Café is open for lunch and dinner daily.

SALSA LOCA $
623–625 Duval St.
(305) 292-1865
www.salsalocakeywest.com
Mexican

Now open in its new location in Cowboy Bill's, Salsa Loca offers freshly made Mexican food in a fun, party atmosphere. Be sure to stop by during happy hour for the two-for-one drink specials. You won't go away hungry: The portions are huge, the menu extensive, and the food is excellent. There are seven different kinds of enchiladas alone, and all come with rice, beans, and a small salad. A local favorite is the mushroom quesadilla served with guacamole, sour cream, salad, and chips and salsa—a vegetarian meal where you won't miss the meat. Salsa Local is open for lunch and dinner daily and delivers to the entire island.

International

A TASTE OF GREECE $
1101 Truman Ave.
(305) 293-6694
Greek

Our weather here in the Keys is a lot like Greece and now there is a restaurant to help set the mood. A Taste of Greece opened in 2007 and with its extensive offerings this is one not to miss. Twenty-one appetizers including hummus and taramosalata, pan-fried squid, spinach pie, stuffed grape leaves, marinated octopus, and one of the local favorites is the sautéed shrimp with tomato, feta scallions, cheese, and ouzo. Many heartier Greek dishes are also on the menu, such as souvlaki, mousaka, and pastitsio. Pita sandwiches and wraps are available for a day in the sun. Desserts also weigh in here: baklava, Easter breads, tiramisu, rice pudding, and cheesecake. This shop also stocks olive oils, olives, cheeses, and vinegars. Everything is available for carryout.

ABBONDANZA $
1208 Simonton St.
(305) 292-1199
Italian
At last, a place to enjoy casual Italian fare in Old Town. The specialty here is pasta, of course, in a variety of shapes and with sauces that range from Alfredo to pomodoro. You'll also find such main dishes as chicken marsala and veal Parmigiana, plus daily specials. The food is quite tasty, the atmosphere is comfortable, and you're sure to discover that the portions at this restaurant live up to its name, which is Italian for "plenty." Abbondanza is a choice place to have dinner for two or a crowd. There is a full bar, and the menu selections are more reasonably priced than some other Italian restaurants in town. Abbondanza is open daily for dinner and offers free parking. No reservations are accepted.

ANTONIA'S RESTAURANT $$
615 Duval St.
(305) 294-6565
www.antoniaskeywest.com
Italian
Stroll by this Northern Italian restaurant on any afternoon, and you can watch pasta in the making along the marble window-front table. Stringy mozzarella also is made fresh

on the premises. Elegant, yet understated, Antonia's is a great place to go if you want to dress up. The menu changes every evening. Past offerings include Linguini Al Gamberi, homemade linguini tossed with Key West pink shrimp, fresh tomato, olive oil, crushed red pepper, garlic, and Italian parsley; and Pesce Del Giorno, pan-sautéed fish of the day served with organic arugula, champagne vinaigrette, salsa verde, and marinated tomatoes. Even with all these spectacular entrees, patrons simply cannot pass up the homemade desserts. Panna cotta features Italian vanilla ice cream with fresh berries and strawberry sauce. Chocolate fondant is served warm with two sauces—raspberry and mango. And of course Key lime pie, which won raves in the *New York Times*. *Bellissimo!* Antonia's maintains an extensive Northern Italian and American wine list. The restaurant is open Mon to Fri for lunch and daily for dinner.

AZUR $$$
425 Grinnell St.
(305) 292-2987
www.azurkeywest.com
Mediterranean
Toss Greek, Italian, and Iberian cuisines in with a tropical setting and you get a creation of a Mediterranean mix called Azur. What you don't get is boring. Step inside the restaurant and you sense the sophisticated air of sleek elegance with an elegant cool edge. The waitstaff is very accommodating and attentive but not overbearing. The pride of Azur is their local fresh fish. Selections to consider are the pan-roasted yellowtail snapper and Key West pink shrimp over braised Swiss chard or the wild-caught fresh seafood and shellfish with sweet peas and saffron infused risotto. Desserts vary but

one standout is crème brûlée infused with lavender and topped with berries. Breakfast and Sunday brunch are not to be missed and showcase equally creative dishes such as the Torta di Granchio, poached eggs on garlic flatbread with house made crab cakes, grilled beefsteak tomatoes, and lemon hollandaise. The wine and beer list is respectable with a varied range of prices. Azur's best ingredient is the innovative talent of the two owners who create memorable dishes in this truly outstanding restaurant. Azur is open for breakfast, lunch, and dinner Mon through Sat, and brunch on Sun.

Pucker Up

It is fascinating when you travel to see the sights, but it is also titillating to try the food of the region you are visiting. In the Florida Keys the influence of Bahamian and Cuban cuisine is in almost every restaurant. One ingredient you will find is sour orange. The fruit is picked from the tree while it is a little green. The juice can be mixed with sugar and made into a drink the Bahamians call "switcher." The Scots harvested the Seville orange that they made famous as marmalade. Another zesty component in Caribbean cooking is Cuban mojo. This is a sour orange, garlic, cumin, olive oil marinade used for pork, beef, or chicken. It's easy to make, but even easier to pick some up, already bottled, in any of our local grocery stores. Take a few bottles home as gifts or try it at your next cookout.

BANANA CAFE $$$
1215 Duval St.
(305) 294-7227
www.bananacafekw.com
French

The exterior of Banana Cafe resembles a quaint Caribbean cottage; the airy interior says French bistro, with pinkish pine wood, artistic black-and-white photography, ceiling fans, and a small bar. Settle into this quiet open-air bistro and choose from more than 40 breakfast and lunch crepes. The thin, pancakelike crepes are stuffed with veggies, fish, and meat, and they are designated either sweet or savory. The most desirable crepe among patrons is the ratatouille, overflowing with sautéed eggplant, zucchini, peppers, extra-virgin olive oil, and garlic and topped with a fried egg sunny-side up. Dinner options include such offerings as local snapper, Parisian gnocchi, lemon-caper brown butter; sliced duck breast served with a sweet-and-sour currant sauce; and yellowtail snapper and crab roulade with tropical mango sauce. Desserts, such as tarte tatin and crème brûlée, are, oh, so French and decadent. Banana Cafe is open for breakfast and lunch daily and dinner from Tues to Sat. Reservations are recommended, particularly on weekends. *Ooh la la!*

FINNEGAN'S WAKE IRISH
  PUB & EATERY $
320 Grinnell St.
(305) 293-0222
www.keywestirish.com
Irish

No need to kiss the Blarney stone at Finnegan's Wake, whose staff guarantees this is one wake you won't want to miss. This Irish pub and eatery sails your spirit across the Big Pond as you toast the legend of the miraculous resurrection of mythical Tim Finnegan. Try authentic Irish fare: bangers and mash (sausages and mashed potatoes, to those of you not wearing the green), shepherd's pie, corned beef and cabbage, Finnegan's Irish Stew, potato pancakes, or the Dublin Chicken Pot Pie. The lip-smacking lovely Irish Potato-leek Soup, a house specialty, is thick and chunky and served with grated cheddar, chopped scallions, and bacon. And be sure to try a black and tan—half Guinness, half lager—or a pint of bottled cider. They also offer 26 draft beers.

Like any good Irish wake, the merriment goes on all day and into the wee hours. Finnegan's Wake is open from lunchtime until 4 a.m. (serving dinner until 10:30 p.m., bar menu until 3 a.m.). You'll find two happy hours here—from 4 to 7 p.m. and from midnight to 2 a.m. Patio dining is available. Reservations will be honored but usually are not necessary. Weekends feature live Irish music.

THE GRAND CAFE $$$
314 Duval St., Key West
(305) 292-4740
www.grandcafekeywest.com
French

Southern French cuisine of Provence in a tropical setting is the ambience of the Grand Cafe. Sit on the patio overlooking Duval Street or inside in the air conditioning amongst vibrant artwork by local artists. A gracious waitstaff orchestrates a fine dance from kitchen to table. The ultimate maestros are the owners and chef who demand nothing short of the best and whose food is consequently at the same level. The sauces are light and represent the flavors of southern French cooking, with fresh herbs and olive oil. Start with the carpaccio of beef tenderloin, served with shaved Parmesan cheese,

red onions, capers, arugula, and white truffle oil or bruschetta, crostini piled high with chopped roma tomatoes and basil pesto. The lunch menu offers crunchy paninis, hot pressed sandwiches served with a small salad of mixed greens with the amazing house vinaigrette dressing. The Grand Cafe prides itself on excellent wine selections and simply grand martinis and is open for lunch and dinner daily. Reservations are recommended. *C'est bon.*

LA TRATTORIA $$$
524 Duval St.
(305) 296-1075
www.latrattoria.us
Italian

This upscale SoHo–style New York bistro rates as a Key West treasure. A romantic taste of old Italy favored by locals, visitors, and Keys residents from as far away as Key Largo, La Trattoria redefines the traditional pasta, veal, chicken, lamb, and seafood dishes of the mother country. The sophisticated decor (linen cloths top intimate tables encircled with black lacquered chairs) belies the fact that you are a stone's throw from the sidewalks of busy Duval Street.

Try Agnello alla Griglia (lamb with fresh rosemary) or Cheese Tortellina alla Romana, with smoked ham and peas in a Parmigiana cream sauce. Penne Arrabbiata, quill-shaped pasta, delivers a bit of a bite, and the traditional Linguine e Vongole does not disappoint. The Insalata Mista will transport your taste buds to Venice for sure. And don't forget dessert—the tiramisu is to die for here. La Trattoria serves dinner nightly. Reservations are suggested, especially in high season. After dinner, retire to Virgilio's, the charming little cocktail lounge with live music just around the corner.

MANGIA MANGIA $$
900 Southard St.
(305) 294-2469
www.mangia-mangia.com
Italian

Off the main drag but definitely on the right track is the pasta lovers' nirvana, Mangia Mangia. Meaning "eat, eat" in Italian, Mangia Mangia bestows a passel of homemade fresh pasta (made daily on the premises with semolina and fresh eggs) and finely seasoned sauces that would excite any palate. The chefs work their macaroni magic in plain view. You can always order the basic sauces—marinara, Alfredo, pesto, meat, and red or white seafood—but for something out of the ordinary, try Bollito Misto di Mare—pappardelle with fresh scallops, shrimp, conch, salmon, mussels, and mahi mahi in a garlic white wine clam sauce. The daily specials will prove difficult to pass up.

Outdoor seating is delightful where the patio area is enclosed with palm trees and flowers. Mangia Mangia serves dinner daily. The restaurant does not take reservations; plan to arrive before 6 p.m. to avoid a wait. You can enjoy selections from Mangia Mangia's extensive wine list. Beer also is served.

MARTIN'S RESTAURANT & LOUNGE $$
917 Duval St.
(305) 296-0111
www.martinskeywest.com
German

Martin's has taken its expansive German menu with its island flair and now shines bright on upper Duval Street. Begin with Pilze a la Martin, toasted bread rounds topped with sautéed mushrooms and herb garlic butter. You'll find classic German dishes such as sauerbraten with spaetzle and red cabbage, and Wiener schnitzel, but Martin's also prepares island seafood creations à la deutsch. Grouper Dijon arrives on a bed of champagne kraut with rosemary potatoes. Yellowtail snapper is encrusted with almonds, flambéed with cognac, and served with a medley of vegetables and wild rice. Choose from a large selection of fine German wines and beers or one of the signature cocktails, like the espresso martini.

Martin's serves dinner nightly, and offers Sunday brunch with dining indoors or out in their tropical garden. Reservations are suggested.

PISCES $$$$
1007 Simonton St.
(305) 294-7100
www.pisceskeywest.com
French

This enduring tropical French establishment has won awards and accolades from Gourmet, Bon Appétit, and Wine Spectator magazines, and the recognition is well deserved. At Pisces, creativity culminates in such delicacies as Lobster Tango Mango, lobster flambéed in cognac with shrimp in saffron butter, mango, and basil; and roast half duckling served with raspberry sauce. One of its finest treasures is Yellowtail Snapper Atocha, sautéed in lemon brown butter with shrimp and scallops. Specials are available nightly. The extensive wine list features some of the best of the vineyards of France and California.

Each of two indoor dining rooms has a distinctive character. The decor features wainscoting; subdued lighting; local acrylic, watercolor, and oil paintings; art by Andy Warhol; and fresh flowers decorating every table. Their rooftop dining area is the perfect romantic setting under the tropical stars, draped in white tablecloths and white chair covers. Candlelight, balmy breezes, and hushed conversations in the epitome of idyllic verve are what makes Pisces, well, Pisces! They are open only for dinner and reservations are recommended.

The Far East

AMBROSIA JAPANESE RESTAURANT $$
1401 Simonton St.
(305) 293-0304

Sake it to me! The sun rises brightly on this wildly popular Japanese restaurant. With a plethora of sushi and sakes, as well as great service, you will understand why it is a locals' top pick. Diverse flavors and textures combined with outstanding sauces will beckon you for a return engagement. Don't forget to explore the drink menu, as they offer a full bar. They will be happy to see you for lunch and dinner.

BENIHANA $$$–$$$$
3591 South Roosevelt Blvd.
(on the Atlantic Ocean)
(305) 294-6400
www.benihana.com

This famous restaurant chain is a contact sport when it comes to the ancient Japanese art of Teppanyaki (literally translated, *teppan* is iron and *yaki* is grilled). I don't know the name for "performance" in Japanese but as a patron of this restaurant you get your money's worth. The menu is vast and appealing while your tableside chef performs his magic. A full bar is available and a private Kimono Room can be reserved for those special occasions with 20 or more people. The view from the front of the building is the Atlantic Ocean while inside you are serenaded by the knife blades chopping on the sizzling grill. Benihana is open for dinner nightly.

CHINA GARDEN WEST $
531 Fleming St.
(305) 296-6177

China Garden West is a quiet, unassuming restaurant. The China Garden West is great for lunch, with chef's specials of pressed duck, subgum wonton, or sea-grass salad. They also have dynamite combo platters offering oriental delights. The China Garden West in Searstown (3300 North Roosevelt Blvd.; 305-296-5618) has the same menu. The China Garden on Big Pine (MM 30 Bayside; 305-872-8861) is located in the Winn-Dixie Shopping Center. Here you get the same excellent Chinese cuisine that they are known for in Key West. Local delivery is available depending on location in the Big Pine area.

All three locations are open seven days a week; takeout is offered, and free delivery is available in Key West with a minimum order of $10.

ORIGAMI JAPANESE RESTAURANT $$
1075 Duval St.
(305) 294-0092

The stark white decor of Origami provides a backdrop for the brightly colored tropical fish adorning the walls. And like the Japanese art of folding paper into decorative or representational forms—origami—the restaurant fashions fresh, local seafood into exquisite sushi and sashimi. The dragon roll must not be missed. Origami also offers traditional Japanese cuisine, such as teriyaki, chicken katsu, steak yakiniku, and tempura.

Sit at the cafe-style tables or at the sushi bar and watch the masters at work. Origami is situated in Duval Square. Free parking is available in the adjoining lot off Simonton Street. Origami is open for dinner daily. Smoking is not permitted inside, but smokers may sit in Origami's lovely outdoor seating area. Beer, wine, and sake are served. Reservations are suggested in high season.

THAI CUISINE $
513 Greene St.
(305) 294-9424
www.keywestthaicuisine.com

The salubrious cuisine of Thailand tingles your palate with the afterglow of Thai curries. Thai curry is a fiery Southeast Asian stew that's not even a kissing cousin to the bland Indian-style powder we Americans associate with the moniker. Thai curry is actually a cooking method, not an ingredient. Together with spices, herbs, and aromatic vegetables, hot chile peppers are ground into a dry paste that infuses Thai curries with heat and passion. At the same time, coconut milk, fish sauce, sugar, and kaffir lime leaves—ubiquitous to every variation of Thai red and green curry—confuse the palate with a riot of sweet-and-sour sensory stimuli.

For another traditional delight, try pad Thai, spicy rice noodles sautéed with shrimp, chicken, and egg, or frog legs with garlic and black pepper. The portions are enormous.

Enjoy a selection of Thai and Japanese beers, house wines, plum wine, and sake. Outdoor seating is available in the evening. Thai Cuisine serves lunch Mon through Fri and is open for dinner every night. Takeout is available, and Thai Cuisine offers free delivery in Key West.

THAI ISLAND $
711 Eisenhower Dr.
(Garrison Bight Marina)
(305) 296-9198
www.thaiislandrestaurant.com

Located at the foot of the bridge in the historic Garrison Bight, Thai Island has become a favorite of locals looking for amazing Thai cooking without the crowds. Dine on their rooftop patio overlooking the Bight as the boats come in with their catches of the day. Start with the tasty Tom Kha Gai or Tom Kha Tofu soup, sour coconut milk blended with chicken (or tofu), mushrooms, lemongrass, scallions, and galanga root. Then opt for one of four different kinds of curry with your choice of seafood, beef, chicken, pork, or tofu that promises to be as spicy as you dare. Thai Island is open daily for lunch and dinner with free parking at Garrison Bight.

SPECIALTY FOODS, CAFES, AND MARKETS

Here in the Florida Keys, we think our fish is pretty special. It's certainly the freshest—sometimes only minutes from line to linen. Its pedigree is elite; most species are not marketed outside South Florida. And the abounding variety of innovative culinary presentations is astounding. Visitors to the Florida Keys, accustomed back home to choosing among cod, halibut, haddock, swordfish, and tuna, are often overwhelmed when confronted with the bountiful selections from our underwater treasure trove.

When you stop at one of our many seafood markets, you will undoubtedly meet the three royal families of our tropical waters: snapper, hogfish, and dolphin, also known as mahi mahi. The famed yellowtail or the equally desirous mangrove or mutton snapper most often represents the moist, sweet snapper dynasty. The firm, mild-flavored hogfish clan competes in popularity with the large-flaked and sweetly moist dolphin fish (not to be confused with the porpoise dolphin, which is a mammal). You won't want to miss our Florida lobster, a delicacy any way you look at it (see the Diving for Lobster Close-up in the Diving and Snorkeling chapter). And if you have never tasted a stone-crab claw, you are in for a treat (see the Close-up in this chapter). To round out your palate, we have provided you with a rundown of delicatessens and shops selling specialty foods.

We have listed our recommended seafood markets and specialty food shops by mile marker (MM) from the top of the Keys in Key Largo to Key West. Key West businesses are listed in alphabetical order.

Most places remain open until at least 5 p.m., with the exception of bakeries, which usually open early and often close in the early afternoon. During high season, December through April, many of these markets and stores extend their hours. The off-season often brings abbreviated hours, so you may want to call before you shop.

UPPER KEYS

**THE FISH HOUSE RESTAURANT &
SEAFOOD MARKET**
MM 102.4 Oceanside, Key Largo
(305) 451-4665
www.fishhouse.com
Primarily a seafood restaurant (see the Restaurants chapter), the Fish House also offers fresh catch of the day from their small seafood market so that you can be the chef of the day if you like. You'll find just-off-the-boat local favorites such as snapper and dolphin as well as other seasonally caught species.

KEY LARGO CONCH HOUSE
MM 100.2 Oceanside, Key Largo
(305) 453-4844
www.keylargocoffeehouse.com

If you're a coffee connoisseur in Key Largo, you'll want to find your way to the Key Largo Conch House, which is housed in a Conch-style house that sits on a lush wooded lot. This shop opened to fill a local demand for a coffee shop, and it fills it well! Choose from among house-blend coffee, gourmet flavors of the day, and espresso drinks. If you prefer a cool drink, how about an iced coffee or a fruit smoothie made with a green-tea base? After making your choice, pick a seat on the wide porch and savor your cup of joe in the fresh air. If you're hungry, the Conch House serves freshly baked pastries as well as breakfast lunch and dinner.

KEY LARGO FISHERIES
MM 99.5 Oceanside, 1313 Ocean Bay Dr., Key Largo
(305) 451-3782 or (800) 432-4358
www.keylargofisheries.com

The family-run Key Largo Fisheries ships wholesale to hundreds of clients throughout the country and also offers retail sales at their Key Largo store and via overnight delivery. At Key Largo Fisheries, customers will find choice seafood, including snapper, mahi mahi, shrimp, and, in season, Florida lobster and stone-crab claws. Conch here is imported from the Bahamas and the West Indies. Key Largo Fisheries is open Mon through Sat.

CHAD'S DELI AND BAKERY
MM 92.3 Bayside, Tavernier
(305) 853-5566

Lots of good food at reasonable prices and quick service! That is not only a winning combo (just like some of their menu items), it is also what makes Chad's Deli and Bakery a success in the Upper Keys. The waitstaff is very friendly and knows all the regulars by name. That goes a long way in a small place like Tavernier and the Keys. Their specialities are four-way sandwiches, speciality pizzas (try the Mombo Combo), calzones, pasta, goulash, and salads. They also serve beer and wine to round out your meal.

SUNSHINE SUPERMARKET
MM 91.8 Oceanside, Tavernier
(305) 852-7216

There isn't a Tavernier resident who doesn't know about the rotisserie chicken and Cuban bread here. Family owned and operated, Sunshine Supermarket offers some tasty Cuban specialties as well: roast pork, ribs, yellow rice, and black beans and rice, all at reasonable prices and huge portions. The pork is marinated in mojo sauce—a Cuban concoction of oil, vinegar, garlic, and other spices. It is available for chicken as well, upon request, and you can buy it by the bottle here.

BOB'S BUNZ RESTAURANT AND BAKERY
MM 81.6 Bayside, Islamorada
(305) 664-8363
www.bobsbunz.com

The banner out front proclaims BEST BUNS IN TOWN, and these oversize cinnamon rolls live up to the hype. Topped with cream-cheese icing, the buns are undoubtedly one of the local favorites. Also available are "gooey" or sticky buns, bagels, muffins, scones, croissants, Key lime pie, cakes, and cookies, which can be ordered online as well. As you might imagine, this restaurant is a wildly popular Islamorada breakfast and lunch spot.

ISLAMORADA FISH COMPANY
MM 81.5 Bayside, Islamorada
(305) 664-9271
www.fishcompany.com

This Islamorada legend operates out of a state-of-the-art, 5,000-square-foot facility in the totally renovated former Green Turtle Cannery building next door to the Islamorada Fish Company's original location. Ten thousand pounds of superfresh fish and seafood find their way through the cutting rooms here, much displayed in a showy 31-foot display case. Everything is temperature controlled at Islamorada Fish Company, so the fish stays extra fresh. You can watch the cutters in action from a glassed-in cutting room.

You'll find all the local favorites, such as dolphin, Florida lobster, snapper, swordfish, stone-crab claws, blue crab, Key West pink shrimp, and tuna. You can liven things up with their extensive selection of hot sauces.

If you prefer to dine in this charming seafood market ambience, the store has a full-service restaurant (see the Restaurants chapter).

THE TRADING POST
MM 81.5 Bayside, Islamorada
(305) 664-2571

This is definitely Islamorada's "super" market. Here you'll discover super grocery selections, supergood deli items, a super meat market, super wine offerings, and super hours. The Trading Post is open 24 hours a day, seven days a week! The store also offers customized catering.

MIDDLE KEYS

THE ISLAND FISH COMPANY
MM 54.5 Bayside, Marathon
(305) 743-4191
www.islandfishco.com

Set your course to this location if you adore oysters! They serve gulf oysters raw, freshly shucked, baked to order with garlic, barbecued, Rockefeller, or Moscow style with sour cream horseradish sauce and black and red caviar. How about a seafood tower that is loaded with oysters, clams, shrimp, and a pound of stone crab claws? Let's not forget clams casino, little neck clams, shrimp cocktail, or peel-and-eat or beer-steamed shrimp. Moving into other seafood arenas, Island Fish Company comes to the table with conch fritters, calamari, mango crab cakes, spinach crab dip, lobster rolls, and Key West shrimp tacos. After just looking at this menu, is there any seafood remaining in the ocean?

FISH TALES MARKET & EATERY
MM 53 Oceanside, Marathon
(305) 743-9196
www.floridalobster.com

This tiny eatery offers fish and seafood baskets and sandwiches, along with a few heartier specials daily. And you'll find Johnny's famous salad and George's popular wasabi and honey or mustard sauces as well. You can even try one of the brothers' homemade bratwurst, which is made with smoked mackerel. Fish Tales will cook your catch if you've had a productive day on the water. The well-stocked seafood market offers Key West shrimp, stone crabs, tuna, swordfish, the Keys trio—snapper, grouper, and dolphin—and more. Fish Tales Market will ship seafood anywhere in the United States. A choice-grade meat counter offers aged steaks, pork tenderloin, and rack of lamb as well.

KEYS FISHERIES MARKET & MARINA
MM 49 Bayside, at the end of 35th St., Marathon
(305) 743-4353 or (866) 743-4353
www.keysfisheries.com

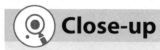

Close-up

Florida Stone Crab Claws

Now, you Yankees can brag about your blue crabs, and you West Coasters may boast of dungeness. But here in the Florida Keys we crow about crab claws like none other—those of the Florida stone crabs.

The stone crabs, large nonswimming crabs found in deep holes and under rocks in the waters surrounding the Keys, have the unusual ability to release their legs or pincers if caught or when experiencing extreme changes in temperature. The separation always occurs at one of the joints to protect the crab from further injury. What is unique about this situation is that the stone crab regenerates the severed appendage, a feat it can accomplish three or four times during its lifetime. This makes it a renewable resource.

The stone crab's two claws serve distinct purposes: The larger claw, or crusher, is used to hold food and fight predators. The smaller claw, known as the ripper, acts as a scissors for cutting food.

The crabs are harvested commercially in the Florida Keys with baited traps. One or both of the crab's claws are removed (it greatly improves the crab's chances of survival if only one claw is taken). The forearm must measure at least 2¾ inches from the tip of the claw to the joint to harvest it legally. The live stone crabs must then be returned to the water, where in 18 months a new claw will have grown to legal size. It is illegal in the state of Florida to harvest whole stone crabs. They are one of our precious resources.

A stone-crab claw has a hard, heavy, porcelainlike shell with a black-tipped pincer. Seafood markets sell stone-crab claws fully cooked. When cooked, the meat inside the shell is sweet and firm-textured. A mild, sweet odor indicates freshness.

The shells must be cracked before serving. If you plan to eat your stone-crab claws within an hour of purchase, have the seafood market crack them for you. It is not recommended that you crack the claws until you are ready to eat them.

If you crack the claws yourself, lightly tap the crockerylike shells with a hammer, a small wooden mallet (available at seafood markets), or the back of a tablespoon. The shells also will crack like a fine china teacup if you hit one claw against the other. Pick the meat from the shell using a small cocktail fork and serve with mustard sauce (cold claws) or clarified butter (resteamed claws).

Stone-crab claws are in season from October 15 until May 15. They do not freeze particularly well, but most seafood markets listed in this chapter will ship iced, fresh stone-crab claws anywhere in the United States.

Fish here is fresh, fresh, fresh, because Keys Fisheries' fishing fleet works out of the marina. You'll find Key West pinks (shrimp), Florida lobster, stone crabs, and all varieties of local fish here, as well as clams, oysters, scallops, squid, conch, and more. Take home homemade soups and seafood salads or spreads if you like. You can also order from the menu of the adjoining eatery (see the Restaurants chapter). They also will fillet, pack, and ship their fish so that you can take your Keys bounty home with you.

LOWER KEYS

BAGEL ISLAND DELI
MM 30 Bayside, Big Pine Shopping Center
(305) 872-9912
www.bagelislandcoffee.com

In a shopping center on Big Pine Key sits a great little bakery and sandwich shop. The folks at Bagel Island bake delectable everyday cakes as well as special-occasion ones, like wedding cakes. For breakfast or morning coffee-break eating, try their homemade bagels, pastries, and Danish. If breakfast is not your thing, stop in for lunch. Try their tuna on a fresh bagel, hot soup, or salads. Sometimes parking is tight, but your search for a space will be well worth the effort.

KEY WEST KEY LIME PIE COMPANY
MM 30 Bayside, Big Pine Key
(305) 872-7400 or (877) 882-7437
www.keywestkeylimepieco.com

Key lime pie, a Florida Keys tradition, is what Key West Key Lime Pie Company is deliciously all about. Lots of people claim to have "award-winning" pie, but the Key Lime Pie Company beat out over 500 other applicants to win best pie for their Key Lime Pie Bar at the American Pie Council Championships in 2009. Each handmade, 9-inch pie (also sold by the slice) is frozen, literally melting in your mouth, bite by bite. The company will ship the pies anywhere in the continental United States overnight or provide you with a frozen travel pack, so you can take a pie on the road with you or back home by airplane. If a fork isn't your style, how about Key lime pie on a stick, dipped in dark chocolate? Messy to eat, but, oh, so yummy. A second delicious location is at 431 Front St. in Key West (305-517-6720).

GOOD FOOD CONSPIRACY
MM 30 Oceanside, Big Pine Key
(305) 872-3945
www.goodfoodconspiracy.com

A full assortment of health foods, homeopathic remedies, vitamins, organic poultry, and organically grown produce is offered at the Good Food Conspiracy. If you browse the shelves, you'll find interesting specialty foods as well. Part of the Conspiracy is a juice and sandwich bar, which features an "outgoing menu" of healthful selections. In addition to the products and produce, Good Food Conspiracy also houses a holistic health center and even a reverend that performs commitment ceremonies and weddings. Talk about one-stop shopping!

MURRAY'S FOOD MARKET
MM 24.5 Oceanside, Summerland Key
(305) 745-3534

This familiar landmark is Summerland Key's lifeline for provisions. Murray's sells most all your food and household needs. Their wonderful fresh deli selection, meat counter, daily baked breads, and beer and wine save all the locals in the area from driving south into Key West or north to Big Pine just for a gallon of milk.

SUGARLOAF FOOD COMPANY
MM 24 Bayside, Summerland Key
(305) 744-0631
www.sugarloaffood.com

This tiny treasure encased in a sunny yellow building is bright and upbeat with goodness galore. Homemade tortellini salad to accompany sandwiches stuffed with homemade meat loaf and red onion mayo is a popular choice. Grab a roast beef and Swiss with horseradish aioli sauce on a baguette, a curry pistachio chicken salad, or classic Cobb for a change. Utterly dreamy chocolate raspberry bread pudding will have you whistling a happy tune!

FANCI SEAFOOD
MM 22.5 Oceanside, Cudjoe Key
(305) 745-3887
www.fanciseafood.com

Shelves and shelves of marinades and seafood sauces will inspire you to try your culinary skills in a new creation when you stop in at Fanci Seafood. The very complete fish and seafood selection lets you choose among the usual Keys finfish (grouper, snapper, and dolphin) and golden crab, stone-crab claws, lobsters, blue crabs, oysters, and mussels.

Love the seafood you eat in the restaurants in the Keys? Then try out those recipes back home with *Ocean Flavors and More!* cookbook. The Florida Keys Commercial Fishermen's Association publishes this collection of favorite recipes from captains, crews, and families. The price is $12, and funds from the book go to the association's scholarship fund for children of fishermen. The cookbooks are sold at various fisheries and specialty shops throughout the Keys, including Key Largo Fisheries, the Island Fish Co., Fanci Seafood, and the Eaton Street Fish Market, among others. You can also order one from their Web site, www.fkcfa.org.

KICKIN' BACK FOOD MART
MM 21.4 Oceanside, Cudjoe Key
(305) 745-2528

Life here in the Keys is really laid back, so why not our grocery stores? This local oasis is easy on and off US 1 offering beer, wine, lottery tickets, ATM machine, and limited groceries. You won't have to worry about finding a parking spot at Kickin'—it's a gravel parking pad. Pretty simple. That's the way folks here like it!

BABY'S COFFEE
MM 15 Oceanside, Key West
(800) 523-2326
www.babyscoffee.com

It's the hottest coffee craze in the Florida Keys, but just who is Baby? The legend lives on: "Late, last century (circa 1991), Gary & O. T. left the Big Bad Apple (NY), looking for a home for their new coffee-roasting company. They set up shop in a small building on the uptown side of Key West's famed Duval Street. In the 1920s an old Cuban family had owned this building and christened it 'Baby's Place,' after the family's youngest son. 'Baby' Rodriguez grew up and ran a cantina there where, legend has it, Ernest Hemingway indulged in the occasional crapshoot with locals, known as 'conchs.' Inspired, Gary and O. T. adopted the Baby's name and let the dice roll one more time."

Lucky for us, Gary and O. T. rolled those dice, 'cause Baby's Coffee is great. And their business grew so large they had to relocate up the Keys on a no-name stretch at MM 15. Baby's roasts only 100 percent Arabica coffee. They ship their coffee fresh within 48 hours; it is not vacuum-packed or freeze-dried. You'll find all their Key West roasts, Hawaiian roasts, specialty roasts, flavored coffees, and decaf roasts on their Web site and can buy it by the pound at Fausto's in Key West.

KEY WEST

BETTER THAN SEX DESSERT CAFÉ
411 Petronia St.
(305) 393-1049
www.betterthansexkw.com

This romantic place will put you in the mood . . . for dessert. Seductive in atmosphere (brown and red velvet decor), vintage in music ('30s and '40s), flirtatious in atmosphere (flickering candlelight), and *wowee wowee* in the dessert department. This cafe serves *only* desserts along with wines and coffees. One such presentation is a Chocolate Cab, a wine goblet coated with lush chocolate then filled with wine! You will be smitten—after all, this is Key West!

BLOND GIRAFFE
1209 Truman Ave.
(305) 295-6776
www.blondgiraffe.com
Key lime pie is indigenous to the Florida Keys. Ask the locals and they'll be happy to tell you their favorite recipe. Rating right up there at the top of the list is the superb blend of flavors produced by the Blond Giraffe. The supertart custard filling and sweet, fluffy meringue sit on a sinfully rich yet delicate pastry crust, reminiscent of an English butter cookie. Check out all their locations, and while you're at it, order pies and have them shipped anywhere in the United States, from Blond Giraffe's Web site.

THE CAFÉ
509 Southard St.
(305) 296-5515
Truly vegetarian and vegan but in no way dull and bland. Large portions, fun staff, and good prices leave you feeling healthy. Simply stated and simply a good place to eat.

COFFEE PLANTATION
713 Caroline St.
(305) 295-9808
www.coffeeplantationkeywest.com

While away on vacation, you might like to check your e-mail, fax a document, or make a copy. Here at the Coffee Plantation, you can do all of the above while enjoying delicious coffee, smoothies, or frappes. They also offer computers with Internet access. Rates and services are reasonable, and the staff is most helpful. The cozy ambience makes this an inviting stop.

COLE'S PEACE ARTISAN BAKERY
1111 Eaton St.
(305) 292-0703
www.colespeace.com
Long a favorite with locals, Cole's Peace Artisan Bakery will become your favorite too. Everything here is authentic from their famous Cuban bread and mango/cranberry bread pudding, to Mexican chocolate cake and ciabatta lotta sandwiches. Load up on the addictive café con leche coffee to wash down the assorted scones, muffins, and cheese croissants. The wonderful owners will cater your party or event with 48 hours' notice.

CORK & STOGIE
1218 Duval St.
(305) 517-6419
www.corkandstogie.com
Just as the name implies, head here to the "closest cigar shop to Cuba," which sells original Key West Cigar Factory cigars and bottles of fine wine. Throughout the year, Cork & Stogie hosts wine tastings, book signings, and live music Fri and Sat nights. Sit inside or outside on the porch and enjoy your purchases. Hemingway would approve.

CROISSANTS DE FRANCE
816 Duval St.
(305) 294-2624
www.croissantsdefrance.com

"Absence makes the heart grow fonder" has significant meaning for Croissants de France. This legendary institution is a phoenix-from-the-ashes story. In 2005, on Valentine's Day, a horrific fire totally destroyed the landmark bakery and restaurant. After the fire, what wasn't burned the owners lost to Hurricane Wilma in 2006. Viva la Croissants—and your waistline! Seduction in broad daylight is what awaits you with their pastry selections. This beloved, tiny treasure also dishes up galettes, quiches, croissants, and brioche sandwiches.

FAUSTO'S FOOD PALACE
522 Fleming St.
(305) 296-5663
www.faustos.com

"Not just a grocery, a social center" reads the slogan in the ads for this gourmet food emporium, which has been serving Key West since 1926. The Fleming Street site is its largest and oldest. Here, in addition to the usual bread, milk, produce, canned goods, and kitchen staples, you will find fresh local seafood, premium meats and poultry, and numerous varieties of wine as well as Beluga caviar, pâtés, rare cheeses, and desserts. A sushi chef is on duty every day, and party platters are available with as little as one hour's notice. The deli counter is especially busy at noontime when the folks who work downtown line up for hot soup, fresh-made sandwiches, and specials like homemade meat loaf and mashed potatoes, Cuban pork, or black beans and rice. The White Street location (1105 White St.; 305-294-5221) is more like a neighborhood grocery, with a smaller deli counter and a limited selection of produce, bread, frozen foods, and canned goods.

FISHBUSTERZ
6840 Front St., Stock Island
(305) 294-6456 or (305) 296-6022
www.fishbusterz.com

Fishbusterz has the happening docks on Stock Island, and it's a great place to get seafood as fresh as if you caught it yourself. You can go watch the boats unload their catch and choose from the day's bounty of fresh shrimp, fish, lobster, conch, stone crabs, and other seafood items. If you prefer, stay and let them prepare the fresh catch from their menu in the open-air, unpretentious Shrimp Shack. This casual eatery offers appetizers, soups, sandwiches, baskets, and dinners. With great views of the working waterfront, harbor, and vessels, you know why everyone chooses this Stock Island find. Fishbusterz is located just down the street from the Hogfish Bar and Grill.

5 BROTHERS
930 Southard St.
(305) 296-5205
5brothersgrocery.tripod.com

If you're headed downtown along Southard Street any weekday morning between 7:30 and 8 a.m., expect to encounter a traffic jam at the corner of Grinnell Street. It's just the locals pulling over to pick up their "fix" at 5 Brothers, which has been serving this island for almost 30 years. This is where Key West goes for buche, that tiny cup of industrial-strength Cuban coffee that satisfies your caffeine habit with a single swig. This tiny corner grocery also makes a mean Cuban mix—that's a combination ham, pork, salami, Swiss, lettuce, and pickle sandwich served on Cuban bread—and great conch chowder (Fri only). For you early birds, 5 Brothers opens at 6 a.m. (closed Sun). The shop is cash only.

FLAMINGO CROSSING
1105 Duval St.
(305) 296-6124
Since 1987 this has been a favorite with locals and visitors alike. Flamingo Crossing is the place to pause for refreshment as you make your way up and down Duval Street. Homemade ice cream is the business here, and it's the closest thing to Italian gelato this side of the Mediterranean. You can choose from such flavors as Cuban coffee, raspberry cappuccino, coconut piña colada, Key lime, passion fruit, and green tea, among others. Or try the ice cream called guanabana/sour sop—two names for the same tasty, delicate fruit. Flamingo Crossing also makes its own sorbet and yogurt. (See the Kidstuff chapter.)

i Harvesting conch (pronounced *konk*) in Florida waters is illegal. Therefore, most seafood markets import conch from the Turks and Caicos Islands. Firmer in texture than that from most other waters, conch from Turks and Caicos waters is some of the best in the world.

GOLDMAN'S BAGEL, SALAD AND SANDWICH DELI
2796 North Roosevelt Blvd.,
Overseas Market
(305) 294-3354
www.goldmansdeli.com
If not for the palm trees outside the door of this full-service restaurant-deli in the Overseas Market, you'd swear you just walked in from the streets of New York or Chicago. Here, the hot corned beef and pastrami sandwiches are sliced thin and piled high in traditional deli style, the bagels are baked fresh daily, and the potato salad is tops. You can carry out such delicacies as chopped liver, potato knishes, smoked whitefish, and kosher franks, along with the bagels and an array of flavored cream cheeses sold by the pound. Try our favorite—the everything bagel "schmeered" with smoked-salmon cream cheese. Breakfast and lunch are served at tables along one side and at the counter. Deli platters and catering are also available.

GRAND VIN
1107 Duval St.
(305) 296-1020
This is *the* place where locals gather to sample fine wines and catch up on the island gossip. Buy a bottle to take back to your hotel room or enjoy a glass (or four) on the porch as you watch the crowds navigate Duval Street. People-watching is a favorite pastime here in Key West and the porch at Grand Vin offers the best views. Friendly, knowledgeable bartenders and wines of every grape variety imaginable make Grand Vin truly toast-worthy.

HELP YOURSELF
829 Fleming St.
(305) 296-7766
www.helpyourselffoods.com
Help Yourself is just that into you! Eating in a healthy way is the way to go and folks come here for the best in natural and organic eats. No dairy, refined sugars, or bad fats allowed and the line outside the door proves one thing—people are helping themselves. Choose your greens (mixed, romaine, spinach), choose your wrap (sprouted grain, gluten-free, whole wheat), your sauce (coconut lime curry, lemon tahini, basil pesto, miso broth), start piling on the proteins (salmon, shrimp, chicken), enjoy a side (sesame noodles, hummus, bean salad, quinoa

tabouli), and top it off with homemade Ginger Aide or organic smoothie. Even their to-go containers are compostable and made from renewable sources. You feel healthy just reading the menu! As an added plus, on Sunday mornings, they have an open-air organic-only produce market.

HOGFISH BAR AND GRILL
6810 Front St., Stock Island
(305) 293-4041
www.hogfishbar.com
One of the last frontiers of true Keys hang-outs, Hogfish Bar and Grill is where the locals go and the fishing boat captains congre-gate—if you can find it. To get there take US 1 North out of Key West and across the Cow Key Channel Bridge. At the third stoplight, bear to the right and onto MacDonald Ave. Follow this for approximately 1 mile and make a right on 4th Ave. (across from Boyd's Campground). Take your next left on Front St. and drive almost to the end—you'll see the Hogfish Bar and Grill on the right. Once you are there, belly up to a picnic table and order the amazing Jason's Lobster Bisque (a favorite of the locals) and the signature Hogfish "Killer" sandwich, which is a fish sandwich smothered with onions and mush-rooms on freshly baked Cuban bread.

KERMIT'S KEY WEST KEY LIME SHOPPE
200 Elizabeth St.
(305) 296-0806 or (800) 376-0806
www.keylimeshop.com
You can't miss this place because Kermit, the Key lime chef (as seen on the Food Network) is usually outside waving you into this Key lime heaven. Everything inside is made with Key lime juice, including oils, cookies, candy kisses, salad dressings, juice concentrate, pie filling, and sweets of all sorts. You'll also find

key lime soaps and lotions here. And be sure to look outside for the authentic Key lime tree—the source of all this pleasure and a rarity these days in the Florida Keys.

MATTHEESSEN'S HOMEMADE
419 Duval St.
(305) 296-8014
www.mattheessens.com
No tourist destination is complete without at least one fudge shop and Mattheessen's proved to be so popular that now there are two. In Key West you'll find more than your fill of this melt-in-your-mouth confection at two Duval Street locations (the second is located at 106 Duval St.; 305-296-1616). Traditional chocolate is always a favorite, of course, but the key lime and maple-pecan varieties are equally tasty and sinful.

MATTHEESSEN'S 4TH OF JULY ICE CREAM PARLOR
1110 White St.
(305) 294-8089
www.mattheessens.com
The original 4th of July restaurant opened its doors in the 1950s and didn't close them until the 1980s. This Key West tradition has been revived by the Mattheessen family, who have remodeled the old eatery with red, white, and blue decor and are now offering ice cream, marble-slab fudge, cookies, and barbecue to old aficionados and enthusiastic newcomers. Gleaming glass cases let your little ones look at their choices of ice cream. Bright blue booths tempt those who want to linger for a while. Slide in and treat yourself to a Cuban sundae, made with Cuban coffee, mocha chips, and dulce de leche ice cream topped with hot fudge and caramel sauce, chocolate-covered espresso beans, whipped cream, and of course, a cherry on top.

MR. Z'S
501 Southard St.
(305) 296-4445
www.mrzskeywest.com
Philly-style, Italian-American fast food, 24/7! This is Mr. Z's claim to fame in Key West. If you have an urge for a cheesesteak at 3 a.m. or pizza at midnight, one call will curb your craving. Locals don't consider an order complete if it doesn't contain cheese fries. Dieters beware! Eat in the small restaurant on one of the few barstools or take it to go. There is also free delivery in Old Town. Cash only.

PEPPERS OF KEY WEST
602 Greene St.
(305) 295-9333 or (800) 597-2823
www.peppersofkeywest.com
Peppers, where chile peppers are the name of the game, bills itself as "the hottest spot on the island." More than 300 varieties of hot sauces already grace the shelves, and more arrive from all over every day. Peppers always has a basket of chips and a few open bottles at the front counter so you can have a taste. Al Roker and Matt Lauer of *The Today Show* barely survived their pepper encounter, so sample if you dare. Peppers bottles its own brands of "hot"— #1, #2, and Goin' Bananas. Look for their Key lime juice as well. And be sure to look around the neighborhood for the chile pepper car. It belongs to one of the owners and can usually be found parked near the shop.

RUSTY ANCHOR FISHERIES
5510 Third Ave., Stock Island
(305) 294-5369
Where's the fish? A little Insider help is needed to negotiate for fish at this place, known to locals as having the freshest at the best prices. The fish market is directly behind Rusty Anchor Restaurant, which is on Third Avenue (see our Restaurants chapter), although no sign on Third Avenue indicates the fishmonger's presence. Simply park at the restaurant and they will show you the way to the fishery. Find out about the catch of the day. Rusty Anchor is known for some of the best prices on jumbo stone-crab claws and colossal shrimp ("under 15s").

SALUTE! ON THE BEACH
1000 Atlantic Blvd.
(305) 292-1117
To "see" Salute is to "see" the "sea"! Right smack dab on Higgs Beach with the Atlantic Ocean as your front yard, Salute has its squatters rights and rightfully so. This locals' hangout is a pet of a restaurant for all of us in the know. Yummy seafood and great Italian choices with the antipasto winning hands down. Perhaps the best part of this place is the free show that goes on at the beach in front of you!

SANDY'S CAFÉ
1026 White St.
(305) 295-0159
Lodged in the same building as the popular M & M Laundry, this hole-in-the-wall Cuban walk-up joint is one of the best places in the Keys for authentic Cuban "fast food." The lines outside the order windows (with a few barstools available for seating) indicate how loyal Sandy's customers are. The cafe con leche, cheese tostada, and Cuban mix sandwiches will have you clamoring for more. Delivery is available in Old Town. No credit cards . . . this is cash and carry only. *Bueno! Bueno!*

SUGAR APPLE NATURAL FOODS
917 Simonton St.
(305) 292-0043
www.sugarapplekeywest.com

A longtime favorite of health-conscious Key Westers, Sugar Apple stocks organic and hard-to-find groceries, vitamins, beauty aids, homeopathic remedies, books, and herbs. A juice bar and deli serve up sandwiches, smoothies, specials, and teas. The owners and staff are very knowledgeable about their products and the benefits of healthy living.

WATERFRONT MARKET
201 William St.
(305) 296-0778
www.naturalretail.com

The serious cooking aficionado and the robust eater will have a ball in this market, located between the Caroline Street side of the Key West Historic Seaport and William Street (parking entrance). You can't miss it as the building is covered in a huge ocean-themed mural by famed Keys artist Wyland. Browsing the shelves reminds us of perusing an international library. All the difficult-to-find ingredients for Japanese, Thai, Chinese, or even Middle Eastern dishes dress the shelves here, often scrutinized by Key West's top professional chefs. This is also a great place to gather everything you need for a day on the water. Waterfront Market features seafood, steaks, a cheese selection to die for, deli, coffee-bean center, and produce section to boot.

NIGHTLIFE

In the Florida Keys, what to do after our famous sunsets is a choice as individualistic as our residents and visitors. But for those revelers who like to party until the wee hours, we take you on a club crawl, tavern tromp, saloon slog—call it what you like. Come promenade our pubs, bars, and nightclubs from Key Largo to Key West, our southernmost city, where a night on the town redefines the cliché.

As a general rule, bars are open later the farther down in the Keys you go, with many establishments in Key West open until 4 a.m. Taverns and pubs in the Upper and Middle Keys are more likely to close between midnight and 2 a.m.

We encourage you to have fun and enjoy our casual Keys pubs, but keep in mind that the DUI limit here is 0.08 percent, less than some other states. Remember, too, that driving-under-the-influence laws apply to all vehicles—scooters, boats, and bikes included. So if you drink, don't drive. Or pedal. Take a cab or take along a designated driver. Pedicabs are also good alternatives and you can usually flag one down in Key West without any hassle.

You'll find the majority of these places open seven nights a week. Exceptions are noted. Remember, however, that hours and entertainment may vary depending on the season or whim of the owners. It is always best to call ahead.

UPPER KEYS

CARIBBEAN CLUB
MM 104.5 Bayside, Key Largo
(305) 451-9970
Bogey and Bacall are alive and well in this famous Key Largo bar and restaurant. The walls are filled with memorabilia from the 1948 classic movie *Key Largo,* even though most of the movie was filmed on Hollywood soundstages and back lots. Great sunset views and live entertainment draw late-night crowds, making this a popular locals' hangout.

BREEZER'S TIKI BAR
MM 103.8 Bayside, Key Largo
(at Marriott Key Largo Bay Beach Resort)
(305) 453-0000
www.marriottkeylargo.com
Breezer's is an elevated gazebo-sheltered bar overlooking the showy property and wondrous waters of the Marriott Key Largo Bay Beach Resort. This fantasy island setting provides the perfect backdrop for the accompanying live island–style music on Fri and Sat.

COCONUTS RESTAURANT & NIGHT CLUB

MM 100 Oceanside, 528 Caribbean Dr.,
Key Largo
(at Marina Del Mar Resort and Marina)
(305) 453-9794
www.coconutsrestaurant.com

A perennial nightclub favorite with a per-colating dance floor, Coconuts has theme nights that keep 'em coming: Mon, disco night; Tues, blues; Wed, ladies' night, with free drinks to all females from 9 to 11 p.m.; Thurs, Fri, and Sat, live Top-40 dance bands; and Sun, karaoke. See our Restaurants chapter for dining options here.

HOLIDAY INN KEY LARGO RESORT AND MARINA

MM 99.7 Oceanside, Key Largo
(305) 451-2121
www.holidayinnkeylargo.com

You'll discover a couple of options at the Holiday Inn Key Largo. Bogie's Café has a piano lounge where you can enjoy the tinkling of the ivories. The outdoor Tiki Bar picks up the pace a bit with live music Thurs through Sat; a mix of reggae, rock, and pop attracts an equal mingling of locals and tourists.

SNAPPER'S WATERFRONT RESTAURANT

MM 94.5 Oceanside, Key Largo
(305) 852-5956
www.snapperskeylargo.com

Snapper's oozes Keys atmosphere, especially on the cypress-and-palm-frond chickees on the outdoor waterside deck. Menu items are innovative (see the Restaurants chapter), and patrons enjoy live entertainment nightly.

HOG HEAVEN SPORTS BAR

MM 85.3 Oceanside, Islamorada
(305) 664-9669
www.hogheavensportsbar.com

The congenial outdoor saloon of Hog Heaven Sports Bar sits unassumingly on the waterfront. You can amuse yourself with televised sports, talk with the locals, or head to the point, where a chickee yields seclusion that may foster romance. As you might expect, the pork here is heavenly.

LORELEI CABANA BAR

MM 82 Bayside, Islamorada
(305) 664-4656
www.loreleifloridakeys.com

This bar not only serves great drinks, but the Lorelei also offers one of the best views of stunning sunsets in the Florida Keys. The bar is a laid-back waterside watering hole and lunch spot all day long, and the views of Florida Bay cannot be beat. See our Restaurants chapter for dining options here.

MIDDLE KEYS

DOCKSIDE BAR & GRILL

MM 53 Oceanside, 35 Sombrero Rd.,
Sombrero Marina, Marathon
(305) 743-0000
www.keysy.com/dockside

The dock rocks during Sunday-night jam sessions, when bands from throughout Florida showcase their talents. New owners brought back the high-energy atmosphere at this open-air harborside hangout. Dockside's Thirsty Thursdays, Fishy Fridays, and Wacky Wednesdays, with the not-to-be-missed RocketMan for entertainment, set this place apart from the others for fun in the sun!

BRASS MONKEY
MM 50 Oceanside, Kmart Plaza, Marathon
(305) 743-4028

This long-established bar and liquor store is a regulars' hangout in Marathon. The Brass Monkey serves up not only lunch and dinner but also live music six nights a week. The lounge opens early and closes in the wee hours. "That Funky Monkey" is still going strong after all these years!

SEVEN MILE GRILL
MM 46 Oceanside, Marathon
(305) 743-4481
www.keysdining.com/7milegrill

You can't miss this watering hole, as it sits off US 1 at the beginning of the Seven Mile Bridge heading south to Key West. When it opens in the morning, you see the many folks lining the bar to sip their favorite beverage and toast the local color that is the Florida Keys. Light fare is on the menu, as are the many drinks of choice.

LOWER KEYS

NO NAME PUB
MM 31 Bayside, North Watson Blvd., Big Pine Key
(305) 872-9115

Wallpapered with dollar bills and full of good cheer and local color, No Name Pub is a must-do, night or day (see the Restaurants chapter for menu offerings and directions). Off the beaten path about as far as you can go in Big Pine, this small saloon sports a funky bar and a pool table.

PARROTDISE WATERFRONT BAR & GRILLE
MM 28.5, Bayside, 183 Barry Ave., Little Torch Key
(305) 872-9989
www.parrotdisewaterfront.com

Perched high above the Big Pine Channel, on the gulf, sits this local haunt. New owners may have changed the name, but the Parrotdise is still a fun, casual meeting hangout for drinks and eats. Easily accessible by car or boat, this bar and grill offers wine and beer along with fabulous water views.

LOOE KEY TIKKI BAR
MM 27.3 Oceanside, Ramrod Key
(305) 872-2215

Alive and kicking in the Keys at this open-air tiki bar is where you will find many locals and ardent dive tourists. Sandwiches and basket dinners accompany a fine sampling of good conversation from the patrons who frequent this no-pretense bar.

KEY WEST

Renowned for its nightlife, Key West boasts of having more bars per capita than anywhere else in the United States. With many of the establishments open seven days a week until 4 a.m., this tiny island lives up to its slightly eccentric reputation. An age-old tradition in Key West is called the "Duval Crawl"—a sampling of libations from all the nightspots on Duval Street, until the only means of moving is to crawl.

In this section we recommend a road map for such a crawl. We start at the Atlantic end of Duval Street, where the pubs are more sparsely located, and move toward the Gulf of Mexico, where the kegs flow freely. NOTE: We do not recommend trying to take in every establishment listed here in one night, but if you do, please take a taxi or pedicab when you finish (see the Getting Here, Getting Around chapter).

Of course, not all the bars in Key West are on Duval Street. We have also included a section called Local Favorites—Key West classics that are a little more off the beaten path but definitely worth checking out. Cheers!

The Quintessential Duval Crawl

LA-TE-DA
1125 Duval St.
(305) 296-6706
www.lateda.com

The La-Te-Da is a combination hotel, cabaret, restaurant, and bar that has been an icon of the party scene since 1978. They not only offer a bar that faces lively Duval Street but also live entertainment in their Cabaret Lounge. There is also a Terrace Bar overlooking the beautiful tropical pool. With the great island drinks and delicious food being served here, you may find it difficult to leave this adult party scene.

THE KEYS KEY WEST PIANO BAR
1114 Duval St.
(305) 294-8859
www.akeywestpianobar.com

This lively spot brings New York City talent to Duval Street, Key West. Pianists provide the music while the bar and waitstaff sing and entertain. On any given night, you might find a Broadway star belting out a tune or a local tickling the ivories on the open mic night. The Keys opens at 5 p.m., there is no cover charge, a light menu is available, and a beverage purchase is required.

801 BOURBON BAR AND CABARET
801 Duval St.
(305) 294-9354
www.801bourbon.com

With a clientele consisting of primarily gay patrons and tourists, the 801 offers a first-floor bar with billiards. A second floor offers live entertainment with Drag Queen Bingo at 5 p.m. every Sunday and drag shows nightly, starring the world famous Sushi. You might have seen her on CNN New Year's Eve counting down the seconds to the new year while being lowered in a giant red high heel. She even managed to make Anderson Cooper blush. If you've never seen a drag show, you may be pleasantly surprised. The professionally choreographed productions here are loads of fun.

AQUA NIGHTCLUB
711 Duval St.
(305) 294-0555
www.aquakeywest.com

Live entertainment at the predominantly gay Aqua Nightclub includes drag shows, karaoke, an "Aqua Idol" competition, poker games Sat and Sun, and a dance club complete with DJs every weekend. No matter what time you stop in at Aqua, there will be something fabulous going on.

COWBOY BILL'S HONKY TONK SALOON
618 Duval St.
(305) 295-8219
www.cowboybillskw.com

The owner of this bar was a real-life cowboy on the rodeo circuit until he came to Key West. Mechanical bull and all, this urban cowboy turned tropical, and patrons are in for one wild ride! Open seven days with happy hour daily, full menu for eats, game room with pool, darts, video games, and 24

TVs a-blaring. Boot scoot across the dance floor to live music, not to mention riding the mechanical bull. Hold on to those cowboy hats—this is not for amateurs!

THE GREEN PARROT BAR
601 Whitehead St.
(305) 294-6133
www.greenparrot.com
Not exactly on Duval Street, but close enough and so quintessentially Key West, the Green Parrot rates a stop on any Duval Crawl. Frequented primarily by locals, and known simply as "The Parrot," this eclectic bar is housed in an 1890s-era building half a block off Duval, down Southard Street. Walls are adorned with unusual oversize portraits and a wall mural of the Garden of Eden. Weekends feature local and national bands playing blues and zydeco, and the large dance floor is usually crowded. The bar also sports video games, billiards tables, darts, a pinball machine, and a jukebox.

VIRGILIO'S
524 Duval St.
(305) 296-8118
www.virgilioskeywest.com
This classy little New York–style bar is not really on Duval; it's actually situated on Applerouth Lane, just around the corner from La Trattoria, one of Key West's best Italian eateries (see the Restaurants chapter). Martinis and their cousins—Gibsons, Manhattans, and cosmopolitans—are the specialty here and on "Martini Mondays," you can pay only $5 for one. Grab a seat at the bar or in one of the overstuffed easy chairs while you sip your cocktail and listen to live light jazz and contemporary music from some of Key West's finest musical talent.

JIMMY BUFFETT'S MARGARITAVILLE CAFE
500 Duval St.
(305) 292-1435
www.margaritavillekeywest.com
Yes, the big man himself does play here once in a while, as do some of the Coral Reefers and bands that have opened for Jimmy on tour. Props from past concerts decorate the walls, ceiling, and even tables. Beginning at 10 p.m. each night and continuing well into the wee hours, a variety of bands and solo artists perform everything from rock 'n' roll to reggae to rhythm and blues. Margaritas are just one of the many frozen drinks offered at the air-conditioned yet open-air bar. You can get a Cheeseburger in Paradise with all the fixin's or pick up some Buffett clothing, recordings, books, and memorabilia at the shop next door (see the Restaurants and Shopping chapters). Country singer/songwriter Kenny Chesney once performed here. Dressed in flip-flops and a T-shirt and drinking beer, this Entertainer of the Year wowed the throng of fans "deep in the heart of the Keys."

THE TOP
430 Duval St.
(at Crowne Plaza Key West La Concha)
(305) 296-2991
www.laconchakeywest.com
High above the city of Key West, with views of the Key West harbor as well as up and down Duval Street, this eagle's-eye perch is one of the most famous bars in all the Keys. The Crowne Plaza Key West La Concha (see Accommodations chapter) was the first upscale lodging facility in the area, and to accommodate its infamous and famous clientele, this bar was developed. Rumor has it Hemingway romanced Ava Gardner and

Marlene Dietrich at La Concha and spent many romantic nights high in the sky (in more ways than one) here at this bar. It offers a great view of Fantasy Fest revelers (see Annual Events chapter) or just a superb sunset aerie. They also have nightly entertainment, which changes weekly. Call to check out the lineup.

> ℹ️ If you can't wait until "it's five o'clock somewhere" for alcohol, in Key West there are two bars that open with the sunrise. Schooner Wharf Bar (see this chapter) has a "Breakfast Club" where regulars show up at 8 a.m. for a beer buzz rather than coffee. Over at Dons' Place, 1000 Truman Ave., at 7 a.m. you can have an espresso martini made with vodka, Kahlua, Tia Maria, and oh, I almost forgot, coffee.

HARD ROCK CAFE
313 Duval St.
(305) 293-0230
www.hardrock.com
A world-renowned classic, Hard Rock Cafe joined the Conch Republic in the summer of 1996. Situated in a renovated, three-story, Conch-style house on Duval Street, Hard Rock Cafe Key West celebrates historic Key West, the preservation of the Florida Keys' fragile environment, and, of course, rock 'n' roll. This 235-seat Hard Rock is open seven days a week and serves up all-American fare.

FAT TUESDAY
305 Duval St.
(305) 296-9373
www.fattuesdaykeywest.com
Stop in at Fat Tuesday and choose from one of 26 flavors of frozen drinks, including margaritas, piña coladas, and 190-octane rum

runners. Our favorite is the Pain in the Ass, a combination piña colada and rum runner. The motto here is "One daiquiri, two daiquiri, three daiquiri, floor," and you can even buy a T-shirt that says it.

BULL & WHISTLE
224 Duval St.
(305) 296-4545
www.bullkeywest.com
This local favorite is actually three bars in one. The Bull is downstairs and features live music in an open-air setting. The Whistle is upstairs and offers pool and video games, along with a great view of Duval Street from the balcony. The Garden of Eden, on the very top, has a great view of Key West . . . and more. It's the only clothing-optional roof garden in town. The Bull & Whistle complex is located at the corner of Duval and Caroline Streets.

RICK'S KEY WEST
202–208 Duval St.
(305) 296-5513
www.ricksanddurtyharrys.com
Rick's Key West offers eight nightspots in one complex including a wine and martini bar, a dance club, a VIP bar and a daquiri bar. In addition, Rick's Downstairs Bar offers live professional entertainment from 4 p.m. until midnight. Then the amateurs take over until 4 a.m. at the karaoke bar. The Tree Bar allows you to sit and sip a spell, all the while watching the sights of Duval Street pass by. The band at Durty Harry's starts playing at 8 p.m. and plays live rock 'n' roll until 4 a.m. Every Tuesday night is Rock-n-Roll Karaoke Night, where you can sing your greatest hits with the full band. This bar also has a television wall, which shows all major sporting events. And for a little more risqué entertainment,

the Red Garter Saloon is a mirror-and-brass adult club. Pick your pleasure.

CAPTAIN TONY'S SALOON
428 Greene St.
(305) 294-1838
www.capttonyssaloon.com
Just half a block off Duval, this watering hole is the site of Hemingway's original barstool and Key West's first hanging tree, which grows through the roof of the bar. Captain Tony's is part of Key West's history as it is the original location of Sloppy Joe's. Once owned by Capt. Tony Tarracino, a friend of Jimmy Buffett and a former Key West mayor, the saloon features walls covered with bras and business cards. Live entertainment is offered nightly.

SLOPPY JOE'S BAR
201 Duval St.
(305) 294-5717
www.sloppyjoes.com
It's no wonder this was Hemingway's favorite watering hole. The upbeat atmosphere of Sloppy Joe's is contagious. The bar opened in 1933 on the site of what is now Captain Tony's Saloon. In 1937 it moved to its current location. Some say that Hemingway did some writing in the back rooms of the bar and kept a few of his manuscripts locked up here. Photos of Hemingway line the walls. Live entertainment is offered from noon to 2 a.m. daily. Country crooner Kenny Chesney has been known to hit the stage here in the spring, so take a close look at who is playing in the live band! Among the brews offered here is Sloppy Joe's beer, which is actually made by Coors. A gift shop sells T-shirts, boxer shorts, hats, and other souvenirs with the Sloppy Joe's logo.

JOE'S TAP ROOM
Behind Sloppy Joe's, Duval and Greene
(305) 294-5717
www.sloppyjoes.com
Located upstairs behind world-famous Sloppy Joe's Bar (see above) on Duval Street, Joe's Tap Room is another venue in this popular hangout. Large-screen TV and porch seating are available here. Doors blow open at noon and they have NFL and college football on HDTV. Gives you a little "home away from home" feeling!

i Take a guided walking tour of the most famous and interesting drinking establishments in Key West, beginning in Old Town and ending on Duval Street. Led by your "professional" guide, you'll be treated to jokes, antics, contests, and stories (Best of the Bars, 305-292-9994; www.keywesthunt .com).

HOG'S BREATH SALOON
400 Front St.
(305) 296-4222
www.hogsbreath.com/key-west
The Hog's Breath features an open-air mahogany bar surrounded by water-sports-related memorabilia, including mounted fish and surfboards. You can try the medium-bodied Hog's Breath beer and sample one of the saloon's famed fish sandwiches. The restaurant (see the Restaurants chapter) is open for lunch and dinner. Live bands play rock, folk rock, blues, and jazz throughout the day and well into the evening. You can purchase T-shirts, hats, and sundry other items emblazoned with the saloon's slogan: "Hog's Breath is better than no breath at all."

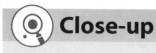

Close-up

The "Fab Four" in the "Fab" Florida Keys

Most folks plan their trip to the Florida Keys months in advance. "Do You Want to Know a Secret"? On Sept. 11, 1964, a group of four young men made an unexpected stop in "Paradise." On that evening, the world-famous **Beatles** were holed up in the old Key Wester Motel on South Roosevelt Boulevard in Key West. Their landmark concert tour, "Beatles in America," was canceled at the Gator Bowl in Jacksonville, Florida, because Hurricane Dora was pounding the east coast of the state. Their private airplane was diverted to the Key West International Airport that evening, where they proceeded to hold an impromptu jam session in the motel bar. Local musician Coffee Butler just finished his evening gig playing piano at a nearby locals hangout when he got word the "Fab Four" were entertaining the pleasantly surprised guests at the motel. Butler rushed over to the Key Wester and asked if he could make it a five-some, playing until the wee hours of the morning until the bartender and the police informed them Florida law stated no music after 4 a.m.

"Good Day Sunshine" allowed the group to depart that morning and continue on their tour. The Key Wester Motel was demolished in 1999 and replaced with a Hyatt time-share complex. The owners salvaged one piece of musical history by restoring the bungalow in which the Beatles had resided and built the Abbey Road snack bar that sits by the swimming pool.

In spring of 2007 a traveling art exhibit featuring more than 100 pieces of John Lennon's drawings came to Key West. The three-day event, *Come Together,* showcased the late Beatle's works, encompassing years 1968 through 1980. John's drawings chronicled family life, with wife Yoko Ono and son Sean, in whimsical drawings, caricatures, and self-portraits.

Before John was a Beatle, he was an art student attending Liverpool Art School in England.

CHART ROOM BAR
Pier House Resort
1 Duval St.
(305) 296-4600 or (800) 327-8340
www.pierhouse.com

You want to experience a slice of Key West history? Step into this tiny bar located in the Pier House Resort and you will be stepping back in time. Tom Corcoran, author of the popular Alex Rutledge Key West mystery series, used to tend bar here while Jimmy Buffett played for tips. The bar has changed little since then and the bartender can regale you with many a story about the duo.

Local Favorites

THE AFTERDECK BAR AT LOUIE'S BACKYARD
700 Waddell Ave.
(305) 294-1061
www.louiesbackyard.com

The deck is large and right on the water. And we do mean *right on* the water. One false step, a few cocktails too many, and . . . splash! Service is friendly and courteous, and the setting is exactly what you were thinking of when you first thought of coming to the Florida Keys. The adjoining restaurant is one of Key West's finest (see the Restaurants chapter under Louie's Backyard).

BLUE MOJITO POOL BAR & GRILL
Hyatt Key West Resort and Spa
601 Front St.
(305) 809-4043
Newly revived interior but with the same fabulous view of the Gulf of Mexico and sunset. This pool bar adds all the ingredients, mixed with a tropical punch, for a romantic setting serving appetizers, salads, and sandwiches for lite bites. Clink!

BOTTLECAP LOUNGE AND LIQUOR
1128 Simonton St.
(305) 296-2807
Every Friday during happy hour at the Bottlecap, the tips go to a local Key West charity. DJs spin on the weekends and the newly renovated bar area has tall tables where you can sit and grab a bite from their new cafe menu. Be sure to order the cheddar and bacon beer burger, one of the best burgers on the island. They take a half pound of Angus ground beef and marinate it in Yuengling Lager with fresh garlic, dry mustard, and herbs, cook it, then top with cheddar cheese, crisp applewood smoked bacon, lettuce, tomato, onions, and dill pickles and serve it on an onion roll. The best news? They serve this delicious burger until midnight every day of the week.

FINNEGAN'S WAKE IRISH PUB & EATERY
320 Grinnell St.
(305) 293-0222
www.keywestirish.com
Exactly like a good Irish public house ought to be, Finnegan's keeps the merriment going until nearly dawn (4 a.m.) and is among a mere handful of Key West establishments serving food into the wee hours (see the Restaurants chapter). You're sure to find your Guinness here, and you can even down a black and tan. Order one and the barkeep will think you just returned from the Emerald Isle. Enjoy live Irish music on weekends and heed their motto: "Come for the food. Stay for the beer. Leave with the staff."

Key West's Burlesque History

Notorious burlesque dancer and actress **Sally Rand** was featured at the 1933 Chicago World's Fair and in the 1934 film, *Bolero*. Sally's claims to fame were her trademark fan dance and bubble dance. Ms. Rand was a Key West winter resident for many years, often visiting the troops at the local Navy Hospital. Her historic gingerbread home on Eisenhower Drive is a far cry from its flamboyant mistress. Also, the world's most famous pin-up model of the 1940s, **Bettie Page,** met and married a young man in Key West prior to her retirement and leaving the area. Her spirit lives on in the **Key West Burlesque Theatre Troupe.** The company puts on performances at various locations around the island and even offers an occasional show and sunset sail. Call (305) 295-7676 or visit www.keywestburlesque.com for more information.

GRAND VIN
1107 Duval St.
(305) 296-1020
Grand Vin is a locals top pick for its bar and wine shop. Not sure which wine suits you best? Sit at the bar and try a tasting flight of wine, three glasses of different varietals that will have your tastebuds singing. And newly expanded seating on the porch or the lower patio is great for people-watching through all hours of the day or night.

POINT 5
915 Duval St.
(305) 296-0669
www.915duval.com
Sleek and sexy is what this lounge announces. In its lofty aerie above chic 915 restaurant, the decor only enhances the drinks. The wine bar is a glowing slab of white onyx; the walls, ceilings, and floors are covered in fabulous Dade County pine while the furniture is straight out of retro 1960 in black and orange. Submit to a cheese plate from the bar menu while relaxing at your table on the open air porch overlooking Duval Street.

SCHOONER WHARF BAR
202 William St.
(305) 292-3302
www.schoonerwharf.com
Dockside at the Key West Historic Seaport is the open-air, thatched-palm Schooner Wharf, which bills itself as "a last little piece of old Key West." The place offers outdoor thatched-umbrella tables, a covered bar, grill, and indoor games, including billiards and darts. Live jazz, rhythm and blues, and island music are featured nightly.

SPORTS PAGE BAR AND GRILLE
610 Greene St.
(305) 296-3230
Watch the game of your choice on one of the eight TVs, two of which are projection, or play the game of pool while enjoying some jalapeño poppers, cheese fries, or potato skins. If the big game is on, the Sports Page is the place to be.

TURTLE KRAALS RESTAURANT AND BAR
231 Margaret St.
(305) 294-2640
www.turtlekraals.com
The lounge portion of this turtle-cannery-turned-restaurant rocks throughout the evening, offering live entertainment (in season) and billiard tables in an open-air, waterfront setting (see the Restaurants chapter). Turtle Kraals's full bar is known for its frozen margaritas, microbrewed beers, and imported beers on tap.

CAMPGROUNDS

Just as the whooping crane, the Florida panther, and green sea turtles are on the endangered species list . . . so are campgrounds in the Florida Keys. The locations of most mobile home parks are on prime real estate. A vast majority of these parks are situated on waterfront/view parcels and are being gobbled up by developers building condos, hotels, or private condotels (condotels are condos privately owned then placed in a pool of properties to be rented by a management company). Whether you enjoy pitching a tent or traveling with a self-contained motor home, the campgrounds of the Keys offer a reasonably priced alternative to motels and resort accommodations. However, you will find that camping rates in the Florida Keys are generally much higher than in other areas of the United States. But all our recommended campgrounds have water access, and many are perched at the edge of the Atlantic or the Gulf of Mexico.

A wide range of amenities distinguishes each campground, but one thing is certain: If you wish to camp in the Keys during January, February, or March—those winter months when the folks up north are dusting off their snow boots—you must reserve your site a year in advance. The Keys have a second high season in the summer months, when Floridians locked into triple-digit temperatures head south to our cooling trade winds and warm, placid waters. During sport lobster season, the last consecutive Wednesday and Thursday of July, it is standing room only in the Keys.

OVERVIEW

We have listed our recommended campgrounds and RV parks by descending mile marker beginning in Key Largo and ending at Stock Island. Key West devotes its land use to megahotels and quaint guesthouses, presenting a dearth of recommendable campgrounds.

If you think you might fancy a really unusual camping experience, be sure to see the "Camping in the Beyond" section in this chapter for information on camping in the Dry Tortugas National Park or Everglades National Park.

You may assume that all our inclusions maintain good paved interior roads, clean restrooms and showers, laundry facilities, and 20- and 30-amp electrical service. Most campgrounds accept pets if they are kept on a leash at all times and walked only in designated areas and never on the beach. Exceptions will be noted.

Rates vary by the type of site you secure. Most campgrounds offer a range of options: tent sites, with or without electricity; RV sites with electricity and water; and sites with electricity, water, and sewer. Waterfront sites or sites with boat dockage will be more costly. Extra people or vehicles at a site will incur additional per-diem charges. All water is municipal, piped down to the Keys from Miami. Cable television and telephone hookups are noted when applicable. Back-in and pull-through dimensions vary. Call the campground if this is critical for your rig. Toll-free telephone numbers, when stated, are for reservation purposes only.

Price Code

Rate ranges are based on a per-diem stay during high season without the 12.5 percent state tax. High season is considered Dec 15 through May. Some campgrounds also consider the summer months as high season. Weekly and monthly rates are usually available at a reduced cost; be sure to inquire when you make your reservation. Major credit cards are accepted unless noted to the contrary.

$..................... $20 to $40
$$ .... $41 to $60
$$$ .... $61 to $80
$$$$ .... More than $81

THE FLORIDA KEYS

Upper Keys

**JOHN PENNEKAMP CORAL
REEF STATE PARK** $
MM 102.5 Oceanside, Key Largo
(305) 451-6300 or (850) 245-2157
www.floridastateparks.org/pennekamp
Aesthetically, the gravel sites at John Pennekamp Coral Reef State Park don't begin to compare with their waterfront siblings at the Keys' other two state parks, Bahia Honda and Long Key, but a canopy of mature buttonwoods shades most of the sites. The wide range of fabulous recreational opportunities within Pennekamp and its proximity to the nightlife in Key Largo more than make up for any lack of romantic oceanfront ambience

(see Beaches and Public Parks in the Recreation chapter). The campground is closed from Aug. 2, 2010 through Mar. 30, 2011 to upgrade camping facilities. The park will remain open thoughout.

**KEY LARGO KAMPGROUND
AND MARINA** $–$$
MM 101.5 Oceanside, Key Largo
(305) 451-1431 or (800) 526-7688
www.keylargokampground.com
Croton and bougainvillea hedges separate the sites in this villagelike campground laden with palm trees. Chickees line the arterial canal that connects the marina to the shallow oceanic bonefish flats beyond. About

Florida Keys Wildfire Safety

The dry season in south Florida is November through April. In the 2006 season more than 128,535 acres were destroyed by wildfires. Be careful when using fire for anything, including campfires and barbecues. Make sure someone is keeping an eye on the flames at all times. If you park your car on high grass, heat from your vehicle can ignite a blaze, especially if papers and debris are around. Be sure to pick up your trash and dispose of it in metal containers to avoid this potential hazard. Watch for sparks that may fly from grinding equipment, torches, and even lawn mowers. For more helpful tips, visit the Florida Division of Forestry Web site at www.fl-dof.com.

one-third of the condo campsites, with full hookups and free cable television, are available for overnighters. Some sites front the canal and have boat slips. Two beaches look out on Newport Bay, and a heated swimming pool and kiddie pool, shuffleboard, horseshoe pits, and volleyball add to the fun. John Pennekamp Coral Reef State Park is only a mile north of the 40-acre campground. Rates are based on four people (two adults and two children younger than age six) and one camping unit per site. There is a maximum of six people allowed per rental unit at any time.

**CALUSA CAMPGROUND RESORT
  AND MARINA $$
MM 101.5 Bayside, Key Largo
(305) 451-0232
www.calusacampground.com**
Escape to this family-friendly camp resort on the Gulf of Mexico with all the relaxation you can handle. Paved interior roads lead to gravel pads with full hookups and pull-through sites. Laundry facilities, clubhouse, LP gas, swimming pool, playground, a boat ramp, and dockage are featured. There is access to the bay and the ocean via Marvin Adams Cut or Tavernier Creek. Tent sites are also counted among the features at Calusa Camp Resort. Pets are welcome as long as they are on a leash.

**BLUE FIN ROCK HARBOR
  MARINA AND RV RESORT $$
MM 97 Oceanside, Key Largo
(305) 852-2025 or (800) 350-6572
www.milemarker97.com**
Relax and retreat as the Atlantic Ocean is steps away at this well-established marina and RV resort. On the property you will find fishing, shuffleboard, swimming pool, boat

ramp with rental boats, and the Mandalay Restaurant and Tiki Bar. A Laundromat is open around the clock. There is 30- and 50-amp service and cable TV. Showers and phone connections are for long-term visitors. There is 24-hour security, and this park can accommodate fifth wheels up to 40 feet.

Middle Keys

**LONG KEY STATE PARK $
MM 67.5 Oceanside, Long Key
(305) 664-4815 or (850) 245-2157
www.floridastateparks.org/longkey**
Every site is oceanfront when you camp at Long Key State Park. You can't get closer to the ocean than this camping in the Florida Keys. Half the 60 sites offer water and electric, and all have picnic tables fronting the shallow saltwater flats. The paved road into the campground parallels the Overseas Highway on one side and the ocean on the other. Each deep site runs from the park road to the ocean.

Like John Pennekamp Coral Reef State Park and Bahia Honda State Park, Long Key State Park follows a strictly regimented reservation policy. Rates are based on four people, one vehicle per site, and include all taxes. Only one camper and one small tent or two small tents are allowed per campsite. The park opens at 8 a.m. and closes at sunset. "Well-behaved" pets are welcome in the campground.

Lower Keys

**SUNSHINE KEY RV RESORT AND
  MARINA $–$$$
MM 39 Bayside, Ohio Key
(305) 872-2217 or (877) 362-6736
www.rvonthego.com**
Sunshine Key RV Resort and Marina occupies an entire key, officially named Ohio Key.

This bustling place, with nearly 400 sites, is more like a small Midwestern town than a camping resort in the Keys. The 75-acre Sunshine Key, with its winding signposted streets and myriad amenities, is friendly and family-oriented. The oceanside portion of Sunshine Key remains a tangle of mangroves, buttonwoods, and palm trees that shields a feathered montage of wildlife popular with bird-watchers.

You will have to rise early to pack in all you can do in a day on Sunshine Key. The large marina, which even has a fishing pier, will shelter your boat, and the experts at the bait and tackle shop will put you on the fish. Tennis courts, a heated swimming pool, volleyball, horseshoes, and a full schedule of adult activities in the clubhouse keep things hopping. A game room, basketball courts, a playground, and water sports occupy the children. Rates are based on two adults and their accompanying children younger than 12.

BAHIA HONDA STATE PARK $
MM 37 Oceanside, Bahia Honda Key
(305) 872-2353 or (850) 245-2157
www.floridastateparks.org/bahiahonda
Claiming the Florida Keys' best natural beach (2½ miles long), the 524-acre Bahia Honda State Park offers campers three kinds of sites but no pull-through sites. The roomy sites at Buttonwood can accommodate large motor homes; Sandspur is limited to tents, vans, and pop-ups. Because these sites sit deep in a tropical hardwood hammock, the park is very selective as to which rigs are allowed to camp here. Only one car and one tent per site are permitted. All these sites have water, and more than half offer electricity. Bayside campsites, accessed by a road passing under the Bahia Honda Bridge, are restricted to tents or small pop-ups. The bridge provides only a 6-foot, 8-inch clearance. These campsites provide water but no electricity.

Three large cabins, each a heated and air-conditioned, two-bedroom duplex with a fully equipped kitchen, a full bathroom, and all linens, literally perch on the water near the bayside campsites. You can throw a baited hook from your front porch, rock a little in the old rocker gracing the deck, and catch your dinner without missing the sunset. Each cabin will sleep six, but you'll have to rough it without television or radio. The cabins can be reserved in person, by telephone, or online (see the Making Reservations for State Park Campsites section in this chapter) up to 11 months in advance. A two-day deposit by credit card, check, or cash will secure the cabin reservation if it's received within 10 days of your making the reservation.

All campsites at Bahia Honda State Park provide a grill and picnic table. The park has a boat ramp, so you may bring your own craft and try your luck at catching a tarpon under the Bahia Honda Bridge, noted as one of the best tarpon-fishing areas in the state (see the Fishing chapter). "You really don't even have to know what you are doing," counsels the assistant park manager. "Put a live mullet on the end of a line and the tarpon will bite."

BIG PINE KEY FISHING LODGE $
MM 33 Oceanside, Big Pine Key
(305) 872-2351
The Big Pine Key Fishing Lodge abuts a natural oceanside inlet that was a by-product of the dredging of Spanish Harbor Channel for Flagler's Railroad. The sites range from rustic grass or dirt tent sites without water or electricity to dockside sites with full hookups.

The boat basin, a part of the Big Pine Fishing Lodge since the late 1950s, accommodates small fishing boats up to 25 feet long for a per-foot daily charge. Ample fish-cleaning stations are provided, so you can ready the spoils of the day for the frying pan. The lodge has an oval swimming pool sunken in a raised deck overlooking a peppering of statuesque coconut palms, all grown from seed.

Rates are based on one or two occupants with one vehicle and one camping unit. Children younger than age six stay free. Air-conditioning, phone outlets, and cable hookups are included in the camping fee.

SUGARLOAF KEY RESORT KOA
KAMPGROUND $$–$$$$
MM 20 Oceanside, 251 County Rd. 939, Summerland Key
(305) 745-3549 or (800) 562-7731
www.thefloridakeys.com/koasugarloaf
Pelicans perched in mangroves near thatched chickees on a palm-speckled beach create an island ambience in this comprehensive KOA on Summerland Key. Nearly 200 gravel, grass, or dirt sites offer a choice of hookups, but no pull-throughs are available. Optional cable hookup is available at an additional charge. The facility offers what you have come to expect from a KOA Kampground—all the necessities plus the amenities of a resort. A full marina covers the gamut of boating and fishing needs. A large heated pool, hot tub, minigolf, horseshoes, and bicycle rentals offer landlubbers relaxing diversions. Volleyball, a game room, and a playground amuse the children. Social activities, crafts, and special events are scheduled during the winter season. Only 20 miles from Key West and near Looe Key National Marine Sanctuary, Sugarloaf Key KOA Kampground

is close to all the action. Rates are based on two occupants; children younger than six stay free. Some RV trailers are available for rent; call to inquire about amenities and pricing.

LAZY LAKES CAMPGROUND
AND RV RESORT $$$
MM 19.5 Oceanside, 311 Johnson Rd., Sugarloaf Key
(305) 745-1079 or (866) 965-2537
www.lazylakesrvresort.com
Off the beaten path, this 28-acre property with a seven-acre saltwater lake is a real Insiders destination for your full-size RV (99 spots available), Big Rigs, tent sites, or to rent a mobile home. Hike the paths leading around the lake or jump into one of the free kayaks and paddle around for a water view. Lazy Lakes offers 30–50 amp service, laundry facilities, restrooms, heated pool, general store, and umbrella tables with lounge chairs. During the year they have activities for their guests that include bingo, horseshoes, darts, potluck dinners, and even holiday celebrations. You may never want to leave!

BLUEWATER KEY RV RESORT $$$
MM 14.5 Oceanside, Sugarloaf Key
(305) 745-2494 or (800) 237-2266
www.bluewaterkey.com
As simple and elegant as a sophisticated ball gown, Bluewater Key RV Resort oozes class. The 80 spacious gravel sites feature metered utility hookups, including telephone and cable television. Uniquely angled toward the water and buffered with palms and shrubbery, each privately owned site has a stone patio with benches and a round cement table. No tents, pop-ups, or vans are allowed at Bluewater Key. All units must be self-contained RVs.

A clubhouse hosts table tennis or informal card games, and the swimming pool attracts sun worshipers from up north. Oceanside flats and deepwater canals surround the property, affording primo fishing for anglers. And if you want a little action at the end of your day of quiet solitude, you are but 14½ miles from the center of Key West. Need we say more?

Those reserving waterfront or canal sites may secure their small boats to the floating docks or bulkhead. The high season at Bluewater Key RV Resort is considered Dec 15 to Apr 15. Although the resort accepts reservations for one day or one week to a month or more depending upon availability, we suggest you book at least a year in advance if you'd like a waterfront spot. Bluewater Key RV Resort has an on-site manager and is protected from intrusion by a 24-hour, phone-operated security gate.

GEIGER KEY MARINA
AND CAMPGROUND $$$–$$$$
MM 10.5 Oceanside, Geiger Key
(305) 296-3553
www.geigerkeymarina.com

Nestled in the mangroves "on the backside of Paradise," you'll discover Geiger Key Marina and Campground. The setting on the Atlantic Ocean is what makes this quiet location a hidden gem. Great white herons patrol the grounds in search of pilchards and pinfish. Pelicans look like ornaments in the mangrove branches as they keep a sharp lookout for snapper, grouper, and parrot fish. Geiger Key Marina and Campground is only 10 miles away from Key West, yet it seems a million miles away with its laid-back 1950s aura. The property has all the updates, however, with RV hookups, laundry facilities, ocean-view private tent sites, transient boat

slips, kayak rentals, and fishing charter boats. Their popular Restaurant and Tiki Bar cooks up pig roasts on Sat night; on Sun, they whip up a chicken and ribs barbecue. Live music is part of the bar's attraction on Fri, Sat, and Sun night. You can get to this jewel by RV or boat. The marina monitors VHF channel 79 for water-mode arrivals.

BOYD'S KEY WEST
CAMPGROUND $$–$$$
MM 5 Oceanside, 6401 Maloney Ave.,
Stock Island
(305) 294-1465
www.boydscampground.com

Although its brochures state a Key West address, Boyd's is actually on Stock Island, just outside the Key West city limits. Most of the level, shaded sites have cement patios. Bordering the ocean, Boyd's offers a boat ramp, a small marina, extensive dock space, heated swimming pool, and four bathhouses. You can catch the city bus into Key West for unlimited diversions, hang out at Boyd's game room, or watch the large-screen television, which is tucked in a tiki hut near the pool. Rates are based on two occupants and one camping unit per site. Small dogs are permitted in hard-shell campers only. Fifty-amp service and modem hookup are available.

LEO'S CAMPGROUND AND
RV PARK $$–$$$
MM 4.5 Oceanside, 5236 Suncrest Rd.,
Stock Island
(305) 296-5260
www.leoscampground.com

Minutes from downtown Key West, you can ride a bike or take the bus from this campground park. Leo's is ideal for a relaxing spot while in the lower Keys. Full RV setup with water, sewer, electric (some up to 50 amp) cable TV, barbecues, and picnic tables. On site also are laundry facilities and a bathhouse. There are tent sites to rent and pets are permitted, but only if traveling in RVs.

CAMPING IN THE BEYOND

If there is a little part of you that longs to forge through uncharted territory and live off the land (or the sea), you can fulfill your fantasies here. Everglades National Park and Dry Tortugas National Park, both daytrip excursions from the Florida Keys, offer unique camping experiences for the adventuresome spirits among you.

i Camping and campfires are not permitted in national wildlife refuges.

Everglades National Park

Canoe or commandeer a small motor craft into the backcountry wilderness of **Everglades National Park.** This 99-mile route, which is recommended for experienced canoeists only, connects **Flamingo** and **Everglades City.** (Allow at least eight days to complete the trip.) The charted routing through such colorfully named spots as **Darwin's Place, Camp Lonesome, Lostman's Five,** and **Graveyard Creek** encompasses 47 primitive campsites of three basic types.

You will need a permit (small fee in season) to camp in one of the backcountry sites. Apply in person at the Gulf Coast or Flamingo Visitor Center up to 24 hours before your trip begins. Everglades National Park also offers camping in two in-park campgrounds. Seasonal reservations (Nov through Apr) can be made for these campsites by calling (800) 365-2267 or at the online reservations

center, accessed by link from the park's Web site at www.nps.gov/ever. Reservations in the winter season are limited to 14 days at one visit, 30 days total per year.

- **Chickees:** These elevated, 10-by-12-foot wood platforms with roofs are placed along interior rivers and bays where no dry land exists. A design originally used by the Miccosukee Indians, these open-air structures allow the wind to blow through, keeping the insects away. A narrow walkway leads to a self-contained toilet. You will need to have a freestanding tent, because stakes and nails are not allowed.

- **Beach Sites:** These are set on coastal beaches that have been built up through time from a conglomeration of fragmented shells. Campers are warned that gulf waters can become extremely rough. Loggerhead sea turtles nest on Highland Beach and Cape Sable in the spring and summer. If you see evidence of their nesting, refrain from lighting a campfire nearby. (Campfires are allowed at beach sites only.)

- **Primitive Ground Sites:** These consist of mounds of earth just a few feet higher than the surrounding mangroves. Willy Willy, Camp Lonesome, and Canepatch are old Indian mound sites. Coastal aborigines, who lived here before the Seminole Indians, constructed mounds of shells or soil as dry dwelling sites amid the mangroves. The ground sites, along interior bays and rivers, have a heavier preponderance of insects than either the beach sites or the chickees. Always be prepared for mosquitoes and tiny biting flies called no-see-ums, especially at sunrise and sunset. Mosquito season corresponds with the rainy season, Apr through Oct. We do not recommend you try to camp in the Everglades during these months.

For more information on park or backcountry camping, visit the aforementioned Everglades National Park Web site, or contact the main park number at (305) 242-7700.

Dry Tortugas National Park

Roughing it takes on gargantuan proportions when you consider camping at **Dry Tortugas National Park,** but it's worth the effort, because this remote bit of Paradise has been preserved in a virginal state. You'll find the 11 palm-shaded tent sites—available on a first-come, first-served basis—in a sandy area on **Garden Key** in front of Fort Jefferson. You must pack in all your supplies, including fresh water; only saltwater toilets,

---

What's Old Is New Again

The Everglades National Park is over 60 years old and the largest subtropical wilderness in the United States. Within this famed park is the historical waterfront village, **Flamingo.** This camping mecca borders Florida Bay to the south that feeds into a sea of sawgrass and pine wilderness. Three plans are now being considered by the state of Florida to rebuild this hurricane-ravaged mecca. On the property is a vintage lodge with cottages and marina. Bringing this famed area back to life will take millions of dollars and time. For more information, visit www.park planning.nps.gov.

---

grills, and picnic tables are provided. There is no food, fresh water, electricity, or medical assistance of any kind on the island.

You must take your chances on securing a campsite, because reservations are not taken for the individual sites. A small fee per person, per night must be paid upon arrival at Fort Jefferson. (The park service says securing a site usually is not a problem.) Campsites accommodate up to eight people. You can reserve a group site for as many as 15 people, however, by contacting the park service, (305) 242-7700. The staff will send you a permit application, which you must mail to: Dry Tortugas National Park, Attn: Group Camping, P.O. Box 6208, Key West, FL 33041. The application requires the following information: name, address, day/night telephone number, group name, date of arrival/departure, number of people in group, primary activities (birding, snorkeling), and mode of transportation to the islands. If the site is available when you submit your completed application, a permit reserving the group site will be issued. You may stay up to 14 days at either individual or group sites, but keep in mind you must bring complete provisioning for the duration of your stay and pack out your trash.

You may have left the civilized world behind you in Key West, but the arena of natural splendor surrounding you in the Dry Tortugas is endless. Tour **Fort Jefferson** (self-guided), America's largest 19th-century coastal fort. The walls of the fort are 50 feet high and 8 feet thick.

A white coral beach, nature-made not man-made, provides a tropical backdrop for doing nothing at all. But you can **snorkel** just 60 yards off the beach or dive the seemingly bottomless blue waters, which, preserved as a sanctuary, are filled with fearless battalions of finfish and squadrons of crawfish that are oblivious to your presence.

Bird-watching is superb. Sooty and noddy terns by the thousands gather in the Dry Tortugas from the Caribbean, nesting on nearby Bush Key. Single eggs are laid in depressions in the sand. Parent birds take turns shading them from the hot sun. The entire colony leaves when the babies are strong enough.

Getting to the Dry Tortugas presents a bit of a challenge—and expense. Seaplane is the fastest means of transportation to the Dry Tortugas, but it's also the most expensive. You can also reach the Dry Tortugas by sea. (See the Recreation chapter for information on the Yankee Fleet Ferry to Fort Jefferson.) The National Park Service provides a list of sanctioned transportation services to the Dry Tortugas, which means they are insured and bonded and they maintain good safety records. The park service advises that the criteria are stringent and the list is constantly monitored. Contact the park service, (305) 242-7700, to get the current recommendations. The Dry Tortugas National Park Web site is www.nps.gov/drto.

BOATING

The voice of the sea speaks to the soul, no more so than in the Florida Keys. Surrounded by the shimmering aquatic prisms of the Gulf of Mexico and the Atlantic Ocean, the Keys volunteer unlimited vistas for watery exploration. Our depths secret famed fishing grounds (see the Fishing chapter) and unparalleled dive sites (see the Diving and Snorkeling chapter). Cruisers from around the world seek out our remote, pristine anchoring-out spots as well as our resort marinas (see the Cruising chapter). And peppering the Keys, from Key Largo to Key West, a proliferation of water-sports facilities afford anyone visiting our shores the opportunity to get out on the water via canoe, sea kayak, water skis, personal watercraft, sailboards, even paddleboats (see the Recreation chapter). The waters surrounding the Florida Keys are protected as part of a marine sanctuary, so regulations concerning the use of personal watercraft are more stringent here than in other parts of Florida. For more information, contact the sanctuary office at (305) 743-2437 or log on to www.floridakeys.noaa.gov.

But the most popular means of wandering our aqueous acres is undoubtedly by boat. The waters encompassing the Florida Keys have been designated a national marine sanctuary since 1990, and the marine zoning plan imposes certain restrictions and responsibilities on all mariners so that our resources may be preserved for all time. (See the Florida Keys National Marine Sanctuary Regulations section of this chapter.) In this chapter we will introduce you to our waters, alert you to the rules of our hydrous highways and byways, and share some safety and navigational tips. We'll provide you with a primer of available public boat ramps, marine supply stores, boat sales and service businesses, as well as motor and sailboat rentals, boat charters, and other sources to enhance your time on the water.

So follow our lighthouse beacon as we illuminate the joys and some of the hazards of boating in the waters of the Florida Keys. The Key West sections give you details of the boating scene in our southernmost city.

BODIES OF WATER

The waters of the Florida Keys conceal multiple habitats that sustain an impressive array of sea life not encountered anywhere else in the United States. Depths range from scant inches (which often disappear altogether at low tide) in the near-shore waters, the flats, and the backcountry of Florida Bay to the fathoms of the offshore waters of the deep blue Atlantic. And buried at sea 4 to 5 miles from our shores runs the most extensive living coral reef track in North America (see the Area Overview, Fishing, Diving and Snorkeling, and Cruising chapters for more information on these waters and the creatures dwelling within).

Flats, Backcountry, and Shallow Near-Shore Waters

Perhaps the most complex of our waters are the shallows of the near-shore waters, those directly off both our coasts, which vary from a few inches to several feet in depth and sometimes stretch for a mile or more from shore. Called "skinny" waters by local captains, these "flats" of the Atlantic and backcountry waters of the Gulf of Mexico and Florida Bay (that portion of the gulf bordered by the Upper Keys and Everglades National Park) prove a challenge to navigate. Popular with anglers searching for bonefish, permit, tarpon, redfish, snook, and sea trout and inhabited by an array of barracuda, sharks, and lobsters, the shallow waters cover meadows of sea grass punctuated with patches of sand, which also function as the nursery waters for many offshore species.

As a boater in the Florida Keys, you should familiarize yourself with the necessary nautical charts before venturing off the dock. Learn to "read" the water (see the Aids to Navigation section in this chapter) because waters are littered with unmarked shoals. Nearshore waters are best traversed in a shallow-draft flatsboat or skiff, by dinghy, canoe, or sea kayak. Operators of personal watercraft should steer clear of the flats to avoid disturbing the aquatic life dwelling below.

If you do happen to run aground here, turn off your motor immediately; the rotating propeller will kill the sea grass. Usually all you need to do is get out of the boat to lighten the load and push the craft to deeper water. Then trim up your motor and proceed. If this doesn't work, wait until the tide rises a bit and try to push off the flat again.

Intracoastal Waterway

The primary navigable waterway in Florida Bay and the Gulf of Mexico is the Intracoastal Waterway. In the Keys it leads from Biscayne Bay at the mainland, under Jewfish Creek, and then parallels the Keys, accommodating boats with drafts of up to 4 to 6 feet. The Intracoastal runs about 2 to 3 miles off the gulfside of our islands, between shallow near-shore waters and the scattered mangrove islands that lie varying distances from the coast. The Intracoastal is well marked to about Big Pine Key, where it meets the Big Spanish Channel and heads north into the Gulf of Mexico. (Red day markers should be kept to the starboard, or right, side of the vessel when traveling down the Keys in the Intracoastal Waterway.) From the Spanish Channel to Key West, boaters must pay close attention to nautical charts to navigate safe passage. Boaters will enter Key West through the well-marked Northwest Channel.

Patch Reefs, Hawk Channel, and the Barrier Reef

Between the near-shore waters of the Atlantic and the barrier reef some 4 to 5 miles offshore lies a smattering of patch reefs submerged at depths as shallow as 3 feet, with some even exposed at low tide. Surrounding waters vary in depth, but generally are much deeper than the flats and near-shore waters.

Hawk Channel—a safely navigable superhighway frequented by recreational boaters and cruisers—runs the length of the Florida Keys, bordering the reef at depths between 11 and 16 feet. Square red and triangular green day markers guide boaters through these waters; red markers should be kept to the starboard, or right, side of the vessel when traveling down the Keys in Hawk Channel.

Outside this marked area, the waters are scattered with dive sites designated with anchor buoys and red-and-white flags, as well as marked and unmarked rocks and shoals. If red-and-white diver-down flags are displayed, boaters should steer clear. These flags indicate that a diver is beneath the water. Lighthouses now mark shallow reef areas, which, at one time, claimed ships that encountered bad weather or navigated carelessly close to the coral mountains. Waters covering the coral reef can run as deep as 20 to 40 feet, but as history attests, depths can vary considerably. Always consult your nautical chart and "read" the water.

The Florida Straits

Outside the reef in the Florida Straits, the water depth of the Atlantic increases dramatically to as much as 80 feet, deepening farther with distance from shore. Although on some days these waters are relatively calm, all offshore boaters should check wind and weather advisories before venturing out.

Creeks and Channels

The channels, or "cuts," between our islands often have extremely strong currents that make traveling between bridge pilings a bit dicey. Current continuously flows from the Gulf of Mexico into the Atlantic because sea level in the gulf is slightly higher than that of the ocean. Exercise caution when boating in these waters.

Key West Harbor

The southernmost city's ports have traditionally been gracious, welcoming tall ships, steamships, ferries, barges, powerboats, and seaplanes. Pirates, wreckers, spongers, shippers, naval officers, and Cuban émigrés all have found shelter here in the midst of their work, play, and quest for worldly wealth and freedom.

Key West's port, the deepest in all the Florida Keys, has a main channel depth of about 33 feet; it is even deeper on the Atlantic side. Passenger cruise ships now include this island among their ports of call. Key West is ranked among the top busiest cruise-ship ports of call in the world. Also in that ranking are the Virgin Islands, Puerto Rico, and the Caymans. Recreational cruisers often head for Key West's bustling harbor to prepare themselves and their boats for a Caribbean journey.

Like the rest of the Florida Keys, Key West is protective of its coral reefs and sea-grass beds, and despite the fact that harbors run deep, waters in the backcountry are shallow everywhere. First-time and novice boaters often run aground here and by Fleming Key and Sand Key west of the harbor.

AIDS TO NAVIGATION

Nautical Charts

Always use nautical charts and a magnetic compass for navigation when boating in the waters of the Florida Keys. Use electronic means of navigation (GPS) only for confirmation of position. Be sure your vessel is equipped with a VHF marine radio.

The U.S. Coast Guard recommends you follow charts issued by the National Oceanic and Atmospheric Administration (NOAA). To secure nautical charts for the entire Florida Keys, you'll need to purchase a chart kit that includes charts for each section. You can also purchase NOAA charts individually. For instance, to navigate the waters surrounding Key West, the U.S. Coast Guard recommends you use navigational chart No. 11441 for the approaches to Key West Harbor and chart No. 11447 for the harbor itself.

Readily available in many marine supply stores throughout the Florida Keys and Key West (see store listings in this chapter), these charts are accurate based on the date marked on them. Store personnel will be able to help you secure the proper, up-to-date chart for the area you will be exploring. Be sure you know how to read the nautical charts before you set off.

Channel Markers

In most waters, boaters follow the adage "red, right, return," meaning that the triangular red channel markers should be kept to the right, or starboard, side of the vessel when heading toward the port of origin. This jingle is confusing at best, for in the Florida Keys it does not appear to apply. Red markers should be kept to the starboard side of the vessel when heading down the Keys, from Key Largo to Key West, through Hawk Channel on the oceanside or the Intracoastal Waterway in the gulf. Conversely, when traveling up the Keys, in either Hawk Channel or the Intracoastal Waterway, square green markers should be kept to your starboard side; keep red markers on your vessel's port, or left, side.

When traversing creeks and cuts from oceanside to the gulf, red markers should be kept on your starboard side, and when coming from the gulf the opposite holds true. In any event, always consult your nautical chart to determine the channel of safe passage and the corresponding positioning of the navigational markers.

Tide Charts

It's important to determine mean low tides within the waters you plan to travel so that

you do not run aground. In the Florida Keys tides typically rise and fall about 1 to 2 feet. During spring, autumn, and a full moon, tides tend to rise to the higher and lower ends of this scale. Boaters should, therefore, rely on a tide conversion chart. Most marinas, bait and tackle shops, and other businesses that cater to boaters can provide tide information for specific areas in conjunction with a current tide chart available from the U.S. Coast Guard.

"Reading" the Water

In the Florida Keys visual navigation often means "reading" the water—that is, recognizing its potential depth by knowing which colors indicate safe passage and which connote danger. As water depth decreases, its underlying sea bottom is indicated by distinctive coloration. Be aware that readings may be difficult in narrow channels and in strong currents where the waters often are murky and restrict visibility. Wear polarized sunglasses to better distinguish one color from another.

The easiest way to remember what each water color signifies is to follow some poetic, but fundamental, guidance:

- **Brown, brown run aground.** Reef formations and shallow sea-grass beds close to the surface cause this color.
- **White, white you might.** Sandbars and rubble bottoms may be in waters much shallower than you think.
- **Green, green nice and clean.** The water is generally safely above reefs or sea-grass beds, but larger boats with deeper drafts may hit bottom. If you are renting a boat, find out what the draft is.
- **Blue, blue cruise on through.** Water is deepest, but changing tides may cause coral reefs to surface. Allow time to steer around them.

WHEN YOU NEED HELP

Although the U.S. Coast Guard and the Florida Marine Patrol work closely together and will make sure you contact the proper party in any event, they do handle different aspects of our waters in the Florida Keys.

Florida Marine Patrol

The Florida Fish and Wildlife Conservation Commission's law enforcement arm is the Florida Marine Patrol. They deal with violations such as environmental crime, fish and crawfish bag limits, and illegal dumping. They also enforce boating safety laws, responding to reports of unsafe boating and wake violations as well as any perceived illegal activity on the water. You can reach the Florida Marine Patrol on a cellular telephone by dialing *FMP or on a regular telephone line at (800) DIAL FMP, (800) 342-5367. The Marine Patrol vessels also monitor VHF channel 16.

i **"*FMP" is a free phone call when you are on your vessel and in need of the Florida Marine Patrol.**

U.S. Coast Guard

The U.S. Coast Guard maintains three bases in the Florida Keys and Key West. Their mission is to ensure maritime safety and handle life-threatening emergencies at sea, such as vessel collisions, drownings, onboard fires, or other accidents at sea. The Coast Guard monitors VHF channel 16 at all times. In an emergency call (305) 743-6388. By cell phone, call *CG. If for some reason you do not have a radio or cellular telephone onboard, flag a passing boat and ask someone on it to radio for assistance.

SeaTow

Run aground? Out of fuel? Motor problems? Instead of calling the Coast Guard, call SeaTow, a nationally recognized boater assistance service that maintains facilities the length of the Keys. Convey the details of your problem and what you think you need. Don't just ask for a tow if you have run out of gas or need only a minor repair. Describe your problem; the difference in cost between having gas delivered to your stranded boat and a multihour tow back to land could be a lot of money. SeaTow also will provide free advice, such as projected weather changes or directions in unfamiliar territory.

SeaTow can be reached on VHF channel 16 at sea by calling "SeaTow, SeaTow." By telephone the offices are (305) 451-3330 in Key Largo; (305) 664-4493 in Islamorada; and (305) 295-9912 in Key West. Visit www.seatow.com for more information.

VESSEL REGULATIONS AND EQUIPMENT

Vessels must be equipped with Coast Guard–approved equipment, which varies according to the boat's size, location, and use (see the Required Equipment section in this chapter). All vessels must either be documented or registered (see below), and the appropriate paperwork must be carried onboard.

Federal, state, and local law enforcement officials may hail your boat so that they can come aboard and inspect it. Among their reasons for imposing civil penalties: improper use of a marine radio and misuse of calling the distress channel VHF channel 16; boating under the influence (a blood alcohol level of 0.10 percent or higher); and negligence. Negligence includes boating in a swimming area, speeding in the vicinity of other boats or in dangerous waters, bow riding, and gunwaling. Boaters without the required Coast Guard–approved equipment on board or with problematic boats that are considered hazardous may be directed back to port.

Vessel Registration

Whether or not you are a resident of the Florida Keys, your vessel must be registered in the state of Florida within 30 days of your arrival if one of our islands is its primary location. Registration renewals require your old registration form and a valid Florida driver's license, if you have one; for registering new boats, bring your manufacturer's statement of origin, dealer's sales tax statement, and bill of sale. If you are registering a used boat you have just purchased, you will need a title signed over to you and a bill of sale, one of which must be notarized, and the previous owner's registration if available.

Boats must be registered annually; only cash is accepted as payment. Excluded from registration requirements are rowboats and dinghies with less than 10 hp motors that are used exclusively as dinghies. All other boats may be registered any weekday between 8:30 a.m. and 4:30 p.m. at one of the following facilities:

- **Plantation Key Government Center,** MM 88.7 Bayside, Plantation Key, (305) 852-7150. Head bayside on High Point Road and turn left into the government center parking lot. Boat registration is handled in the tax collector's office in the annex building.
- **Monroe County Tax Collector's Office,** MM 47 Oceanside, Marathon, (305) 743-5585. The office is on the Overseas Highway just past the Monroe County Sheriff's Department.

- **Harvey Government Center at Historic Truman School,** 1200 Truman Ave., Key West, (305) 295-5010. Follow the Overseas Highway until it becomes Truman Avenue. Proceed south on Truman until it intersects with White Street. The Harvey Government Center is on the corner of Truman and White. Head for the tax collector's office.

Required Equipment

The U.S. Coast Guard requires that vessels using gasoline for any reason be equipped with a ventilation system in proper working condition. With the exception of outboard motors, gasoline engines must also be equipped with a means of backfire flame control. In addition, Coast Guard–approved fire extinguishers are required for boats with inboard engines, closed or under-seat compartments with portable fuel tanks, and other characteristics. There are additional requirements for vessels of more than 39 feet and boats used for races, parades, and other specific purposes.

Personal flotation devices, night distress signals, and navigation lights are other required equipment. Contact the U.S. Coast Guard at (305) 743-6778 or (305) 664-8078 for specific requirements for your size and style of boat.

Recommended Equipment

Regardless of your boat's size, location, and use, the U.S. Coast Guard recommends that you have the following equipment onboard: VHF radio, visual distress signals, anchor and spare anchor, heaving line, fenders, first-aid kit, flashlight, mirror, searchlight, sunscreen and sunburn lotion, tool kit, ring buoy, whistle or horn, fuel tanks and spare fuel, chart and compass, boat hook, spare propeller, mooring line, food and water, binoculars, spare batteries, sunglasses (polarized to see water color variations better), marine hardware, extra clothing, spare parts, paddles, and a pump or bailer.

THE FLORIDA KEYS NATIONAL MARINE SANCTUARY REGULATIONS

The Florida Keys fall within the boundaries of the Florida Keys National Marine Sanctuary, created by the federal government in 1990 to protect the resources of our marine ecosystem. And while, for the most part, visitors can freely swim, dive, snorkel, boat, fish, or recreate on our waters, there are some regulations to guide these activities. For a complete copy of the regulations and marine coordinates of the areas, contact the sanctuary office at (305) 743-2437, or visit www.floridakeys.noaa.gov.

i Both boat safety and personal watercraft (PWC) safety courses are offered online by the Florida Fish and Wildlife Commission. The courses teach boat safety and Florida boating laws. Upon successfully completing a course, you will receive a Florida Boating Safety Education ID card, which will make you eligible for a discount on boat or PWC insurance. For more information: www.boat-ed.com/fl.

Sanctuarywide Regulations

These mandates focus on habitat protection, striving to reduce threats to water quality and minimize human impact of delicate resources. The following are prohibited in our waters:

- Moving, removing, injuring, or possessing coral or live rock.
- Discharging or depositing trash or other pollutants.
- Dredging, drilling, prop dredging, altering, or abandoning any structure on the seabed.
- Operating a vessel in such a manner as to strike or injure coral, sea grass, or organisms attached to the seabed, or cause prop-scarring.
- Anchoring a vessel on living coral in water less than 40 feet deep when you can see the bottom. Anchoring on hard-bottom surfaces is allowed.
- Operating a vessel at more than idle speed within 100 yards of residential shorelines, stationary vessels, and navigational aids marking reefs.
- Operating a vessel at more than idle speed within 100 feet of a diver-down flag.
- Diving or snorkeling without a dive flag.
- Operating a vessel in such a manner as to endanger life, limb, marine resources, or property.
- Releasing exotic species.
- Damaging or removing markers, mooring buoys, scientific equipment, boundary buoys, and trap buoys.
- Moving, removing, injuring, or possessing historical resources.
- Taking or possessing protected wildlife.
- Using or possessing explosives or electrical charges.
- Collecting marine life species—tropical fish, invertebrates, and plants—except as allowed by Florida Marine Life Rule (46-42 F.A.C.).

Marine Zoning Restrictions

The sanctuary's marine zoning regulations focus protection on portions of sensitive habitats, while allowing public access in others. Only about 2 percent of the sanctuary's waters fall into the five zoning categories. All sanctuarywide regulations apply in the special zones as well as a number of additional rules and restrictions.

With certain exceptions, the following activities are prohibited in the Ecological Reserves (ERs), Sanctuary Preservation Areas (SPAs), and Special Use (research-only) Areas:

- Discharging any matter except cooling water or engine exhaust.
- Fishing by any means.
- Removing, harvesting, or possessing any marine life.
- Catch and release fishing by trolling are allowed in Conch Reef, Alligator Reef, Sombrero Reef, and Sand Key SPAs only.
- Touching or standing on living or dead coral.
- Anchoring on living or dead coral, or any attached organism.

Additional regulations for Tortugas South ER:

Vessels may only enter if they remain in continuous transit with fishing gear stowed. Diving and snorkeling are prohibited.

Additional regulations for Tortugas North ER:

- Access permit required to stop or use a mooring buoy.
- Anchoring is prohibited.
- Mooring vessel(s) more than 100 feet in total or combined length overall is prohibited.

- No access permit is necessary if vessel remains in continuous transit with fishing gear stowed.

Wildlife Management Areas (WMAs):

Public access restrictions in these areas include idle speed only/no wake, no access buffer, no motor, and limited closures, and are marked as such.

Special Use Areas:

There are four Special Use Areas designated within the sanctuary as research-only areas. These areas are closed to all activities. They are located in the vicinity of: Conch Reef, Tennessee Reef, Looe Key (Hawk Channel patch reef), and Eastern Sambo Reef.

Activities prohibited in the Key Largo and Looe Key Existing Management Areas:

Removing, taking, spearing, or otherwise damaging any coral, marine invertebrate, plant, soil, rock, or other material. However, commercial taking of spiny lobster and stone crab by trap and recreational taking of spiny lobster by hand or hand gear consistent with applicable state and federal fishery regulations are allowed.

Spearfishing and possession of spearfishing equipment is prohibited, except while passing through without interruption.

PUBLIC BOAT RAMPS

If you trailer your boat to the Florida Keys, you can launch it at any number of public ramps. Here is a list of boat-launching sites maintained year-round for your use. Parking is limited except at park sites. Please note that for those listings noted with a $, you must pay a launch fee.

Upper Keys

MM 110 Bayside, Key Largo
MM 102 Oceanside, John Pennekamp
Coral Reef State Park, Key Largo, $
MM 92.5 Oceanside, Harry Harris County
Park, Key Largo, $ (weekends and
holidays)
MM 86 Bayside, Founder's Park,
Islamorada, $ (except for locals)
MM 79 Bayside, Islamorada, Indian Key Fill
MM 71 Bayside, Islamorada

Middle Keys

MM 54 Bayside, Marathon
MM 49 Bayside, Marathon Yacht Club,
33rd Street, Marathon

Lower Keys

West of Seven Mile Bridge Bayside,
Little Duck Key
MM 37 Oceanside, Bahia Honda State
Recreation Area, $
MM 33 Bayside, Spanish Harbor Key
MM 27.5 Bayside, SR 4A, Little Torch Key
MM 22 Oceanside, Cudjoe Key
MM 11 Bayside, Big Coppitt Key
MM 10 Oceanside, Shark Key Fill

Key West

BOAT U.S. TOWING SERVICES
MM 5 Oceanside, Stock Island
End of Route A1A, Smathers Beach
(305) 664-7495 or (800) 888-4869
Being stranded in a vessel on the water is not fun! Never pay a towing charge again when you join this marine towing and salvage service with 24-hour assistance. Call their 800 number for membership and protect yourself for any marine assistance.

MARINE SUPPLY STORES

Marine supplies and NOAA charts recommended by the U.S. Coast Guard may be purchased at the following facilities.

Upper Keys

WEST MARINE
MM 103.4 Bayside, Key Largo
(305) 453-9050 or (800) 685-4838
www.westmarine.com
West Marine is an expansive store that carries a variety of supplies for sailboats and powerboats. Hardware and electric, safety, plumbing, and maintenance needs can be met at West Marine. There are three additional locations at MM 48.5 Oceanside in Marathon (305-289-1009 or 800-685-4838); 5790 Second St. on Stock Island (305-294-2025 or 800-685-4838); and 725 Caroline St. in Key West (305-295-0999 or 800-685-4838).

CURTIS MARINE
MM 92 Oceanside, Tavernier
(305) 852-5218
Curtis Marine offers complete marine and sailing supplies as well as batteries, wire, and riggings. They can help with davit cables, and there's a nice selection in their ship's store.

Middle Keys

See West Marine entries in the Upper Keys section for their Middle Keys locations.

HARBOUR POINT MARINE
MM 46 Oceanside, Marathon
(305) 289-0505
www.keysmako.com
Marathon Harbour Point Marine is a Premier Level MerCruiser and Mercury Outboard dealership. Its full sales and service

facility sells Mako and SeaCraft boats with an excellent staff to assist with all your boating needs.

Lower Keys

SEA CENTER
MM 29.5 Oceanside, Big Pine Key
(305) 872-2243
www.sea-center.com
Sea Center offers boat sales, services, and supplies, including hardware, electric, and maintenance needs.

Key West

See West Marine in the Upper Keys section for their lower Keys and Key West locations.

KEY WEST MARINE HARDWARE INC.
818 Caroline St.
(305) 294-3519
This is the place to go for every cleat, bolt, snap, or thingamajig your powerboat or sailboat requires, because Key West Marine Hardware has it all. You'll find the complete set of official NOAA nautical charts to the Keys and Caribbean waters along with cruising, fishing, and sailing publications of every description. The stock of fishing tackle is limited, but you really can dress your boat in style with all the add-on amenities offered here. You can also dress yourself. Key West Marine carries a large selection of stylish boating togs.

BOAT SALES, REPAIRS, FUEL, AND STORAGE

Facilities throughout the Florida Keys carry a wide variety of new and used boats. For boat owners, most of these sales centers provide all the necessary services, including local hauling, repairs, bottom painting, and fuel.

Upper Keys

UNIQUE MARINE
MM 93 Bayside, Tavernier
(305) 853-5370
www.uniquemarine.com
For more than 10 years, Unique Marine has been the established dealer for EdgeWater, ProKat, ShreaWater, SeaQuest, Venture, and Yamaha. This dealership takes pride in educating the public about Catamaran fishing boats. They are there for you long after the sale, as they value long-term relationships with their loyal customers. Stop in and see why Unique Marine continuously receives prestigious customer-service awards from various boat manufacturers year after year.

PLANTATION BOAT MART & MARINA, INC.
MM 90 Bayside, Tavernier
(800) 539-2628
www.plantationboat.com
Plantation Boat Mart sells Glacier Bay, Palmetto Custom, Jupiter, Sea Pro, and Hydrasport brand boats and is a Hurricane dealer. You may also buy Yamaha, Johnson, and Evinrude engines here. Plantation Boat Mart maintains a full-service repair department.

SMUGGLERS COVE RESORT AND MARINA
MM 85.5 Bayside, Islamorada
(305) 664-5564 or (800) 864-4363
www.smugscove.com
Nice package the folks at Smugglers Cove Resort and Marina have developed in the Upper Keys. Their building at the marina has stationary docks that berth up to 70-foot boats in the slips and is located in a lovely nautical setting. Fuel docks are available along with a great ship's store including live bait and tackle inside. You can rent boats

here or hang out with one of the captains and go on a charter for backcountry or off-shore fishing.

CARIBEE BOAT SALES
MM 81.5 Bayside, Islamorada
(305) 664-3431
www.caribeeboats.com

Offshore anglers shop at Caribee for Grady Whites, Pursuits, and Contenders 20 to 36 feet in length. For fishing the backcountry, the facility carries 16- to 21-foot Hewes, Path-finder, and Maverick boats as well as Boston Whalers. Yamaha and Mercury engines are sold here. Indoor and outdoor storage is available, and certified mechanics are on duty seven days a week. Bottom painting and boat hauling are provided; Caribee car-ries 89-octane fuel and sells live bait, frozen bait, and ice. Mobile service is available.

Middle Keys

THE BOAT HOUSE MARINA
MM 53.5 Oceanside, Marathon
(305) 289-7979
www.theboathousemarina.com

New, state-of-the-art dockage has emerged in Marathon. Owned by the Singh Company (see Accommodations chapter, Tranquility Bay Beach House Resort and Parrott Key Resort), this complex is like no other in the Keys. It was constructed to withstand 155 mph winds and has high-tech security, online Web cams, and auto fire suppression. They offer 40-foot wet and 36-foot dry storage with full-service boat sales and repairs on site.

QUALITY YACHT SERVICE
MM 52 Bayside, 10701 Fifth Ave.,
Marathon
(305) 743-2898

Quality Yacht Service offers marine fuel cleaning and tank cleaning for both diesel and gasoline engines. It also provides mobile service.

MARATHON BOAT YARD
MM 48.5 Oceanside, Marathon
(305) 743-6341 or (888) 726-9004
www.marathonboatsandyachts.com

Marathon Boat Yard has become the first in the Florida Keys to be designated as a "Clean Boatyard." This ensures that the normally messy job of working on boats doesn't harm the environment. This boat yard is a full-service marine yard, and on their two-acre site they handle new boats, yacht brokerage, sportfishing boats, center consoles, cocktail cruisers, flat boats, and more. To reach them by boat: N 24 42.441, W 81 06.268.

KEYS BOAT WORKS INC.
MM 48.5 Bayside, 700 39th St., Marathon
(305) 743-5583
www.keysboatworks.com

Keys Boat Works provides a comprehensive range of services for boats up to 67 feet in length and maintains 15-ton and 50-ton travel lifts. This full-service yard offers fiberglass work, carpentry, and Awlgrip topside painting. A variety of on-premises businesses contribute to the one-stop shopping for boat service, including: diesel mechanics, an electronics specialist, a yacht refinisher, sign painter, and fiberglasser. Keys Boat Works can store vessels up to 60 feet, either in or out of the water. The facility has a capacity for 180 boats.

Lower Keys

SEA CENTER
MM 29.5 Oceanside, Big Pine Key
(305) 872-2243
www.sea-center.com

Sea Center carries new ProLines and Angler and services Johnson and Evinrude engines. Bottom painting and limited boat hauling are available. The facility carries 93-octane fuel and maintains a complete marine store with parts and accessories.

Key West

FISH AND RACE
5555 College Rd., Sunset Marina, Stock Island
(305) 292-2291
www.fishandrace.com
Three mechanics with one goal in mind: "When you go out on your boat, we want you to come back." Their expert mechanical skills with decades of combined experience help them keep this motto. An extensive inventory of repair parts and a vast selection of new Mercury and Honda outboard engines offer top-of-the-line tune-ups to powerhead and gear-case rebuilding on engines that range in size from 2 to 300 horsepower.

i If you see a red-and-white diver-down flag displayed while you are boating, stay at least 100 feet away. Divers or snorkelers are in these waters. Motoring between 100 feet and 300 feet from a diver-down flag must be at idle speed.

GARRISON BIGHT MARINA AND BOAT RENTAL
Garrison Bight Causeway
711 Eisenhower Dr., Key West
(305) 294-3093 or (305) 294-5780
www.garrisonbightmarina.net
This full-service marina offers both long- and short-term dry or in-water storage. Unleaded fuel may be purchased here, too. Garrison Bight Marina also rents powerboats (15 to 22 feet) by the hour, half day, full day, or full week. Garrison Bight Marina is a sales and service dealer for Yamaha, Johnson, Evinrude, and Suzuki engines.

i Tycoon Henry Flagler was not only famous for his overseas railroad from Miami to Key West, but also operated three cargo ships that sailed from Key West to Havana, Cuba. Measuring up to 350 feet in length, each one held a capacity of 30 refrigerated railroad cars on board.

KING'S POINTE MARINA
5950 Peninsula Ave., Stock Island
(305) 294-4676
www.cortexcompanies.com
King's Pointe Marina is a kind of one-stop storage and service facility for boaters. Outside dry storage and inside storage are available. Oceanside sells fuel and has a mechanic on staff, a fully stocked tackle shop, a pump-out facility, and a bathhouse.

PROP DOCTOR OF KEY WEST
MM 5 Oceanside, Stock Island
(305) 292-0012
The owners go by the creed of "Boats need to be on the water, not out of the water." A lot of boat owners know that if you shear a prop or damage it by striking something, you could be landlocked for weeks. Now at Prop Doctor, you can be back on the high seas in a few days. They do all the work themselves on Stock Island and do not send the repairs to the mainland. You can call them and they will send a driver out to the marina to pick up the damaged prop and bring it back to you, sometimes in only a matter of hours. Prop Doctor can also handle shafts, struts, and rudders. They plan on keeping you fishing!

KAYAKS

The first kayaks were created by Artic Indians, the Inuit. Constructed of wooden frames covered in sealskin, the kayak's varied by design from region to region. Today, kayaks are equally creative and beautiful in design. Using one of these ancient forms of water transportation in the eco-sensitive Florida Keys is one way to reduce our carbon footprint and further protect this fragile spot on Earth. A wonderful and impressive book on kayaking is *Florida Keys Paddling Atlas* published by this book's publisher, Globe Pequot Press, and written by Mary and Bill Burnham.

Upper Keys

FLORIDA BAY OUTFITTERS
MM 104 Bayside, Key Largo
(305) 451-3018
www.kayakfloridakeys.com
One of south Florida's largest kayak and canoe dealers with loads of accessories in stock. This place will have you sport paddling in no time! Knowledgeable and dedicated staff, these folks know their business. Offering sales and rentals with full- and half-day water trips for one or more. Check out their Kids Summer Kayak Camp (see the listing in the Kidstuff chapter).

BACKCOUNTRY COWBOY OUTFITTERS
MM 82.2 Bayside, Islamorada
(305) 517-4177
www.backcountrycowboy.com
Living large in the Florida Keys but not wrestling herds of cattle, Backcountry Cowboy Outfitters kayaks a different range and gathers customers to paddle and explore the beautiful waters here. Noted for their guided kayak tours, camping, and kayak equipment, these folks fill your every request and they are open seven days a week. Ask about their sunset and sunrise trips as well as their full-moon excursions.

THE KAYAK SHACK
MM 77.5 Oceanside, at Robbie's Marina, Islamorada
(305) 664-4878
www.kayakthefloridakeys.com
Explore the backcountry waters by renting a kayak from the Kayak Shack. You can paddle into the unknown by yourself or take one of several guided tours through mangrove canals, to Lignumvitae or Indian Key (see the Attractions chapter), or across the saltwater flats at sunset.

REFLECTIONS NATURE TOURS
(305) 872-4668
www.floridakeyskayaktours.com
Reflections Nature Tours is a mobile nature tour company that trailers their kayaks to a number of tour locations in the Lower Keys to take advantage of the tides and the prevailing winds. With more than 20 favorite kayaking spots, they can always find a favorable paddling site in any wind condition. Marine life, birds, plant life, and indigenous Keys animals can be viewed up close and personal. Guides will teach you kayaking techniques and give you the lowdown on the flora and fauna of the Keys.

Middle Keys

MARATHON KAYAK
MM 50.5 Oceanside, Marathon
(305) 395-0355
www.marathonkayak.com
Well-known for kayaking tours throughout the Keys, Marathon Kayak is a top-notch group to outfit and guide you in your journey. After purchasing your gear, their demo

center lets customers get the feel for their equipment and product line to ensure satisfaction. Marathon Kayak offers multiple locations for outings including the Seven Mile Bridge, Bahia Honda State Park, fishing tours, and sunset tours. For paddlers, they also rent for half, full day, multiday, and weekly.

Lower Keys

REELAX CHARTERS
MM 17 Oceanside, Sugarloaf Key
(305) 744-0263 or (305) 304-1392
www.keyskayaking.com
Enjoy backcountry trips on the water in the mangroves of the tranquil Lower Florida Keys. The captain has a boat with a 10-foot beam to accommodate kayaks, a grill, cooler, and beach chairs. It is wheelchair accessible.

Key West

BLUE PLANET KAYAK
(305) 294-8087
www.blue-planet-kayak.com
Join in the fun with Blue Planet Kayak and take one of their informative and lively kayak tours. Everything from ecotours to sunset, starlight, birding, and custom tours, these folks know their business. They also rent kayaks for half- and full-day on-your-own paddling adventures. They will pick you up at your lodging location or meet you in the Publix Shopping Center on North Roosevelt Boulevard in Key West for your convenience and to help you find their marina on Stock Island.

LAZY DOG KAYAKING
MM 4.2 Bayside, Stock Island
(305) 295-9898
www.lazydog.com

Stop by the Lazy Dog shack and sign up for a two- or four-hour kayak tour around Key West. You can rent a single or double kayak or try your hand (and balance) in a standup paddleboat.

POWERBOAT RENTALS

The following rental facilities offer U.S. Coast Guard–approved, safety-equipped vessels complete with VHF marine radios. Rental boat sizes vary from 15 to 27 feet, in a number of configurations: center consoles, bowriders, cuddy cabins, and pontoon boats. The boats feature options such as compasses, depth finders, Bimini or T-tops, dry storage, swim ladders, and dive platforms. You can rent a powerboat for either a half day or full day. Call the establishments to inquire about specific boats offered, their features, and prices. (Prices are usually quoted without tax or gasoline.)

Purchase the nautical chart you need (see the Aids to Navigation section in this chapter) and bring it with you to the boat rental facility of your choice. Most facilities will provide you with an operational briefing and a nautical chart review before you set off. Some of these facilities require that you remain within a specific locale at all times; others base this decision on weather conditions.

Upper Keys

ROBBIE'S BOAT RENTALS & CHARTERS
MM 77.5 Bayside, Islamorada
(877) 664-8498
www.robbies.com
One of the Florida Keys' more interesting boat rental facilities, Robbie's is behind the Hungry Tarpon Restaurant. Visitors come to Robbie's just to feed the many tarpon that lurk close to shore (see the Kidstuff chapter). Boat rentals, too, are popular, since Robbie's

is only half a mile from historic Indian Key (see the Attractions chapter). Robbie's rents boats from 14 feet to 27 feet in length.

Key West

BOAT RENTALS OF KEY WEST
The Galleon Marina
617 Front St.
(305) 294-2628
www.boatrentalsofkeywest.com
You can rent Wahoos and Wellcrafts of 20 to 26 feet, as well as Jet Boats and Jet Skis. Navigational charts are provided and reviewed, along with an overview of local waters and suggestions (based on weather conditions) of directions to take and places to see. A questionnaire and verbal review ensure that boaters are experienced. Jet Ski tours are also available.

i The Florida Circumnavigational Saltwater Paddling Trail was inaugurated in the Florida Keys in 2006. The 26 segments allow kayakers to explore waters from Big Lagoon State Park, south of Pensacola, around the Keys, to Fort Clinch State Park, north of Jacksonville—with a kayak support network, recommended campsites, and motel stays. For more information, visit www.dep.state.fl.us/gwt/paddling/saltwater.htm.

GARRISON BIGHT MARINA
711 Eisenhower Dr. (corner of Palm Avenue and Eisenhower Drive)
(305) 294-3093
www.garrisonbightmarina.net
Open seven days a week, Garrison Bight Marina offers a modern fleet of boats to

rent ranging from 15 to 22 feet. They rent by the hour, half day, or full day; weekly charters with guides are also available. You can rent diving equipment here too as well as fish finders and GPS for your boat. Happy boating!

i In town for the 2009 Key West International Sailing Regatta, Denmark's Crown Prince Frederik was at the helm of *Nanoq*. More than 150 boats in 13 classes competed in this exciting race (see Annual Events chapter).

SAILING

With an abundance of protected anchorages, harbors, and marinas and warm tropical waters, the Florida Keys are often described by sailors as the "American Caribbean." Our offshore barrier reef provides protection from swells. Our bayside is so sheltered that many skippers with low-draft boats (typically catamarans or small, monohull sailboats) can trim up their sails and guide their crafts through the Intracoastal Waterway. Catamarans and monohulls with drafts of 4 or 5 feet fare best along the sometimes shallow Intracoastal; monohulls with 6-foot drafts have difficulty getting out of bayside marinas. These boats may also run aground here. Most oceanside marinas and harbors typically run deep enough to accommodate virtually any type of sailboat (see the Cruising chapter).

Within the Florida Keys, local sailing clubs organize their own informal races. Sailing in the Florida Keys can include cruising, limited bareboat charters, and a combination of snorkeling, fishing, diving, or gunkholing. Many head out simply to enjoy the sail. In order to sail the diverse waters of the

Florida Keys, however, boaters must know a rig from a right-of-way.

Sailing Courses

Several facilities throughout our islands offer sailing courses for beginner through advanced levels, along with bareboat certification and brush-up sessions. Prices vary greatly depending upon the duration and complexity of the courses and the number of people participating. Be sure to ask about all your options when you call to book your instruction.

FLORIDA KEYS SAILING
MM 49 Bayside, Marathon
(305) 731-8105
www.sailfloridakeys.com
You'll find a wide variety of sailing operations at Florida Keys Sailing, located at Keys Fisheries and Marina. The sailing school offers everything from half-day and full-day day sailing classes to advanced bareboat sailing courses, and almost everything in between.

The basic introductory three-day, Learn-to-Sail keelboat course is designed to provide the new sailor with a solid foundation. In the basic cruising course, students learn to responsibly skipper and crew an auxiliary-powered cruising sailboat within sight of land in moderate wind and sea conditions. Bareboat cruising is the advanced cruising course.

Racing clinics aboard J/24 sloops are offered on short windward–leeward courses. Students learn the techniques of starting, luffing, positioning on the racecourse, covering an opponent to win, and defending position.

Bareboat rentals also are available. Boats include a 14-foot Day Sailer, J/24 Race Ready, Irwin 34 Basic Cruiser, and a Catalina 30-foot Keys Cruiser.

Bareboat Charters

If you already know how to sail or you prefer to explore our waters on your own, the Florida Keys also offers captained and bareboat charters for anywhere from two hours to several weeks. Prices vary depending upon the size of the vessel and the length of the bareboat excursion.

TREASURE HARBOR MARINE INC.
MM 86.5 Oceanside
200 Treasure Harbor Dr., Islamorada
(305) 852-2458 or (800) 352-2628
www.treasureharbor.com
Treasure Harbor maintains a fleet of 12 sloops and ketch rigs ranging in size from 19 to 41 feet by Cape Dory, Watkins, Hunter, and Morgan. Skilled sailors can charter any one of these boats on their own, and written and verbal "exams" will test your sailing experience. Professional captains will provide nautical charts, overviews of Florida Keys waters, and suggestions of places to visit from John Pennekamp and the Everglades to Key West and the Bahamas. Skippers are available. A two-day minimum is required for all boats greater than 25 feet in length. Security deposits are required. Power trawler yachts are also available.

Treasure Harbor Marine also offers charters on an Antigua 37 catamaran or a 47-foot Marine Trader, which must be rented with an accompanying captain. Advance reservations for all vessels are suggested.

SOUTHERNMOST SAILING
6810 Front St., Key West
(at Safe Harbor Marina)
(305) 766-4683
www.southernmostsailing.com
Southernmost Sailing maintains a fleet of charter catamarans and monohull sailboats,

including Hunter, Ticon, Jeanneau, Gemini, PDQ, Tobago, and J/24. They range in size from 24 to 42 feet. Qualified sailing captains are permitted to sail virtually anywhere except Cuba, including Shark River, Florida's west coast, the Marquesas, and the Dry Tortugas. A charter-boat captain is available at an additional cost.

If boats are not out on a multiday charter, customers may rent them for a per-diem cost or charter them with captain for the additional fee. All boats are equipped for cruising and have auxiliary engines that reduce fuel consumption.

Reservations are recommended. In the off-season you probably won't have any trouble securing a boat as little as one week out. However, for high-season sailing, make your reservations at least three to six months in advance.

Sailing Clubs and Regattas

Avid sailors throughout our islands have formed sailing clubs, which sponsor casual regattas. These are not your upscale yacht clubs, but membership does have its privileges—discounted race entry fees and dinners, and the opportunity to meet individuals who share your interests.

UPPER KEYS SAILING CLUB
MM 100 Bayside, 100 Ocean Bay Dr., Key Largo
(305) 451-9972
www.upperkeyssailingclub.com
Established in 1973, the Upper Keys Sailing Club is based in a club-owned house on the bay and comprises Upper Keys residents of all ages. Races on Buttonwood Bay are held on a regular basis. Spectators watch from clubhouse grounds. Two offshore races take place over a two-week period.

As a community service, members provide free two-day sailing seminars four times a year. Seminars combine two hours of classroom instruction with extensive time on the water aboard the club's 19-foot Flying Scots. Boaters with Sunfish and Hobie Cats are welcome. Membership requires a onetime initiation fee and annual dues.

THE FLORIDA KEYS DRAGON BOAT CLUB
Locations vary
(305) 304-5100
www.floridakeysdragonboat.com
In 277 B.C., the Chinese tried to save a poet from being eaten by fish and dragons by beating the water with their paddles. Here in Key West, this primal teamwork is all fun and games. Twenty-two paddlers are on board, including one helmsman and one rummer, who sets the cadence. The boat design originates from ancient China with its brightly colored scales, fierce horned head, and a dragon tail. The Loch Ness Monster gone Disneyland? This muscle-aching sport is one vicious work out!

KEY WEST SAILING CLUB
Sailboat Lane, off Palm Avenue
Garrison Bight Causeway, Key West
(305) 292-5993
www.keywestsailingclub.org
Key West Sailing Club is a private organization open to anyone for membership. The club itself is located at the base of the Garrison Bight Bridge. The club has four Sunfish boats and a Hobie Cat, as well as four Optimists, two lasers, a Snipe, an American Day Sailer, and a Cape Dory. In addition, a sizable fleet of privately owned JY15s is available for members to use on race days. The club sponsors monthly offshore races for boats

20 feet and larger; call for more information. During daylight saving time, small boat (20 feet or less) races are held every Wed at 6 p.m. Group and private instruction is available for both adults and juniors (younger than age 18). Dates and times of courses change seasonally; call for details.

Membership requires a onetime initiation fee and annual dues. The membership year begins in Jan, but dues are prorated so anyone who joins later doesn't pay for a full year. A membership entitles members to use club facilities seven days a week between 6 a.m. and midnight. Membership also grants possible dockage in a wet or dry slip; rates are based on boat length. Information on courses, boat races, and membership is available on the club's information line listed above.

MARATHON SAILING CLUB
(305) 743-4917

The Marathon Sailing Club, a young, informal group, meets the second Wednesday of each month. Typically the club holds monthly regattas on courses around Marathon. The club's three major regattas each year attract sailors from across the Keys: Marathon to Key West; a two-day Sombrero Cup race; and the bay-to-ocean race, a course running bayside from Marathon to Channel Five and then back oceanside. A Lady Skipper's trophy puts only women at the helm. Membership requires annual dues. Call Bruce Palmenberg for meeting locations and more information.

HOUSEBOAT RENTALS

Florida Keys houseboats provide all the comforts of home combined with a camplike experience. Whether you seek a weekend excursion or a gently rocking place to spend your vacation, these rentals may very well float your boat.

HOUSEBOAT VACATIONS OF THE FLORIDA KEYS
MM 85.9 Bayside, Islamorada
(305) 664-4009
www.floridakeys.com/houseboats

Houseboat Vacations of the Florida Keys offers live-aboard vessels that range from two 42-foot-long catamarans that sleep six or eight adults to a 44-foot-long houseboat that accommodates eight. You must have some boating experience to rent one of these floating homes. Boaters must venture no farther than 8 miles offshore along 25 miles of surrounding coastline in Florida Bay. You may not take the houseboats into the ocean. Each houseboat offers a full galley and air-conditioning and features a gas grill on deck. There is a three-day minimum; weekly rentals are available. Call for current pricing.

CRUISING

Regarded as America's out-islands by seasoned cruisers of motor and sailing yachts, the Florida Keys can justifiably boast about the sheltered harbors and easily navigated waters enveloping the serpentine stretch. Our waters are well marked; our charts, up to date; and the U.S. Coast Guard keeps channels dredged to the proper depth. The Atlantic's Hawk Channel runs along the ocean side of the Keys, protected by the only coral reef in the continental United States. The Intracoastal Waterway—called the Big Ditch in the North's inland waters—cuts through the causeway from the mainland at Jewfish Creek and then parallels the Keys through Florida Bay and the Gulf of Mexico. Keys waters are most accessible to boats with drafts of up to 4½ feet, but you can cruise the Keys with 5½- to 6-foot drafts if you're careful.

If you covet first-class creature comforts, put into one of our comprehensive marinas and enjoy the perks of staying at a luxury resort. Do you relish seclusion? Anchor out on the leeward side of a remote, uninhabited key. Or take the best of both worlds and plan a combination of the two.

To help you plan your Keys cruising adventure, we guide you on a tour of our preeminent marinas and little-known anchoring-out destinations (in descending order from the Upper to Lower Keys). Be sure to read our Key West and Beyond section, where the junket continues.

THE FLORIDA KEYS

Marinas

All marinas listed in this chapter take transient boaters, but we suggest you make reservations at least a month in advance during the popular winter season from Dec through Mar. You may assume unless otherwise stated that all our recommended marinas supply hookups for both 30-amp and 50-amp service as well as fresh water. You'll find that provisioning is easy along the 120-mile stretch of the Florida Keys. Most marinas have ship's stores or are within walking distance of a convenience market. The occasional exception is noted.

The marinas keep an active list of expert marine mechanics who are generally on call to handle any repair needs that might develop during your cruise. We highlight fuel dock facilities and availability of laundry, showers, and restrooms. We also point out restaurants and the hot spots for partying while ashore.

There are no restrictions against bringing children and pets unless specifically noted. Keep your pet on your vessel or on a leash at all times.

Dockmasters monitor VHF channel 16, but they will ask you to switch channels once you've established contact. They will give you detailed directions to the marinas.

i "Wet-foot, dry-foot" is the name of the 1995 revision of the Cuban Adjustment Act of 1996. The revision designates that any Cuban caught on the waters between two nations ("wet feet") would be sent back to their country. Make it ashore ("dry feet"), one would get a chance to remain in the United States.

THE MARINA CLUB AT BACKWATER SOUND
MM 104 Bayside, Key Largo
(305) 453-7800 or (866) 734-1524
www.marinaclubkeylargo.com
The future of boat storage is deeded racko-miniums, and the Marina Club at Backwater Sound has these newest entries in water-front ownership. These dry racks are rented through the marina, and the amenities include showers, a lounge, fuel, boat care, restaurant, Wi-Fi access, concierge, diving, and spa services.

MARINA DEL MAR
MM 100 Oceanside, 527 Caribbean Dr., Key Largo
(305) 451-4107 or (800) 451-3483
www.marinadelmarkeylargo.com
Plan ahead if you want to stay at one of the 137 slips at Marina Del Mar marina, which lies within the underwater boundaries of John Pennekamp Coral Reef State Park and the Key Largo National Marine Sanctuary. All but a select few are usually booked far in advance from Jan through Mar, so plan ahead. The slips will accommodate vessels with a 6-foot draft (mean low tide) and up to 70 feet in length, but depth at the mouth of

the channel drops drastically at low tide, to about 4½ feet, so exercise caution. A short walk to the Overseas Highway will satisfy provisioning requirements. Laundry, shower, and restroom facilities are provided on the premises. Marina rates do not include water and electricity; a minimum daily charge will be levied. Marina Del Mar Resort (see the Accommodations chapter) has tennis courts, a swimming pool, and a hot tub for your use. Gorge yourself at the hotel's continental breakfast for a nominal charge. And don't miss Coconuts, a popular restaurant and percolating nightspot.

Marina Del Mar is accessed via Hawk Channel, Marker Red No. 2.

THE PILOT HOUSE MARINA
MM 100 Oceanside, Key Largo
(305) 451-3142
www.pilothousemarina.com
Sitting alongside the Pilot House Restaurant (see the Restaurants chapter), this marina offers an array of services to boaters. Deep dockage with slips that can accommodate up to 60-foot-long boats, repairs for your boat, 30- and 50-amp, restrooms, showers, laundry facilities, cable TV, Wi-Fi, bait for fishing, diesel, and gas are available. Enjoy the tiki bar at the restaurant next door.

PLANTATION YACHT HARBOR MARINA
MM 87 Bayside, Islamorada
(305) 852-2381
www.pyh.com
You can grab a slip close to the Keys' fabled backcountry at the bayside Plantation Yacht Harbor, a municipal marina located at Islamorada Founder's Park (see the Recreation chapter). This 88-slip marina can accommodate vessels up to 60 feet in length, drawing 5 feet. Mobile marine mechanics are on call to

service needy vessels, and a fuel dock supplies both diesel fuel and gasoline. Plantation Yacht Harbor does not have a ship's store, but a 1-mile walk up the Overseas Highway will put you at a convenience store. You may use the on-site laundry, showers, and restroom facilities. Tennis courts, a swimming pool, a small beach, skate park, playground, dog park, and sports field await your pleasure.

Plantation Yacht Harbor Marina is accessed via the Intracoastal Waterway, between Markers No. 78 and No. 78A, or via Snake Creek from the Atlantic.

i Due to the city of Key West's bay-bottom lease, cruise ships may only dock at Mallory Square Pier 12 times a year during sunset. The ships must either moor elsewhere the rest of the year or leave at least one hour before sunset so as not to block the view!

WATERMARK MARINA OF ISLAMORADA
MM 80.5 Bayside, Islamorada
(305) 664-8884 or (888) 232-6287
www.watermarkmarina.com
Facing Florida Bay, the location of Watermark Marina of Islamorada provides clear passage into the flats and bay of the Florida Keys, Everglades National Park, and the Atlantic Ocean. If you are water-oriented to fishing, kayaking, or just pure enjoyment, then this marina is for you.

HAWK'S CAY RESORT AND MARINA
MM 61 Oceanside, Duck Key
(305) 743-7000 or (800) 432-2242
www.hawkscay.com
Probably the best all-around marina in the Keys, Hawk's Cay offers a totally protected boat basin and all the amenities of its fine resort hotel (see our Accommodations and Restaurants chapters). Dock your boat at one of the 52 full-service marina slips (5-foot draft) with 30 and 50 amp service, fresh water, cable TV, and phone. If you come in a vessel less than 35 feet, you can dock it at one of 32 small-boat slips and stay at the resort. These slips have no shore power, and you may not stay aboard your boat overnight. Rates will be the same as for the other transient slips, except there is no minimum.

Hawk's Cay maintains an extensive list of qualified marine mechanics in the area and has divers on call. The full-service ship's store sells everything, including groceries, fine wines, boating hardware, fishing tackle, clothing, and paperback books. It also offers video rentals. A full-service fuel dock pumps regular and premium gasoline and diesel fuel. Showers and restrooms are in the ship's store, and the marina is equipped with a pump-out station at the fuel dock. Laundry facilities are coin-operated. Cable television hookup is available at an extra fee.

Hawk's Cay Marina is accessed via Hawk Channel at Marker No. 44 when traveling down the Keys or at Marker No. 45 when approaching from Key West.

DOLPHIN MARINA
MM 28.5 Oceanside, Little Torch Key
(305) 872-2685 or (800) 553-0308
www.dolphinmarina.net
Quiet Little Torch Key is the safe harbor for this delightful marina. Dolphin Marina offers not only boat rentals and dockage but also quaint lodging. The lodging quarters consist of small cottages overlooking Newfound Harbor and cozy apartments with one or two bedrooms. All offer refrigerators, coffeemakers, and cable TV. You do not have

to enjoy fishing or water activities to stay here! Just minutes from luxurious Little Palm Island (see Accommodations chapter), this down-to-earth marina offers all you need for a day afloat on the open waters of the Atlantic. Dolphin Marina has a fleet of Angler boats that you can rent. Alternatively, you can venture out in your own vessel with an experienced fishing or diving guide. The marina and ship's store can stock you with all the supplies for your outing. Boat launching and trailer storage are available if you tow your own boat. Located at 24.39.95 north latitude and 81.23.28 west longitude.

LITTLE PALM ISLAND
MM 28.5 Oceanside, Little Torch Key
(305) 872-2524 or (800) 343-8567
www.littlepalmisland.com

Arriving at Little Palm Island by sea, you will be certain you missed your tack and landed in Fiji, because this exquisite jewel is more reminiscent of the South Seas than South Florida. Little Palm Island, the westernmost of the Newfound Harbor Keys, lies 4 nautical miles due north from Looe Key Light. And while the average bank account strains at the tariffs charged for villa accommodations on the island (see the Accommodations chapter), staying at the marina is a real deal, even though it is the most expensive marina in the Florida Keys. As marina guests you're invited to use all the recreational facilities: sailboards, day sailers, fishing gear, canoes, snorkeling gear, beach, lagoonal swimming pool, and the sauna.

Little Palm's marina, though small, maintains slips on Newfound Harbor for boats up to 120 feet in length, with a draft up to 6 feet. Smaller boats can be accommodated at 575 feet of dock space on a protected lagoon. The controlling depth coming into

the harbor is 6 feet, but the dockmaster will help you navigate around the tides. The dockmaster monitors VHF channels 9 and 16 at all times. Dockhands are available to assist with lines. Hookup for one 50-amp service is included in dockage fees; additional connections depend upon availability. Boats docked at the T-dock enjoy 100-amp service.

Because you're staying on an out-island, offshore from the contiguous Keys and their more plentiful water supply, you will be allowed only one gallon of water per foot per day. However, the resort offers you use of guest showers and restrooms in the quarterdeck and a laundry facility during your stay, so this water conservation is not a hardship.

Little Palm Island's renowned gourmet restaurant welcomes you for breakfast, lunch, and dinner. You may choose to cook aboard your vessel, but be advised that you're prohibited from consuming your own food or beverages in island public areas. Children younger than age 16 are not permitted at Little Palm Island; nor are villa guests allowed to bring pets. Little Palm does accommodate pets of overnight marina guests, but you must keep them on a leash and walk them only in designated areas. In keeping with the tranquil ambience of the island, motorized personal watercraft also are banned. Discounts are offered to members of Boat US.

Little Palm Island is accessed via the Atlantic at the entrance to Newfound Harbor, Marker Red No. 2.

SUGARLOAF MARINA
MM 17 Bayside, Sugarloaf Key
(305) 745-3135

Housed next to the Sugarloaf Lodge, this marina has ramp access, fuel, beer, soda, bait, tackle, and ice. It may be rugged and rough looking, but locals give it a thumbs up.

Anchoring Out

Barefoot elegance, breathtakingly beautiful, and peaceful all describe anchoring out in the pristine waters lacing the Florida Keys. From the northernmost keys of Biscayne Bay to Loggerhead Key at the end of the line, remote havens remain unspoiled, many reachable only by boat. Ibis, white pelicans, and bald eagles winter among select out-islands, and whole condominiums of cormorants take over the scrub of tiny mangrove islets. Gulf waters simmer with snapper, redfish, lobster, and stone crabs. The Atlantic Ocean sparkles with the glory of the living coral reef beneath. So pack up and push off for an Insiders' bareboat cruise of the Florida Keys, from top to toe.

Elliott Key

On the eastern side of Biscayne Bay, the island of Elliott Key, which has the ranger station for Biscayne National Park, guards a complex ecosystem from the ocean's battering winds. Anchor on the leeward side of Elliott Key just off the pretty little beach north of Coon Point. This anchorage—good in northeast to east to southeast winds—is usually accessed via the Intracoastal Waterway.

A strong current rushes through the shallow channel between Sands Key and Elliott Key, and small-boat traffic is heavy on weekends. Although the fishing and diving here are first rate, take care. At the southern tip of Elliott Key, Caesar Creek—named for notorious pirate Black Caesar, who dipped in to stay out of sight in the 1600s—offers dicey passage to Hawk Channel for boats carefully clearing a 4-foot draft at high tide.

The more forgiving Angelfish Creek, farther south at the north end of Key Largo, is the favored route from Biscayne Bay to the ocean in this wild and deserted area. Angelfish Creek is the Intracoastal Waterway's last outlet to the ocean until after Snake Creek Drawbridge for large boats or those heading for Hawk Channel.

Pumpkin Key

Safe anchorage surrounds Pumpkin Key, making this island an ideal choice for winds coming from any direction. Be sure to test your anchorage, because Pumpkin Key's waters cover a grassy sea bottom. Nearby Angelfish Creek—filled with grouper, snapper, and angelfish—almost guarantees dinner. Scoot out the creek to take advantage of the diving at John Pennekamp Coral Reef State Park. Approachable from Hawk Channel or the Intracoastal, this area remains virginal even though it rests in the shadow of Key Largo.

Blackwater Sound

As you anchor in the placid ebony waters of Blackwater Sound, the twinkling lights of Key Largo remind you that civilization is but a dinghy ride away. Anchor along the southeast shoreline of Blackwater Sound for a protected anchorage in east to southeast winds. The Cross Key Canal, which connects Blackwater Sound to Largo Sound, passes under a fixed bridge at the Overseas Highway in Key Largo. If your boat clears 14 feet safely, traverse the canal to dive or snorkel in John Pennekamp Coral Reef State Park.

Tarpon Basin

Enter Tarpon Basin through Dusenbury Creek or Grouper Creek. Both passages teem with snapper and grouper.

ℹ️ The Atlantic Intracoastal Waterway begins in Boston, Massachusetts, and ends in Key West, Florida. This 3,000-mile scenic and historic course takes you through man-made canals, bays protected by barrier reefs, natural river channels, and estuaries. It is used extensively by commercial and recreational boaters and "snowbirds" heading south for the winter.

Largo Sound (John Pennekamp Coral Reef State Park)

John Pennekamp Coral Reef State Park and the adjacent Key Largo National Marine Sanctuary encompass the ocean floor under Hawk Channel from Broad Creek to Molasses Reef. Exit the Intracoastal Waterway at Angelfish Creek and enter Hawk Channel to proceed to Largo Sound. Enter Largo Sound through South Sound Creek. Park staff supervise this anchorage, which is completely sheltered in any weather. Call on VHF channel 16 to reserve a mandatory mooring buoy in the southwest portion of the sound; anchoring is prohibited. A nominal fee for the moorings entitles boaters to full use of park facilities and its pump-out station.

The reefs of John Pennekamp Coral Reef State Park shine brighter than others in the Keys. The bulk of Key Largo's landmass has inhibited development of the erosive channels that cut between the other Keys, preserving shallower waters. More sun filters through the shallow water, causing the coral to flourish. Much of this reef breaks the surface of the water during low tide.

Butternut Key and Bottle Key

Don't worry. Those baby sharks you see in the waters surrounding Butternut Key won't hurt you. The skittish infants leave this nursery area when they reach 2 to 3 feet in length. Prevailing winds will determine anchorage sites near these islands, which offer good holding ground. On the Florida Bay side of Tavernier, Butternut Key and Bottle Key showcase voluminous birdlife. Roseate spoonbills breed on Bottle Key, feeding upon the tiny killifish of the flats. A pond on the island attracts mallard ducks in the winter. And amid this gunkholers' paradise, the elusive bald eagle rewards the patient observer with a fleeting appearance.

Cotton Key

Approach Cotton Key from the Intracoastal Waterway. This anchorage, protected from north to southeast winds, offers the best nightlife in the Keys north of Key West. Take your dinghy around the entire island of Upper Matecumbe and the community of Islamorada. Catch the action at the Lorelei or Atlantic's Edge at Cheeca Lodge (see the Restaurants chapter). Check out the fishing charters at Bud n' Mary's Marina (see the Fishing chapter). Stop in at the Islamorada Fish Company and take ready-to-eat stone crabs back to your boat for a private sunset celebration (see the Specialty Foods, Cafes, and Markets chapter). Dinghy through Whale Harbor Channel to the Islamorada Sand Bar, which at low tide becomes an island beach. And, if you'd just like to commune with nature, the forested northeast section of Upper Matecumbe Key hosts a rookery for good bird-watching. NOTE: There is a no-motor zone on the tidal flat.

Lignumvitae Key

Government-owned Lignumvitae Key stands among the tallest of the Keys, at 17 to 18 feet above sea level. A virgin hammock sprinkled with lignum vitae trees re-creates the feeling of the Keys of yesteryear, before mahogany forests were cut and sold to Bahamian ship-builders. From 1919 to 1953 the Matheson family, of chemical company notoriety, owned the island, where they built a large home and extensive gardens of rare plantings.

Hug the northwest side of the island for good anchorage in east to southeast winds.

Dinghy to the Lignumvitae Key dock for guided tours conducted by the state park service. You can also dinghy through Indian Key Channel to historic Indian Key (see the Attractions chapter). Nearby Shell Key almost disappears at high tide, so exercise caution. Pods of playful dolphins romp in Lignumvitae Basin, and a sighting of lumbering sea turtles is not unusual. But be sure to bait a hook—fishing is prolific.

Matecumbe Bight

If winds are not good for anchoring near Lignumvitae, Matecumbe Bight provides good holding ground, except in a north wind. Two miles south, Channel Five—east of Long Key—offers a good crossover between Florida Bay and Hawk Channel for large sailboats. Strong currents run in the channel beneath the bridge, which is a fixed span with a 65-foot overhead clearance.

Long Key Bight

Anchor in Long Key Bight, which is accessed via Hawk Channel oceanside or through Channel Five from the Intracoastal Waterway. Bordering Long Key State Park—a 300-acre wilderness area with a good campground, tables, and grills—the Bight is protected yet open. Dinghy through Zane Grey Creek for good gunkholing. Legendary author Zane Grey angled at the former Long Key Fishing Club during the days of Flagler's Railroad. Beachcomb for washed-up treasure on the southeast shores of Long Key.

Boot Key Harbor

Boot Key Harbor in Marathon serves as a good, safe port in a bad blow, but, crowded with live-aboards, it is a bit like anchoring out in Times Square. Enter this fully protected harbor from Sister's Creek or at the western entrance near the beginning of the Seven Mile Bridge.

NOTE: Moser Channel goes under the hump of the Seven Mile Bridge, creating a 65-foot clearance. The draw-span of the old bridge has been removed, but the rest remains. A portion on the Marathon end now functions as the driveway to Pigeon Key (see the Attractions chapter). A stretch on the Bahia Honda end is maintained for bridge fishing and is referred to locally as the "longest fishing pier in the world." The Moser Channel and the Bahia Honda Channel (with 20-foot clearance) are the last crossover spots in the Keys. You must decide at Marathon if you will travel the Atlantic route or via the gulf to Key West. If you need fuel, note that the marina at Sunshine Key is the last bayside marina until Key West.

Big Spanish Channel Area

Leave all traces of civilization behind and head out the Big Spanish Channel toward the out-islands. Proceed with care, for this remote sprinkling of tiny keys is part of the Great White Heron National Wildlife Refuge. Before venturing into this backcountry area, secure a Public Use Regulations Map from the Lower Keys Chamber of Commerce (305-872-2411, 800-872-3722). Obey no-entry, no-motor, and idle-speed zones. Get your Florida bird guide out of the cabin and count the species. Then treat yourself to a swim with the dolphins, which travel in pods throughout these gulf waters.

ℹ️ Before venturing into the Great White Heron National Wildlife Refuge, secure a Public Use Regulations Map from the Lower Keys Chamber of Commerce, MM 31 Oceanside, Big Pine Key, (305) 872-2411.

Little Spanish Key

The western side of Little Spanish Key provides the best protection from northeast to southeast winds. Explore the surrounding clear waters by dinghy where the endangered green turtles, which weigh between 150 and 450 pounds, have been spotted feeding on sea grass. Catch your limit in snapper and share your bounty with the friendly pelicans.

Newfound Harbor

Newfound Harbor—formed by the Newfound Harbor Keys and the southern extension of Big Pine Key—stars as the premier oceanside harbor between Marathon and Key West. Dinghy to exquisite Little Palm Island, the setting for the film *PT-109*, the story of John F. Kennedy's Pacific experience during World War II. Newfound Harbor lies within easy reach of Looe Key National Marine Sanctuary, a spur and groove coral reef ecosystem popular with divers and snorkelers.

KEY WEST AND BEYOND

Welcome to the ultimate cruising destination: Key West. Full of history and histrionics, this vibrant, intoxicating port pumps the adrenaline, pushes the envelope, and provides a rowdy good time for all. And when you signal a turn back into the slow lane again, dust off your charts and head out to the wild beyond of the Dry Tortugas, the end of the line.

Marinas

All of our suggested marinas take transient boaters, but the multiplicity of celebrated special events in Key West dictates that you prudently reserve a slip as far in advance as possible. You may assume unless otherwise stated that all our recommended marinas supply hookups for both 30-amp and 50-amp service as well as fresh water. Some marinas impose a minimum charge. Key West offers extensive self-provisioning facilities ranging from supermarkets to gourmet take-out shops (see the Specialty Foods, Cafes, and Markets chapter). The city also supports a variety of good marine mechanics, which the marina dockmasters will contact on your behalf should the need arise. Contact the dockmaster on VHF channel 16 for directions and read your charts closely.

A&B MARINA
700 Front St.
(305) 294-2535 or (800) 223-8352
www.aandbmarina.com
A&B Marina is situated in the heart of Old Town, right in the middle of all the action. Most of its 50 transient slips will accommodate vessels with up to 7-foot drafts. A&B offers dockage for vessels up to 140 feet in length. Cable television hookup is included in dockage fees. A&B maintains a diesel fuel dock.

A&B has a convenience store, air-conditioned shower facilities, a laundry room, a 24-hour (10 months of the year) bar and grill, and the Commodore Waterfront Steakhouse and Alonzo's Oyster Bar. A&B Lobster House, upstairs, has been feeding hungry cruisers since 1947 and still welcomes one and all. And people-watching is great from the dockside bar.

A&B Marina is accessed from the Atlantic via the Main Ship Channel (S.E. Channel), at Markers Nos. 24 and 25. From the gulf take the N.W. Channel to the Main Ship Channel.

THE GALLEON RESORT AND MARINA
619 Front St.
(305) 296-7711 or (800) 544-3030
www.galleonresort.com

Cruisers love the Galleon, probably the most popular of Key West's marinas. The carbonated excitement of Duval Street pulsates only a few blocks away, but the ambience at the Galleon remains unhurried and genteel. The 91 dockage slips will accommodate vessels up to 140 feet, 9-foot drafts. One 50-amp service is included in the daily dockage rate, but you can secure another for an additional fee. Cable and telephone hookups are available for a minimal charge. Fuel is available in Key West Bight or at Conch Harbor Marina.

The Galleon indulges you with all the amenities and then some: shower and restroom facilities, a laundry, pump-out station, deli, swimming pool, tiki bar, private beach, fitness center, sauna, patio, and picnic tables. And if that is not enough, book an afternoon of snorkeling at the on-premises dive shop or plan a fishing expedition with one of the charter boats at the dock. Rent a moped or bicycle and explore Key West, or just kick back and relax on the sundeck. Pets are welcome in the marina but not on the adjoining resort property. The Galleon is accessed via the Main Ship Channel at Marker No. 24.

KEY WEST BIGHT MARINA
Key West Historic Seaport
201 William St.
(305) 809-3983
www.keywestcity.com

Situated in the heart of the Key West Historic Seaport, Key West Bight Marina has 33 deepwater transient slips that will accommodate vessels up to 140 feet in length with a maximum draft of 12 feet. Dockage includes 30-, 50-, and 100-amp power; cable TV, water, and phone hookups; 24-hour security; a pump-out station; trash removal; ice; and bath, shower, and laundry facilities. Docking rates are the most reasonably priced in Key West. Key West Bight Marina is accessed by entering Key West waters via the N.W. Channel to the Main Ship Channel to Marker Red No. 4 from the Gulf of Mexico, or from the Atlantic via Hawk Channel to the Main Ship Channel to Marker Red No. 4.

KING'S POINTE MARINA
5950 Peninsula Ave., Stock Island
(305) 294-4676
www.cortexcompanies.com

This top-drawer marina, occupying a finger of Stock Island, offers a Key West alternative for peace and solitude, for it is tucked far away from the fray. Its slips will accommodate vessels up to 80 feet in length with 12-foot maximum drafts. Access to the marina is directly from Hawk Channel. Reservations are suggested 30 days in advance during the winter season. Gas- and diesel-qualified marine mechanics work on the premises. King's Pointe provides all the essentials: gas and diesel fuel dock, ship's store and tackle shop, laundry, showers and restrooms, and free cable hookups. An additional charge is levied for telephone hookup. Your pet is welcome if kept on a leash.

King's Pointe Marina is accessed via the Atlantic at the entrance to Safe Harbor Channel, Marker Red No. 2.

THE WESTIN KEY WEST RESORT AND MARINA

245 Front St.
(305) 294-4000 or (866) 837-4250
www.westinkeywestresort.com

The Westin Key West Resort and Marina offers transients all the perks of its lavish property: pool, hot tub, and weight room as well as Bistro 245 restaurant and Latitudes restaurant on Sunset Key. About one-quarter of the marina's dock space is available to transients. The south basin offers floating slips that accommodate vessels with 30-foot drafts; the north basin's 600 feet of rigid dock space handles craft with 15-foot drafts or less.

Make reservations up to six months in advance to dock at the Westin Key West Resort and Marina. Only 1 block off famed Duval Street, its location can't be beat and it fills up quickly. In addition to daily transient rates, a power fee is levied. Cable television hookup is included in the dockage fee, and the requisite laundry, shower, and restroom requirements are supplied on the premises. Fuel may be obtained half a mile up the channel at Key West Bight.

The Westin Key West Resort and Marina owns the private offshore Sunset Key. Guests of the hotel or marina may take a day trip to the island and enjoy its pristine beach, away from the fray of Key West.

The Westin Key West Marina is accessed via the Main Ship Channel at Marker Red No. 14 if coming from the south, or, from the north, via the N.W. Channel at Marker Green No. 17.

Anchoring Out

The highway may stop in Key West, but the path to adventure continues into the sunset.

The Dry Tortugas, the brightest gems in the necklace, mark the real end of the line in the Florida Keys. Once you leave Key West Harbor, you join the ranks of the swashbucklers who have abandoned the safety of civilization to explore the vast unknown.

Be sure you know the range and capabilities of your craft, because only self-sufficient cruising vessels can make the 140-nautical-mile trek to the Dry Tortugas and back. There is no fuel, fresh water, provisioning, or facilities of any kind once you leave Key West. Unpredictable foul weather could keep you trapped at sea for days, so make sure you are fueled for 200 miles, and stock the larder for extenuating circumstances.

Key West

If you want to anchor out in busy Key West Harbor, look for a spot west of Fleming Key in about 10 to 15 feet of water. You'll find less current, good holding ground, and less fishing-vessel traffic than around Wisteria Island. The municipal dinghy dock at the foot of Simonton Street is the only official place to land your dinghy, but you might want to arrange secured short-term dockage for your dinghy from one of the marina dockmasters.

Boca Grande Key

A string of shoals and keys snakes west from Key West, offering unparalleled diving and fishing opportunities. Beyond Man and Woman Keys—popular snorkeling spots—Boca Grande Key offers a good day anchorage on the northwestern side with a beautiful white-sand beach. The current is too swift to anchor overnight, but snorkel the small wreck visible just north of the island. Be alert to the constantly shifting shoals around the entrance channel. Note also that this

Close-up

Lighthouses of the Florida Keys

Nostalgic memories are aroused when you think of lighthouses. Rugged, isolated, beautiful in strength and haunting in their history, these beacons of light hold anyone's imagination if you are interested in sea navigation. General George Gordon Meade's first career may have been a commander of Union forces but his interest and real love was in pharology. His genius in marine engineering led him to Delaware Bay and the building of lighthouses along that body of water. Known for his screwpile design in lighthouses, most of his structures remain standing today. Meade came to the Florida Keys where he designed and built Carysfort, Sombrero, Rebecca, and Sand Key Lighthouses. To end his dignified career, he went on to design the beautiful Fairmount Park in Philadelphia.

Carysfort Reef Lighthouse: Placed on the National Register of Historical Places in 1984, this red lighthouse was built in 1825 and first lit in 1852. Carysfort is the oldest iron screwpile lighthouse still functioning in the U.S. and the first type in the Florida Keys. Named for the HMS *Carysfort* which ran into the reef in 1770, automated in 1960, it stands at 112 feet and is shaped in a skeletal octagonal pyramid.

Alligator Reef Lighthouse: This still functioning lighthouse was built in 1873 and sits 4 miles east of Indian Key off Islamorada. Automated in 1963, this old beauty is an iron pile with a platform and painted white and black. The height is 136 feet and is skeletal in its shape.

Sombrero Key Lighthouse: Built in 1858 in the skeletal octagonal pyramidal design, brown in color, automated in 1960, Sombrero still helps boats navigate the waters off Marathon. Not open to the public, this 160-foot lighthouse is operated by the U.S. Coast Guard.

American Shoal Lighthouse: Built in 1880, it sits in the Atlantic off Sugarloaf Key. This brown-and-white sentinel was automated in 1963. It reaches a height of 103 feet and was constructed in the skeletal octagonal pyramidal shape.

Key West Lighthouse: Located at 938 Whitehead Street in historic Old Town, this 86-foot black-and-white structure is a real gem. Built in 1847 for the purpose of help-

---

island is a turtle nesting ground—all or parts of it are off-limits during specific times of the year, and fines are possible.

Marquesas Keys

About 24 miles from Key West, a broken collar of low-lying, beach-belted islands forms the Marquesas Keys. If you pass Mooney Harbor Key on your way into the inner sanctum, watch for coral heads about 1,100 yards offshore. Prevailing winds will determine at which side to anchor, but you should be able

to achieve a protected anchorage. Many a ship crashed on the coral heads in this area, leaving interesting wrecks, but check with the Coast Guard before you dive, because the U.S. Navy has been known to use the area west of the Marquesas as a bombing and strafing range. Explore the big rookery of frigatebirds or take aim with a little spearfishing. This pit stop on the way to the Dry Tortugas rates as an end point in itself. NOTE: A 300-foot no-motor zone is established around the three smallest islands, a ing ships navigate the perilous reefs off the lower Keys, it was listed on the National Register of Historical Places in 1998. It was automated in 1915, then deactivated in 1969. Built in the West Indian vernacular style, it now is open as a museum and operated by the Monroe County and City of Key West Historical Society.

Loggerhead Key Lighthouse: Used as an active aid for navigating the Dry Tortugas National Park off Key West, this black-and-white structure was built in 1858 and was automated in 1988. Standing 157 feet, this lighthouse is operated by the National Park Service and is open to the public.

Tortugas Harbor Lighthouse: In Garden Key, off Key West, operated by the National Park Service, proudly stands this hexagonal shaped black beauty that is open to the public. Built in 1876, activated in 1912 and deactivated in 1921, this lighthouse sits in the Fort Jefferson Dry Tortugas National Park and is only accessible by boat or seaplane.

Sand Key Lighthouse: Seven miles southwest off Key West, this lighthouse with its red and black colors stands 120 feet out of the water. Built in 1826, automated in 1938, and deactivated from 1989 to 1998, it's not open to the public. Built in the square skeletal with center column design, it is listed on the National Register of Historical Places.

Rebecca Shoal Lighthouse: The original skeletal iron structure was assembled in Key West, disassembled, then erected onsite in 1886. This structure was named after the lighthouse keeper Rebecca Flaherty and her five children, who were killed in the 1836 hurricane. Forty-three miles off Key West, where the Gulf of Mexico and the Atlantic meet, this is the most remote of all the lighthouses on our list. Totally destroyed by the August 2004 Hurricane Charlie, all that remains today is a small beacon with an effective beam range seen 9 miles away. You pass this marker on the way to the Dry Tortugas.

The Florida Keys have plenty of lighthouses to help navigate your boat safely. Most are owned and operated by the U.S. Coast Guard and some are open to the public. Go to www.lighthousestovisit.com to see which ones they are.

300-foot no-access buffer zone is established around one mangrove island, and an idle-speed-only/no-wake zone is established in the southwest tidal creek.

Dry Tortugas

Open water stretches like a hallucination from the Marquesas to our southernmost national park, the Dry Tortugas. Ponce de León named these islands the Tortugas—Spanish for "turtles"—in 1513, presumably because the waters teemed with sea turtles, which he consumed as fresh meat. Lack of fresh water rendered the islands dry.

The first sight of the massive brick fortress of Fort Jefferson, the colorful history of which began in 1846, is breathtaking (see the Attractions chapter).

Unparalleled diving exists in these unsullied waters. Colors appear more brilliant because the waters are clearer than those bordering the inhabited Keys. The entire area is a no-take zone, so don't be alarmed if you spot a prehistoric-size lobster or jewfish. Be sure to snorkel the underwater nature trail. From your dinghy, watch for the nesting sooty and noddy terns in their Bush Key sanctuary (landing is forbidden).

In 2007 federal regulation went into effect establishing a 46-square-mile Research Natural Area (RNA) in Dry Tortugas National Park. Fishing and anchoring are strictly prohibited in this RNA; boaters are allowed to anchor during daylight hours on sand bottoms until mooring buoys are in place. Overnight anchoring can only occur on sand bottoms within 1 nautical mile of the Harbor Light at Fort Jefferson. Combined with the Tortugas Ecological Reserve and now the RNA, this is the largest no-take marine reserve in the continental United States. The popular fishing area in the Dry Tortugas—the anchorage around Fort Jefferson and Garden Key—will remain open for recreational fishing.

Loggerhead Key

Just beyond Garden Key dozes Loggerhead Key, called the prettiest beach in the Keys by those in the know. A good day anchorage with a legion of interesting coral, this is literally the end of the line for the Florida Keys. Nothing but 900 miles of water lies between this point and the Mexican coast. Hope you remembered to fuel up in Key West!

FISHING

A ngling in the Florida Keys approaches a religion to many. The very essence of the Keys is embodied in gleaming packages of skin and scales, for a day fishing the cerulean waters that lap our islands creates a sensory memory not quickly forgotten. Long after the last bait is cast, tales of captured prizes or the ones that got away evoke visions of the sun, the sea, and the smell of the salt air.

Anglers fish here with an intensity rarely seen anywhere else in the United States . . . the world, even. Eavesdrop on a conversation anywhere in the Keys, and someone will be talking about fishing. As you drive down the Overseas Highway and look out at our acres of shimmering waters, you will feel an overwhelming urge to join in the battle of power and wits—fish against angler—that makes the Keys so special.

The Florida Keys have more than 1,000 species of fish; most are edible, all are interesting. Six of them—bonefish, permit, tarpon, redfish, snook, and sailfish—have earned game-fish status, meaning they may not be sold. To pursue these and other species, you will need a saltwater fishing license (see the Fishing Licenses section in this chapter). You must obey catch and season restrictions and size limits. These regulations change often. Ask for an up-to-date listing when you purchase your fishing license.

The Florida Keys falls within the boundaries of the Florida Keys National Marine Sanctuary, created by the federal government in 1990 to protect the resources of our marine ecosystem. And while, for the most part, visitors freely swim, dive, snorkel, boat, fish, or recreate on our waters, some regulations took effect in July 1997 to guide these activities. Refer to the Boating chapter for information on these regulations before you venture into our waters. For a complete copy of the regulations and marine coordinates of the areas, contact the sanctuary office, (305) 743-2437, or check their Web site, www.floridakeys.noaa.gov.

CATCH-AND-RELEASE ETHICS

Preserve our natural resources. "A fish is too valuable to be caught only once," the U.S. Department of Commerce, the National Oceanic and Atmospheric Administration, and the National Marine Fisheries Service maintain. We agree. The spirit behind the catch-and-release policy is to enjoy the hunt and the score, but take a photograph of the fish home with you, not the quarry itself. Taxidermists do not need the actual fish to prepare a mount for you; they only need the approximate measurements. Take home only those food fish you plan to eat.

To properly release a fish, keep the fish in the water and handle it very little whenever possible. Dislodge the hook quickly with a hookout tool, backing the hook out the opposite way it went in. If the hook can't be removed quickly, cut the leader close to the mouth. Hold the fish by the bottom jaw or lip—not the gills—with a wet hand or glove so that you don't damage its mucus or scales. Have your photo taken with the fish, then cradle the tired fish, rocking it back and forth in the water until it is able to swim away under its own power. This increases the oxygen flow through its gills, reviving the fish and thereby augmenting its chances for survival against a barracuda or shark.

WHERE TO FISH

To introduce you to our complex watery ecosystem and the species of fish dwelling therein, we have divided fishing destinations into four distinct sections: the flats, the backcountry, the bluewater, and the bridges.

The Flats

The continental shelf is nature's gift to the Florida Keys. Stretching from the shoreline like a layer of rippled fudge on a marble slab, it lingers for many shallow miles before plunging to the depths of the bluewater. In the Keys we rather reverently call this area the flats. Waters ranging from mere inches to several feet in depth cover most of the flats, but some areas completely surface during low tide, exposing themselves to the air and intense sunlight. Changing winds, tides, temperatures, and barometric pressure ensure that conditions in the flats fluctuate constantly.

An unenlightened observer might think the flats uninteresting, for most of this watery acreage is covered with dense turtle grass, shell-less sand, or muddy muck. But far from being a wasteland, the flats are the **feeding grounds** and **nursery** for a city of marine families whose members inspire dramatic tales of daring and conquest from every person who has ever baited a hook here.

The **4,000 square miles** of flats—from Key Biscayne to Key West and beyond—yield a trio of prize game fish—**bonefish, permit, and tarpon**—which, when caught in one day, we refer to as the **Grand Slam.** And keeping company in the same habitat are the bonus fish—**barracuda** and **shark**—that regularly accommodate anglers with exciting runs and fights. Fishing the flats is really a combination of angling and hunting, for you must first see and stalk the fish before you ever cast the waters. The hunt for bonefish, permit, and tarpon requires patience and unique angling skills, but most essentially, you must be at the right place at the right time.

We cannot even begin to teach you how to fish for these formidable fighters of the flats in this chapter. You should hire a **professional guide,** for which there is no substitute—at least while you are a novice. Guides know the local waters well and keep detailed records of where to find fish under every condition, saving you precious hours and money in the pursuit of your mission (see the Guides and Charters section of this chapter). But we will introduce you to the exciting species you will encounter on our flats, relate their personalities, tattle about their habits, and point you in the right direction so you can learn all you wish to know and share in the angling experience of a lifetime: fishing the flats in the Florida Keys.

First in the **see-stalk-cast** sequence so important in fishing the skinny waters of the flats is the visible interpretation of the watery hallucination under the surface. To see the fish of the flats, you must have polarized sunglasses to cut the sun's glare so that you can concentrate on looking through your reflection on the top of the water, to the shallow bottom. Under the water, fish often look like **bluish shadows,** or they may appear as **indistinct shadings** that simply look different from the waters surrounding them.

Most waters of the flats in the Keys are fished from a **shallow-draft skiff,** or **flatsboat,** although you can wade out from shore in many areas if you prefer. Never motor onto a flat; the fish can hear the engine noise and spook easily. Use an electric trolling motor or, better yet, **pole in,** using a push pole. A push pole is a fiberglass or graphite dowel, 16 to 20 feet long with a V-crotch on one end, for traversing the soft bottom of the flats and a straight end on the other, for staking out. Using it requires body power and coordination and more than a little practice. A flatsboat has a raised poling platform that gives the poler or guide a height advantage to more readily distinguish the fish from its shadowy surroundings, in preparation for an accurate cast.

i In April 2008, former President George H. W. Bush landed a monster 130-pound tarpon in Lignumvitae Channel off Islamorada. After a 45-minute fight with this trophy catch, he tagged the fish and released it back into the wild.

At the turn of the tide, the fish begin to move into the flats, grazing like sheep in a pasture. Guides know where the fish congregate during an incoming (flood) tide and an outgoing (ebb) tide. While it may prove dangerous for the fish to come up on the flats—they expose themselves to predators—the concentration of food is too enticing for them to resist. The fish prefer feeding during the low, incoming tide; the food is still easy to find, but they won't risk becoming stranded on the flats.

Bonefish: Phantom of the Flats

A sighting of the glistening forked tail of the **Gray Ghost**—alias of the famed **bonefish** (*Albula vulpes*) haunting our flats—has been known to elevate the blood pressure of even the most seasoned Keys angler to celestial heights. This much-respected, skittish silver bullet is considered the worthiest of all opponents, a wily, suspicious street fighter, here one moment, gone the next. The bonefish's **superior eyesight, acute hearing, keen sense of smell,** and **boundless speed** routinely befuddle anglers, some of whom dedicate their lives to thwarting the fish's Houdini-like escape attempts.

You can spot a bonefish three ways: **tailing, mudding,** or **cruising.** When the slender, silvery bonefish feeds, it looks like a washerwoman leaning over to get her laundry out of the basket—head down, bottom up. The fork of the tail will break the surface of the water—a tailing fish. The bonefish feeds into the current because its food source is delivered in the drift. As the fish puts its mouth down into the sand and silt, rooting around on the bottom of the flats, looking for shrimps, crabs, and other crustaceans, the water clouds up. This is called **"making a mud."** As the mudding bonefish continues feeding, the current takes the cloudy water away so it can see its prey once again. Bonefish require water temperatures of 70 degrees and higher for feeding on the flats.

Spotting a cruising fish takes some practice. Look for **"nervous water."** The bonefish pushes a head wake as it swims, which sometimes shows as an inconsistency on the surface of the water. On other occasions, a mere movement by the fish under water will cause the surface water to appear altered. Most of the time that the bonefish is cruising, however, it is swimming in deeper water; you will have to spot it. The back and sides of the bonefish are so silvery they act as a mirror. The fish swims right on the bottom of the flats in 8 or more inches of water. The sun shining through the water causes the bottom to reflect off the sides of the fish. So if you think you have seen a ripple of weeds, the image may actually be a bonefish.

The best **bait** for bonefishing is **live shrimp.** A guide with an experienced eye will put you on the fish by calling out directions like the hands of a clock. The bow of the boat will always be 12 o'clock. You will be instructed by the guide to look in a direction—for instance, 2 o'clock—and, at a specified distance, to spot the bonefish in preparation for a cast. The **cast** is the most crucial part of successfully hooking a bonefish. You should be able to cast 30 feet quickly and accurately. A cast that places the bait too close to the fish will spook it and cause the bonefish to dart away at breakneck speed. If the bait is cast too far away, the fish won't find it at all. The bait should land 2 to 3 feet in front of the fish and be allowed to drift to the ocean floor.

Many times the bonefish will smell the bait prior to seeing it because the fish is downcurrent of the bait and swimming into the current. The bonefish begins to dart back and forth and goes in circles, looking for the scented prey. Once the fish locates the source of the scent, it tends to suck in the bait. You, the angler, must make sure there is **no slack** in the line and that your **rod tip** is low to the water. Then firmly but gently lift up to **set the hook.** Hold on tight and

raise your rod straight up in the air, holding your arms as high above your head as possible. Once the fish realizes something is wrong—that it's hooked—it will peel away in an electrifying run, taking out 100 to 150 yards of line in a heartbeat. This whole process—from sighting to hooking—explodes in adrenaline-pumping nanoseconds. Ten to 30 minutes later, after the bonefish makes several pulse-pounding sprints, you can reel in the tired fish to the side of the skiff, where the guide will photograph both victor and spoils. Then quickly **release** the bonefish so that it may rest up and thrill another angler on yet another day (see the previous section in this chapter on Catch-and-Release Ethics).

i Please watch for manatees in the waters of the Florida Keys. If you see one of these gentle creatures and it appears to be injured, call (800) DIAL-FMP, *FMP, or use VHF channel 16. Stay in deep water and avoid running your motor over sea-grass beds. Obey speed zone and sanctuary signs. Look, but don't touch; please do not feed or give the manatees water. For more information, visit www.savethemanatee.org.

Bonefishing is a major playing card of the fishing deck we so lavishly deal here in the Florida Keys. Bonefish usually range in size from **5 to 10 pounds,** but the size of this fish belies its strength. A 5-pound bonefish fights like a 20-pound wannabe. The Keys are the only place in the continental United States where an angler can fish for bonefish. Locals boast that the Keys have the biggest and best-educated bonefish this side of the Gulf Stream. Expect bonefish to grace our flats during Apr, May, June, Sept, Oct, and occasionally into Nov. Cool weather and cold fronts push them into deeper waters from Dec through Mar. The hot weather of July and Aug drives them to cooler, deeper waters as well, although some will stay all year.

Permit: Ultimate Flats Challenge

Though sharing the same waters as the bonefish and stalked in the same manner, the **permit** (*Trachinotus falcatus*) proves to be a more elusive catch. **Spooky, skittish, and stubborn,** this **finicky eater,** which can take out line like a **long-distance runner,** is so difficult to catch that most anglers never even see one. Three or four times the size of a bonefish—averaging **20 to 30 pounds**— the silvery, platter-shaped permit forages in the safety of slightly deeper waters, not risking exposure of its iridescent blue-green back. Its sickle-shaped, black-tipped tail pokes out of the water as it feeds on bottom-dwelling crabs and shrimps, often tipping off its location. The permit's shell-crushing jaws, rubbery and strong, can exert 3,000 pounds of pressure per square inch, enabling it to masticate small clams and crustaceans and dash many an angler's expectations.

The permit will **tail** or **mud** like a bonefish. In fact, both fish have been known to rub their snouts so raw from repeatedly rooting around in the mud, looking for food, that they caricature W. C. Fields. But unlike a bonefish, the permit is often spotted lazily cruising near the surface of the water. Many times its wispy black dorsal fin will break the water, looking like a drifting piece of weed.

The best days to find permit are those glorious, cloudless sunny smiles from Mother Nature, cooled by a slight ocean breeze. Schools of permit will graze the top of the flats and near rocky shorelines in higher tides and poke around in basins and channels during low tides, searching for a meal of small crabs and crustaceans. They often hover above submerged objects such as lobster pots. If you pass above an area littered with sea urchins, be on the lookout for permit searching for gourmet fixings.

Not easily duped, a tailing permit will make you forget all about a bonefish because, if you manage to hook one, you've got a street brawl on your hands that could last an hour or more. When hooked, the permit instinctively heads for deeper water. In the transition zone between the flats and the bluewater, the permit will try to cut the line by weaving through coral heads, sea fans, and sponges. The fish will pause in its run to bang its head on the bottom or rub its mouth in the sand to try to dislodge the hook. If you manage to follow the permit through this obstacle course, you may actually catch it a quarter mile from where you hooked it.

Tarpon: The Silver King

It is little wonder that the **tarpon** (*Megalops atlanticus*) is dubbed the **"silver king,"** for it wins 9 out of every 10 encounters with an angler. The tarpon's lunglike gas bladder allows it to take a gulp of atmospheric air from time to time, enabling the fish to thrive in oxygen-depleted water. This magnificent superhero of the sea, ranging in size from **50 to 200 pounds,** will break the surface and **"roll"** with a silvery splash as it steals an oxygen jolt and powers on for an intensified fight. The tarpon frequents the **deeper flats** of 4 to 8 feet or hangs out in the rapidly moving waters of channels, or under one of the many bridges in the Keys. Live mullet, pinfish, and crabs will entice this **hungry but lazy** despot, which faces into the current, effortlessly waiting for baitfish to be dragged into its mouth. The tarpon's toothless lower jaw protrudes from its head like an overdeveloped underbite, filled with bony plate that crushes its intended dinner.

The successful angler will use **heavy tackle** and a **needle-sharp hook.** Hold the rod with the tip at 12 o'clock and wait. When the fish strikes and eats the bait, let the **rod tip drop** with the pressure, giving minimal resistance. When the rod is parallel to the water and the line is tight, **set the hook** through the bony structure with a series of short, very strong jabs. Once hooked, the stunned fish **runs** and **leaps** repeatedly, with reckless abandon, entering the water headfirst, tail-first, sideways, belly-flopped, or upside down, an Olympian confounding its rod-clutching judge. It is important to have a **quick-release anchor** when fishing for tarpon because, once the action starts, you must be on your way, chasing the cavorting fish. Be prepared to duke it out, for it is often a standoff as to who tires first, the angler or the tarpon.

Exciting to catch on light tackle is the schooling baby tarpon, which, at up to 50 pounds, sprints and practices its aerobatics like its older siblings. Look for baby tarpon in channels and in harbors.

Tarpon season generally begins in Apr and continues until mid-July. Because the tarpon is primarily a **nocturnal feeder,** the best fishing is at daybreak and dusk or during the night.

This magnificent creature grows very slowly, not reaching maturity until it is at least 13 years old. Since the tarpon is **not an edible fish,** some people consider killing it akin to murder.

If you want a simulated mount of your catch, take an estimate of the length and girth for the taxidermist, take a photograph

with your prize, and release the fish quickly and carefully.

Barracuda: Tiger of the Flats

Look for the **barracuda** (*Sphyraena barracuda*), which packs a wallop of a fight, anywhere the water is about 2 feet deep, especially grassy-bottom areas. This **toothy, intelligent** predator has **keen eyesight** and moves swiftly. The barracuda's inquisitive nature causes it to make investigative passes by your boat, where it is oft tempted to sample your baited offerings intended for other species. Pilchards make good bait for catching barracuda. Cut off part of the tail fin of a pilchard before baiting the hook. This injury causes the bait to swim erratically, attracting the insatiable 'cuda. When casting to a barracuda, your bait should land at least 10 feet beyond the fish and be retrieved across its line of sight. A cast that lands the bait too close—5 feet or less—will frighten the 'cuda into deep water. If you are using artificial baits such as a tube lure, be sure to retrieve the bait briskly to pique the barracuda's interest.

Humans eat barracuda in some tropical areas, but not in the Keys. The flesh is sometimes toxic, and it is not worth the risk. You are better off quickly **releasing** the fish so that it might fight another round.

Sharks

Several **shark** species (order *Selachii*) roam our flats looking for a free meal. **Sand sharks** and **nurse sharks** are relatively docile, but **bonnetheads** and **black-tip** sharks readily will take a shrimp or crab intended for a bonefish or permit, putting up a determined fight. If you happen to catch a shark, wear **heavy gloves** and cut the leader with **pliers.** The shark will swim away and will be able to work the hook loose from its mouth. Digestive acids and saltwater will corrode the hook in mere days, causing the fish no permanent harm.

The Backcountry

When Mother Nature bestowed the prolific oceanside saltwater flats on the Florida Keys, she didn't stop at our rocky isles. As the Gulf of Mexico meets mainland Florida, a lively ecosystem flourishes in a body of water known as **Florida Bay.** Hundreds of tiny uninhabited keys dot the watery landscape, referred to locally as the backcountry. Loosely bordered by the Keys—from Key Largo to Long Key—and Everglades National Park, backcountry waters offer a diverse habitat of **sea grass** or **mudflats, mangrove islets,** and **sandy basins.** The southernmost outpost of the Everglades National Park is at **Flamingo,** which maintains a marina, boat rentals, houseboats, and guide services.

You'll usually be able to find **snappers, sheepshead, ladyfish,** and the occasional **shark** along the grass-bed shorelines, the open bays, and in the small creeks flowing out of the Everglades. And the silver king, the mighty **tarpon,** frequents backcountry creeks and channels, flats, and basins and is rumored to be particularly partial to the **Sandy Key Basin** in the summer months. But beckoning anglers to these waters is another sporting trio—**redfish, snook,** and **spotted sea trout**—which when caught in one day is boasted far and wide as the Backcountry Grand Slam.

Redfish, aka Red Drum

The coppery **redfish,** or red drum (*Sciaenops oceallatus*), all but disappeared in the 1980s from overfishing, but conservation measures by the state of Florida and the federal government caused a rebirth. This fast-growing fish migrates offshore to spawn when it reaches about **30 inches** (four years). It is a protected species in federal waters. Regulations open a scant 9-inch window for anglers to keep one captured redfish per day, which must measure between 18 and 27 inches. All redfish measuring less than 18 inches or more than 27 inches must be released, always. Because it grows so rapidly, the redfish is exposed to harvest for only one year of its life.

As with fishing for bonefish or permit, you will look for redfish on an incoming tide, when they will be rooting for crabs on the shoals and flats. As the water gets higher, the fish work their way up on the flats. You will want to use a **shallow-draft boat** with a **push pole** or **electric trolling motor** and be prepared with **polarized sunglasses** for enhanced vision in spotting a tailing fish. You'll hear experienced anglers say, "**A tailing red is a feeding red.**" The reddish, squared-off profile of the redfish's tail can be spotted from several hundred feet. When the fish is really hungry, you may see its entire tail exposed, even the shady eyelike spot at the base. Cruising redfish will push a head wake similar to that of a bonefish.

Although a redfish isn't nearly as easily spooked as a bonefish, you should still stay as far away from the fish as possible while still casting a right-on winner. Live shrimps or crabs will entice the fish, which, with **poor eyesight,** hits almost any bait coming its way. The hooked redfish often sticks around and puts up a **hard fight.** Attracted to its discomfort, other redfish swim to the scene of the accident. You can often catch another redfish if you can get another baited hook into the water fast enough. The redfish is highly coveted for eating, put on the culinary map by New Orleans's Chef Prudhomme and his famed Cajun blackening process.

The backcountry of the Florida Keys is one of the few places in the world where you can fish for redfish year-round, although they prefer cooler waters. It is illegal, however, to buy or sell our native redfish, and they must be kept whole until you reach shore. You are forbidden to gig, spear, or snatch the red drum.

Snook

The second member of the Backcountry Grand Slam, the **snook** (*Centropomus undecimalis*) likes to tuck against the shady mangrove shorelines to feed on baitfish that congregate in the maze of gnarled roots. A falling tide will force the baitfish out of their rooted cages and into deeper holes where the snook can get at them. But the baitfish aren't the only ones getting snookered. This cagey, sought-after game fish, once hooked, has buffaloed many an angler, vanishing back into the mangroves and snapping its tenuous connection to the rod-wielder like a brittle string. If you win the battle of the bushes or find the snook pushing water in the open or at the mouth of a creek, you still haven't won the war. Once hooked, the snook thrashes about violently, trying to dislodge the barbed intruder. Its hard, **abrasive mouth** and **knife-sharp gill covers** can dispense with your line in a flash.

This silvery, **long-bodied** fish—thickened around the middle—faces its foes with a depressed snout and a protruding lower jaw. A distinctive lateral, black racing stripe extends the length of its body, all the way to its divided dorsal fin. The snook is unable to tolerate waters colder than 60 degrees. And while some anglers feel snook is the **best-tasting** fish in the Keys, Florida law

mandates that in Monroe County you may not fish for snook from Dec 15 through Jan 31, nor in the months of May, June, July, and Aug. The fish must measure between 26 inches and 34 inches. Limits are one snook per person, per day. Snook may not be bought or sold, and you must purchase a $2 snook stamp for your saltwater fishing license in order to fish for them.

Spotted Sea Trout, aka Spotted Weakfish

Even though this backcountry prize is called a **weakfish,** it can be a challenging catch. The weakfish moniker derives from its clan's easily torn mouth membranes. The **spotted sea trout** (*Cynoscion nebulosus*)—actually a member of the fine-flavored drum family—nevertheless resembles a trout, with shimmering iridescent tones of silver, green, blue, and bronze.

The sea trout's lower jaw, unlike a true trout's, projects upward, and a pair of good-size canine teeth protrude from the upper jaw. These predatory, **opportunistic feeders** enjoy a smorgasbord of offerings but are particularly fond of live shrimp. The sea trout makes a distinctive **splash** and **popping sound** when it feeds on a drift of shrimp. These weakfish are easily spotted in the shallow backcountry waters, popular with **light-tackle** enthusiasts who enjoy the stalk-and-cast challenge.

Sea trout prefer temperatures between 60 and 70 degrees. Each must measure at least 12 inches to be fished, and the catch is limited to four fish per person, per day. They are highly ranked as a table food because they are so delicately flavored, but the flesh spoils rapidly. Ice it quickly, and fillet the fish immediately upon returning to shore.

The Bluewater

The Gulf Stream, or Florida Current, moves through the Florida Straits south of Key West and flows northward, along the entire coast of Florida, at about 4 knots. This tropical river, 25 to 40 miles wide, maintains warm temperatures, hosting a piscatorial bounty from the prolific Caribbean that constantly restocks the waters of the Keys. The **bluewater** encompasses deep water from the reef to the edge of the Gulf Stream and is particularly prolific at the humps, which are underwater hills rising from the seafloor. The **Islamorada Hump** is 13 miles offshore from Islamorada. The **West Hump** lies 23 miles offshore from Marathon and rises from a depth of 1,100 feet to 480 feet below the surface.

Bluewater fishing is synonymous with offshore fishing here in the Keys. To an angler, it means big game: **tuna, billfish, dolphin, cobia, wahoo,** and **kingfish.** Also offshore, at the edge of the coral reef and the near-shore patch reefs, you will find a palette of **bottom fish, snappers,** and **groupers** coveted more for their table value than their fighting prowess, and a grab bag of bonus fish—some good to eat, all fun to catch.

Until you are experienced in our waters, you will need a **guide.** To troll for big game fish in the bluewater, you should book a **private charter,** which will put you on the fish and supply everything you need, including the professional expertise of the captain and mate, who know when to hold 'em . . . and when to fold 'em. These charters usually accommodate six anglers and, though pricey, provide the most instruction and individual attention. You can divide the cost with five other anglers or join with another party and split the tab (see the Guides and Charters section of this chapter).

Alternately, sign on to a **party boat,** or **head boat,** which usually accommodates 50 or more anglers. These boats usually take anglers to the reef for bottom fishing, where you can drop a line and try your luck for snapper, grouper, and even kingfish and some of their sidekicks. Mates on deck untangle lines, answer questions, and even bait your hook. And although it is a little bit like taking the bus during rush hour instead of a limousine, at $30 to $40 per day—rods, tackle, and bait included—a party boat remains the most economical means of fishing offshore.

Billfish: Marlin and Sailfish

Before you head out to the bluewater to hunt for **sailfish** and **marlin,** you might want to have a cardiac workup and check your blood pressure because, if your trolled bait takes a hit, it will prove a battle of endurance.

The **cobalt-blue marlin** (*Makaira nigricans*), largest of the Atlantic marlins, migrates away from the equator in warmer months, enigmatically gracing the Keys waters on its way northward. **Females** of the species often reach trophy proportions—**1,000 pounds or more**—but **males** rarely exceed **300 pounds.** Tuna and bonito provide the mainstay of the blue marlin's diet, but some blue marlin have been found with young swordfish in their stomachs. Anglers trolling ballyhoo or mullet have the chance of latching onto a blue marlin, especially in tuna-infested waters. A fighting blue marlin creates a specter of primitive beauty: A creature the size of a baby elephant plunges to the depths, then soars in gravity-defying splendor, only to hammer the water once again and shoot off in a torpedo-like run.

Less often caught in our waters is the **white marlin** (*Tetrapturus albidus*), which is much smaller than the blue, averaging **50** to **60 pounds** and rarely exceeding **150 pounds.** Both marlin use their **swordlike bills** to stun fast-moving fish, which they then consume. Unlike other members of its family, the dorsal and anal fins of the white marlin are rounded, not sharply pointed. The upper portion of its body is a brilliant green-blue, abruptly changing to silvery white on the sides and underslung with a white belly. White marlin will strike trolled **live bait, feathers,** and **lures,** hitting hard and running fast with repetitive jumps. The white marlin begins its southward migration as the waters of the North Atlantic cool in the autumn.

A shimmering dorsal fin, fanned much higher than the depth of its streamlined steel-blue body, distinguishes the **sailfish** (*Istiophorus platyperus*) from its billed brethren. Fronted with a long, slender bill, this graceful creature—averaging **7 feet long** and **40 pounds** in Florida waters—is meant to be captured and **released** but stuffed no more. Probably the most popular mount of all time—the flaunted mark of the been-there, done-that crowd—the sailfish, at least in the Florida Keys, is generally allowed to entertain, take a bow, and go back to the dressing room until the next show. Taxidermists now stock fiberglass blanks, so you need only phone in the prized measurements to receive your representative mount.

The migration of the sailfish coincides with that of the snowbirds, those northerners who spend the frigid months in the balmy Florida Keys. In late autumn and early winter, the sailfish leave the Caribbean and gulf waters and head up the Gulf Stream to the Keys. A fast-growing fish—4 to 5 feet in one year—the sailfish seldom lives more than five years. Feeding on the surface or at mid-depths on small fish and squid, the sailfish also is amenable to trolled appetizers of outrigger-mounted live mullet or ballyhoo that will wiggle, dive, and skip behind the boat like rats after the Pied Piper. The sailfish, swimming at up to **50 knots,** will give you a run for your money, alternating dramatic runs and explosions from the depths with catapults through the air. The sailfish delights novice and expert alike. The inexperienced angler can glory in the pursuit with heavy tackle, while the seasoned veteran can lighten up, creating a new challenge. Both will savor the conquest.

Florida law allows you to keep one billfish per day and mandates size limitations. Sailfish must be at least 63 inches; blue marlin, 99 inches; and white marlin, 66 inches. We recommend, however, that you follow the ethical considerations of catch-and-release, recording your conquest on film instead.

Blackfin Tuna

Highly sought by anglers and blue marlin alike, the **blackfin tuna** (*Thunnus atlanticus*) is set apart from the other six tunas of North America by its totally black finlets. Rarely exceeding **50 pounds,** this member of the mackerel family is not as prized as the giant bluefin of North Atlantic waters, but Keys anglers still relish a substantial battle and the bonus of **great eating.** Primarily a **surface feeder,** the blackfin terrorizes baitfish from below, causing them to streak to the surface and skitter out of the water like skipping stones, a move that attracts seabirds. A sighting of diving gulls will tip off the presence of tuna at the feed bag. Blackfin tuna are partial to a chumming of live pilchards but will also attack feathers and lures trolled at high speeds. Tuna fishing on the humps is usually good in the spring months.

Dolphin: Schoolies, Slammers, and Bulls

Anyone who has ever seen a rainbow of schooling **dolphin** (*Coryphaena hippurus*), **aka mahi mahi,** knows the fish's identity crisis is unfounded. Nothing about this prismatic fish suggests the mammal sharing its name. The dolphinfish resembles a Technicolor cartoon. Its bright green, blue, and yellow wedgelike body looks like the fish just crashed into a paint cabinet, and its high, blunt, pugnacious forehead and Mohawk-style dorsal fin evoke a rowdy, in-your-face persona not wholly undeserved. Once out of the water, however, the brilliant hues ebb like a fading photograph, tingeing sweet victory with fleeting regret.

Second only to billfish and tuna, dolphin are prized by bluewater anglers. **Frantic fights** follow **lightning strikes,** and the dolphin often throws in some **aerobatics** besides. This unruly fighter rates as a delicacy at the table as well, celebrated as moist white-fleshed dolphin fillets in the Keys and South Florida, but marketed as mahi mahi elsewhere. Dolphinfish are **surface feeders,** attracted to the small fish and other tasty morsels associated with floating debris or patches of drifting sargassum weed. Flying fish, plentiful in the Gulf Stream waters, form a large portion of their preferred diet. A school of dolphin will actually attack a trolled bait of small, whole mullet or ballyhoo, streaking from a distance in a me-first effort like schoolboys to the lunch gong. It is not unusual for three or four rods to be hit at one time, an all-hands-on-deck effort that approaches a marathon. And as long as you keep one hooked dolphin in the water, alongside the boat, its buddies will hang around and wait their turn for a freshly baited hook.

Dolphins are rapidly growing fish, living up to five years. The young are called schoolies, generally in the **5- to 15-pound range.** Slammers make an angler salivate, as they each weigh **25 pounds** and more, and an attacking school can get your heart pumping. Doing battle with the heavyweight, the bull dolphin, quite often happens by accident while you are trolling for some other species. But the bull can hold his own in any arena. Dolphin season is generally considered to be from March until Aug, but the fish tend to stay around most of the year. Limit is 10 per person, per day.

Cobia: The Crab Eater

The **cobia** (*Rachycentron canadum*), the orphan of the piscatory world, enjoys no close relatives and is in a family by itself. Excellent on the table or on the troll, the adult cobia is a favorite bonus fish, often caught during a day in the bluewater looking for sailfish. Particularly partial to crabs, the cobia also feeds on shrimp, squid, and small fish. The young cobia is found often in the flats of near-shore **bays** and **inlets** around the **mangroves** and around **buoys, pilings,** and **wrecks.**

Wahoo

A fine-eating bonus fish, generally caught by fortunate accident while trolling for sailfish or kingfish, the **wahoo** (*Acanthocybium solandri*) is far from an also-ran. One of the **fastest** fish in the ocean, the wahoo is a bona fide member of the mackerel family, similar in many ways to the Spanish mackerel. Its long, beaklike snout and slender silver-and-blue-striped body contribute to its prowess as a speed swimmer, for when hooked, the wahoo runs swiftly, cutting and weaving like a tailback heading for a touchdown. This loner rarely travels in schools.

Wahoo season is in May, but the fish are here year-round.

Kingfish, aka King Mackerel

Here in the Florida Keys, we call the **king mackerel**—which goes by assorted aliases in other parts of the country—the **kingfish.** At the turn of the 20th century, kingfish was the most popular catch off the Keys. Sailfish, then unrevered, were considered pests because they crashed the kingfish bait. The streamlined kingfish (*Scomberomorus cavalla*) travels in large schools, migrating up and down the coast in search of warm waters. Kingfish commonly frequent the waters of the Keys during the winter months, heading north in the spring.

Kings can be caught by drift fishing, where anglers cut the boat's engines and drift, fishing over the schools. Alternately, you can troll for kingfish with whole mullet or ballyhoo. Some captains prefer to anchor and chum, lacing the slick from time to time with live pilchards. Any method you use, a wire leader is essential when angling for kingfish because the fish displays razor-sharp teeth it is not reluctant to use. King-fish caught in our waters commonly weigh in at about **20 pounds,** although the fish have been recorded reaching upward of **40 pounds.** The kingfish is a good sport fish and also makes a fine meal. Limit is two per person, per day.

Amberjack

When all else fails in the bluewater, you can always find a deep hole and battle an **amberjack** (*Seriola dumerili*). This powerful, bottom-plunging fish—nicknamed AJ—guarantees a good brawl. Bringing in an amberjack is like pulling up a Volkswagen Beetle with light tackle.

i Just over 20 miles out, southeast of the Middle Keys, is a favorite fishing spot called Marathon's West Hump. This is an underwater seamount that comes up within 480 feet of the surface and is located in waters twice as deep. The constant easterly flow of the Gulf Stream creates the "hump" that draws baitfish, fish, and fishing enthusiasts!

The Reef Elite: Snapper and the Mackerels

Inhabiting the edge of the barrier reef that extends the length of the Florida Keys and in the smaller patch reefs closer in to shore, several finned species noteworthy for their **food value** coexist with the brightly painted tropicals and other coral-dwelling creatures. Like a well-branched family tree, these fish encompass many clans, all entertaining to catch and most delectable to eat. Startled anglers have even brought in permit while fishing the wrecks along the reef line. The brooding presence of the barracuda is always a strong possibility on the reef because the 'cuda is partial to raw snapper "stew" or grouper "tartare" when given the opportunity. It thinks nothing of stealing half the hooked fish in one mighty chomp, leaving the angler nothing but a lifeless head.

You will need a boat at least 20 feet long to head out to the reef, some 4 to 5 miles offshore. But with a compass, your NOAA charts, GPS, tackle, chunked bait, and some information gathered locally at the nearest bait and tackle shop, you should be able to find a hot spot on your own. Then all you need to do is fillet the captives, find a recipe, and fry up the spoils.

The snapper family is a popular bunch in the Florida Keys. The prolific cousins—all pleasurable to eat, delightful to catch, and kaleidoscopic to see—confuse Northerners with their dissimilarity. Snappers travel in schools and like to feed at night. Most common on the Keys table is probably the sweet, delicate **yellowtail snapper** (*Ocyurus chrysurus*), which usually ranges from 12 to 16 inches in length. Big yellowtails, called **flags,** approach **5 to 6 pounds** and 20 inches in length and are prevalent from late summer through Oct. The yellowtail's back and upper sides shade from olive to bluish with yellow spots. A prominent yellow stripe begins at the yellowtail's mouth and runs midlaterally to its deeply forked tail, which, as you would expect, is a deep, brilliant yellow. The yellowtail is skittish, line-shy, and tends to stay way behind the boat. The fish's small mouth won't accommodate the hooks most commonly used in the pursuit of the other snappers. Successful anglers use **light line, no leaders,** and **small hooks** buried in the bait.

The **mangrove snapper,** or **gray snapper** (*Lutjanus griseus*), though often haunting the coral reef, also can be found inshore in mangrove habitats. Grayish in color with a red tinge along the sides, the mangrove snapper displays two conspicuous canine teeth at the front of the upper jaw. The mangrove is easier to catch than the yellowtail or the mutton snapper. Live shrimp and cut bait, added to a small hook, will induce these good fighters to strike. Anglers enjoy taking the mangroves on light tackle.

The brightly colored **mutton snapper** (*Lutanus analis*) shades from olive green to red, with a bright blue line extending from under its eye to its tail and a black spot below the dorsal fin marking its side. Mutton snappers are most often caught in blue holes, so called because the water color of these deep coral potholes appears bluer

than the surrounding waters. You will also find muttons in channels and creeks and occasionally even on a bonefish flat. The fish range in weight from **5 to 20 pounds.** Mutton snappers are rumored to be shy and easily spooked by a bait that is cast too closely, but they love live pilchards. Usually caught in cloudy, churned-up water, the muttons provide a fierce confrontation. Limit for snappers is 10 per person, per day.

Ergonomically designed for speed, the torpedo-shaped **Spanish mackerel** (*Scomberomorus maculatus*) distinguishes itself from the king and the cero with a series of irregular, buttercup-yellow spots on its stripeless sides, which look like the freckles on the Little Rascals. Cherished by light-tackle enthusiasts, the Spanish mackerel averages less than **2 pounds** and 20 inches in length. Its razorlike teeth dictate you carefully consider your choice in terminal tackle, for slashing your line rates at the top of the Spanish mackerel's getaway tactics. Spanish mackerel migrate into Florida Bay in Feb. Limit is 15 per person, per day.

Larger than its Spanish cousin, the **cero mackerel** (*Scomberomorous regalis*) displays yellow spots above and below a bronze stripe that runs down its silvery sides, from the pectoral fin to the base of its tail. The cero is the local in our visiting mackerel lineup, not straying far from the waters of South Florida and the Keys, where it feeds on small fish and squid. The cero makes excellent table fare when consumed fresh, but fillets do not freeze well.

You may encounter the **tripletail** (*Lobotes surinamensis*) if you fish around wrecks, buoys, or sunken debris. Nicknamed the **"buoy fish,"** the tripletail has been known to reach **40 pounds** and a length of 3 feet. The fish's dorsal and anal fins are so long that they resemble two more tails, hence the name tripletail. The tripletail is a mottled palette of black, brown, and yellow, looking like an autumn leaf. Young tripletails, which like to stay close to shore in bays and estuaries, often are spotted floating on their sides at the surface, mimicking a leaf on the water. The tripletail will put up a valiant fight, and, though not seen on a restaurant menu, it will make a tasty dinner. You must catch tripletail with a hook and line only, no snatch hooks.

The Bridges

The **bridges** of the Florida Keys attract fighting **game fish** and flavorful **food fish** like magnets draw paper clips. The state of Florida replaced many of the original bridges of the Overseas Highway with wider, heavier spans in the late 1970s and 1980s, subsequently fitting many of the old bridges, no longer used for automobile traffic, for use as fishing piers. These bridges are marked with brown-and-white signage depicting a fish, line, and hook. (Many of the old bridge structures have been closed because lack of maintenance has left them unsafe. Be sure to fish only from those bearing the county signage.) The fishing bridges offer the general public free fishing access to many of the same species that frequent more far-flung areas of our waters. Parking is provided at the fishing-pier bridges. The Seven Mile Bridge, the Long Key Bridge, and the Bahia Honda Bridge have been designated historical monuments.

The waters beneath the bridges host a lively population of **tarpon, mangrove snappers, snook, baby groupers,** and **yellowtails** (see the Flats, Backcountry, and Bluewater sections of this chapter for information on these fish). **Grunts** (*Haemulon plumieri*) also are commonly caught at the bridges. Though little respected in other Keys waters, this small, bluish-gray fish is, nevertheless, fun to catch and makes a tasty meal. The grunt's name is derived from the sounds escaping the fish's bright orange mouth when it is captured. This grunting sound is actually the grinding of the pharyngeal teeth, which produces an audible noise amplified by the air bladder.

Night fishing is popular from the bridge piers, too. An outgoing tide with a moderate flow inspires the fish to continue feeding after dark. Baitfish and crustaceans, a temptation too great for many of the finned predators to pass up, are funneled through the pilings and out to sea.

Stop in at one of the local bait and tackle shops to get rigged out for bridge fishing. The local fishing experts working in these shops are encyclopedias of knowledge and will be able to guide you as to times, tides, and tackle. Locals recommend you use stout tackle when fishing from one of our bridges. You not only have to retrieve your catch while battling a heavy current, but you also must lift it a great distance to the top of the bridge.

Live shrimp, cut bait, or live pinfish will attract attention from at least one of the species lurking below. You will need to keep your shrimp alive while fishing from the bridge. Put the shrimp on ice in a five-gallon bucket with an aerator or in a large Styrofoam cooler with an aerator. You can also lower a chum bag (filled with a block of chum, available at all bait shops) into the water. Tie a couple of dive weights to a long rope, lower the chum bag down the surface of a piling on the downcurrent side of the bridge, and tie it off to the railing. Then fish the slick. The chum will drift with the current, attracting **sharks** and any **finfish** in the neighborhood.

You will need sinkers on your line in order for your baited hook to drop to the bottom because a swift current pulses under the bridges. Don't launch your cast away from the bridge. Drop your bait straight down, near a piling or downcurrent, at the shoreside of the bridge. Rubble from past construction sometimes piled here creates a current break, allowing the fish a place to rest, feed, or hide in the swirls or eddies. Don't forget to buy a fishing license.

FISHING LICENSES

Florida law states you must possess a **saltwater fishing license** if you attempt to take or possess marine fish for noncommercial purposes. This includes finfish and such invertebrate species as snails, whelks, clams, scallops, shrimps, crabs, lobsters, sea stars, sea urchins, and sea cucumbers.

Exempt from this law are individuals younger than age 16 and Florida residents age 65 and older. You are also exempt if you are a Florida resident and a member of the U.S. armed forces not stationed in Florida and home on leave for 30 or fewer days, with valid orders in your possession.

Florida residents who are fishing in saltwater or for a saltwater species in fresh water, from land, or from a structure fixed to land need not purchase a license. Land is defined as "the area of ground located within the geographic boundaries of the state of Florida that extends to a water depth of 4 feet." This includes any structure permanently fixed to land such as a pier, bridge, dock or floating dock, or jetty. If you use a vessel to reach ground, however, you must have a license. And if you are wading in more than 4 feet of water or have broken the surface of the water wearing a face mask, you also must have one.

You are not required to have a license when you fish with one of our licensed captains on a charter holding a valid vessel saltwater fishing license or if you are fishing from a pier that has been issued a pier saltwater fishing license. Other, more obscure exemptions also apply. Check www.florida fisheries.com for more information.

A Florida saltwater fishing license is available from most bait and tackle shops and from any **Monroe County tax collector's office.** You can also obtain a license over the telephone by dialing (888) 347-4356. Licenses are now available online at www .myfwc.com. Residents and nonresidents pay differing amounts for this license. The state defines a resident as anyone who has lived in Florida continuously for at least six months; anyone who has established a domicile in Florida and can provide evidence of such by law; any member of the U.S. armed forces who is stationed in Florida; any student enrolled in a college or university in Florida; or an alien who can prove residency status.

The penalty for fishing without the required license or stamps is $50 plus the cost of purchasing the proper documentation. A $51.50 tarpon tag is required if you insist upon keeping and therefore killing a tarpon instead of releasing it (see the Catch-and-Release Ethics section in this chapter).

TOURNAMENTS

If you're an angler who would like to compete against your peers instead of just yourself, the Florida Keys offers a plethora of exciting tournaments—more than 50 a year—encompassing most of the finned species enriching our waters. These tournaments, scheduled year-round from Key Largo to Key West, award prizes, cash, or trophies in a variety of categories ranging from heaviest or longest to most caught and released in a specified time period.

Generally, the tournaments fit into one of three categories, although some tournaments have multiple divisions. The **billfish tournaments**—white marlin, blue marlin, and sailfish—are the most prestigious and the most expensive. Billfish tournaments are catch-and-release events. Proof of the catch usually requires a photograph and a sample of the leader, which will be tested for chafing. Scoring follows an intricate point system. A catch of a white marlin, a blue marlin, and a sailfish in one day—not your average day, even in the Keys—constitutes a slam.

Dolphin tournaments are more family-type competitions. Anglers use their own boats without guides, and if the dolphin exceeds prespecified poundage, it may be brought in and weighed. Anglers can keep the fish, which are excellent eating.

Flats tournaments—tarpon, bonefish, and permit—are always catch-and-release, usually scored by a point system. A catch on a fly rod scores more points than one retrieved on light tackle. The fish must be measured, a photo must be taken, and the process must be witnessed. We recommend you book one year in advance for tarpon tournaments.

Some of our tournaments are restricted to a specific category of angler—women only or juniors only, for instance—or to a particular type of tackle, such as light tackle or fly rods. Others award a mixed bag of catches ranging from game fish to groupers to grunts. Many of the tournaments donate at least a portion of their proceeds to a charitable organization.

In the following section we introduce you to a sampling of the most important fishing tournaments held annually in the Keys. For a complete listing, visit www.fla-keys.com/fishing.

BAYBONE CELEBRITY TOURNAMENT
Sheraton Beach Resort, Key Largo
(305) 664-2002
www.redbone.org
Event No. 2 in the Celebrity Tournament Series, the prestigious catch-and-release Baybone tournament is in late Sept or early Oct. The Celebrity Tournament Series, which includes the Mercury S.L.A.M., donates 100 percent of its proceeds to the Cystic Fibrosis Foundation for research. The stalked catch for the Baybone is bonefish and permit, which are photographed against a measuring device and released. Points are awarded for catches on fly, spin/plug, or general bait; nothing heavier than 12-pound test may be used in all divisions. An intricate point system determines the winners, who receive original paintings and sculptures as prizes. Anglers can fish as a two-person team, or one angler can be paired with a celebrity.

CHEECA LODGE & SPA PRESIDENTIAL SAILFISH TOURNAMENT
MM 82 Oceanside, Islamorada
(305) 664-4651 or (800) 327-2888
www.cheeca.com/fishing-and-recreation
Perhaps the most prestigious of all tournaments in the Florida Keys is this tournament, held in Feb. The former president, George Bush himself, competes in this event. Preceded by a kickoff meeting, two days of intense fishing are followed by an awards banquet at Cheeca Lodge. Fifty boats participate, two anglers per boat. Other than those included in the most-catches category, bonefish must weigh at least eight pounds to qualify. All must be released. Trophies are

awarded to winners. Proceeds benefit a variety of Keys environmental groups.

COCONUTS DOLPHIN TOURNAMENT
Key Largo
(305) 453-9794
www.coconutsrestaurant.com
The largest dolphin tournament in the Florida Keys, Coconuts Dolphin Tournament at Marina Del Mar in mid-May regularly hosts more than 700 anglers. This three-day tournament, which awards prizes, runs from 8 a.m. to 3 p.m. each day. The 2010 prize for a dolphin weighing over 63.9 pounds was a two-year lease on a Honda Ridgeline truck. You can book a charter to fish the tournament or use your own boat. The director says there has been no proven advantage to having a charter. Scoring is determined by weight of the fish. Since this is a food-fish tournament, anglers may bring in all dolphin of more than 10 pounds.

i The most famous bluewater angler in Key West's collective consciousness remains Ernest Hemingway, who augmented his famous writing with a passion for fishing these waters. Photographs of Hemingway with his prized, monster-size tarpon and sailfish cause many a covetous angler to turn green with envy.

DON HAWLEY INVITATIONAL TARPON TOURNAMENT
Islamorada
(305) 664-2444
www.islamoradasailfishtournament.com
The oldest tarpon-on-the-fly tournament in the Keys and the first all-release tournament, the Don Hawley event is a five-day fishing extravaganza of all-fly, all-tarpon, and all-release. Anglers are awarded 1,000 points for

a catch-and-release on 12-pound tippet; 750 points on 16-pound. Winners amassing the most points secure original Keys art by such notables as Al Barnes, Bill Elliott, and Kendall Van Sant. Proceeds of the tournament benefit the nonprofit Don Hawley Foundation, which supports the study of tarpon fishery and preservation in the Florida Keys and provides assistance to guides and their families in time of need. The tournament, held in Dec, is limited to 25 anglers.

ISLAMORADA FISHING CLUB SAILFISH TOURNAMENT
Islamorada
(305) 664-4735
The historic fish club offers a large cash prize to the winning team in dolphin and tarpon tournaments thoughout the year.

KEY WEST FISHING TOURNAMENT
Key West
(305) 295-6601
www.keywestfishingtournament.com
This unusual tournament must have been designed for the angler who just can't fish enough. It lasts from Mar to Nov, and encompasses a potpourri of divisions and species. Both charters and individuals can register for the tournament and also participate in a two-day kickoff tournament-within-a-tournament, which in itself awards cash prizes. Anglers weigh their food-fish catches or record their releases at participating marinas and are awarded citations for their efforts. At the grand finale of the tournament, the tabulated results are announced, and all prizes are presented.

LADIES TARPON TOURNAMENT
Marathon
(305) 289-2248

The waters under the Seven Mile Bridge and the Bahia Honda Bridge are invaded by tarpon-seeking women each year in late Apr or early May in this ladies-only tarpon tournament. The number of tarpon caught and released in the two-day tournament determines the winners of a cache of rods and reels, trophies, and an assortment of jewelry. Points are awarded for catches on 12-pound test and 30-pound test.

LEON SHELL MEMORIAL SAILFISH TOURNAMENT
Key Colony Beach
(305) 289-1310
www.leonshelltournament.com
This is two days of fishing, with the proceeds benefiting the Keys Hospice and Visiting Nurses Association of the Florida Keys. The tournament is named after Leon Shell, best known as the inventor of the Leon Lure, an artificial lure regarded as one of the top bubble-creating lures ever invented. With well over $100,000 donated since the tournament's inception, this draws a huge crowd. In the yearly tourney, cash prizes are awarded and the prize for the boat releasing the most sailfish is given out at an awards dinner. Weight fish divisions are given for dolphin, tuna, wahoo, and kingfish. Also, there is a junior division for youngsters ages 9 to 15½ years old.

MERCURY CELEBRITY S.L.A.M. TOURNAMENT
Key West
(305) 664-2002
www.redbone.org
First in the Celebrity Tournament Series each year is the S.L.A.M. (Southernmost Light-tackle Anglers Masters) event in early September, for the benefit of cystic fibrosis research (see the Baybone tournament event). Participants in this two-day fishing event angle to score a Grand Slam: the catch and release of a bonefish, permit, and tarpon in two days. Points are awarded for each release in categories of fly, spin/plug, and general bait. Each release is photographed against a measuring device.

Like the other tournaments in this series, the S.L.A.M. awards original art and sculpture to its winners. Anglers can fish as a two-person team, or one angler can opt to fish with a celebrity.

i Never discard your fishing line in the water. It can injure marine life, sea turtles, or seabirds.

GUIDES AND CHARTERS

There are many **captains** and **guides** in the Florida Keys offering their services on the flats, bluewater, or backcountry. Our guides are the most knowledgeable in the world—licensed captains who maintain safe, government-regulated watercraft. Hiring a guide allows the first-time visitor or the novice angler an opportunity to learn how to fish the waters of the Florida Keys and catch its bounty without having to spend too much time learning about the fish's habits. And guides will be your best teachers, for they usually have a lifetime of experience. Once you fish our waters, however, you will be the "hooked" species, for this unforgettable angling experience is addictive.

Book a guide as soon as you know when you are coming to the Keys, because the guides here book up quickly, especially during certain times of the year. If you hope to fish our waters with a guide during tarpon season, especially the months of May and June, plan a year ahead. Holidays such as Christmas and New Year's book up quickly also. Traditionally, the months of Aug through Nov are a bit slower. You may be able to wing it during those months, but we wouldn't advise it. Even if you don't take a charter trip, stop at a fishing marina about 4 p.m. and check out the catch of the day.

Bluewater or **offshore fishing charters** can accommodate six anglers. The captain guides the vessel to his or her favorite hot spots, which are anywhere from 6 to 26 miles offshore and usually closely guarded secrets. Often he or she will stop on his bluewater trek so the mate can throw a cast net for live bait. The mate will rig the baits, ready the outriggers, and cast the baited hooks for you. **Big game fish** are usually stalked by trolling, as are dolphin. You need do nothing but relax, soak in the sea air, and wait for the call, "Fish on!" Then the action is up to you.

Bluewater charter boats range in size from 35 to 50 feet. Each generally has an enclosed cabin and a head (toilet) onboard. Everything you need for a day's fishing is provided except your refreshments, lunch, and any personal items you may need. It is customary to tip the mate 10 to 15 percent in cash if you have had a good day.

Guides for **flats fishing** or **backcountry angling** usually take a maximum of two anglers per boat. The guide will pole the skiff or flatsboat through the skinny water, attentively looking for fish from atop the poling platform. This sight fishing dictates both guide and anglers stand alert, all senses engaged. The angler, whether fly fishing or spin casting, casts to the desired location directed by the guide.

Flatsboats measure 16 to 18 feet. They are not outfitted with any shading devices, nor do they have a head. Be aware, you may have to use rather primitive facilities. Many

of the guides will dip into shore for a pit stop, but others will not, so inquire before you leave the dock. All fly or spin rods, reels, tackle, and bait are provided. Some guides even tie their own flies, providing special furry or feathery creations proven to entice the fish. It is customary to tip the guide 10 to 15 percent in cash if you were happy with the excursion.

When booking a charter, inquire about penalties for canceling your reservations. No-shows frequently will be charged the full price.

Always bring sunscreen, polarized sunglasses, a cap with a long bill lined with dark fabric to cut the glare, and motion-sickness pills (even if you've never needed them before). Anglers are responsible for providing their own lunches and refreshments. Keys tradition is to bring lunch for the captain and mate on a bluewater charter or for the guide on a flats trip.

Many guides are known only on a word-of-mouth basis, but we have compiled a source list of fishing marinas and outfitters you may call to secure an offshore charter or flats or backcountry guide. The chambers of commerce in Key Largo, Islamorada, Marathon, the Lower Keys, and Key West also act as referral sources (see subsequent listings).

Perhaps even more than the rest of the Keys, you'll need a guide to find the fish in the waters surrounding Key West. A busy harbor for centuries, **Key West's marinas** and **bights** are a bustling maze to the uninitiated. Many of the more than 60 charter boats in the Key West fleet dock at the City Marina at Garrison Bight, which is accessed on Palm Avenue, just off North Roosevelt Boulevard. This marina is locally referred to as Charter Boat Row. From 7 to 7:30 a.m. and 3:30 to 5 p.m. the captains are available at their vessels to take direct bookings. You can meet them and their crews, see the offshore vessels, and save money to boot. Booking a charter directly with the captain instead of a charter agency nets you a sizable discount. Other charter boats dock at Key West Bight, in the Key West Historic Seaport.

Some guides are willing to captain your private vessel at a much-reduced charter rate. If this interests you, inquire when you call one of these booking sources. Often hotels maintain a source list of guides or charter captains they will recommend. Inquire when you reserve your accommodations.

i For all the Keys fishing news, go to www.fishingthefloridakeys .com. This site gives you great info from seaworthy captains to the latest on where the fish are biting to what's new in fishing gear.

Offshore and Backcountry Guide Booking Sources

Establishments acting as booking services will determine your needs and book your flats/backcountry guide or bluewater/off-shore charter directly. Cancellation policies vary and change from year to year, so be sure to inquire about procedures and penalties before you book your charter. The top guides in the Florida Keys book out of the establishments listed below. Be sure to log on to their Web sites to find out more information on the guides they represent.

Upper Keys
BAY AND REEF COMPANY
MM 82 Oceanside, Islamorada
(305) 393-1779
www.bayandreef.com

WHALE HARBOR DOCK & MARINA
MM 81.9 Oceanside, Islamorada
(305) 664-9888
www.whaleharborcharters.com

WORLD WIDE SPORTSMAN INC.
MM 81.5 Bayside, Islamorada
(305) 664-4615 or (800) 227-7776
www.basspro.com

SANDY MORET'S FLORIDA KEYS OUTFITTERS
MM 81.2 Oceanside, Islamorada
(305) 664-5423
www.floridakeysoutfitters.com

BUD N' MARY'S FISHING MARINA
MM 79.8 Oceanside, Islamorada
(305) 664-2461 or (800) 742-7945
www.budnmarys.com

Middle Keys
CAPTAIN HOOK'S MARINA
MM 53 Oceanside, Marathon
(305) 743-2444 or (800) 278-4665
www.captainhooks.com

WORLD CLASS ANGLER
MM 49 Bayside, Marathon
(305) 743-6139
www.worldclassangler.com

Lower Keys
STRIKE ZONE CHARTERS
MM 29.5 Bayside, Big Pine Key
(305) 872-9863 or (800) 654-9560
www.strikezonecharter.com

Key West
In addition to the limited number of fishing marinas and outfitters booking guides or charters, Key West's fishing excursions are

put together by charter agencies operated out of booths peppering Mallory Square, Duval, and other major streets of Key West. You also can book party boats at these booths.

KING'S POINTE MARINA
MM 5, 5950 Peninsula Ave., Stock Island
(305) 294-4676
www.cortexcompanies.com

THE SALTWATER ANGLER
Westin Key West Resort & Marina
243 Front St., Key West
(305) 296-0700
www.saltwaterangler.com

Chambers of Commerce
KEY LARGO CHAMBER OF COMMERCE & FLORIDA KEYS VISITOR CENTER
MM 106 Bayside, Key Largo
(305) 451-1414 or (800) 822-1088
www.keylargo.org
This chamber will provide names of guides who either belong to the Key Largo Chamber of Commerce or those from other areas of the Keys who pay a fee to the Florida Keys Visitor Center for representation.

ISLAMORADA CHAMBER OF COMMERCE
MM 82.5 Bayside, Islamorada
(305) 664-4503 or (800) 322-5397
www.islamoradachamber.com
This chamber maintains an active list of guides in the Islamorada area.

GREATER MARATHON CHAMBER OF COMMERCE
MM 53.5 Bayside, Marathon
(305) 743-5417 or (800) 262-7284
www.floridakeysmarathon.com

Upon request, this chamber will send you a list of guides belonging to the Marathon Guides Association. (The list is also posted on their Web site.) The list specifies the guide's name, address, telephone number, type of fishing (such as bluewater or flats), fishing specialties (spin or fly), and size and make of boat. If you don't have time to wait for this list by mail, the chamber will provide several selections over the telephone. The visitor center maintains a reservation line at (877) 934-FISH.

LOWER KEYS CHAMBER OF COMMERCE
MM 31 Oceanside, Big Pine Key
(305) 872-2411 or (800) 872-3722
www.lowerkeyschamber.com
The Lower Keys Chamber goes beyond its membership list to refer you to a wide range of guides and captains in the area.

KEY WEST CHAMBER OF COMMERCE
510 Greene St., Key West
(305) 294-2587 or (800) 648-6269
www.keywestchamber.org
The staff at the Key West Chamber of Commerce will mail you a list of guides or captains who are chamber members.

i More than 10 percent of the International Game Fish Association (IGFA) saltwater line-class and fly-fishing world records have been set in the Florida Keys.

Party Boats

Party boats, sometimes called **"head boats,"** offer a relatively inexpensive way to fish the waters of the Keys. The party boats, U.S. Coast Guard–inspected and certified vessels, generally hold **50 passengers** or more, but most average no more than 25 to 30 anglers. Party boats take anglers out to the reef, where they anchor or drift and bottom fish for more than 40 species of fish. Spring and summer seasons sport a plethora of **groupers, snappers, dolphinfish,** and **yellowtails,** while **kingfish** and **cobia** are more apt to make an appearance in the winter months. **Porgies, grunts,** and some species of **snappers** and **groupers** show up all year. Occasionally even a **sailfish** or a **big shark** has been caught from a party boat here.

The party boat offers **rod and reel rental** at a nominal fee per trip. This includes your terminal tackle—hook, line, and sinker—and all bait. If you bring your own fishing gear, bait is included in the excursion fee. You do not need a fishing license on a party boat. While most party-boat information mentions your license is included in the excursion fee, this actually is only a temporary license, good for the duration of your fishing trip only. Two or more mates will be working the boat, helping you bait hooks, confiding fishing tips, and untangling the inevitable crossed lines.

Most of the party boats have seats around the periphery of the lower deck and a shaded sundeck up top. You are advised to wear shorts rather than swimsuits and durable sneakers or deck shoes, not thongs or sandals. Remember, there will be a lot of anglers and many flying hooks on the boat. Put some sturdy cloth between your skin and that accidental snag. Most captains recommend bringing a lightweight long-sleeved shirt for protection against the sun and a jacket to ward off cool breezes. Bring sunglasses, sunscreen, a hat, and motion-sickness pills (many people who never suffered from seasickness before find drifting in the swells causes them *mal de mer*). Also bring a fishing rag or towel to wipe your hands on during the day.

After you land a fish, a mate will help you take it off the hook and will check the species to make sure it is not one of those protected by law, such as Nassau grouper. The mate then will measure the fish to ensure it meets the required size limit, tag it with your name, and place it on ice. At the end of the fishing trip, you may reclaim your catch. The mate will clean your fish, usually for tips. Party boats with a set cleaning-fee policy will be noted in the descriptions. Mates work for tips aboard party boats, the standard tip being 10 to 15 percent if you had a good day and if the mate was helpful.

The following party boats may be booked for **day** or **evening charters.** It is always a good idea to arrive at the docks 30 minutes before departure to stow your gear on the boat and secure a good position on deck. All boats have restrooms onboard. Most have an enclosed cabin and offer a limited snack bar, beer, and soda. Exceptions will be noted.

In all cases, you are allowed to bring your own cooler filled with lunch and refreshments. All party boats recommended in this section take credit cards unless otherwise stated. Children's rates for youngsters age 12 and younger are often available.

i Before green turtles were placed on the endangered and protective list and no longer allowed to be caught, they were once a source of food throughout Florida's history. The "pens" that held the turtles were called "kraals."

Upper Keys
SAILOR'S CHOICE
Holiday Inn Marina, MM 100 Oceanside, Key Largo
(305) 451-1802
www.sailorschoicefishingboat.com
Sailor's Choice, a 65-foot, aluminum, custom-built craft with an air-conditioned lounge, offers plenty of shade and seating for anglers on its daily fishing excursions. Children are welcome on both day and evening trips. During the day, they can easily see the big fish in the water and seabirds, porpoises, and sea turtles. The two daily excursions are from 9 a.m. to 1 p.m. and 1:30 to 5:30 p.m.

MISS ISLAMORADA
Bud N' Mary's Marina
MM 79.8 Oceanside, Islamorada
(305) 664-2461, (800) 742-7945
www.budnmarys.com
Miss Islamorada is a 65-foot air-conditioned party/fishing boat that entertains up to 45 people. All tackle is provided with an experienced crew. Catering onboard is available for fishing, sunset cruises, corporate meetings, memorial services, and weddings. This boat is quite the "lady!"

CAPTAIN MICHAEL
MM 77.5 Bayside, Islamorada
(305) 664-9814, (877) 664-8498
www.robbies.com
If you just can't get enough fishing, the *Captain Michael* offers a money-saving option: Fish the morning excursion, and go out again in the afternoon at a reduced price. Rates for children younger than age five, who will only be "assisting" Mom and Dad, are further reduced. The 65-foot *Captain Michael*, with spacious decks and an air-conditioned

cabin, is available for private charters, sunset cruises, and wedding receptions.

Middle Keys
MARATHON LADY
Marathon Lady Dock at the Vaca Cut Bridge
MM 53 Oceanside, Marathon
(305) 743-5580
www.fishfloridakeys.com/marathonlady
Children fish for significantly reduced rates aboard the *Marathon Lady*. Inquire when you make your reservations. If you rent a rod and reel for the excursion, your tackle is included, but if you prefer to bring your own gear, terminal tackle is available for a nominal fee. The mates will clean your catch for a small fee. A cooler with lunch and refreshments is allowed on all-day winter excursions. However, on summer evening excursions, which replace the all-day winter ventures, the captain prefers you bring your refreshments in a plastic bag; the crew will put them on ice for you.

From Oct through May they offer daily trips, and from June through Aug they run daily trips. *Marathon Lady* does not run during the month of Sept.

Lower Keys
SEA BOOTS
MM 24.5 Oceanside, Summerland Key
(305) 745-1530, (800) 238-1746
www.seaboots.com
With a Coast Guard Masters License under his belt, Captain Jim Sharp has been on the water most of his life. His vast experience fishing the cool blue waters of the Florida Keys and the Bahamas makes an outing with Jim a thrilling experience. On his six-passenger boat, *Sea Boots*, you are provided fishing license, tackle, bait, and ice for the trip.

Key West

Key West party boats are docked at Charter Boat Row on Palm Avenue off North Roosevelt. You can call the numbers listed to make reservations, book a space at one of the booths on Duval Street and in the Mallory Square area, or simply come down to the docks and make arrangements directly with the captain. Vessels usually operate at far less than maximum capacity during most seasons, so finding a spot should not present a problem.

ANDY GRIFFITHS CHARTERS
7007 Shrimp Rd., Stock Island
(305) 296-2639 or (305) 292-2277
www.fishandy.com
Climb aboard any one of six vessels for half-day, full-day, or overnight fishing trips. This seasoned captain, with over 30 years' experience, and his crew take you fishing day and night. Snorkeling, kayaking, or swimming is also part of the fun while in the beautiful Dry Tortugas and Marquesas Keys.

GREYHOUND V
Charter Boat Row, City Marina,
Garrison Bight
(305) 296-5139
Daily trips are from 11 a.m. to 4 p.m. Passengers who would like to ride along and use the sundeck instead of fishing may do so for a lesser charge. In July and Aug two excursions are offered daily. The party boat does not operate in the month of Sept. Mates charge a nominal fee to clean your fish.

GULF STREAM III AND IV
Charter Boat Row, City Marina,
Garrison Bight
(305) 296-8494, or (888) 745-3595
www.keywestpartyboat.com

The *Gulf Stream III* and *IV* provide a full-service lunch counter offering sandwiches, beer, and soda. Ever prepared, the crew will provide free motion-sickness pills if the need arises. The mates will clean your catch for a small fee. Daily excursions are Sept through June. Evening outings are conducted in July and Aug only. Sunbathers may come along on these party boats for half price.

OUTFITTERS

Upper Keys

WEST MARINE
MM 103.4 Bayside, Key Largo
(305) 453-9050 or (800) 685-4383
www.westmarine.com
West Marine is your one-stop shop for all of your boating and fishing needs. Great inventory, large selection, and helpful sales folks are available to assist with questions. Check out their Web site for other locations in the Upper Keys.

WORLD WIDE SPORTSMAN INC.
MM 81.5 Bayside, Islamorada
(305) 664- 4615 or (800) 227-7776
www.basspro.com
Anglers will discover nirvana at World Wide Sportsman, a 29,000-square-foot super store in Islamorada (see the Shopping chapter). Owned by Johnny Morris of Bass Pro Shops, World Wide is stocked to the rafters with a wide assortment of fishing tackle, such as Billy Pate, Tibor, Penn, Sage, Daiwa, Shimano, Orvis, and many more. You'll find fly-tying materials and a huge assortment of flies here. A rod and reel repair center is on premises. Ex Officio, Woolrich, Bimini Bay, Sportif, Tarponwear, and Columbia fishing clothes for both men and women are just a few of the many brands offered.

The facility also features a full-service marina of 40 to 50 slips, accommodating boats up to 42 feet in length. Many of the area guides launch from these facilities. The marina offers a fuel dock (both gas and diesel) as well as frozen, live, and fresh bait. All things considered, this fishing emporium is every angler's dream store.

SANDY MORET'S FLORIDA KEYS OUTFITTERS
MM 81.2 Oceanside, Islamorada
(305) 664-5423
www.floridakeysoutfitters.com
This shop made *Field and Stream's* top 10 list as selected by the magazine's editors. The focus here is on fly fishing, and this outfitter's personnel rank as some of the most experienced in the sport. You'll find such brands as Orvis, Sage, G. Loomis, and Scott fly rods and Tibor, Orvis, and Abel fly reels, plus a wide selection of flies and fly-tying materials. In addition to Columbia, Sage, Patagonia, and Orvis clothing, Florida Keys Outfitters sells Teva sandals and Sebago and Columbia boat shoes.

Middle Keys

WORLD CLASS ANGLER
MM 49 Bayside, Marathon
(305) 743-6139
www.worldclassangler.com
World Class Angler sells anything and everything you'll need for saltwater fishing, stocking 37 brand names of reels, rods, and fishing gear. The facility specializes in the tarpon worm lure, a must-have if you are lucky enough to witness the annual worm hatch in our waters. The tarpon worm hatches at night for two nights in a row, and then in two weeks another worm hatch takes place. No one can predict exactly when the hatchings will happen, usually in June, but the tarpon go wild over the worms. So, we are told, do the anglers. Even if you don't fish, the sign outside this store always draws chuckles for the owner's wit and humor.

This Isn't Kansas

The months of June through Nov make up hurricane season in south Florida. Here in the Florida Keys, summer alerts us to keep a watchful eye peeled on the skies over open water for yet another weather concern. This concern is water spouts. Water spouts are tornadoes or vortexes that form over open water and here in the Keys there are as many as 400 to 500 each year. We hold the title of the most frequent spot on earth for water spouts to form. The reason for this is our islands and shallow water heat the air; add to the mix our high humidity. With that heat, the air rises and the water in the humidity forms water droplets that make up clouds. As the water vapor condenses, more heat is released thus causing the air to rise faster. Then throw in the east-to-northeast "trade winds" and boom—the perfect water spout. Ranging in height from 18,000 to 20,000 feet they are dramatic to witness. Rarely do they come ashore, but nevertheless, they bear keeping a watchful eye on, especially if you are in or on the water.

Lower Keys

REEF LIGHT TACKLE
MM 29.7 Oceanside, Big Pine Key
(305) 872-7679
www.reeflighttackle.com

Stop in and swap fish stories about the one that did not get away because you came here for your fish outfitting! They have it all including a live bait room. The crew call their inventory "fish candy." There are lures by Hank Brown, Hookup, C & H, and Calcutta; jigs and spoons by Tormentor and Williamson Trolling Lures; terminal tanks with accessories; and reels by Avet and Shimano. Also in stock are shirts, hats, and polarized eyewear.

i In 2008, two fishermen anchored in the reef off Marathon spotted a 19-foot juvenile whale shark. These are the largest sharks in the ocean with adults measuring 33 feet long and weighing up to 60 tons. Their identifying marks are spotted backs with broad, flat faces. They scoot along feeding on whatever they can filter through their giant mouths. They are gentle and the only danger is getting slapped with their fins or tail. You just never know what you will see in the sea in the scenic Florida Keys!

Key West

CONCHY JOE'S MARINE & TACKLE, INC.
2300 North Roosevelt Blvd.
(305) 295-7745
www.conchyjoeskw.com

Conchy Joe's offers Biscayne, Diamondback, Falcon, and Star rods, as well as Billy Baits and Chaos Lures. You'll find Daiwa, Penn, and Shimano reels and fly fishing supplies. On-site rod and reel repair is also available along with custom-built rods and reels.

THE SALTWATER ANGLER
243 Front St.
(at Westin Key West Resort and Marina)
(305) 296-0700
www.saltwaterangler.com

The Saltwater Angler specializes in fly tackle. Look for Sage, G. Loomis, Orvis, and Scott rods and Orvis, Lamson, Sage, Loop, Fin-Nor, Tibor, and Abel reels. The store also stocks a full assortment of flies and fly-tying materials. You can also select from a complete line of top-brand fishing apparel by Ex Officio, Orvis, Patagonia, and Columbia. Books and artwork with an angling theme round out their offerings.

FLY-FISHING SCHOOLS

SANDY MORET'S FLORIDA KEYS FLY FISHING SCHOOL
MM 81.2 Oceanside, Islamorada
(305) 664-5423
www.floridakeysoutfitters.com

Founded and directed by veteran saltwater fly-fisherman Sandy Moret, this school brings freshwater fly-anglers back to school in droves to learn saltwater fly-fishing skills and techniques. Moret, who also owns and operates Florida Keys Outfitters, is a multitime grand champion of the Gold Cup Tarpon Tournament. With more than a dozen fly-rod Grand Slams and four world records to his credit, he has assembled an outstanding team of world renowned anglers to teach both novices and veterans the tricks of the trade.

DIVING AND SNORKELING

Ranking as the third largest reef system and one of the most popular dive destinations in the world, the Florida Keys' reef runs 192 miles from Virginia Key in Biscayne Bay all the way to the Dry Tortugas in the Gulf of Mexico. A fragile symbiotic city of sea creatures crowds our reef—fish, sponges, jellyfish, anemones, worms, snails, crabs, lobsters, rays, turtles, and, of course, both soft and stony corals—sometimes mixing it up with sunken bounty of a different kind: shipwrecks of yesteryear.

Although our coral reef appears sturdy, this toothsome barrier is actually made up of colonies of tiny living animals. These coral polyps develop so slowly it can take years for some species to grow just one inch. The careless toss of an anchor or slightest touch can destroy decades of coral growth in just seconds. When polyps are damaged or killed, the entire colony becomes exposed to the spread of algae or disease, and the reef is at risk.

To protect and preserve our marine ecosystem, Congress established the Florida Keys National Marine Sanctuary in 1990. Extending on both sides of the Florida Keys, the 2,800-square-nautical-mile sanctuary is the second largest marine sanctuary in the United States (see the Area Overview chapter). The sanctuary encompasses two of the very best diving areas in the reef chain of the Keys: the Key Largo National Marine Sanctuary, which in turn envelops John Pennekamp Coral Reef State Park; and the Looe Key National Marine Sanctuary.

The state of Florida adjusted its offshore boundaries from 7 miles to 3 miles. This means many of the underwater dive and snorkel sites that used to be referred to as John Pennekamp Coral Reef State Park are now actually part of the Key Largo National Marine Sanctuary. To clear up the confusion, remember: Key Largo National Marine Sanctuary encompasses the waters of John Pennekamp Coral Reef State Park, but Pennekamp is not synonymous with the sanctuary.

OVERVIEW

In this chapter we provide you with a rundown of great reef and wreck dives and snorkel adventures from Key Largo to the Dry Tortugas. Our reefs are not within swimming distance of the shore, so you will need to make your way by boat. If you plan to venture out on your own craft or in a rental boat, be sure to stop at a dive center or marine supply store and purchase a nautical map that denotes the exact coordinates for dive and snorkel sites (see the listings in this chapter). Motor to the reef only if you know the waters, are an experienced boat handler, and can read the nautical charts well. You are financially liable for damage to the reef, so always anchor only at mooring buoys when provided or on sandy areas of the sea bottom. Florida law dictates you fly the diver-down flag, which is red with a diagonal white stripe, to warn other boaters that divers are under water within 100 feet of your craft.

Probably the most popular and hassle-free way to dive or snorkel in the Florida Keys is to go out with a dive charter. Most reputable dive centers in the Keys belong to the Keys Association of Dive Operators, which sets standards of safety and professionalism. Crews are trained in CPR, first-aid, and handling dive emergencies. Emergency oxygen supplies are kept onboard. The dive captains, who must be licensed by the U.S. Coast Guard, judge weather conditions and water visibility each day and select the best sites suited to your experience level. Often their coveted knowledge of little-visited patch reefs and wrecks affords you an experience you could not duplicate on your own. We offer you a guide to dive centers, noting the comprehensive services ranging from instruction and underwater excursions to equipment rentals and sales.

In the Florida Keys, usually neither the crew nor the dive master accompanies divers in the water. Divers spread out across a shallow reef, two by two, swimming in a buddy system. The dive master stays onboard and watches everyone from the boat. You must prove your experience level by showing current dive certification and your dive log before you may go out on a dive charter. If you have not made a comparable dive within the past six months, you must hire an instructor to accompany you in the water. Be sure you are comfortable with the sea conditions and that they are consistent with your level of expertise. If this is your first dive, alert the crew so that they can help you.

i Funded by Sanctuary Friends Foundation of the Florida Keys, Ken Nedimeyer and a group of volunteers have successfully propagated and transplanted native staghorn corals in the wild. Some of the corals Ken "baby-sat" for 12 years, and by using polyps that settled on his "livestock," the staghorn thickets have been successfully established. Contact the Foundation at (305) 289-2288 or visit www.sanctuary friends.org for more information.

Whether you dive on your own or go out to the reef with a charter, you should be aware of the strong current of the outgoing tidal flow and in the Gulf Stream. It is easy to overlook the current in the fascination of your dive until, low on both energy and air, you must swim against it to get back to the boat. Begin your dive by swimming into the current. To determine the direction of the current, watch the flow of your bubbles or lie back into a float position and see which way the current carries you.

Be careful around bridges. The tremendous energy of the tides passing through the pilings of our bridges creates coral outcroppings that would not normally be so close to shore. Divers and snorkelers without boat transportation to the patch reefs or the gulf waters like to take advantage of this underwater terrain to look for lobsters. Be forewarned: It is very dangerous to dive or snorkel under and around our bridges. The currents are swift and the tidal pull is strong. Boat traffic is often heavy. If you do decide to dive or snorkel here, be sure to carry a diver-down flag with you on a float, and follow the buddy system. The best and safest time to tackle these turbulent waters is just before slack tide, during slack tide, and immediately following slack tide. The time of this cycle varies with wind, the height of the tide, and the phase of the moon.

Whether you'd like to spend a few hours, days, weeks, or a lifetime exploring our coral reefs and wrecks, you'll find in this chapter all you need to know to "get wet," as divers like to say, in the Florida Keys.

IN EMERGENCIES

Divers in the Florida Keys are in good hands in the face of a recompression emergency. The Florida Keys Hyperbaric Center (305-853-1603) is located at Mariners Hospital in the Upper Keys (see the Health Care chapter).

Dive shop personnel, instructors, dive masters, and boat captains have joined with members of the local EMS, U.S. Coast Guard, Marine Patrol, NOAA, Monroe County Sheriff's office, and the Florida State Highway Patrol to develop a coordinated evacuation program to get injured divers off the water and to the hyperbaric chamber quickly. In case of a decompression injury, call 911 and get the victim to the nearest emergency room as rapidly as possible.

The Keys to the Reef

Most diving and snorkeling takes place on the barrier reefs of the Florida Keys. These linear or semicircular reefs, larger than the inner patch reefs, have claimed a graveyard of sailing vessels, many laden with gold and silver and other precious cargo. Salvaged by wreckers for centuries, the remains of these wrecks entice experienced divers, some of whom still hope to discover a treasure trove. Lighthouses were erected on the shallower, more treacherous sections of the barrier reef during the 19th century as an aid to

---

Great Annual Fish Count

The Reef Environmental Education Foundation (REEF), headquartered in Key Largo, invites divers to participate in the Great Annual Fish Count. First begun in California's Channel Islands in 1992, it now extends beyond U.S. borders into the Caribbean and Canada. More than 105,000 volunteer surveys have been submitted. This survey is used for fish population, studies of marine protected areas, artificial reefs, and to see if a particular species is being overfished. No wildlife is harmed in this effort, and to date, nearly 10,000 divers have contributed. Visit www.fishcount.org or www.reef.org to learn more.

---

navigation. They now also mark popular dive and snorkel destinations.

The coral reef system of the Florida Keys is distinctively known as a spur-and-groove system. Long ridges of coral, called spurs, are divided by sand channels, or grooves, that merge with the adjoining reef flat, a coral rubble ridge on the inshore edge of the reef. The ridges of elkhorn coral thrive in heavy surf, often growing several inches a year. The spurs extend 100 yards or more, with shallower extremities sometimes awash at low tide while the seaward ends stand submerged in 30 to 40 feet of water. Small caves and tunnels wind through to the interior of the reef, home to myriad species of marine plants and animals. The white grooves separating the spurs are covered with coarse limestone sand, a composite of coral and mollusk shell fragments and plates from green calcareous algae. The wave action passing between the spurs of coral creates furrows in the sand floor of the grooves.

Generally, the shallower the reef, the brighter the colors of the corals, because strong sunlight is a prerequisite for reef growth. Legions of fish sway back and forth keeping time with the rhythm of the waves. While deep dives yield fascinating discoveries—such as long-lost torpedoed ships—for those with advanced skills, sport divers will not be disappointed with the plethora of sea life within 60 feet of the surface. Night dives reveal the swing shift of the aquatic community. While the parrotfish may find a cave, secrete a mucous balloon around itself, and sleep the night through, sparkling corals blossom once the sun sets, and other species come out of hiding to forage for food.

Supplementing our coral barrier and the broken bodies of reef-wrecked ships, artificial reefs have been sunk to create underwater habitats for sea creatures large and small. The Florida Keys Artificial Reef Association, a nonprofit corporation of Keys residents, banded together in 1980 to capitalize on putting to use the many large pieces of concrete that became available during the removal of some of the old Keys bridges. More than 35,000 tons of rubble were deep-sixed throughout the Keys' waters between 1981 and 1987, creating acres of artificial reefs. In recent years, steel-hull vessels up to 350 feet long have been scuttled in stable sandy-bottom areas, amassing new communities of fish and invertebrates and easing the stress and strain on the coral reef by creating new fishing and diving sites. You'll find a comprehensive list of the artificial reef locations at the Florida Fish and Wildlife Conservation Commission Web site: www.state.fl.us/fwc/marine.

Always use a mooring buoy if one is available. The large blue-and-white plastic floats are drilled directly into the sea bottom and installed with heavy chains or concrete bases. They are available on a first-come, first-served basis, but if you are a small craft, it is courteous to tie off with other similar boats, allowing larger vessels use of the mooring buoys. Approach the buoy from downwind against the current. Secure your boat to the pickup lines using a length of your own rope. Snap shackles provide quick and easy pickup and release. Large boats are advised to give out extra line to ensure a horizontal pull on the buoy. If no mooring buoys have been provided, anchor only in a sandy area downwind of a patch reef, so that your boat's anchor and chain do not drag or grate on nearby corals.

DIVE SITES

In the Keys parts of this section, we highlight some of the better-known and most enchanting dive and snorkel sites, listed in descending order from the top of the Keys in the Key Largo National Marine Sanctuary to the Looe Key National Marine Sanctuary in the Lower Keys.

In Key West our coral reef system heads west into the sunset as it swings by Cayo Hueso into the untamed and isolated but charted waters leading to the Marquesas and the Dry Tortugas. (The half-day dive excursions based in Key West do not venture as far as these outer, uninhabited Keys. You will have to charter private overnight dive excursions or travel the distance in your own motor or sailing yacht if you wish to explore these waters; see the Cruising chapter.) In the Key West and the And Beyond parts of this section, we highlight 19 of the most interesting dive and snorkel sites from Key West to the Dry Tortugas National Park.

Underwater History

In August 2008, underwater archaeology students from across the country took part in a deep mystery 25 feet below the surface off Key Largo. Their discovery of weathered metal bands of a paddle wheel, parts of a smokestack, and boilerplates helped them solve the puzzle of the shipwrecked *Menemon Sanford*. This 237-foot side-paddle steamship sank in 1862 while on a secret Civil War mission. The vessel was built in 1854 and named after Captain Sanford, founder of the Sanford Independent Line that later became Royal Caribbean Cruise Line.

Upper Keys

Carysfort Reef

Situated at the extreme end of Key Largo National Marine Sanctuary, Carysfort Reef appeals to both novice and intermediate divers. British vessel HMS *Carysfort* ran aground here in 1770. The reef, now marked by the 100-foot steel Carysfort Lighthouse, undulates between 35 and 70 feet. Lush staghorn corals, which look like bumpy deer antlers, and masses of plate coral, which overlap each other like roofing tiles, cascade down the 30-foot drop to the sandy bottom. Schools of algae-grazing blue tang and

pin-striped grunts circulate among the coral heads of a secondary reef. The HMS *Winchester*, a British man-of-war built in 1693, hit the reef in 1695 after most of her crew died of the plague while en route from Jamaica to England. The wreck, discovered in 1938, was cleaned out by salvagers in the 1950s. It rests southeast of Carysfort Light in 28 feet of water. Location: North Carysfort: Lat. 25° 13.80, Long. 80° 12.74; South Carysfort: Lat. 25° 13.00, Long. 80° 13.06.

The Elbow

Aptly named, the Elbow looks like a flexed arm as it makes a dogleg turn to the right. Prismatic damselfish and angelfish, so tame they will swim up and look you in the eye, belie this graveyard of sunken cargo ships, the bones of which litter the ocean floor. The 191-foot *Tonawanda*, built in 1863 in Philadelphia, ended its short career as a tug and transport vessel in 1866 when it stranded on the reef. The ca. 1877 passenger/cargo steamer *City of Washington*, cut down and sold as a barge, piled up on the Elbow Reef in 1917 as it was towed by the Edgar F. Luchenbach. Dynamited so it would not impede navigation, the barge's scattered remains rest near the *Tonawanda* in about 20 feet of water covered with purple sea fans and mustard-hued fire coral trees. The unidentified Civil War wreck, now nothing more than wooden beams held together by iron pins, sits in 25 feet of water. A search of the area may yield a sighting of an old Spanish cannon, probably thrown overboard to lighten the load when one of the ships ran aground. The Elbow, marked by a 36-foot light tower, provides good diving for the novice. Depths at this spur-and-groove reef range between 12 and 35 feet, and currents vary. Location: Lat. 25° 08.82, Long. 80° 15.19.

Christ of the Deep *Statue*

Perhaps one of the most famous underwater photographs of all time is of the *Christ of the Deep* statue, which stands silhouetted against the sapphire-blue ocean waters bordering Key Largo Dry Rocks. This 9-foot figure of Christ, arms upraised and looking toward the heavens, was donated to the Underwater Society of America by Egidi Cressi, an Italian industrialist and diving equipment manufacturer. Designed by Italian sculptor Guido Galletti and cast in Italy, the statue is a bronze duplicate of the Christ of the Abysses, which stands under water off Genoa. Surrounded by a flotilla of nonchalant skates and rays, the statue's left hand appears to be pointing to the massive brain corals peppering the adjoining ocean floor. With depths ranging from shallow to 25 feet, snorkeling is outstanding. Schools of electric-blue neon gobies congregate in cleaning stations, waiting to service other fish that wish to be rid of skin parasites. A slow offer of an outstretched arm may net you a goby-cleaned hand. Location: Lat. 25° 07.45, Long. 80° 17.80.

Grecian Rocks

This crescent-shaped patch reef, which ranges in depth from shallow to 35 feet, ranks as a favorite among snorkelers and novice divers. Colonies of branched elkhorn corals, resembling the racks of bull moose or elk, provide a dramatic backdrop for the curious cruising barracudas, which often unnerve divers by following them about the reef but rarely cause a problem. Colossal star corals dot the area, which is populated by a rainbow palette of Spanish hogfish and a scattering of protected queen conch. An old Spanish cannon reportedly is concealed in one of the more luminous of the star coral,

placed there some time ago by rangers of John Pennekamp Coral Reef State Park. Look for a small patch of reef near Grecian Rocks where old cannon and fused cannonballs litter the landscape. At low tide this reef rises out of the water. Location: Lat. 25° 06.70, Long. 80° 18.55.

San Pedro Underwater Archaeological Preserve

This shipwreck park named after the Spanish ship *San Pedro* lies in 18 feet of water approximately 1.25 nautical miles south of Indian Key. The ship went down in 1773, and the remains can be found on the white sand bottom. Visit www.floridastateparks.org for more information.

USS **Spiegel Grove**

The USS *Spiegel Grove,* a decommissioned landing ship dock (LSD 32), was scuttled as an artificial reef in May 2002 in the waters off Key Largo. The largest vessel ever sunk as an artificial reef in the United States, the *Spiegel Grove* did not go down without a fight, however. The ship unexpectedly began to sink ahead of schedule, turtling and sinking upside down and at an angle that kept it from completely submerging. The ship's bow stuck up out of the water for three weeks before a Resolve Marine Group salvage crew rolled it onto its starboard side, allowing it to sink completely on June 10, 2002. The Spiegel Grove rests at a depth of 130 feet, midway between the *Benwood* wreck and the Elbow reef.

Benwood *Wreck*

The English-built freighter *Benwood*, en route from Tampa to Halifax and Liverpool in 1942 with a cargo of phosphate rock, attempted to elude German U-boats early in World War II by running without lights. Unfortunately, the American freighter *Robert C. Tuttle* also took a darkened route. In their ultimate collision, the American ship ripped the *Benwood*'s starboard side open like a can opener. As it limped along, a fire broke out on deck and attracted a German U-boat, which finished her off with two torpedo hits. A memorable first wreck for novice divers, the bow of the ship remains in about 50 feet of water, while the stern rests in but 25 feet. It lies in line with the offshore reef about 11/2 miles north of French Reef. Location: Lat. 25E 03.16, Long. 80E 20.02.

French Reef

Even novice divers can negotiate the caves at French Reef. Swim through the 3- to 4-foot limestone ledge openings or just peer in for a glance at the vermilion-painted blackbar soldierfish, which often swim upside down, mistakenly orienting themselves to the cave ceilings. Limestone ledges, adorned with tub sponges, extend from the shallows to depths in excess of 35 feet. Follow the mooring buoys for the best route. A mountainous star coral marks Christmas Tree Cave where, if you swim through the two-entrance passage, trapped air bubbles incandescently flicker in the cave's low light. Hourglass Cave sports a shapely column of limestone that divides the space in half, and White Sand Bottom Cave, a large swim-through cavern, shelters a potpourri of groupers, dog snappers, moray eels, and copper-colored glassy sweepers. Location: Lat. 25° 02.06, Long. 80° 21.00.

White Bank Dry Rocks

A garden of soft corals welcomes snorkelers and novice divers to these patch reef twins. With calm waters and depths ranging from shallow to 25 feet, White Bank Dry Rocks extends north and south along Hawk Channel at the southern end of Key Largo National Marine Sanctuary. You will feel as if you are swimming in a giant aquarium, for the lacy sea fans, feathery sea plumes, and branching sea whips create surreal staging for the fluttering schools of sophisticated black-and-yellow French angelfish. Bring an underwater camera. Location: 1¼ miles inshore of French Reef.

Molasses Reef

Shallow coral ridges of this well-developed spur-and-groove reef radiate from the 45-foot light tower that marks Molasses Reef. Mooring buoys bob in deeper water, about 35 feet. Just off the eastern edge of the tower lies a single windlass, all that remains of the so-called Winch Wreck, or Windlass Wreck. Look for Christmas tree worms among the masses of star coral. The conical whorls, resembling maroon and orange pine trees, are actually worms that reside in living coral. If you slowly move a finger toward these faux flowers, they will sense your presence within half an inch and disappear like Houdini into their coral-encased tube homes. Location: Lat. 25° 01.00, Long. 80° 22.53.

USCG Bibb *and* USCG Duane

Advanced divers will relish the exploration of the two U.S. Coast Guard cutters sunk as artificial reefs 100 yards apart near Molasses Reef. Both these vessels, ca. mid-1930s, saw action in World War II and the Vietnam War. Both did search and rescue in their later peacetime years and were decommissioned in 1985. A consortium of dive shops and the Monroe County Tourist Development Council bought the cutters, which were subsequently stripped of armament, hatches, and masts, then cleaned. In 1987 the Army Corps of Engineers sank the 327-foot vessels on consecutive days. The *Bibb* rests on her side in 130 feet of water with her upper portions accessible at 90 feet. The upright *Duane* sits in more than 100 feet of water, but you can see the wheelhouse at 80 feet and the crow's nest in 60 feet of water. Location: *Bibb*—Lat. 24° 59.71, Long. 80° 22.77; *Duane*—Lat. 24° 59.38, Long. 80° 22.92.

Pickles Reef

Pickles Reef got its name from the coral-encrusted barrels strewn about the ocean floor near the remnants of a cargo ship, called the Pickles Wreck, that carried them to their demise. The kegs are said to resemble pickle barrels, hence the name of the reef, but more likely were filled with building mortar bound for burgeoning construction in Key West. Look for the distinctively marked flamingo tongue snails, which attach themselves to swaying purple sea fans, grazing for algae. Flamboyantly extended around the outside of the flamingo tongue's glossy cream-colored shell is a bright orange mantle with black-ringed leopardlike spots. Don't be tempted to collect these unusual creatures, for the colorful mantle is withdrawn upon death. With depths between 10 and 25 feet and a moderate current, Pickles Reef is a good dive for novice to intermediate skill levels. Location: Lat. 24° 59.23, Long. 80° 24.88.

Conch Reef

Dive charters usually anchor in about 60 feet of water at Conch Reef, but the area actually offers something for everyone. With depths ranging from shallow to 100 feet and currents varying from moderate to strong, beginners as well as intermediate and advanced divers will be entranced here.

The shallow section, festive with swirling schools of small tropicals, extends for a mile along the outer reef line. Conch Wall steeply drops from 60 to 100 feet, where sea rods, whips, fans, and plumes of the gorgonian family's deepwater branch congregate with an agglomeration of vaselike convoluted barrel sponges. The coral of Conch Reef was nearly decimated by heavy harvesting in bygone eras; dead stumps of pillar corals can still be seen. Location: Lat. 24° 57.11, Long. 80° 27.57.

Hens and Chickens

A brood of large star coral heads surrounds a 35-foot U.S. Navy light tower within 7 feet of the water's surface on this inshore patch reef, bringing to mind a mother hen and her chicks. Less than 3 miles from shore, this easily accessed 20-foot-deep reef remains popular with novice divers. Plumes, fans, and candelabra soft corals intermingle with skeletons of the coral graveyard (almost 80 percent of the reef died in 1970 after an unusually cold winter). Jailhouse-striped sheepshead mingle with shy notch-tailed grunts and the more curious stout-bodied groupers, but don't be tempted; spearfishing is not allowed here. Remains of the Brick Barge, a modern casualty, and an old steel barge torpedoed during World War II lie among the coral heads. Location: Lat. 24° 55.9, Long. 80° 32.90.

Eagle

In 1985 an electrical fire disabled the 287-foot *Aaron K*, a freighter that carried scrap paper between Miami and South America. Declared a total loss, she was sold to the Monroe County Tourist Council and a group of local dive shops and then scuttled her for use as an artificial reef. The vessel was renamed the *Eagle* after the Eagle Tire Company, which provided much of the funding for the project. A must-do for advanced divers, the *Eagle* landed on her starboard side in 120-foot waters, though her upper portions lurk within 65 feet of the surface. Densely packed polarized schools of silversides flow and drift within her interior. The tiny fork-tailed fish will detour around divers swimming through the school. Location: Lat. 24° 52.18, Long. 80° 34.21.

Middle Keys

Alligator *Reef*

Launched in 1820 in Boston, the USS *Alligator* hunted pirates in Florida as part of the West Indies Squadron. A 136-foot light tower now marks her namesake, Alligator Reef, which claimed the copper- and bronze-fitted warship in 1825. The navy stripped the ship's valuables and blew her up. The *Alligator* rests offshore from the 8- to 40-foot-deep reef, now a bordello of brilliant tropicals, corals, and shells. Location: Lat. 24° 51.07, Long. 80° 37.21.

American, Maryland, and Pelican Shoals

American, Maryland, and Pelican shoals lie just off shore of the Saddlebunch Keys. They are east of Summerland and Cudjoe Keys where dive boats depart. Teeming with fish, these reefs are less visited than others in the Florida Keys.

Coffins Patch

Gargantuan grooved brain corals join staghorns and toxic fire corals at Coffins Patch, a 1½-mile reef popular with Middle Keys divers. A drift of yellow-finned French grunts and festive angelfish join an escort of mutton snappers, each distinctively branded with a black spot below the rear dorsal fin, as they guard the remains of the Spanish galleon *Ignacio*, which spewed a cargo of coins across the ocean floor in 1733. Location: Lat. 24° 40.60, Long. 80° 58.50.

Thunderbolt

In 1986 the artificial reef committee bought the *Thunderbolt*, a 188-foot cable-laying workboat, from a Miami River boatyard. The vessel was cleaned and her hatches removed. She then was towed south of Coffins Patch, where she was sunk as an artificial reef. Sitting majestically upright in 115 feet of water, the *Thunderbolt*'s bronze propellers, cable-laying spool, and wheelhouse are still recognizable. A stainless-steel cable leads from the wreck to a permanent underwater buoy. Current is strong at this wreck. Clip a line to the eye on the buoy and walk down the line. This dive is suitable for those with advanced certification. Location: Lat. 24° 39.48, Long. 80° 57.90.

Delta Shoals

This shallow 10- to 20-foot shoal claimed many an unsuspecting ship through the centuries. Perhaps the most colorful history is that of an old vessel that ran aground in the 1850s. The ship yielded no treasure, but recovery of unique relics and elephant tusks led to the name Ivory Wreck. Among the wreckage were leg irons and brass bowls, leading historians to believe this was a slave ship from Africa. Location: Lat. 24° 37.78, Long. 81° 05.49.

Sombrero Reef

A 142-foot lighthouse tower marks this living marine museum. Coral chasms, ridges, and portals support a proliferation of fuzzy, feathery, or hairy gorgonians as well as a salad bowl of leafy lettuce coral. A battalion of toothy barracuda swims reconnaissance, but don't be alarmed. You are too big to be considered tasty. Location: Lat 24° 37.50, Long. 81° 06.50.

Lower Keys

Looe Key National Marine Sanctuary

In 1744 Captain Ashby Utting ran the 124-foot British frigate HMS *Looe* hard aground on the 5-square-mile Y-shaped reef now bearing her name. Remains of the ship are interred between two fingers of living coral about 200 yards from the marker in 25 feet of water. The ballast and the anchor remain camouflaged with centuries of vigorous coral growth. Preserved as a national marine sanctuary since 1981, the 5- to 35-foot-deep waters surrounding Looe Key protect the diverse marine communities from fishing, lobstering, or artifact collecting, all forbidden.

The sanctuary, like Key Largo National Marine Sanctuary in the Upper Keys, offers interesting dives for novice, intermediate, and advanced divers alike. The spur-and-groove formations of Looe Key National Marine Sanctuary are the best developed in the Keys, and you can observe a complete coral reef ecosystem within the sanctuary's boundaries (see the Area Overview chapter).

Take a laminated reef-creature guide sheet (readily available in dive shops) on your dive to identify the senses-boggling array of sea life at Looe Key. Look for some of these interesting species: The yellowhead jawfish excavates a hole in the sand with its mouth and retreats, tail-first, at the first sign of danger. The wary cottonwick sports a bold black stripe from snout to tail. The prehistoric-looking red lizardfish rests camouflaged on rocks and coral. The occasional blue-spotted peacock flounder changes color, chameleonlike, to match its surroundings.

Commercial dive charters provide excursions to Looe Key from Big Pine Key, Little Torch Key, and Ramrod Key. Location: Lat. 24° 32.70, Long. 81° 24.50.

The Adolphus Busch

Scuttled in 1998 between Looe Key and American Shoal, this 210-foot freighter is

Astronauts Under the Sea

NASA's National Oceanic and Atmospheric Administration's Aquarius underwater laboratory is the site for "splash down." This is tech talk for astronaut training underwater. The lab at Aquarius is a 45-foot-long complex that rests 62 feet beneath the surface, 3 miles off Key Largo in the Florida Keys National Marine Sanctuary. This setting provides a habitat for astronauts training for possible assignments to missions in space. During the NASA Extreme Mission Operations, astronauts imitate moonwalks, testing for mobility using specially designed space suits and weights to simulate lunar gravity.

Aquarius is also the world's only undersea science facility. In 2007 a Saudi Arabian prince, Khaled bin Sultan, financed the underwater SeaCAMEL Webcast made available to universities and institutions around the United States and England.

named for one of the founders of the brewing industry. The *Adolphus Busch* sits upright in 100 feet of water. A tower comes within 40 feet of the surface and can be penetrated. *Adolphus Busch* is rapidly becoming a thriving tenement of fish and marine organisms. Location: Lat. 24° 31.81, Long. 81° 27.64.

Key West

Eastern Sambo

An underwater ridge at 60 feet dropping off sharply to the sand line at 87 feet goes by the name of Eastern Drop-off in this immensely popular reef area southeast of Key West. Reddish-brown honeycomb plate corals encrust the sloping reef face while boulder corals pepper the base at the outer margin of the reef. The Hook, a long spur-and-groove canyon, extends south from the Eastern Sambo reef marker. Look for cruising tarpon during the summer months. West of Eastern Sambo is a site commonly referred to as No. 28 Marker, where sea turtles and nurse sharks make their rounds of the elkhorn coral. Location: Lat. 24° 29.50, Long. 81° 39.80.

Middle Sambo

Coral heads and soft corals cover the sand beneath the 30- to 40-foot depths of Middle Sambo. You won't be alone as you observe the prolific lobsters haunting this area, especially in the summer months. Look for squadrons of tarpon and snook. Location: Lat. 24° 29.71, Long. 81° 41.79.

Western Sambo

Mooring buoys mark this popular reef area with a variety of dives to 40 feet. Fields of branch coral stretch into the blue infinity while mountains of sheet, boulder, star, and pillar corals cover the dramatic drop from 28 to 40 feet. Small yellow stingrays, which are actually covered with dark spots and can pale and darken protectively when the environment dictates, lie on the bottom with their stout, venomous tails buried in the sand. In the protected midreef area of the Cut, goggle-eyed blennies mill about with a colony of yellowhead jawfish, retreating tail-first into their sand holes when frightened.

Half a mile south of Western Sambo, the remains of the *Aquanaut*, a 50-foot wooden tugboat owned by Chet Alexander, were scuttled in 75 feet of water as an artificial reef. Scattered about amid drifts of mahogany snappers and nocturnal glasseyes, the wreck is alive with spiderlike yellow arrow crabs. Location: Lat. 24° 29.38, Long. 81° 42.68.

Cayman Salvager

The 187-foot-long, steel-hulled buoy tender *Cayman Salvager*, built in 1936, originally sank at the Key West docks in the 1970s. Refloated and innards removed, she went back down in 1985 for use as an artificial reef, coming to rest on her side. Hurricane-force waves later righted her, and she now sits in 90 feet of water on a sandy bottom. Look for the fabled 200-pound jewfish and 6-foot moray eel residing in her open hold. Location: 6 miles south of Key West, 1 mile southwest of Nine Foot Stake, which is 1 mile west of No. 1 Marker.

Joe's Tug

Sitting upright in 60 feet of water, *Joe's Tug*, a 75-foot steel-hulled tugboat, was scuttled as an artificial reef in 1989. The boat rests inshore from the *Cayman Salvager* on a bed of coral. This is one of the most popular wreck dives in the Key West circuit. Look for Elvis, the resident jewfish, who hangs out at the tug with yet another large moray eel. Location: 6 miles south of Key West.

Eastern Dry Rocks

Shells, conchs, ballast stones, cannonballs, and rigging of disintegrating wrecks litter the rubble zone, coral fingers, and sand canyons of Eastern Dry Rocks. With depths between 5 and 35 feet and only light current, this dive is suited to novices. Location: Lat. 24° 27.50, Long. 81° 50.44.

Rock Key

Twenty-foot cracks barely as wide as a single diver distinguish Rock Key from nearby cousins at Eastern Dry Rocks. A 19th-century ship carrying building tiles from Barcelona went aground on Rock Key, scattering her bounty about the ocean floor. Tiles carrying the Barcelona imprint are reportedly still occasionally recovered. Location: Lat. 24° 27.21, Long. 81° 51.60.

Stargazer

Billed as the "world's largest underwater sculptured reef," *Stargazer* stands 22 feet below the surface, 5 miles off Key West between Rock Key and Sand Key. The creation of artist Ann Lorraine Labriola, *Stargazer* mimics a primitive navigational instrument, its giant steel sections—ranging between 2,000 and 8,000 pounds—emblazoned with constellation symbols and emblems. A "mystery chart" sends divers on an underwater treasure hunt with a series of puzzles that require a certain amount of celestial knowledge to solve. Location: Lat. 24° 27.49, Long. 81° 52.09.

Sand Key

Originally called Cays Arena by early Spanish settlers, Sand Key, 6 miles south of Key West, is partially awash at low tide. Topped by a distinctive 110-foot red iron lighthouse, Sand Key's shape, composed of shells and ground coral, changes with each hurricane and tropical storm. Sand Key shines as a good all-weather dive and, with depths ranging to 65 feet, appeals to all skill levels. The shallows of the leeward side provide good snorkeling. In spring and summer the Gulf Stream movement over the shallows provides great visibility and vibrant colors. You can easily reach Sand Key on your own in a 17- to 18-foot boat on a calm day. Location: Lat. 24° 27.19, Long. 81° 52.58.

Ten-Fathom Bar

Advanced divers peruse a gallery of deep dives on the western end of the outer reef system, which is nearly 4 miles long. The southern edge, Fennel Ridge, begins at about 60 feet deep, giving the site its name, then plunges to the sand line, undulating between 90 and 120 feet. Encrusted telegraph cables at 45 to 55 feet, apparently snaking a line to Havana, cut across the eastern end of the Ten-Fathom Bar, competing with man-size sponges and dramatic black coral.

Near the cable, Eye of the Needle sports a plateau of coral spurs. Deep, undercut ledges shelter the spotted, white-bellied porcupinefish. Divers can swim under a ledge and up through a broad "eye" to the top of the plateau. Depths max out at 120 feet, but you'll see much more between 40 and 80 feet. Be prepared for a sea squadron of fin-driven tropicals to shadow your every move. Location: Half a mile due south of Sand Key.

Toppino's Reef (#1 Marker Reef)

Four and a half miles south of Boca Chica Channel and 5 miles south of Key West is one of the most beautiful shallow dive spots in the Keys. Famous for 8- to 10-foot high coral fingers rising from the bottom, marine life congregate to eat off the hard and soft coral. This is a very popular nighttime dive spot in 25 feet of water. The U.S.S. *Vandenberg* was sunk near this spot in 2009 (see below, this chapter).

Western Dry Rocks

Experts will love the unusual marine life at Western Dry Rocks. Novices and snorkelers will, too, because this site ranges in depth from 5 to 120 feet, averaging 30 feet with lots of light. Coral fingers with defined gullies and coral formations laced with cracks and caves showcase species normally found more in the Bahamas than in the Keys. The deep-dwelling candy basslets hide themselves away at 90 feet, while their more gregarious cousins, the orangeback bass, hang out in the open. The dusky longsnout butterflyfish prefer dark recesses, though they will sometimes curiously peer out to see what's happening. Sharks have been witnessed regularly enough to prompt advice against spearfishing. Location: 3 miles west of Sand Key.

Alexander's Wreck

Commercial salvor Chet Alexander bought a 328-foot destroyer escort from the U.S. Navy at the bargain price of $2,000 and sank her (still sporting her deck guns) in about 40 feet of water west of Cottrell Key as an artificial reef in 1972. Though the current fluctuates from moderate to strong, the relatively shallow depths here allow conscientious novices a chance to swim among fascinating sea creatures: The bodies of the prison-bar-striped spadefish resemble the spade figures in a deck of playing cards.

Zebra-striped sheepshead are so curious that if you remain stationary, they may come over to investigate. The flashy metallic gold- and silver-striped porkfish is apparently the victim of a cruel creator—two bold, black, diagonal bands slash across its glittery head. Location: Lat. 24° 36.97, Long. 81° 58.91.

Cottrell Key

A snorkeler's paradise at 3 to 15 feet, Cottrell Key, on the gulf side, saves the day for divers when the weather is foul on the Atlantic. The grassy banks of the adjoining lakes protect the reef in east-southeast to southwest winds. Ledges and solution holes run for several miles amid intermittent coral heads and swaying gorgonians. The pits, crevices, and coral caves hold great treasures: encrusting orange sponges, which look like spilled cake batter; lustrously mottled cowries camouflaged by their extended mantles; the Florida horse conchs, which will venture out of their long conical spire if you wait patiently; and the spindle-shaped freckled tulip snails. Location: Gulf side, 9 miles out of N.W. Channel.

USS Vandenberg

Key West has its newest artifical reef—a 13,000-ton, 520-foot-long, 100-foot-tall, decommissioned vessel, the *General Hoyt S. Vandenberg*. Located near mile marker 32, in 140 feet of water, 6 miles off the coast of Key West, in the Florida Keys National Marine Sanctuary at a cost of nearly $6 million, the *Vandenberg* is one of the premier dive sites in the world. Experts boast you can dive there for days and not see it all. Suitably trained and equipped deep divers can penetrate the superstructure using the multi-horizontal and vertical swim-through flooding and venting holes that are cut into the ship. The

Vandenberg is a retired U.S. Air Force missile tracking ship and was decommissioned in 1983. The ship also tracked U.S. space missions in the early 1960s. Local videographers from Digital Island Media won an Emmy for their work on filming the sinking of the *Vandenberg*.

> **i** Local honorary conch and ocean explorer Sylvia Earle convinced Google executives to launch Google Ocean in February 2009. Using existing maps and databases to reveal parts of the ocean world beneath surfaces, Google's downloadable programs allow views under the Florida Keys of marine protected areas, dive sites, and shipwrecks. All this without getting your hair wet! Visit www.earth.google.com/ocean.

And Beyond

The Shipwrecks of Smith Shoals

Between June and Aug 1942, four large ships met their demise near Smith Shoals, apparent unwary victims of American military mines. The USS *Sturtevent,* a 314-foot-long four-stack destroyer, was only two hours out of port escorting a convoy when two consecutive explosions ripped her apart. She rests in 65 feet of water. The 3,000-ton American freighter *Edward Luchenbach*, en route from Jamaica to New Orleans with a cargo of tin, zinc, and tungsten, joined the *Sturtevent* after hitting the same minefield. The *Bosiljka* also made a navigational misstep, succumbing to an American mine as she carried her pharmaceutical cargo from New Orleans to Key West. Groupers, jewfish, snappers, and cobia populate the sunken 277-foot Norwegian ship *Gunvor*, taken by a mine on her way to Trinidad from Mobile,

Alabama. The wreckage is scattered in 60 feet of water. Location: Lat. 24° 45.30, Long. 81° 01.18.

Marquesas Keys

This group of 10 mangrove islands surrounded by shallow waters has alternately been called the remains of a prehistoric meteor crater and an atoll. The ring of keys was named for the Marquis de Cadierata, commander of the 1622 Spanish fleet that included the wrecks *Atocha* and *Santa Margarita*. The wrecks were partially salvaged until 1630 by the Spanish, who enticed slave divers to search the remains, promising freedom to the first diver to recover a bar of silver from the site. Mel Fisher rediscovered the ships in 1985. Fisher, the famous 20th-century salvor, found a mother lode of treasure in the holds. The islands evidence little human influence, for they remain uninhabited. Clusters of coral heads shrouded in groupers and snappers mark the southern edge of the islands. Twenty-five miles from Key West, the Marquesas appeal to divers cruising in their motor yachts or on an overnight charter or to hale and hearty day-trippers. West of the Marquesas several wrecks dot the suboceanic landscape. Exercise caution before diving, however, because the U.S. Navy has been known to use them as bombing and strafing targets from time to time. Before you strap on your tanks, check your radio for a Coast Guard bulletin regarding this area. Location: 25 miles west of Key West.

Northwind

The *Northwind*, a large metal tugboat belonging to Mel Fisher's Treasure Salvors Inc., tragically sank in 1975 while working on the *Atocha* project. Said to have a malfunctioning fuel valve and a leaky bulkhead, the *Northwind* capsized while at anchor, taking Fisher's son and daughter-in-law to a watery grave. The vessel lies on her side in 40 feet of water 3½ miles southwest of the Marquesas.

Cosgrove Shoal

A 50-foot skeletal lighthouse marks the northern edge of the Gulf Stream, 6 miles south of the western Marquesas. This rocky bank runs for miles, a prehistoric dead reef where caves and ledges support gardens and forests and social clubs of marine fin and flora. A contingent of giant barracuda patrols the shallows, and black coral grows up from the depths, which extend beyond recreational diving capacities. Be sure to take the strong outgoing tide into consideration before you dive here. Location: 6 miles south of the western edge of the Marquesas.

The lionfish, a small fish with spines that are venomous, is prolific and voracious and has been spotted in the Florida Keys waters. The lionfish is native to the Pacific Ocean and has been known to upset local ecosystems off the coast of North Carolina as well as in the Bahamas. If you see one, do not touch the lionfish. Immediately contact REEF at (305) 852-0030.

Marquesas Rock

Moderate to strong currents and depths to 120 feet dictate that this dive is only suited to advanced skill levels. A can-buoy marks the rocky plateau of Marquesas Rock, the cracks and crevices of which reveal a potpourri of sea life. A school of jacks, apparently attracted by your bubbles, may make a swing past. Saucer-eyed reddish squirrelfish, with elongated rear dorsal fins resembling squirrel tails, mind their own business in the shaded bottom crevices. Occasional sightings of sailfish, sperm whales, and white sharks have been reported. Keep in mind that when diving at Marquesas Rock you are 30 miles from the nearest assistance.

Dry Tortugas National Park

The end of the line in the Florida Keys, the Dry Tortugas lie some 60 miles beyond Key West. Small boats are discouraged from making the trip because strong tidal currents flowing against prevailing winds between Rebecca Shoals and the reef of the Tortugas can be treacherous. There is no fuel, fresh water, or facilities offering provisions, nor will you find any emergency assistance. Nonetheless, if your vessel is self-sufficient, if you are with a charter out of Key West, or you have traveled to the Dry Tortugas by seaplane or ferry to camp on Garden Key (see the Recreation and Campgrounds chapters), you are in for the treat of a lifetime.

The eight-island chain is guarded as our southernmost national park. All living creatures below are protected from collection or capture, so a virtual mega-aquarium exists beneath the sea. The constant Gulf Stream current cleanses the waters, allowing visibility of 80 to 100 feet over the 100-square-mile living coral reef. Just off the beach on the west side of Loggerhead Key slumbers a snorkeler's paradise. About a mile offshore lies the remains of a 300-foot, steel-hulled French wreck. Divers report that a monster-size jewfish estimated to be 150 years old resides under the wreck. Other wrecks are littered about the ocean floor, claimed by the reef during centuries past.

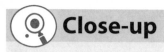

Close-up

Diving for Lobster

Now, you Easterners may conjure up scarlet visions of the mighty Maines, but when we say lobster here in the Florida Keys, a totally different creature comes to mind. Equally delectable and much in demand, the **Florida lobster,** or spiny lobster, is actually a crustacean whose relatives include crabs, shrimp, and crawfish. Unlike its Downeast cousin, the Florida lobster is clawless. Ten spiderlike legs support its spiny head and hard-shell body, and radarlike antennae make up for bugged eyes and weak eyesight. But its best defense, and the one most coveted by hungry humans, remains its powerful tail muscle, which propels the lobster backward at breakneck speed.

Diving for lobster is a popular sport in the waters of the Florida Keys. Like any other hunt, you will need to understand your intended prey, for self-preservation will be their only consideration. Nocturnal feeders, spiny lobsters hide underwater in crevices, between rocks, in caves, under artificial reefs, near dock pilings, or in dead coral outcroppings during the day. They are not easy to spot. They occasionally peek out from their protective holes, but most often only a single antenna will be visible. The good news is that a whole gang may be hiding out together.

So how do you catch these potentially tasty morsels locals call "bugs"? We have found a few basic tools—and tricks—to help swing the scales in your favor:

- **You will need a pair of heavy-duty dive gloves,** for the two large horns on the lobster's head and the sharp spines of its whipping tail can draw blood.

- **To store your captive prizes, get an easy-to-open mesh game bag** that has a fastener that you can hook to your weight belt. Be sure this bag does not drag over the reef, which would damage coral and other marine life.

- A probe, or "tickle stick," which is a **long metal or fiberglass rod with a short, 90-degree bend on one end,** allows you to wisely restrain from poking your arm into a crevice or hole in order to coax out a lobster. That hole could just as easily house a moray eel as a lobster.

- And finally, **a lobster net is a must** if you hope to capture the tickled lobster.

Florida law mandates lobster hunters carry a device to measure the **carapace** of each lobster. (The carapace is that portion of the lobster shell beginning between the eyes and extending to the hard end segment just before the tail.) The carapace should measure at least 3 inches; otherwise, the lobster—deemed a "short"—must be returned to the sea. The measuring device is most often made of plastic or metal and can be attached to a string and secured to your game bag. Measure the lobster before you put it in your bag; do not bring it to the boat to be measured.

To harvest lobsters in the Florida Keys recreationally, you must possess a valid **Florida saltwater fishing** license with a current **crawfish stamp** (see the Fishing chapter).

Look for lobsters in the **patch reefs** on the ocean side. Patch reefs can usually be found by using the **NOAA navigational charts.** Look for relatively shallow areas (15 to 20 feet) surrounded by deeper water (25 to 30 feet). If your boat is equipped with a chart recorder, use this device to detect bottom contours and the presence of fish. Look for irregular bottom areas, which will usually mean coral outcroppings and sponges. When you find the suspected patch reefs, check them out with a quick dive to the bottom before anchoring your boat. You will need to scuba dive for lobsters in the patch reefs.

Alternately, look for lobster **"holes"** in the shallow gulfside waters and, wearing mask, fins, and snorkel, **free-dive** for the crustaceans—a one-breath challenge for sure. These areas will appear as patches of brightness in the turtle-grass floor as you skim across the water in your skiff. Sandy sea bottom looks bright also, so you must slow to idle speed and look for a hunk of coral. It helps to throw a buoy marker at this spot (connect a dive weight to a Styrofoam buoy with a length of line), because these coral outcroppings are few and far between. Send a dive scout over the side to bird-dog the outcropping for antennae, and with a little luck, the hunt will begin.

These crusty crustaceans are a wily group. When frightened, the lobster will contract its powerful tail and propel itself like a bullet backward to the far recesses of its shelter or deep into the sea grass. Tickle your way to victory. Slowly slide your **tickle stick** behind the lobster and tap its tail. Bothered from behind, the lobster is persuaded to slowly leave its shelter to investigate. Once the lobster is out of the hole, place the net behind (yes, behind!) the lobster with the rim firmly resting on the sandy bottom if possible. Tap the lobster's head with the tickle stick. This time, irritated, the lobster will propel backward into your net. Quickly slam your net down on the seafloor so the lobster cannot escape. Then secure the net closed with your other hand. The lobster may thrash and become tangled in the net.

Holding the netted lobster firmly with one hand, measure the carapace. Carefully remove the lobster from the net. If the lobster is a short, release it to be captured another day. If it is legal size, place it securely in your game bag, tail-first. One thrust of the vigorous tail could negate all your efforts. Also, be careful not to release any other "bugs" you have already bagged. If you see a dark spot or reddish orange nodules under the tail, this lobster is an egg-bearing female. By Florida law you must release her.

Place your captured lobsters in the **saltwater-filled bait well** of your boat or store them on ice in a cooler with a lid. Do not wring the tails from the lobsters until you get back to shore. It is against Florida law to separate the tail from the body while on Florida waters. Once on dry land you may pull the tails, which by law must measure more than 5½ inches. There is negligible meat in the body of the Florida spiny lobster, so it may be discarded unless you want to boil it to make lobster stock. After wringing the tail, break an antenna from the severed body of the crawfish. Insert the antenna, larger end first, into the underside base of the tail and then pull it out. The spiny thorns of the antenna will snag the intestinal tract, which will be removed with the antenna. If you wish to freeze the lobster tails, place several in a small plastic zipper bag, fill the bag with fresh water, and place the bags in the freezer for up to six months.

We think the best way to cook Florida lobster tail is on the **grill.** First, with a sharp knife or kitchen scissors, butterfly the tail by cutting through the outer shell and meat. Spread the tail open and sprinkle with melted butter, salt, pepper, and onion powder or garlic powder if desired.

Place the tail on a double-thick piece of aluminum foil and fold the foil envelope style, sealing tightly. Grill over hot coals for 15 to 20 minutes or until the shell is bright red and the meat is no longer translucent. Serve grilled lobster tail with clarified butter or a slice of Key lime.

DIVE CENTERS

As you drive down the Overseas Highway from Key Largo to Key West, you will notice banner-size, red-and-white diver-down flags heralding one dive shop after another. More than 100 such establishments are listed in the phone book alone. To help you navigate this minefield of choices, we supply you with the best ammunition: information.

Many of the dive operations offer the same basic services and will take you to similar, if not the same, spots. But each also differs in many ways. Snorkelers and divers often are taken to the reef in the same excursion, for the varied depths of our spur-and-groove reefs can be experienced with multiple levels of expertise. Snorkel-only trips also are an option. The size of dive excursions varies greatly, ranging from 20 individuals or more to a small-boat group called a six-pack.

Dive rates are based on a two-tank, two-site daylight dive. If you don't have your own equipment, full-gear packages—generally including two tanks, buoyancy compensator, weight belt, regulator, octopus breathing device, gauges, and occasionally mask, fins, and snorkel—are available. A wet suit is advisable in winter. Always ask exactly what is included if you need a full-gear package. All our recommended dive centers make a one-tank, night-dive excursion on request unless otherwise specified.

Virtually all of our listed dive centers offer optional dive packages, either for multiple days of diving or for hotel-dive combinations. If you plan to dive on several days of your holiday, you will save money with a package, but you will be limited to diving with one exclusive dive center.

You may assume, unless otherwise noted, all featured dive centers rent full equipment and maintain a retail dive shop where you can purchase equipment, accessories, and underwater camera housings if needed. You may also count on the fact that all recommended dive centers offer a one-day "let's give it a try" resort course. These courses are based on participation of two or more people. Private courses also are available at a considerably higher fee. Many of our recommended dive centers offer a wide selection of Professional Association of Diving Instructors (PADI), National Association of Underwater Instructors (NAUI), and other advanced classes.

You will be required to show your certification card and logbook, and you must wear a buoyancy compensator and a submersible pressure gauge. Snorkels are required equipment for all divers. To dive deeper than 60 feet, considered a deep dive, you must hold advanced certification or a logbook entry showing dives to equivalent depths within the last six months. If you cannot meet these specifications, you will be required to be accompanied by an instructor or guide, which often requires an additional fee. You must wear an octopus (an emergency breathing device to share air with your dive buddy) or carry spare air for a deep dive, and you must be equipped with a depth gauge or a timing device. You do not need advanced certification to participate in a night dive, but you must own or rent a dive light and carry a Cyalume stick as a backup lighting system.

All dive centers request you check in at least 30 minutes prior to the excursion's departure. Allow even more time if you are renting a full-gear package. We list the dive centers in descending mile marker order from Key Largo through the Lower Keys to Key West, where the listings are alphabetical.

Upper Keys

CAPTAIN SLATE'S ATLANTIS DIVE CENTER
MM 106.5 Oceanside, 51 Garden Cove Dr., Key Largo
(305) 451-3020 or (800) 331-3483
www.captainslate.com

You can watch Captain Slate feed baitfish to a barracuda, mouth to mouth, and see him cuddle with a moray eel on the weekly Friday-morning "Creature Feature" dive trip with Captain Slate's Atlantis Dive Center, when the captain himself performs these fearless feats under water. Divers from all skill levels enjoy outings with the Atlantis Dive Center. Snorkelers can make a snorkel-only excursion to one destination aboard a glass-bottomed boat, or they can accompany divers to two reef locations. Snorkeling rates here include mask, fins, snorkel, and safety vest.

A special feature of Captain Slate's is the custom underwater wedding package. Divers are married in front of the Christ of the Deep statue at Key Largo Dry Rocks. Vows are made via underwater slates as guest-divers watch the ceremony from the ocean floor and guest-snorkelers view the proceedings from overhead. Guest landlubbers are accommodated in the glass-bottomed boat, where the perspective varies yet again. Videos and still-photography of the blessed event are also available.

AMY SLATE'S AMORAY DIVE RESORT
MM 104.2 Bayside, Key Largo
(305) 451-3595 or (800) 426-6729
www.amoray.com

From this resort, you can hop out of bed onto the deck and take off for a scuba excursion. The Amoray Dive Resort's villa lodging options, complete with hot tub and pool, cater to your every diving whim (see the Accommodations chapter). Amoray's catamaran will whisk you to the reefs of the Key Largo National Marine Sanctuary for a two-tank dive. Night dives are available.

SILENT WORLD DIVE CENTER INC.
MM 103.2 Bayside, Key Largo
(305) 451-3252 or (800) 966-3483
www.silentworldkeylargo.com

Silent World regularly visits the Elbow, Key Largo Dry Rocks, the *Benwood*, French Reef, Carysfort Reef, and other popular sites within Key Largo National Marine Sanctuary.

HORIZON DIVERS
MM 102.5 Oceanside, Ocean Drive, Building #1, Key Largo
(305) 453-3535 or (800) 984-3483
www.horizondivers.com

Horizon Divers offers a full hour of bottom time studying large varieties of fish species found in the waters off Key Largo. Videotape or photograph the sea life in these waters while polishing your diving skills. Whether you're novice or advanced, Horizon Divers have instructors to help you hone your skills. Advanced divers can dive in the area wrecks and in waters up to depths of 140 feet.

JOHN PENNEKAMP CORAL REEF STATE PARK BOAT RENTALS & DIVE CENTER
MM 102.5 Oceanside, Key Largo
(305) 451-6300 or (800) 326-3521
www.floridastateparks.org/pennekamp

Pennekamp State Park Dive Center prides itself on being the "only authorized dive center" in John Pennekamp Coral Reef State Park, although all the Key Largo dive centers advertise themselves as diving Pennekamp State Park. The only dive center actually situated inside Pennekamp's grounds, this company's scuba shuttles regularly visit such novice sport dives as Molasses Reef, French Reef, Christmas Tree Cove, the wreck of the *Benwood*, and the Christ of the Deep statue. All dives are less than 60 feet, and certification requirements are stringent. If you have not dived in the past two years, you must hire a guide. If you have not dived in three years, you will have to take a review course. Pennekamp does not offer night dives.

CORAL REEF PARK COMPANY
MM 102.5 Oceanside, John Pennekamp Coral Reef State Park, Key Largo
(305) 451-6300 or (800) 326-3521
www.pennekamppark.com

Snorkel-only excursions in John Pennekamp Coral Reef State Park leave the docks three times daily. The shallow-reef sites vary, depending upon where the least current, least wave action, and best visibility conditions exist. The snorkel trip lasts two and a half hours, with an hour and a half of actual snorkeling time at Molasses Reef, White Bank Dry Rocks, Grecian Rocks, Key Largo Dry Rocks, or Cannon Patch.

Another option is a four-hour sail and snorkel aboard a 38-foot catamaran. If you want to stay close to shore, you can rent mask, fins, and snorkel and paddle around in the water off Cannon Beach, where, yes, there really are a couple of sunken cannon and ancient anchors.

OCEAN DIVERS
MM 100 Oceanside, 522 Caribbean Dr., Key Largo
(305) 451-1113 or (800) 451-1113
www.oceandivers.com

Ocean Divers has had over 500,000 divers come through their dive center. Diving with Ocean Divers, which opened in 1977, brings a different adventure, because this company tries to maintain a rotating schedule of set dive sites if conditions allow. Visiting the popular sites within the Key Largo National Marine Sanctuary, Ocean Divers slips into Eagle Ray Alley and Fire Coral Cave at Molasses Reef, and between the stands of the rare day-feeding pillar coral. Divers who enjoy wreck dives can visit the *Bibb*, the *Duane*, and the *Spiegel Grove*. Night dives are regularly offered and upon request.

Ocean Divers is adjacent to Marina Del Mar Resort. It maintains two dive shops. The second is located at MM 105.5 Bayside, Key Largo.

RAINBOW REEF
MM 100 Oceanside, Key Largo
MM 83.4 Oceanside, Islamorada
(305) 664-4600 or (800) 457-4354
www.rainbowreef.us

Rainbow Reef, with two locations, offers extensive dives to coral and artificial reefs, ledges, walls, and centuries-old wrecks. Oh, and don't forget the fish! Depths range from 18 feet to 120 feet, with each dive site offering its own unique qualities. The charters hit all the spectacular spots from Pennekamp State Park down to Alligator Reef. Rainbow Reef has small (12 persons max) boats to help make your dive personal and pleasurable. They are a full-service PADI 5 Star Gold Palm Instructor. See you beneath the sea!

DIVERS DIRECT
MM 99.6 Oceanside, Key Largo
(305) 451-0118 or (800) 348-3872
www.diversdirect.com

This water lover's emporium, Divers Direct, with six locations in the state of Florida (see the Web site for details) offers one of the largest selections in men's, women's, and children's clothing along with dive gear, kayaks, surfboards, wakeboards, snorkeling, kids equipment, scuba gear, videos, books, and a repair service. In business since 1984, the owners are divers as well. They have trained their staff to be knowledgeable of their products and make sure their customers have the right gear for the right dive.

FLORIDA KEYS DIVE CENTER
MM 90.5 Oceanside, Tavernier
(305) 852-4599 or (800) 433-8946
www.floridakeysdivectr.com

The Florida Keys Dive Center is one of the few that offers technical diving. This refers to diving beyond the limits that apply to recreational diving. New compressors blend trimex, a gas containing varied blends of helium, nitrogen, and oxygen. Partial pressure blending puts 100 percent oxygen into special scuba tanks in addition to pre-blended enriched. The Florida Keys Dive Center is also one of only two 5 Star PADI Career Development Centers in the Keys.

The Florida Keys National Marine Sanctuary has devised a Shipwreck Trail that directs you to nine historic shipwreck sites along our coral reef. Underwater site guides for each of the wrecks are available at local dive shops. The guides provide shipwreck and mooring-buoy positions, history of the wrecked ships, a site map, and information on marine organisms you may encounter.

Middle Keys

ABYSS DIVE CENTER
MM 54 Oceanside, Marathon
(at the Holiday Inn Marina)
(305) 743-2126 or (800) 457-0134
www.abyssdive.com

The Abyss Dive Center in Marathon subscribes to the less-is-more theory of diving, which guarantees lots of personal attention. The company takes a maximum of six divers or snorkelers to 48 sites spread over the reefs at Sombrero Key, Coffins Patch, Yellow Rocks, and Delta Shoals. Abyss will take you to the *Thunderbolt* if your certs are current or your dive experience warrants, or you can hire an instructor and explore the wreck with a guide.

TILDEN'S SCUBA CENTER
MM 49.5 Bayside, Marathon
(at the Blackfin Resort and Marina)
(305) 743-7255 or (888) 728-2235
www.tildensscubacenter.com

Long known as a top-notch dive center in the Florida Keys, Tilden's heads to such reef locations as Coffins Patch, Porkfish Reef, and Shark Harbor and takes advanced divers on guided excursions to the *Thunderbolt* and the *Adelaide Baker* wrecks. Tilden's reports that the Middle Keys reef tracts are very healthy. Tilden Scuba Center operates the largest dive vessels in the Middle Keys—it's licensed to carry 40 passengers—but limits its excursions to 24 divers and snorkelers.

HALL'S DIVING CENTER
MM 48.5 Bayside, Marathon
(305) 743-5929 or (800) 331-4255
www.hallsdiving.com

If you are an advanced certified diver or have an 80-foot dive under your weight belt, head out to the *Thunderbolt* with Hall's. Divers of other skill levels will enjoy diving the Middle Keys' 25- to 90-foot reef specialties, from Looe Key to Coffins Patch and especially around Sombrero Reef. Snorkelers may accompany divers at shallow reef locations.

In addition to standard equipment, a deluxe full-gear package, featuring top-of-the-line Nitrox clean gear, is available. Hall's also rents and provides certification in the use of a rebreather and offers such specialty dives as marine interaction dives and diver propulsion vehicles. Or you can rent mask, fins, and snorkel and explore the shallow gulf waters or the Atlantic Ocean off Sombrero Beach with a buddy.

Lower Keys

UNDERSEAS INC.
MM 30.5 Oceanside, Big Pine Key
(305) 872-2700
www.flkeysdiving.com
In the Lower Keys, when you've said, "Looe Key National Marine Sanctuary," you've said it all. And when you need a dive center, Underseas will take you to depths to satisfy all levels from snorkelers and novice divers to those with advanced skills. Looe Key is endlessly fascinating. Departures are at 8:30 a.m. and 1:30 p.m.

STRIKE ZONE CHARTERS
MM 29.6 Bayside, Big Pine Key
(305) 872-9863 or (800) 654-9560
www.strikezonecharter.com
Docked out back, Strike Zone Charter's glass-bottomed catamarans are ready to transport you to the Looe Key National Marine Sanctuary for a spectacular two-tank dive. Strike Zone now also visits one of the Keys' newest artificial reefs, the *Adolphus Busch*.

LOOE KEY REEF RESORT & DIVE CENTER
MM 27.5 Oceanside, Ramrod Key
(305) 872-3786 or (800) 942-5397
www.diveflakeys.com
The friendly crew at Looe Key Reef Resort whisks you off to the Looe Key National Marine Sanctuary, where you will visit three sites with at least an hour of bottom time at each location. On Wed and Sat divers visit two reef sites plus the wreck of the *Adolphus Busch*. The other days divers will visit three reef sites. Snorkelers may accompany divers.

Looe Key Reef Resort and Dive Center offers dive/lodging packages at its adjoining motel. The dive boat leaves from its mooring directly behind the motel so schlepping your gear is not a burden here.

i Soldiers Undertaking Disabled Scuba (SUDS) is a nonprofit organization designed to help improve the lives of injured soldiers returning from Iraq and Afghanistan. As part of soldiers' physical rehab, SUDS takes them to Key Largo to finalize their scuba certification. For more information, visit www.sudsdiving.org.

Key West

CAPTAIN'S CORNER DIVE CENTER
125 Anne St.
(305) 296-8865 or (305) 304-0437
www.captainscorner.com
Captain's Corner Dive Center's reef and snorkel excursions feature wreck and reef dives, and double wreck dives are available by special arrangement.

During daylight saving time months you can dive the twilight wreck and reef dive on Tues, Thurs, and Sat. First you dive a wreck, then watch the sunset from the deck of the boat. After dark, experience the after-hours sea life during a reef dive.

Private trips may be booked to the wreck of the *Nuestra Señora de Atocha*, 30 miles west of Key West. Captain's Corner always has instructors in the water with you, so you can sign on even if you are a novice diver. The boat departs from 631 Greene St., corner of Greene and Elizabeth Streets at the Conch Republic Seafood Restaurant.

Pin Wreck

Off Grassy Key, in 14 feet of water, archaeological divers from the Florida State Division of Historical Resources and Florida Keys National Marine Sanctuary discovered a timeworn pile of rubble known as the Pin Wreck (named after the shiny copper alloy and wooden fastening pins found on the ocean bed floor). The 130-foot wreck is one of a few found in Hawks Channel that flows between Marathon and Grassy Key. Divers also confirmed, from further examining the wreck, that turtles have used the old posts and alloy fasteners to scratch themselves. By doing so, they have kept corrosion off the metal parts.

DIVE KEY WEST INC.
3128 North Roosevelt Blvd.
(305) 296-3823 or (800) 426-0707
www.divekeywest.com
Dive Key West offers "reef du jour," customizing the schedule based on diver demand and weather conditions. It concentrates on the 30-foot reef lines where the light is better and the colors are more brilliant, allowing you more bottom time. The inner reefs have large stands of coral and a high concentration of tropical fish, while at the outer reefs you will see less coral, more big sea fans, sponges, and larger finfish. For your two-dive combo you can choose between a wreck and a reef or two reefs. Dive Key West visits the wrecks of the *Cayman Salvager*, *Joe's Tug*, and the *Alexander* wreck, which, at 90 feet, 60 feet, and 30 feet, respectively, offer a skill level for everyone.

If you do not have the skill level for the wreck dive of your choice, you may hire an instructor to accompany you. Snorkelers will be custom-fitted with gear at no extra charge, and free instruction is available. Night dives, scheduled upon request, are always accompanied by an instructor. Departure times for the night dive vary by daylight saving time.

LOST REEF ADVENTURES
261 Margaret St. on Key West Bight
(305) 296-9737 or (800) 952-2749
www.lostreefadventures.com
Lost Reef Adventures customizes its dive trips one day before departure based upon the skill levels and dive-site desires of interested divers. Excursions visit the celebrated *Joe's Tug*, *Cayman Salvager*, and *Alexander* wreck sites and reefs from the Western Sambos to the Western Dry Rocks. Lost Reef offers night pilgrimages seasonally. First you can pay homage to the sun as it sinks into the water; then you will take the plunge for a one-tank twilight dive.

SUBTROPIC DIVE CENTER
1605 North Roosevelt Blvd. on
Garrison Bight
(305) 296-9914 or (800) 853-3483
www.subtropic.com
Mornings find Subtropic's dive boat exploring two wrecks or two reefs. Wrecks visited include *Joe's Tug*, the *Cayman Salvager*, and the *Alexander* wreck, whose shallower depths invite exploration by those of all experience levels.

Subtropic offers trips to a wreck and a reef or two reefs in the afternoons. These excursions visit the Sambos, Rock Key, Sand Key, and the Dry Rocks. Snorkelers are welcome on the afternoon excursions, or they may opt for a snorkel-only trip. Night dives are offered regularly.

RECREATION

If you want to scuba dive, fish, sail, or motor in our abundant waters, see the related chapters in this book. For a plethora of other stimulating diversions, read on. We show you where the action is—from skydiving, parasailing, and water sports to sunset cruises, gunkholing ecotours, and bicycling. You'll find out about our beaches and public parks in this chapter. And if the weather isn't fine—which is rare—or you would just like to stay indoors, look here, too, for billiards, bowling, bingo, and movie theaters.

OVERVIEW

Expect to pay a fee for your recreational choices. We will indicate which diversions are free. Recreation facilities are organized by category from Key Largo to Key West.

AIR TOURS AND SKYDIVING

ISLAND AEROPLANE TOURS
Key West International Airport
3469 South Roosevelt Blvd.
(305) 294-8687
www.keywestairtours.com

For a bird's-eye view of Key West and beyond, take a ride in a vintage open-cockpit biplane. Island Aeroplane Tours sightseeing biplane rides take you over the coral reef, to view shipwrecks in Fleming Key Channel, along the south shore of Key West, to Boca Grande Key, across the backcountry waters, and up the Keys as far as Little Palm Island (see the Accommodations chapter). Tours range from six minutes to more than an hour. Prices are based on two people riding in the front seat. Island Aeroplane Tours also offers aerobatic rides.

SKYDIVE KEY WEST
MM 17 Bayside, Lower Sugarloaf Airport, Sugarloaf Key
(305) 745-4386
www.skydivekeywest.com

Try tandem skydiving from 10,000 feet over the Lower Keys and Key West with Skydive Key West. First-timers are welcome. Allow one hour per person for this venture, including training and the jump. Soft landings are provided on Lower Sugarloaf Key. Skydive expeditions aboard a Cessna 182 depart Sugarloaf Airport between 10 a.m. and sunset seven days a week. Skydivers are advised not to scuba dive for 24 hours before their jump. Videos and photographs are available for purchase as souvenirs. Jumps are by reservation only, and you must be at least 18 years of age to take the plunge.

BEACHES AND PUBLIC PARKS

Life's a beach, the T-shirts say, but first-time visitors to the Keys who expect to find soft, white, endless sand along the ocean are bound to be disappointed. The coral reef protects the Keys from the pounding surf that grinds other shorelines into sand, and so most of ours must be carted in by the truckload. Nevertheless, if stretching out in the sand tops your recreational must-do list, humans and nature have teamed up here to bring you a stretch or two. Some of our parks and beaches charge admission fees, and most have specific hours of accessibility.

Keys beaches do not maintain lifeguard stations. Riptides are rare here, but jellyfish are not. Swim at your own risk and never venture out alone or after dark.

Upper Keys

DAGNY JOHNSON KEY LARGO HAMMOCK BOTANICAL STATE PARK
MM 106 Oceanside, Key Largo
(305) 451-1202
www.floridastateparks.org/keylargo-hammock
Situated on nearly 2,500 acres and stretching for nearly 11 miles of north Key Largo, this state park is a jewel. The park is located in a tropical jungle of mangrove swamp, coastal rock barren, and a rockland hammock. Some of the resident species are rare tree snails, the Schaus swallowtail, the silver-banded hairstreak, and mangrove and hammock skippers. There is a guided walk every Thurs and Sun on a beautiful half-mile nature trail. A backcountry permit, obtained at the John Pennekamp Coral Reef State Park (see listing below), gives you access to an additional 6 miles of tranquil Keys flora and fauna.

JOHN PENNEKAMP CORAL REEF STATE PARK
MM 102.5 Oceanside, Key Largo
(305) 451-1202
www.floridastateparks.org/pennekamp

Well known to divers and snorkelers as the first underwater state park in the United States, John Pennekamp also serves a wide palette of diversions within its land-based boundaries. You can explore most of the fascinating habitats of the Florida Keys here (see the Area Overview chapter). Enjoy campfire programs, guided walks, and canoe trips. The park offers a nature trail, beaches, picnic areas, campsites (see the Campgrounds chapter), restrooms, showers, and water-sports concessions (see listings in this chapter) where you can rent any equipment you might desire, from scuba gear to sailboats.

Expect to pay a nominal admission fee per person and per vehicle. The park is open from 8 a.m. to sunset.

FRIENDSHIP PARK
MM 101 Oceanside, Key Largo
This park sports a playground, a Little League field, swings, and a basketball court. It's perfect for those lazy afternoons with children in tow, and it's especially inviting for picnics. The park is open from 8 a.m. until dusk or when a Little League game is scheduled. Admission is free.

KEY LARGO COMMUNITY PARK
MM 99.6 Oceanside, Key Largo
www.fla-keys.com/keylargo/children.htm
This huge community park offers playgrounds, ball fields, a skate park, and tennis and volleyball courts and is co-located with Jacob's Aquatic Center (see listing in this chapter). The park is free but you must have a permission slip signed by the Key Largo Family YMCA to skate here.

HARRY HARRIS PARK
MM 92.5 Oceanside, Tavernier
(305) 852-7161

Bring the kids along to Harry Harris, where a small beach fronts a tidal pool protected by a stone jetty. You'll find a playground, ball field, volleyball net, in-line skating park, and picnic grounds. Restrooms are available. To reach the park, follow signs leading toward the coast along the oceanside by mile marker 92.5 (Burton Drive). Stay on Burton Drive about 2 miles and follow the signs to the left. Admission is free, except on weekends and federal holidays when nonresidents (persons residing outside Monroe County) must pay a per-person admission fee as well as a docking fee to use the boat ramp. The park is open from 8 a.m. to sunset.

FOUNDERS PARK
MM 87 Bayside, Plantation Key
(305) 853-1685
www.islamorada.fl.us/newsite/
founderspark

Islamorada, Village of Islands, is proud of its green spaces. One of its gleaming examples is the 40-acre municipal Founders Park on Plantation Key. This multipurpose park offers fun for the entire family—including the family dog! The park features playgrounds, sandy beaches, a dog park, baseball diamonds, picnic areas, an Olympic-size pool with restrooms, bocce ball, and tennis courts, a vita course with 18 exercise stations, a skate park, and unforgettable views of the Gulf of Mexico. Various community events are held here throughout the year, so check local publications. Some fees may apply to some areas.

KITE BEACH
MM 83.8 Oceanside, Islamorada
(305) 664-9814

Behind Whale Harbor Marina, experienced kite boarders are allowed to take to the air. Check in at the marina dock and pay a fee to use this launch point.

BEACH BEHIND THE LIBRARY
MM 81.5 Bayside, Islamorada

This stretch of beach has no more official name than its general location, but it does offer a playground, restrooms, and showers. There is no admission charge.

LIGNUMVITAE KEY BOTANICAL
STATE PARK
MM 78.5 Bayside, Islamorida
(305) 664-9814

The only way to get to this park is by boat. The trails here provide real insight to an almost untouched tropical spot. Tours are available by calling the number above.

INDIAN KEY BEACH
MM 78 Oceanside, Islamorada

Although there isn't much of a beach here, a swimming area and boat access are available. Admission is free.

SEA OATS BEACH
MM 74 Oceanside, Islamorada

Featured on the front page of *USA Today* after Hurricane Wilma flooded this part of US 1, Sea Oats Beach has now been refurbished to the tune of $5.4 million. This long stretch of beach offers a full mile of open water with grass flats for wade fishing for bonefish and tarpon. It is not unusual for a flats skiff to go poling by or to see folks just hanging out on the beautiful white sand with the sea oats blowing in the Atlantic breeze.

ANNE'S BEACH
MM 73.5 Oceanside, Islamorada

At low tide, tiny Anne's Beach holds enough sand to accommodate several blankets, but it attracts sun worshipers by the dozens. Swimming waters are shallow. A wooden boardwalk meanders for about 0.3 mile along the water, through the mangroves. Five picnic pavilions jut out from the boardwalk. Parking is limited. To find Anne's Beach, slow down along the Overseas Highway southwest of Caloosa Cove Resort and look toward the ocean for two small parking lots. The boardwalk connects the lots. Blink and you'll miss it. There is no charge.

LONG KEY STATE PARK
MM 67.5 Oceanside, Long Key
(305) 664-4815
www.floridastateparks.org/longkey

A long, narrow sand spit makes up the "beach" at this state park, which is fronted by a shallow-water flat. This park was once the site of the Long Key Fishing Club. This area was a magnet for the world's finest saltwater fishermen during Henry Flagler's era. In 1929 President-elect Herbert Hoover arrived by train from Miami to fish here. The hurricane of 1935 destroyed both the club and the railroad. Today, you can rent a canoe and enjoy the calm, easily accessible waters while you bird-watch and fish in ideal conditions. The picnic area is equipped with charcoal grills. Long Key State Park offers superb oceanfront campsites (see the Campgrounds chapter), restrooms, and shower facilities. Expect to pay a nominal admission fee per person and per vehicle. Long Key State Park is open from 8 a.m. to sunset.

Middle Keys

CURRY HAMMOCK STATE PARK
MM 56.2 Oceanside, Marathon
(850) 245-2157

The newest addition to the state park scene in the Florida Keys is Curry Hammock, at Little Crawl Key just north of Marathon Shores. Exuding an untouched charm all its own, the park offers a mix of tropical hammock, mangrove swamp, and a wide expanse of the coral rock sand that passes for a beach in the Keys. Grills and picnic tables abound, many tucked beneath shady buttonwood trees. The kids will enjoy the swings and slides. And anglers will like the shallow, productive bonefish flat that fronts the shoreline. A cut of deeper water on the north side of the park affords the chance for a "real" swim and maybe some snorkeling as well. Changing rooms and restrooms are fresh, clean, and new. A number of roofed pavilions protect picnic tables and grills from the elements. A nominal fee for entry is charged by honor system. Camping is not allowed here. So far, this little gem remains relatively undiscovered.

SOMBRERO BEACH
MM 50 Oceanside, Sombrero Beach Road, Marathon
(305) 289-3000

This spacious, popular public beach offers a picnic area, playground, and sweeping views of the Atlantic. Swimming waters run deep off Sombrero Beach. Restrooms are available. Marathon Chamber of Commerce, and volunteer organizations, work to keep this gem of a beach in pristine condition. There is no admission charge, and parking is plentiful.

MARATHON COMMUNITY PARK
MM 49 Oceanside, Marathon

The city of Marathon can be very proud of their 23-acre public park, which offers two softball fields, four tennis courts, playgrounds, picnic area, three basketball courts that are also used as a roller-hockey rink, a jogging path, a pavilion, band shell, and restrooms. The park is free.

Lower Keys

LITTLE DUCK KEY BEACH
MM 39 Oceanside, Little Duck Key
With restrooms and picnic shelters, this beach makes for an ideal lunch spot. The small beach provides a swimming area but no lifeguards. Open from 8 a.m. until dusk, the beach is free to the public. And don't be confused by the name. This beach is on Little Duck Key, not Duck Key. You will find it on the left side of the Overseas Highway, just this side of Bahia Honda, as you are traveling south toward Key West.

BAHIA HONDA STATE PARK
MM 37 Oceanside, Bahia Honda
(305) 872-2353
www.floridastateparks.org/bahiahonda
Across the Seven Mile Bridge from Marathon, Bahia Honda State Park sparkles like a diamond and boasts the best natural beach in all of the Florida Keys. Narrow roads wind through the mangrove thickets, many of which have been fitted as campsites (see the Campgrounds chapter). Tarpon fishing beneath the Bahia Honda Bridge attracts seasoned anglers and novices alike, and the park has its own marina with boat ramps and overnight dockage.

At the dive shop in the concession building, you can rent snorkeling equipment or book a trip to Looe Key National Marine Sanctuary. Groceries, marine supplies, and souvenirs are sold here, too.

Bahia Honda offers picnic facilities, restrooms, guided nature walks, and charter boat excursions. Expect to pay a nominal admission fee per person and per vehicle. The park is open 8 a.m. to sunset.

BIG PINE KEY PARK
MM 31, Oceanside, End of Sands Road, Big Pine Key
Monroe County spent $5 million on this community park that includes a playground, baseball field, basketball and roller hockey courts, plus a skate park and a central building containing a concession stand. Located on the property is an all-purpose field for other sports programs plus jogging trails circling the park.

Key West

BAYVIEW PARK
Truman Avenue and Jose Martí Drive
You will definitely notice Bayview Park if you are driving into Key West on North Roosevelt Boulevard, which becomes Truman Avenue. On your left as the road narrows and you head into Old Town, Bayview Park is one of the few free green spots still left in Key West. Look for the gazebo. Several picnic tables are strewn throughout the park and come highly recommended for a shady afternoon lunch.

FORT ZACHARY TAYLOR HISTORIC
  STATE PARK
Truman Annex at the end of
Southard Street
(305) 292-6713
www.floridastateparks.org/forttaylor
Look to the left of the brick fort for a pleasant, although rocky, beach with picnic tables and barbecue grills. The locals call this place "Fort Zach"; this is where they come in droves to sunbathe and snorkel. The water is clear and deep, and you're likely to see many colorful fish congregating around the limestone-boulder breakwater islands constructed just offshore. When it gets too hot on the beach, head for the shade—there's

plenty of it available under the lofty pine trees in the picnic area. The beach area is open 8 a.m. to sunset. An admission fee to the park is charged.

HIGGS BEACH AND C. B. HARVEY REST BEACH
Atlantic Boulevard

These twin beaches are so close together they are often mistaken for each other. Higgs Beach offers a playground, picnic tables, and nearby tennis courts. It is between White and Reynolds Streets on Atlantic Boulevard. The beach is open sunrise to 11 p.m. Admission is free.

Rest Beach is smaller than Higgs Beach and is dwarfed by the massive White Street Pier. This pier is a favorite with anglers and dog walkers and is sometimes called the "unfinished road to Cuba." Rest Beach has the same hours as Higgs Beach. Right across the street is an extensive playground called Astro City, a favorite with the kids.

SMATHERS BEACH
South Roosevelt Boulevard

Across from Key West International Airport, Smathers is a long strip of sand that bustles with food vendors, water-sports concessions, and beautiful bods in itsy-bitsy, teeny-weeny suits. Admission here is free, but bring plenty of quarters for the streetside parking meters. If you don't mind carting your beach gear a few extra yards, free parking is available on the far side of South Roosevelt. The beach is open sunrise to 11 p.m.

BICYCLING

You'll be able to get a "wheel" deal when you rent a bike and cycle the Keys. Rentals are offered by the day, 24 hours, multiple days, week, or month. Most of these establishments sell parts and new bicycles, do repairs, and rent helmets and other gear. Remember, Florida state law requires helmets for cyclists younger than age 16.

Upper Keys

Among the best places to bike the Upper Keys are Harry Harris Park, where bicycle lanes are provided, and on the bicycle paths in the median and along the ocean side of the Overseas Highway in Key Largo. Down the Keys, you may safely cycle through Islamorada's Old Highway, which borders the Overseas Highway on the ocean side. A bike path on the bay side finishes a tour through Upper Matecumbe Key and on through Lower Matecumbe Key, thereby making it possible to safely cycle from about mile marker 90 to approximately mile marker 72.

BILL'S DISCOUNT BIKE SHOP
MM 102 Oceanside, Key Largo
(305) 453-4070

Mostly new, high-end bikes at discount prices for all of your biking needs. Nice shop offering service with a smile.

TAVERNIER BICYCLE AND HOBBIES
MM 92 Bayside, Tavernier
(305) 852-2859
www.tavernierbikes.com

Tavernier Bicycle and Hobbies rents cruisers (one-speed bicycles) for men, women, and children by the day, week, or month. Per-day prices decrease with multiple-day rentals.

Middle Keys

In Marathon you'll need to cycle on the old Seven Mile Bridge to Pigeon Key (a good 2-mile-plus jaunt), use the Key Colony Beach bicycle lane (turn onto the Key Colony

Causeway at mile marker 53.5 to get to Key Colony), or pedal along the relatively traffic-free streets of the Sombrero residential area (turn onto Sombrero Beach Road, MM 50, next to Kmart).

OVERSEAS OUTFITTERS
MM 48 Bayside, Marathon
(305) 289-1670

To make that active lifestyle come alive, Overseas Outfitters is the place in the Middle Keys. They carry Oakley and Maui Jim sunglasses and Adidas active wear for women, along with bike sales, service, and rentals. If wheezing down the road on roller blades is your ticket to ride, they have those here as well.

Lower Keys

The Lower Keys span 30 miles, but toward the end of the Keys you will have the best luck finding rental bikes on Stock Island and Key West (see section below).

BIG PINE BICYCLE CENTER
MM 31 Bayside, Big Pine Key
(305) 872-0130

This is the best source for bicycle rentals in the upper portion of the Lower Keys.

Key West

A & M RENTALS
523 Truman Ave.
(305) 896-1921
www.amscooterskeywest.com

A & M Rentals provide their customers free pick-up and drop off in the city of Key West. Here you can rent bikes by the day or week, scooters by the hour or the week, and electric cars for two- or four- hour rides.

THE BIKE SHOP
1110 Truman Ave.
(305) 294-1073
www.thebikeshopkeywest.com

The Bike Shop rents one-speed cruisers with baskets and locks.

EATON BIKES
830 Eaton St.
(305) 295-0057
www.eatonbikes.com

Ever fall in love with a bicycle? If not, this may be a first! The guys at Eaton Bikes are two hip entrepreneurs who will *ooh* and *aah* you with their artistic, intricate designs on bicycles, choppers, low riders, and electrical bikes. The Eaton Bike boys will even custom design one to ensure you are a true pedal pusher! Their cycles are as beautiful to look at as they are to ride. Walk in and pedal out—I promise that!

ISLAND BICYCLES
929 Truman Ave.
(305) 292-9707
www.islandbicycle.com

Island Bicycles offers a full selection of bicycles for sale and rent. Repairs and accessories are also available here.

MOPED HOSPITAL
601 Truman Ave.
(305) 296-3344
www.mopedhospital.com

Moped Hospital rents single-speed bicycles with coaster brakes, baskets, high-rise handlebars, soft seats, balloon tires, and locks by the hour, day, and week.

RECYCLE BICYCLES
MM 4.5 Oceanside, Stock Island
(305) 294-7433

The screaming green building gets your attention even if you don't need a bike. Inside the folks offer a full-service bicycle shop and free pickup and delivery on bike repairs.

BOAT EXCURSIONS AND SUNSET CRUISES

Our crowning glory rests in our encompassing waters. Explore the backcountry and the waters of the Everglades National Park on group gunkholing ecotour expeditions (see the Area Overview chapter) or take a glass-bottomed boat trip to the reef to view the fascinating creatures residing there. Relax aboard a sunset cocktail cruise or fire up for a casino cruise. Expect to pay a fee for all these adventures.

i For your safety, Florida has warning flags posted on our public beaches statewide. Double red lines: No swimming at all. Yellow: Medium hazard, moderate surf and/or currents. Green: Low hazard, calm conditions, but exercise caution. Purple: Dangerous marine life.

Upper Keys

JOHN PENNEKAMP CORAL REEF STATE PARK
MM 102.5 Oceanside, Key Largo
(305) 451-1621
www.floridastateparks.org/pennekamp
Pennekamp's glass-bottomed catamaran, the *Spirit of Pennekamp*, carries as many as 150 people on two-and-a-half-hour tours of the reef. Tours are offered three times daily. The 38-foot catamaran *Salsa* departs the park marina twice daily for a sailing/snorkeling adventure.

CAPT. STERLING'S EVERGLADES ECO-TOURS
MM 102 Bayside, Dolphin Cove, Key Largo
(305) 853-5161, (888) 224-6044
www.pennekamp.com/sterling
Venture 17 miles into the waters of the Everglades National Park, in and around mangrove and bird rookery islands (see the Area Overview chapter) aboard a 23-foot pontoon boat. Tours are limited to six passengers and depart twice daily. The Key Largo Flamingo Express charter takes you through Crocodile Dragover, the Dump Keys, and 38 miles to Flamingo in Everglades National Park. And then there's the Crocodile Tour, a nighttime adventure that takes you in search of the elusive Florida saltwater crocodile.

AFRICAN QUEEN
MM 100 Oceanside, Holiday Inn Docks, Key Largo
(305) 451-2121 or (800) 465-4329
www.holidayinnkeylargo.com
Board the legendary *African Queen*—featured in the Humphrey Bogart and Katharine Hepburn movie of the same name—in Key Largo for daily one-hour cruises and sunset or charter excursions during the autumn and winter months.

KEY LARGO PRINCESS GLASS BOTTOM BOAT
MM 100 Oceanside, at the Holiday Inn Docks, Key Largo
(305) 451-2121 or (800) 465-4329
www.keylargoprincess.com
This princess carries passengers on narrated two-hour tours that drift above the reef. A full bar is onboard, and guests can buy hot dogs and snacks. *Key Largo Princess* tours are offered three times daily. Family rates and

private charters are available. The boat is wheelchair accessible.

QUICKSILVER CATAMARAN
MM 100 Oceanside, Holiday Inn Docks, Key Largo
(305) 451-0105, (800) 347-9972
www.quicksilversnorkel.com
Daily sails through the sanctuary waters of John Pennekamp Coral Reef State Park vary with the season aboard this 50-foot catamaran, *Quicksilver*. Discounts and family rates are available on snorkel/sunset sail combinations. Private and group charters also can be arranged. Gear rental is extra.

SUNCRUZ CASINO
MM 100 Oceanside, Holiday Inn, Key Largo
(305) 451-0000 or (800) 474-3423
www.suncruzcasino.com
Sports betting, blackjack, slot machines, dice, roulette, and video poker are among the many diversions onboard *SunCruz Casino*. A full bar and à la carte sandwich menu satisfy hungers of another kind; a welcome-aboard cocktail and hors d'oeuvres are served to all free of charge. Guests at Key Largo's Holiday Inn, Ramada, or Marriott sail for free as often as they desire. The general public may board the more-than-100-foot vessel's gambling sails for a small admission fee. The actual casino is moored each day 3 miles offshore in federal waters. Water taxis take guests to and from the casino vessel every two hours.

CARIBBEAN WATERSPORTS ENVIRO TOURS
MM 97 Bayside, at the Key Largo Grande Resort and Beach Club, Key Largo
(305) 852-5553 or (800) 445-8667
www.caribbeanwatersports.com
Glide through the Everglades with Caribbean Watersports' two-hour guided Hobie Sailing Safaris and explore uninhabited mangrove islands all along Florida Bay. Environmental gunkholing tours (see the Area Overview chapter) provide the same guided ride in a 17-foot rigid inflatable Zodiac that has a fiberglass hull, stabilizing inflatable side pontoons, and a quiet electric trolling motor. Tours are limited to six people; you must call ahead to reserve a spot.

THE NAUTILIMO
MM 82 Bayside, Islamorada
(305) 942-3793
www.nautilimo.com
To see a 1983 Cadillac stretch limousine on the sea is a trip—literally. Giving the boat its shape is a wood-rib frame mounted on a 23-foot Carolina skiff, powered by a 100-horsepower engine. After the fiberglass covering was installed, the details brought the boat to life. Salvaged from a discarded Cadillac, the dashboard, mirrors and grill are authentic. To complete the look, the *NautiLimo* was generously covered in pink paint. A trip out on this one-of-a-kind boat lasts two hours and covers 9 miles of beautiful Florida Bay country. All that is missing is Elvis!

Middle Keys

HAWK'S CAY RESORT AND MARINA
MM 61 Oceanside, Duck Key
(305) 743-7000 or (888) 313-5749
www.hawkscay.com
Sail aboard the 40-foot custom sailing catamaran at up to 20 knots or sign on for a more leisurely sunset cruise. Or rent a sea kayak for a self-guided ecotour of the out-islands near Duck Key. All these excursions may be booked at Hawk's Cay.

Many other water-related activities are available at Hawk's Cay, including chartered fishing excursions to the backcountry or the reef. For those with other interests, many other amusements are available, including personal watercraft and small-boat rentals, water-skiing, pontoon party barge rentals, and parasailing.

KEY LIMEY CHARTERS
MM 61 Oceanside, Duck Key
(305) 293-1814
www.keylimey.com
This is the only private gunkholing charter that will whisk you away at 35 knots into the backcountry waters of Florida Bay to the Arsnicker Keys, 7 miles northwest of Lower Matecumbe, to see the fabulous white pelicans. These ultimate snowbirds winter in the Keys from Nov until about the end of Mar. The flock often numbers 500 or more around the tiny islets of the Arsnicker. Captain John Skidmore stealthily poles his flatsboat through the shallows so as not to alert the birds to your presence. Bring your camera! Captain Skidmore is also an expert flats fishing guide, specializing in bonefish, permit, tarpon, redfish, snook, and other backcountry species. You can combine the bird-watching gunkholing excursion with some guided backcountry fishing if you like.

TURTLE ISLAND WATERSPORTS
MM 50 Oceanside, Marathon
(305) 289-0888
www.tranquilitybay.com/adventure/
watersports.htm
Located at Tranquility Bay Beach House Resort (see Accommodations chapter for both), Turtle Island Watersports can equip you for fun activities, both above and beneath the water. They offer snorkeling, parasailing, kayaks, boat rentals, fishing charters, Hobie Cats, sunset cruises, Waverunner rentals, island tours, and scuba diving.

SMORGASBOAT HARBOR TOURS
MM 50 Oceanside, Marathon
(305) 318-9725
www.smorgasboat.com
Fun time on a boat ride aboard the Smorgasboat Harbor Tour in their electric boat! Take in scenic vistas in Boot Key Harbor, go bar hopping to local nightspots, or use their services as a water taxi to and from your own boat. The owners offer one-and-a-half-hour harbor tours, sunset cruises, or ecotours. Bring your own food and drinks or they can arrange refreshments for you.

SPIRIT CATAMARAN CHARTERS
MM 47.5 Oceanside, 56223 Ocean Dr.,
Marathon
(305) 289-0614
A 40-foot catamaran named *Spirit* takes passengers snorkeling to popular Middle Keys reefs twice a day, makes family charter cruises to Pigeon Key, offers marine biology tours with classrooms of children, and sets off for a daily sunset cruise at the end of the day. Call in advance to make reservations.

Lower Keys

STRIKE ZONE CHARTERS
MM 29.5 Bayside, Big Pine Key
(305) 872-9863 or (800) 654-9560
www.strikezonecharter.com
This five-hour, backcountry out-island excursion, which includes a fish cookout on a secluded island, will entice your entire family (see the Kidstuff chapter for more details and see the Diving and Snorkeling chapter for Strike Zone's underwater offerings).

Key West

ADVENTURE CHARTERS
MM 5.5 Oceanside, 6810 Front St., Safe
Harbor Marina, Stock Island
(305) 296-0362
Looking for an alternative to the traditional
party-boat booze cruise? Adventure Charters offers half-day snorkel cruises, half-day
backcountry nature excursions, and full-day
backcountry adventures that combine kayaking, snorkeling, fishing, and beachcombing
through tidal streams and along mangrove
islands that are unreachable by larger boats.
To find Adventure Charters, turn at MacDonald Avenue near Chico's Cantina.

APPLEDORE CHARTER WINDJAMMER
201 William St.
(305) 304-9222
Daily snorkel trips aboard this 85-foot, oak-
framed pine schooner head for the reef.
The excursion includes a full lunch, a fruit
platter, snacks, and beverages, plus beer
and wine for after-snorkeling libation. Gear
is provided, and passengers need bring only
towels and sunscreen. A nightly sail-only
excursion includes beer and wine (champagne during sunset).

During the high season the *Appledore*
fills up quickly; call with a credit card to confirm reservations in advance. The *Appledore*,
which has circumnavigated the world,
summers in Maine, and is in Key West Oct
through May.

DANGER CHARTERS
407 Caroline St.
(305) 296-3652
www.dangercharters.com
Don't let the moniker fool you: *Danger*
and *Danger Cay* are the names of the two
Chesapeake Bay Skip Jack sailboats, not any

situation you will encounter on this adventurous charter. Up to six people board the
skipjack and right away owner and captain
Wayne Fox assigns one of his new crew as
first mate. The fun begins as the new mate
learns the intricacies of tending to a sailboat and tacking into the wind. The boat
soon travels to the backcountry, where the
crew disembarks into three double kayaks and journeys through the mangrove
islands. Then the sailboat moves to another
location, where snorkeling gear is donned.
Finally, after much adventure, the boat sails
back home. Excursions last about five hours.
Full-day trips, sunset cruises, and specialized bird-watching trips are also available.
Call for details and pricing. Their traditional
wooden power yacht, *Roamer*, takes you to
a pristine reef, where the staff serves you a
picnic lunch. Kayak to an out-island in the
backcountry and enjoy your yacht-for-a-day.

DISCOVERY UNDERSEA TOURS
251 Margaret St.
(305) 293-0099 or (800) 262-0099
www.discoveryunderseatours.com
This company offers the Keys' only "underwater viewing room," which the tour claims is a
reverse aquarium. See firsthand living coral,
tropical fish, and marine life without getting
a drop of water on you. They offer three daily
trips on a 78-foot vessel equipped with A/C
and a snack bar serving sodas, beer, wine,
and champagne on their sunset cruise. The
boat is handicapped accessible.

DREAM CATCHER CHARTERS
5555 College Rd., Bayside, Key West
(305) 304-0497 or (888) 362-3474
www.chartersofkeywest.com
How romantic for a couple or great fun
with a group of six—cruising the Key West

harbor in your own personal 29-foot power boat. Your captain handles all the navigating as you enjoy the company and the lovely view of Key West from the water. The trip is approximately two hours. Sodas and water are provided. The sunset is free!

FURY CATAMARANS
237 Front St.
(305) 294-8899 or (877) 994-8898
www.furycat.com

Climb aboard one of Fury's 65-foot catamarans for a sail by day or night. Fury offers two three-hour trips to the reef daily for snorkeling—one in the morning, one in the afternoon—plus a two-hour champagne sunset sail each evening. You can buy separate tickets for day snorkeling or sunset sailing, or purchase a combination snorkeling/sunset sail ticket. Fury also offers snuba excursions. (Snuba, a cross between scuba diving and snorkeling, involves a cylinder of compressed air attached to a raft and connected to two 20-foot-long regulator hoses that participants use for breathing.) Beer, white wine, sodas, and snorkeling/snuba gear are included in the price of your ticket. In addition, Fury offers parasailing as well as a land/sea excursion package that includes a trip to the reef and a tour of Key West aboard either the Conch Tour Train or Old Town Trolley.

LIBERTY FLEET OF TALL SHIPS
202 William St., Docks at Schooner Wharf
(305) 292-0332
www.libertyfleet.com

The 80-passenger schooner *Liberty* now resides full-time in Key West, offering two-hour morning, afternoon, and sunset sails year-round. Sunset sails include complimentary beer, wine, and champagne. Passengers are invited to participate in hands-on sailing,

but it's perfectly okay if you just want to sit back and let the captain do all the work.

The 125-foot, 115-passenger *Liberty Clipper* plies the waters off the Florida Keys and Dry Tortugas from Nov through May. On Tues, Thurs, and Sun nights, passengers can dine on Caribbean-style favorites while they listen to reggae music and watch the sun sink into the gulf. During the summer months, the *Liberty Clipper* offers a variety of adventure cruises along the Atlantic coast. Check the Web site for details. Not to be missed is Joe Universe and his "Stargazer" night sails.

MOSQUITO COAST ISLAND OUTFITTERS
MM 4.2 Oceanside, Stock Island
(305) 295-9898
www.mosquitocoast.net

The gang at this outfitters offers guided backcountry tours that include a narration of the trees, birds, fish, coral, sponges, sea grass, and sea creatures (see the Area Overview chapter). Single and double kayaks are available; half the trip is devoted to snorkeling. Gear, snacks, and bottled water are included in the fee. They even have a two-hour paddle tour with you and your dog! Children are welcome but must be at least nine years old to participate.

RESTLESS NATIVE CHARTERS
201 William St.
(305) 394-0600
www.restlessnative.com

Sail away for the day on this luxurious 50-foot catamaran yacht while you enjoy a gourmet lunch with wine, beer, or soda. Sailing aboard this beauty, with her 28-foot beam, you can expect a smooth and unforgettable time on the water. Onboard are two kayaks for individual pursuits, swinging air chairs, and hammocks, or you can get dragged from the cargo net, snorkel on the reef, or walk the sandbar. The *Restless Native* can only carry six passengers, with crew, so this is like having your own private vessel to explore the waters off Key West.

SEBAGO CATAMARANS
201 William St., at the Key West Historic Seaport
(305) 292-4768 or (800) 507-9955
www.keywestsebago.com
Head out to the reef for a snorkeling/sailing adventure aboard Sebago's 60-foot catamaran or cruise Key West Harbor at sunset. Complimentary drinks are served on both excursions. Sebago also offers parasailing as well as a six-hour "Island Ting" trip that includes kayaking, snorkeling, and sailing, plus a luncheon buffet. Call for details.

SUNNY DAYS CATAMARAN
Key West Historic Seaport
(305) 296-5556, (800) 236-7937
www.sunnydayskeywest.com
Sunny Days could once boast of having the only "high-speed catamaran service" to Dry Tortugas National Park. Although that's no longer true, with the launching of its *Fast Cat II* in May 1999, Sunny Days does continue to have the fastest ferry service. The 100-passenger, high-speed *Fast Cat II* makes the voyage from Key West to Fort Jefferson in just less than two hours. As a result of the time saved, passengers aboard *Fast Cat II* can get in a little extra snorkeling at Garden Key or even squeeze in a snorkeling side trip to the *Windjammer* wreck (there's an extra charge per person for the side trip).

A continental breakfast and lunch are included in the fare, along with snorkeling gear and instruction and a guided tour of Fort Jefferson. Campers pay an extra fee to accommodate their gear.

In addition to its daily run to Fort Jefferson, Sunny Days also offers twice-daily cruises aboard their *Caribbean Spirit*. The excursions go to the reef for snorkeling, a combination snorkeling/sunset cruise, and a champagne sunset cruise. Reef Express thrills you with snorkeling in two locations, with half-day outings with sunset combos. Dolphin Tours lets you go to the backcountry to observe dolphins at play. Cruzan Cat puts you onboard a 43-foot catamaran and powers you out, in 20 minutes, to a coral reef. All prices vary depending on the length of the cruise and the time of day.

WHITE KNUCKLE THRILL BOAT RIDE
MM 4.5 Oceanside, Hurricane Hole Marina, Stock Island
(305) 797-0459
www.whiteknucklethrillboatride.com
Hold on to your head, keep your arms inside the boat, and your feet on the footboards—you are in for one wild ride! This is not a boat ride for the faint of heart nor your elderly relatives. With a velocity of about 50 mph, this boat is a mix of an Everglades airboat and a Jet Ski with a screaming group of about 12 on board. Twisting, turning, and spraying saltwater every which way, you return to the dock exhilarated and soaking wet. A photographer is on hand to capture that look on your face as the "White Knuckle" makes a 360-degree turn—priceless.

YANKEE FLEET FERRY TO FORT JEFFERSON AND DRY TORTUGAS NATIONAL PARK
Key West Historic Seaport
(305) 294-7009 or (800) 322-0013
www.yankeefreedom.com

A voyage to Dry Tortugas National Park, 70 miles west of Key West, requires a full day. But if you have the time, be sure to include the adventure in your itinerary. Not only is this a spectacular ride back in history, it's a chance to experience what the Florida Keys are truly all about.

Ponce de León named the seven islands Las Tortugas (the Turtles) in 1513. The word Dry was later incorporated into the title to let seafarers know that there is no fresh water available here.

You'll be able to take a tour of the massive and historical Fort Jefferson on Garden Key and enjoy calm seas, pristine natural sand beaches, and some of the best snorkeling anywhere. The protected waters surrounding the Tortugas sparkle with all the sea creatures of the coral reef, plus a few shipwreck remains. And because this area has been designated a no-take zone, the creatures you see get a chance to grow larger than those you might otherwise encounter. Do remember, however, that there is no food, fresh water, electricity, or medical assistance at Fort Jefferson. There are public restrooms.

The *Yankee Freedom II,* a 100-passenger, high-speed catamaran, whisks passengers from Key West to Fort Jefferson in less than two and a half hours. *Yankee Freedom II* departs promptly at 8 a.m. and returns at 5:30 p.m. daily. Fare includes round-trip transportation; snorkeling gear; en route commentary by a naturalist-historian; a 45-minute guided tour of Fort Jefferson; continental breakfast of bagels, doughnuts, cold cereal, and juice; and lunch consisting of cold salads and a make-your-own sandwich bar. Coffee, iced tea, and water are complimentary; you can buy sodas, beer, wine, and mixed drinks onboard. Passengers are not permitted to carry alcohol to the Dry Tortugas.

Only campers staying the night on Garden Key may bring large coolers (see the Campgrounds chapter). Campers pay slightly higher fees for passage aboard *Yankee Freedom II* to accommodate their gear.

i There are six beaches in the Key West area. South Beach: end of Duval Street and the Atlantic Ocean (no facilities); Dog Beach: next to Louie's Backyard restaurant (no facilities); Higgs Beach: end of Reynolds Street (facilities); Rest Beach: home to White Street Pier (facilities within walking distance); Smathers Beach: South Roosevelt Boulevard (facilities); and Fort Zachary Taylor: entrance through Truman Annex at Southard Street (facilities).

GOLF AND TENNIS

Putters and players drive the Keys links, and racqueteers of all ages love our courts. Read on and be on the ball. Expect to pay for court time by the hour. Greens fees are reasonable at the public course in Key West, and if you belong to a country club back home, be sure to contact Sombrero Country Club to see about reciprocal privileges.

Upper Keys

ISLAMORADA TENNIS CLUB
MM 76.8 Bayside, Islamorada
(305) 664-5340
www.islamoradatennisclub.com
This facility maintains four clay and two hard courts, five of which are lit for extended play into the evening hours. Private lessons, clinics, round-robins, and tournaments are offered to the general public, and Islamorada Tennis Club will arrange games at

all levels. A pro shop and boutique are on premises. Same-day racquet stringing is available.

Middle Keys

KEY COLONY BEACH GOLF AND TENNIS
MM 53.5 Oceanside, Eighth Street, Key Colony Beach
(305) 289-1533
Greens fees at Key Colony Beach's nine-hole, par-3 public course are a real deal. And you can rent clubs and a pull cart inexpensively as well. Tee times are not required. The course is open 7:30 a.m. to sunset. Key Colony Beach Golf Course is the only public course in the Keys outside Key West. Tennis players can enjoy the two lit hard courts, which are open from 8 a.m. to 9 p.m. To find the golf course, turn toward the ocean onto Key Colony Beach Causeway at the traffic light at MM 53.5.

WONDERLIN TENNIS
MM 50 Oceanside, 19 Sombrero Blvd., at Sombrero Country Club, Marathon
(305) 743-2250
Marathon's favorite pro, Tim Wonderlin, together with the Sombrero Country Club, offers a tennis package that is difficult to beat. A per-day guest fee entitles you to unlimited tennis and pool privileges at the resort; you can also purchase a seasonal membership. The four hard courts are lit so play commences at 7 a.m. and can continue until 10 p.m. During the high season (Nov 15 through Apr 15), Wonderlin offers morning two-hour special clinics and organized round-robin play: women's day, men's day, or mixed doubles. Expect to pay an additional charge for these events. Private lessons may be scheduled.

BOONDOCKS MINI-GOLF
MM 27.5 Bayside, Ramrod Key
(305) 872-4094
www.boondocks.us.com
Boondocks Mini-Golf is a family-fun park that allows kids of all ages to enjoy a round of miniature golf. Some of the larger hotels offer mini golf for their clients, but this is the only public mini-golf course in the Keys. The large rock formation is shaped like a huge boulder with a state-of-the-art 18-hole course complete with waterfalls, tunnels, ponds, tiki hut clubhouse, and towering, giant cavemen. The lush tropical landscaping at this attraction gives it Keys believability. Boondocks Mini-Golf is a fun place to hold birthday parties, tournaments, or fund-raisers. This family-friendly destination is a "must do" while here.

Key West

BAYVIEW PARK TENNIS
1310 Truman Ave.
(305) 294-1346
The tennis courts at Bayview Park are open to all on a first-come, first-served basis. Reservations are neither required nor accepted. There are no court fees, and courts are lit until 10 p.m.

ISLAND CITY TENNIS
1310 Truman Ave.
(305) 294-1346
These public tennis courts are owned by the city of Key West and keep the lights on till 9 p.m. Island City Tennis is right on Truman Avenue that leads to Duval Street. It is first-come, first-served and is very popular with visitors as well as locals. There is a pro-shop on premises operated by a father and son team that are a delight. In fact, the father teaches tennis at Key West High School.

KEY WEST GOLF CLUB
MM 5 Bayside, Stock Island
(305) 294-5232
www.keywestgolf.com
The only public 18-hole course in the Keys, this par-70 course designed by Rees Jones offers a clubhouse, pro shop, and lessons. Greens fees are hefty in high season but about a third less in the off-season. For late-afternoon golfers, special "twilight" fees are available after 2:30 p.m. Monroe County residents receive discounts, but you must reside here year-round to qualify. Call for details.

KEY WEST TENNIS TOO
811 Seminole Ave.
(305) 296-3029
Affiliated with the Casa Marina Resort and adjacent to it, Key West Tennis Too utilizes the hotel's three hard-surface courts. Tournament lights make nighttime play possible. A pro offers lessons by appointment, you can rent a ball machine, and a complete pro shop carries top-brand racquets and offers in-house stringing. Guests of the Casa Marina or Reach Resort play for about half the court fees that the public pays. Tennis clinics are held daily.

RADICAL DIVERSIONS

Jumping out of perfectly good airplanes, parasailing, kiteboarding, waterskiing, wingsuit flying, or free diving underwater without an oxygen tank some of the many extreme sports. Here is a list of shops that provide thrill seekers a source and means for their fix of over-the-edge athletic thrills. Hold your breath—you are now in the deep end so get ripping!

SEVEN SPORTS KITEBOARDING
MM 88 Bayside, Plaza 88, Islamorada
(305) 853-5483
www.sevensports.com
Private instructions from PASA-certified instructors for beginners, intermediate or advanced boarders in the thrilling sport of kiteboarding keeps Seven Sports busy. You can also test your nerve on a SUP board and master the art of paddleboarding. That's standing *up* on a board in case you didn't know!

OTHERSIDE BOARDSPORTS
MM 87.7 Oceanside, Islamorada
(305) 853-9728
This shop offers board-sports-minded athletes a chance to skateboard, kiteboard, wakeboard, and wakeskate. With knowledgeable instructors, you will be off and skating in no time.

EXTREME SPORTS FLORIDA KEYS
MM 81.9 Oceanside, Whale Harbor Dock Marina, Islamorada
(305) 664-4055
www.extremesportsfloridakeys.com
Located on the premises of Coconut Cove Creek Resort on Windley Key, Extreme Sports offers a variety of thrilling activities. You can get ultralight flight instructions here as well as kiteboard lessons, guided or self-guided ecotours, or rent a Jet Ski, Waverunner, or boat.

THE KITE HOUSE
1801 North Roosevelt Blvd., Key West
(305) 294-8679
www.thekitehouse.com
Ten years ago perhaps only 10,000 people were involved with the sport of harnessing the wind. Today, over 500,000 agile folks

partake in this exhilarating hobby. Kiteboarding is not for the amateur, so the owner of this business urges anyone to take a few lessons with a PASA (Professional Airsport Association) instructor. After the lessons, these instructors give you practice runs, get into your power zone, and you're off!

WATER SPORTS

Pick your pleasure and make a splash—parasailing, waterskiing, and kayaking. You'll find personal watercraft and paddleboat rentals in this section. For a rundown of scuba diving/snorkeling trips to the reef, see our Diving and Snorkeling chapter. Expect to pay a fee for these watery endeavors.

Upper Keys

IT'S A DIVE WATERSPORTS
MM 103.8 Bayside, Marriott Key Largo
Bay Beach Resort, Key Largo
(305) 453-0000 or (800) 809-9881
www.marriottkeylargo.com
It's a Dive offers personal watercraft and kayak rentals. Parasailing, waterskiing, and scuba instruction are available, and snorkeling trips aboard a glass-bottomed boat depart twice daily.

CORAL REEF PARK COMPANY
MM 102.5 Oceanside, John Pennekamp
Coral Reef State Park, Key Largo
(305) 451-6300 or (800) 326-3521
www.pennekamppark.com
Coral Reef Park Company rents snorkeling equipment at Pennekamp Park for unguided exploration of the near-shore Pennekamp waters off Cannon Beach, or you can sign on with one of the snorkeling tours to the reef (see the Diving and Snorkeling chapter for details). Rent canoes or kayaks here and paddle the mangrove water trails. Small boats also are available for hire.

JACOB'S AQUATIC CENTER
MM 99.6 Oceanside, Key Largo
(305) 453-7946
www.jacobsaquaticcenter.org
Jacob's Aquatic Center is a three-pool complex with a 25-meter, eight-lane competition pool and contiguous diving pool with 1- and 2-meter diving boards. This facility is suitable for scuba and Red Cross certification, synchronized swimming, youth swim teams, masters swimming, swim lessons, water aerobics/Pilates, gymnastics, and water polo. They also have an interactive pool/water park featuring a pirate ship, "spray" gym, and "beachfront" entry. Co-located with the Key Largo Community Park (see listing in this chapter).

H2O SPORTS
MM 84.5 Oceanside, at Pelican Cove,
Islamorada
(305) 664-4435 or (800) 445-4690
www.pcove.com
On the beach at Pelican Cove, hook up with H2O Sports personal watercraft and 16-foot skiffs for round-trip visits to the Sand Bar (a popular snorkeling and swimming site). A reef boat takes snorkelers on excursions, and 16-mile, guided personal watercraft tours depart before sunset and head through the backcountry.

OVER UNDER ADVENTURES
MM 82 Oceanside, Islamorada
(305) 852-8015 or (800) 682-8862
www.overundercharters.com
This company offers on-the-water vacation packages and they will even pick you up in Miami or Fort Lauderdale and bring you to

the Florida Keys. Come join the fun for a full week of fishing, backcountry exploration, or diving. If you drive or fly into the Keys, they have boat locations all the way from Islamorada to Key West for clients.

Middle Keys

HAWK'S CAY RESORT AND MARINA
MM 61 Oceanside, Duck Key
(305) 743-7000 or (888) 313-5749
www.hawkscay.com
The water-sports facility at Hawk's Cay offers parasailing, pontoon or center-console boat rentals, personal watercraft, and kayak rentals, as well as water-ski and wakeboard rentals, scuba center, and instruction. A sailing school is also on the premises.

Key West

ISLAND WATERSPORTS
245 Front St., Westin Key West Resort and Marina
(305) 296-1754 or (888) 382-7864
www.island-watersports.com
Personal watercraft and Jet boats are available for rental by the half hour or hour. This business also boasts the largest riding area in Key West. If you like, wet suits and goggles are also offered. The guided tour aboard a personal watercraft offers you one and a half to two hours of island sightseeing.

KEY WEST WATER SPORTS
714 Seminole St., at the Casa Marina Resort
(305) 294-2192
www.keywestwatersports.com
A wide variety of water-sports gear is ready and waiting for you here. Feel like a lazy afternoon just drifting? Try a Sun Cat floating lounge chair. Or maybe a Sea Peeper—a

two-person glass-bottomed boat—is more your style. Key West Water Sports is also home to high-performance shortboards and quality sailboarding equipment. If you've never tried the sport before, climb aboard the Cat Surfer—the folks here guarantee that anyone can learn to sailboard on this baby. Hobie Cats, personal watercraft, baby-seat bikes, double-seater scooters, waterskiing, and parasailing are also available.

THE KEYS TO KEY WEST
5555 College Rd., Bayside
(305) 292- 7212 or (888) 362-3474
www.gotothekeys.com
The Keys to the Keys claim they throw the largest island party in the Keys. This inclusive package is billed as "do it all in one day" and even their Web site comes with a warning label: "This trip will wear you out!" The package trip involves Wave Running, sunfish sailboating, banana boat rides, kayaking, knee boarding, snorkeling, windsurfing, and parasailing. Trips are from 10 a.m. to 4 p.m. with lunch, sodas, and water served. Be sure and eat a hearty breakfast before this outing!

PARAWEST WATERSPORTS INC.
700 Front St. at A&B Lobster House
(305) 292-5199
This parasailing enterprise prides itself on offering excursionists the most free falls and dips in Key West. Regular rides of 8 to 10 minutes include heights of 300 feet with one free fall and one dip; longer, higher rides of 10 to 12 minutes reach 600 feet and include several free falls and dips. Most parasailing is done behind Christmas Tree Island and Sunset Key. Single and double personal watercraft also are available for rent. Renters must remain within a limited riding area.

SUNSET WATERSPORTS
Smathers Beach
(305) 296-2554

This outfit offers something for everyone. Parasailing, Hobie Cats, kayaks, and sailboards are all provided on Smathers Beach. For an all-inclusive day trip, take the "Do It All." From the Key West Seaport, a 44-foot catamaran takes you out about 3 miles to a shallow wreck. From there, take turns exploring with personal watercraft, waterskiing, and just about anything else they can imagine.

LET'S GO TO THE MOVIES

Cinema buffs can screen the latest flicks here. The theaters offer matinees on Sat and Sun and sometimes on weekdays at a reduced ticket price.

Upper Keys

TAVERNIER TOWNE CINEMAS
MM 92 Bayside, Tavernier
(305) 853-7003 (movie hotline),
(305) 853-7004
www.taverniercinemas.com

This is a five-plex theater that features first-run films with Dolby-enhanced sound and the latest technology. Matinees daily, late-night shows on weekends. Located in the Tavernier Towne Center.

Middle Keys

MARATHON COMMUNITY CINEMA
MM 50 Oceanside, Marathon
(305) 743-0288
www.marathontheater.org

This is no average movie theater. Owned and operated by the Marathon Community Theater, the cinema is small and intimate, although the screen is large. Seating is informally arranged in comfy barrel chairs around cocktail-style tables. A single movie is shown twice nightly. Matinees are offered on Sat and Sun. The theater is tucked behind Marathon Liquors.

Key West

CINEMA KEY WEST 6
3338 Roosevelt Blvd., Searstown
Shopping Center
(305) 296-7211
www.regalcinemas.com

Six movies run concurrently at the Florida Keys' first multiplex cinema. All tickets for shows before 6 p.m. are discounted. Listening devices for the hearing impaired are available here as well.

TROPIC CINEMA
416 Eaton St., Key West
(305) 295-9493
www.keywestfilm.org

This movie theater is a show unto itself. Historical and beautifully renovated with loving care to detail (see Arts and Culture chapter), this is one magical setting for any film being shown. In the lobby, beer, wine, soda, and treats can be ordered to take into the shows. Tropic Cinema houses four screening rooms. The newest one is the Peggy Dow Theater, named after the actress who starred with James Stewart in *Harvey*.

PHYSICAL FITNESS

Upper Keys

PILATES IN PARADISE
MM 98.8, Bayside, Key Largo
(305) 453-0801
www.pilatesinparadise.net

Owner and instructor Christi Allen is a certified Romana's Pilates instructor with over 1,500 hours of training in the Pilates method from teachers all over the country. Allen is also a certified nutrition and lifestyle coach and therefore takes a holistic approach to fitness, which is reflected in her classes. Pilates in Paradise offers classes in mat, tower, reformer, and combo, which is a little bit of everything. Classes are small—some only have room for three or four participants due to the equipment—and some require you to have prior Pilates experience, so make sure you inquire before booking. The mat class is for all levels—no experience necessary. Private instruction is also available.

KEY LARGO YOGA
Key Largo
(305) 879-0377
www.keylargoyoga.com
Yoga teacher Kathy Shirley will come to your home, hotel, or even meet you at Founders Park for a private, semi-private, or group yoga session. She has been practicing yoga for over 10 years and completed the 200-hour training for Vinyasa yoga. If you've never taken yoga, but always wanted to try, a private or semi-private session in the great outdoors will let you experience the beauty in the heart of the Keys while doing some good for your heart as well.

FROGGY'S FITNESS
MM 91.8 Bayside, Tavernier
(305) 852-8623
www.froggysfitness.com
Froggy's Fitness is a 6,500-square-foot fitness center that features free weights, treadmills, stairmasters, elliptical machines, and more. In addition to customized personal training, Froggy's offers yoga, boot camp, Pilates, aerobics, and kick boxing classes as well as indoor cycling. The center provides individualized diet and nutrition plans and body-fat

testing. You can purchase gym wear, aerobics footwear, and vitamins, protein supplements, and other health foods here, too.

Middle Keys

BODIES IN MOTION
MM 50.5 Oceanside, Marathon
(305) 292-2331
www.bodiesinmotiononline.com
Head to this "little studio with a lot of heart" for yoga, fitness, and flexibility classes. Yoga is taught every Mon, Wed, Fri, and Sat at 9:30 a.m. and Tues at 7 p.m. Private sessions are available and all levels are welcome. Body work and massage therapy are also offered, as well as Cranial Release Technique, a hands-on process that creates the relaxation of nervous system, fascial, and muscle tissue tension throughout the entire body. Breathe out already!

KEYS FITNESS CENTER
MM 49.5 Oceanside, Marathon
(305) 289-0788
www.floridakeysfitness.com
Offering fitness equipment by Paramount, Life Fitness, and Nautilus, Keys Fitness Center also sports a separate free-weights room for the serious workout addict. The facilities offer private showers and a relaxing sauna. Personal trainers are bilingual. Keys Fitness Center is open Mon to Fri from 6 a.m. to 9 p.m., Sat from 8 a.m. to 6 p.m. and Sun from 9 a.m. to 4 p.m.

YOGA BY THE SEA
Spirit Snorkeling
MM 47.5 Bayside, Marathon
(305) 289-0614
www.spiritsnorkeling.net
How many people can say they've done yoga on the ocean? Calling all yogis! Spirit

Snorkeling offers a yoga sunset cruise aboard their 34-foot catamaran taught by an Ananda instructor. No need to worry about the motion of the ocean as the construction of the watercraft is such that it is almost as wide as it is long, allowing for much more stability than other crafts. All levels are welcome. Call for schedules and availability. *Namaste* indeed!

Lower Keys

PIRATE WELLNESS CENTER
MM 21.4 Oceanside, Cudjoe Key
(305) 744-3348
www.piratewellnesscenter.com
Pirate Wellness Center houses a multi-use studio, treatment rooms, a steam room, and locker rooms in their comfortable 5,000-square-foot building. The studio is the location for classes including step aerobics, yoga, cardio, and strength training. There are also treadmills, recumbent and upright bikes, rowers, free weights, and Smart Strength training machines. Personal training is also available as are day, week, and "snowbird" passes.

Key West

BIKRAM YOGA STUDIO OF KEY WEST
927 White St.
(305) 292-1854
www.bikramyogakeywest.com
This is the real thing and is not for wimps. Classes are 90 minutes long and you will need to bring or rent a yoga mat for $1 on the premises. At Bikram Yoga, the room is kept warm so your muscles will stretch more easily. To that end, it is recommended that ladies wear leotards and men wear bathing suits. Renowned yoga experts often give seminars here and classes are held daily; call for details.

BODY ZONE SOUTH
2740 North Roosevelt Blvd.,
Overseas Market
(305) 292-2930
www.bodyzonefitnessclub.com
A full range of exercise equipment is available here, including Nautilus equipment, treadmills, stationary bikes, stair climbers, and plenty of free weights. Classes include indoor cycling, yoga, and core strength. Personal training and massage are available. The juice bar and play care for children are both convenient services. Body Zone South is open daily.

COFFEE MILL DANCE & YOGA STUDIO
916 Pohalski St.
(305) 296-9982
www.coffeemilldance.com
The Coffee Mill is the place in Key West to get moving! Instructors include members of the Key West Contemporary Dance Company and classes are taught for beginners and advanced dancers (or wannabe dancers) of all ages. Coffee Mill's extensive class list includes yoga, ballet for beginner adults, aerobics, Pilates, Capoeira, Zumba, jazz, and even belly dancing. Classes are held daily, and visitors are welcome.

ISLAND GYM
1119 White St.
(305) 295-8222
www.keywestislandgym.com
This facility is open seven days for serious athletes. Island Gym hosts a full range of free weights as well as indoor and outdoor workout spaces. Personal training and group fitness sessions are also available, and wireless headsets allow you to watch TV on flat screens while working out on the elliptical or treadmill.

PARADISE HEALTH AND FITNESS
1706 North Roosevelt Blvd.
(305) 294-4120
www.paradisehealthandfitness.com
In addition to a full-circuit weight room, Paradise offers a wide range of group classes, including yoga, Pilates, extreme fitness, and lower and upper body challenges for all ages and fitness levels. They also offer ballroom and salsa classes on the weekends for beginners or advanced dancers. Personal trainers are on staff to assist you and will make home visits if you're so inclined. Short- or long-term memberships as well as daily rates are available.

STAY FIT STUDIO
804 White St.
(305) 294-0693
www.stayfitstudiokeywest.com
Start off another perfect day in paradise with an invigorating workout with Stay Fit Studio. They have classes in spinning, Pilates, boot camp, and yoga, among many others. Stay Fit Studio will also come to you. Want to try yoga on the beach? Or a poolside boot camp? Whatever your fitness level, they will work with you. Their certified personal trainers are experts in their fields and through their Weekly Wellness Package, Stay Fit will tailor a workout specifically for your needs. Stay Fit also offers massages and facials so you can truly relax post-workout.

JUST PLAIN FUN

THE BLAKE FERNANDEZ SKATE PARK
Corner of Flagler and Kennedy Drive
(305) 809-3765
Costing more than $229,000, this high-profile skate park is awesome! The 7,500-square-foot park includes grind rails, half and quarter pipes, jump boxes, half bowl ramps of varying pitches, a small staircase, and open spaces for skating and in-line skating. Good place to go for your kick-flips and ollies! Children under 17 must have written permission signed by a guardian. No consent needed to observe—you'll lose a few pounds just by watching these exciting athletes in motion! Super cool!

KEY WEST SPEEDWAY
218 Whitehead St.
(305) 296-8268
www.keywestspeedway.com
Racers, start your engines, fasten your seat belts, and get ready to drive at 200 mph on NASCAR courses from Daytona, Charlotte, Atlanta, or Indy. With four cars, full-motion racing simulators, 180-degree screen runs by 26 computers, and the chance to sit in an actual race car, this is exciting family entertainment. Bump draft your way to the front of the pack and take home a checkered flag. Dale Earnhardt, Jr., eat your heart out!

KEY WEST WATER TOURS
MM 4.5 Oceanside, Stock Island
(305) 294-6790
www.keywestwatertours.com
Ride a Waverunner or take in an aerial view of Key West—you can do them both at Key West Water Tours. Take a Waverunner on a 27-mile guided tour around Key West or ride for an hour in a 4-square-mile play area. Parasail to see dolphins, sharks, sting rays, and other marine life from a lofty perch. Both activities will be a Kodak moment!

MORE THAN JUST JEEPS OF THE KEYS
(305) 367-1070 or (866) 587-8533
www.morethanjustjeeps.com
Hot wheels for cruising the Hot Keys! This company promises you a cool car like

custom Jeeps and S-T-R-E-T-C-H-E-D Jeeps, SUVs, and Hummers. You could tone it down a bit and rent a convertible or sedan. They also provide transportation to and from Miami and Fort Lauderdale airports. Call for delivery to you.

OLD SCHOOL BOARD SHOPPE
614 Greene St., Key West
(305) 292-1600
www.oldschool.com

It all started in California when this husband and wife flipped out over all things board related. Their shop handles classic long and drop boards for tricks and the owners suggest their products make great commuter transportation. Also on hand are trucks, bearings, wheels, and skate apparel.

ATTRACTIONS

Our landmass is but a drizzle of frosting across our seas, but this yummy confection of coral yields some tantalizing attractions. Don't wait for a rainy day (you might not have one) to explore our historical sites, out-islands, museums, nature preserves, and marine research centers.

We've organized the attractions described in this chapter by mile marker in descending order down the Keys, beginning in Key Largo. You'll find the majority of our most popular land-based diversions bordering the Overseas Highway, for our string of islands is not very wide. In our Key West section, we offer several categories of attractions scattered throughout our southernmost city. Many are free or charge a nominal amount for admission.

Don't miss this chapter's final section, "And Beyond . . . ," where we reveal the hidden treasures of Dry Tortugas National Park.

So put on your sandals, grab your hat, and look for those car keys. Dally with us on an Insiders' tour of Paradise's distractions.

Price Code
Codes are based on adult admission.

$	$5 or less
$$	$6 to $10
$$$	$11 to $20
$$$$	More than $21

THE FLORIDA KEYS

Upper Keys

DOLPHIN COVE   **$$$$**
MM 101.9 Bayside, Key Largo
(305) 451-4060 or (877) 365-2683
www.dolphinscove.com
Dolphin Cove, situated on a five-acre lagoon in Key Largo, offers an in-water encounter with bottlenose dolphins in addition to myriad other water activities. The dolphin program is offered daily. Participants must be age 7 and older and, if younger than age 18, must be accompanied by an adult. The encounter is preceded by a 30-minute boat ride in the waters of the backcountry, where you will receive an orientation briefing about the dolphins and about the interactions you will experience.

Dolphin Cove also offers Natural Swim dolphin encounter, which is a freestyle snorkel program. In this unstructured encounter, the dolphins do not exhibit trained behaviors, instead choosing to freely swim and interact with human participants. Participants must be at least age 8 for this encounter, and a participating adult or guardian must accompany anyone younger than age 13. Participants ages 13 to 17 must be observed by a parent or guardian.

Dolphin Cove also offers guided ecological tours of the Everglades National Park backcountry waters and Florida Bay, where you'll learn the mysteries of the mangrove habitat and probably encounter many of the species of birds and sea life discussed in our Area Overview chapter. Other interesting trips into Florida Bay are offered on request, such as guided snorkel trips, kayak tours, sunset cruises, and even a private nighttime crocodile search in the near-shore waters of the Everglades. Call Dolphin Cove to arrange one of these customized trips.

DOLPHINS PLUS INC. $$$$
MM 100 Oceanside, Ocean Bay Drive, Key Largo
(305) 451-1993, (866) 860-7946
www.dolphinsplus.com
This marine mammal research and education facility offers you the opportunity to learn the fascinating habits and lifestyles of the bottlenose dolphin and enter its world for a compatible swim. The two-and-a-half-hour natural swim, offered twice daily, teaches you all about dolphins, including their social pod structure, communication methods, and anatomy. You'll learn how to conduct yourself in the water for your 30-minute swim with the dolphins. Participants must be comfortable in water above their heads and know how to use a mask, fins, and snorkel. Participants who do not wish to swim are also welcome. Individuals age 8 and older may swim with the dolphins, but a participating adult must accompany those younger than age 13. Participants ages 13 to 17 may swim alone but must be accompanied by an observing parent or guardian.

Dolphins Plus also offers a two-hour, structured interaction program three times daily where you can be in the water and involved directly with the dolphins. After an educational briefing, you will experience a structured water session encompassing platform behaviors and in-water behaviors. Interaction varies in each session, depending on the dolphin and the instructor. Sessions for the structured orientation program are offered daily. Participants must be age 7 or older, and a participating parent or guardian must accompany anyone younger than age 13. Pregnant women may not participate in either program.

Participants in all programs must call for reservations. Directions to Dolphins Plus are complicated. Call the center or check the Web site for detailed instructions.

FLORIDA KEYS WILD BIRD CENTER FREE
MM 93.6 Bayside, Tavernier
(305) 852-4486
www.fkwbc.org
Dedicated to the rescue, rehabilitation, and release of ill, injured, and orphaned wild birds, the Florida Keys Wild Bird Center will fascinate visitors of all ages. Artificial environmental hazards such as entanglement with anglers' lines or fishhooks also can render the birds injured and helpless. This rapid-care aviary treats the wounds, supervises the convalescence, and releases the birds back into the wild. Meanwhile, you may walk along a boardwalk path through the birds' natural habitats, which have been discreetly caged with wire enclosures. Signage and brochures provide environmental education of Keys habitats.

The Wild Bird Center is open daily during daylight hours. The center is funded by public donations; there are no admission fees. Look for the Florida Keys Wild Bird Center signs as you drive down the Keys.

WINDLEY KEY FOSSIL REEF STATE GEOLOGIC SITE $
MM 85.5 Bayside, Windley Key
(850) 245-2157
www.floridastateparks.org/windleykey

Quarried long ago by workers building Flagler's East Coast Railroad Extension, the fossilized coral reef that forms the bedrock of the Keys (see the Area Overview chapter) is exposed here for all to see. Borrow the in-house trail guide, which interprets what you'll discover on Windley Key's four trails. The state site is open Thurs through Mon. Guided tours are offered at 8 a.m. and 5 p.m.

THEATER OF THE SEA $$$–$$$$
MM 84.7 Oceanside, Islamorada
(305) 664-2431
www.theaterofthesea.com

With continuous performances offered daily, Theater of the Sea is the Florida Keys' showiest marine entertainment facility. The natural saltwater lagoons, created by excavations for Flagler's Railroad, are home to a potpourri of popular marine creatures: dolphins, stingrays, sharks, sea turtles, game fish, and more.

Special programs are offered for an additional fee, which includes park and show admission. The Trainer-for-a-Day program, open to those age 10 and older, allows you to assist the trainers in feeding and caring for the dolphins and sea lions. You'll learn about nutrition and food preparation behind the scenes, then interact with the mammals in this three-hour session, but you will not swim with the dolphins or sea lions.

The Swim with the Dolphins program and Swim with the Sea Lions sessions are offered to visitors ages five and older. (Children ages five to seven must have a parent or legal guardian swim with them.) The programs include 30 minutes of instruction

and 30 minutes in the water snorkeling and swimming with the dolphins or the sea lions. The Swim with the Stingrays program includes 15 minutes of instruction and 30 minutes in the water snorkeling with the stingrays, sea turtles, and other marine life. Swimmers must be age five and older to participate. (Minors must be accompanied by a parent or legal guardian in the swim area.)

Youngsters age three and older will enjoy the Wade with a Dolphin program. The one-hour session includes an orientation and 30 minutes interacting with a dolphin while standing in shallow water. Interaction includes such dolphin behaviors as cradles and kisses.

All participants in the special swim programs must be competent swimmers, must not be pregnant, and must speak and understand English. Call for reservations.

FLORIDA KEYS HISTORY OF DIVING MUSEUM $$
MM 83 Bayside, Islamorada
(305) 664-9737
www.divingmuseum.org

Making a grand ingress in 2006, the Florida Keys History of Diving Museum displays historic diving equipment and research documents representing more than 3,000 years of underwater exploration from around the world as well as the Florida Keys. The self-guided tours begin with "Timeline of Diving" (starting with breath-holding diving), an "Art McKee Exhibit" (regarded as the father of recreational diving), "Parade of Nations" (a collection of historic hard-hat dive helmets from around the world), a gallery featuring underwater lighting and communication (which led to today's scuba sport diving), and the gallery "Into the Abyss" (showcasing diving suits). World-renowned maritime-life artist Guy Harvey, along with David Dunleavy and local schoolchildren, have created a breathtaking sea life mural to catch your eye on the exterior of the museum.

PIONEER CEMETERY   FREE
MM 82 Oceanside, at Cheeca Lodge, Islamorada

Their gravestones defiled in the hurricane of 1935, the founding fathers and mothers of Islamorada—the Parkers, Pinders, and Russells—still rest in the Pioneer Cemetery, now a part of the extensive grounds of Cheeca Lodge. A schoolhouse and the Methodist church, both destroyed in the hurricane, once bordered the cemetery. The angel statue marking the grave of Etta Dolores Pinder was found on the highway, miraculously intact except for a broken arm and wing. In 1989 Cheeca Lodge and University of Miami historian Josephine Johnson researched the cemetery, leading to the designation of the Pioneer Cemetery as a historical site by the Historical Association of Southern Florida. A plaque at the cemetery gate commemorates the event. You'll find the tiny Pioneer Cemetery surrounded by a white picket fence near the beach on the Cheeca Lodge grounds. The cemetery is open for free viewing by the general public.

HURRICANE MONUMENT   FREE
MM 81.6 Oceanside, Islamorada

Honoring the hundreds of residents and railroad workers in Islamorada who lost their lives in the Labor Day hurricane of 1935, this monument depicts the fury of nature's elements with a bas-relief of high seas and wind-battered palm trees. Carved out of local coral limestone, the Hurricane Monument may be freely viewed just off the Overseas Highway.

GREEN TURTLE HAMMOCK
MM 81 Bayside, Islamorada

A historic eight-acre property is now a passive park. The area provides a natural outdoor recreation and education setting including nature trails, a wildlife observation platform, and a launch with dockage for kayaks and canoes to paddle across Florida Bay. A historic cottage doubles as an interpretive center as well as an amenity for the adjacent Florida Keys Overseas Heritage Trail.

INDIAN KEY STATE
HISTORICAL SITE $
MM 77.5 Oceanside, Indian Key
(850) 245-2157
www.floridastateparks.org/indiankey

A colorful history paints Indian Key, a 10-acre oceanside island about ¾ of a mile offshore from Lower Matecumbe Key. Now uninhabited, this tiny key has yielded archaeological evidence of prehistoric Native American cultures. Once visited by Spaniards and pirates alike, the island was purchased in 1831 by Jacob Housman, who established a thriving settlement. Indian Key became the Dade County seat in 1836. Physician Henry Perrine sat out the Second Seminole War here, which proved a misguided decision, for Indians attacked the island in 1840, and he lost his life after all. Fires destroyed all the structures except for the foundations. Although some people returned after the assault, by the early 1900s the key supported only burgeoning vegetation.

Indian Key is accessible only by boat. Limited private dockage is available for small boats, but the site has no restrooms or picnic facilities. The historical site is open from 8 a.m. to sundown. Ranger-led tours are at 9 a.m. and 1 p.m.

Robbie's Marina, MM 77.5 Bayside, (305) 664-9814, or www.robbies.com, offers the only regularly scheduled tour transportation to the island. Reservations are preferred. And while you are waiting for the boat, buy a cup of bait and feed the tarpon that come around the docks regularly.

LIGNUMVITAE STATE
BOTANICAL SITE $
MM 77.5 Bayside, Lignumvitae Key
(850) 245-2157
www.floridastateparks.org/lignumvitae

Named for the lignum vitae tree, Lignumvitae Key—our highest island at 17 feet above sea level—supports one of the best examples of a virgin hardwood hammock in the Florida Keys (see the Hardwood Hammocks section in the Area Overview chapter). Also on the island is the 1919 home of the Matheson family, of chemical company fame, who owned the island for many decades. The stilt-style home sports two storm hatches—bedroom and porch—so doors would not be blown off their hinges in a bad blow. The screened porch enabled the Mathesons to leave via the hatch, keeping the mosquitoes at bay.

One-hour ranger-guided walks at 10 a.m. and 2 p.m. allow visitors to tour the house and the hardwood hammock. You may not enter the hammock unless accompanied by a ranger. Park officials suggest you come equipped with mosquito repellent and sturdy shoes. Like Indian Key, Lignumvitae Key may be accessed only by boat, and limited private dockage for small craft is available (see previous write-up for information on Robbie's Marina, which offers transportation to the key). Lignumvitae Key is closed Tues and Wed.

i Get out of the hotel or house, stop the shopping and fishing, and take a nature call at the Key West Botanical Garden and Tropical Forest (see this chapter). There are exciting events going on all the time. Some of the highlights are Hot Havana Nights, their annual summer party; Brunch With Mom in the Garden blooms in May; and Jewels of the Tropical Forest glitters in Feb. In Apr, Migration Mania offers kids the thrilling experience of bats, birds, butterflies, and reptiles up close and personal! This stuff is better than Disney!

Middle Keys

THE DOLPHIN CONNECTION $$$$
MM 61 Oceanside, at Hawk's Cay Resort, Duck Key
(305) 743-7000, (888) 814-9154
www.dolphinconnection.com

Dolphin Connection's Dolphin Discovery provides an interactive, 25-minute, in-water encounter with the most famous of our Florida Keys marine creatures, bottlenose dolphins. You will not actually swim with the Connection's dolphins, but you'll get to know them up close and personal. You'll be able to touch, feed, pet, and play with them from the security of a submerged platform (great for nonswimmers or those people with physical limitations).

After a short classroom orientation reviewing dolphin and people etiquette, you will sit in the water on a shallow platform, where the trainer will familiarize you with the dolphin's anatomy. Trainers enlighten participants about the dolphins and their marine environment as well as the Florida Keys' ecosystem.

The 45-minute Dolphin Discovery program is open to participants who are 4 feet, 6 inches or taller. The encounters are held several times daily. There is a maximum of six people per program, with the intimate ratio of three people to one trainer and one dolphin.

Adults who do not wish to get wet in the Discovery program can participate in Dockside Dolphins, as can pregnant women, who are not allowed to join in the in-water Dolphin Discovery. Dockside Dolphins is a 30-minute, behind-the-scenes look at dolphin training sessions. Participants learn how the professionals at Dolphin Connection train the dolphins and then, from the dock, take part in an actual training procedure. You'll be able to feel, feed, and pet the dolphins but not have to get into the water. Adults and children love this experience (children age five and younger must be accompanied by a paying adult). Dockside Dolphins is offered daily.

Kids have a ball as participants in the unique 30-minute Dolphin Detectives program. From the dry docks, the children learn how to be dolphin trainers. (Children age five and younger must be accompanied by a paying adult.) The kids learn the trainer's hand signals and get to try them out on the playful dolphins during a supervised training session. The participants are taught how to feed the dolphins—touching, weighing, and preparing those fish the mammals like so much.

Dolphin Detectives kicks off daily. Advance reservations are required for all programs. Bookings are accepted up to three months in advance.

AQUA RANCH $$$$
MM 59.3 Oceanside, Grassy Key
(305) 743-6135
www.aquaranch.org

Featured on Animal Planet, this seven-acre saltwater lake on Grassy Key gives visitors an opportunity to interact with cobia and snapper. Cobias weigh in between 50 and 100 pounds and these gentle creatures look a whole lot smaller from the shore than when you descend down the swim ladder and get in the water. Ask about "Old Man Winter," the 115-pound favorite at the ranch. If you fall in love with one of the fish, you can adopt one for $20. Makes a great gift to a child for a birthday or holiday and it helps the planet too! For the more timid visitor you can feed the cobia or snapper, travel around the lake in a canoe, rent a tent site (no RVs or campers allowed), or tour the facility for a small donation. Rustic and real makes this one of the Insiders' favorite attractions.

DOLPHIN RESEARCH
CENTER $$$–$$$$
MM 59 Bayside, Grassy Key
(305) 289-1121 or (305) 289-0002 (for reservations)
www.dolphins.org

Look for the giant statue of a dolphin and her calf that heralds the Grassy Key home of the Dolphin Research Center. Once the lodging for Flipper, the famed television star of yesteryear, the Dolphin Research Center offers a variety of fascinating encounters with these smart marine mammals.

One-hour, narrated walking tours introduce you to the dolphins in their natural environments, where you'll witness their training sessions. Walking tours are offered five times daily. Children younger than age four are admitted free with a paying adult.

The half-day Dolphin Encounter enables you to learn how people interact with the dolphins. You'll attend a workshop, take the walking tour, and then spend 20 minutes in the water with two dolphins and up to five other people. The ratio of people to dolphins is never more than three to one. Children ages 5 to 12 must be accompanied in the water by a paying adult. Life jackets will be supplied to participants of all ages who desire them. This program is very popular, and access is limited. For reservations, you must call on the 1st or 15th day of the month preceding the month you'd like to swim. (For example, call Oct 1 if you'd like to reserve a dolphin swim from Nov 1 to Nov 14; call Oct 15 if you'd like a reservation from Nov 15 to the end of the month.)

In the DolphinSplash program, you can meet the dolphins in the water without swimming. Participants stand on a submerged platform, waist-deep in water, and the dolphins swim up to say hello. You'll receive 15 minutes of instruction, enjoy 15 minutes in the water, and then take one of the guided walking tours. Make reservations following the same procedures as Dolphin Encounter. For DolphinSplash, however, a few spots are saved every day for walk-ins, so you might get lucky. Participants must be at least 44 inches tall; children below this height must be held in the arms of a parent or guardian. Children younger than age three are admitted free. A participating adult must accompany children younger than age eight.

Programs at the Dolphin Research Center include Meet a Dolphin, where you can observe a dolphin behavior session and then join the trainer at the dock for a personal introduction to the dolphin; and Paint with a Dolphin, where you can help a dolphin actually paint a T-shirt for you in your choice of two colors. Unlike the other interactive programs at the center, you can purchase tickets for these after you arrive.

Exciting additions at the DRC are Researcher for a Day, where you interact with instructors with hands-on responsibilities, help collect data, and learn how dolphins and sea lions are trained to understand tasks. All About Babies is a presentation in the Dolphin Theater, then walk with the staff to the maternity lagoon for a closer look at mothers and their calves. Dolphin Conversations let you eavesdrop on dolphin communication below the water's surface via a hydrophone. Secret Lives of Dolphins, again in the Dolphin Theater, offers a look at dolphin social structures and behaviors. Dolphins and the Deep Blue Sea allows students to explore the Florida Keys marine life for a five-day in-depth fun experience.

You can immerse yourself in a dolphin world and earn college credit at the one-week DolphinLab, a series of dolphin behavior seminars and hands-on encounters. You'll live on the premises in the center's dormitory and enjoy side trips to Key West and snorkeling at Looe Key National Marine Sanctuary. Summer programs for middle school, junior high, and teens are also available. Call for more information.

MARATHON WILD BIRD CENTER   FREE
MM 50.5 Bayside, Marathon
(305) 743-8382
www.marathonwildbirdcenter.org

Safely protected on a wooded 64-acre park of the Crane Point Hammock, the Marathon Wild Bird Center is a licensed wildlife rehabilitation facility that specializes in migratory birds. Incorporated in 1998, they work with local veterinarians and other caring individuals who are concerned with the rescue, rehabilitation, and return of wild birds back into their natural setting of the Florida Keys. Their

Web site gives step-by-step detailed instructions on the care of orphaned baby birds.

MUSEUMS OF CRANE POINT $$
MM 50.5 Bayside, Marathon
(305) 743-9100
www.cranepoint.net

The small, interesting Museum of Natural History and the adjoining Florida Keys Children's Museum (see the Kidstuff chapter) sit on the skirt of the Crane Point hammock, which covers a bit of history in itself. The museum houses a potpourri of Keys icons and exhibits. Creatures of the reef have been authentically re-created in tropical splendor and are accompanied by an audio of the sounds of the deep. You'll see the inhabitants of the pinelands habitat—slash pines, red mangroves, silver buttonwood, key deer, and miniature raccoons; ancient shipwreck memorabilia; shells of giant sea turtles; tree snails of the tropics; even a stuffed osprey, great white heron, egret, frigatebird, and the like.

Between the two museum structures, a fish-filled lagoon attracts fin fanciers, and the wild-bird rescue flight cage fascinates bird lovers of all ages. You'll see a Caribbean-style sailing canoe, paddled here in 1989 by three Guatemalan refugees, and an authentic Cuban freedom raft. Children enjoy the outdoor osprey nest exhibit, in which they really get a bird's-eye view of the museum. They can climb right up into the nest. Guided tours of the museum are offered weekdays from Dec through Apr.

After you tour the exhibits, traipse down the nature trails that loop through Crane Point hammock, which is named for the Cranes, who owned the property until the early 1970s. The Cranes protected the area from development and preserved the

forested land as a good example of our rare hardwood hammock habitat (see the Area Overview chapter). A ¼-mile boardwalk trail, which leads through a mangrove habitat, allows the visitor an up close and personal view of the lush tropical foliage on the property.

The museum provides a self-guided tour pamphlet that also lists some of the unusual tropical hardwoods you'll see along the nature trails. The Adderley House walk, about half a mile long, leads to the restored Bahamian-style house built around 1905 by George Adderley, a black Bahamian settler of the Middle Keys. The concretelike walls of the one-room structure are constructed from ground shells.

Crane Point is open daily. One admission charge allows access to both trails and museums. Children age six and younger get in free.

PIGEON KEY NATIONAL HISTORICAL SITE $$
Old Seven Mile Bridge,
Bayside, Pigeon Key
(305) 289-0025, (305) 743-5999 (gift shop), (305) 743-5999 (ferry ride)
www.pigeonkey.net

Though undoubtedly Pigeon Key was known to Native Americans and Bahamian fishermen in the early days of the Keys, it was Henry Flagler's East Coast Railroad Extension that put the tiny five-acre key on the historical map. And it is the volunteer-staffed Pigeon Key Foundation that keeps it there. The island is connected to the mainland by a bridge that was originally built for the railroad and which served as a construction and maintenance site for the railroad from 1908 to 1935. The hurricane of 1935 flooded Pigeon Key and caused so much damage to the railroad that the company decided not to rebuild (see the History chapter). When the Seven Mile Bridge was built over the railroad spans in the late 1930s, Pigeon Key became headquarters for the Bridge and Toll District.

Over the ensuing decades the key was used as a fishing camp, a U.S. Navy site, a park, and a marine biology center for the University of Miami. In 1982 the new Seven Mile Bridge was constructed, bypassing Pigeon Key from auto traffic. The Pigeon Key Foundation, a nonprofit local organization with the stated mission "to preserve the history and environment of the Florida Keys" was established in 1993, securing a long-term lease to the island from Monroe County.

Pigeon Key is a living testament to the Florida Keys of 1912 to 1940. The foundation has restored eight of the island village's buildings dating from the early 1900s. Automobiles are not allowed on the Old Seven Mile Bridge.

In 2008, the old bridge was finally closed to all vehicle traffic and a new ferry service has begun to carry passengers to Pigeon Key. At MM 47, oceanside, behind the gift shop, is where the dock for the trip is located.

Lower Keys

THE BLUE HOLE   FREE
MM 31 Bayside, Key Deer Boulevard, Big Pine Key
(305) 872-2411
You may wonder why all those cars are parked on the side of Key Deer Boulevard, for from the roadside the area looks like an uninhabited stand of slash pines. Park your vehicle and join the crowd. A few steps into the thatch palm understory you'll see a large, water-filled barrow pit, known as the Blue

Hole. Inhabiting this incongruous water hole are a couple of resident alligators, the only known 'gators in the Keys. If you're lucky, you may catch a glimpse of one of these elusive reptiles.

Ducks and wading birds stay out of the alligators' path. The Blue Hole is ¼ mile north of the intersection of Key Deer and Watson Boulevards. There is no charge for visiting the Blue Hole.

NATIONAL KEY DEER REFUGE AND
   WATSON NATURE TRAIL   FREE
MM 30.5 Bayside, Key Deer Boulevard, Big Pine Key
(305) 872-2239
www.fws.gov/nationalkeydeer
The National Key Deer Refuge protects the pineland habitat frequented by the key deer, a small species—not much larger than a German shepherd—that is found nowhere else in the world (see the Area Overview chapter). Some areas of the refuge, which encompasses a large portion of Big Pine Key, are off-limits to visitors and are so marked. National wildlife refuge signs, depicting a flying bird, mark the boundaries of the refuge, which is open for daytime public access on designated trails.

You can find the ⅓-mile Watson Nature Trail 1.3 miles north of the intersection of Key Deer and Watson Boulevards. The trail winds throughout the pineland habitat of the refuge (see the Area Overview chapter). The short Mannillo Trail, ⅕ mile, traverses pine rockland and freshwater wetland habitats.

The key deer are protected by law—even feeding them is a misdemeanor offense. Roadkill remains a primary hazard to the key deer. Speed limits on US 1 through Big Pine Key are reduced to 45 mph during the day and 35 mph at night and are strictly enforced. The best time to look for key deer is early in the morning or at dusk.

You can sometimes spot key deer beside US 1, but you are more likely to see them along the back roads and especially on No Name Key, where there are fewer human inhabitants. To reach No Name Key, turn right at the intersection of Key Deer and Watson Boulevards. The road will take you through a residential neighborhood and across a cement bridge to No Name Key, ending abruptly at a pile of boulders.

PERKY BAT TOWER   FREE
MM 17 Bayside, Sugarloaf Key

Richter Perky may have had bats in his belfry in 1929 when he decided to build this Sugarloaf Key tower, but such are dreams that lay the foundations for legends. Perky believed that the uniquely designed, louvered pine tower, when laced with the proper bait, would attract a Keys population of mosquito-loving bats, thus solving his insect-infestation problem. Alas, the nocturnal fliers bypassed his offering, and Perky had to go back to the drawing board. The structure has withstood the tests of time and the elements, however. Perhaps Perky should have called it a hurricane shelter.

To find Perky Bat Tower, turn right (bayside) at the Sugarloaf Airport sign just beyond Sugarloaf Lodge when heading down the Keys. When the road forks, bear to the right.

KEY WEST

Key West's historic Old Town district is perfect for a leisurely stroll to take in the history and eccentricity of this tiny island. How about visiting an aquarium, a cemetery, or a garden? Or maybe a tour of haunted houses or an old wrecker's house filled with antiques? We've checked out all the high points for you, including a few "only in Key West" attractions guaranteed to keep you entertained.

Key West attractions have been divided into three categories: Historic Homes and Museums, One of a Kind, and Guided and Self-Guided Tours. Within each category, attractions are listed in alphabetical order.

Historic Homes and Museums

AUDUBON HOUSE &
TROPICAL GARDENS $$
205 Whitehead St.
(305) 294-2116 or (877) 294-2470
www.audubonhouse.com

It was 12 years before the house was built, but in 1832 John James Audubon did spend time on the grounds of John Geiger's huge garden. Legend has it that Audubon sketched the white-crowned pigeon and the geiger tree he found in the garden here. During his stay in the Keys, Audubon produced 18 sketches of native wildlife. Original lithographs of these drawings are on display at the Audubon House. The house and environs, however, are more reminiscent of the family of Captain John Geiger, a wrecker who built the house and lived here with his family. Set your own tour pace with a free pair of headphones and a tape that brings the house alive. Audubon House is open daily. Children younger than age six are free.

CURRY MANSION INN $
511 Caroline St.
(305) 294-5349 or (800) 253-3466
www.currymansion.com

This imposing home evokes images of an opulent old Key West, although the three-story Conch house now serves as the focal point for a bed-and-breakfast inn and a museum. Built in 1905 by Milton Curry, Florida's first homegrown millionaire, the inn's public rooms display a selection of antiques and memorabilia. Poke around in the attic, and you'll find an 1899 billiard table among the old dresses and luggage. From the attic you can climb the widow's walk for a panoramic view of Key West Harbor. Self-guided tours are available daily. See the Accommodations chapter for information on overnight stays in the adjacent buildings.

EAST MARTELLO MUSEUM $$
3501 South Roosevelt Blvd.
(305) 296-3913
www.kwahs.com

This enchanting, artifact-filled former fort will bring you up to speed on Key West history. Built during the Civil War, the brick fortress was never completely finished because the circular Martello design became antiquated before it was ever armed. Operated today as a museum and gallery by the Key West Art and Historical Society, the 8-foot-thick walls support pictures, artifacts, and historical documents. Featured in the small gallery are the charming wood carvings of Key West's Mario Sanchez and the funky welded sculptures by the late Stanley Papio of Key Largo, fabricated from bedsprings, toilet fixtures, and other so-called junk. You can climb the citadel to the lookout tower for an unobstructed view of the Atlantic coast.

East Martello Museum is open daily. Kids younger than age six get in free. Adults may purchase a combination ticket that allows admission to this museum, the Key West Lighthouse Museum, and the Key West Museum of Art and History at the Custom House (see descriptions later in this chapter). Visits to all three facilities need not be made on the same day.

FLORIDA KEYS HISTORICAL MILITARY MEMORIAL   FREE
One Mallory Square, Key West

Flush with military history, Key West honors its best with this handsome memorial dedicated to those who have proudly served their country and the military events directly affecting Key West and the Keys. Beginning in 1822, when the U.S. Navy raised the American flag over Key West, the era of the Spanish-American War, through World War I and World War II, Korea, the Cuban missile crisis, Vietnam, Desert Storm, Iraq, and the ongoing war on drugs, this simple, elegant display stands proud as a sentinel reflecting a community paying homage to these historical events and brave souls.

HARRY S. TRUMAN LITTLE WHITE HOUSE $$
111 Front St.
(305) 294-9111
www.trumanlittlewhitehouse.com

Ordered by his doctor to retreat to a stress-free climate and recover from a lingering cold, President Harry S Truman came to Key West for the first time in 1946. Like so many others, he was instantly smitten with the island and spent 11 working vacations in the commandant's quarters, dubbed the Little White House. Built in 1890, the house was renovated for its famed visitor in 1948. Opened to the general public as a museum dedicated to "Give 'Em Hell Harry" in 1991, the home has once again been restored to its 1948 splendor. You'll be able to view Truman's Winter White House as it looked when he spent his 175 working vacation days here. The family quarters, poker porch, dining room, and living room (complete with Truman's piano) are open to the public.

The guided tour takes you into the rooms and lives of Harry and Bess. The Exhibition Room displays a permanent collection of photographs of Presidents Eisenhower and Kennedy. Eisenhower spent two weeks here recuperating from his second heart attack, and Kennedy held a summit meeting here before the Bay of Pigs action. Jimmy Carter visited with his family in 1996, and again in 1997 for New Year's Eve. Former President Bill Clinton and wife Hillary spent a weekend here in 2005. A 10-minute video recounts the history of the home, and a collection of presidential memorabilia is on display in the museum gift shop. Guided tours are conducted daily. Children younger than age four are admitted free.

HEMINGWAY HOME AND MUSEUM $$
907 Whitehead St.
(305) 294-1136
www.hemingwayhome.com
Once the home of Key West's most famous writer, Ernest Hemingway, the Hemingway Home and Museum ranks at the top of any must-do list and is Key West's most popular attraction. Built by wrecker Asa Tift in 1851, the home took on historical significance when Ernest and Pauline Hemingway moved in. Pauline spearheaded extensive remodeling, redecorating, and refurnishing and fitted her backyard with the island's first swimming pool. Hemingway wrote several of his most celebrated works, including *For Whom the Bell Tolls*, *Death in the Afternoon*, *The Green Hills of Africa*, and *To Have and Have Not*, from his pool house office out back. The Hemingways lived in this Key West home from 1931 to 1939. Guided tours lasting approximately 45 minutes are offered every 10 minutes, daily. Children younger than age six enter free. Be sure to look for the infamous six-toed cats!

i Looking for a quiet, tranquil place to catch your breath? Just a few blocks off the hustle and bustle of Duval Street is the serene Stations of the Cross Gardens on the grounds of historic St. Mary Star of the Sea Catholic Church. This half-acre garden is open to travelers and islanders alike.

HERITAGE HOUSE MUSEUM AND ROBERT FROST COTTAGE $$
410 Caroline St.
(305) 296-3573
www.heritagehousemuseum.org
The memorabilia in the Heritage House Museum pays tribute to Jessie Porter, a cultured, well-traveled woman at the center of Key West society in the mid-1900s. Visitors to the house included Tallulah Bankhead, Thornton Wilder, Gloria Swanson, Tennessee Williams, Pauline Hemingway, and, of course, regular visitor Robert Frost, who stayed in the small cottage in the rear garden when he wintered in Key West, which he did off and on from 1945 through 1960. Visitors are invited to make themselves at home in the comfortable original surroundings and even to play the antique piano. Children younger than age 12 get in free.

KEY WEST LIGHTHOUSE AND KEEPER'S QUARTERS MUSEUM $$
938 Whitehead St.
(305) 294-0012
www.kwahs.com
This 1847 structure, inland on a Key West street just across from the Hemingway Home, affords visitors a bird's-eye view of Key West from atop its 90-foot light tower (88 steps to the top). Why a lighthouse so far from the water? It was positioned here to avoid the fate of its predecessor on Whitehead Point,

which toppled in a hurricane the previous year. The keeper's quarters houses maritime memorabilia and a gift shop.

The lighthouse museum is open daily for self-guided tours. Children younger than age six are free. Adults may purchase a combination ticket for admission to this museum, the East Martello Museum, and the Key West Museum of Art and History at the Custom House (see descriptions elsewhere in this chapter).

THE KEY WEST MUSEUM OF ART AND HISTORY AT THE CUSTOM HOUSE $$
281 Front St.
(305) 295-6616
www.kwahs.com

Even if it contained no exhibits, this lovely building just off Mallory Square, where Front and Whitehead Streets come together, would be worth a stop. With its 20-foot ceilings, arched windows, 12 fireplaces, and magnificently restored staircase, the structure itself is a work of art. Designed by the renowned architect Henry Hobson Richardson and completed in 1891 at a cost of less than $110,000, the building required 917,000 bricks from New York, iron from Pennsylvania, dozens of masons from Massachusetts, and more than 100 carpenters, plasterers, and other skilled construction workers from throughout the United States. Although it was officially called the U.S. Custom House, this structure also housed the U.S. Postal Service and the U.S. District Court. Here, in the second-floor courtroom, the official inquiry into what caused the sinking of the USS Maine was conducted. The Custom House served the city well for four decades, but as government needs changed and the various agencies moved to larger quarters elsewhere

on the island, the building was deemed "superfluous property" and abandoned in the 1960s. Fortunately, it was not targeted for demolition. Today it is on the National Register of Historic Places and remains one of the finest examples of Richardsonian/Romanesque Revival architecture in existence.

For close to 30 years, the Custom House stood empty and forlorn. In 1990 the Key West Art and Historical Society acquired the building and began a restoration that would take nine years and nearly $9 million to complete. It was finally reopened to the public as a museum of national stature in August 1999.

Inside you will find seven galleries and a gift shop. Exhibits of artwork and historical artifacts change periodically; however, those on the second floor traditionally focus on the history of Key West. Be sure to continue up the stairs to the third floor. There are no exhibit galleries here, but the works of folk artist Mario Sanchez, which line the walls between the closed office doors, are worth the climb. There's a great view from the arched window overlooking Sunset Key and the harbor here, too.

The museum is open daily. Children younger than age six enter free. Adults may purchase a combination ticket that allows admission to this museum as well as to the East Martello Museum and the Key West Lighthouse Museum (see descriptions elsewhere in this chapter).

MEL FISHER MARITIME HERITAGE SOCIETY AND MUSEUM $$
200 Greene St.
(305) 294-2633
www.melfisher.org

For 16 years, "today's the day" was the hope of treasure salvor Mel Fisher, who finally struck pay dirt on July 20, 1985. Finding the *Nuestra Señora de Atocha*, which Fisher estimated to be worth $400 million, ensured his legacy as treasure hunter extraordinaire. Heavy gold chains, jeweled crosses, and bars of silver and gold are among the artifacts on display at the permanent first-floor exhibit. In 2007, Mel Fishers' Treasures subcontracted a company to salvage the shipwreck site of the *Santa Margarita*. Their discovery of this 1622 Spanish galleon yielded a metal box full of pearls, gold artifacts, and chains. The second-floor exhibit changes frequently—call for details. A museum shop offers a variety of pirate and nautical gifts. The museum is open daily. Children younger than age six are admitted free.

SAN CARLOS INSTITUTE   **FREE**
516 Duval St.
(305) 294-3887
www.institutosancarlos.org
Founded in 1871 by Cuban exiles, the San Carlos Institute was established to preserve the language and traditions of the Cuban people. Dubbed "La Casa Cuba" by legendary poet and patriot José Martí, the institute helped unite the exiled Cuban community. The current building was completed in 1924 and operated as an integrated school until the mid-1970s, when deteriorating conditions necessitated its closing. With the perseverance of the Hispanic Affairs Commission, a state agency headed by Rafael Penalver, restoration of the San Carlos was completed and the institute reopened on Jan. 3, 1992, 100 years to the day after José Martí's first visit in the late 19th century. Today the San Carlos Institute is a museum, library, school, art gallery, theater, and conference center. The institute is open weekends. Admission is free.

The Schooner Western Union Maritime Museum

The *Schooner Western Union* is one of the oldest working wooden schooner ships in the United States. The Schooner Western Union Preservation Society is the not-for-profit corporation founded for the purpose of restoring, maintaining and operating the historic **Schooner Western Union Maritime Museum** in Key West. In addition to the restoration of the schooner, they operate the boat as a maritime museum with an educational outreach program that includes historical tours, children's activities, and private excursions. This proud 130-foot vessel is built of mahogany timbers and Dade County pine. The beam is 23.5 feet, draft is 8 feet, and the sail area is a whopping 4,800 square feet. Even though the *Schooner Western Union* is a sailing vessel, the ship has two engines to steady it at sea. Book her for day, sunset, or stargazing sails. You can also reserve the *Schooner Western Union* for weddings and special events. Contact (305) 292-1766, 202 William St., Key West. Visit www.schoonerwesternunion.org for more information.

WEST MARTELLO TOWER JOE ALLEN
  GARDEN CENTER   **$**
Atlantic Boulevard and White Street
(305) 294-3210
www.keywestgardenclub.com

Built in 1862, the West Martello Tower, like the other forts on the island, was never involved in an actual war. It was, however, used for target practice by the U.S. Navy, which accounts for its somewhat shabby condition. Today the tower is also the Joe Allen Garden Center, and the Key West Garden Club operates here. Use the self-guided tour to spot local flora, including a key lime tree, or just find an inviting spot to relax. West Martello is open Tues through Sat in season. The schedule may vary; call for more information. Admission is free, but note that shirt and shoes are required.

WRECKER'S MUSEUM $
322 Duval St.
(305) 294-9502
www.oirf.org
Built in 1829, this museum is known as the "oldest house in Key West." The Conch cottage was the home to Captain Francis B. Watlington and consists of three buildings: the main house, a kitchen house, and exhibit building. Peek into the life of a wrecking family with documents and memorabilia from the salvage trade. The Wrecker's Museum is open daily. The tours are self-guided, but a docent is always available on the premises to answer questions.

One of a Kind

AFRICAN CEMETERY AT
HIGGS BEACH FREE
Atlantic Boulevard, Key West
In 1860, the slave trade brought thousands of young slaves from West Africa to the New World. Hundreds were brought to Key West to be eventually shipped back home to West Africa. Unfortunately, many died in transit and the bodies were buried in mass graves in the Higgs Beach area. In 1993, these events come to the attention of a local historical researcher and in 2007, a concrete slab was poured over the grave site and the "African Cemetery at Higgs Beach" sign erected as a first step in creating a lasting memorial.

FLORIDA KEYS ECO-DISCOVERY
CENTER $
35 East Quay Rd., Truman Waterfront
(305) 292-0311, (305) 809-4700
www.floridakeys.noaa.gov/eco-discovery.html
With a $6 million price tag, the 6,400-square-foot Eco-Discovery Center in Old Town is operated by the National Oceanic and Atmospheric Administration's Florida Keys National Marine Sanctuary, the National Park Service, and the U.S. Fish and Wildlife Service. Located at historic Truman waterfront, the center's high points are a 22-minute film by David Talbot, the award-winning director of *Free Willy* fame. Talbot takes you on an exciting trip from land to under the sea. In the Eco-Discovery Center you can utilize touch-screen computers to learn more about the Keys and conservation for this part of the planet, coral reefs, Keys habitats, and a walk-through version of the Aquarius Undersea Lab (see the Diving and Snorkeling chapter). In 2008, a new 2,400-gallon coral reef aquarium exhibit opened to feature hard and soft corals to educate the public about preserving our coral reefs. Stop in on Saturday mornings when kids kindergarten through grade five can attend the "Discovery Saturdays" programs. To add to the marvels of this complex, there is a "green" roof that covers the main structure—talk about being eco-friendly!

FORT ZACHARY TAYLOR HISTORIC
STATE PARK $
Truman Annex at Southard Street
(305) 292-6713
www.forttaylor.org
Although not fully completed until 1866, this Key West military bastion served the Union well during the Civil War, when it guarded against Confederate blockade runners. So impressive were its defenses, the fort was never attacked. It saw continuous usage by the military until the federal government deeded the structure to the state of Florida for use as a historic site. The Florida Park Service opened Fort Zachary Taylor to the public in 1985.

The surrounding park offers a beach for fishing, swimming, or snorkeling, as well as picnic areas equipped with tables and grills, outside showers, snack bar, and restroom facilities. It also offers one of the best, unobstructed views of the sunset. Fort Zachary Taylor is open daily from 8 a.m. to sunset. Hang on to your ticket stub; you may leave the park and return at any time throughout the same day by simply showing your ticket to the booth attendant. Hint: Come here to watch the sunset away from the craziness going on at Mallory Square (see description later in this chapter).

KEY WEST AIDS MEMORIAL FREE
Foot of White Street and Atlantic
Boulevard
www.keywestaids.org
The names of many of the victims of the AIDS epidemic are inscribed on this memorial, which consists of flat granite slabs embedded in the walkway approaching White Street Pier. Built with private funds and dedicated on World AIDS Day, Dec. 1, 1997, the memorial has room for 1,500 names. At the unveiling, it contained 730. New names are engraved annually and dedicated in a ceremony that takes place each December on World AIDS Day. Members of a volunteer group—Friends of the Key West AIDS Memorial—maintain and protect this site.

KEY WEST AQUARIUM $$
1 Whitehead St. at Mallory Square
(305) 296-2051 or (800) 868-7482
www.keywestaquarium.com
Key West's oldest tourist attraction (built in 1934) and still one of the most fascinating our southernmost city has to offer, the Key West Aquarium affords you a diver's-eye view of the marine creatures of our encompassing waters. Stroll at your leisure alongside the backlit tanks re-creating our coral reefs, but don't miss the guided tours offered four times daily, when you'll witness the feeding of the species. You'll marvel at the feeding frenzy of the sharks and saw-tooths; the nurse sharks and stingrays flipping and splashing for their rations; and the tarpon, barracuda, game fish, and sea turtles recognizing the hands that feed them in the outdoor Atlantic Shores Exhibit, created to look like a mangrove lagoon.

A highlight for kids is the "touch tank" just inside the front door. Here, they can reach in and grab hold of horseshoe crabs, hermit crabs, conchs, sea cucumbers, and many other creatures that populate the waters surrounding Key West. Be sure to bring your camera—you'll want to capture the expression on your child's face when the horseshoe crab in his or her hand suddenly flexes its legs. The aquarium is open daily. Children age three and younger are admitted free. Discounts are available.

Close-up

Marriage, Keys Style

Jet Skiing, skydiving, horseback rides, scuba diving, yachts and schooners, light-houses, sunset on the beach, historic sites, private gardens, fabulous mansions, theme characters. Sounds like a delightful tour of the Florida Keys, but actually these are ideas for getting married in the fabulous Florida Keys!

Florida always ranks high for honeymoon destinations, and the Keys offer wedding planners who can orchestrate a wedding you and your wedding party will always remember. Whether getting married, renewing your vows, or sharing commitment ceremonies, using the Florida Keys as a backdrop will make for a day like no other—in more ways than one.

Most wedding coordinators offer free consultations and will help orchestrate all the details from the ceremony site to florists, photographers, caterers, music, and the reception. There are a wealth of Web sites to help you, but http://keywest.com/weddings is a good place to start. To marry in the Keys one must be 18 years of age. A public notary can perform the ceremony as well as a minister. Out-of-state residents do not have to undergo blood tests, and there is no waiting period for non-Florida residents or residents from other countries.

THE KEY WEST BUTTERFLY & NATURE CONSERVATORY $$
1316 Duval St.
(305) 296-2988 or (800) 839-4647
www.keywestbutterfly.com

The Key West Butterfly & Nature Conservatory was opened in January 2003 by Sam Trophia and George Fernandez, the proprietors of the perennially popular Wings of Imagination: The Butterfly Gallery. The conservatory celebrates the lives of butterflies around the globe. Visitors first stop at the Learning Center for a brief introductory film on the wonders of the butterflies' world before proceeding to the Miracle of Metamorphosis exhibit. Here you can watch the actual butterfly-hatching process and observe the stages of development from egg to caterpillar to chrysalis. All the butterflies are bred in captivity on butterfly farms in North, Central, and South America, as well as

Southeast Asia and Africa. When mature, the butterflies are released into a 5,000-square-foot glass-enclosed greenhouse featuring more than 3,500 tropical trees and plants. The gardens are a horticulturalist's nirvana—lush and tropical vegetation inhabited by 30 to 50 species of exotic butterflies, such as blue morpho and emerald swallowtail, and myriad birds from all over the world. A gallery displays Trophia's original butterfly designs. The conservatory is open daily. Children younger than age four are free.

KEY WEST CITY CEMETERY FREE
Bordered by Angela, Frances, and Olivia Streets, and Windsor Lane
(305) 292-8177
www.keywestcity.com/cemetery

Built in 1847 after the horrific hurricane the year before washed out the sand sanctuary at the island's southernmost point, Key West

City Cemetery, right in the center of town, adds a human element to the history of Key West. The marble monuments of the wealthy were shipped to the island; local markers were generally produced from brick or coral-based cement. Carved with symbols and prosaic sayings, such as I TOLD YOU I WAS SICK and DEVOTED FAN OF JULIO IGLESIAS, the gravestones are a living legacy for those lying beneath. Some of the tombs are "bunked," or stacked, because digging in the coral rock proved difficult and seawater percolates just under the surface.

The Historic Florida Keys Foundation makes it easy to explore the Key West City Cemetery, which was recognized by the state as a Florida Heritage Site in 2006. The organization's self-guided tour pamphlet lists graves of 42 of Key West's most prominent or notorious deceased citizens, with brief personality profiles and a translation of the meaning of the carved symbols on the gravestones. Pick up a free Historic Key West City Cemetery Self-Guided Tour pamphlet in the Florida Room at the Monroe County Public Library, 700 Fleming St., or at the Key West Chamber of Commerce, Mallory Square.

If you'd like a little help with your meandering, an hour-long guided tour of the cemetery is available every Tues and Thurs, courtesy of the Historic Florida Keys Foundation. Tours leave at 9:30 a.m. from the cemetery's main gate, which is located at the corner of Margaret and Angela Streets. Reservations are required. A donation of $10 is requested. For reservations, phone (305) 292-6718. Historic preservationist Sharon Wells also conducts cemetery tours by reservation only (see the Guided and Self-Guided Tours section of this chapter).

KEY WEST HISTORIC SEAPORT AND HARBORWALK — FREE
201 William St., at the Key West Bight
(305) 294-1100
www.keywestcity.com

Formerly known as Key West Bight, this once-seedy piece of prime waterfront real estate was where shrimpers, spongers, and turtle traders came to unload their daily catch, tell tall tales of the sea, quaff a few brews, and just generally hang out. With the relocation of the shrimp boats to Stock Island and the demise of sponging and turtle hunting, this area has undergone a complete metamorphosis. In January 1999 it was officially opened as the Key West Historic Seaport and HarborWalk.

Tall ships still tie up here, but so do million-dollar yachts. Trendy shops, restaurants, and raw bars now line a pristine wooden boardwalk that follows the bend of the coastline here from the foot of Front Street to the foot of Margaret Street. Despite gentrification, this remains a busy working marina. Vessels bound for the Dry Tortugas leave from here, as do many of the snorkel and sunset cruises and fishing charters (see our Recreation chapter for details). You even can catch an occasional glimpse of the old Key West in places like Turtle Kraals, a turtle-cannery-turned-restaurant, and Schooner Wharf Bar.

The seaport area bustles with activity on a daily basis; it's also home to numerous special events throughout the year. For a complete listing of seaport shops, services, activities, and attractions, pick up a free copy of the Historic Seaport Log. This quarterly publication can usually be found at several locations along the HarborWalk, at the Key West Chamber of Commerce on Mallory Square, and at stores throughout Key West. Look for it wherever you see stacks of free weekly newspapers.

KEY WEST HISTORICAL MEMORIAL SCULPTURE GARDEN   FREE
Mallory Square
(305) 294-4142

Located on Key West's original shoreline just behind Mallory Square, this tiny fenced-in "garden" pays homage to three dozen men and women whose lives and deeds have had tremendous impact on the southernmost city. Here you will find the stories and likenesses of such former influential citizens as wreckers Asa Tift and Captain John Geiger; Ernest Hemingway, writer; Harry S Truman, former U.S. president; railroad magnate Henry Flagler; Sister Louise Gabriel, whose Grotto to Our Lady of Lourdes is said to have protected Key West from hurricanes for more than 75 years; and Charley Toppino, land developer. All of the bronze busts, as well as the imposing wreckers sculpture, are the works of sculptor James Mastin of Coral Gables, Florida.

As you wander through the garden, be sure to look down, too—the walkways are paved with commemorative bricks purchased by individuals and families in remembrance of their friends and relatives. Proceeds from the sale of these bricks help support construction and maintenance of the garden. The sculpture garden is open daily during daylight hours.

KEY WEST SHIPWRECK HISTOREUM $$
1 Whitehead St., Mallory Square
(305) 292-8990
www.shipwrecktours.com

Relive the days of wreckers, lumpers, and divers at the Shipwreck Historeum—part museum, part theater—where actors, video footage, and interactive presentations recreate vestiges of Key West's once-lucrative wrecking industry. During the 1800s about 100 ships passed by the port of Key West daily, many running aground on the reef. Asa Tift, a 19th-century wrecker and the original owner of what would one day become the Hemingway Home, tells his story of salvaging the goods of the SS *Isaac Allerton*, which was downed by a hurricane in 1856 (see our Kidstuff chapter). Shows run every 30 minutes, daily. Children younger than age four are admitted for free.

The Historium now offers a 90-minute Historic Walking Tour of Key West. "Meet" colorful characters and famous faces who helped make the southernmost city the destination it is today.

KEY WEST TROPICAL FOREST AND BOTANICAL GARDEN   FREE
5210 Jr. College Rd., Stock Island
(305) 296-1504
www.keywestbotanicalgarden.org

Follow Jr. College Road, then turn right just past Bayshore Manor, to find this little-known slice of serenity tucked between the Florida Keys Aqueduct Authority plant and the Key West Golf Course. Maintained by volunteers from the Key West Botanical Garden Society and funded by donations since 1935, this 11-acre garden represents the last undeveloped native hardwood hammock in the environs of Key West and is the only frost-free tropical humid forest and botanical garden in the continental United States. Despite its proximity to US 1 and a busy public golf course, the garden features exotic and native plants that can be viewed from a series of walking trails and is surprisingly peaceful. The garden is home to numerous birds and butterflies, especially during the spring and fall migration seasons. On any given day, you're apt to see a turtle sunning itself on a log or an egret searching for food in Desbiens Pond. You can also sit in the quiet, restored Toppino Nature Chapel.

The garden took a hard hit from Hurricane Georges in 1998 and was hit again in 2005 by Hurricane Wilma, which dropped 4 feet of saltwater into the gardens. The efforts of dedicated volunteers helped save a lot of the property. Volunteers were also able to save the 10,000,000th tree planted in the United States by the National Tree Trust. In 2005 the Key West Tropical Forest and Botanical Garden acquired 7.5 additional acres that nearly doubled its size. Open every day of the week and, even though entry is free, a donation is graciously accepted.

KEY WEST WILDLIFE CENTER   FREE
Atlantic Boulevard and White Street
(305) 292-1008

This is a branch of the Marathon Wild Bird Center (located at the Museums of Crane Point, see listing in this chapter) treating sick, injured, and orphaned animals with a mission to educate the public about birds and other wildlife in the Keys. This shelter lies on the grounds of the McCoy Indigenous Park, full of rare and native species of flora. At any given time approximately 100 animals, ranging from seabirds to raccoons to chickens, are recovering here; you can see them during visiting hours. Key West Wildlife will rescue animals anywhere from the Seven Mile Bridge to the Dry Tortugas. The park is open daily from sunup to sundown. Admission is free, but donations are appreciated, and volunteers are always needed.

MALLORY SQUARE
SUNSET CELEBRATION   FREE
1 Whitehead St.
(305) 292-7700
www.sunsetcelebration.org

A do-not-miss event during any visit to Key West is the famous (perhaps infamous) sunset celebration. Buskers and street players, vaudevillians and carny wannabes strut their stuff every day as the sun sinks into the Gulf of Mexico over Sunset Key off Mallory Square. Beverage and nosh vendors hawk refreshments while the entertainers compete for your attention. From fire-eaters to furniture jugglers, tightrope walkers to sword swallowers, you'll rarely see the same routine two nights in a row. A footbridge links Mallory Square to the pier at the adjacent Hilton Resort and Marina, where the likes of vaudevillian Jeep and his dog Moe and Dominique's high-flying cats delight the crowd.

This daily event, a Key West tradition since 1984, is free to all, but pack your pocket with small bills because the performers play for tips. The fun starts approximately one hour before sunset at Mallory. Check page three of the morning *Key West Citizen* for daily sunset times.

MILE MARKER 0   FREE
Corner of Whitehead and
Fleming Streets

Key West is truly the last resort and here's the proof: The official green-and-white Mile Marker 0 signifying the end of US 1 is posted at this corner. Have someone snap a picture of you in front of the sign that reads "end—US 1." It will make a wonderful reminder of that very moment you finally arrived at the end of your road . . . that's providing some souvenir hunter hasn't made off with the sign, which happens with great regularity. Tampering with highway signs (including those enticing green mile markers) is against the law, by the way. If you must own one, replicas of Mile Marker 0 are available for purchase in many Key West shops.

NATIONAL WEATHER SERVICE STATION   FREE

1315 White St.
(305) 295-1316
www.srh.noaa.gov/eyw

Weather observation in Key West dates back at least as far as 1832, when rainfall measurements were taken at the Sand Key Lighthouse. In 1870, the first observation station was opened on Duval Street. The National Weather Service relocated to different spots during the 1900s. In 2006 a new $5.1 million station opened on White Street, bringing the art and technology of weather reporting into the 21st century.

Key West sits in a prime location between the Gulf of Mexico and the Atlantic Ocean, making it an important stop along international shipping lanes. Forty percent of the world's shipping relies on the Key West Weather Station for weather data. Tours of this architectural marvel are available Mon to Fri by appointment only.

THE SOUTHERNMOST POINT   FREE

Corner of Whitehead and South Streets

Look for the traffic jam at the Atlantic end of Whitehead Street and you'll see the giant red, white, green, and yellow marker buoy that designates the southernmost point of the continental United States. And standing in front of it, in the street, blocking traffic trying to turn left onto South Street, preens a never-ending stream of Key West visitors, trying to capture the moment they stood closer to Cuba than anyone else in the country. Call it touristy, even tacky, if you like, but the crowds seem to love it.

USS *MOHAWK* COAST GUARD CUTTER MEMORIAL MUSEUM $

Truman Waterfront, Old Navy Pier
(305) 292-5072
www.ussmohawk.org

This historic floating museum opened in 2006 and is a one-of-a-kind attraction in the Florida Keys, and one of only 55 in the United States. The 165-foot-long ship is docked at the waterfront, beyond Truman Annex at the Florida Keys National Marine Sanctuary's Environmental Center (see the entry in this chapter). This unique memorial is sure to please landlubbers as well as naval historians. Launched in 1934, the USS *Mohawk* was commissioned to patrol the Hudson and Delaware Rivers to break up ice formations on these two major waterways. The ship was one of the first to be fitted with sonar and was later involved in 14 attacks against Nazi U-boats while on patrol along the Atlantic Ocean. Tours allow guests to visit six decks, including the radio and sonar rooms, galley, crew quarters, and officers' staterooms.

Guided and Self-Guided Tours

CONCH TOUR TRAIN $$$

301 Front St. at Mallory Square
Flagler Station, 901 Caroline St.
(305) 294-5161, (800) 213-2474
www.conchtourtrain.com

Some folks might think a narrated motor tour spells "tourist" with a capital T, but the quirky little Conch Tour Train is a great way to garner an overview of Key West in the shaded comfort of a canopied tram. You'll pass by most of the attractions we've written up in this chapter, sometimes twice, because in tiny Key West the train weaves a circuitous route that often changes from one hour to the next depending on road construction and special events that necessitate street closures. Regardless of the path, you're sure to enjoy the ride as your guide recounts fact and legend, tall tales, and sad stories about life in Key West.

Tours start at Mallory Square or Flagler Station on Caroline Street. Children younger than age four ride free. The tour lasts 90 minutes, with one 10-minute rest break at the Conch Tour Train ticket station, 501 Front St. Train passengers can also get off at Land's End Village at the foot of Margaret Street to explore the historic seaport area on foot, then reboard another train to complete the tour.

GHOSTS & LEGENDS OF
KEY WEST $$
(305) 294-1713
www.keywestghosts.com

Each evening at 7 and 9 p.m., Ghosts & Legends of Key West leads visitors to our southernmost city on a shadowy saunter down the narrow lanes of Old Town. The second ghostly attraction in Key West (see Ghost Tours of Key West below), Ghosts & Legends meets at the corner of Duval and Caroline Streets at the Porter Mansion. Guides share dark narratives of haunted mansions, voodoo superstitions, a secret leper colony, and pirate lore, hitting such "low" spots as the old city morgue and St. Paul's Cemetery. This 90-minute jaunt may put you in touch with Key West's restless spirits.

GHOST TOURS OF KEY WEST $
(305) 294-9255
www.hauntedtours.com

Love a good ghost story? Key West's No. 1 haunted attraction, Ghost Tours, offers you the chance to get an in-depth introduction to the most famous ghosts of our island. Highlights include a visit to the city's original hanging tree. Tales of Robert, a haunted doll said to have been possessed by an evil spirit, intensify the mystery. Disbelief and awe surround the deeds of the German count who dug up the body of his true love, dressed her in a bridal gown, and serenaded her for seven years. Narrated by a spooky, caped, lantern-bearing guide, this 1-mile

tour wends its way through Key West after dark and lasts about 90 minutes.

Tours leave nightly from the lobby of the Crowne Plaza La Concha, 430 Duval St. Plan to arrive approximately 15 minutes in advance to purchase your tickets, and do bring cash or traveler's checks; no credit cards are accepted. Groups of six or more may purchase tickets in advance in the lobby of the La Concha hotel. You will need to make reservations for this popular tour. Space is limited, so book early by phoning the number shown above.

GO GPS TOURS $$$
414 Greene St.
(305) 293-8891
www.gogpstours.com

Saunter the streets of Key West with a handheld interactive device that allows you to choose where you want to go and what to see. Entertaining and educational, this GPS tour is available in multiple languages and is both an audio and video system offering the latest technology for sightseeing at your own pace.

LLOYD'S TROPICAL BIKE TOUR $$
(305) 294-1882
www.lloydstropicalbiketour.com

Lloyd is one of the island's most colorful characters and will lead you on a leisurely two-hour bike tour of the island, machete in hand. He is an expert on all things Key West, having lived on the island for over 35 years. Lloyd also has access to many tucked away places you won't find on any map. Don't worry—if you haven't been on a bike since before you had your first margarita, you will still be able to enjoy yourself. In the two hours it takes Lloyd to show you around the historic Old Town area of Key West, just a few blocks off the crowded main street of Duval, but seemingly worlds away, you will stop at Nancy Forrester's Secret Garden (see below), an acre of foliage in the middle of Old Town that houses rescued exotic parrots, Cuban tree frogs, and plant life as colorful as Lloyd. You also might stop along the way to hear stories from other locals, and sample the local fruits. As Lloyd says, "There is always some kind of fruit in season, perhaps something you've never tried before, like a sapodilla, a Surinam cherry, a sugar apple, or . . . let me surprise you. Just sit back, pedal along effortlessly on our flat island, and relax. It all makes so much sense." And we couldn't agree more.

NANCY FORRESTER'S
SECRET GARDEN $$
One Free School Lane
(off the 500 block of Simonton between Fleming and Southard Streets)
(305) 294-0015
www.nfsgarden.com
On an acre lot in downtown Key West, this treasure trove of magic awaits a visitor's discovery. Open to the public since 1944, this botanical and horticultural garden thrives and blooms. This frost-free spot charges a minimal amount and showcases exotic tropicals such as orchids, bromeliads, aroids, ferns, palms, bog plants, and over 150 species of palms. On the property is an art gallery selling antique botanicals and zoological prints.

OLD TOWN TROLLEY TOURS OF KEY
WEST $$$
3840 North Roosevelt Ave.
Key West Welcome Center
(305) 395-4958 or (800) 213-2474
www.historictours.com
Join the Old Town Trolley Tour for an informative, convenient entry into Key West. The trolley stops at most major hotels, handy if you're staying in the southernmost city. Day-trippers will appreciate the free parking at the Key West Welcome Center, where you can pick up the tour. The trolleys depart every 30 minutes, and you can get off at any of the nine stops and reboard the same day. All along the way the tour guide will treat you to a Key West history lesson, full of anecdotes and legends. Old Town Trolley Tours run daily. For children younger than age four, it's free.

PELICAN PATH FREE
Key West Chamber of Commerce
510 Greene St.
(305) 294-2587
Visitors who like to wander on their own should be sure to first pick up a copy of the Pelican Path brochure at the chamber of commerce on Greene Street. This handy compact walking guide and map offers a short history of Key West as well as a suggested route that will take you past 50 of our most prominent historic structures. Most of the buildings described in this brochure are now private homes and guesthouses. Those that are open for touring are highlighted in yellow. Don't be surprised, however, if you can't spot those yellow-and-blue Pelican signs described in the brochure as path markers; many of them have disappeared over the years. Even so, the Pelican Path remains relatively easy to follow and is a great way to get acquainted with island history.

RIPLEY'S BELIEVE IT OR
NOT MUSEUM $$
108 Duval St.
(305) 293-9939
www.ripleyskeywest.com
Ripley's Believe It or Not is world-famous for strange, fantastic, weird, and just

hard-to-believe artifacts. The Ripley's museums have always been noted for oddities such as the world's heaviest man, the biggest human nose, and the person with the most tattoos. In the Ripley's Key West location, they house a Key West gallery with items from Ernest Hemingway (reading glasses, typewriter, and a shrunken torso) and Count Von Cossel (who stole the body of his beloved and kept her in the fuselage of a plane in his backyard). There is also a Boutique of Weird Clothing showing a vest made of human hair, a giant pair of shoes, and even a pair of Madonna's underwear. And if all that weren't enough, they also have a portrait of Vincent Van Gogh made from butterfly wings. You know you're not in Kansas anymore!

WILD DOLPHIN ADVENTURES $$
William Street, Old Historic Key West Bight
(305) 304-8000
www.wilddolphinadventures.com
Relax and get away from the crowds of Key West: take an adventure on the *Coral Reefer* out onto the Gulf of Mexico and interact with beautiful wild Atlantic bottlenose dolphins. This is an ecology tour watching a Key West resident pod of dolphins in their natural habitat where they live and play. On your outing you will see local marine life, birds, coral reefs, sponges, 'rays, and more. Snorkeling is also available on these trips. Seating is limited and reservations are recommended.

And Beyond . . .

DRY TORTUGAS NATIONAL PARK
National Park Service
(305) 242-7700
www.nps.gov/drto

Visit Dry Tortugas National Park, the end of the line in the Florida Keys, for a spectacular ride back in history. Accessible only by boat or seaplane (see the Cruising, Campgrounds, and Recreation chapters for transportation options), the Dry Tortugas, 70 miles west of Key West, harbor a rich history and an even more prolific underworld. (No admission charge is levied to visit the park, but transportation charges can be substantial.)

Ponce de León named the seven islands "Las Tortugas" in 1513, presumably for the multitude of sea turtles (tortugas). The "Dry" moniker was added later to indicate the islands' lack of fresh water. You'll be able to take a self-guided tour of Fort Jefferson on Garden Key, America's largest 19th-century coastal fort, which was started in 1846 but never completed. The walls are 50 feet high and 8 feet thick. For years the fort operated as a military prison. Fort Jefferson's most famous inmate was Dr. Samuel Mudd, who was convicted of conspiracy after he set the broken leg of President Lincoln's assassin, John Wilkes Booth.

The protected waters surrounding the Tortugas sparkle with all the sea creatures of the coral reef as well as a good many shipwreck remains. With natural sand beaches and calm seas, snorkeling and swimming are a must. All the waters of the Dry Tortugas National Park are designated a no-take zone, so you may see fish and lobsters of gargantuan proportions. There is no food, fresh water, electricity, or medical assistance at Fort Jefferson. Saltwater toilets, grills, and picnic tables are provided. No lodging exists out here in the beyond. Campers pay slightly more than day-trippers for passage to Fort Jefferson, mostly to cover the cost of transporting the gear they must carry in and out.

KIDSTUFF

Get ready, get set, go! It's time to explore the alphabet soup of things to do in the Florida Keys and Key West, especially for kids. But we have to warn you. Your parents will want to come along.

We deviate from our usual geographic arrangement in this chapter, but all the attractions we list include addresses and phone numbers. Look to related chapters for a comprehensive listing of hours of operation, admission-cost ranges, and Web sites.

Tell Mom, Dad, and any one else in your family, if they want to find out more details of our ABCs (and 1, 2, 3s in Key West), they can look in the Recreation and Attractions chapters, where they'll find lots more fun things to do.

THE FLORIDA KEYS

Fun from A to Z

A is for . . .
affectionate sea lions that may try to kiss you at **Theater of the Sea** at MM 84.7 Oceanside, Islamorada, (305) 664-2431—so be prepared. You can pet the sharks in the touch tank and touch the dolphins in another tank. In the main lagoon, created by excavations for Henry Flagler's Railroad (see the Historical Evolution chapter), the dolphins put on quite a show. Watch them walk on their tails and jump high in the air. You'll see tropical fish and game fish, stingrays, and sea turtles. There is even a boat ride through the lagoon (for more on Theater of the Sea, see the Attractions chapter).

B is for . . .
baiting a hook. Go fishing on one of our group party boats (see the Fishing chapter for complete information). You may catch the prismatic dolphinfish, which has a blunt forehead like Bart Simpson's. Or reel in some yellowtail snappers; they really have yellow tails. Almost certainly you'll catch grunts. They make a funny grunting sound when you take them out of the water. Keep a lookout for the playful mammal dolphins and sea turtles.

C is for . . .
the hermit crabs at the **Florida Keys Children's Museum at the Museums of Crane Point,** MM 50.5 Bayside, Marathon, (305) 743-9100. You can learn all about the hermit crabs (and even hold one!) then dress up in pirate clothes and hop aboard a pirate ship. Ahoy matey! There is also a lagoon where you can feed the fish and look for sharks, a honeybee display complete with honeybees and honeycomb, and a huge seashell exhibit. Oh, and don't miss looking for the resident wild iguanas! (For more, see the Attractions chapter).

D is for . . .
"Don't touch!" If you touch the sap of the poisonwood tree when you walk through

the **nature trails at Crane Point,** MM 50.5 Oceanside, Marathon, (305) 743-9100, it will make you itch like poison ivy does. This tropical Keys forest is full of interesting sinkholes, red mangroves, thatch palms, and lots of cool lizards, land crabs, and birds. One fee covers admission to the hammock and the Florida Keys Children's Museum. And you'll enjoy the adjoining Museum of Natural History, too (see the Attractions chapter).

E is for . . .
examining the fossilized imprints of ancient shells and marine organisms you'll find in the coral quarry walls of **Windley Key Fossil Reef Geologic Site,** MM 85.5 Bayside, Windley Key, (305) 664-2540. If you bring a paper and crayon, you can make a crayon rubbing (see the Attractions chapter for more on the geologic site).

F is for . . .
feeding the giant tarpon that swim in the waters at **Robbie's Marina,** MM 77.5 Bayside, Islamorada, (305) 664-9814, (877) 664-8498. You can purchase a cup of baitfish, the tarpon's favorite snack, at the marina. These giant "silver kings" will swim in a frenzy before your very eyes, jockeying to be first in line when you throw the fish in the water.

G is for . . .
grabbing some rays at the beach. Play in the sand or look for crabs and crustaceans at **Sombrero Beach** in Marathon, MM 50 Oceanside, Sombrero Beach Road, which even has picnic tables so you can make a day of it. There is no admission fee. **Bahia Honda State Park,** MM 37 Oceanside, has two beaches. A small one near the concession stand at the south end of the park is calm, sheltered, and roped off for safety. The

other, the Sandspur, is much longer. You can wade in the soft sand through waters that vary from several inches to 3 feet deep looking for sea creatures and washed-up treasure (see the Recreation chapter for more on beach options).

H is for . . .
hopping aboard a glass-bottomed boat for a five-hour ecological tour of the Lower Keys backcountry with **Strike Zone Charters,** MM 29.5 Bayside, Big Pine Key, (305) 872-9863, (800) 654-9560. You'll learn the history of the key deer and the tiny out-islands, the hurricanes, the wreckers, and the Indians. You'll see bald eagle nesting sites, great white herons, egrets, and dolphins feeding in the wild. You can snorkel and fish a little too. And to top it all off, you'll enjoy a fish cookout picnic on a private island (see the Recreation chapter for more information).

i Mel Fisher Maritime Museum offers a summer kids program, Mer Academy, at Fort Zachary Taylor State Park. Parents may sign their children up for one to four weeks. Class size is limited and students must have completed the fifth grade to participate. Call the Mel Fisher Maritime Museum Education Department at (305) 294-2633 for more information.

I is for . . .
investigating the Blue Hole—but don't feed the alligators. This freshwater sinkhole at MM 30.5 Bayside, Key Deer Boulevard, Big Pine Key, is home to a couple of curious 'gators, and they'll swim almost up to the viewing platform. Keep your puppy on a leash because its barking will ring the alligators' dinner bell. You'll see turtles in the Blue

Hole, and key deer come 'round at dusk. There is no admission charge.

J is for . . .

jumping into a good book. Visit one of our Keys public libraries: Key Largo, MM 101.4 Oceanside, Tradewinds Shopping Center, (305) 451-2396; Islamorada, MM 81.5 Bayside, across from the Hurricane Monument, (305) 664-4645; Marathon, MM 48.5 Oceanside, next to Fisherman's Hospital, (305) 743-5156; Big Pine, MM 31 Bayside, 213 Key Deer Blvd., (305) 289-6303; Key West, 700 Fleming St., (305) 292-3595. Visitors to Monroe County can pay $15 for a library card valid for one year, or they can read a book in the library for free.

K is for . . .

kicking your finned feet as you practice snorkeling in the shallow waters of the protective U-shaped jetty called **The Horse-shoe,** MM 35 Bayside, just over the Bahia Honda Bridge as you head down the Keys. You'll see a natural aquarium of colorful tropical fish with no danger from sharks or barracuda 'cause they can't get in. It's free.

L is for . . .

looking a great white heron in the eye at the **Florida Keys Wild Bird Center,** MM 93.6 Bayside, Tavernier, (305) 852-4486, (888) 826-3811. Although some of the birds you'll see are permanent residents at the shelter because they can't exist in the wild anymore, others are recovering from injuries and will leave the center once healed. All the birds live in natural habitats that have been enclosed by huge wire cages. You can even go into the pelican cage by yourself (see the Attractions chapter for more on the center).

M is for . . .

meeting friendly dolphins up close and personal at the **Dolphin Research Center,** MM 59 Bayside, Grassy Key, (305) 289-1121. The dolphins' behavior trainers will put them through learning exercises in the saltwater lagoon. You can swim with dolphins in the Dolphin Encounter if you are between 5 and 12 years old and your mom or dad goes with you (see the Attractions chapter for more information).

N is for . . .

navigating your way through marked mangrove trails on the Largo Sound of **John Pennekamp Coral Reef State Park,** MM 102.5 Oceanside, Key Largo, (305) 451-1621, in a two-person kayak rented from Coral Reef Park Company. Take a grown-up with you and then paddle the kayak and spy on all the neat fish and sea creatures that are under the water (for more information, see the Recreation chapter).

i Become a "star" of the Florida Keys Eco-Discovery Center. Your donation purchases a sea star inscribed with your name, the name of a friend, or a tribute to a loved one. It will be embedded in concrete as a permanent part of the Florida Keys Eco-Discovery Center walkway. For more information, visit www.nmsfocean.org.

O is for . . .

observing the catch of the day when you visit one of our fishing marina docks between 3:30 and 4 p.m. (see the Fishing chapter). That's when the charter boats come back in from offshore, and if their luck held, so will yours. You'll see giant dolphin, tuna, snapper, wahoo, grouper, and cobia. But you probably won't see sailfish and marlin because, since they aren't good to eat, we prefer to release them back into the ocean so they may continue to live. This is free fun.

P is for...
planning on joining the Pigeon Key's Marine Science Center Education staff for a one- or two-week summer camp. This is a hands-on science expedition into the living history of Pigeon Key and the Florida Keys. Students ages eight years and older will learn about habitats, marine life, and the fragile ecosystem we live in. Parents can sign up their student in a PADI scuba certification program as well. Classes are usually at the end of June through mid-July. Lunch is served daily. MM 47 Oceanside, Marathon. Call (305) 289-0025 or visit www.pigeonkey.net.

Q is for...
qualifying as a super sleuth when you participate in the **Dolphin Connection's Dolphin Detectives Program.** If you are at least five years old, you can learn how to be a dolphin trainer. You'll get your hands all fishy preparing the dolphins' food. And you might get splashed as you supervise a dolphin training session from the dry docks. You'll find Dolphin Connection at Hawk's Cay Resort, MM 61 Oceanside, (888) 814-9154 (see the Attractions chapter).

R is for...
riding out Watson Boulevard in **Big Pine Key** and crossing the bridge to **No Name Key.** If you come just as the sun is setting, you'll probably see our miniature key deer— they're only 3 feet tall—wandering along the roadside. To get to No Name Key, go to MM

31 Bayside. Turn right onto Key Deer Boulevard, then right onto Watson and across the bridge. This is a free ride.

S is for...
swimming in the tidal pool at Key Largo's **Harry Harris Park,** MM 92.5 Oceanside, (305) 852-7161, if you get tired of swinging or playing on the slide. This state park has a small beach collared by a stone jetty so the waters are always calm. When the tide goes out, you can look for sea creatures (for more information, see the Recreation chapter).

T is for...
taking in a movie matinee. Visit one of the Keys' cinemas: **Tavernier Towne Cinemas,** MM 92 Bayside, Tavernier, (305) 853-7004; **Marathon Community Cinema,** MM 50 Oceanside, Marathon, (305) 743-0288; or **Regal Cinema 6,** Searstown Shopping Center, 3338 Roosevelt Blvd., Key West, (305) 294-0000.

U is for...
unlocking the mysteries of a hardwood hammock on a nature walk with a naturalist on **Lignumvitae Key,** (305) 664-2540. You'll have to take a boat trip from Robbie's Marina, MM 77.5 Bayside, Islamorada, (305) 664-9814, for Lignumvitae is out in Florida Bay. This is the way all the Keys looked long ago. You'll see the red bark of the gumbo-limbo tree, called the "tourist tree" because the bark peels like a sunburned vacationer. You'll also encounter leafy trees with such unusual names as mastic, strangler fig, and pigeon plum. The lignum vitae tree (its name means "wood of life") grows very slowly (see the Attractions chapter for more information).

V is for . . .
visiting Perky Bat Tower, MM 17, Sugarloaf Key. Mr. Perky built this tower many years ago thinking he could attract lots of bats to eat the mosquitoes that were bothering him. His plan didn't work, but the tower is still standing. To find Perky's crazy tower, turn right (bayside) at the Sugarloaf Airport sign just beyond Sugarloaf Lodge when heading down the Keys. When the road forks, bear to the right.

W is for . . .
watching skilled artisans at **Bluewater Potters** work the clay by hand to form creative and functional shapes for spoon rests, dinnerware, lamps, and fun decorative pieces. You'll find their studio at MM 102.9 Oceanside, Key Largo, (305) 453-1920; www.bluewaterpotters.com.

X is for . . .
eXtreme dolphin watching! Book a trip with Key West's original dolphin charter, **Dolphin Watch,** and observe the wild dolphins as they play and frolic in their natural habitat. The boat is a custom-made 31-foot catamaran and they only book six people per trip, so you and your family will have no trouble viewing the magnificent creatures, along with other sea life including turtles, rays, fish, and maybe even a manatee or two. Dolphin Watch is located in the Key West Harbour. Call (800) 979-3370 or visit www.dolphinwatchusa.com for more information.

Y is for . . .
"Yow!" That's what you'll say when you see a shark really close up. Stop at **Captain Hook's Marina,** MM 53.1 Oceanside, Marathon, (800) 278-4665, and look at their 48,000-gallon outdoor aquarium. Every day

at 4 p.m. you can watch the sharks—and lots of other big fish, too—receive their evening meal. Keep your fingers out of the tank so you don't become dessert. It's free fun.

Z is for . . .
zipping on over to the City of Marathon Parks and Recreation to sign up for **Camp Adventure** for kids ages 6 to 13. For seven weeks, beginning in June till mid-July, the weekly camp, with exciting themes that change each week, will keep youngsters entertained, educated, and active. Parents can register children for single or multiple weeks. Because of the camp's popularity, it is first-come, first-serve to sign up. To find out more, call (305) 743-6598 or visit www.marathonflorida.org.

i Sign up for a summer Kayak Camp with Florida Bay Outfitters. These camps, beginning in June, offer kids ages 8 through 12 an introduction to the fun and exciting adventure of paddle sports. For more information, visit www.kayakfloridakeys.com or call (305) 451-3018.

FUN IN THE KOOL TROPICAL KEYS

There are so many fun and exciting things to do while here, they don't register on any scale. The following are off the charts and just plain fun.

BOONDOCKS MINI-GOLF
MM 27.5 Bayside, Ramrod Key
(305) 872-4094
www.boondocks.us.com
Come one, come all to this family-oriented miniature golf park. The formation of the course is in the shape of a huge boulder

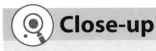 **Close-up**

Things that Go Bump in Plain Sight . . . Robert the Doll

This straw-filled toy doll was a gift, given to Key West resident Eugene Otto as a child by his Jamaican nurse in the early 1800s. The nurse, upset for being dismissed by Eugene's mother, handmade the stuffed doll in the likeness of young Master Otto, and some say it was voodoo cursed. The doll was even given young Mr. Otto's first name of "Robert." With his unblinking eyes, faded sailor suit, and the mysterious stories surrounding him, Robert has become a legend in his own right. Living in their family home on the corner of Eaton and Simonton streets (see Accommodations chapter, the Artist House), young Eugene became very attached to Robert and even blamed the doll for mishaps and unusual events, saying "Robert did it!" Eventually, the toy was banned to the attic and, as the story goes, he would taunt schoolchildren from the upstairs window so much that the kids would take a different route to school. When Mr. Otto died in the 1970s, Robert was given a home in a glass case at the **East Martello Museum** (see Attractions chapter) where he resides today. Despite rumors of ruined photographs and unexplained events at the museum from time to time, Robert is the most popular exhibit in the museum. In the summer of 2008, Robert took a road trip, leaving Key West for the first time in more than 100 years. He was featured at the Atlantic Paranormal Society Convention in Clearwater, Florida. Trick or treat any time of the year. . . .

with 18 state-of-the-art holes complete with waterfalls, tunnels, ponds, tiki hut clubhouse, and one giant caveman that towers over the fun.

KIDS ART CENTER
727½ Fort St., Key West
(305) 345-3456
www.just4kidsart.com
Established in 1999, this nonprofit community-based arts project is first class. Their mission statement is giving families, especially children, the opportunity to enhance their artistic talents. Just 4 Kids holds classes for all ages including Mommy & Me, Teen Night, Graffiti Art, drawing techniques, sewing, and ceramic projects. Parents and grandparents

can tag along on various dates to join in on the fun. As the old saying goes, the family that creates together has more fun together!

KEY WEST SAILING CLUB
Sailboat Lane, off Palm Avenue
Garrison Bight Causeway, Key West
(305) 292-5993
www.keywestsailingclub.org
Small sailors get a large charge out of the youth program offered at the Key West Sailing Club. Each summer for two weeks in June and July, youngsters 8 through 16 can sign up for beginners and advanced courses in sailing. The beginners class teaches how to launch boats, about safety on the water, confidence on the water, and all points of

sailing and seamanship. In the advanced class, they learn to sail various boats and the fine points of racing and cruising. There are family sessions as well.

OTHERSIDE BOARDSPORTS
MM 87.7 Oceanside, Islamorada
(305) 853-9728
www.othersideboardsports.com
Most outdoor enthusiasts come to the Keys for sky and water sports. Now there is something for the board-sports minded at Otherside Boardsports. If you dig skateboarding, kiteboarding, wakeboarding, and wakeskating you have found your haven. The owners are kiteboard instructors and located their shop midway between Key Largo and Marathon because of the two skate parks in those areas with Islamorada in between offering great kiteboarding off Whale Harbor and Anne's Beach. The store is loaded with gear including "decks," "trucks," and "wheels." If you have to ask what these are, you have no business on one of these sports boards!

SEACAMP ASSOCIATION
MM 30 Oceanside, Newfound Harbor Road and 1300 Big Pine Ave.,
Big Pine Key
(305) 872-2331 or (877) 732-2267
www.seacamp.org
This scuba and marine science camp for children ages 12 through 17 has been in Big Pine Key since 1966. Children from around the world sign up for Seacamp's 18-day program to experience scuba diving, sailing, snorkeling, and sailboarding. Marine science classes teach about such subjects as exploring the seas, animal behavior, and Keys critters. Scuba certification is available.

The camp operates from June through Aug and offers a day camp in summer for children ages 10 through 14. In addition, Seacamp is affiliated with the Newfound Harbor Marine Institute, which hosts three-day winter field trips for teachers and students from fourth grade through high school.

ANNUAL EVENTS

No one knows how to throw a party better than residents of the Florida Keys. Come dress with us in period attire as we relive eras of our past. Or join locals and folks from across the world in a challenging road race on a bridge spanning miles of open sea.

We also have boat parades, bikini contests, battle reenactments, and our own unplugged, underwater concert. Or try your angling skills in one of our many fishing tournaments (see the Fishing chapter for an expanded listing). Immerse yourself in Florida Keys arts and culture at our historical observances, music festivals, or arts and crafts fairs.

And my, how we love to eat. From Key Largo to Key West, food festivals abound. These events provide an inexpensive means of sampling incredibly fresh seafood and menu items from leading local restaurants.

OVERVIEW

The following selection of festivals and events is a sampling of what we offer annually in the Florida Keys, organized by month, from Key Largo to Key West. Additional events occur sporadically from year to year. Dates and locations often change from year to year, and admission prices vary. Call the local chambers of commerce for details: Key Largo, MM 106 Bayside, (305) 451-1414, (800) 822-1088; Islamorada, MM 82.5 Bayside, (305) 664-4503, (800) 322-5397; Marathon, MM 53.5 Bayside, (305) 743-5417, (800) 262-7284; Lower Keys, MM 31 Oceanside, (305) 872-2411, (800) 872-3722; Key West, 510 Greene St., (305) 294-2587, (800) 527-8539. You can pick up the annual *Attractions & Events* brochure at any of these chambers. You also will find annual event information on the official Web site of the Monroe County Tourist Development Council: www.fla-keys.com.

JANUARY

ART UNDER THE OAKS
MM 89.5 Bayside, Plantation Key, Islamorada
(305) 852-5372
www.artundertheoaks.com
Begun in 1982, Art under the Oaks, held in the gardens on the grounds of San Pedro Church, is always a tremendous community gathering. This one-day celebration in mid-Jan is held in a natural setting under a lovely canopy of oak trees. It offers homemade crafts, fine art from local artists, specialty food booths, self-guided nature tours of the gardens, children's arts and crafts, raffle items, and live music. Because of the large turnout, free shuttle bus service runs from the Plantation Key School's parking lot to the event.

CHEECA LODGE PRESIDENTIAL SAILFISH TOURNAMENT
MM 82 Oceanside, Cheeca Lodge, Islamorada
(305) 664-4651, (800) 327-2888
www.cheeca.com/sailfish
In 1989 when George H. W. Bush was our president, he came to Islamorada on holiday and to fish. This exciting three-day tourney, in mid-Jan, is part of the Florida Keys Gold Cup Sailfish Championship and world Billfish Series. Cash prizes and trophies are awarded in this catch-and-release event.

KEY WEST HISTORIC HOUSE AND GARDEN TOURS
Various Key West sites
(305) 294-9501
www.oirf.org
Olde Island Restoration, a nonprofit organization that encourages preservation of Key West's many historical structures, sponsors this popular tour—spanning Dec, Jan, Feb, and Mar—to show off some of the city's finest private properties. Typically, each event features five or six privately owned homes. Tours explore shotgun-style cottages, Conch-style mansions, and everything in between.

The tours are self-guided, but participants may meet at the Olde Island Restoration offices along Mallory Square and then embark on a Conch Train bound for the tour site. Scheduled dates vary from year to year. There is an admission fee.

KEY WEST LITERARY SEMINAR
516 Duval St., San Carlos Institute, Key West
(888) 293-9291 or (888) 293-9291
www.kwls.org
Originated in 1983 and dedicated to the celebration of the written word, the Key West Literary Seminar is a very important gathering of noteable authors and their admiring public. Key West's San Carlos Institute serves as the home base for these sessions. Writing workshops, tours of legendary local authors' homes, and cocktail parties also are offered to seminar participants. Included in the core seminar price, these parties offer the opportunity to mingle with panel guests. Workshops and tours cost an additional fee. The four-day event is typically held during the second week of Jan. Call for information on registration and workshop fees, but reserve early. These events are typically sold out up to a year in advance. The 2011 headliners are Roy Blount, Jr., Frank Bruni, Gael Greene, and Daniel Halpern.

SCULPTURE KEY WEST
Fort Zachary Taylor Park, Key West
(305) 295-3800
www.sculpturekeywest.com
Sculpture Key West may be viewed by land, seen by boat, and observed by air. Showcased from mid-Jan till mid-Apr, this annual event has grown from a handful of Key West locals to a nationally and internationally prominent exhibition showcasing world-renowned contemporary sculptures.

KEY WEST CRAFT SHOW
Whitehead Street, Key West
(305) 294-1241
www.keywestartcentercom
Key West ends the month of Jan with a weekend-long exhibit of original crafts. Among the one-of-a-kind items offered for sale, you'll find handmade jewelry, leather goods, wood carvings, kitchen accessories, and beach and lounge chairs. Exhibitors come from throughout the United States. The crafts show takes place in the street—on

Whitehead Street between Eaton and Greene. Admission is free.

i If you are "road tripping" south to the Florida Keys, remember that Florida's Turnpike (built in 1957) is a toll road. If you travel on I-95 or US 1 in Florida, there are no tolls.

FEBRUARY

GIGANTIC NAUTICAL FLEA MARKET
MM 87 Bayside, Islamorada
(305) 664-4503, (800) 322-5397
www.giganticnauticalfleamarket.org
In 1995 the Upper Keys Rotary Club began this giant flea market. New and used boats, clothing, marine equipment, electronics, dive gear, antiques, fishing gear, and nautical arts and crafts are just some of the items available. Held at the end of Feb in Founders Park (see the Recreation chapter) on Plantation Key, entrance to the market is free, with all proceeds from the sale of items to benefit local area youth. There is a free shuttle from Coral Shores High School at MM 90 due to limited parking.

PIGEON KEY ART FESTIVAL
MM 49 Oceanside, Marathon
(305) 743-5999
www.pigeonkey.net
Hundreds of artists from throughout the country apply to display their works in this annual early Feb show, but only 70 are selected by the judges to participate. *Sunshine Artist Publication* rated this festival among the top 100 art shows in the nation. The festival is generally scheduled for the first weekend in Feb, at the Marathon Community Park. At weekend's close, judges bestow awards for the best artwork in categories such as watercolor, oil and acrylic painting,

jewelry, photography, sculpture, glass, pottery, and graphics. Live entertainment features the music of steel-drum bands, jazz groups, classical ensembles, and country-and-western performers. Local restaurants sell food, and raffle drawings include original artwork donated by each participating artist.

All proceeds are donated to the Pigeon Key Foundation for restoration of the island (see the Attractions chapter). Artists pay entry fees, and half the show's work has a Florida theme.

THE WINTER STAR PARTY
MM 23.8 Oceanside, West Summerland Key
(386) 362-5995
www.scas.org
Each year in early Feb, for over 20 years, more than 600 amateur astronomers have flocked to the Florida Keys for one of the largest stargazing gatherings in the world. The Winter Star Party, sponsored by the Southern Cross Astronomical Society, is a weeklong celebration and an opportunity to gaze at the clear skies offered here. Participants also attend lectures and workshops and learn from special guest speakers. This get-together is not just for well-versed astronomers but also for beginners. There are no walk-in tickets, so purchase yours in advance on the Web site listed above.

CIVIL WAR HERITAGE DAYS
Fort Zachary Taylor, at Truman Annex at Southard Street, Key West
(305) 294-2587 or (800) 648-6269
www.forttaylor.org
History comes alive at Fort Zachary Taylor (see the Recreation and Attractions chapters) during the first two weeks in Feb, when the fort is the setting for a Civil War

battle reenactment. During the event, the fort is filled with activity as many enthusiasts gather while wearing the uniforms of Union and Confederate soldiers. Other participants in period attire portray merchants and citizens. Events include the capture of a blockade runner, with the captain of the vessel standing trial. Key West was the only southern city that stayed in the Union throughout the Civil War, with the fort being a key point in guarding the shipping lanes to Union ports.

OLD ISLAND DAYS ART FESTIVAL
Whitehead Street, Key West
(305) 294-1241
www.oirf.org

If you appreciate art, your heart is bound to beat faster at the sight of several blocks of exhibits by talented local artists. Inspired by this southernmost city, they take this opportunity to showcase their vivid creations. Virtually all artistic media are represented in this juried, weekend-long show, including oil, watercolor, and acrylic paintings; graphics; wood, metal, and stone sculptures; glasswork; and photography. Judges provide merit awards within each category. Old Island Days Art Festival exhibits line Whitehead Street from Greene Street to Caroline and into Truman Annex. No charge for browsing. Usually held at the end of Feb.

MARCH

KEY WEST GARDEN CLUB FLOWER
SHOW AT WEST MARTELLO TOWER
Atlantic Boulevard and White Street,
Key West
(305) 294-3210
www.keywestgardenclub.com

Established in 1949 by former Key West politician Joe Allen, the Garden Club organizes monthly educational seminars for the public. Plant-swapping sessions also are popular. The group holds a prejuried show every other year. Held at the Joe Allen West Martello Tower, home of the Key West Garden Club, the show features some 800 entries of floral arrangements, potted plants, palms, rare tropical flowers, and hybrids. Judges from garden clubs throughout the state of Florida award ribbons and prizes in several categories. The flower show is typically held during the spring, not necessarily always in Mar. There are admission costs.

CONCH SHELL BLOWING CONTEST
Sunset Pier at Ocean Key House,
Duval Street, Key West
(305) 294-9501
www.oirf.org

Come to this fun "Conch Honk." The Conch Shell Blowing Contest offers adults and children the opportunity to sound off. Prizes are awarded to the loudest, the funniest, and the most entertaining conch-shell blowers in several divisions. This one-day, springtime event takes place on the waterfront and on various dates each year, but usually in Mar or Apr. Participation is free.

APRIL

SEVEN MILE BRIDGE RUN MARATHON
(305) 395-7040
www.southernmostrunners.com

Men and women from across the world flock to this 7-mile roadway, which spans the open water between Marathon and Bahia Honda. In the wee morning hours, these spirited individuals participate in the most scenic competition of its kind: a run across one of the world's longest bridges. Organized by the Marathon Runners Club, sponsored by a number of Florida Keys businesses, and designed to raise money for local schools and youth groups, the run is said to be the only one in the world held completely over and surrounded by water. Postrace prizes are awarded in various categories, and runners gather for what is likely the world's largest early-morning celebratory bash. Usually, the run is held on the second Sat in Apr and begins on the Marathon end of the Seven Mile Bridge. Expect to pay an entry fee. Spaces are limited, so if you plan to run, reserve your spot early.

WORLD SAILFISH CHAMPIONSHIP
(305) 294-4000
www.worldsailfish.com

Presented in mid Apr, this three-day sailfish challenge is one of South Florida's most illustrious tourneys. Winners of previous sailfish tournaments, elite anglers, and celebrity participants are challenged in this event. VIP registration is available for teams wanting to rub elbows with the likes of Don Shula, Johnny Bench, or Norman Schwarzkopf (past attendees) and sometimes even fish with a celebrity teammate. Cash prize money, reaching six figures, is awarded to the team for the largest confirmed number of sailfish caught and released during this hard-fought championship.

CONCH REPUBLIC INDEPENDENCE
   CELEBRATION
Various Key West sites
(305) 296-0213
www.conchrepublic.com

Key West has always been marked by an independent spirit, and this 10-day festival exalts it. It officially commemorates the city's attempt to secede from the United States on Apr 23, 1982, after the U.S. Border Patrol established roadblocks at the end of the mainland to screen for drugs and illegal aliens. Independent Key Westers rebelled, creating their own flag and attempting to secede from the United States.

The secession fizzled, of course, but locals here find the brief attempt at independence a reason to party nevertheless. Around this same time every year, officials of the fictitious Conch Republic—secretary general, prime ministers, navy, air force, and all—host a picnic, fashion show, buffet, and pirates' ball. Events also include Conch cruiser car shows, the Red Ribbon Bed Race down Duval Street, and what has been dubbed "the world's longest parade"—spectators lining the route simply join in the fun as the floats pass by.

One final word on emancipation in the southernmost city: Duck! During the Great Battle of the Conch Republic, all forms of food whiz through the air and ultimately find their marks on participants and spectators. The battle engages the Conchs and the U.S. Coast Guard in a water fight held at sea just off Mallory Square. Conch Republic Celebration events are held throughout the island and on the water.

MAY

CINCO DE MAYO FESTIVAL
202 William St., Schooner Wharf Bar
(305) 292-3302

In 1994, the first Cinco de Mayo Fiesta kicked off with all the sizzle and salsa anyone could handle. Still going strong, this zany festival is usually held the first week of May. In honor of the victory of the Mexican army over the French at the Battle of Pueblo in 1862, current revelers pay homage with everything from a taco eating contest to taking shots of tequila, eating hot jalapeño peppers, and drinking beer in record time. The ancestors would be proud! *Olé*, and don't forget your sombrero! Ay, Chihuahua!

HARRY S. TRUMAN LEGACY SYMPOSIUM
111 Front St.
(305) 294-9911
www.trumansymposium.com
From 1945 to 1953, President Harry S. Truman spent 11 working vacations on the Key West Navy Base in what was to be the Little White House. The annual Truman Legacy Symposium, held in mid-May, offers a reception and lunch with a VIP tour of the house. Guest speakers discuss various roles Truman played in shaping our nation's history. Topics change each year as do the speakers. His grandson, Clifton Truman Daniel, usually is in attendance and gives one of the keynote addresses.

KEY WEST SONGWRITERS FESTIVAL
400 Front St., Key West
(305) 292-2032
www.kwswf.com
You may not recognize the names of the performers at this annual event in early May, but if you're a country music fan, you'll almost certainly know their songs. This festival, launched in 1996, brings some of the country's foremost performing songwriters to the Key West stage.

The four-day festival includes intimate concerts by all the songwriters, held at different venues throughout Key West.

JUNE

DON HAWLEY INVITATIONAL TARPON TOURNAMENT
Islamorada
(305) 664-3864
www.donhawleyfoundation.org
This Don Hawley event is the Keys' oldest tarpon-on-the-fly tournament and the original all-release event. Proceeds benefit the nonprofit Don Hawley Foundation, which supports the study of tarpon fishery and preservation in the Florida Keys. Usually held in early June. See the Fishing chapter for details.

THE ORIGINAL FKCC SWIM AROUND KEY WEST
(305) 809-3562
www.fkccswimaroundkeywest.com
Sponsored by the Bone Island Masters Club, this USMS-sanctioned event is a 12.5 mile swim clockwise around the island of Key West. Age groups 18 through 65 and older can register.

i The Monroe County Tourist Development Council maintains an online calendar of events. For the latest month-by-month listings of festivals, gallery showings, and theater productions, visit www.fla-keys.com.

JULY

FOURTH OF JULY FIREWORKS
Bayside, Key Largo
(305) 451-1414, (800) 822-1088
View this 30-minute fireworks display from land or, if you are a boater, by sea. Funded by local merchants, the show typically begins at 9 p.m. The best coastal viewing spots are the Caribbean Club, Señor Frijoles, Sundowners, and Marriott Key Largo Bay Beach Resort. Some of these facilities host barbecues with live entertainment. Admission is free, but you must be a patron to enjoy the view from a private business. Food and drinks are sold separately.

STAR SPANGLED EVENT AT SOMBRERO BEACH

MM 50 Oceanside, Marathon
(305) 743-5417, (800) 262-7284

On July 4 follow a parade to the beach, where fireworks decorate the sky, and enjoy all-American hot dogs, hamburgers, and fish sandwiches. Live entertainment is provided; games are available for the kids, and an afternoon volleyball tournament welcomes last-minute sign-ups. Many people see the fireworks display from the decks of their boats, anchoring offshore for the extravaganza. The traffic jam at sea rivals the one on land. No admission or entry fee is required. Food and games are priced individually.

JULY 4TH FIREWORKS

White Street Pier, White Street and Atlantic Boulevard, Key West
(305) 294-2587, (800) 648-6269

The Key West Rotary Club sponsors this pyrotechnic extravaganza every July 4 beginning at 9 p.m. and lasting approximately 30 minutes. Best viewing spots are Higgs Beach and the Casa Marina. There is no admission charge; the fireworks are funded strictly by donations.

UNDERWATER MUSIC FESTIVAL

MM 31 Oceanside, Big Pine Key
(305) 872-2411, (800) 872-3722
www.lowerkeyschamber.com

Whether you dive, snorkel, or merely swim, here is an unplugged series of concerts that beats music videos fins-down. Enjoy six hours of prerecorded, commercial-free music—from Beethoven to the Beatles to the humpback whale song—in synchronicity with tropical fish swimming across the reefs of the Looe Key National Marine Sanctuary. Dance the day away under water, and

look out for surprises such as mermaids and the Keys' very own Snorkeling Elvises. Typically, the music fest runs from midmorning to midafternoon and is broadcast live on WWUS/US 1 radio, 104.1 FM. Landlubbers and those who have danced up an appetite can enjoy this same music plus a variety of foods, arts and crafts, and family games at the Lower Keys Chamber of Commerce, MM 31 Oceanside. Admission to both the concert and the food festival, usually held the second Sat in July, is free. See the Diving and Snorkeling chapter for a list of dive and snorkel charters that will take you to the reef.

HEMINGWAY DAYS FESTIVAL AT HEMINGWAY HOME AND MUSEUM

907 Whitehead St., Key West
(305) 294-2587
www.fla-keys.com

Celebrate the legendary author's birthday with residents of the old man's former hometown by the sea. There's a street fair, a short-story competition, and a Hemingway look-alike contest at what was one of his favorite haunts, Sloppy Joe's (see the Nightlife chapter). This weeklong event centers on the author's July 21 birthday. Fees for some events are required. Call for more information.

REEF AWARENESS WEEK

631 Greene St., at Reef Relief, Key West
(305) 294-3100
www.reefrelief.org

Reef Relief is one of the best known and largest of the organizations whose sole purpose is to protect North America's only living coral reef. And when these folks throw a party, they invite everyone. This weeklong event in mid-July offers all sorts of information to those who want to learn about the coral reef. Visit the art auction and poetry readings, or become a member of this worthy organization during the kickoff week. For more information, call Reef Relief, or visit the organization's retail store at the address listed. Admission is usually free, but some events may carry an entry fee.

i Heading into "love bug" territory is not an invite for Valentine's Day. In the months of late May and early June, heading north from the Florida Keys, you run smack dab into these pesky critters—literally—which splat all over windshields, hoods, and grills of cars, not to mention your sunglasses and body parts if you are cycling.

SEPTEMBER

BAYBONE CELEBRITY TOURNAMENT
Sheraton Beach Resort, Key Largo
MM 97 Bayside, Key Largo
(305) 664-2002
www.redbone.org
Event No. 2 in the Celebrity Tournament Series is a catch-and-release tournament in pursuit of bonefish and permit. Proceeds benefit the Cystic Fibrosis Foundation. See our Fishing chapter or call the number above for more information. Usually held in late Sept or early Oct.

FLORIDA KEYS BIRDING AND WILDLIFE FESTIVAL
MM 56.2 Bayside, Marathon
(305) 289-2690
www.keysbirdingfest.org
Held at Curry Hammock State Park in Marathon, this exciting annual event celebrates with guided kayaking tours, birding talks, field trips, and astronomy. There are guest speakers throughout the event offering expert presentations on various bird-related topics. The festival is usual held the last weekend of Sept, which coincides with Florida wildlife at the peak of the birding season.

WOMENFEST KEY WEST
Various Key West sites
(305) 294-2587
www.womenfest.com
They are women; hear them roar. Each week after Labor Day, thousands of women from all over the country gather in Key West for a bit of female bonding. They include women from diverse races, religions, professions, and sexual orientations; the motto is "Free to Be You with Me in Key West." This seven-day celebration includes women-only water sports, cocktail comedies, and concerts. Organizers host wine-tasting dinners, parties, and picnics, and women ship off together on sunset sails.

Many events are free, including the "Sisters for Brothers" blood drive to compensate for the gay male population not being permitted to donate blood. Discounted party passes are available for groups of events that come at a cost, such as the Old Town Trolley Tour that highlights infamous Key West women.

Gay male and female guesthouses and mainstream hotels provide accommodations, and some of the island's "all-boys" houses (see the Accommodations chapter) become all-women for this week instead.

FLORIDA KEYS POKER RUN
Miami through Key West
(305) 294-2587
www.keyspokerrun.com
Revved up in 1972, bikers have traveled our roads into Key West, for this highly successful

and popular motorcycle run. For this event in early Sept, more than 10,000 motorcyclists ride from Miami to Key West, stopping at various points within our islands to pick up playing cards. At the end of the ride, the player with the best poker hand wins, and all enjoy live bands, field events, and runs-within-a-run on Duval Street. Bikers can also get their machines blessed before returning home. Entry is free; each poker hand costs a nominal fee.

S.L.A.M. CELEBRITY TOURNAMENT
Key West
(305) 664-2002
www.redbone.org
First of the annual Celebrity Tournament Series is the Southernmost Light-tackle Anglers Masters (S.L.A.M). Anglers try to score a Grand Slam by catching and releasing a bonefish, permit, and tarpon in two days. Proceeds benefit the Cystic Fibrosis Foundation. Usually held in early Sept. See the Fishing chapter for details or call the number listed above.

OCTOBER

FANTASY FEST
Various Key West sites
(305) 296-1817
www.fantasyfest.net
This is Key West's biggest party of the year—a citywide celebration similar to Mardi Gras in New Orleans (see the Close-up in this chapter). Usually held in late Oct.

GOOMBAY FESTIVAL
Petronia Street, Key West
(305) 294-2587 or (800) 648-6269
www.goombay-keywest.org
Designed to showcase the cultural customs of the city's Bahamian community through food, music, and crafts, this grassroots affair has grown to include African, Filipino, and Latin traditions, too. Food booths dish up typical festival fare such as gyros, sausages, peppers, and Thai selections, but tucked among them are the treasures of this event: Jamaican jerk chicken and pork, Bahamian cracked conch, conch salad, fried fish, and pigeon peas and rice, all highly seasoned. Dance in the streets to the music of African and steel drummers or calypso bands. Stop by the simulated Nassau straw market to see straw hats and fruit baskets being woven.

The festival stretches from the corner of Petronia at Duval down to Emma Street and now encompasses many of the streets that make up a good share of the neighborhood known as Bahama Village. Held the first weekend of Fantasy Fest (see the Close-up in this chapter), Goombay sets the stage for an even wider segment of society to flaunt their heritage. There is no admission charge.

NOVEMBER

AMERICAN POWERBOAT ASSOCIATION WORLD CHAMPIONSHIP RACE
Waters off Key West
(305) 296-6166
www.superboat.com
Just as Key West begins to recover from Fantasy Fest, the big boats roar into town to compete in a week's worth of offshore races that culminate in the naming of the world's champ. These are no little, putt-putt motorboats; they are high-performance ocean racers costing more than $1 million each and boasting speeds of 125 to 150 mph. Close to 50,000 fans line the waterfront to view the competition, which generally takes place the second week of Nov. There's no charge to watch, and the best viewing spots are along Mallory Square and at the

 **Close-up**

Fantasy Fest

Kookier than Carnival and merrier than Mardi Gras, Fantasy Fest is Key West's own decadent decibel of dreamy delight.

Fantasy Fest was originally conceived as a way to boost tourism in an otherwise soft season. It succeeded—and how! Today, more than two decades after its conception, this event more than doubles the island's population for one week in October, culminating with the arrival of some 70,000 revelers on Duval Street for the Saturday-night parade.

Fantasy Fest is a nine-day adult Halloween celebration that commences on a Friday night with the Royal Coronation Ball, where the King and Queen of Fantasy Fest are crowned. The competition is open to all, and campaigning for the titles begins as early as late August. The winners are the ones who "buy" the most votes (translation: They raise the most money for AIDS Help Inc.). The closer it gets to Fantasy Fest, the fiercer the competition becomes and the more creative the candidates are.

The final tally takes place at the Coronation Ball. The man and woman—or man and man-in-drag—are dubbed "royalty" only after emerging from a field of entrants. The King and Queen receive regal robes, crowns, and scepters and preside over all official Fantasy Fest events. The real winners in all of this, however, are the people served by AIDS Help Inc.

The festivities continue throughout the weekend as captains seek the winner's cup in the Fantasy Yacht Race's Victory at Sea. On Masked Monday fines are imposed on anyone (including any unsuspecting tourist) who does not comply with the loony law of the land: You must be masked to meander Duval Street, or the Mask Rangers will make an example of you.

Each year, Fantasy Fest features a new theme, which is emblazoned on posters and T-shirts promoting the events—all of which are for sale, of course. In keeping with Key West's penchant for parties, a poster-signing celebration is held on Masked Monday. The following night you can enjoy a preview of some courageous/outrageous costumes at the Masked Madness and Headdress Ball. Then on Wednesday, be sure to enter your pet (and yourself) in the Pet Masquerade and Parade. No species is excluded. Visit www.fantasyfest.org or call (305) 296-1817 for more information.

harborside hotels—the Pier House, Ocean Key House, Hyatt, and Westin. Even if you're not a particular fan of powerboats, these are something to see.

DECEMBER

CHRISTMAS BOAT PARADE
Bayside, Key Largo
(305) 451-1414 or (800) 822-1088
www.keylargo.org

Deck the boats with boughs of holly . . . Come watch a festive parade of between 30 and 50 lighted boats glow its way through Blackwater Sound. Prizes are awarded in various categories. At recent events, we've spotted Santa Claus catching a sailfish and Frosty the Snowman water-skiing. As with the Fourth of July Fireworks, the best coastal viewing locations are the Caribbean Club, Señor Frijoles, Sundowners, and Marriott Key

Largo Bay Beach Resort. Some of these facilities host barbecues with live entertainment. Admission is free, but you must be a patron at any of these facilities to enjoy the view. Usually held in early Dec.

POPS IN THE PARK
Founders Park
MM 87 Bayside, Plantation Key
(305) 853-7294
www.islamorada.fl.us
Come one and all to the Pops in the Park performance held in mid-Dec. Enjoy this free outdoor concert featuring the music of Christmas and Hanukkah. Bring a blanket or lawn chair for this family gathering and capture the true spirit of the holiday season.

LIGNUMVITAE CHRISTMAS
Islamorada
(305) 664-2540
www.keyshistory.org
A historic Keys coral rock home from the 1900s (see Attractions) is decorated inside and out with all the floral blossoms in bloom on the island. See angels created out of palm fronds with grape vines in place of holly. If you are talented, you may spend time creating your own ornaments using such things as grape leaves, sea beans, and shells. Travel by boat and you will be greeted by guides at the dock dressed in period costumes to enhance the magical spell of an era gone by. Robbie's Marina (see Boating chapter) provides the transportation for this two-day event.

KEY COLONY BEACH BOAT PARADE
MM 53.5 Oceanside, Key Colony Beach
(305) 743-5417 or (800) 262-7284
www.floridakeysmarathon.com
A more intimate, equally spectacular version of the Key Largo boat parade, this one is held along the landmark canals of Key Colony Beach. Usually held in early Dec. Admission is free.

BOOT KEY HARBOR CHRISTMAS BOAT PARADE
Marathon
(305) 743-5417 or (800) 262-7284
www.floridakeysmarathon.com
Sponsored by the Marathon Power Squadron, this parade begins at sundown on the first Sat in Dec. The best public viewing areas include Faro Blanco Marina, Boot Key Harbor Bridge, and the Dockside Lounge on Sombrero Road, where judging ceremonies are held immediately following the parade.

CHRISTMAS AROUND THE WORLD AT MARATHON GARDEN CLUB
MM 50 Bayside, Marathon
(305) 743-4971
www.marthongardenclub.org
This month-long, annual display by the Marathon Garden Club features more than a dozen Christmas trees, each decorated in the traditional style of a different country. Expect to pay an admission fee.

KEY WEST LIGHTED BOAT PARADE
Various Key West sites
(305) 294-2587, (800) 648-6269
www.keywestcity.com
Lighted boat parades are common throughout our islands, and Key West is no exception. In addition to the magical entourage of skiffs, schooners, and cruisers, viewers may enjoy the preparade sunset activities at Mallory Square. The boat parade begins at Schooner Wharf Bar at the foot of William Street, but you can get the best view from Mallory Square and the pier beside the Hilton Resort and Marina. The boat parade

is typically held in early Dec. Participation is free, but call Schooner Wharf at (305) 294-2587 to reserve your spot.

NUTCRACKER KEY WEST
Tennessee Williams Theatre
5901 West College Rd., Stock Island
(305) 295-7676
www.nutcrackerkeywest.org
www.keystix.com

Paradise Ballet Theatre and the children of Key West, under the direction of founder Joyce Stahl, will leave you breathless with their annual artistic production of the *Nutcracker*. This classic ballet is all done with fabulous professionalism, but with a Keys twist. King Neptune, the queen, and her cavaliers perform their magic along with local kids who dance as baby chicks, toy soldiers, angel fish, reef fish, and tiny shrimp. Worthy of a standing ovation every time, performances are scheduled from the last week of Nov through the first week of Dec.

PIRATES IN PARADISE FESTIVAL
Various Key West locations
(305) 296-9694
www.piratesinparadise.com

Each year in early Dec, this rip-roaring event draws buccaneer aficionados and reenactors "living" pirate history. Part of the excitement is pirate encampments, tall ship pirate attacks, swashbuckling events for kids, a Village Thieves Market, and the staged recreation of the trial of Anne Bonny and Mary Read, those two infamous female pirates. A plank walking contest and pirate costume judging round out this boisterous festival. Can Johnny Depp and the Pirates of the Caribbean be somewhere in the crowd? Admission is free.

KEY WEST HOLIDAY PARADE
Begins on Truman Avenue
(305) 294-2587 or (800) 648-6269
www.keywestcity.com

Fun for kids and grown-ups as well, this street parade has floats from various businesses around the area. Lots of color and music, and some even toss candy canes for a sweet taste of holiday spirit. Santa and Mrs. Claus appear at the end of the line so as not to disappoint the sleepyheads in the crowd dreaming of sugar plums. This event is usually held the second weekend in Dec.

KWANZAA CELEBRATION
Various Key West locations
(305) 294-0884
www.bahamaconchclt.org

Celebrations presented by the Bahama Conch Community Land Trust begin on Dec 26 and continue through Jan 1 each year. Events revolve around family-oriented values. Food, festivities, and faith are the highlights featured throughout this weeklong observance.

KEY WEST TRIKW TRIATHOLON
www.trikw.com

The first annual triatholon consists of a swim in the warm Gulf of Mexico waters on the first leg, biking the overseas highway, then running along the Atlantic Ocean to the finish line. There will also be an expo with information booths on all things healthy in the Keys. Start training now!

NEW YEAR'S EVE ON DUVAL STREET
Key West
(305) 294-2587 or (800) 648-6269
www.keywestcity.com

Times Square has nothing on us when it comes to knowing how to ring in a new year.

ANNUAL EVENTS

We close off the street and, in typical Key West style, party outdoors till the bars close down at 4 a.m. So come New Year's Eve, grab your hat and horn and head for Duval to watch the conch shell drop from the top of Sloppy Joe's Bar at the stroke of midnight (or the red high heel at Bourbon Street Pub). Just don't wear your best silks and satins for this celebration because it will be raining champagne for sure! Round out your New Year's revelry with an "ooh" and an "ah" as you watch the fireworks explode above Key West Harbor. CNN television network televises this countdown, so be on your best behavior as you smile at the cameras.

ARTS AND CULTURE

Creative juices flow freely in the Florida Keys. Is it the sunshine? Or maybe the profusion of riotous colors everywhere you look? Perhaps our pervasive nothing-is-impossible, sky's-the-limit attitude is a contributing factor. Or maybe it's the fact that when you're in the Keys, you take the time to smell the bougainvillea.

Key West is the cultural center of the Florida Keys. This scintillating port has long attracted free spirits and adventurers—wreckers, sailors, spongers, shrimpers, and pirates—who played an enormous role in Key West's settlement and development. An enigmatic quality inherent in the essence of Key West draws fertile minds and searching souls to its inner sanctum like moths to a flame. From Ernest Hemingway to earnestly trying, Key West has hosted for a time the famous, the infamous, and the obscure.

Join us for an Insiders' look at the arts, from Key Largo to Key West, some traditional, others not so. Enjoy our music, theater, and dance while you are here and tour our myriad galleries. Or, if your timing is right, catch an arts festival, literary seminar, or theater gala for a creative night out. Be sure to check the Annual Events chapter for descriptions of special arts festivals and events.

ARTS ORGANIZATIONS

The Florida Keys Council of the Arts (www .keysarts.com) is considered the official arts organization of the Florida Keys. They provide services to visual and performing artists in the Keys by offering grants, showcasing art in public places, and sponsoring various festivals and events throughout the year. This and other arts organizations are listed alphabetically.

FLORIDA KEYS COUNCIL OF THE ARTS
1100 Simonton St., Key West
(305) 295-4369
www.keysarts.com

The Florida Keys Council of the Arts acts as the "chamber of commerce" of arts throughout the Keys. The council's stated mission is "to connect artists and arts organizations with each other, with local audiences, and with the important tourism economy." They maintain an artist registry and Web site on which you'll find complete, year-round listings of the arts and entertainment events in the Keys. In addition, they get the cultural word out to the public via a weekly calendar in five local newspapers and a quarterly brochure of events.

One of the council's most prominent projects is the ongoing "Art in Public Places" program, in which the group displays the works of local artists in changing exhibits at such places as the Key West airport.

The arts council both writes and provides grants that benefit individual artists, arts organizations, schools, and libraries. It is supported by Monroe County and private donations and has several hundred members throughout the Florida Keys. A referral and support service, the arts council provides thousands of artists throughout the Keys with a means of political clout.

LOWER KEYS ARTISTS NETWORK
MM 30.5 Bayside, 221 Key Deer Blvd., Big Pine Key
(305) 872–1828
www.artistsinparadise.com
Formed in 1994, the Lower Keys Artists Network has about 50 members, and anyone in the Lower Keys interested in art is welcome to join. Meetings are held from Dec to May at Artists in Paradise, a co-op gallery in Big Pine. Members assist in judging student art competitions and work with the public library to provide arts and crafts programs for children. The group raises funds for art scholarships through corporate sponsorships. Lower Keys Artists Network also provides demonstrations and seminars on all forms of art, including watercolor, wood sculpture, food sculpture, stained glass, and etching.

PURPLE ISLES ART GUILD
MM 101.4 Oceanside, Key Largo
(305) 451-2396
www.purpleislesartguild.com
First executed in 1966, the Purple Isles Art Guild has over 1,000 visitors viewing its annual event, held in the Key Largo Public Library from mid-Feb through the first part of Mar. You can vote for "Best in Show" in watercolors, oils, acrylics, sculpture, 3-D, photography, digital art, and student art. In addition to the show, the guild meets once a month in the Library Community Room and invites anyone to join them for the camaraderie and to enhance their talents.

SOUTH FLORIDA CENTER FOR THE ARTS
(305) 304-9059
www.sfca-arts.org
After Hurricane Andrew tore through South Miami and Dade County in 1992, the South Dade Center for the Arts moved to Key Largo and established itself as the South Florida Center for the Arts (SFCA). A private, nonprofit organization, SFCA provides a community concert series and some years offers jazz and chamber music programs as well as concerts for children.

Local fund-raisers support Arts for Youth, which encourages young audiences to participate in the arts. Members also provide workshops, plays, and arts programs in local schools. Between its arts and concert association members, this organization has approximately 350 members, many of whom reside in the Upper Keys.

THEATER

ICE (ISLAMORADA COOL ENTERTAINMENT)
MM 87 Bayside, Founders Park, Islamorada
MM 89.9 Oceanside, Coral Shores High School, Plantation Key
(305) 395-6344
www.keysice.com
"Stars above . . . stars onstage" is the bill for bringing great dance, music, and theater to the Upper Keys. These venues invite friends, neighbors, and visitors to enjoy wonderful performances in the Founders Park amphitheater or in the Coral Shores High School of the Performing Arts. The calendar sparkles with concert series, special events, and plays for every age and artistic taste.

MARATHON COMMUNITY THEATRE
MM 49.5 Oceanside, Marathon
(305) 743-0994
www.marathontheater.org

Providing top-notch live theatrical entertainment to locals and visitors for decades, the Marathon Community Theatre annually stages four to six productions, such as *Music Man, Ravenscroft,* and *Applause!,* which each run Thurs through Sat for a month.

Productions utilize full sets and full costuming, and actors hail from all throughout the Keys, from Key Largo to Key West. The group also hosts other productions, ranging from art shows and concerts to the Lovewell Foundation's summer theater program for children.

RED BARN THEATRE
319 Duval St. (rear), Key West
(305) 296-9911 or (866) 870-9911
www.redbarntheatre.com

Quaint and charming, the restored carriage house that hosts the Red Barn Theatre has stood in the shadows of one of Key West's oldest houses, now the Key West Women's Club, for more than 50 years. Up from its humble beginnings as an animal stable, the building hosted the Key West Community Players for a time and also was the venue for puppet shows and piano concerts. Lovingly restored in 1980, the 88-seat structure shines with professional regional theater at its finest. And because of its size and layout, there isn't a bad seat in the house.

The Red Barn Theatre does five or six shows each year, including original comedies, musicals, and dramas by published writers. Its season runs from late Nov through June. Past productions have included plays by Key West's own, the late Shel Silverstein. Full sets, costumes, and orchestrated scores are featured.

TENNESSEE WILLIAMS FINE ARTS CENTER
5901 West College Rd., Stock Island
(305) 296-1520 or
(305) 295-7676 (tickets)
www.tennesseewilliamstheatre.com

The Tennessee Williams Fine Arts Center (TWFAC) opened in January 1980 on the campus of Florida Keys Community College with the world premiere of Tennessee Williams's unpublished play *Will Mr. Merriwether Return from Memphis?* Named for one of Key West's most illustrious writers, this 478-seat, air-conditioned theater features a thrust stage extending 8 feet in front of the curtain line, a fly system, and a state-of-the-art lighting and sound system.

The Tennessee Williams Fine Arts Center produces a full season of dance, theater, chamber music, and shows by nationally known performing artists. It is also home to the Key West Symphony Orchestra (see separate listing later in this chapter). In-house productions involve amateur actors from the community and feature students working toward associate of science degrees in acting and theater production. Professional touring companies bring a wave of nationally and internationally recognized artists to the Florida Keys. In 2010, Patti LuPone, Chita Rivera, and Lily Tomlin all performed their cabaret shows here. Chamber music concerts are sprinkled throughout the copious performance calendar of the Tennessee Williams Fine Arts Center, which runs from late Nov through Apr.

Most of the productions are held in the evening, but some events offer matinees on weekends as well. The Florida Keys Community College Chorus, which is coed, performs here three times each year, including early Dec and mid- to late Mar.

WATERFRONT PLAYHOUSE
Mallory Square, Key West
(305) 294-5015
www.waterfrontplayhouse.org
Community theater at its finest shines from an unlikely thespian arena on the waterfront. Once the site of Porter's warehouse, the physical structure served as an icehouse in the 1880s, storing blocks of ice cut from New England ponds and brought to Key West as ships' ballast. The Waterfront Playhouse restored the old warehouse into the current theater, infusing the crumbly stone walls with enduring creativity and talent. In 2007, a $300,000 major transformation of the most public parts of the buildings space gave the structure both a modern and intimate feel while staying true to its historic roots.

The Waterfront Playhouse, dedicated to expanding knowledge of dramatic works to the general public, presents a variety of musicals, comedies, dramas, and mysteries each season. Past productions have included *The Full Monty, Twelve Angry Men,* and Terrence McNally's *Lips Together, Teeth Apart.* The community thespians also offer a children's theater workshop in the summer and other participatory theater experiences to Key West schoolchildren throughout the year. The performance season is from Nov through Apr.

i **For listings of current shows in Key West or to purchase tickets, visit www.keystix.com or call (305) 295-7676.**

CINEMA

TROPIC CINEMA
416 Eaton St., Key West
(305) 295-9493
www.keywestfilm.org

Until 1998 there was no creative film representation in the Keys. In that year the Key West Film Society formed to bring the area the best of independent, foreign, and alternative movies. Since then Tropic Cinema has shown more than 150 films. Highlights have included the Cuban musical *Buena Vista Social Club*, Pedro Almodovar's Oscar-winning *All About My Mother*, and for the avant-garde, *The Celebration*—an ultimate in contrast: no lighting, no music, and shot on video. The purpose of the Key West Film Society and Tropic Cinema is to showcase film in Key West and be a magnet for this cutting-edge art.

MUSIC

KEY WEST SYMPHONY ORCHESTRA
5901 College Rd., Key West
(305) 292-1774
www.keywestsymphony.com
On a laid-back island like Key West, where Duval Street rocks until 4 a.m. with the beat of calypso and soca, blues and Buffett wannabes, you might not expect to find many hard-core classical music fans. But they are here, all right. And in enough numbers, it seems, to support a symphony orchestra.

Thanks to the enthusiasm, not to mention the untiring fund-raising efforts, of a small but dedicated corps of classical music fans, the Key West Symphony Orchestra made its debut in fall 1998. Under the musical direction of native Key Wester Sebrina Maria Alfonso, the orchestra plays to standing room only at the Tennessee Williams Fine Arts Center on three weekends between Nov and Apr. The critically acclaimed symphony consists of more than 40 classical musicians, many from major metropolitan symphonies throughout the United States, who come together to perform under the baton of conductor Alfonso. In addition to a regular concert series, selected members of the orchestra also participate in community outreach programs, taking their music directly into the Monroe County schools and participating in question-and-answer sessions at a variety of fund-raising events.

Performances by the Key West Symphony Orchestra take place throughout the year at the Tennessee Williams Fine Arts Center on the campus of Florida Keys Community College. Tickets may be purchased at the TWFAC box office.

THE MIDDLE KEYS CONCERT ASSOCIATION, INC.
www.marathonconcerts.com
Every year since 1969, the Middle Keys Concert Association has brought live concert artists to the Florida Keys for the cultural enrichment of our residents and visitors. Four to six concerts are held annually at Marathon venues, quite often San Pablo Catholic Church (MM 53.5 Oceanside). A well-balanced season of offerings includes classical and semiclassical music, encompassing voice, strings, brass, and organ.

You may purchase a subscription to all concerts or buy tickets at the door. Children are admitted for free. Pick up a current brochure at the Marathon Chamber of Commerce, MM 53.5 Bayside, (305) 743-5417 or (800) 262-7284.

Seven "New Friends," by renowned sculptor J. Seward Johnson, greet travelers at the Key West International Airport. The group stands atop the airport terminal eagerly awaiting your arrival. Johnson's other works are showcased at the Key West Museum of Art and History at the Custom House (see Attractions chapter).

ART GALLERIES

Unique galleries dot the Florida Keys, often tucked amid commercial shops in a strip mall or gracing a freestanding building off the beaten track. In Key West, galleries abound along Duval Street, and you'll also find small lofts and garrets secreted off the beaten track down narrow lanes. Come along for a gallery crawl through the high spots of the Florida Keys' art scene, from Key Largo to Key West. The Florida Keys section is organized by descending mile marker. Listings are alphabetical in the Key West section. Consult www.keysarts.com/culture/galleries.cfm for even more information.

The Florida Keys
KEY LARGO ART GALLERY
MM 103 Bayside, Key Largo
(305) 451-0052
www.keylargoartgallery.com
The theme of the Key Largo Gallery is to provide a creative haven for the artists and educate the community on various art forms. The camaraderie of the group of artists housed here allows an explosion of creative talent. On the last Friday of each month, the gallery features a different artist during a wine-and-cheese evening. The building is filled with colorful pieces, all with South Florida themes. In 2007 one of the original "Highwaymen" was featured at the gallery. The Florida African Highwaymen were given that name in the 1950s because they traveled the roads and used their vehicles as showcases for their art, selling alongside highways.

BLUEWATER POTTERS
MM 102.9 Oceanside, Key Largo
(305) 453-1920
www.bluewaterpotters.com

High-fire stoneware and functional pottery set the theme for Bluewater Potters. Husband-and-wife owners Corky and Kim Wagner demonstrate their work right on the premises. The Wagners' inventory includes everything from spoon rests to full dinnerware and architectural pieces. Some work is brought in by outside artists. Among the pieces offered are wine goblets and baking dishes. All glazes are oven-, microwave-, and dishwasher-safe. Custom dinnerware is a specialty of the Wagners.

THE GALLERY AT KONA KAI
MM 97.8 Bayside, Key Largo
(305) 852-7200 or (800) 365-7829
www.konakairesort.com
The Gallery at Kona Kai secrets away a small yet exquisite changing exhibit of fine art treasures. The gallery showcases prominent South Florida artists such as Clyde Butcher, who is known for his hauntingly surreal black-and-white photography of the Everglades and Big Cypress National Preserve. Also featured is Gregory Sobran, a watercolorist who chronicles quintessential scenes of the Keys in a spectrum of pastel hues.

Kona Kai Gallery once partnered with a Paris gallery, so they now also represent some fine contemporary French artists whose works in oils and bronze sculptures feature interpretations of flower fields of the French countryside, landscapes of Provence, and depictions of the French people. Italian minimalist Franco Passalaqua and painters Jonny, of Venezuela, and Reuther, of Brazil, have joined the ranks of featured artists. The Gallery at Kona Kai represents these three artists exclusively in America.

RAIN BARREL VILLAGE OF ARTISTS AND CRAFTSPEOPLE
MM 86.7 Bayside, Islamorada
(305) 852-3084
www.keysdirectory.com/rainbarrel
The infamous Betsy the Lobster stands to greet shoppers at the entrance to this artist colony. At 30 feet tall and 40 feet in length, she is a show stopper! The Rain Barrel Village of Artists and Craftspeople is a garden complex of creativity. The 2,000-square-foot front mixed-media gallery features an array of paintings, sculpture, woodwork, and decorative glass. You'll find an eclectic assortment of art and craft creations, including whimsical ceramics and an expansive wind chime collection. There is a small café inside the complex that serves ready-to-go wraps, sandwiches, salads, key lime pie, and ice cream.

THE STACIE KRUPA STUDIO GALLERY OF ART
MM 82.9 Oceanside, Islamorada
(305) 517-2631
www.staciekrupa.com
You can watch Stacie Krupa, artist in residence, as she creates her huge, vibrant, mixed-media works on canvas at this contemporary, SoHo-style gallery. A powerful combination of bright colors and massive images, some of which depict Florida Keys birds and fish, Krupa's expressive creations will knock your sandals off.

REDBONE ART GALLERY
MM 81 Oceanside, Islamorada
(305) 664-2002
www.redbone.org
The Ellis family of Islamorada began this nonprofit organization as a means of raising funds for research for cystic fibrosis, a disease

that afflicts their daughter. Each year the Ellises hold a trilogy of celebrity backcountry fishing tournaments in order to raise these funds (see the Tournaments section of the Fishing chapter), and their art gallery defrays the cost of office expenses.

The gallery sports a variety of saltwater and marine art and sculptures from local artists and others noted for their works related to sportfishing, such as Don Ray, Diane Peebles, James Harris, Jeanne Dobie, and C. D. Clarke. Redbone Art Gallery exclusively showcases the original watercolors of Chet Reneson in South Florida.

ARTISTS IN PARADISE
MM 30.5 Bayside, 221 Key Deer Blvd., Big Pine Key
(305) 872-1828
www.artistsinparadise.com
Artists in Paradise is a cooperative gallery in Big Pine run by those artists from the Lower Keys Artists Network who use the gallery to display their work (see the listing in this chapter). More than 30 artists currently show works done in a variety of media: sculpture, oils, watercolors, acrylic, pen and ink, pottery, copper, and stained glass. The gallery is open daily.

Key West

ALAN S. MALTZ GALLERY
1210 Duval St.
(305) 294-0005
www.alanmaltz.com
Using the mystical nature of light, Alan S. Maltz, a world-renowned fine-art photographer, is an inspiration with his haunting and magical images. When you enter his gallery and view the art on the walls, you feel as though you are not looking at a piece of artwork hanging there but rather

upon the actual scene he photographed. His pieces are large and compelling. Alan's framing technique is as unique as his talent because he has the ability to keep his audience involved in the piece as a whole. Maltz is the author of *Key West Color*, *Miami: City of Dreams,* and *Florida: Beyond the Blue Horizon.*

ART@830 GALLERY AND STUDIO
830 Caroline St.
(305) 295-9595
www.art830.com
The gallery owners have been on the Key West art scene since 1993. Their Art@830 showcases photography, paintings, ceramics, contemporary glass art, turned wood art, and body painting. All of the works are from local artist and feature emerging artists and their talent.

FLORIDA KEYS COMMUNITY COLLEGE
5901 West College Rd., Stock Island
(305) 296-9081
www.fkcc.edu
Florida Keys Community College stages four art shows a year in the Library Gallery. Invitational shows are held in Oct and Feb, and the Florida Artist series is showcased in Jan and Feb. Student work is exhibited during the month of Apr.

THE GALLERY ON GREENE
606 Greene St.
(305) 294-1669
www.galleryongreene.com
Think you can't afford fine art? Think again. This gallery prides itself on displaying original art priced for every pocketbook—from $10 to $25,000! Among the offerings here are works by former part-time Key West resident the late Jeff MacNelly (he drew the cartoon strip "Shoe") and Henry La Cagnina, the last survivor

of 12 artists brought to Key West in the 1930s by the WPA. This gallery also supports working artists. You can usually expect to find at least one artist in residence, bent over his or her work, in a corner of the gallery.

GINGERBREAD SQUARE GALLERY
1207 Duval St.
(305) 296-8900
www.gingerbreadsquaregallery.com
Billed as Key West's oldest private art gallery, established in 1974, Gingerbread Square Gallery on upper Duval features sculptures, art glass, one-person shows, and ongoing presentations of the highly acclaimed works of Key West's favorite artists. Sal Salinero's oils depict the treasures of the rain forest. John Kiraly's fanciful paintings capture the spirit of locales real and imagined.

GLASS REUNIONS
825 Duval St.
(305) 294-1720
www.glassreunions.com
Glass is the business here, and you can get it in almost any form or color imaginable. Lamps, vases, and mirror wall hangings all showcase the talents of the various artists. For the traditionalist, a wide selection of stained-glass art is available.

GUILD HALL GALLERY
614 Duval St.
(305) 296-6076
www.guildhallgallerykw.com
More than 20 local artists display their work here, presented in a vast array of media. Most of the pieces focus on island life, with a definite Bahamian and Caribbean influence thrown in. Head upstairs for more unusual, and larger, works of art. This is Key West's original artists' co-op.

GUY HARVEY'S ISLAND SHOP AND GALLERY
511 Greene St.
(305) 295-0019
www.guyharveysislandshop.com
The gallery of Guy Harvey, a renowned Keys artist-angler, focuses on his art. Always obsessed with the sea and the creatures dwelling within, Harvey taught college biology for years before becoming a full-time marine wildlife artist in 1988. In addition to original works of art, the gallery sells wearable art that features imprints of his famous paintings. Watch your back . . . or that of the next guy going down the street. Harvey's paintings are showcased on the back of many a T-shirted visitor to the Florida Keys.

HAITIAN ART COMPANY
600 Frances St.
(305) 296-8932
www.haitian-art-co.com
Bold, wild colors and primitive designs mark the artistic offerings of Haiti, displayed in the multiple rooms of Haitian Art Company. The intricate paisley-style designs often weave an image of a serpent or wild animal within the overall picture. The work of Haiti is a study of form and color not readily encountered in this country. All pieces are originals. This gallery is tucked into a residential neighborhood at the corner of Frances and Southard Streets, way off Duval, but it's definitely worth the walk.

HANDS ON
1206 Duval St.
(305) 296-7399
www.handsongallery.com
The loom in the front of this attractive shop says it all. Here you will find the ever-changing, always exquisite creations of owner Ellen

Steiniger. Her handwoven scarves, jackets, and shawls are as beautiful to see as they are enjoyable to wear. Shop here, too, for handcrafted earrings, bracelets, and beads to accessorize your wearable art as well as an array of other fine American-made crafts. The gallery is also home to the work of 50-plus artists, each with a unique style.

HARRISON GALLERY
825 White St.
(305) 294-0609
www.harrison-gallery.com
Sculptor Helen Harrison and her husband Ben, a musician and author, have operated this charming gallery since 1986. Helen's spirit is discovered in a calabash, a palm frond, and gourds. Her pieces are just glorious! In addition to Helen's own work, ever-changing exhibitions highlight local artists. Open daily, but please ring the bell.

ISLAND ARTS
1128 Duval St.
(305) 292-9909
www.island-arts.com
This co-op of local artists fashions itself after a Caribbean bazaar, and many of the items herein illuminate just how fertile the imagination can be. Welded sculptures created out of scrap iron, metal junk, old screws, and tools turn up as a rooster, ostrich, duck, or dinosaur. Paper Smash is sculpted recycled paper made into snakes, pelicans, fish, and manatees. You'll also find a potpourri of handpainted tiles, stained-glass pieces, and ceramics, all with an island theme.

ISLAND NEEDLE POINT
527 Fleming St.
(305) 296-6091
www.islandneedlepoint.com

Julie Pischke is one of a handful of needlepoint designers who specialize in tropical designs. Her award-winning creations draw from the colors and textures of her home in the Florida Keys. She offers her art on pillows, bags, belts, shoes, rugs, and footstools. Julie's bold, bright, colorful, and eclectic motifs befit their inspiration. Long after your trip has ended, a bright, handmade memento reminds you of your hot days in the sun and your cool tropical nights in Paradise.

JOY GALLERY
1124-A Duval St.
(305) 296-3039
www.joy-gallery.net
A little sign that hangs amid the surreal paintings of out-of-body experiences by Lucie Bilodeau in the Joy Gallery reads: WARNING—THE PURCHASE OF FINE ART IS NOT NECESSARILY A LOGICAL DECISION. Bilodeau's brooding pieces are joined by limited editions by Irma Quigley and Gretchen Williams. A must-see is the rooster art by Thomas Easley.

KEY WEST ART BAR
901 Caroline St.
(305) 304-9001
www.keywestartbar.com
Set up in Flagler Station, the owner has opened a whole new venue for art. Featuring fine art, a jewelry bar, her Art Slut line and an area out back to enjoy a glass of vino with a Surprize Cinema. Stop by on the Loungee-aoke nights and bring out your lounge lizard qualities! Fun and dizzy and well worth a stop!

KEY WEST ART CENTER
301 Front St.
(305) 294-1241
www.keywestartcenter.com

This nonprofit organization is devoted to encouraging local talent by giving artists a canvas for their talents. Dues and commissions for their works keep this artistic colony thriving. Housed in a historic building that was once a grocery store near the waterfront, the Key West Art Center helps the arts stay glowing in a city that fans the flames of talent.

KATE'S GALLERY
930 Eaton St.
(305) 294-8451
www.justpeachey.com
"Art that is fun and art off the beaten path." Gallery owner Kate Peachy lives this verve. Inside this playful studio you'll find paintings, sculpture, furniture, and pottery. Looking around you'll see a fisherman painted on a piece of driftwood, a young Picasso illustrated on a four-string guitar, a 3-foot fountain crafted from chrome bumpers and artistically shaped into a dolphin, and a 3-foot sculpture made from cigarette packs. This shop gives new meaning to whimsical and fanciful.

KEY WEST LIGHT GALLERY
1203 Duval St.
(305) 294-0566
www.kwlightgallery.com
The size of the gallery is small in comparison to the multiple offerings inside. Sharon Wells's Key West Light Gallery features exhibits of photography and original paintings, including luminous watercolors. Some pieces are so full of light you think there is special lighting behind the art. There's no limit to Sharon's talent or her themes: Key West, Cuba, architecture, cemeteries, Mexico, flowers, and more. This is a not-to-be-missed shop if you love electrifying art.

LUCKY STREET GALLERY
1130 Duval St.
(305) 294-3973
Contemporary fine art of the cutting-edge variety is the focus here. Sculptures by John Martini and the works of artists Roberta Marks, Susan Rodgers, Lincoln Perry, and others are featured. New shows are staged approximately every two weeks.

MARY O'SHEA'S GLASS GARDEN
613 Eaton St.
(305) 293-8822
www.keywestglass.com
The ancient Egyptians get credit for discovering glass fusion 5,000 years ago, but Mary O'Shea is the artist who brought it to Key West. Her gallery, opened in 1999, features a profusion of original and colorful sculpture, masks, bowls, plates, and jewelry—all made from fused glass and each taking three days to complete.

Each piece of glass must be cut and layered to form a double thickness, then melted in a kiln. The piece is then cooled for a day, melted again, transposed, and formed into the desired shape. The resulting pieces are not only beautiful but also durable, and dishwasher- and microwave-safe. Don't be afraid to touch and don't hesitate to ask Mary about custom designs.

MONKEY APPLE ART FACTORY
1022 Duval St.
(305) 296-4100
www.monkeyappleartfactory.com
Rock your walls with this great-looking art. Art by the square foot from the artist's original paintings to portraits of Marlene Dietrich and Greta Garbo to cats and landscapes. If you can't get to the Keys any time soon, check out their Web site—it will make you want to redecorate your palace today!

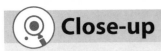

Close-up

Art Here, Art There, Art Everywhere

The Florida Keys Council of the Arts created "Art in Public Places" in 2000 to visually maintain the character, identity, and history of our island community. This public display of creative talent charges no admission fees for events; some works are permanently mounted in or on buildings, and the pieces are appropriate for all age groups.

Walk or drive around our hometowns and see for yourself why so many artist draw inspiration from this "Paradise." Beginning in Key Largo, inside the Murray Nelson Government Building at MM 102 bayside, there are various rotating art exhibits. Press onward to Plantation Key, where photographer Debra Yates's murals grace the walls of the Roth Building located at MM 88, bayside. Head down to Key West and go along Junior College Road on Stock Island, where you can locate three works by Jae DeVoe, Chod Stine, and Dick Moody. While in this part of town, turn at 5525 on the same road and check out Jay Grogin's tile and ceramic fountain at the Key West City Public Safety Building. Journey to Caroline Street and view Christian Wilson's "Underwater Creation" on Harbor House condos. Wander back into town and roam by the Key West City swimming pool to marvel at Duke Rood's wooden sculpture. Make your next stop at the end of Seminole Avenue where the lovely floor design by J. T. Thompson is part of the Mary and John Spottswood Waterfront Park. Traverse to Wall Street in Old Town to appreciate the children's tile mural that is priceless. Finally, head out to the White Street Pier and gaze at the planters by Wally McGregor at the AIDS Memorial.

At the Key West International Airport, check out the art on the walls and listen to the sounds being played, featuring original music recorded by local musicians. The Lower Keys Medical Center and the Freeman Justice Center also offer various artists on display. So much art and so little time! Visit www.keysarts.com for more information.

SODU GALLERY
1102 Duval St.
(305) 296-4400

An unrestricted window display showcases amazing local artists, enabling them to strut their stuff in grand style. Jewelry, acrylics, paintings, and pencil drawings, with painting on furniture, dinnerware, and fabrics, fill the shop with excitement and fun.

SOUTH POINTE GALLERY
1201 Duval St.
(305) 295-9354
www.authenticvintageposters.com

The owner of South Pointe Gallery travels extensively in pursuit of authentic vintage posters to add to her collection. The striking works are primarily French with a mix of American, German, and Italian. Decorating with posters is not a unique idea, but very appealing for their bold images and their less expensive prices than other art forms.

THE STUDIOS OF KEY WEST
600 White St., Key West
(305) 296-0458
www.tskw.org

A nonprofit artist colony located in the old historic Armory building (built in 1891) evolved after many talented artists could not find affordable space to house their creations. Located in the already popular, art-filled neighborhood of White Street, the Studios of Key West has attracted writers, painters, and poets among their eclectic virtuoso. The Studios offer workshops and lectures that are open to the public. This is their El Dorado in the tropics. Fun to try: for $5, you place a token into a cigarette machine that has been revived into a Southern-Art-O-Mat and out pops an art object. Twenty artists share in this unique venture.

WILD SIDE GALLERY
291 Front St., Clinton Square Market
(305) 296-7800

From carved wood walking sticks to ceramics, jewelry, and watercolors, all objets d'art in this interesting and affordable gallery depict some element of nature. Artists and craftspeople represented here are from throughout the United States.

WYLAND GALLERIES
MM 81 Oceanside, Islamorada
(305) 664-4720
www.wylandkw.com

The first East Coast display venues of Wyland, the world's leading marine-life artist, the galleries display a wide range of the environmental artist's work. His world-renowned, life-size whaling wall murals, one of which adorns the Kmart building in Marathon and another on the Waterfront Market building at the Key West Historic Seaport, reflect Wyland's unshakable commitment to saving the earth's oceans and thereby its marine creatures. Also displayed are several paintings from the "above and below" series, for which Wyland collaborated with other talented artists to create a scene looking beneath and above the sea concurrently. In 2007 Wyland painted his 95th and final "Whaling Wall" in the United States at MM 99.2 in Key Largo. The mural covers 7,500 square feet and wraps completely around a building (a whaling cube). A time-lapse view can be seen at www.wylandfoundation .org. In addition to the Islamorada location, there are two other Wyland Galleries at 102 Duval St. (305-294-5240, 888-294-5240) and 623 Duval St. (305-292-4998, 888-292-4998) in Key West.

SHOPPING

Stretched along our 100 miles of Overseas Highway is every diversion imaginable for the serious (and not-so-serious) shopper. Scuba aficionados find nirvana here, reveling in state-of-the-gear offerings from our plethora of dive shops (see the Diving and Snorkeling chapter). Anglers, who may readily concede that you might be able to be too thin or too rich, staunchly maintain that you can never have too many fishing rods or an excess of tackle (see the Fishing chapter). And boaters, who all know that a vessel is really a floating hole into which you pour money, find a virtual smorgasbord of shopping options guaranteed to fertilize their needs exponentially (see the Boating chapter).

But what about the rest of us, free spirits who like to see the ocean through the rim of a glass, preferably while lying prone by the swimming pool in the shade of a coconut palm? We know we don't require much in the way of clothing here in the Keys' tropicality, just a suit (small and stringy), shoes (light and strappy), and a hat (woven and floppy), but we have pent-up shopping desires, too.

OVERVIEW

So here is the ultimate road map to the shops. We describe our favorite shops in geographic order by mile marker, from Key Largo to Key West. Our Key West section is divided into four sections. Best of Duval is organized by numerical address, from upper Duval (oceanside) to lower Duval (gulfside), so you can stroll the street and take in all the shops. Off Duval, the not-to-be missed shops on surrounding streets, is organized in alphabetical order. Lastly, we give you information on noteworthy shops Way Off Duval and in New Town. Be sure to scope out the Arts and Culture chapter for descriptions of galleries selling creative works, many by local artists. And turn to our Specialty Foods, Cafes, and Markets chapter to find piscatory treasures and other palate pleasers.

Many of our shops are open daily, especially in Key West, but many close on Sunday. Some close on alternate days, so it is best if you call before venturing out, as hours and days of operation can vary season to season.

UPPER KEYS

SHELL WORLD
MM 106 Bayside, Key Largo
(305) 451-9797 or (888) 398-6233
www.shellworldflkeys.com
At Shell World, you'll think you've been beached with every type of shell in existence. Yes, they have your typical clam, oyster, and mussel shells, but they also carry a tremendous variety of other shells from throughout the world. In the aisles throughout the store are conch, abalone, cone, and nautilus shells,

as well as wind chimes, jewelry, and flowers made from various shells. This is a great place for kids to see what nature develops under the oceans. A second location is at MM 97.5 in the median, Key Largo (305-852-8245, 888-398-6233).

ISLAND SMOKE SHOP
MM 103.5 Bayside, Pink Plaza, Key Largo
(305) 453-4014 or (800) 680-9701
www.islandsmokeshop.com

With a 1,000-square-foot walk-in humidor and over 3,000 square feet of retail space, the Island Smoke Shop is one of the largest in south Florida. Showcasing a full line of cigars, lighters, and accessories, it has one of the largest selections of pipes in the area, as well as some wonderful house blends of tobacco. The shop also exclusively sells El Originale cigars, voted best in the United States by both *Smoke* and *Cigar Aficionado* magazines. On Saturday, Island Smoke Shop has live cigar-rolling demonstrations; the rollers come down from Miami. You can order by mail here.

LARGO CARGO
MM 103.1 Oceanside, Key Largo
(305) 451-4242
www.largocargo.com

The can't-miss landmark for Largo Cargo is a large cannon pointing at US 1 with "magic" smoke being propelled from the barrel. Inside this bright blue dwelling is some pretty cool stuff for your souvenir collection. They have pirate flags and windsocks with skulls and crossbones; key lime products of juice, oils, jellies, chutneys, and barbecue sauces for culinary buffs; tropical apparel with the big favorite—mens' khaki beer-can shorts (need I say more?); nautical jewelry handcrafted from silver and sea glass; metal

sculptures of fun "Pelican Pete" for your yard; and the all-time favorite, a message in a bottle—perfect to mail home (in a small box) in lieu of a postcard.

EXOTIC ISLAND DÉCOR AND GIFTS
MM 103 Bayside, Key Largo
(305) 451-4140

A Balinese-inspired home and furniture store has come to the Florida Keys. The owners travel to the exotic lands of Bali and Indonesia, Singapore and Malaysia to stock the store with hand-crafted tropical Asian designs all showcased in a 4,500-square-foot building. Some of their interior furnishings include lamps, silk trees, plants, and fountains. Call it feng shui meets Jimmy Buffett land.

FLORIDA KEYS GIFT COMPANY
MM 103 Oceanside, Key Largo
(305) 453-9229

This bright, entertaining gift shop is loaded with a wide array of Florida Keys treasures. Dazzling glass jewelry; men's, women's, and children's island wear; hats; postcards; and T-shirts for the whole family (one comes with markers so the kids can color in a pre-printed pattern). Cute, unusual gifts with a friendly staff to make stopping here a pleasure.

SANDAL FACTORY OUTLET
MM 102.4 Oceanside, Key Largo
(305) 453-9644 or (800) 736-5397

These sandal outlets allow you to fit yourself. Pick from a copious sea of ladies' sandals—strappy, sport, and utilitarian. Men and children can be accommodated here, too. You won't find every style in every size, but you can choose from hundreds of designs. A second location is at MM 82 Oceanside in Islamorada (305-664-9700).

CAPTAIN'S IMPORTS
MM 99 Bayside, Key Largo
(305) 453-1800
www.captainsimports.com
There is no need for neon signs to alert you to Captain's Imports, especially at night. In front of this shop are pulsating, colorful, 24-foot palm trees! The first time you see these delightful symbols of tropical living come to life in orange, purple, red, and blue, you'll promise yourself you will not party so hard anymore! Inside the store is equally a Technicolor joy. You'll find steel drum art and wall art featuring fish, iguanas, and seahorses. Captain's Imports also carries Talavera pottery, the beautiful art form originating in 16th-century Moorish Spain and now made in Mexico. There is one fish pattern named "Key West." This is not a store you'll find on Main Street back home.

PINK JUNKTIQUE
MM 98 Oceanside, Key Largo
(305) 853-2620
You can't miss this unusual building going north on US 1. It is hot pink with giant flamingos out front. Inside is an inviting, nostalgic collection of vintage clothing, housewares, bedding, jewelry, and collectibles. The inventory changes constantly, so it is a great place to browse and recall those "happy days" of whatever era you remember.

KEY LIME PRODUCTS AND TROPICAL GIFTS
MM 95 Oceanside, Key Largo
(305) 853-0378 or (800) 870-1780
www.keylimeproducts.com
From tangy edibles and thirst-quenching beverages, to soothing lotions and luscious bath products, Key Lime Products and Tropical Gifts offers a cornucopia of Florida Keys products at its two locations in the Upper Keys. Here at Key Lime Products you can even purchase lawn and patio ornaments as well as a tiki hut for your yard! Have no fear about getting this stuff home: They ship worldwide.

COVER TO COVER BOOKS
MM 91.5 Bayside, Tavernier
(305) 853-2464
Cover to Cover Books is owned by two sisters who graduated from nearby Coral Shores High School. Being from the Keys, they know their customers like family and will brew up a yummy cup of latte while you browse their store. During the year, best-selling authors cruise through the Keys offering book signings and readings, making this store one of the stops.

GERRY DRONEY TROPICAL GARDENS
MM 88.7 Bayside, Tavernier
(305) 852-4715
A riot of orchids, bromeliads, anthuriums, gingers, and other exotic tropical plants greets you as you wander through Gerry Droney's Tropical Gardens. This is tropical browsing at its finest. You'll find pots galore of every shape, size, and color as well as a full line of insecticides, fertilizers, and soil additives. Even if you eventually have to hop a plane for home, stop in here to see how Paradise blooms.

RAIN BARREL VILLAGE OF ARTISTS AND CRAFTSPEOPLE
MM 86.7 Bayside, Islamorada
(305) 852-3084
www.keysdirectory.com/rainbarrel
Can't miss this place with the famous sculpture of Betsy the Lobster greeting shoppers. At 30 feet tall and 40 feet long, it's a great photo opportunity. Inside is a lush, tropical

hideaway housing artists and crafters who work in retail shops that are peppered beneath the gumbo-limbos and amid the bougainvillea. Refer to the Arts and Culture chapter for a rundown of the galleries and studios at the Rain Barrel.

GARDEN OF EDEN
MM 82.3 Oceanside, Islamorada
(305) 664-5558
The show-stopping tropical fish atop a coral reef is the "can't miss" feature outside Garden of Eden. In fact, it was featured on the cover of this guide book's 10th edition! Have you noticed those manatee mailboxes along the Overseas Highway? Well, this is the place to find them. Garden of Eden is filled with silk flowers and arrangements, including orchids, bromeliads, and many other faux tropicals. Look for the hand-carved bottle stoppers; the caricatures are a riot and sure to remind you of someone back home.

MILK AND HONEY
MM 82.2 Oceanside, Keys Plaza,
Islamorada
(305) 304-9107
www.milknhoneystore.com
This sweet jewelry store sells select designer pieces that will make you feel very special. Known for unique styles that are very feminine and fun to wear, they also carry handbags and shearling boots—to boot!

ISLAND SILVER & SPICE
MM 82 Oceanside, Islamorada
(305) 664-2714
Billed as the Keys' department store, Island Silver & Spice offers a quality sampling of many things. The men's department is tucked away in the rear of the store, allowing the much larger ladies' section to predominate. Dressing

rooms, looking like tiny pastel conch houses, are sprinkled throughout the store. Fine jewelry is offered as well as a limited selection of shoes, children's clothing, books, and games. The peach-and-green building also houses an eclectic assortment of gourmet kitchen items, bath and household accessories, and an upstairs bargain corner.

ICHTHYOPHILE
MM 82 Bayside, Islamorada
(305) 664-8960
www.ichthyophile.com
This unique shop with an even more unique name is sure to hook your attention. Ichthyophile (one who enjoys and studies fish) is lovingly stocked with rare, historic prints of sea life that have been preserved from books that are up to 200 years old. The owner was a backcountry guide for 13 years, and his interest led him to open this entertaining and interesting shop. Look for the Kids' Corner, with toys and books with a water or fish subject; it's a great way to interest kids in becoming anglers.

SEA DRAGON
MM 82 Oceanside, Islamorada
(305) 664-0048
www.seadragonfurniture.com
Billing itself as "exotic island decor," Sea Dragon will help you create your own Shangri-la. The owners travel to Bali each season to make selections that help their customers create a tropical Asian look in their "crib." Indonesian artwork and teak furniture with unusual pieces make this shop a must-see.

ANGELIKA
MM 81.9 Bayside, Islamorada
(305) 664-9008
www.angelikaclothing.com

Upmarket ladies' fashions with an old-fashioned twist, natural fabrics, and whimsical designs mark the merchandise at Angelika's. Look for Angelika's great hats and handbags.

BLUE MARLIN JEWELRY
MM 81.9 Oceanside, Islamorada
(305) 664-8004 or (888) 826-4424
www.bluemarlinjewelry.com
Discover gold in this interesting jewelry shop. Blue Marlin sports a great selection of gold charms, depicting most of the species of our ecosystem. Especially striking are the black coral fish. Many pieces are also offered in sterling silver.

HOOKED ON BOOKS
MM 81.9 Oceanside, Islamorada
(305) 517-2602
www.hookedonbooksfloridakeys.com
Hooked on Books is filled to the rafters with used books and paperbacks. You can trade in your used paperback books two-for-one. For every two paperbacks you bring in, you can take one used paperback with you. Or for the hardback books, bring the book in for a 25 percent credit based on the publisher's price. (If the hardcover book has been printed in paperback, you will receive only a $1 credit.) Accumulate credits to buy other used hardcover books. This is a great deal for avid readers and book collectors.

SUNNY EXPOSURES
MM 81.9 Bayside, Islamorada
(305) 664-8445
See suits, suits, and more suits here—for surf and sun, not the office. Ladies' swimsuits of every style and description, for every imaginable body type, join ranks with cover-ups, lotions, and sunglasses. Sunny Exposures even carries some men's and kids' suits.

WORLD WIDE SPORTSMAN INC.
MM 81.5 Bayside, Islamorada
(305) 664-4615 or (800) 227-7776
www.basspro.com
Don't miss a stop at World Wide Sportsman, the massive fishing emporium that is an Islamorada must-see. Housed in a former in-and-out storage building renovated with an old-fashioned, exposed-brick exterior and surrounded by native trees and shrubs, World Wide showcases the exact replica of Hemingway's 42-foot ship, the *Pilar*. Visitors can climb aboard and examine Hemingway's chair and even his typewriter. Rumor has it that he wrote at least one novel while fishing on the *Pilar*. A 6,000-gallon saltwater aquarium presents the creatures of our reef, including baby tarpon, bonefish, and redfish. A small art gallery upstairs features works of local artists.

Memorabilia aside, World Wide is stocked to the rafters with a wide assortment of fishing tackle (see the Outfitters section in the Fishing chapter), and a full line of men's and women's technical clothing is offered, including Ex Officio, Woolrich, Sportif, Columbia, and much more.

If your stamina runs out before your money does, sit a spell in one of the rocking chairs lining the back porch and watch the action on the Gulf of Mexico. Or pop up to the Zane Grey Bar; sink into a leather chair; look at the vintage fishing photos of Grey and his cronies; and sip a tall, cool one. Even if you don't like to fish, World Wide Sportsman is one place you won't want to pass by.

BANYAN TREE ANTIQUES
MM 81.2 Oceanside, Islamorada
(305) 664-3433 or (877) 453-9463
www.banyantreegarden.com
A shaded courtyard is the cool, unruffled invite greeting you at Banyan Tree Antiques.

The proprietors are a knowledgeable couple who know their stuff with an ever-changing inventory, making the Banyan Tree Antiques a find! An eclectic mix of antiques and contemporary items for home and garden abound.

BABYCAKES
MM 80 Oceanside, Islamorada
(305) 664-2996

Cute name for a cute store for cute bambinos! From newborn to size 7, Babycakes offers hip, trendy clothes and gifts for the upscale Keys youngsters. The most popular item is a diaper bag—it's eco-friendly because it is made from recycled water bottles.

MIDDLE KEYS

KEY BANA RESORT APPAREL
MM 53.5 Oceanside, Key Colony Beach
Causeway, Key Colony Beach
(305) 289-1161
www.keybana.com

Ladies, you are sure to find a new swimsuit or tropical cotton item here that you can't pass up. And Key Bana has a roomful of shorts and shirts for men, too. Check out the solar tan-through bathing suits or the beer-can shorts.

YE OLDE ENGLISH FLY SHOP
MM 53 Bayside, Marathon
(305) 743-8595
www.yeoldeenglishflyshop.com

Do you know the difference between a "creel" and a "reel"? The owner of this shop does! Ye Olde English Fly Shop specializes in British fishing memorabilia for collectors and decorators with outstanding vintage rods and reels from the 1800s. Showcasing lures, flies, nets, rods, and gaffs makes this shop a nautical history lesson as well as pleasing to the eye.

MAROONED IN MARATHON
MM 53 Bayside, Marathon
(305) 743-3809

Definitely cast yourself ashore and hurry into this charming shop so you can be marooned in Marathon too! This is a fun gift shop for the young and young at heart. As they say to their customers, "Everything you want, some things you need, and many things you can't live without when you're not marooned on this tiny tropical island." They offer T-shirts, kid stuff, Atocha jewelry, Beach Bum novelties, and other things you can't live without!

D'ASIGN SOURCE
MM 52.7 Bayside, Marathon
(305) 743-7130
www.dasignsource.com

This wonderful home furnishing and design center oozes class. You'll find the very latest and very best in materials, fixtures, finishes, and designs for home remodeling, building, and furnishing. Even if you aren't in the market for a home makeover, make your way to D'Asign Source's megastore, with home ideas for both indoors and out. Browsing the 25,000-square-foot showroom is an inspiration.

BAYSHORE CLOTHING AND SMALL WORLD
MM 52 Oceanside, Marathon
(305) 743-8430
www.bayshoreclothing.com

Bayshore caters to men's and women's tropical garment needs, a guaranteed attitude adjustment from the busy workaday world up north. The little people's shop beckons parents and especially grandparents with a cute selection of swimsuits, warm-weather togs, and toys.

WICKER WEB
MM 52 Oceanside, Marathon
(305) 743-3696

Across from the Marathon Airport runway, in the Southwind Building, you'll discover the Wicker Web, three showrooms chock-full of tropically inspired items for every room in your house. You'll find a wide selection of baskets, wall hangings, wicker items, lamps, plasticware, and bath accessories.

GOOFY GECKO, LAZY LIZARD, AND KRAZY LARRY'S LAST STORE
MM 50.3 Oceanside, in the Publix
Shopping Center, Marathon
(305) 289-4228
www.keysgiftsonline.com

This combo store, actually three stores in one rambling space, stocks unique tropical "stuff." The store meanders from room to room, chockablock with palmy treasures—furniture, rugs, pillows, items for entertaining, soaps and lotions, garden items, even swishy, Keysy clothes. You'll have a ball just looking around here, even if tropical isn't your decorating motif up north.

KEYKER'S BOUTIQUE & GALLERY
MM 50.3 Oceanside, 67 53rd Street,
Marathon
(305) 743-0107
www.keykers.com

Keyker and other local clothing designers create custom island clothing for women and children, unusual yet flattering styles using exquisitely fine cottons. You'll find them displayed at this cooperative establishment, along with interesting jewelry, accessories, craft items, and paintings.

PATIO & HOME FURNITURE GALLERIES: ORIGINAL FURNITURE ART GALLERY
MM 50 Oceanside, Marathon
(305) 743-2740

TROPICAL FURNITURE GALLERY
MM 49.5 Oceanside, Marathon
(305) 289-2038
www.patiohomefurnituregalleries.com

Sometimes we stroll through the enormous Furniture Art Gallery just to see what wild new things they've added to the collection. Besides offering the most complete selection of quality furniture in the Keys—such as Lexington, Tommy Bahama, Natuzzi Leather, and Cabana Joe—the Furniture Art Gallery peppers the showroom with accessories that range from the sublime to the outrageous. Tropical Furniture Gallery sells upmarket bamboo, wicker, and rattan furniture.

BP CARGO
MM 49.5 Oceanside, Marathon
(305) 743-0555

Jimmy Buffett is alive and well in this shop! Everything imaginable (except the main Parrothead himself) is sold here. His music plays continuously. Buffett trinkets and rack after rack of his Buffett apparel line, Caribbean Soul, can take you away to Margaritaville.

MARATHON DISCOUNT BOOKS
MM 48.2 Oceanside, Marathon
(305) 289-2066

Marathon Discount Books offers all books at 10 to 90 percent off retail prices. Selling primarily publishers' overstock, the store also offers best sellers, local-interest books, and books on tape. The staff also will place special orders. Open daily.

EQUIPMENT LOCKER SPORT & BICYCLE
MM 48 Bayside, Marathon
(305) 289-1670

This is where you'll find a great selection of bicycles and related biking gear. Here is where you'll also pick up exercise equipment and the gamut of necessities for every sport, from hoops to weight lifting to in-line skating. Top-brand athletic shoes line the walls.

PIGEON KEY FOUNDATION GIFT SHOP
MM 47 Oceanside, Pigeon Key Visitors Center, Marathon
(305) 743-5999
www.pigeonkey.net

Look for the old railway car, still sitting on the tracks of Flagler's Railroad at MM 47 Oceanside. Hidden unassumingly inside resides the Pigeon Key Visitor Center Gift Shop, a potpourri of Keys memorabilia and gift items. The gift shop, like everything on Pigeon Key, is run by a contingent of loyal volunteers, and all proceeds go to the Pigeon Key Foundation.

i Not enough space in your luggage for your shopping purchases? Several mail shops in the Keys will ship your treasures home. Visit the UPS Store in Key Largo (305-453-4877), in Marathon (305-743-2005), or in Key West (305-292-4177); the Package Solution in Key Largo (305-451-5461); the Mail Spot in Key West (305-296-5333); or PakMail, 4th Street in Key West (305-295-1491).

LOWER KEYS

LITTLE PALM ISLAND GIFT SHOP
MM 28.5 Oceanside, Little Torch Key
(305) 872-2524 or (800) 343-8567
www.littlepalmisland.com

Stop at this mainland substation of Little Palm Island and visit the gift shop. You'll find interesting glassware, sculptures, and handpainted plates, in addition to upscale clothing and straw hats. If you go out to Little Palm Island itself, for lunch or dinner or to stay the night, don't miss the island shop. The tropical ambience will tempt you to discard your shorts and don an island caftan.

KEY WEST

For shoppers, Key West lives up to its reputation as Paradise. Colorful, funky, one-of-a-kind shops abound on our fair island. To aid your search-and-purchase mission, we have taken the best of Key West—a little of this, a little of that—and presented it in a simple format. Our shop-till-you-drop tour of Key West begins on Duval Street with the Best of Duval section. Other little treasures are tucked in and about the narrow, quiet streets of Old Town, and although sometimes tough to find, they are definitely worth the search. We've categorized them as Off Duval. And finally, we lead you to Way off Duval, for some interesting offerings, with a mention of New Town, where you'll find the major retail chains, which stock all the basics for living in Paradise.

i Scan local newspapers and look for yard sales. This is a fun way to get out into the neighborhoods, up and down the Keys, and see how the natives live! The houses and streets of this vacation mecca are beautiful and charming.

The Best of Duval is arranged by numerical address order, from the Atlantic to the gulf. Off Duval and Way off Duval are organized alphabetically. If your tastes lean more toward original artwork and handcrafted jewelry, be sure to check the Art Galleries section of our Arts and Culture chapter for additional shopping suggestions.

Best of Duval

ARCHEO GALLERY
1208 Duval St.
(305) 294-3771
www.archeogallery.com
Not everyone can trek to Timbuktu, Ouaga-dougou, Djenne, or Paris, but at this shop you can! The owners fly halfway around the world to bring one-of-a-kind beads, ceremonial pieces, sculptures, and artifacts to their customers. Also in their emporium a visitor will locate "village" furniture from the island of Java in Indonesia. A shopper might feel the need for a passport here!

CUBA! CUBA!
814 Duval St.
(305) 295-9442
www.cubacubastore.com
Get a little "Libre!" in your life with this quaint little shop that espouses a passion for all things Cuban. Art is very much a part of the selection evidenced by nostalgic wood carvings, depicting a typical Cuban kitchen. Cookbooks and authentic jams and marmalades line the shelves, and guitars and maracas are just begging to be played. A selection of cigars is also on display.

COCKTAILS! KEY WEST
808 Duval St.
(305) 292-1190
To think there is a shop that celebrates drinking but without one real bottle of spirits in sight! This distinctive atelier has all of the accent pieces to fashionably enhance bending your elbow. Hand-painted martini glasses, coasters, towels, cocktail shakers,

wine holders, and the most unique of all—old doorknobs and pool balls made into wine stoppers.

TOWELS OF KEY WEST
806 Duval St.
(305) 292-1120, (305) 294-1929,
(800) 927-0316
www.towelsofkeywest.com
Towels in all shapes, sizes, and budgets fill this simple store. Get the best-selling, colorful print terry robe, or immerse yourself in big, warm, oversize, colorful beach and bath towels.

ARIA KEY WEST
718 Duval St.
(305) 517-7347
Step into this open, bright boutique but hold on to your wallet—this place is a shopper's Holy Grail! Super good-looking funky costume jewelry, handbags, hats, and vintage pieces are everywhere—every available space is covered. If the owner is minding the store, you are in for a treat. She is a delight and effervescent. The gals from *Sex in the City* would surely approve!

i Duval Street is 14 blocks long and runs from the Atlantic to the Gulf of Mexico. It is known as the longest main street in the world because it goes from coast to coast.

THE BEACH HOUSE SWIMWEAR
714 Duval St.
(305) 292-9300
www.thebeachhouseswimwear.com
You can spend your whole vacation in this shop just trying on bathing suits because they have more than 4,000 from which to choose. This tiny shop with the big selection has been on Duval since 1977. At the Beach

House Swimwear, you will find designer and name brands for women, men, and kids.

ACA JOE
617 Duval St.
(305) 294-1570

Need some cargo shorts? A pair of deck shoes? A lightweight jacket for your sunset cruise? ACA Joe has a wide assortment of cool, comfortable cotton clothing for men and women as well as shoes that are perfect for boating and beachcombing. You'll find a nice selection of tropical print camp shirts here, too—tasteful enough to wear even when you return home.

HOT HATS
613 Duval St.
(305) 294-1333

If you're heading out into the midday sun, you'd best wear a hat. And you're sure to find a flattering one at this shop devoted entirely to headgear, including everything from canvas caps to straw boaters. There's even a rack full of multicolored baseball caps with propellers for catching those island breezes in a whimsical way.

BIRKENSTOCK OF OLD TOWN
612 Duval St.
(305) 294-8318 or
(800) 330-2475 (orders)
www.birkenstore.com

With sandals being essential apparel for island life, it makes good sense for Birkenstock to have a large, full-service store right in the middle of it all. Although Birkenstocks don't come cheap, the shoes are exceptionally durable and comfortable. Rare is the local who doesn't own at least one pair. Count on paying upward of $50 for yours, but do watch the sale rack here. You can sometimes get a

pretty good deal on discontinued styles. This store also does in-house repairs.

THE SOLE MAN
610 Duval St.
(305) 292-2505

Everyone who lives here, or visits for any length of time, winds up buying clever, glitzy, fun sandals. The Sole Man has something for every "sole," and you will end up tossing those socks in the back of your drawer or suitcase.

FAST BUCK FREDDIE'S
500 Duval St.
(305) 294-2007
www.fastbuckfreddies.com

If there weren't literally hundreds of stores to explore in Key West and you never reached the bottom of your pockets, Fast Buck Freddie's, at the southeast corner of Duval and Fleming, would be your one-stop shop. Their window displays are as much to gawk at as is the merchandise inside. Their Christmas windows are so elaborate that their designers begin the transformation in August. FBF's carries men's and women's clothing in metropolitan and tropical styles. Just around the bend from the megastore's clothing section are imported items from around the world, such as clocks, candleholders, picture frames, and some of the most unusual home furnishings you'll see anywhere. Look to Freddie's kitchenware department for an extensive selection of cookbooks, gourmet kitchen accessories, herb-flavored oils, and Godiva chocolates. And be sure to check out the unusual toys, novelty items, and greeting cards in the back of the store. But beware—some may be X-rated.

See the listing later in this chapter for Half Buck Freddie's, Fast Buck Freddie's discount store, and Fast Buck's at Home, elegant and island furniture and accessories.

MARGARITAVILLE STORE
500 Duval St.
(305) 296-9089 or (800) 262-6835
www.margaritavillestore.com
Everything here is tuned to one thing—the works of Key West's favorite son, Jimmy Buffett. All his albums are available here, along with tons of shirts, books, photos, and other Parrothead paraphernalia. Spend some time perusing the walls—they're packed with photos and memorabilia related to events in the life of the man from Margaritaville. This place is a must-stop for Buffett fans old and new.

NEPTUNE DESIGNS
301 Duval St.
(305) 294-8131
Most of the jewelry filling this shop has an oceanic motif and is wrought in gold or silver. Leaping silver dolphins frolic with golden, gliding sea turtles on necklaces displayed on a black background. Noah's Ark figurines are on display—tiny ships decked with all manner of wildlife.

CONGRESS JEWELERS
129 Duval St.
(305) 296-5885
www.congressjewelers.com
Congress Jewelers might have only a small store on Duval, but boy, do they have the jewelry. They are one of only two authorized Rolex dealers in the Keys, so if glamorous watches are your bling-bling, get your eye candy here. Congress also has breathtaking gold, silver, precious-gem, and semiprecious-gem pieces to tempt you.

i "Shop till you drop" can be taken literally here in the tropical heat of the Florida Keys. Give yourself a gift by pampering your body with a spa treatment for an hour or a full day. Some therapists are mobile and will even come to you! The local Yellow Pages or hotel concierge can assist you in locating this service.

Off Duval

ABACO GOLD
418 Front St.
(305) 296-0086
A honeymoon voyage to the Abaco Islands prompted owners John and Angela to dub their store Abaco Gold. The jewelry line here is exclusive—like no other in the Florida Keys, or elsewhere for that matter. Abaco Gold specializes in unique, nautical designs featuring mermaids, dolphins, and tropical themes. If you love jewelry, you'll love this store.

ASSORTMENT, INC.
514 Fleming St.
(305) 294-4066
This chic men's clothing store, just a few steps off Duval Street, carries the latest in men's casual fashions with a dressy flair. Handsome jackets, shirts, slacks, and shoes are tastefully displayed. Polo by Ralph Lauren, Barry Bricken, and Cole-Haan shoes are just a few of the lines you'll find here. Assortment, Inc., also offers great-looking gifts and accessories for that special guy in your life.

BESAME MUCHO
315 Petronia St.
(305) 294-1928
www.besamemucho.net
Step into this tastefully decorated shop, and you will feel as though you have stepped

back in time. This place is for "the person who has everything, needs nothing, but loves gifts." Ceiling fans stir the air, and the CD playing softly in the background is reminiscent of Old Havana. The shelves are filled with items that look as though they belong on a movie set, ca. 1940. Here you'll find an assortment of picture frames, desk accessories, tableware, lucky tokens, tropical cards and books, baskets, Tahitian bath oils—in short, what the owners lovingly refer to as "essential island provisions."

BLUE
MM 82.2 Oceanside, Islamorada
(305) 517-9225
www.blueislandstore.com
Shop here for classic linen skirts, tops, jackets, pants, and dresses that will look just as appropriate on Fifth Avenue as they do on Duval. Be sure to check out the accessories here, too. The bead jewelry is handmade, and the colors are a perfect complement to the easy-fitting, understated styles. A second location is at 718 Caroline St. (305-292-5172).

COMMOTION
800 Caroline St.
(305) 292-3364
www.localcolorkeywest.com
Stylish island separates that are as fun to wear as they are practical to own await you here. These natural, washable linen and flax fabrics will help you keep your cool—a definite must in the Florida Keys. Best of all, unlike some island designs that look out of place outside the Tropics, these will look just as great when you get back home.

DUCK AND DOLPHIN ANTIQUES
601 Fleming St.
(305) 295-0499

This elegant shop—reminiscent of the antiques shops we've seen in Europe—is filled with ornate furnishings and accent pieces that can only be called trés chic. You'll find everything from a grand piano to a crystal chandelier. These items are in mint condition, with price tags to match.

FAST BUCK AT HOME
726 Caroline St.
(305) 294-1304
Freddy decided the Florida Keys needed an elegant island furniture and accessory store and this one is it! Woven textured sofas and chairs, stunning wood dining tables with tropical print covered chairs, dreamy throw pillows, dazzling light fixtures, and interesting accessories to "wow" any decor and decorator.

HALF BUCK FREDDIE'S
920 Caroline St.
(305) 294-5047
www.fastbuckfreddies.com
Slightly dated, overstocked, or slow-moving merchandise from Fast Buck Freddie's (see earlier listing in this section) never dies. It simply ends up across Duval and down a few blocks, at Half Buck Freddie's on Caroline. Everything here, from clothing to calendars to kitchen gadgets, was once on sale at Freddie's. Now it's moved out and marked down 50 percent from its original price. The stock changes regularly, and the hours are limited. Half Buck Freddie's does not have a phone number. The number listed above is for Fast Buck Freddie's; the folks there can answer all your questions.

IN ONE ERA
1118 White St.
(305) 293-0208
www.rubylane.com/shops/in1era

This tiny shop has a large selection of delightful estate jewelry, old period costumes (great for Fantasy Fest), vintage lighting, chandeliers, and small antiques. Their inventory also includes Cuban and Key West memorabilia.

KEY ACCENTS
804 Caroline St.
(305) 293-8555
www.keyaccents.net
New England in feel but Key West in style, Key Accents is like a breath of fresh air. Nicely displayed inside an old home, you will find furniture, pictures, lamps, and home accessories. The inventory is not large, but the pieces they do offer show very well.

KEY WEST ALOE
540 Green St.
(305) 293-1885, or
(800) 445-2563 (orders)
www.keywestaloe.com
Step into Key West Aloe on Front Street for a showroom of the only perfumes, skin-care products, and cosmetics to boast a "made in Key West" label. Their products are shipped throughout the world.

KEY WEST CONCH TRADERS
Clinton Square Market
(305) 296-2369, (888) 592-6624
www.conchtraders.com
You can take home, mail, or order almost anything that reminds you of your visit to the Florida Keys from this shop. The owners of Conch Traders have tapped into the local retail vendors offering art, books, music, Key lime products, jewelry, and any other items they can add to their inventory. Get home and wish you had bought that wall hanging? Or that great bracelet? Call or go to their Web site and it can still be yours!

KEY WEST ISLAND BOOKSTORE
513 Fleming St.
(305) 294-2904
This shop sells everything from the classics to the best sellers, along with topical nonfiction and the works of Florida Keys and Key West writers—often at below-market prices. This store is especially supportive of Florida authors and often hosts book-signing events that generate lots of local excitement and a party atmosphere. Carl Hiaasen, James Hall, Jimmy Buffett, Philip Caputo, James Dickey, and Thomas McGuane have all signed books here. Be sure to check the rare-book room in the back.

KEY WEST KITE COMPANY
409 Greene St.
(305) 296-2535
The Key West Kite Company is just waiting to make windy days wondrous with flags, banners, and flying tours. The first kite store to set up shop in all of Florida, Key West Kites offers everything from handmade to high-performance sport kites. There's a great selection of yo-yos here, too, plus juggling supplies and instructions.

KEY WEST WINERY, INC.
103 Simonton St.
(305) 292-1717, (866) 880-1717
www.thekeywestwinery.com
This is wine like you've never tasted before. Not one variety is made from grapes! These wines live up to Key West's tropical image—laid-back, funky, and packed with pizzazz. All the wines are made from a potpourri of fruits, such as Eleganta, a semisweet red raspberry variety that won a silver medal at the Indiana International Wine Competition in 1999. Also medal winners: Hot Sun, a dry white wine with a slight tomato taste and a

hint of peppers; Orange Sunshine, a semi-sweet wine made from 100 percent fresh-squeezed Florida orange juice; and 40 Karats, a buttery semidry white wine that is similar to a Chardonnay, but 100 percent carrot and much more flavorful. You'll find many, many more interesting fruit wines here, and best of all, you can stop in and taste as many wines as you want, seven days a week.

KINO SANDALS
107 Fitzpatrick St.
(305) 294-5044
www.kinosandalfactory.com
When Roberto "Kino" and Margarite Lopez immigrated from Cuba they had no idea their Kino sandals would be so well received. Roberto had a factory in Cuba and after working several odd jobs in Key West, he opened a sandal factory here in 1966. Using his nickname, Kino, for the business, he built a lovely Cuban-style factory that is still in operation today. The high ceilings in the factory allow the heat to drift outside while the terra-cotta tiled floors remain cool. Here you pick from a variety of leathers and colors for your custom sandals. Prices are very reasonable, and they make a terrific souvenir. A constant reminder of your trip to the Florida Keys, there's nothing like happy feet!

LILLY PULITZER
600 Front St.
(305) 295-0995
www.lillypulitzer.com
In 1960 a young socialite, Lilly Pulitzer, opened a juice stand in West Palm Beach. When her uniform seemed more popular than her juice, the famous "Lillys" were created. Jackie Kennedy was photographed in Life magazine wearing one, and from then on everyone had to have the Florida shift.

Today, Lilly Pulitzer shops offer the signature piece in tropical green and hot pink, along with bright and fun prints in various other tantalizing colors. She has also extended her line to include jewelry, shoes, home accents, and a clothing line for children.

LOCAL COLOR
274 Margaret St., Key West Historic Seaport
(305) 292-3635
www.localcolorkeywest.com
The Margaret Street shop is where locals and tourists alike come to purchase the colorful, comfortable clothing that fits the Key West lifestyle. In addition to casual apparel for men and women, you'll find fun hats, handbags, and costume jewelry to complete

"KW" Jewelry

Created in Key West for Key Westers and visitors, this jewelry design has made a huge hit with men, women, and kids. The design features the initials "KW" hooked together, with a braided nautical wrap signifying the tribute to Key West and the islands' connection to the sea. For those who wear such pieces, this symbol means they will always return here. A lot of stores carry these items, but to insure you are getting the real thing, the following list is a good guide: Local Color, 276 Margaret St. (305-292-3635) and 425 Greene St. (305-296-0151); Commotion, 800 Caroline St. (305-292-3364); Lili's, 424 Greene St. (305-292-2343); or www.keywestbracelet.com.

your island look. The Greene Street location (425 Greene St.; 305-296-0151) is the place to shop for inexpensive, fun jewelry to adorn your neck, ears, wrists, fingers, even ankles and toes.

MACINTOSH SYSTEMS SOLUTIONS
1011 Truman Ave.
(305) 293-1888
www.macintoshsolutions.biz
Offering a wide range of Apple hardware, software andaccessories, Macintosh Solutions makes the Florida Keys tech savvy. The owners have been serving our community since 2000 as a mobile support and service company, and with their brick and mortar location, we don't have to drive all the way to Miami to get our Mac fix—or get our Mac fixed, for that matter!

MILLIE'S
425 Front St.
(305) 294-6877
Want to be in the UK and Key West at the same time? Stop in at Millie's and you will have done just that. Everything British is here from Spotted Dick Pudding to British daily newspapers to Cadbury chocolates. Why, the Queen mum herself greets you (in a comical depiction) at the front door!

PELICAN POOP SHOP
314 Simonton St.
(305) 292-9955
www.pelicanpoopshoppe.com
This eclectic collection of artwork includes originals from all over the Caribbean. If you're in the market for a life-size, stone Mayan deer dancer or a Haitian oil-drum sculpture, this is the place to come. For a small purchase or a nominal admittance fee, you can tour the private Casa Antigua gardens out back,

linked forever to Ernest Hemingway by a quirky twist of fate. He completed A Farewell to Arms here while awaiting delivery of his new Ford back in 1928.

Long after Hemingway left Key West, this building became a hotel, then later the island's largest brothel, and its first drag club. Today it is home to City Commissioner Tom Oosterhoudt and his mother, Mary Ann Worth. On your visit to the gardens, you will hear Tom himself recount the colorful history of the building in a six-minute audio presentation.

THE RED CHANDELIER BOUTIQUE
1075 Duval St., #18 Duval Square
(305) 294-6227
www.redchandelierkw.com
You've heard the phrase "dress for success." Well, here at the Red Chandelier you can "dress for Key West." Light, breezy and affordable dresses, tops, skirts, shoes, jeans, and accessories are geared toward the tropical shopper. Don't forget to say "hi" to the resident mascot, Mambo, and no, the darling is not for sale!

REEF RELIEF ENVIRONMENTAL CENTER & STORE
631 Greene St.
(305) 294-3100
www.reefrelief.org
You can learn about our fragile coral reef here at the Reef Relief Environmental Center. Continuous videos, displays, and free information will heighten your awareness of what you can do to protect North America's only living coral reef. Merchandise on sale includes coral reef books, educational products for both adults and children, and informational videos.

THE RESTAURANT STORE
1111 Eaton St.
(305) 294-7994
www.keywestchef.com
The Restaurant Store is chock-full of kitchen and cooking gear to feed 5 or 50. You'll discover state-of-the-art utensils, pots and pans, and accessories for culinary aficionados and chefs alike. This store is nirvana for foodies.

SCRUBS OF KEY WEST
MM 87.8 Oceanside, Islamorada
(305) 853-1700
www.scrubskeywest.com
Scrubs are not necessarily just for surgeons anymore. Nor do the loose-fitting shirts and drawstring pants have to be hospital green. Scrubs of Key West stitches them up in all manner of tropical prints—fish, palm trees, lizards, and the like. And although plenty of local doctors, nurses, dentists, and hygienists shop here, nonmedical types have discovered that this is a great place to buy casual wear and gifts—like soft fabric handbags, keychains, and eyeglass cases. A second location is at 720 Caroline St. (305-295-7232).

STYLE KEY WEST
313 Margaret St.
(305) 292-4004
www.stylekeywest.com
The sweetness and enchantment of this shop are a reflection of the husband and wife team that owns Style Key West. The furniture pieces, accessories, and colors that grace the walls, including items tastefully placed around the shop, make you want to go home and replace all that you own with everything they showcase. They offer classic tropical pieces with such appeal that you

can decorate your castle in the tropics or your chateau back home.

VOLTAIRE BOOKS
330 Simonton St.
(305) 296-3226
www.voltairebooks.com
This boutique bookstore greets customers with a cozy, friendly, welcoming atmosphere. Comfy upholstered seating and fresh-brewed java are part of the charm of Voltaire Books. Great resource for tropical reading as most of their inventory is Florida Keys themes by local authors, past and present.

> **i** Monroe County (which is all of the Florida Keys) was created in 1823 and named for the fifth U.S. president, James Monroe. Duval Street, in Key West, is named after William Pope Duval, Florida's first territorial governor, serving from April 1822 to April 1834. He was appointed by President James Monroe.

Way off Duval

BARGAIN BOOKS AND NEWSSTAND
1028 Truman Ave.
(305) 294-7446
South Florida's largest retailer of pre-read books is right here on our tiny island. Wander through room after slightly dusty room of fiction, sci-fi, romance, and other literature. A couple of cats may find your lap a cozy spot to take a nap as you sit in one of the comfortable chairs and peruse a favorite title. If you love books and you love a bargain, you won't be disappointed. But be prepared to spend some time here. Half the fun of finding your bargain book is in the search for it.

BORDERS EXPRESS
2212 North Roosevelt Blvd.
(305) 294-5419
www.borders.com

Not surprisingly, this is Key West's largest bookstore and, perhaps, its most visible. It's a stand-alone shop on US 1 with plenty of free parking. On the inside, the store looks much like every other Borders Express you've ever been in, with a notable exception: Right up front, there's a huge display of titles by Key West authors as well as an impressive array of books on a variety of Florida-related subjects. In addition to several guides to Key West and Florida Keys attractions, you'll find island cookbooks, maps, history tomes, and nature guides to help you identify our native flora and fauna. You'll also find especially helpful clerks here as well as frequent book signings and sales, the proceeds of which are often earmarked for local charities.

DOG 30
1025 White St.
(305) 296-4848
www.dogthirty.com

The Florida Keys residents love their animals, and here at Dog 30 they show how much they care. The owners carry healthy dog food, homemade bakery treats, dog beds, carriers, and even catnip. Stop in and check out the resident pooch, Blue, a Catahoula Leopard Hound that is bred to hunt wild boar.

ISLE STYLE
1204 Simonton St.
(305) 292-4000

Step inside this diminutive cocoon packed with designs from local jewelry artisans,

one-of-a-kind clothing, and vintage handbags and meet an owner who is a "stylist." The stock changes frequently, so one visit may not fill your shopping bag. On the property is also a spa. So, you can shop till you drop, be revived, and do it all over again.

LILO SURF SHOP
813 North Roosevelt Blvd.
Kmart Shopping Center
(305) 294-1800

The Keys might not be known for surfing waters, but you can still look the part. Located at the Hurricane Hole Marina, the Lilo Surf Shop has the coolest selection of surf apparel. The owner stocks everything from Reef and Rainbow sandals, T-shirts, shorts, and swimsuits to skim boards, skateboards, hats, and, of course, surfboards. Just about everything for you cool surfer-dudes!

i The New Town area along North Roosevelt Boulevard is often overlooked by shoppers enamored with the funky shops of Old Town. But this is where the locals shop. A series of strip malls or plazas—Kennedy Drive, Key Plaza, Luani Plaza, Overseas Market, Searstown—are within blocks of each other and feature the staples of everyday life as offered by major retail chain stores.

SEAM SHOPPE
1114 Truman Ave.
(305) 296-9830
www.tropicalfabricsonline.com

This fabric shop offers a fabulous selection of tropical fabrics for fashion, quilting, and home decor. Patterns include fish, shells, Hawaiian themes, nautical, palm trees, and tropical foliage. You'll find batiks and bark cloth here as well.

TIMMY TUXEDOS
812 Fleming St.
(305) 294-8897
www.timmytuxedos.com
In spite of what you may think about the Keys dress code of flip-flops and T-shirts, we do dress up occasionally, and Timmy's Tuxedos is the only formal attire shop in the Keys. Here you can buy all the "dress-up" garb you need, plus rent jackets and tuxedos. They also carry beautiful Keys prints for ties and cummerbunds, to make that formal gathering tropical.

LIVING HERE

In this section we feature specific information for residents or those planning to relocate here. Topics include real estate, education, health care, and much more.

RELOCATION AND VACATION RENTALS

Most snowbirds and full-time residents of the Florida Keys (except for the native-born Conchs) first rented homes, condominiums, or mobile homes while on vacation in Paradise. Rentals primarily are classified as short-term and long-term. Short-term rental agreements range from a weekend to six months; anything exceeding six months is considered a long-term rental. However, to preserve the integrity of our residential communities, the Monroe County Planning Commission has prohibited short-term rentals of 30 days or less throughout residential areas of unincorporated Monroe County. Incorporated areas such as Islamorada, Layton, Key Colony Beach, Marathon, and Key West can opt for differing regulations. Few short-term rental options are currently available in the Florida Keys, and the competition is fierce for those that are. The best advice we can offer is to work through a rental agent who knows what's legally available and always book your accommodation early.

OVERVIEW

Unlike long-term tenants, short-term tenants are required by the state of Florida to pay an 12.5 percent sales tax. Generally not incorporated into the price quoted for short-term rentals, this tax includes the same tourist bed tax charged by hotels, motels, inns, and resorts for maintaining, advertising, and promoting our facilities and attractions. Quotes for short-term rentals do, however, typically include furnishings and utilities, with the exception of long-distance phone calls.

Owning a parcel of Paradise in the Florida Keys can be summed up in two words: very expensive. Real estate prices in the Florida Keys depend largely upon access to the water. Direct oceanfront or bayfront property garners the highest prices, followed by property on a canal with an ocean or bay

view, and by property on a canal with access to the ocean or bay. Other areas, such as Ocean Reef, Duck Key, and Sunset Key, have special features that make homes desirable—such as gated security, golf courses, swimming pools, strict building covenants, and other community amenities—and owning a home there is pricey, indeed.

Some relief is available for certain owners in the form of a homestead exemption. In Florida this exemption allows $25,000 of the assessed value of a house purchased as a primary residence to be exempt from property tax. Real estate taxes in Monroe County are based on a millage rate that changes annually with the county budget and are some of the highest in the state. In addition, besides homeowner's insurance, homeowners must factor in the cost of windstorm and flood insurance to guard against our ever-threatening hurricanes.

Those of us who have chosen to live in the Florida Keys think the price of Paradise is worth it. To assist you in your search for a piece of the rock, we provide you with a general overview of the communities of the Florida Keys, as well as the types of homes you'll encounter in our neighborhoods. At the end of the chapter, we include listings of real estate professionals who can assist you in finding a rental property or a home of your own. Look to our Key West section of this chapter for vacation rental and real estate information in our southernmost city.

RENTAL PROPERTIES

The Role of Real Estate Agents

Real estate agents handle most short-term rental properties. The exceptions are condominiums that act as hotels and employ on-site managers (see the Accommodations chapter) and homeowners who market rentals on their own. Because of changes in laws as indicated above, the latter choice is becoming more and more scarce.

Depending upon its size and specialty, an agency that handles rentals may list anywhere between 10 and 200-plus short-term rental options. Most large agencies employ sales associates who specialize in short-term rentals. Except for Key West, where agents handle much of the entire island, Florida Keys agents typically specialize within the region of their office (see the Real Estate Companies section in this chapter).

Finding a rental property through an agency has its advantages. Rental agencies almost always offer descriptions and photographs of available properties and advice on the best option for your needs and desires.

Most of them, in fact, maintain Web sites, which allow you to peruse the options at your leisure and, in most cases, actually see the property you are booking. Agents ensure that a home is clean and that its grounds are maintained.

In order to manage short-term rentals for stays of fewer than 30 days, real estate agencies and/or property owners and managers of condominium complexes must be licensed by the state of Florida. Units rented for fewer than 30 days are considered resort dwellings, and agents and/or owners and managers must therefore abide by a Florida statute that applies to hotels and restaurants. Depending upon the category of accommodation (condominium or single-family home, for instance), safety and health standards set by this statute may require fire extinguishers, electric smoke detectors in sleeping areas, mattress covers on all beds, and deadbolt locks on doors.

Seasonal Rates

As Old Man Winter rolls around, travelers flock to the Florida Keys seeking respite from cold and snow. Referred to locally as "snowbirds," these visitors drive rental rates up between the months of December and April, the high season.

Summertime is when diving is typically best (see the Diving and Snorkeling chapter). It's also the time of year when residents throughout Florida head to the Keys for the relief of the ocean breezes. However, the rest of the mass market moves back home, so rents may be a bit lower than high season during the months of May through August.

September through November is relatively quiet tourism-wise, because autumn is the prime season for hurricanes in the Florida Keys. During this period you'll find reduced rates, and, as long as you keep a watchful eye on the forecasts, you'll be able to enjoy uncrowded shops, attractions, and streets.

Minimum Stays

Most short-term tenants rent a home or condominium in the Florida Keys for a week to three or four months. The bulk of the short-term rental market consists of two-week vacationers, but our islands are also popular with northern residents and retirees who retreat here for the winter. Virtually no private homes are available for rent on a daily basis (see the Accommodations chapter).

During holidays, such as Christmas and Easter, and special events, including sport lobster season and Fantasy Fest, minimum stays range from four days to two weeks. Individual property owners establish these policies. Inquire of your rental agent or property owner/manager.

Options and Restrictions

Owners designate their rental properties as smoking or nonsmoking. The number of nonsmoking properties is growing.

Children are generally welcome, but some condominium complexes restrict the number of children allowed in a single unit. One adults-only facility, Silver Shores, a mobile-home park in Key Largo catering to senior citizens, exists in the Florida Keys.

Condominiums typically do not allow pets, but some single-family homes and mobile-home parks do accept them. An additional security deposit or a fee (sometimes both) is often required. The fee covers the cost of spraying the home for fleas, which ensures accommodations free of pesky insects. Tending to pets outside

the rental facility, however, is the owner's responsibility, and fleas can be abundant on hot and humid days.

i In the 1950s, Philip Toppino built houses on Summerland Key for avid pilots. The homes sit along the airstrip and you can park your private plane underneath the house.

Reservations and Payment Options

Naturally, the most desirable rental properties tend to book the earliest, and many tenants book the same home for the same weeks year after year. To achieve the greatest selection of rentals, we suggest that you reserve at least six months to a year in advance. During holidays, the demand for short-term rentals can exhaust the supply. If you plan to travel to the Florida Keys during the high season (Dec through Apr) and holidays (especially Christmas week or during Fantasy Fest), you would be wise to reserve one to two years in advance.

Payment options vary according to how far in advance you book and when you check in. Typically, an initial deposit of 10 to 25 percent of the total rental cost, made with a personal check or a credit card, will hold a unit. If you book a rental unit one year in advance, you frequently can opt for an installment plan. The balance typically is paid 30 to 60 days prior to your arrival. Some agents allow you to pay with cash or credit card upon arrival, provided that you check in during office hours, which vary from agency to agency. Ask about these specifics when you call.

When you book a unit, your real estate agent will mail you a lease application and reservation agreement that must be completed and returned with a rental deposit.

Reservation agreements will list the address and telephone number of the property so you can notify family and friends accordingly.

Security Deposits

Your rental agreement holds you responsible for any damage to the dwelling and its contents. Security deposits provide the homeowner with added protection and a means of paying any telephone charges not billed to your credit card. As a general rule, count on supplying 50 to 75 percent of one week's rent (slightly more for a monthly rental). Security deposits on large homes with expensive furnishings can be much higher.

If you have opted for an installment plan, you will pay the security deposit with your final payment when you check in. The deposit often is returned in the mail two weeks to one month after your departure, or after the homeowner's telephone bill is received and a damage assessment completed.

Cancellation Policies

Homeowners set monetary penalties for cancellations anywhere between 30 days in advance of reservations, with a nominal cancellation fee for administrative services, to 60 days in advance, with a full refund. Don't assume that an impending hurricane or other emergency beyond your control will warrant a refund of your payment. In such cases, some homeowners may be generous in providing full or partial refunds or offering credit toward accommodations at a future date—but don't bank on it. Generally, you forfeit your deposit when weather emergencies cancel your vacation plans.

Refund policies are negotiated among the tenant, real estate agency, and property owner and usually are not included in lease agreements. Many real estate agencies sell trip insurance, whereby a third party will refund the full cost of a vacation rental for which you have paid a portion but not used. These policies typically cost 5 percent of the total dollars at risk.

REAL ESTATE: COMMUNITY OVERVIEWS

Upper Keys

Key Largo

Key Largo is popular with divers interested in the abundant reefs within John Pennekamp Coral Reef State Park and the Florida Keys National Marine Sanctuary. And because Key Largo is within 20 miles of the mainland, property here often is in great demand by weekday commuters and South Floridians purchasing weekend retreats. In real estate terms, Key Largo generally includes the exclusive, members-only Ocean Reef subdivision at the extreme northeast edge and encompasses all land southwest to Tavernier.

Ocean Reef

A luxury subdivision in North Key Largo, Ocean Reef is a private, all-inclusive gated community of large single-family homes, condominiums, and town houses. Properties here attract buyers seeking privacy, exclusivity, and the opportunity to fish, dive, snorkel, swim, shop, and dine out without ever leaving the complex. This community has three golf courses, a marina, and other amenities open only to residents.

Tavernier

Toward the southern end of Key Largo is Tavernier, one of the Florida Keys' oldest settlements. Some Tavernier homes date from the early farming settlements at the turn of the past century. Plantation Key (its northern end also maintains a Tavernier postal designation) has a wide range of real estate opportunities, with single-family subdivisions primarily bayside. The Snake Creek Drawbridge makes Plantation Key an ideal homesite for owners of large yachts and sailboats.

Islamorada

In 2008, *National Geographic* placed Islamorada on their list of top 12 cities in which to live and play. No other city in Florida even made it in the top 50! Islamorada, which was incorporated in 1998, stretches from Plantation Key to Lower Matecumbe. Lot sizes in Islamorada typically are larger than those in other areas of the Florida Keys, a factor intended to attract builders of large, impressive homes. Upper Matecumbe Key is the heart of Islamorada, commercially developed but with homes tucked along the waterfront in quiet residential areas. Lower Matecumbe Key is Islamorada's predominantly residential island, with a bike path, tennis club, and private beach.

Layton

The late Del Layton, a Miami grocery store owner, developed tiny Layton into a subdivision in the 1950s. Later he incorporated it as the Florida Keys' smallest city. Except for several oceanfront homes, all single-family residences in Layton are on oceanside canals, with the nearby Channel 5 Bridge allowing access to the bay. Fifteen miles from Marathon and Islamorada, Layton is largely a community of retirees, with a population of approximately 250.

Middle Keys

Duck Key

Duck Key is composed of five islands connected by white Venetian-style bridges. A series of flow-through canals encircle each island, ensuring that nearly half the homes or lots offer canalfront dockage or open-water views. The uniquely situated islands allow direct access to both the ocean and the Gulf of Mexico. The Duck Key Property Owners Association, an active group, maintains rights-of-way and public area plantings, has established distinctive signage, and sponsors social events throughout the year. Duck Key Club, a private swim and tennis club, is located on Center Island and also sponsors myriad social activities for its members. Residents pay a small out-of-pocket tax to employ a private security firm to supplement county services. Hawk's Cay Resort is on the first island, Indies Island, which is zoned differently from the rest. The other four islands—Center, Plantation, Harbour, and Yacht Club—are designated for single-family residential housing only. All homes must be of concrete-block-style (CBS) construction.

Grassy Key

Grassy Key, a sleepy, rural island with a few oceanfront bungalow courts and several restaurants, is distanced from Marathon by preservation lands. With no canals on Grassy Key, there is no pricing middle ground. The area has single-family homes on dry lots or waterfront estates along the Gulf of Mexico and the Atlantic. Grassy Key is now a part of incorporated Marathon.

Key Colony Beach

Incorporated in 1957, Key Colony Beach—a 285-acre peninsular finger surrounded by incorporated Marathon—developed its property with a row of condominiums directly on the Atlantic and single-family homes built on a series of canals. Key Colony Beach employs its own police and enforces its own signage and zoning ordinances. Accessed by a causeway from US 1, Key Colony Beach has a post office and a few small shops and restaurants.

Marathon

Marathon was heavily developed in the 1950s, when dredging was relatively commonplace. This area probably has more canals and waterways—and thus more canalfront properties—than any other region of Monroe County; however, with no active zoning ordinances for all these years, in some neighborhoods it is not uncommon to find a run-down mobile home situated next to an upscale canalfront dwelling. Marathon was incorporated in 1999 and now has its own mayor and city commission, as well as the ability to levy citywide property taxes. Marathon is the commercial hub of the Florida Keys, featuring supermarkets, a movie theater, Home Depot, Office Depot, Kmart, and other shops and restaurants.

Lower Keys

Big Pine Key

This rural, semi-isolated island has acres of open space and limited development potential. Home to the National Key Deer Refuge, this island is popular with many Key West and Marathon workday commuters. This area probably offers the best value for the money in affordable housing.

Little Torch and Ramrod Keys

Little Torch Key and Ramrod Key have a rural feeling, with homes on both the Atlantic and the Gulf of Mexico as well as on dry lots. These communities aren't far from Key West.

Summerland, Cudjoe, and Sugarloaf Keys

Heading closer to Key West and into the more exclusive subdivisions of Summerland, Cudjoe, and Sugarloaf Keys, you'll find luxurious properties. Summerland features a number of waterfront homes, along with a small airstrip that allows residents to park their private airplanes directly beneath their homes.

Baypoint, Shark Key, Big Coppitt, and Key Haven

Shark Key is a gated community developed with strict architectural guidelines. Large open-water lots on Shark Key are beautifully landscaped, and houses set on them typically are very expensive. Baypoint, Big Coppitt, and Key Haven are in demand for their convenient location, only minutes from Key West.

KINDS OF PROPERTIES

Condominiums

Condominiums are scattered throughout the Upper and Middle Keys, and many home buyers find them to be a low-maintenance way to keep up a part-time residence. For full-time residents, condos commonly offer amenities not always available in a single-family home, such as swimming pools, fitness facilities, saunas, hot tubs, boat dockage, and covered parking.

During our peak tourist season (generally Dec through Apr), condominiums often are teeming with activity, affording residents the opportunity to meet renters from across the country. When the low season rolls around and occupancy typically drops to 30 percent or less at any given time, full-time residents have the facilities nearly all to themselves. If you plan to become a full-time Florida Keys resident in a condominium, be sure to check on whether the complex you have your eye on maintains an active rental program. You may not enjoy living alongside transient residents.

What you'll pay for a condo depends on the size of the unit, its location, and its view. You also need to factor monthly maintenance fees into the overall cost; these increase with unit sizes and cover maintenance of the common area, a reserve account for future major repairs, and insurance for damage by flood, wind, storm, peril, and salt air. (See the Close-up in this chapter.)

Mobile Homes

First the good news: A mobile home is the least expensive real estate you can buy in the Florida Keys. The bad news? Most vulnerable to hurricane damage, mobile homes are the first properties ordered for evacuation during severe-storm watches in the Florida Keys. Zoning ordinances restrict mobile homes to specific communities.

Often the least expensive mobile homes are those that have existed in residential subdivisions since before zoning ordinances were established. These mobile homes, which have individual septic tanks, lack the recreational and service-oriented amenities typically offered in mobile-home communities here.

Buyers who purchase property in a mobile-home community pay more but frequently enjoy a clubhouse atmosphere complete with a swimming pool, shuffleboard court, boat ramp, dockage, on-site manager, sewage treatment, and a convenience store. The price of any mobile home increases with

a concrete or wood-frame addition—an elevated Florida room, built-up gravel roof, poured concrete slab, and other features.

Single-Family Homes

Dry-lot homes—those not fronting a water view or canal—are the least expensive single-family home option in the Keys. Canal-front homes generally sell for much more, with homes on the open water usually in the millions. Because many real estate purchases here are made by boaters, homes that sit closer to a bridge—providing access to both the ocean and the bay—sell more quickly.

Since 1975, the county has required that most homes be constructed of concrete block, be positioned on stilts, and have hurricane shutters. Nonconforming structures built before the 1975 ordinance took effect have been grandfathered, but if 50 percent or more of the dollar value of a nonconforming use structure is destroyed and requires rebuilding, new zoning laws and building restrictions apply.

Much of a buyer's decision to purchase a home in the Florida Keys depends upon the structure's ability to withstand a hurricane. Concrete-block-style (CBS) homes are considered more solid than those made of wood. Most are elevated on stilts to avoid potential flooding. CBS stilt homes typically cost more than ground-level CBS homes of comparable sizes. CBS homes typically command higher prices than all-wood frame structures.

A large percentage of Lower Keys homes are factory-built, wood-frame modulars. Because they are constructed under controlled circumstances and designed to withstand 135 mph winds, some homeowners believe they're stronger than wood-frame homes built on the site.

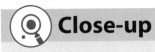

Close-up

Hot—It's Not

Key Wester and famed playwright Tennessee Williams' *Cat on a Hot Tin Roof* is a slinky, sensual, artistic play and movie. In the real world of tin roofs, the title could not be further from the truth. Thomas Jefferson was an advocate of tin roofs and used one for his home, Monticello (construction began in 1768 and ended in 1809).

Prior to tin roofs, copper was imported from England until the end of the 18th century, when rolling sheet metal was developed in America. Corrugated, stiffened sheets allowed greater span over lighter framework, thus decreasing installation time and labor. In 1857, one of the first metal roofs in the south was on the U.S. Mint in New Orleans. In the late 19th century, patterned tin roofs were all the rage as they are today. The durability of these roofs proves they hold up during hurricanes, heat from the sun reflects off the metal, and lightning discharges over the metal thus helping to prevent the spread of fires. Long used on barns and rural out structures, they hold an authentic simplistic charm of another era. Resurgence in metal roofing in newer homes is on the increase due to attractive designs, the distinctive look to be more compatible with historic neighborhoods, and the fact that the metals may be recycled. Wend the streets on foot or trolley (one should be *A Street Car Named Desire*) of Old Town in Key West, cast your eyes skyward, over the delicious cakelike, gingerbread trimmed, historic homes, and marvel at the icing of tin on the roofs of these beautiful ladies. The Tennessee Williams home on Duncan Street still sports a metal roof and is as charming today as when the famous owner was in residence in this southernmost city. As Maggie or Blanche will attest, tin roofs on vintage homes are "hot" commodities in the ever-sizzling south Florida real estate market.

If you are considering buying a home in the Florida Keys, landscaping also may influence your decision. Some buyers prefer intricate vegetation, which requires costly irrigation, while others want low-maintenance pearock and xeriscaping (landscaping using indigenous plantings that require no irrigation).

REAL ESTATE COMPANIES

Though all Florida Keys agents share a multiple listing service (MLS) with properties available throughout Monroe County, each agency tends to specialize in its own territory. We describe some of the largest agencies for sales and rentals in the sections that follow. This is not meant to be a comprehensive listing by any means. For a complete list, consult the Yellow Pages for the appropriate communities, or pick up copies of the many real estate guides available free of charge at supermarkets and other locations throughout Monroe County. See our Key West section for real estate companies in that city.

Upper Keys

COLDWELL BANKER SCHMITT REAL ESTATE
MM 100 Bayside, Key Largo
(305) 451-4422 or (877) 289-0035
www.realestatefloridakeys.com

Coldwell Banker Schmitt covers the Florida Keys' real estate sales and rental market from one end of US 1 to the other. In addition to these two offices, which serve the Upper Keys, the firm also maintains offices in Marathon, Big Pine Key, and Key West (see separate listings below).

> **i** Driving along our residential streets, our neighborhoods look like any small town. But every once in awhile you see a house or building that is completely entombed in a red and yellow circus-like tent. These are signs that the exterminators are at work! In the tropical Florida Keys, we have all sorts of critters that a can of bug spray just won't eradicate.

MARR PROPERTIES
MM 100 Bayside, Key Largo
(305) 451-4078 or (800) 277-3728
www.floridakeysproperties.com

Serving the Keys since 1965, this office offers sales of commercial and residential properties and a knowledge of the upper Keys real estate market.

EXIT REALTY FLORIDA KEYS
MM 91 Oceanside, Tavernier
(305) 852-4442 or (888) 881-3948
www.exitfloridakeys.com

Residential and commercial sales are the thrust of this company. They also offer annual and vacation rentals as well as property management services. Two other locations are at MM 50 Bayside in Marathon (305-743-9292, 888-825-9292) and MM 31 Bayside in Big Pine Key (305-872-1133, 888-288-1133).

FREEWHEELER REALTY
MM 98.5 Bayside, Key Largo
(305) 852-4400 or (877) 852-4450
www.freewheeler-realty.com

Freewheeler deals in property management, rentals, and sales for homes, condos, villas, and efficiencies on the beach, bay, and canal. Another location is at MM 86 Bayside in Islamorada (305-664-4444, 866-664-2075).

AMERICAN CARIBBEAN REAL ESTATE INC.
MM 81.8 Bayside, Islamorada
(305) 664-4966
www.americancaribbean.com

American Caribbean handles over 100 properties for sale or rent from Duck Key to Key Largo.

Middle Keys

THE WATERFRONT SPECIALIST
MM 54 Oceanside, 80th St. Station, Marathon
(305) 743-0644 or (800) 342-6398
www.waterfrontspecialists.com

Despite its name, this agency can direct you to sales and rental opportunities both on and off the water.

COLDWELL BANKER SCHMITT REAL ESTATE
MM 52.5 Bayside, Marathon
(305) 743-5181 or (800) 366-5181
www.realestatefloridakeys.com

Sales and vacation rentals in the Middle Keys are the focus at this office of a firm that covers the real estate market from one end of the Keys to the other (see other listings in this section).

AMERICAN CARIBBEAN REAL ESTATE INC.
MM 52 Oceanside, Marathon
(305) 743-7636 or (800) 940-7636
www.acresales.com
American Caribbean specializes in Middle Keys sales and rental properties from Duck Key to Key Largo.

RE/MAX KEY TO THE KEYS
MM 49.5 Bayside, Marathon
(305) 743-2300 or (800) 743-2301
www.wilkinsonteam.com
Agents handle sales and rental properties from Long Key to Big Coppitt.

Lower Keys

COLDWELL BANKER SCHMITT REAL ESTATE
MM 30.5 Oceanside, Big Pine Key
(305) 872-3050 or (800) 488-3050
www.realestatefloridakeys.com
Sales and vacation rentals in Big Pine and the Lower Keys are the focus of this office.

ERA LOWER KEYS REALTY
MM 30 Oceanside, Big Pine Key
(305) 872-2258 or (800) 859-7642
www.eralowerkeysrealty.com
This establishment deals with sales and rentals in the Lower Keys.

ACTION KEYS REALTY, INC.
MM 24.8 Oceanside or Summerland Key
(305) 745-1323, (800) 874-1323
www.actionkeysrealty.com
In addition to residential sales throughout the Lower Keys, this agency handles vacation rentals, primarily on Summerland, Ramrod, and Little Torch Keys.

PRIVATE ISLANDS, HOMES, AND HIDEAWAYS

Picture yourself in the following locations and soon you will know the meaning of "lost in paradise." Vacationing at its finest, these properties will leave you not believing: You were where? On an island? Out in the middle of the ocean? On a helicopter pad? Aboard a private skiff? Only one word can sum it up: fabulous.

ALLIGATOR REEF
MM 86 Bayside, Islamorada
(305) 664-2075 or (866) 664-2075
www.floridavacations.com
Need 10 bedrooms, 4 kitchens, 2 heated pools, 8 bathrooms, and accommodations for 25 people? Then Alligator Reef compound is for you! With an observation deck overlooking the Atlantic Ocean, you can relax or enjoy all of the amenities on the property. Go kayaking, play Ping-Pong, swim, or swing in the hammocks. Do it all or nothing—this getaway packs a true "tropical punch."

EAST SISTER ROCK ISLAND
MM 50 Oceanside, Marathon
(305) 446-7377 or (305) 446-7377
www.valuevacationrentals.com
Piloting your own 21-foot Carolina skiff to and from the mainland of Marathon, you travel to your island in the sun, East Sister Rock Island. Completely surrounded by a moat, the house sits on a coral reef. A 12-foot veranda swings around the 5,000-square-foot home. This a diver's and snorkeler's haven. If that isn't your bag, then you can swim in the pool or a bigger "pool"—the Atlantic Ocean! If the skiff is too slow for your entrance—or exit—there is a helicopter pad on the grounds.

TERRA'S KEY
MM 79.3 Oceanside, Islamorada
(305) 664-2361
www.terraskey.com

Located off Islamorada is Terra's Key (also known as Tea Table Key). This sun-drenched seven-acre private island is connected to US 1 by a causeway. Five bedrooms, six bathrooms, tennis court, heated pool with a wet bar, and inspiring vistas of the Atlantic Ocean make this a setting for a vacation you will never forget.

VIVA ON DUVAL
1224 Duval St.
(305) 294-7358 or (800) 404-2802
www.vivaonduval.com

Built in 1935, and named after the late Key West City Commissioner Jose Valdes' wife "Viva," this gleaming white home glows in the bright Key West sun. In 2007, the heirs of the estate beautifully restored this piece of Key West–Cuban architectural history that now awaits your arrival. The design is neoclassic, with triangular pediment, wraparound porches, stately columns at the main entrance, and a widow's walk atop the home. First greeting you, inside the impressive entrance hall, are polished wood floors and a grand banister winding to the second floor. Twelve-foot ceilings in the downstairs area open into the living room, dining room, laundry room, and kitchen. Outside the kitchen is a private pool and landscaped garden. Upstairs there are three bedroom suites with two king-size beds and one queen-size bed, and all bedrooms have plasma TVs. This stately home is smoke free and no pets allowed. Once here, you can walk to many shops, restaurants, and attractions as Viva On Duval is in the hub of things to do. This elegant vintage mansion is ideal for a family vacation or executive retreat.

KEY WEST

Despite the fact that Key West is heavily developed, with both old and new homes on generally small lots throughout the city, real estate agents report that the demand for homes far outstrips the island's supply. Also, while waterfront property is a prime attraction for home buyers throughout the rest of the Florida Keys, it is rarely found in Key West, because commercial development lines all waterfront areas. Nevertheless, real estate in the southernmost city is expensive.

The island of Key West is an incorporated city governed by local elected representatives as well as by Monroe County. Consequently, the property tax structure here includes both city and county government expenses. Key West has its own land-use plan with zoning ordinances, permitting units, density requirements, and building height and setback minimums. Within the historic district of Old Town, another layer of control and review exists. The five-member Historical Architecture Review Commission (HARC) reviews applications for improvements and new construction. Established in 1986, HARC works to ensure the integrity of the historic district.

Key West offers a selection of styles in single-family homes, town houses, and condominiums. The island has few mobile home parks, and the only mobile-home communities here are small and hidden away. There are also several on Stock Island.

Town houses, typically adjoining structures with a common wall, allow homeowners to own the ground beneath them. The center of the common wall is the dividing line, and party wall agreements determine who maintains responsibility in cases of repair or destruction.

If you wish to purchase beachfront housing, owning a condominium is without a doubt the way to go. Along the south side of Key West are several relatively new, multistory beachfront condominiums with elevators, enclosed parking, pools, tennis courts, and hot tubs. Units range in size from one bedroom, one bath to three or four bedrooms and two or three baths. Only a few units have waterfront or partial water views, however.

The majority of single-family homes in Key West are in areas known as Old Town, Mid Town, and New Town, and real estate agents further break two of these regions into "old" and "new" Old Town and "old" and "new" New Town. Boundaries are roughly established, with some overflow, and within all Key West areas you'll discover a diverse array of properties dating from between the early 1800s and the late 1900s.

Convenience to the water or to touristy Duval Street is not usually a factor in the cost of Key West property. Rather, prices generally depend on the size and condition of the house, its lot, and its location. The island itself is only 2 miles long by 4 miles wide, so beaches and harbors are never far away. Some home buyers seek property as far from the busy roadways and attractions as possible.

Community Profiles

Old Town

Settled in the early to late 1800s and the early 1900s, Old Town is characterized by large wood-frame houses of distinctive architectural styles. Typically built by shipbuilders and carpenters for New England sea captains, many of these homes feature Bahamian and New England influences and high ceilings. Several historic district homes are

now exquisite guesthouses (see the Accommodations chapter).

In addition to its obvious aesthetic qualities, Old Town is desirable because it is within walking distance of just about everything Key West has to offer, including shops, restaurants, nightlife, and galleries. Among the community's residents are a large number of artists and writers. Toward the southern end of Whitehead Street and west of Duval on Petronia Street, about a block from the Ernest Hemingway Home and Museum, lies **Bahama Village.** This community now is undergoing gentrification as home buyers purchase and renovate existing properties here.

One of Key West's more recent developments in Old Town is **Truman Annex,** where private homes, town houses, and condominiums all boast features of Key West's distinctive architecture. This self-contained development once was an extension of the island's Bahama Village section and later a portion of the Key West naval base. Truman Annex was constructed and renovated according to a unified plan reminiscent of Old Town but with more green space and winding streets. Because of the charm that this gated development exhibits, even the hubbub created by large cruise ships entering the nearby harbor does not affect its pricey real estate values. Condominiums in the Harbour Place complex of Truman Annex are almost directly on the water and are well in seven figures. Single-family homes are in the multimillion-dollar price range.

Mid Town and New Town

Stretching from White Street all the way east to Kennedy Boulevard, Mid Town boasts a mix of wood-frame and concrete-block ground-level homes built in the late 1950s and 1960s. New Town, developed a bit later, spreads out along North Roosevelt Boulevard, and is largely commercial on its perimeter.

Recently completed in the Mid Town area is **Roosevelt Annex,** a gated community of 25 single-family homes and town houses fronting the Gulf of Mexico on the former county fairgrounds along North Roosevelt Boulevard. Billed as the last developable site in Key West with open-water views, Roosevelt Annex was constructed by the developer of Truman Annex and the Key West Golf Club.

The **Key West Golf Club community,** on Stock Island, looks a lot like Truman Annex. Here, single-family homes, town houses, and condominiums display elements of Conch-style architecture. Each residence overlooks the Florida Keys' only 18-hole public golf course, along with surrounding lakes and ponds. If you are not in the market to buy at this time, a variety of long-term rental options is available. All residents have free access to tennis courts, nature walks, several swimming pools, and, of course, golf.

Sunset Key

If you would truly like to live on a secluded island—but not too far from civilization—consider a home on Sunset Key. Formerly known as Tank Island (the navy once stored its fuel in huge tanks here), Sunset Key is just a stone's throw across the harbor from Mallory Square. About half of the island is devoted to guest cottages and a beachfront restaurant-bar operated by the **Westin Key West Resort and Marina** (see the Accommodations chapter); the rest is reserved for single-family homes. Interior building lots begin at one and a half million. In addition to fabulous open-water

sunset views, homeowners on Sunset Key enjoy such amenities as a health club, pool, tennis courts, and putting green. Their cars, however, must remain behind at the Westin parking garage on Key West; only golf carts and bicycles are permitted on Sunset Key. Regular ferry service is available from the Westin Marina.

Real Estate Companies

We describe some of the largest Key West agencies for sales and rentals in this section. However, this is not meant to be a comprehensive listing. For a complete list, consult the Yellow Pages.

BASCOM GROOMS REAL ESTATE
1110 Truman Ave.
(305) 295-7511 or (888) 565-7150
www.bascomgrooms.com
In addition to residential sales, this agency also handles commercial properties and vacation rentals.

BEACH CLUB BROKERS INC.
1075 Duval St., Suite C-11
(305) 294-8433 or (800) 545-9655
www.kwreal.com
Specializing in the sale, purchase, and management of local and international property, Beach Club Brokers also has a separate rental division, Rent Key West Vacations Inc. (see separate listing).

CENTURY 21 ALL KEYS
1720 North Roosevelt Blvd.
(305) 294-4200 or (800) 373-4200
www.c21allkeys.com
Century 21 deals with real estate sales and rentals in our southernmost city.

COLDWELL BANKER SCHMITT REAL ESTATE
1201 White St.
(305) 296-7727 or (800) 598-7727
www.realestatefloridakeys.com
Sales and rentals from Key Largo to Key West are the focus of this office.

COMPASS REALTY
201 Front St., Suite 101
(305) 292-1881 or (800) 884-7368
www.compass-realty.com
Compass Realty sells property throughout Key West but also focuses on the sale and rental of Truman Annex properties as well as those in the Key West Golf Club and Roosevelt Annex communities.

ISLAND GROUP REALTY
2409 North Roosevelt Blvd., Suite 10
(305) 295-7110 or (800 225-4277
www.isellkw.com
This real estate company offers any of the services you might need for relocating to the Florida Keys. If your needs are residential, commercial properties, or rentals, the sales associates at Island Group Realty can assist with your request.

KEY WEST REALTY INC.
1109 Duval St.
(305) 294-3064 or (800) 654-5131
www.keywestrealty.com
In addition to real estate sales, this agency is very heavily into the rental business with a wide variety of vacation options.

PREFERRED PROPERTIES COASTAL REALTY, INC.
520 Southard St.
(305) 294-3040 or (800) 462-5937
www.realkeywest.com
This agency offers residential and commercial property sales as well as vacation rentals, investment properties, and long-term property management.

PRUDENTIAL KNIGHT & GARDNER REALTY
336 Duval St.
(305) 294-5155 or (800) 843-9276
www.keysrealestate.com
Prudential Knight concentrates sales efforts on the purchase, sale, rent, or lease of properties and boat slips from Key West to Marathon.

RENT KEY WEST VACATIONS, INC.
1107 Truman Ave.
(305) 294-0990 or (800) 833-7368
www.rentkeywest.com
This agency handles rentals exclusively. Rent Key West offers extensive listings, with properties ranging from studio apartments to four-bedroom homes.

TRUMAN & COMPANY
1205 Truman Ave.
(305) 292-2244
www.trumanandcompany.com
This is a highly professional company with a great knowledge of the Key West and Monroe County real estate market. Most of the principals in this company are long-time residents and handle with first-hand knowledge the unique residential and commercial aspects of buying and selling property in the Florida Keys.

VACATION KEY WEST
(305) 295-9500 or (800) 595-5397
www.vacationkw.com
This agency will help you choose a great location for a few days or for an extended visit here in the tropics. They can place you in an historic inn, romantic hideaway, condo, or cottage.

RETIREMENT

If we are to believe Noah Webster, retirement means "withdrawing from active life." Not so in the Florida Keys. Our retirees are anything but retiring. Each year, about the time Jack Frost starts whistling up north, the influx of snowbirds to our sun-kissed islands begins, and the collective pulse of our communities quickens.

Unlike other retirement areas in Florida, our seniors usually don't keep to themselves in preplanned communities. You'll find them living in residential neighborhoods and condominiums, RV parks, and mobile-home villages. Our seniors contribute an added dimension to our communities. They form a much-needed core of volunteers for many of our public services, including the county libraries, local hospitals, and area schools.

The American Association of Retired Persons (AARP) accepts individuals age 50 and older into membership, which means the first wave of baby boomers has already reached "senior" status, and some are taking the Florida Keys by storm. These prime-of-lifers have taken a career-course detour, leaving that corporate 9-to-5 (or, more likely, 9-to-9) grind to venture off the track into uncharted territory.

Regardless of age, the retirees in the Florida Keys remain youthful. Our warm, tropical climate is kind to old bones (young ones, too!). The pace of our lifestyle moves to a different drummer . . . well, more of a reggae beat. Some people even feel we live longer down here . . . and they're in their 90s. Our energetic retirees enjoy fishing and scuba diving, golf and tennis, boating, and bridge. They are active in myriad special-interest organizations the length and breadth of the Keys. Many pursue artistic hobbies long put on the back burner while the rest of their lives simmered. Some go back to school, developing new skills and honing others.

OVERVIEW

At the heart of the retirement community in the Florida Keys are the senior citizen centers, which serve as cohesive units of companionship and support to retirees of all ages and circumstances. The centers were constructed and are maintained as a joint venture between Monroe County and the local chapters of AARP. The county nutrition sites are in the centers (see Nutrition Services in the Senior Services section in this chapter).

Membership in AARP is not a prerequisite for most activities of the senior citizen centers, but anyone age 50 or older may pick up an application to AARP at any of the centers. Because our seniors participate in activities based all throughout the Keys, we have organized this chapter by interest group, incorporating all areas of the Keys from Key Largo to Key West.

SENIOR CENTERS

PLANTATION KEY SENIOR CENTER
Various Locations
(305) 852-7133
www.monroecounty-fl.gov
This active group of seniors in the Upper Keys has a series of fund-raisers, such as its annual rummage sale, to raise money for community organizations, including the fire department, the ambulance corps, and the local Red Cross chapter. Besides monthly meetings, this Upper Keys group enjoys bingo; members donate the money raised to Hospice. During the winter season, when the ranks swell by some 60 to 75 percent, classes such as Spanish are offered at the center. Puzzles, crafts, and cards are favorite impromptu activities.

Many of the retirees in the Upper Keys are active in conservation and preservation organizations, fraternal organizations, the Florida Keys Council of the Arts, and the Key Players (see the Arts and Culture chapter), and human service groups such as Hospice and the Domestic Abuse Shelter. The center is next to the sheriff's substation.

MARATHON SENIOR CENTER
MM 48.8 Bayside, 535 33rd St., Marathon
(305) 743-3346
www.monroecounty-fl.gov
This lively bunch in the Middle Keys maintains a whirlwind of activities, especially during the winter season, such as bridge, crafts, weekly bingo, and regular exercise sessions. A balanced meal is served at the center every weekday at noon. The seniors trip the light fantastic with special events, such as the Valentine Sweetheart Dance and the St. Patrick's Day party. They charter buses and go on special excursions to the Monkey Jungle or Everglades National Park,

to Homestead or Miami, even an overnight to Busch Gardens in Tampa. The trips usually cost a nominal fee and include entrance fees and dinner.

The center offers Arrive Alive instruction for seniors several times throughout the year. Arrive Alive is a bookwork driving course that, when passed, nets the senior citizen a discount on auto insurance. The crafting groups hold boutiques where they display and sell their creations. The seniors have a series of yard sales throughout the year to make money to maintain the center. Volunteers also go to the elementary schools several times a week and, like grandparents, assist children in reading or math, or just talk to the child and give a hug when needed.

The Marathon Senior Center has a large lending library. It also has free income tax preparation when that dreaded time rolls around. Free flu shots and blood pressure checks are available on a regular basis.

BIG PINE KEY SENIOR CENTER
MM 31 Bayside, 380 Key Deer Blvd.,
Big Pine Key
(305) 872-3990
www.monroecounty-fl.gov
Not to be outdone by the other Keys centers, the seniors in the Lower Keys boogie in a bevy of activities like their compatriots up the Keys. The winter season finds them country line dancing and exercising, taking French lessons, and attending classes in hatha yoga. The center shows classic movies and hosts potlucks and bingo. The group has an active barbershop quartet and a serious chess club. Two times each month seniors can get free blood pressure checks.

The Lower Keys Big Pine Senior Center, which is right behind the Big Pine Key firehouse, is open every day for card playing and puzzle making. The seniors sponsor 55 Alive driving classes (much like the group in the Middle Keys) as well as computer instruction. During the winter season the center often holds dances, playing recorded Big Band music.

KEY WEST SENIOR CENTER
1016 Georgia St., Truman School at the Harvey Government Center
(305) 295-5165
www.monroecounty-fl.gov
The seniors in Key West often go their own way, we are told, so not as many organized activities emanate from this center as from others in the rest of the Keys. The seniors are active in the Key West Garden Club, the Art and Historical Society, the Maritime History Society, the Key West Yacht Club, the Power Squadron, and fraternal organizations such as Moose and Elk. More than 50 seniors regularly come to the center for the county-supplied hot meals each day (see Nutrition Services in this chapter), staying to play bingo or cards afterward. Bridge is popular, too.

COLLEGE COURSES

The Florida Keys Community College offers a selection of courses of interest to seniors, but there is no tuition break for senior citizens. Check the FKCC Web site for current course offerings and tuition charges. The academic year is divided into three terms. The fall class session runs from Aug through Dec. The spring term is Jan to May. Summer classes are held from the beginning of May through mid-Aug. Class offerings change often, so call the college branch of your choice for a course catalog and the most recent class schedule.

UPPER KEYS CAMPUS
MM 89.9 Oceanside, Coral Shores High School, Tavernier
(305) 852-8007
www.fkcc.edu
Seniors and retirees particularly enjoy the computer classes offered at this branch of Florida Keys Community College. They also sign up for such classes as conversational Spanish, watercolor painting, beginning drawing, creative writing, and American and English literature.

MIDDLE KEYS CAMPUS
MM 50 Oceanside, 900 Sombrero Beach Rd., Marathon
(305) 743-2133 or (305) 743-0749
www.fkcc.edu
The Middle Keys branch of FKCC offers general-interest classes in foreign language and computer science as well as more unusual fare, such as nature walks, tours of the Everglades, conservation classes, and photography instruction.

FLORIDA KEYS COMMUNITY COLLEGE
5901 West College Rd., Stock Island
(305) 296-9081
www.fkcc.edu
The main campus of the Florida Keys Community College offers many more classes of interest to seniors than the other branches up the Keys. Art classes in ceramics, stained glass, jewelry making, lettering and calligraphy, drawing, wheel throwing, print making, photography, graphic arts, painting, and sculpture will intrigue the artistically inclined. Courses in computerized photography and graphic arts are also offered. Many foreign languages are available, and the selection of literature courses includes one on Florida Keys writers and literature. Seniors

can try their hands at creative writing and dabble in the natural sciences with marine data collection, marine archaeology, and the culture and environment of the Florida Everglades. Vocational courses include marine propulsion technology (good for those with boats to repair) and electronic engineering technology (to fix DVD players and the like).

FKCC has a beautiful swimming pool and offers classes in water aerobics and fitness swimming. Seniors can take classes as non-degree-seeking students or work toward an associate of arts or associate of science degree.

Lifelong learning doesn't necessarily mean that you must enroll in a degree program or semester-long course. FKCC also offers a variety of continuing education workshops, seminars, and classes devoted to a single subject such as stock-market investment, custom rod making, accessing the Internet, or bookbinding. These classes may meet for a single session or several weeks depending on the complexity of the subject matter.

PUBLIC LIBRARIES

The Monroe County libraries are popular reading-room destinations with seniors in the Keys. They all maintain ever-growing large-print collections and a wide selection of current magazines. In addition, most of the libraries have a burgeoning number of videotapes and books on tape that may be checked out. Electronic catalogs in each of the libraries list all the materials in the system. Your local library will be able to get information from other branches for you upon request. The Key West library maintains a well-stocked Florida History Room that provides a fascinating look back through the centuries in Key West and all of the Keys.

Volumes of old photographs are housed here.

The libraries also host special events, such as lectures and film screenings, throughout the year. The library system has a strong volunteer program as well.

The Monroe County library system includes the following branches: Key Largo, (305) 451-2396, MM 101.4 Oceanside, Tradewinds Shopping Center, Key Largo; Islamorada, (305) 664-4645, MM 81.5 Bayside, Islamorada; Marathon, (305) 743-5156, MM 48.5 Oceanside, next to Fishermen's Hospital, Marathon; Big Pine, (305) 872-0992, MM 31 Bayside, 213 Key Deer Blvd., Big Pine Key; and Key West, (305) 292-3595, 700 Fleming St., Key West. Visit www.monroecounty-fl.gov for more information.

SPECIAL-INTEREST ACTIVITIES

It is not uncommon here in the Florida Keys to hear a senior citizen complain, "Since I've retired, I've never been so busy in my life!" Seniors get involved in civic clubs and fraternal organizations such as the Elks, Eagles, Moose, and Shriners. They work with human service organizations such as Big Brothers/Big Sisters, Florida Keys Children's Shelter, Domestic Abuse Shelter, and the AIDS Prevention Center. Retirees donate valuable time to the Florida Keys Council of the Arts, the American Cancer Society, and Guardian Ad Litem. And they participate in activities helping the Florida Keys themselves such as Reef Relief, Florida Keys Wild Bird Rehabilitation Center, and Friends of the Everglades.

Contact the chamber of commerce in your area for a complete listing of the special-interest organizations of the Florida Keys. Area chambers include those in Key Largo, (305) 451-4747, (800) 822-1088; Islamorada, (305) 664-4503, (800) 322-5397;

Marathon, (305) 743-5417, (800) 262-7284; Lower Keys, (305) 872-2411, (800) 872-3722; and Key West, (305) 294-2587, (800) 527-8539. Visit www.monroecounty-fl.gov for more information.

i Each month the Florida Keys Southernmost Car Club holds a "Show and Shine" event. The excitement of these shows allows the general public to behold dream classic autos from an era long gone, up close and personal. All makes and models, including trucks, low-riders, and chrome motorcycles, are on display. The Car Club chooses various locations throughout the Keys, so call ahead for dates and times at (305) 942-1758 or visit www.southernmostcarclub.com.

Garden Clubs

Some of the most popular organizations in the Florida Keys are its garden clubs, perhaps because we have so many days of glorious sunshine or because our subtropical climate fosters the growth of such exotic flowering foliage and palms.

UPPER KEYS GARDEN CLUB
MM 94 Bayside, Tavenier
www.upperkeysgardenclub.com

The Frances Tracy Garden Center (next to the Red Cross Building) hosts members of the Upper Keys Garden Club on the third Tuesday of every month. The group often hears a lecturer speak on some phase of subtropical horticulture. They hold a Plant Ramble sale as a fund-raiser and sponsor a garden walk through lovely private gardens of the Upper Keys each year.

The Upper Keys Garden Club is affiliated with the Florida Federation of State Garden Clubs and the National Council of State Garden Clubs.

Members support the community's landscaping needs by donating plants and labor in landscaping the Coast Guard Station, Coral Shores High School, and Plantation Key Elementary School.

MARATHON GARDEN CLUB
MM 50 Bayside, Marathon
(305) 743-4971
www.marathongardenclub.org

The Marathon Garden Club was organized in March 1955, when the Keys were in desperate need of beautification. Beginning as a small grassroots group that held meetings in each other's homes, the ranks have burgeoned. Much of the lovely landscaping gracing public areas of Marathon is the work of the Marathon Garden Club. You'll notice the group's creative handiwork at the American Legion, the chamber of commerce building, the firehouse, Fishermen's Hospital, the public library, the Key Colony Causeway, along the Overseas Highway, and at Marathon High School.

Since the 1970s the group has sponsored successful house tours, plant and crafts fairs, and flower shows. Each year in March they sponsor a house and garden tour in Marathon that is open to the public. In December they stage Christmas Around the World (see the Annual Events chapter). Garden club members take their collective expertise into the Monroe County schools, where they teach the children about plants and trees as well as flower arranging.

The Marathon Garden Club meets the third Fri of each month from Oct through May. The public is invited. The gift shop, which offers a changing selection of unusual specialty gift items, is open year-round from Mon through Sat, 10 a.m. to 2 p.m.

KEY WEST GARDEN CLUB
Atlantic Boulevard and White Street at
West Martello Tower, Key West
(305) 294-3210
www.keywestgardenclub.com
The Key West Garden Club maintains the gardens of West Martello Tower, an old Civil War fort at Higgs Beach on Atlantic Boulevard. The club meets once a month for a short business meeting followed by a presentation by a guest speaker, often a visiting horticulturist. These events are open to the general public. Twice a year the group holds a plant sale at its West Martello Tower headquarters. You can walk away with beautiful plants at bargain prices and a wealth of free gardening tips and information to boot. In March of alternating years, the Key West Garden Club sponsors a garden tour during which the general public can visit five private gardens in Key West (see the Annual Events chapter for details).

i Looking for something to do? Why not call Habitat for Humanity in the Keys and volunteer your talents. Three locations serve this county: Upper Keys, (305) 453-0050 or (305) 453-7855; Middle Keys, (305) 395-1386; and Lower Keys, (305) 872-4456. Ongoing projects include fishing tourneys, raising money for hurricane season, spelling bees, an annual gala, and a ReStore offering furniture, appliances, and building supplies in their redistribution center located at mile marker 30.5 in Big Pine Key. Visit www.habitatlowerkeys .org for more information.

American Contract Bridge League

Duplicate bridge passes muster as the game of choice among those addicts of the sport.

"If there's a game in town, we'll find it," says one duplicate player. The play is recognized by the National American Contract Bridge League, and you can earn Life Master's points. The games are open to all. If you don't have a partner, don't worry; the director will pair you with a partner for the day's game. A nominal fee is charged to play.

It is best to call the director before the day of play to make sure the schedule has not been changed. The groups are listed here by location.

- **Civic Club,** MM 99.5 Oceanside, Key Largo; (305) 451-9833. Play is year-round on Mon and Fri afternoons and on Tues evening.
- **San Pablo Catholic Church,** MM 53.5 Oceanside, 550 122nd St., Marathon; (305) 743-4687. Play is year-round on Thurs afternoons.
- **Kirk of the Keys,** MM 51 Oceanside, Marathon; (305) 743-4256. Play is on Mon, Wed, and Fri afternoons.
- **Senior Center,** Harvey Government Center, 1016 Georgia St., Key West; (305) 295-5165. Play is on Tues, Thurs, and Sun afternoons.

Golf and Tennis

Two of the most popular sports among seniors are golf and tennis. See our Recreation chapter for information on facilities in the Florida Keys.

SENIOR SERVICES

AARP
Upper Keys, (305) 852-7132
Middle Keys, (305) 743-4008
Big Pine Key, (305) 872-3990
Key West, (305) 295-5156
www.aarp.org

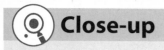 **Close-up**

Mix It Up

BINGO

The Florida Keys is not all about fishing and sunsets. If you enjoy bingo, check out the game at the **801 Club** (801 Duval, 305-293-9644) or at **La-Te-Da** (1125 Duval, 305-296-6706). Neither has a cover, and all proceeds go to charity. Bingo can also be played at the **Key West Senior Center** (305-295-5165) and at **Sons of Italy at the American Legion** (305-294-7374).

DANCE

If you like salsa, swing or ballroom, you can dance your way up and down the **Keys: Paradise Health and Fitness** in Key West, (305) 294-4120; **Big Pine Senior Center,** (305) 872-3990; **Marathon Community Theatre** (Tropical Tappers meet for classes), (305) 743-3346; and **Theo and Ganies Dance Center** in Marathon (for training like a pro), (305) 743-0660.

SCRABBLE

Tax your brain power at the **Scrabble Club for Scrabbleholics** at the Key Largo Coffeehouse, (305) 451-3664.

WALKING

The **"I Hate to Exercise" walking group** meets at Founders Park MM 87, Islamorada. For information on the Key Largo Hammock Nature Walks, call (305) 451-1202.

QUILTING

For information on the **Quilter's Club,** call the Chamber of Commerce numbers for Key Largo, Big Pine, and Key West.

BOCCE

Bocce is a game of Italian origin similar to lawn bowling. The sport is played at the **Indigenous Park,** and the season begins in October. Call (305) 297-3595 for information.

PHOTOGRAPHY

Make that a Kodak moment and join the **Upper Keys Photography Club.** The club meets monthly with all levels of expertise welcomed. Call (305) 852-4533.

BIKING

Bike paths are plentiful in the lower Keys. Try the one at MM 17 Sugarloaf Road. You can park at the Sugarloaf Lodge, across US 1. The round-trip is approximately 15 miles. MM 19.5 on Sugarloaf Key takes you on Crane Boulevard to the bay. MM 27.8 Middle Torch and Big Torch is just off US 1. Park on Middle Torch Road. The scenic trip is about 15.5 miles.

The nationally known organization of the American Association of Retired Persons has local chapters in most cities. Here in the Florida Keys there are four offices from Plantation Key to Key West. Each chapter offers their own programs in areas of interest to their members. The membership dues are $3 a year, and you must be at least 50 years of age. For that nominal sum members can select from line dancing and computer classes to county services. Helpful folks with helpful information.

THE AMERICAN RED CROSS OF GREATER MIAMI AND THE FLORIDA KEYS
5450 McDonald Ave., Unit 11, Stock Island
(305) 296-4033
www.miamiredcross.org

Clara Barton founded the American Red Cross in 1881 and now there are more than 1,300 chapters nationwide. Everyone knows what this humanitarian organization means to any community, near and far. The services rendered on a local basis range from emergency relief to health and safety education and everything in between.

COMMUNITY SUPPORT SERVICES
Upper Keys, (305) 852-7125
Middle Keys, (305) 289-6016
Lower Keys/ Key West, (305) 292-4408

Monroe County, which encompasses the Florida Keys, has the highest cost of living of any county in the state of Florida. Yet no adjustment is made in eligibility requirements for aid for senior citizens, who are usually managing on fixed incomes. This county agency works with seniors on a case-by-case basis as an interim assistance agency, helping solve unexpected crises that put them at temporary financial risk. The agency also aids seniors in matters of lost checks, robbery, chairs, and walkers; and helps out with short-term medical needs such as prescriptions, eyeglasses, and hearing aids. This help is designed to restore the individuals to self-sufficient status or to refer them to the appropriate state or federal agencies for more long-term support. Documentation of need is required to qualify for assistance.

IN-HOME SERVICES
Key West, (305) 292-4481

In-Home Services networks information and referrals between the private and public sector for family members, friends, and other agencies seeking services on behalf of impaired elderly persons. Participants must be at least age 60. The program is designed so the elderly may maintain quality of life while remaining in their homes.

The information and referral telephone line (800-273-2044) is staffed by case managers from 8 a.m. to 5 p.m., Mon through Fri. They will specifically target the needed assistance and refer the caller to the resources available. Case management provides a social worker to support and help those requiring assistance.

Chore services for impaired elderly who can no longer accomplish the tasks for themselves are available. These include yard work, heavy-duty cleaning services, and small minor household repairs. Homemaking support with light housekeeping, meal preparation and planning, shopping, laundry tasks, and other essential errands assist clients in need. Personal care, in-home respite aides will help with bathing, dressing, and other personal needs, providing relief for caregivers. A fee schedule assessment based on the person's income will determine what or if he or she will have to pay for these services.

MONROE COUNTY EXTENSION SERVICES
1100 Simonton St., #2-260, Key West
(305) 292-4501
www.ifas.ufl.edu
The Monroe County Extension Services, in partnership with the University of Florida, has been empowering citizens since 1987. This enormously beneficial agency creates an objective of educating the folks in their community on a variety of topics: agriculture, the environment, lawn and garden, relationship to ocean waters in this community, 4-H programs, hurricane preparedness, families, and consumers.

MONROE COUNTY SOCIAL SERVICES
www.monroecofl.virtualtownhall.net
The Florida Keys offers senior citizens a wide range of services through the Monroe County Social Services Agency, whose main administrative offices are in Key West. We also have listed the branch office locations in the Upper and Middle Keys and the contact numbers of each department in the individual descriptions below. Note that services in the Middle Keys also include Big Pine Key, which ordinarily is included with the Lower Keys throughout the book. The rest of the Lower Keys are handled from the offices in Key West.

Alternately, you can call the Elder Helpline (800-273-2044) and describe your problem or need; you will be referred to the proper agency. Monroe County Social Services office locations include: in the Upper Keys, Plantation Key Government Center Annex, MM 88.8

Bayside, Tavernier; in the Middle Keys, Marathon Government Annex, MM 50.5 Oceanside, 490 63rd St., Suite 190, Marathon; and, in the Lower Keys, Public Service Building, Wing III, 5100 College Rd., Key West.

To find information on Monroe County Services online, consult www.monroe county-fl.gov.

i Bet you didn't know . . . The official Florida state symbols are: the Cracker horse (brought here 500 years ago by Spanish explorer Ponce de Leon), the loggerhead turtle, the alligator, the panther, the manatee, the mockingbird, oranges (and their juice), and last and the tastiest—Key lime pie!

NUTRITION SERVICES
Upper Keys, (305) 852-7133
Middle Keys, (305) 743-3346
Lower Keys, (305) 872-3617
Key West, (305) 295-5166
Funded by the Older Americans Act of 1960 and the Alliance for Aging for Miami-Dade and Monroe Counties, and aided with a 10 percent cash match by the Monroe County Board of Commissioners, this service offers many county nutrition programs to seniors age 60 and older. Homebound persons can receive a daily hot meal from Meals on Wheels. The senior centers throughout the Keys offer a low-cost, noontime, complete balanced meal (see the Senior Centers section in this chapter). The midday repast is supplemented with instruction on nutrition, hygiene, health-care concerns, and hurricane preparedness, and the group also participates in card games and organized activities.

VETERANS AFFAIRS
88820 Overseas Hwy., Tavernier
(305) 453-8777
www.va.gov
This office is a liaison between veterans and the Veterans Administration, providing services for more than 21,000 vets in Monroe County. This office helps in locating education benefits, outpatient and hospitalization needs, insurance claims, social security appeals, transportation to the Miami VA, and other services. A second and third location are at 490 63rd St. in Marathon (305-289-6009) and 1200 Truman Ave in Key West (305-295-5150).

HEALTH CARE

We have included information on health-care options, ranging from full-service hospitals and specialty care providers for patients in need of cancer or dialysis treatments to physical therapy clinics and mental health services. And don't miss the information on veterinary-care options. We care about Spot and Fluffy, too!

Please be reminded, however, that this is not intended to be a comprehensive listing of all possible health services. The Florida Keys and Key West are served by physicians in nearly every specialty as well as by osteopaths, chiropractors, podiatrists, dentists, and optometrists. So if, while visiting our islands, you should develop a sudden toothache from downing one too many frozen coladas or drop a contact lens somewhere in the sand, don't despair. One of our many health-care providers will be available to help you, even on short notice. Ask your hotel concierge for a referral to the appropriate specialist or consult the Yellow Pages.

And should your situation call for medical expertise that is not available in the Florida Keys, rest assured that you will still be able to receive state-of-the-art treatment in a timely manner. The University of Miami's renowned Jackson Memorial Medical Center as well as other mainland hospitals and trauma facilities are just a helicopter ride away.

OVERVIEW

This chapter lists health care options by category in descending mile marker order from Key Largo to Key West, then alphabetically in Key West.

ACUTE-CARE CENTERS

Upper Keys

SELECT PHYSICAL THERAPY
MM 100 Bayside, Key Largo
(305) 453-0409
www.novacare.com
Select Physical Therapy maintains a network of therapists throughout the Florida Keys, specializing in physical, speech, and occupational therapy. Some locations also offer orthopedist, family physician, and internist referrals. A location in Key West is at 3156 Northside Dr. (305-292-1805).

THE GOOD HEALTH CLINIC
MM 91.5 Oceanside, Tavernier
(305) 853-1788
www.thegoodhealthclinic.org
This upper Keys clinic opened for the specialized and primary care of the uninsured population. This medical facility offers X-rays, general orthopedic surgery, and the services of doctors in Miami who specialize in hematology, oncology, back surgery, ophthalmology, and more. Local doctors associated with the clinic include dermatologists, mental health practitioners, pediatricians, and optometrists.

MARINERS HOSPITAL
MM 91.5 Bayside, Tavernier
(305) 434-3000
www.baptisthealth.net

Mariners Hospital, established as a nine-bed physicians' clinic in 1959, today is a state-of-the-art hospital facility, completed in the late 1990s. Among the services provided here are 24-hour emergency care, surgery (including outpatient), respiratory therapy, pulmonary rehabilitation, cardiac rehabilitation, and radiology (including MRI, CT scans, and mammography). Mariners maintains a sleep diagnostic center, laboratory, and pharmacy and has a hyperbaric, or decompression, chamber (see the Diving and Snorkeling chapter). Mariners has a helicopter pad for transfer of severe cases to mainland hospitals.

The hospital is a part of Baptist Health South Florida, a nonprofit health-care organization. Mariners Hospital also maintains and operates a state-of-the-art physical therapy center in a separate location at MM 100.3 Bayside, Key Largo, (305) 451-4398.

Middle Keys

FISHERMEN'S HOSPITAL
MM 48.7 Oceanside, Marathon
(305) 743-5533
www.fishermenshospital.com

The medical staff at Fishermen's Hospital offer care in the areas of cardiology, cardiac rehabilitation, family practice, general surgery, gynecology, oncology, internal medicine, neurology, pathology, radiology, rheumatology, and plastic/reconstructive surgery. A CT scanner, known as a helical scanner, provides three-dimensional images with extraordinary clarity. Emergency service and same-day surgery also are available.

A helicopter pad allows for emergency chopper services, and a hyperbaric emergency response team is on call for divers. Fishermen's Overnight Guest program provides testing and pre-surgery (the night prior to surgery) room and board. Also licensed to provide home health care, Fishermen's accepts most forms of insurance. Other hospital resources include a certified diabetes educator and nutritional support services. Fishermen's Hospital also offers physical therapy services at two separate locations: at MM 54, on Marathon Key, and at the Big Pine Key Plaza at MM 29.7. For information on either of these physical therapy centers, phone (305) 289-9950. This hospital is a for-profit organization.

MARATHON HEALTH CENTER
MM 48.5 Oceanside, Marathon
(305) 743-4000

The Marathon Health Care facility is a CareNet discount health program for residents and visitors to the Florida Keys. They provide affordable, comprehensive, primary care, dental, obstetrics, and gynecology services for the insured and uninsured in Monroe County as well as visitors. No appointments needed and walk-ins are accepted.

Lower Keys

BIG PINE MEDICAL AND MINOR EMERGENCY CENTER
MM 30 Oceanside, Big Pine Key
(305) 872-3321

This emergency-care center, conveniently located on Big Pine Key, treats minor illnesses and emergencies (broken bones, cuts, insect bites, and so on). Although appointments are encouraged, walk-ins are welcome. The clinic is generally open Mon through Fri from 8 a.m. to 5 p.m. and some

Sat mornings. However, hours may vary with the season and patient demand, so it is best to phone ahead.

Key West

21ST CENTURY ONCOLOGY
3426 North Roosevelt Blvd.
(305) 296-0021
www.21stcenturyoncology.com
This health care treatment center opened in 2006, providing a full spectrum of radiation therapy services to cancer patients. A portion of their treatments are conventional external beam treatments and advanced services such as prostate seed implants, 3-D conformed treatment planning, intensity modulated radiation, and image-guided radiotherapy.

BODY OWNERS
5450 MacDonald Ave., Stock Island
(305) 294-8866
www.keywestphysicaltherapy.com
The knowledgeable staff and compassionate care make this physical therapy and wellness center a popular one with patients and physicians. Everyone goes out of their way to make sure your therapy sessions are comfortable and informative. They offer sessions for children with special needs as well.

KEY WEST URGENT CARE
1503 Government Rd.
(corner of Flagler Avenue and Seventh Street)
(305) 295-7550
Not feeling so hot? Need to see a doctor in a hurry? This is the place to go. No appointment necessary.

Treatment for minor illnesses and injuries is available six days a week, from 8 a.m. to 3:30 p.m., and credit cards are accepted. Some local insurance plans may also be accepted.

LOWER FLORIDA KEYS HEALTH SYSTEM
5900 Junior College Rd., Stock Island
(305) 294-5531
www.lkmc.com
This accredited primary-care hospital is the only hospital in the Florida Keys to offer maternity services. Lower Florida Keys Health System maintains 169 beds, a 24-hour emergency room, a clinical lab, and a heliport. Added services include pediatrics, inpatient and outpatient psychotherapy, physical therapy, radiation therapy, chemotherapy, and cardiovascular and ambulatory care. The hospital offers substance-abuse assistance and comprehensive wellness programs.

TRUMAN MEDICAL CENTER
540 Truman Ave.
(305) 296-4399
Truman Medical Center makes no appointments but is open seven days. This walk-in clinic will see patients from 9 a.m. to 4:30 p.m. Mon through Fri, 9:30 a.m. to noon on Sat, and noon to 2 p.m. on Sun.

MOBILE MEDICAL CARE

RURAL HEALTH NETWORK OF MONROE COUNTY
2901 Overseas Hwy., Marathon
(305) 289-8917
www.rhnmc.org
The Rural Health Network was established to provide primary medical care and dental services to the uninsured and underinsured residents of Monroe County. Two fully equipped RVs travel up and down the Keys to provide medical services to folks who are uninsured and might not otherwise seek primary-care treatment.

A combined effort of the Monroe County Health Department, the three Keys hospitals, the Health Foundation of South Florida, Catholic Charities of the Archdiocese of Miami, HUD, FEMA, HRSA, and the Florida Keys Area Health Education Center in conjunction with the University of Miami, this mobile medical service covers Key Largo to Key West.

The vans are equipped like doctors' offices. Each has two small examination rooms and a cab that doubles as a triage area. Each mobile unit is staffed by a registered nurse, a nurse practitioner, and a health educator, as well as nursing and medical students. Patients needing care beyond the scope of the Medi-Van staff may be referred to specialists and area hospitals.

Appointments are available and walk-ins are welcome. The Medi-Vans charge a co-pay for their services.

HOME HEALTH SERVICES

HOSPICE OF THE FLORIDA KEYS/ VISITING NURSE ASSOCIATION
MM 92 Oceanside, Tavernier
(305) 852-7887
www.hospicevna.com

Hospice provides care for terminally ill patients with six months or less to live. Services are provided in private homes and nursing homes throughout the Keys by a staff of registered nurses, patient-care managers, and social workers. Certified nursing assistants tend to personal needs such as bathing, grooming, and bedding. All home-care patients must be referred to the agency by a physician. Comfort Care, which is private-duty nursing care, is also available. Hospice's purpose is to ensure patients' comfort so that the last days of their lives are quality ones.

Within this same nonprofit organization, the Visiting Nurse Association (VNA) provides more aggressive home care for patients still undergoing various treatments or who need blood tests or care for wounds. This service also is provided upon a physician's request. Both Hospice and VNA are on call 24 hours a day, seven days a week. Medicare and Medicaid are accepted. There are two additional Hospice locations at MM 50.5 Oceanside in Marathon (305-743-9048), and 1319 William St. in Key West (305-294-8812).

LIFELINE HOME HEALTH CARE
MM 53 Oceanside, Marathon
(305) 743-9817
www.lhcgroup.com

As the name implies, Lifeline Home Health Care provides registered nurses, home health aides, physical therapists, rehabilitation, and hospice. An RN is on call 24/7 through their call center. Lifeline Home Health Care also installs personal response (lifeline) devices. Medicare and private insurances are accepted for their services.

MEDICAL/HOSPITAL EQUIPMENT

CORAL MEDICAL HOME EQUIPMENT
MM 88 Oceanside, Islamorada
(305) 852-4393
www.coralmedical.com

This long-established Keys business gives customers first-rate delivery of their medical equipment needs, including 24-hour emergency service, home IV provisions, respiratory and oxygen supplies, and the usual variety of crutches, walkers, and various medical apparatus.

ALTERNATIVE HEALTH CARE

Many of the people who reside full time in the Florida Keys are laid-back types who

Emergency Numbers

While we sincerely hope you won't ever need to use the following telephone numbers, it is a good idea to keep this information in a convenient place.

Police, Fire, or Rescue	911
Florida Poison Information Center	(800) 282-3171
U.S. Coast Guard Marine and Air Emergency	(305) 295-9700 or
	CG/VH channel 16
Florida Marine Patrol of the FWCC	*FMP or (800) DIAL FMP
Florida Highway Patrol	*FHP or (800) 240-0453
Monroe County Emergency Management	(305) 289-6018
Hurricane Preparedness	(800) 427-8340
Emergency Information Hotline	(800) 955-5504

were drawn to our islands by a desire to pursue a less-than-conventional lifestyle. In many cases their approach to health care is as nontraditional as their approach to life.

The Florida Keys, and Key West in particular, boast a wealth of options in the alternative health care category. These include everything from yoga classes and massage therapy on the beach to acupuncture, homeopathic medicine, organic foods, and herbal remedies. For a complete list of alternative health care options and practitioners throughout the Florida Keys, consult the local Yellow Pages under the following categories: Acupuncture, Health Clubs, Health and Diet Food Products, and Massage Therapists.

ISLAND DOLPHIN CARE
150 Lorelane Place, Key Largo
(305) 451-5884
www.islanddolphincare.org
Island Dolphin Care specializes in working with special-needs children interacting with dolphins. This not-for-profit facility provides assisted therapy to children with critical illnesses, disabilities, and special needs who come from all over the world.

VETERINARY SERVICES

Your four-legged friends and "family" sometimes need health care, too. These pet clinics cater to their needs from the top of the Keys to Key West.

Upper Keys

ANIMAL CARE CLINIC
MM 100.6 Bayside, Key Largo
(305) 453-0044
www.drfredpeacock.com

Boarding and grooming are small parts of the operation at Animal Care Clinic. The clinic maintains oxygen-intensive critical-care units and offers surgery, lab testing, X-rays, EKG, and ultrasound dentistry, as well as emergency on-call service, 24 hours a day, seven days a week.

GRANNIE'S BED AND BONE
MM 88.5 Oceanside, Islamorada
(305) 853-0056

Upper Keys families with pets now have a place to have their animals lovingly boarded. Here at Grannie's 700-square-foot facility, your pet can stay for a day or a longer extended visit. The services provided include walking, play time, administering medications, bathing, and grooming.

VCA UPPER KEYS ANIMAL HOSPITAL
MM 87.8 Oceanside, Islamorada
(305) 852-3665
www.vcaupperkeys.com

This clinic provides comprehensive services for all types of animals, including dogs, cats, birds, reptiles, ferrets, and exotics. Twenty-four-hour emergency care is offered seven days a week. Boarding is provided for clients.

Middle Keys

ANIMAL HOSPITAL OF THE KEYS
MM 52.5 Bayside, Marathon
(305) 743-2287

This veterinary hospital offers a full range of services, including 24-hour emergency care

and boarding. (Note that the last four digits of their telephone number spell "cats.")

MARATHON VETERINARY HOSPITAL
MM 52.5 Oceanside, Marathon
(305) 743-7099, (800) 832-7694
www.marathonvethospital.com

Marathon Veterinary Clinic is small, but the vets here offer full services, including 24-hour emergency care, for dogs, cats, and all exotics.

Lower Keys

CRUZ ANIMAL HOSPITAL
MM 27 Bayside, Ramrod Key
(305) 872-2559
www.cruzanimalhospital.com

A variety of medical services for virtually all pets, plus 24-hour emergency service, is available at Cruz Animal Hospital. Military and senior citizen discounts are available.

DOC SYN'S VETERINARY CARE
MM 22.7 Bayside, Cudjoe Key
(305) 744-0074

At Doc Syn's the motto is, "We treat your pets as if they were our own." The facility offers complete medical and surgical care for dogs, cats, birds, ferrets, and reptiles. Evening hours are available.

Key West

ALL ANIMAL CLINIC
5505 Fifth Ave., Stock Island
(305) 294-5255
www.allanimalclinic.com

This clinic offers medicine, surgery, dentistry, an in-house laboratory, X-rays, and emergency care. They offer house calls by appointment and also have an air-conditioned boarding facility.

ANIMAL HOSPITAL OF OLDE KEY WEST & STOCK ISLAND
6150 Second St., Stock Island
(305) 296-5227

Veterinary services for dogs, cats, birds, and small exotics are provided in a modern, full-service facility that offers a yearly health-care plan. A complete boarding facility is on the premises. Twenty-four-hour emergency service is also available.

i *Sylvilagus palustres hefneri* is not the name of a *Playboy* centerfold, but it is the name of a marsh rabbit found on Big Pine Key in 1980. Hugh Hefner, founder and editor of *Playboy* magazine, funded a study that identified the species as endangered. In 2007, feral cats were killing the marsh rabbits, and Hef once again stepped in and donated funds to Stand Up For Animals to capture the cats and to ensure they would not be euthanized.

HOUSE CALL VET
(305) 294-9551

House Call Vet is exactly what this name implies! If you are visiting Key West and have a pet that needs a veterinarian, this is the doc to call. If you get a recording, leave a message and someone will get back to you to discuss your animal's needs and arrange a time to visit. Too bad we humans don't have the same service!

LOWER KEYS ANIMAL CLINIC
1456 Kennedy Dr., Key West
(305) 294-6335

This facility treats small exotics but mostly sees cats and dogs. The staff offers regular check-ups, surgery, dentistry, vaccinations, X-rays, and general medical treatment for pets.

EDUCATION AND CHILD CARE

The Florida Keys and Key West are served by public and private schools, preschools, and a community college. Thanks to a visiting institute and college degree programs at the Boca Chica Naval Air Station in the Lower Keys, students can earn bachelor's, master's, and even doctoral degrees without ever leaving our islands. In addition, several institutions of higher education in Miami are within commuting distance.

In addition to the following information on education options is a comprehensive look at the child-care scene in the Florida Keys and Key West. We explore traditional child-care services along with other handy (sometimes vacation-saving) options such as drop-in care, babysitting, sick-child and respite care, family child-care homes, and public after-school programs.

EDUCATION

Public Schools

The Monroe County School District oversees schools from Key Largo to Key West, including three high schools. Some elementary and middle schools within our county occupy the same building; other middle and high schools share facilities. Stretching more than 100 miles, traversing 42 bridges, with more than 8,000 students attending 17 schools and centers in its jurisdiction, the Florida Keys is a unique and stimulating classroom setting.

The school system operates on a school year that runs from late Aug through early June.

An elected board headed by an elected superintendent, who oversees five district representatives, governs our public schools. Board members serve four-year terms. School funding comes from Monroe County property taxes. For more information on Monroe County Public Schools, consult their Web site at www.monroe.k12.fl.us.

Charter School
BIG PINE ACADEMY
MM 30.2 Oceanside, Big Pine Key
(305) 872-1266
www.monroe.k12.fl.us
This small charter school on Big Pine Key is for preschool through fourth grade. Their curriculum is to ensure a safe and nurturing school environment teaching basic skills that will enrich and challenge children's lives and prepare them for their next grade levels.

> **i** Promenade down to 1302 White St. in Key West to gaze at the front of the Glynn Archer Elementary School. Before you stands a beautiful explosion of flowers. In 2007 a group of citizens led by the Tropia Butterfly Foundation created this garden to attract more butterflies to our tiny island, embellishing public spaces with color and piquing the interest of schoolchildren.

EDUCATION AND CHILD CARE

Private Schools

Private schools typically offer smaller student-teacher ratios and a variety of learning curricula. The following list includes private schools operating in the Florida Keys and Key West.

MONTESSORI ISLAND SCHOOL
MM 92 Oceanside, Tavernier
(305) 852-3438
Montessori Island School offers guidance for infants and toddlers up to pre-kindergarten in a natural setting. There is no air-conditioning in the building and the use of natural light brings the environment closer to the classroom.

TREASURE VILLAGE MONTESSORI SCHOOL
MM 86.7 Oceanside, Islamorada
(305) 852-3482
www.treasurevillagemontessori.com
Montessori schools across the country work on the principle of self-pacing for children. This Montessori school, established in 1996, works on the same idea of purposeful action. The school provides education for preschool through elementary children with Montessori-certified teachers.

ISLAND CHRISTIAN SCHOOL
MM 83.4 Bayside, Islamorada
(305) 664-2781
www.islandchristian.org
Established in 1974 by a group of parents from Island Community Church, Island Christian began with 54 students. As grade levels were added and the school became accredited, enrollment increased to 300. Island Christian today teaches pre-kindergarten through high school students in a traditional college-preparatory curriculum

that incorporates the Abeka and Bob Jones Christian teachings. The school offers a full interscholastic sports program to junior and senior high school students.

MARATHON LUTHERAN SCHOOL
MM 53.3 Bayside, 325 122nd St., Marathon
(305) 289-0700
www.lutheransonline.com/mlc2
A service of Martin Luther Chapel and the Lutheran Church Missouri Synod, a national Lutheran organization, Marathon Lutheran School offers education from kindergarten through sixth grade. Using the School of Tomorrow PACE program, Marathon Lutheran offers its students the opportunity to learn at their own speeds with several class levels combined. Established in 1987, the school requires students to attend weekly chapel service and take religion classes.

GRACE LUTHERAN SCHOOL
2713 Flagler Ave., Key West
(305) 296-8262
www.gracekw.ctsmemberconnect.net
Established in 1952 and designed for pre-kindergarten three-year-olds through second-graders, Grace Lutheran offers computers and teaches Spanish in all but pre-kindergarten classes. During "God Time," students learn about Christian ideals and how to live them.

THE HOMESCHOOL HIGH SCHOOL
5901 College Rd., Key West
(305) 292-0075
www.hs2kw.org
In 1997, the HomeSchool High School (HS2) was launched by parents and educators seeking a challenging education for their children. The privately run, nonprofit college preparatory high school is located on

the campus of the Florida Keys Community College in Key West. Classes offered at HS2 are math, science, English, civics, chemistry, global history, and additional subjects as demand arises. Student-instructor is a 7 to 1 ratio. The students participate in sports and band at the Key West High School.

MARY IMMACULATE STAR OF THE SEA
700 Truman Ave., Key West
(305) 294-1031
www.keywestcatholicparish.org
Mary Immaculate follows a pre-kindergarten through eighth-grade curriculum outlined by the Archdiocese of Miami, including religious instruction. The school's mission is to provide opportunities for all Lower Keys families to experience a Catholic education. Within a Christian environment, the instructors foster spiritual, academic, and social development.

MONTESSORI CHILDREN'S SCHOOL OF KEY WEST
1221 Varela St., Key West
(305) 294-5302
www.keywestmontessori.com
This private Montessori school educates children in pre-kindergarten through kindergarten. Here teachers guide students without unnecessary interference—all furnishings are child-size, and photos are hung at a child's viewing level. Allowed freedom within certain guidelines, Montessori children work at their own pace on their own projects.

MONTESSORI ELEMENTARY CHARTER SCHOOL
1127 United St., Key West
(305) 294-4910
www.keywestmontessori.com

The Key West Montessori Elementary Charter School is a nonprofit, public school teaching children in grades one through five. The school utilizes the work of Maria Montessori, who developed a method of educating children focusing on the child as the foundation for learning.

I Spy . . .

In 2004 two students doing a survey for moths in the Key West Tropical Forest and Botanical Gardens (see the Attractions chapter) looked up in an Arjuna almond tree, *Terminalia arjuna,* the only one of its kind in the garden, and discovered a *Phyllops falcatus,* better known as a Cuban fig-eating bat or white-shouldered bat. This was an exciting discovery because these bats have only been known to exist in Cuba, Hispaniola, and on Grand Cayman. The appearance of the Cuban fig-eating bat is the first recorded in Florida and the first in the United States.

Additional Educational Opportunities

Residents and visitors to the Florida Keys may participate in a number of hands-on educational opportunities listed below.

MARINELAB, MARINE RESOURCES DEVELOPMENT FOUNDATION
51 Shoreland Dr., Key Largo
(305) 451-1139 or (800) 741-1139
www.mrdf.org
Since 1972 the nonprofit Marine Resources Development Foundation (MRDF) has

offered students an in-depth introduction to the ecology of the Keys. The MRDF provides customized programs for students, who learn about sea life in the Emerald Lagoon or explore the MarineLab Undersea Laboratory. Customized programs also include scuba certification, coral reef ecology, mangrove ecology, or a trip to the Everglades.

SEACAMP ASSOCIATION
**MM 30 Oceanside, Newfound Harbor Road
and 1300 Big Pine Ave., Big Pine Key
(305) 872-2331 or (877) 732-2267
www.seacamp.org**
This scuba and marine science camp for children ages 12 through 17 has been in Big Pine Key since 1966. Children from across the world sign up for Seacamp's 18-day program to experience scuba diving, sailing, snorkeling, and sailboarding. Marine science classes teach about such subjects as exploring the seas, animal behavior, and Keys critters. Scuba certification is available.

The camp operates from June through Aug and offers a day camp in summer for resident children ages 10 through 14. In addition, Seacamp is affiliated with the Newfound Harbor Marine Institute, which hosts three-day winter field trips for teachers and students from fourth grade through high school.

SAN CARLOS INSTITUTE
**516 Duval St., Key West
(305) 294-3887
www.institutesancarlos.org**
In keeping with its century-old mission of promoting Cuban culture and democratic ideals, the historic San Carlos Institute offers Spanish-language classes for adults in two terms: winter and summer. Taught by native

speakers, these eight-week sessions are available at three levels: beginner, intermediate I, and intermediate II.

Higher Education

FLORIDA KEYS COMMUNITY COLLEGE
**5901 West College Rd., Key West
(305) 296-9081
www.fkcc.edu**
When Florida Keys Community College (FKCC) began operation in fall 1965, it became the first institution of higher education in the Florida Keys. FKCC was established through funding provided to Monroe County by the Florida state legislature after parents and teachers had expressed concerns over the lack of a college in the Keys. Today FKCC offers associate of science and arts degree programs in such fields as business administration, computer programming and analysis, nursing, multimedia technology, and marine environmental technology.

FKCC's performing and visual arts programs are enhanced by the college's Tennessee Williams Fine Arts Center (see the Arts and Culture chapter). Its marine environmental technology and dive programs are especially popular. Certificate programs are offered at FKCC in business data processing, marine propulsion technology, small-business management, addiction studies, and more. Vocational training is also available for law enforcement and correctional officers. In 1995 FKCC opened the Mario F. Mitchell Aquatic Safety Center for dive technology and a state-of-the-art oceanfront pool.

In addition to its main campus on Stock Island, Florida Keys Community College also offers a limited number of classes at two other Keys locations: the Middle Keys Center at 900 Sombrero Beach Rd., MM 50,

Marathon, (305) 743-2133; and the Upper Keys Center at MM 89.9, Tavernier, (305) 852-8007.

SAINT LEO COLLEGE–KEY WEST CENTER
Boca Chica Naval Air Station, Key West
(305) 293-2847
www.saintleo.edu
Saint Leo College offers the only regionally accredited bachelor's degree program in the Florida Keys. Located in Key West since 1975, Saint Leo is a private college that offers associate of arts and bachelor of arts degrees in business administration, criminology, human services, and/or human resource administration. Situated at the naval air station, Saint Leo College is open to all civilian and military personnel and their families in the Florida Keys. Classes are designed for the working adult.

CHILD CARE

Gone are the days of Ward and June, Ozzie and Harriet, and Lucy and Ricky, those televised icons of the 1950s nuclear family. In their TV Land, Pop went to the office while Mom stayed home with the children. Nowadays, when fathers go off to work, most mothers are right behind them on their way to jobs; grandparents work, too. Child care has become a necessity, and the Florida Keys' scenario differs little from this national norm.

The problem of finding good, competent child care is compounded here by a shortage of available providers at any cost. According to the National Association for the Education of Young Children, child care is the fourth-largest item in the family budget after food, housing, and taxes. Infant care (birth to age one) and weekend and evening care are in particularly short supply in Monroe County, which encompasses the Keys.

Day-to-day child care in the county generally falls into two categories: center-based care and family child-care homes.

In this section we provide information on types of child-care programs, and contacts for centers that serve the Florida Keys and Key West.

Resources

WESLEY HOUSE FAMILY SERVICES COORDINATING AGENCY
1304 Truman Ave., Key West
(305) 809-5000 or (877) 595-5437
www.wesleyhouse.org
With offices in Key West and serving all of the Florida Keys, Wesley House assists families in making the best of a difficult situation. The Wesley House Resource & Referral Network (WHR&RN) is perhaps the most important resource in the Keys for parents looking for appropriate, quality child care. (Wesley House is a national division agency of the United Methodist Church and a United Way of Monroe County agency.) WHR&RN acts as a link between families and the child-care services they seek. It can recommend affordable child care for children up to 5 years old and after-school and summer care for children up to 12 years old. Families may access services at three locations in the Florida Keys: 175 Wrenn St., Tavernier, (305) 853-3518; 2796 Overseas Highway, Marathon, (305) 289-2675; and 1304 Truman Ave., Key West, (305) 809-5000.

WHR&RN offers other assistance in the forms of subsidized child care, scholarships, and help in obtaining legal aid, medical aid, food stamps, and other services. The network conducts classes for parents in money management, parenting skills, nutrition, and handling everyday pressures. It provides personal help for families with at-risk children, assisting them in filling out paperwork to meet eligibility requirements. Wesley House also offers transportation to and from child-care centers for children in at-risk situations.

Wesley House will provide referrals for families needing sick care or in-home nursing specialists. Some child-care centers will offer drop-in care.

Baby Chicks Rental

It's hard to travel on a plane (or in a car for that matter) and bring along cribs, strollers, high chairs, and all the gear for the little one. By calling the owner of this come-to-your-door baby equipment rental business, you can travel with just your luggage and baby! Call (305) 879-3340 or visit www.babychicksrental.com for more information.

Types of Programs

This section describes the center- and home-based child-care options available to parents in Monroe County.

Child-Care/Preschool Centers

The minimum state licensing requirements dictate that a child-care center must hold a valid license from the Health and Rehabilitative Services (HRS) Department of the state of Florida. The license must be posted in a conspicuous place within the center.

The center must adhere to the number of children for which it is licensed, and it must maintain the minimum staff-to-child ratio for each age level: Younger than age one, 1 teacher for every 4 children; age one,

1 to 6; age two, 1 to 11; age three, 1 to 15; age four, 1 to 20; and age five, 1 to 25. We stress that this is the minimum ratio. It may not be sufficient to give your child the level of care you desire.

Licensing standards mandate health and safety requirements and staff training requirements. These include: child abuse and neglect training, a 20-hour child-care training course, a 10-hour specialized training module, and 8 hours of in-service training annually. In addition, there must be one CPR- and first-aid–certified person on-site during business hours. Some centers are prepared to accept infants; others are not.

Some child-care centers are exempt from HRS licensing. They are accredited and monitored by religious agencies, the school board, or the military.

Unfortunately, no child-care centers are open weekends or evenings in the Keys.

Contact Wesley House for a list of HRS-licensed and license-exempt child-care/preschool centers in the Florida Keys and Key West.

Family Child-Care Homes

Family child-care is considered by the state of Florida to encompass home-based child care with five or fewer preschool-age children from more than one family unrelated to the caregiver. Any preschool children living in the home must be included in the maximum number of children allowed. The adult who provides the child care is usually referred to as a family child-care home operator.

Some counties in Florida require that family child-care homes be licensed. Monroe Country, which includes the Florida Keys, requires only registration with the Department of Health and Rehabilitative Services.

Every adult in the household must be screened. Registration requires no on-site inspection of the home for minimum health, safety, and sanitation standards, however. Nor is there a requirement that the family child-care operator have CPR or first-aid training.

Military programs are exempt from this registration. They have their own accreditation procedures and are available only to family members of military personnel.

Wesley House actively recruits for and offers a three-hour course covering basic health and safety issues to persons who wish to operate registered family child-care homes.

Public After-School Programs

Many public schools in the Florida Keys and Key West run their own after-hours programs for school-age children from 2:15 to 5:30 p.m. and also on school holidays and summer weekdays. Most schools charge for this service. Contacts at the schools are: Key Largo Elementary School, MM 104.8, Key Largo, (305) 453-1255; Plantation Key School, 100 Lake Rd., Tavernier, (305) 853-3281; Switlik Elementary, MM 48.8 Bayside, 33rd St., Marathon, (305) 289-2490; Big Pine Key Neighborhood School, Palomino Horse Trail, Big Pine Key, (305) 872-1266; Sugarloaf Elementary/Middle School, 255 Crane Road, Sugarloaf Key, (305) 745-3282; Poinciana Elementary School, 1407 Kennedy Dr., Key West, (305) 293-1630; Sigsbee Elementary, Sigsbee Naval Base, Key West, (305) 294-1861 (military families only); Gerald Adams Elementary School, 5855 West Junior College Rd., Key West, (305) 293-1609.

i In 2009, Kent Denver School students raised monies to buy high-tech cameras and equipment to offer a live feed from a Web camera off the Bahia Honda bridge. The purpose was to empower students and teens to be good stewards for oceans through science, research, and philanthropy. Visit http://teens4oceans.org for more information.

Babysitting

Personal knowledge of the person you choose to care for your child in your absence is the best of all possible worlds, but it isn't always a reality. If you are a visitor to the Florida Keys or Key West or a newly relocated resident, you may have to take a leap of faith and entrust your child to someone you do not know. Therefore, you should check references. For referrals, contact Wesley House (see listing under Resources) or ask the concierge at your hotel.

You can also contact local chambers of commerce, which often keep lists of local residents who babysit: Key Largo, (305) 451-1414, (800) 822-1088; Islamorada, (305) 664-4503, (800) 322-5397; Marathon, (305) 743-5417, (800) 262-7284; Lower Keys, (305) 872-2411, (800) 872-3722; and Key West, (305) 294-2587, (800) 527-8539. Be sure to ask by what criteria these referrals have been checked for more insight as to who best suits your needs.

MEDIA

Even after Henry Flagler's extension of the Florida East Coast Railroad provided Florida Keys residents access to the mainland, communications on our islands were limited. To receive local news and news outside the South Florida area, residents relied on radio broadcasts from Miami, sporadic postal service, and what was probably their most effective and timely means of dispatch: word of mouth, or what is jokingly referred to as "the Conch telegraph."

Today two dailies and a contingent of weeklies and free papers tie the Keys together. Both AM and FM radio stations are still restricted by wattage, and residents must subscribe to satellite or cable service to get television reception.

NEWSPAPERS

In addition to home delivery, our newspapers are often sold in curbside vending racks, grocery stores, pharmacies, convenience stores, and bookstores. A handful of shops carry national and international newspapers. Because the Florida Keys are considered a remote distribution site, some national newspapers, such as the *New York Times*, are sold at a higher newsstand price. A rule of thumb: Get to the newsstand early. The farther you travel from the mainland, the more quickly the out-of-town papers sell out.

Dailies

KEY WEST CITIZEN
3420 Northside Dr., Key West
(305) 292-7777
www.keysnews.com
In 1904 a small, weekly newspaper known as the *Citizen* appeared on the newspaper scene in Key West; it was later consolidated with the 1899 *Inter-Ocean* to form the *Key West Citizen*. Cooke Communications now owns the *Key West Citizen*, along with weekly *Solares Hill* (now published in the Sunday edition of the *Citizen*), the *Free Press* Community Newspapers, and Florida Keys News Service.

The *Citizen* shares editorial coverage and classified advertisements with its sister publications and features a significant amount of syndicated material and lifestyles coverage.

The *Citizen's* editorial focus is primarily on features. *Paradise*, a tabloid appearing in Thursday's edition, is a comprehensive compendium of what's currently happening in the theaters and at the clubs and galleries around town. Free copies of *Paradise* are available at newsstands, hotels, guesthouses, restaurants, and other businesses throughout Key West. The *Citizen* also publishes "The Menu," a free quarterly guide containing menus from many area restaurants.

THE MIAMI HERALD
1 Herald Plaza, Miami
(305) 350-2111 or (800) 437-2535
www.miamiherald.com

The largest-circulation daily newspaper in the southeastern United States, this Pulitzer Prize–winner has maintained Key West correspondents for decades and now has a bureau in the southernmost city, Key West. The *Miami Herald* features crisp writing and tends to favor features over hard news except when issues are pressing. The *Herald* is widely available throughout the Keys. There is a Key West location at 619 Eaton St. (305-294-5131).

i Prior to 1917, the Florida Keys were a much more peaceful place. It was in that year the first long-distance phone connection linked the Keys to Miami.

Weeklies and Biweeklies

THE REPORTER
MM 91.6 Oceanside, Tavernier
(305) 852-3216
www.keysnet.com
When the *Reporter* began in the early 1900s, the newspaper, which was based in Key Largo, was mimeographed. As the publication grew, its owners bought what was at the time a top-of-the-line printing press—a monumental event in Keys publishing, since few newspapers were actually printed in this stretch of Monroe County. **The** *Reporter* is published by the McClatchy Company, which also publishes the *Miami Herald* and the *Florida Keys Keynoter*.

Published each Thurs, this tabloid packages community news from south Miami-Dade County to Marathon in a traditional black-and-white format and is available in stores throughout the Upper Keys.

FREE PRESS COMMUNITY NEWSPAPERS
MM 81.5 Oceanside, Islamorada
(305) 664-2266 or (800) 926-8412
www.keysnews.com
Formerly known as the *Islamorada Free Press,* this group of weekly tabloid newspapers has grown to include five separate editions, each serving a segment of the Florida Keys population, from Ocean Reef to Big Pine Key. Owned by Cooke Communications since August 2000, the *Free Press* community newspapers cover local news and sports in each area. The newspapers are published each Wed and are available free in grocery and convenience stores as well as in curbside racks from Homestead to Big Coppitt Key. A second location is in Marathon at MM 52 Oceanside (305-743-8766).

FLORIDA KEYS KEYNOTER
MM 48.6 Oceanside, Marathon
(305) 743-5551

KEY WEST KEYNOTER
2720A North Roosevelt Blvd., Key West
(305) 296-6989
www.keysnet.com
The *Florida Keys Keynoter* is owned by the McClatchy Company and is considered the *Miami Herald*'s sister newspaper. The *Keynoter* is Monroe County's second-oldest publication. With a weekly television news program and a separate Key West edition, the twice-weekly *Keynoter* offers comprehensive local coverage of the Florida Keys. Known for its in-depth coverage of the Keys' political scene, once a week the *Keynoter* also features "L' Attitudes," an arts and entertainment section that includes complete television listings for the area, special features, and upcoming Keys events.

This tabloid-style newspaper is published each Wed and Sat and is widely available in shops, newsstands, and curbside racks throughout the Keys.

> **i** Handy Web sites for visitors and locals: General information: www.fla-keys.com. Cities: www.islamorada.fl.us, www.keywestcity.com, www.keycolonybeach.net, and www.ci.marathon.fl.us.

CONCH COLOR
314 Simonton St., Key West
(305) 294-7566
www.conchcolor.com
Publisher and editor Tom Oosterhoudt's *Conch Color* showcases his exciting and entertaining life. Tom is everywhere and is invited to everything that is anything. He has taken this lifestyle and turned it into a fun and colorful photographic chronicle. This is the Keys version of *People* magazine. The paper is published weekly, covers Marathon to Key West, is free, and can be picked up at most commercial locations.

KEY WEST THE NEWSPAPER
422 Fleming St., Key West
(305) 292-2108
www.kwest.net/~kwtn
Since its debut in Jan 1994, *Key West The Newspaper* has found its niche in the realm of politics and entertainment. While the paper boasts a hearty entertainment section full of live music listings, reviews, and local color, it is perhaps best known for its investigative reporting. This free weekly's motto is "journalism as a contact sport." It is distributed every Fri morning in Key West and Stock Island.

SOLARES HILL
3420 Northside Dr., Key West
(305) 294-3602
www.solareshill.com
Founded in 1971, the free weekly *Solares Hill* ceased its independent status in 1998 when it was acquired by the publishers of the *Key West Citizen* and the *Free Press* community newspapers. Although the newspaper's former slogan, "The straight truth plainly stated," has been replaced with the words, "The way a newspaper should be," its focus remains primarily on politics and business, along with a smattering of restaurant, theater, and book reviews. *Solares Hill* is inserted in the Sunday edition of the *Citizen* newspaper.

> **i** Everyone knows Jimmy Buffett can sing, but did you know he also wrote three books that made the *New York Times* best-seller list? Three were fiction: *Tales from Margaritaville, Where is Joe Merchant?*, and *Swine Not.* His nonfiction book is titled *A Pirate Looks at Fifty.* Buffett is one of only six authors in the list's history to have number-one titles in both fiction and nonfiction. The others were Ernest Hemingway, Dr. Seuss, Mitch Albom, William Styron, and John Steinbeck. Wanna bet those five couldn't sing?

RADIO

Radio reception in the Florida Keys is heavily influenced by factors such as weather and distance from the transmitter. Clear skies and sunshine will optimize good reception; luckily, we have plenty of both most of the time. Some of our more popular radio stations include:

- **WEOW Today's Hits,** 92.7
- **Key-Z FM,** 93.5
- **Conch Country,** 98.7
- **Sun Classic Rock,** 99.5
- **US-1 Radio,** 104.1
- **Island,** 107.1

TELEVISION

Florida Keys residents must pay for cable television service in order to receive network channels. Our cable provider is Comcast, (866) 288-3444.

In addition to national programming, local-origination programming is offered on channels 5, 24, and 75 through 79. This public service programming includes live coverage of city commission and local political meetings, as well as real estate listings and local-interest shows on a variety of topics such as health care and fishing. Channel 5 also offers interesting and informative infomercials during the day and evening, highlighting many of the Keys' attractions found in this book.

Satellite communication is an alternative to cable service. Check the Yellow Pages for companies offering satellite dishes and service.

INDEX

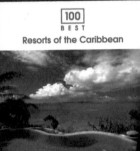

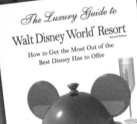

INSIDERS' GUIDE ®

The acclaimed travel series that has sold more than 2 million copies!

Discover: Your Travel Destination.
Your Home. Your Home-to-Be.

Albuquerque

Anchorage &
  Southcentral
  Alaska

Atlanta

Austin

Baltimore

Baton Rouge

Boulder & Rocky Mountain
  National Park

Branson & the Ozark
  Mountains

California's Wine Country

Cape Cod & the Islands

Charleston

Charlotte

Chicago

Cincinnati

Civil War Sites in
  the Eastern Theater

Civil War Sites in the South

Colorado's Mountains

Dallas & Fort Worth

Denver

El Paso

Florida Keys & Key West

Gettysburg

Glacier National Park

Great Smoky Mountains

Greater Fort Lauderdale

Greater Tampa Bay Area

Hampton Roads

Houston

Hudson River Valley

Indianapolis

Jacksonville

Kansas City

Long Island

Louisville

Madison

Maine Coast

Memphis

Myrtle Beach &
  the Grand Strand

Nashville

New Orleans

New York City

North Carolina's
  Mountains

North Carolina's
  Outer Banks

North Carolina's
  Piedmont Triad

Oklahoma City

Orange County, CA

Oregon Coast

Palm Beach County

Palm Springs

Philadelphia &
  Pennsylvania Dutch
  Country

Phoenix

Portland, Maine

Portland, Oregon

Raleigh, Durham &
  Chapel Hill

Richmond, VA

Reno and Lake Tahoe

St. Louis

San Antonio

Santa Fe

Savannah & Hilton Head

Seattle

Shreveport

South Dakota's
  Black Hills Badlands

Southwest Florida

Tucson

Tulsa

Twin Cities

Washington, D.C.

Williamsburg & Virginia's
  Historic Triangle

Yellowstone
  & Grand Teton

Yosemite

**To order call 800-243-0495
or visit www.Insiders.com**

Getaway ideas for the local traveler

Need a day away to relax, refresh, renew?
Just get in your car and go!